Lecture Notes in Computer Science 3223

Commenced Publication in 1973
Founding and Former Series Editors:
Gerhard Goos, Juris Hartmanis, and Jan van Leeuwen

D1392749

Konrad Slind   Annette Bunker
Ganesh Gopalakrishnan (Eds.)

Theorem Proving
in Higher Order Logics

17th International Conference, TPHOLs 2004
Park City, Utah, USA, September 14-17, 2004
Proceedings

 Springer

Volume Editors

Konrad Slind
Ganesh Gopalakrishnan
University of Utah
School of Computing
50 South Central Campus Drive, Salt Lake City, Utah, UT84112, USA
E-mail: {slind;ganesh}@cs.utah.edu

Annette Bunker
Utah State University
Electrical and Computer Engineering Department
4120 Old Main Hill, Logan, UT 84341, USA
E-mail: bunker@helios.ece.usu.edu

Library of Congress Control Number: 2004111288

CR Subject Classification (1998): F.4.1, I.2.3, F.3.1, D.2.4, B.6.3

ISSN 0302-9743
ISBN 3-540-23017-3 Springer Berlin Heidelberg New York

Springer is a part of Springer Science+Business Media

springeronline.com

© Springer-Verlag Berlin Heidelberg 2004
Printed in Germany

Typesetting: Camera-ready by author, data conversion by Olgun Computergrafik
Printed on acid-free paper   SPIN: 11319238   06/3142   5 4 3 2 1 0

Preface

This volume constitutes the proceedings of the *17th International Conference on Theorem Proving in Higher Order Logics* (TPHOLs 2004) held September 14–17, 2004 in Park City, Utah, USA. TPHOLs covers all aspects of theorem proving in higher-order logics as well as related topics in theorem proving and verification.

There were 42 papers submitted to TPHOLs 2004 in the full research category, each of which was refereed by at least 3 reviewers selected by the program committee. Of these submissions, 21 were accepted for presentation at the conference and publication in this volume. In keeping with longstanding tradition, TPHOLs 2004 also offered a venue for the presentation of work in progress, where researchers invited discussion by means of a brief introductory talk and then discussed their work at a poster session. A supplementary proceedings containing papers about in-progress work was published as a 2004 technical report of the School of Computing at the University of Utah.

The organizers are grateful to Al Davis, Thomas Hales, and Ken McMillan for agreeing to give invited talks at TPHOLs 2004.

The TPHOLs conference traditionally changes continents each year in order to maximize the chances that researchers from around the world can attend. Starting in 1993, the proceedings of TPHOLs and its predecessor workshops have been published in the Springer Lecture Notes in Computer Science series:

1993 (Canada)	Vol. 780	1999 (France)	Vol. 1690
1994 (Malta)	Vol. 859	2000 (USA)	Vol. 1869
1995 (USA)	Vol. 971	2001 (UK)	Vol. 2152
1996 (Finland)	Vol. 1125	2002 (USA)	Vol. 2410
1997 (USA)	Vol. 1275	2003 (Italy)	Vol. 2758
1998 (Australia)	Vol. 1479	2004 (USA)	Vol. 3223

We would like to thank Amber Chisholm and Perry Hacker of University of Utah Conference Services for their help in many aspects of organizing and running TPHOLs.

Finally, we thank our sponsors: Intel and the National Science Foundation.

June 2004

Konrad Slind,
Annette Bunker,
and Ganesh Gopalakrishnan

Program Committee

Mark Aagaard (Waterloo)
David Basin (Zurich)
Ching-Tsun Chou (Intel)
Peter Dybjer (Chalmers)
Jean-Christophe Filliâtre (Paris Sud)
Mike Gordon (Cambridge)
Elsa Gunter (NJIT)
Jason Hickey (Caltech)
Doug Howe (Carleton)
Bart Jacobs (Nijmegen)
Matt Kaufmann (AMD)
Tom Melham (Oxford)
Tobias Nipkow (München)
Christine Paulin-Mohring (Paris Sud)
Frank Pfenning (CMU)
Sofiène Tahar (Concordia)

Clark Barrett (NYU)
Yves Bertot (INRIA)
Thierry Coquand (Chalmers)
Amy Felty (Ottawa)
Jacques Fleuriot (Edinburgh)
Jim Grundy (Intel)
John Harrison (Intel)
Peter Homeier (DoD, USA)
Paul Jackson (Edinburgh)
Sara Kalvala (Warwick)
Thomas Kropf (Bosch)
César Muñoz (NASA)
Sam Owre (SRI)
Lawrence Paulson (Cambridge)
Konrad Slind (Utah)
Burkhardt Wolff (Freiburg)

Additional Referees

Stefan Berghofer
Sylvain Conchon
Christophe Dehlinger
Lucas Dixon
Alfons Geser
Ali Habibi
Felix Klaedtke
Mohamed Layouni
Nicolas Magaud

Holger Pfeifer
Sylvan Pinsky
Tom Ridge
Norbert Schirmer
Carsten Schürmann
Radu I. Siminiceanu
Laurent Théry
Luca Viganò
Martin Wildmoser

Table of Contents

Error Analysis of Digital Filters
Using Theorem Proving

Behzad Akbarpour and Sofiène Tahar

Dept. of Electrical & Computer Engineering, Concordia University
1455 de Maisonneuve W., Montreal, Quebec, H3G 1M8, Canada
{behzad,tahar}@ece.concordia.ca

Abstract. When a digital filter is realized with floating-point or fixed-point arithmetics, errors and constraints due to finite word length are unavoidable. In this paper, we show how these errors can be mechanically analysed using the HOL theorem prover. We first model the ideal real filter specification and the corresponding floating-point and fixed-point implementations as predicates in higher-order logic. We use valuation functions to find the real values of the floating-point and fixed-point filter outputs and define the error as the difference between these values and the corresponding output of the ideal real specification. Fundamental analysis lemmas have been established to derive expressions for the accumulation of roundoff error in parametric Lth-order digital filters, for each of the three canonical forms of realization: direct, parallel, and cascade. The HOL formalization and proofs are found to be in a good agreement with existing theoretical paper-and-pencil counterparts.

1 Introduction

Signal processing through digital techniques has become increasingly attractive with the rapid technological advancement in digital integrated circuits, devices, and systems. The availability of large scale general purpose computers and special purpose hardware has made real time digital filtering both practical and economical. Digital filters are a particularly important class of DSP (Digital Signal Processing) systems. A digital filter is a discrete time system that transforms a sequence of input numbers into another sequence of output, by means of a computational algorithm [13]. Digital filters are used in a wide variety of signal processing applications, such as spectrum analysis, digital image and speech processing, and pattern recognition. Due to their well-known advantages, digital filters are often replacing classical analog filters. The three distinct and most outstanding advantages of the digital filters are their flexibility, reliability, and modularity. Excellent methods have been developed to design these filters with desired characteristics. The design of a filter is the process of determination of a transfer function from a set of specifications given either in the frequency domain, or in the time domain, or for some applications, in both. The design of a digital filter starts from an ideal real specification. In a theoretical analysis of the digital filters, we generally assume that signal values and system coefficients

K. Slind et al. (Eds.): TPHOLs 2004, LNCS 3223, pp. 1–17, 2004.
© Springer-Verlag Berlin Heidelberg 2004

are represented in the real number system and are expressed to an infinite precision. When implemented as a special-purpose digital hardware or as a computer algorithm, we must represent the signals and coefficients in some digital number system that must always be of a finite precision. Therefore, arithmetic operations must be carried out with an accuracy limited by this finite word length. There is a variety of types of arithmetic used in the implementation of digital systems. Among the most common are the floating-point and fixed-point. Here, all operands are represented by a special format or assigned a fixed word length and a fixed exponent, while the control structure and the operations of the ideal program remain unchanged. The transformation from the real to the floating-point and fixed-point forms is quite tedious and error-prone. On the implementation side, the fixed-point model of the algorithm has to be transformed into the best suited target description, either using a hardware description or a programming language. This design process can be aided by a number of specialized CAD tools such as SPW (Cadence) [3], CoCentric (Synopsys) [20], Matlab-Simulink (Mathworks) [16], and FRIDGE (Aachen UT) [22].

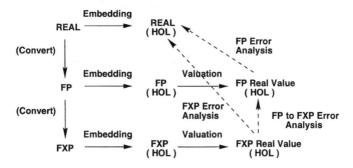

Fig. 1. Error analysis approach

In this paper we describe the error analysis of digital filters using the HOL theorem proving environment [5] based on the commutating diagram shown in Figure 1. Thereafter, we first model the ideal real filter specification and the corresponding floating-point and fixed-point implementations as predicates in higher-order logic. For this, we make use of existing theories in HOL on the construction of real numbers [7], the formalization of IEEE-754 standard based floating-point arithmetic [8,9], and the formalization of fixed-point arithmetic [1,2]. We use valuation functions to find the real values of the floating-point and fixed-point filter outputs and define the errors as the differences between these values and the corresponding output of the ideal real specification. Then we establish fundamental lemmas on the error analysis of the floating-point and fixed-point roundings and arithmetic operations against their abstract mathematical counterparts. Finally, we use these lemmas as a model to derive expressions for the accumulation of the roundoff error in parametric Lth-order digital filters, for each of the three canonical forms of realization: direct, parallel, and cascade [18].

Using these forms, our verification methodology can be scaled up to any larger-order filter, either directly or by decomposing the design into a combination of internal sub-blocks. While the theoretical work on computing the errors due to finite precision effects has been extensively studied since the late sixties [15], it is for the first time in this paper, that a formalization and proof of this analysis for digital filters is done using a mechanical theorem prover, here the HOL. Our results are found to be in a good agreement with the theoretical ones.

The rest of this paper is organized as follows: Section 2 gives a review of the related work. Section 3 introduces the fundamental lemmas in HOL for the error analysis of the floating-point and fixed-point rounding and arithmetic operations. Section 4 describes the details of the error analysis in HOL of the class of linear difference equation digital filters implemented in the three canonical forms of realization. Finally, Section 5 concludes the paper.

2   Related Work

Work on the analysis of the errors due to the finite precision effects in the realization of the digital filters has always existed since their early days, however, using theoretical paper-and-pencil proofs and simulation techniques. For digital filters realized with the fixed-point arithmetic, error problems have been studied extensively. For instance, Knowles and Edwards [14] proposed a method for analysis of the finite word length effects in fixed-point digital filters. Gold and Radar [6] carried out a detailed analysis of the roundoff error for the first-order and second-order fixed-point filters. Jackson [12] analyzed the roundoff noise for the cascade and parallel realizations of the fixed-point digital filters. While the roundoff noise for the fixed-point arithmetic enters into the system additively, it is a multiplicative component in the case of the floating-point arithmetic. This problem is analyzed first by Sandberg [19], who discussed the roundoff error accumulation and input quantization effects in the direct realization of the filter excited by a deterministic input. He also derived a bound on the time average of the squared error at the output. Liu and Kaneko [15] presented a general approach to the error analysis problem of digital filters using the floating-point arithmetic and calculated the error at the output due to the roundoff accumulation and input quantization. Expressions are derived for the mean square error for each of the three canonical forms of realization: direct, cascade, and parallel. Upper bounds that are useful for a special class of the filters are given. Oppenheim and Weinstein [17] discussed in some details the effects of the finite register length on implementations of the linear recursive difference equation digital filters, and the fast Fourier transform (FFT) algorithm. Comparisons of the roundoff noise in the digital filters using the different types of arithmetics have also been reported in [21].

In order to validate the error analysis, most of the above work compare the theoretical results with corresponding experimental simulations. In this paper, we show how the above error analysis can be mechanically performed using the HOL theorem prover, providing a superior approach to validation by simulation.

Our focus will be on the process of translating the hand proofs into equivalent proofs in HOL. The analysis we propose is mostly inspired by the work done by Liu and Kaneko [15], who defined a general approach to the error analysis problem of digital filters using the floating-point arithmetic. Following a similar approach, we have extended this theoretical analysis for fixed-point digital filters. In both cases, a good agreement between the HOL formalized and the theoretical results are obtained.

Through our work, we confirmed and strengthened the main results of the previously published theoretical error analysis, though we uncovered some minor errors in the hand proofs and located a few subtle corners that are overlooked informally. For example, in the theoretical fixed-point error analysis it is always assumed that the fixed-point addition causes no error and only the roundoff error in the fixed-point multiplication is analyzed [17]. This is under the assumption that there is no overflow in the result and also the input operands have the same attributes as the output. Using a mechanical theorem prover, we provide a more general error analysis in which we cover the roundoff errors in both the fixed-point addition and multiplication operations. On top of that, for the floating-point error analysis, we have used the formalization in HOL of the IEEE-754 [8], a standard which has not yet been established at the time of the above mentioned theoretical error analysis. This enabled us to cover a more complete set of rounding and overflow modes and degenerate cases which are not discussed in earlier theoretical work.

Previous work on the error analysis in formal verification was done by Harrison [9] who verified the floating-point algorithms such as the exponential function against their abstract mathematical counterparts using the HOL Light theorem prover. As the main theorem, he proved that the floating-point exponential function has a correct overflow behavior, and in the absence of overflow the error in the result is bounded to a certain amount. He also reported on an error in the hand proof mostly related to forgetting some special cases in the analysis. This error analysis is very similar to the type of analysis performed for DSP algorithms. The major difference, however, is the use of statistical methods and mean square error analysis for DSP algorithms which is not covered in the error analysis of the mathematical functions used by Harrison. In this method, the error quantities are treated as independent random variables uniformly distributed over a specific interval depending on the type of arithmetic and the rounding mode. Then the error analysis is performed to derive expressions for the variance and mean square error. To perform such an analysis in HOL, we need to develop a mechanized theory on the properties of random variables and random processes. This type of analysis is not addressed in this paper and is a part of our work in progress. Huhn et al. [11] proposed a hybrid formal verification method combining different state-of-the-art techniques to guide the complete design flow of imprecisely working arithmetic circuits starting at the algorithmic down to the register transfer level. The usefulness of the method is illustrated with the example of the discrete cosine transform algorithms. In particular, the authors have shown the use of computer algebra systems like Mathematica or Maple at the algorithmic level to reason about real numbers and to determine certain error bounds for the results of numerical operations. In contrast to [11], we propose an error analysis for digital filters using the HOL theorem prover. Although the computer algebraic systems such as Maple or Mathematica are much more popular and have many powerful decision procedures and heuristics, theorem provers are more expressive, more precise, and more reliable [10]. One option is to combine the rigour of the theorem provers with the power of computer algebraic systems as proposed in [10].

3 Error Analysis Models

In this section we introduce the fundamental error analysis theorems [23, 4], and the corresponding lemmas in HOL for the floating-point [8, 9] and fixed-point [1, 2] arithmetics. These theorems are then used in the next sections as a model for the analysis of the roundoff error in digital filters.

3.1 Floating-Point Error Model

In analyzing the effects of floating-point roundoff, the effects of rounding will be represented multiplicatively. The following theorem is the most fundamental in the floating-point rounding-error theory [23, 4].

Theorem 1: If the real number x located within the floating-point range, is rounded to the closest floating-point number x_R, then

$$x_R = x(1 + \delta), \text{ where } |\delta| \leq 2^{-p} \tag{1}$$

and p is the precision of the floating-point format.

In HOL, we proved this theorem in the IEEE single precision floating-point format for the case of rounding to nearest as follows:

```
Lemma 1: FLOAT_ROUND_RELATIVE_ERROR
⊢  normalizes x ⟹  ∃ e. abs (e) < (1 / 2 pow ((fracwidth X) + 1)) ∧
   (Val (float (round X To_nearest x)) = x * (1 + e))
```

where the function *normalizes* defines the criteria for an arbitrary real number to be in the normalized range of floating-point numbers [8], *fracwidth* extracts the fraction width parameter from the floating-point format X, *Val* is the floating-point valuation function, *float* is the bijection function that converts a triple of natural numbers into the floating-point type, and *round* is the floating-point rounding function [9].

To prove this theorem [4], we first proved the following lemma which locates a real number in a binade (the floating-point numbers between two adjacent powers of 2):

```
Lemma 2: REAL_IN_BINADE
⊢  normalizes x ⟹  ∃ j. j ≤ ((emax X) − 2) ∧
   (2 pow (j + 1) / 2 pow (bias X)) ≤ abs x ∧
   abs x < (2 pow (j + 2) / 2 pow (bias X))
```

where the function *emax* defines the maximum exponent in a given floating-point format, and *bias* defines the exponent bias in the floating-point format which is a constant used to make the exponent's range nonnegative. Using this lemma we can rewrite the general floating-point absolute error bound theorem (ERROR_BOUND_NORM_STRONG) developed in [9] as follows:

```
Lemma 3: ERROR_BOUND_NORM_STRONG_NORMALIZE
⊢  normalizes x ⟹
     ∃ j. abs (error x) ≤ (2 pow j / 2 pow (bias X + fracwidth X))
```

which states that if the absolute value of a real number is in the representable range of the normalized floating-point numbers, then the absolute value of the error is less than or equal to $2^j/2^{(bias\ X\ +\ fracwidth\ X)}$. The function *error*, defines the error resulting from rounding a real number to a floating-point value which is defined as follows [9]:

```
⊢_def   error x = (Val (float (round X To_nearest x)) − x)
```

Since $(2^{(j+1)} / 2^{(bias\ X)}) \leq |x|$ for the real numbers in the normalized region as proved in Lemma 2, we have $(|error\ x| / |x|) \leq (2^j / 2^{(bias\ X\ +\ fracwidth\ X)}) / (2^{(j+1)} / 2^{(bias\ X)})$ or $(|error\ x| / |x|) \leq (1 / 2^{((fracwidth\ X)\ +\ 1)})$. Finally, defining $e = (error\ x\ /\ x)$ will complete the proof of the floating-point relative error bound theorem as described in Lemma 1.

Next, we apply the floating-point relative rounding error analysis theorem (Theorem 1) to the verification of the arithmetic operations. The goal is to prove the following theorem in which floating-point arithmetic operations such as addition, subtraction, multiplication, and division are related to their abstract mathematical counterparts according to the corresponding errors.

Theorem 2: Let $*$ denote any of the floating-point operations $+, -, \times, /$. Then

$$fl\ (x * y) = (x * y)(1 + \delta), \quad \text{where } |\delta| \leq 2^{-p} \qquad (2)$$

and p is the precision of the floating-point format. The notation $fl\ (.)$ is used to denote that the operation is performed using the floating-point arithmetic.

To prove this theorem in HOL, we start from the already proved lemmas on the absolute analysis of rounding error in the floating-point arithmetic operations (FLOAT_ADD) developed in [9]. We have converted these lemmas to the following relative error analysis version, using the relative error bound analysis of floating-point rounding (Lemma 1):

```
Lemma 4: FLOAT_ADD_RELATIVE
⊢  Finite a ∧ Finite b ∧ normalizes (Val a + Val b)
    ⟹  Finite (a + b) ∧ ∃ e. abs e ≤ (1 / 2 pow ((fracwidth X) + 1))
        ∧ (Val (a + b) = (Val a + Val b) * (1 + e))
```

where the function *Finite* defines the finiteness criteria for the floating-point numbers. Note that we use the conventional symbols for arithmetic operations on floating-point numbers using the operator overloading in HOL.

3.2   Fixed-Point Error Model

While the rounding error for the floating-point arithmetic enters into the system multiplicatively, it is an additive component for the fixed-point arithmetic. In this case the fundamental error analysis theorem can be stated as follows [23].

Theorem 3: If the real number x located in the range of the fixed-point numbers with format X', is rounded to the closest fixed-point number x'_R, then

$$x'_R = x + \epsilon, \quad \text{where} \quad |\epsilon| \leq 2^{-fracbits\ (X')} \tag{3}$$

and *fracbits* is a function that extracts the number of bits that are to the right of the binary point in the given fixed-point format.

This theorem is proved in HOL as follows [1]:

```
Lemma 5: FXP_ROUND_ABSOLUTE_ERROR_BOUND
⊢ (validAttr X') ∧ (representable X' x) ⟹
   abs (Fxp_error X' x) ≤ (1 / 2 pow (fracbits X'))
```

where the function *validAttr* defines the validity of the fixed-point format, *representable* defines the criteria for a real number to be in the representable range of the fixed-point format, and *Fxp_error* defines the fixed-point rounding error.

The verification of the fixed-point arithmetic operations using the *absolute* error analysis of the fixed-point rounding (Theorem 3) can be stated as in the following theorem in which the fixed-point arithmetic operations are related to their abstract mathematical counterparts according to the corresponding errors.

Theorem 4: Let $*$ denote any of the fixed-point operations $+$, $-$, $\times$, $/$, with a given format X'. Then

$$fxp\ (x * y) = (x * y) + \epsilon, \quad \text{where} \quad |\epsilon| \leq 2^{-fracbits\ (X')} \tag{4}$$

and the notation *fxp (.)* is used to denote that the operation is performed using the fixed-point arithmetic. This theorem is proved in HOL using the following lemma [1]:

```
Lemma 6: FXP_ADD_ABSOLUTE
⊢ (Isvalid a) ∧ (Isvalid b) ∧ validAttr (X') ∧
   representable X' (value a + value b) ⟹  (Isvalid (FxpAdd X' a b)) ∧
   ∃ e. abs e ≤ (1 / 2 pow (fracbits X')) ∧
   value (FxpAdd X' a b) = (value a + value b) + e
```

where *Isvalid* defines the validity of a fixed-point number, *value* is the fixed-point valuation, and *FxpAdd* is the fixed-point addition.

4   Error Analysis of Digital Filters in HOL

In this section, the principal results for the roundoff accumulation in digital filters using the mechanized theorem proving are derived and summarized. We shall employ the models for the floating-point and fixed-point roundoff errors in HOL presented in the previous section. In the following, we will first describe in details the theory behind the analysis and then explain how this analysis is performed in HOL.

The class of digital filters considered in this paper is that of linear constant coefficient filters specified by the difference equation:

$$w_n = \sum_{i=0}^{M} b_i \, x_{n-i} - \sum_{i=1}^{L} a_i \, w_{n-i} \tag{5}$$

where $\{x_n\}$ is the input sequence and $\{w_n\}$ is the output sequence. L is the order of the filter, and M can be any positive number less than L. There are three canonical forms of realizing a digital filter, namely the direct, parallel, and cascade forms (Figure 2) [18].

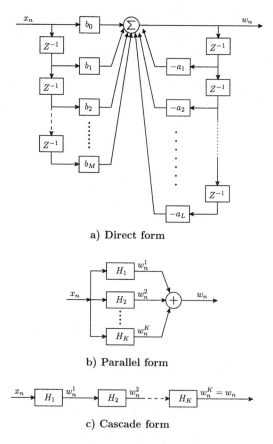

a) Direct form

b) Parallel form

c) Cascade form

Fig. 2. Canonical forms of digital filter realizations

If the output sequence is calculated by using the equation (5), the digital filter is said to be realized in the direct form. Figure 2 (a) illustrates the direct form realization of the filter using the corresponding blocks for the addition, multiplication by a constant operations, and the delay element.

The implementation of a digital filter in the parallel form is shown in Figure 2 (b) in which the entire filter is visualized as the parallel connection of the simpler filters H_i of a lower order. In this case, K intermediate outputs $\{w_n^i\}$, $i = 1,2,\ldots,K$ are first calculated and then summed to form the total output $\{w_n\}$. Therefore, for the input sequence $\{x_n\}$ we have:

$$w_n^i = f_i x_n + g_i x_{n-1} - c_i w_{n-1}^i - d_i w_{n-2}^i \tag{6}$$

where the parameters f_i, g_i, c_i, and d_i are obtained from the parameters a_i and b_i in equation (5) using the parallel expansion. The output of the entire filter w_n, is then related to w_n^i by:

$$w_n = w_n^1 + w_n^2 + \cdots + w_n^K \tag{7}$$

The implementation of a digital filter in the cascade form is shown in Figure 2(c) in which the filter is visualized as a cascade of lower filters. From the input $\{x_n\}$, the intermediate output $\{w_n^1\}$ is first calculated, and then this is the input to the second filter. Continuing in this manner, the final output $w_n^K = w_n$ is calculated. Since the output of the ith section (w_n^i) is the input of the $(i+1)$th section, the following equation holds:

$$w_n^{i+1} = w_n^i + k_i w_{n-1}^i + l_i w_{n-2}^i - c_i w_{n-1}^{i+1} - d_i w_{n-2}^{i+1} \tag{8}$$

where the parameters k_i, l_i, c_i, and d_i are obtained from the parameters a_i and b_i in equation (5) using the serial expansion.

There are three common sources of errors associated with the filter of the equation (5), namely [15]:

1. **input quantization:** caused by the quantization of the input signal $\{x_n\}$ into a set of discrete levels.
2. **coefficient inaccuracy:** caused by the representation of the filter coefficients $\{a_k\}$ and $\{b_k\}$ by a finite word length.
3. **round-off accumulation:** caused by the accumulation of roundoff errors at arithmetic operations.

Therefore, for the digital filter of the equation (5) the actual computed output reference is in general different from $\{w_n\}$. We denote the actual floating-point and fixed-point outputs by $\{y_n\}$ and $\{v_n\}$, respectively. Then, we define the corresponding errors at the nth output sample as:

$$e_n = y_n - w_n \tag{9}$$
$$e_n' = v_n - w_n \tag{10}$$
$$e_n'' = v_n - y_n \tag{11}$$

where e_n and e'_n are defined as the errors between the actual floating-point and fixed-point implementations and the ideal real specification, respectively. e''_n is the error in the transition from the floating-point to fixed-point levels.

It is clear from the above discussion that for the digital filter of the equation (5) realized in the direct form, we have:

$$y_n = fl \left(\sum_{k=0}^{M} b_k \, x_{n-k} - \sum_{k=1}^{L} a_k \, y_{n-k} \right) \tag{12}$$

and

$$v_n = fxp \left(\sum_{k=0}^{M} b_k \, x_{n-k} - \sum_{k=1}^{L} a_k \, v_{n-k} \right) \tag{13}$$

The notations fl (.) and fxp (.) are used to denote that the operations are performed using the floating-point and fixed-point arithmetics, respectively. The calculation is to be performed in the following manner. First, the output products $a_k \, y_{n-k}$, $k = 1,2,\ldots,L$ are calculated separately and then summed. Next, the same is done for the input products $b_k \, x_{n-k}$, $k = 0,1,\ldots,M$. Finally, the output summation is subtracted from the input one to obtain the main floating-point output y_n. Similar discussion can be applied for the calculation of the fixed-point output v_n. The corresponding flowgraph showing the effect of roundoff error using the fundamental error analysis theorems (Theorems 2 and 4) according to the equations (2) and (4), is given by Figure 3, which also indicates the order of the calculation.

Formally, a flowgraph is a network of directed branches that connect at nodes. Associated with each node is a variable or node value. Each branch has an input

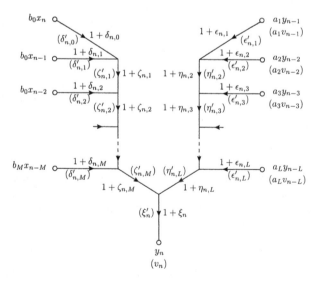

Fig. 3. Error flowgraph for Lth-order filter (Direct form)

signal and an output signal with a direction indicated by an arrowhead on it. In a linear flowgraph, the output of a branch is a linear transformation of the input to the branch. The simplest examples are constant multipliers and adders, i.e., when the output of the branch is simply a multiplication or an addition of the input to the branch with a constant value, which are the only classes we consider in this paper. The linear operation represented by the branch is typically indicated next to the arrowhead showing the direction of the branch. For the case of a constant multiplier and adder, the constant is simply shown next to the arrowhead. When an explicit indication of the branch operation is omitted, this indicates a branch transmittance of unity, or identity transformation. By definition, the value at each node in a flowgraph is the sum of the outputs of all the branches entering the node. To complete the definition of the flowgraph notation, we define two special types of nodes. *(1) Source nodes* that have no entering branches. They are used to represent the injection of the external inputs or signal sources into a flowgraph. *(2) Sink nodes* that have only entering branches. They are used to extract the outputs from a flowgraph [18].

The quantities $\delta_{n,k}, k = 0,1,\ldots,M$, $\epsilon_{n,k}, k = 1,2,\ldots,L$, $\zeta_{n,k}, k = 1,2,\ldots,M$, $\eta_{n,k}, k = 2,3,\ldots,L$, and ξ_n in Figure 3 are errors caused by the floating-point roundoff at each arithmetic step. The corresponding error quantities for the fixed-point roundoff (shown in parentheses) are $\delta'_{n,k}, k = 0,1,\ldots,M$, $\epsilon'_{n,k}, k = 1,2,\ldots,L$, $\zeta'_{n,k}, k = 1,2,\ldots,M$, $\eta'_{n,k}, k = 2,3,\ldots,L$, and ξ'_n. Note that we have used one flowgraph to represent both the floating-point and fixed-point cases, simultaneously. For floating-point errors, the branch operations are interpreted as constant multiplications, while for fixed-point errors the branch operations are interpreted as constant additions. We have surrounded the fixed-point error quantities and output samples by parentheses to distinguish them from their floating-point counterparts. Therefore, the actual outputs y_n and v_n are seen to be given explicitly by:

$$y_n = \sum_{k=0}^{M} b_k\, \theta_{n,k}\, x_{n-k} - \sum_{k=1}^{L} a_k\, \phi_{n,k}\, y_{n-k} \tag{14}$$

where

$$\theta_{n,0} = (1+\xi_n)(1+\delta_{n,0}) \prod_{i=1}^{M}(1+\zeta_{n,i})$$

$$\theta_{n,j} = (1+\xi_n)(1+\delta_{n,j}) \prod_{i=j}^{M}(1+\zeta_{n,i}), \quad \text{where } j = 1,2,\ldots,M$$

$$\phi_{n,1} = (1+\xi_n)(1+\epsilon_{n,1}) \prod_{i=2}^{L}(1+\eta_{n,i})$$

$$\phi_{n,j} = (1+\xi_n)(1+\epsilon_{n,j}) \prod_{i=j}^{L}(1+\eta_{n,i}), \quad \text{where } j = 2,3,\ldots,L$$

and

$$v_n = \sum_{k=0}^{M} b_k \, x_{n-k} - \sum_{k=1}^{L} a_k \, v_{n-k} + \sum_{k=0}^{M} \delta'_{n,k} + \sum_{k=1}^{M} \zeta'_{n,k} + \sum_{k=1}^{L} \epsilon'_{n,k} + \sum_{k=2}^{L} \eta'_{n,k} + \xi'_n \quad (15)$$

For the error analysis, we need to calculate the y_n and v_n sequences from the equations (14) and (15), and compare them with the ideal output sequence w_n specified by the equation (5) to obtain the corresponding errors e_n, e'_n, and e''_n, according to the equations (9), (10), and (11), respectively. Therefore, the difference equations for the errors between the different levels showing the accumulation of the roundoff error are derived as the following error analysis cases:

1. *Real to Floating-Point Error Analysis:*

$$e_n + \sum_{k=1}^{L} a_k \, e_{n-k} = \sum_{k=0}^{M} b_k \, (\theta_{n,k} - 1) \, x_{n-k} - \sum_{k=1}^{L} a_k \, (\phi_{n,k} - 1) \, y_{n-k} \quad (16)$$

2. *Real to Fixed-Point Error Analysis:*

$$e'_n + \sum_{k=1}^{L} a_k \, e'_{n-k} = \sum_{k=0}^{M} \delta'_{n,k} + \sum_{k=1}^{M} \zeta'_{n,k} + \sum_{k=1}^{L} \epsilon'_{n,k} + \sum_{k=2}^{L} \eta'_{n,k} + \xi'_n \quad (17)$$

3. *Floating-Point to Fixed-Point Error Analysis:*

$$e''_n + \sum_{k=1}^{L} a_k \, e''_{n-k} = \sum_{k=0}^{M} \delta'_{n,k} + \sum_{k=1}^{M} \zeta'_{n,k} + \sum_{k=1}^{L} \epsilon'_{n,k} + \sum_{k=2}^{L} \eta'_{n,k} + \xi'_n - \quad (18)$$

$$\sum_{k=0}^{M} b_k \, (\theta_{n,k} - 1) \, x_{n-k} + \sum_{k=1}^{L} a_k \, (\phi_{n,k} - 1) \, y_{n-k}$$

Similar analysis is performed for the parallel and cascade forms of realization based on the error flowgraphs as shown in Figures 4 and 5, respectively.

In HOL, we first specified a parametric Lth-order digital filters at the real, floating-point, and fixed-point abstraction levels, as predicates in higher-order logic. The direct form is defined in HOL using the equation (5). For the real specification, we used the expression $sum\ (m, n)\ f$ denoting $\sum_{i=m}^{m+n-1} f(i)$, which is a function available in the HOL real library [7] and defines the finite summation on the real numbers. For the floating-point and fixed-point specifications, we defined similar functions for the finite summations on the floating-point ($float\_sum$) and fixed-point (fxp_sum) numbers, using the recursive definition in HOL. For the parallel form, we first specified the ith parallel path using the equation (6). Then, we specified the entire output as defined in equation (7), using the finite summation functions. Finally, we specified the cascade form of realization as defined in equation (8), using recursive definitions in HOL. For the error analysis of the digital filters in HOL, we first established lemmas to compute the output

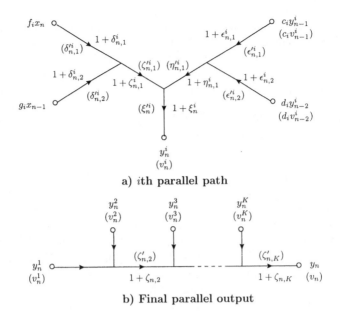

a) ith parallel path

b) Final parallel output

Fig. 4. Error flowgraph for Lth-order filter (Parallel form)

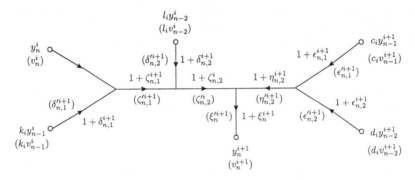

Fig. 5. Error flowgraph for Lth-order filter (Cascade form)

real values of the floating-point and fixed-point filters according to the equations (14) and (15), for the direct form of realization. For this, we need to define the finite product on the real numbers. We defined this function in HOL recursively as the expression $mul\ (m,n)\ f$ denoting $\prod_{i=m}^{m+n-1} f(i)$. Finally, we defined the errors as the differences between the output of the real filter specification, and the corresponding real values of the floating-point and fixed-point filter implementations ($Real\_To\_Float\_Error, Real\_To\_Fxp\_Error$), and the error in transition from the floating-point to fixed-point levels ($Float\_To\_Fxp\_Error$), according to the equations (9), (10), and (11), respectively. Then, we established lemmas for the accumulation of the round-off error between the different levels, according to the equations (16), (17), and (18). Finally, we proved these lemmas using the fundamental floating-point and fixed-point error analysis lemmas, based on the error models presented in Section 3. The lemmas are proved by induction on the parameters L and M for the direct form of realization. Similar analysis is performed in HOL for the parallel and cascade realization forms. For these cases, we proved the corresponding lemmas by induction on the parameter K which is defined as the number of the internal sub-filters connected in parallel or cascade forms to generate the final output. The corresponding error analysis lemmas in HOL for the direct form of realization are listed in Appendix A.

5   Conclusions

In this paper, we describe a comprehensive methodology for the error analysis of generic digital filters using the HOL theorem prover. The proposed approach covers the three canonical forms (direct, parallel and cascade) of realization entirely specified in HOL. We make use of existing theories in HOL on real, IEEE standard based floating-point, and fixed-point arithmetic to model the ideal filter specification and the corresponding implementations in higher-order logic. We used valuation functions to define the errors as the differences between the real values of the floating-point and fixed-point filter implementation outputs and the corresponding output of the ideal real filter specification. Finally, we established fundamental analysis lemmas as our model to derive expressions for the accumulation of the roundoff error in digital filters. Related work did exist since the late sixties using theoretical paper-and-pencil proofs and simulation techniques. We believe this is the first time a complete formal framework is considered using mechanical proofs in HOL for the error analysis of digital filters. As a future work, we plan to extend these lemmas to analyse the worst-case, average, and variance errors. We also plan to extend the verification to the lower levels of abstraction, and prove that the implementation of a digital filter at the register transfer and netlist gate levels implies the corresponding fixed-point specification using classical hierarchical verification in HOL, hence bridging the gap between the hardware implementation and high levels of the mathematical specification. Finally, we plan to link HOL with computer algebra systems to create a sound, reliable, and powerful system for the verification of DSP systems. This opens new avenues in using formal methods for the verification of DSP systems as a complement to the traditional theoretical (analytical) and simulation techniques. We are currently investigating the verification of other DSP algorithms such as the fast Fourier transform (FFT) which is widely used as a building block in the design of complex wired and wireless communication systems.

References

1. B. Akbarpour, S. Tahar, and A. Dekdouk, "Formalization of Cadence SPW Fixed-Point Arithmetic in HOL," In Integrated Formal Methods, LNCS 2335, Springer-Verlag, pp. 185-204, 2002.

2. B. Akbarpour, and S. Tahar, "Modeling SystemC Fixed-Point Arithmetic in HOL," In Formal Methods and Software Engineering, LNCS 2885, Springer-Verlag, pp. 206-225, 2003.

3. Cadence Design Systems, Inc., "Signal Processing WorkSystem (SPW) User's Guide," USA, July 1999.

4. G. Forsythe, and C. B. Moler, "Computer Solution of Linear Algebraic Systems," Prentice-Hall, 1967.

5. M. J. C. Gordon, and T. F. Melham, "Introduction to HOL: A Theorem Proving Environment for Higher-Order Logic," Cambridge University Press, 1993.

6. B. Gold, and C. M. Radar, "Effects of Quantization Noise in Digital Filters," In Proceedings AFIPS Spring Joint Computer Conference, vol. 28, pp. 213-219, 1966.

7. J. R. Harrison, "Constructing the Real Numbers in HOL," Formal Methods in System Design, 5 (1/2): 35-59, 1994.

8. J. R. Harrison, "A Machine-Checked Theory of Floating-Point Arithmetic," In Theorem Proving in Higher Order Logics, LNCS 1690, Springer-Verlag, pp. 113-130, 1999.

9. J. R. Harrison, "Floating-Point Verification in HOL Light: The Exponential Function," Formal Methods in System Design, 16 (3): 271-305, 2000.

10. J. R. Harrison, and L. Théry, "A Skeptic's Approach to Combining Hol and Maple," Journal of Automated Reasoning, 21: 279-294, 1998.

11. M. Huhn, K. Schneider, T. Kropf, and G. Logothetis, "Verifying Imprecisely Working Arithmetic Circuits," In Proceedings Design Automation and Test in Europe Conference, pp. 65-69, March 1999.

12. L. B. Jackson, "Roundoff-Noise Analysis for Fixed-Point Digital Filters Realized in Cascade or Parallel Form," IEEE Transactions on Audio and Electroacoustics, AU-18: 107-122, June 1970.

13. J. F. Kaiser, "Digital Filters," In System Analysis by Digital Computer, F. F. Kuo and J. F. Kaiser, Eds., pp. 218-285, Wiley, 1966.

14. J. B. Knowles, and R. Edwards, "Effects of a Finite-Word-Length Computer in a Sampled-Data Feedback System," IEE Proceedings, 112: 1197-1207, June 1965.

15. B. Liu, and T. Kaneko, "Error Analysis of Digital Filters Realized with Floating-Point Arithmetic," Proceedings of the IEEE, 57: 1735-1747, October 1969.

16. Mathworks, Inc., "Simulink Reference Manual," USA, 1996.

17. A. V. Oppenheim, and C. J. Weinstein, "Effects of Finite Register Length in Digital Filtering and the Fast Fourier Transform," Proceedings of the IEEE, 60 (8): 957-976, August 1972.

18. A. V. Oppenheim, and R. W. Schafer, "Discrete-Time Signal Processing," Prentice-Hall, 1989.

19. I. W. Sandberg, "Floating-Point-Roundoff Accumulation in Digital Filter Realization," The Bell System Technical Journal, 46: 1775-1791, October 1967.

20. Synopsys, Inc., "CoCentric^{TM} System Studio User's Guide," USA, August 2001.

21. C. Weinstein, and A. V. Oppenheim, "A Comparison of Roundoff Noise in Floating Point and Fixed Point Digital Filter Realizations," Proceedings of the IEEE (Proceedings Letters), 57: 1181-1183, June 1969.

22. H. Keding, M. Willems, M. Coors, and H. Meyr, "FRIDGE: A Fixed-Point Design and Simulation Environment," In Proceedings Design Automation and Test in Europe Conference, pp. 429-435, February 1998.

23. J. H. Wilkinson, "Rounding Errors in Algebraic Processes," Prentice-Hall, 1963.

A   Digital Filter Error Analysis Lemmas in HOL

Lemma 7: L_ORDER_FILTER_DIRECT_FORM_REAL_TO_FLOAT_THM

⊢ L_Order_Filter_Direct_Form_Ideal_Spec a b x w M L ∧
L_Order_Filter_Direct_Form_Float_Imp X a′ b′ x′ y M L ⟹
∃ t f.
if (L = 0) then
    (Real_To_Float_Error n = sum (0,SUC M) (λ i. Val (b′ i) *
    (t i − 1) * Val (x′ (n − i))))
else
    ((Real_To_Float_Error n + sum (1,L) (λ i. a i *
    Real_To_Float_Error (n − i)) = sum (0,SUC M) (λ i. Val (b′ i) *
    (t i − 1) * Val (x′ (n − i))) − sum (1,L) (λ i. Val (a′ i) *
    (f i − 1) * Val (y (n − i))))) ∧
∃ k d p e z.
(abs k ≤ (1 / 2 pow ((fracwidth X) + 1))) ∧
(∀ i. (i ≤ M) ⟹ (abs (d i) ≤ (1 / 2 pow ((fracwidth X) + 1)))) ∧
(∀ i. (i ≤ M) ⟹ (abs (p i) ≤ (1 / 2 pow ((fracwidth X) + 1)))) ∧
(∀ i. (i ≤ L) ⟹ (abs (e i) ≤ (1 / 2 pow ((fracwidth X) + 1)))) ∧
(∀ i. (i ≤ L) ⟹ (abs (z i) ≤ (1 / 2 pow ((fracwidth X) + 1)))) ∧
(t 0 = (1 + k) * (1 + d 0) * (mul (1,M) (λ i. (1 + p i)))) ∧
(∀ j. (1 ≤ j ∧ j ≤ M) ⟹ (t j = (1 + k) * (1 + d j) *
(mul (j,(M − (j − 1))) (λ j. (1 + p j))))) ∧
(f 1 = (1 + k) * (1 + e 1) * (mul (2,(L − 1)) (λ i. (1 + z i)))) ∧
(∀ j. (2 ≤ j ∧ j ≤ L) ⟹
(f j = (1 + k) * (1 + e j) * (mul (j,(L − j + 1)) (λ j. (1 + z j)))))

Lemma 8: L_ORDER_FILTER_DIRECT_FORM_REAL_TO_FXP_THM

⊢ L_Order_Filter_Direct_Form_Ideal_Spec a b x w M L ∧
L_Order_Filter_Direct_Form_Fxp_Imp X′ a″ b″ x″ v M L ⟹
∃ k′ d′ p′ e′ z′.
abs k′ ≤ (1 / 2 pow (fracbits X′)) ∧
(∀ i. (i ≤ M) ⟹ abs (d′ i) ≤ (1 / 2 pow (fracbits X′))) ∧
(∀ i. (i ≤ M) ⟹ abs (p′ i) ≤ (1 / 2 pow (fracbits X′))) ∧
(∀ i. (i ≤ L) ⟹ abs (e′ i) ≤ (1 / 2 pow (fracbits X′))) ∧
(∀ i. (i ≤ L) ⟹ abs (z′ i) ≤ (1 / 2 pow (fracbits X′))) ∧
if (L = 0) then
    (Real_To_Fxp_Error n = sum (0,SUC M) (λ i. d′ i) +
    sum (1,M) (λ j. p′ j) + k′)
else
    (Real_To_Fxp_Error n + sum (1,L) (λ i. a i * Real_To_Fxp_Error
    (n − i)) = sum (0,SUC M) (λ i. d′ i) + sum (1,M) (λ j. p′ j) +
    sum (1,L) (λ i. e′ i) + sum (2,(L − 1)) (λ j. z′ j) + k′))

Lemma 9: L_ORDER_FILTER_DIRECT_FORM_FLOAT_TO_FXP_THM

⊢ L_Order_Filter_Direct_Form_Ideal_Spec a b x w M L $\wedge$
   L_Order_Filter_Direct_Form_Float_Imp X a′ b′ x′ y M L $\wedge$
   L_Order_Filter_Direct_Form_Fxp_Imp X′ a″ b″ x″ v M L $\implies$
   $\exists$ t f k′ d′ p′ e′ z′.
   if (L = 0) then
        (Float_To_Fxp_Error n = sum (0,SUC M) (λ i. d′ i) +
        sum (1,M) (λ j. p′ j) + k′ − (sum (0,SUC M)
        (λ i. Val (b′ i) * (t i − 1) * Val (x′ (n − i)))))
   else
        (Float_To_Fxp_Error n + sum (1,L) (λ i. a i * Float_To_Fxp_Error
        (n − i)) = sum (0,SUC M) (λ i. d′ i) + sum (1,M) (λ j. p′ j) +
        sum (1,L) (λ i. e′ i) + sum (2,(L − 1)) (λ j. z′ j) + k′ −
        sum (0, (SUC M)) (λ i. Val (b′ i) * (t i − 1) * Val (x′ (n − i)))
        + sum (1,L) (λ i. Val (a′ i) * (f i − 1) * Val (y (n − i)))))

Verifying Uniqueness in a Logical Framework

Penny Anderson[1] and Frank Pfenning[2,*]

[1] Department of Computer Science, Lafayette College
penny@cs.lafayette.edu
[2] Department of Computer Science, Carnegie Mellon University
fp@cs.cmu.edu

Abstract. We present an algorithm for verifying that some specified arguments of an inductively defined relation in a dependently typed λ-calculus are uniquely determined by some other arguments. We prove it correct and also show how to exploit this uniqueness information in coverage checking, which allows us to verify that a definition of a function or relation covers all possible cases. In combination, the two algorithms significantly extend the power of the meta-reasoning facilities of the Twelf implementation of LF.

1 Introduction

In most logics and type theories, unique existence is not a primitive notion, but defined via existence and equality. For example, we might define $\exists!x.A(x)$ to stand for $\exists x.A(x) \land \forall y.A(y) \supset x = y$. Such definitions are usually made in both first-order and higher-order logic, and in both the intuitionistic and the classical case. Expanding unique existence assertions in this manner comes at a price: not only do we duplicate the formula A, but we also introduce two quantifiers and an explicit equality. It is therefore natural to ask if we could derive some benefit for theorem proving by taking unique existence as a primitive.

In this paper we consider an instance of this problem, namely verifying and exploiting uniqueness in a logical framework. We show how to establish uniqueness of certain arguments to type families in the logical framework LF [7] as implemented in the Twelf system [15]. We further show how to exploit this uniqueness information to verify meta-theoretic properties of signatures, thereby checking proofs of meta-theorems presented as relations in LF. In particular, we can automatically verify the unique existence of specified output arguments in a relation with respect to some given input arguments. Our algorithm will always terminate, but, since the problem is in general undecidable, will sometimes fail to establish uniqueness even though it holds.

Our algorithm extends prior work on coverage checking [24] and mode checking [18], which in combination with termination checking [16], can verify meta-theoretic proofs such as cut elimination [12], the Church-Rosser theorem [19], logical translations [13], or the soundness of Foundational Typed Assembly Language [3,4]. The specific motivation for this work came mostly from the latter, in which a significant portion of the development was devoted to tedious but

---

* This research has been supported by NSF Grant CCR-0306313.

K. Slind et al. (Eds.): TPHOLs 2004, LNCS 3223, pp. 18–33, 2004.
© Springer-Verlag Berlin Heidelberg 2004

straightforward reasoning about equality. Our algorithms can automate much of that.

We believe that our techniques can be adapted to other systems of constructive type theory to recognize properties of relations. In that direction, the research can be seen as an extension of the work by McBride [11] and Coquand [2], who present procedures for deciding whether a definition by pattern matching of a dependently typed function consists of cases that are exhaustive and mutually exclusive. Here, we permit not only inputs containing abstractions, but also relational specifications, which are pervasive and unavoidable in constructive type theories. Like the prior work on functions, but unlike prior work on coverage checking [19, 24], we can also verify uniqueness and unique existence.

The remainder of the paper is organized as follows. In Section 2 we briefly introduce the notation of the LF type theory used throughout. In Section 3 we describe our algorithm for verifying uniqueness of specified arguments to relations, and we prove its correctness in Section 4. In Section 5 we briefly review coverage checking, one of the central algorithms in verifying the correctness of meta-theoretic proofs. In Section 6 we show how to exploit uniqueness information to increase the power of coverage checking. We conclude in Section 7 with some further remarks about related and future work.

2   The LF Type Theory

We use a standard formulation of the LF type theory [7]; we summarize here only the basic notations. We use a for type families, c for object-level constants, and x for (object-level) variables. We say *term* to refer to an expression from any of the three levels of kinds, types, and objects.

$$
\begin{array}{rll}
\text{Kinds} & K ::= \text{type} \mid \Pi x{:}A.K \\
\text{Types} & A, B ::= a\, M_1 \ldots M_n \mid \Pi x{:}A.B \\
\text{Objects} & M, N ::= c \mid x \mid \lambda x{:}A.M \mid M\,N \\
\text{Signatures} & \Sigma ::= \cdot \mid \Sigma, a{:}K \mid \Sigma, c{:}A \\
\text{Contexts} & \Gamma, \Delta ::= \cdot \mid \Gamma, x{:}A \\
\text{Substitutions} & \theta, \sigma ::= \cdot \mid \theta, M/x
\end{array}
$$

Contexts and substitutions may declare a variable at most once; signatures may declare families and constants at most once. We do not distinguish terms from any of the three levels that differ only in the names of their bound variables. Our notion of definitional equality is $\beta\eta$-conversion, and we tacitly exploit the property that every kind, type, and object has a unique long $\beta\eta$-normal form [1, 8] which we call *canonical*. The relatively simple nature of this definitional equality avoids some thorny issues regarding intensional and extensional equality in constructive type theories [10, 9] that would complicate our analysis. We omit type-level λ-abstractions from the syntax since they do not occur in canonical forms. The principal judgments we use are:

$$\Gamma \vdash_\Sigma A : \text{type} \qquad \text{Type } A \text{ is valid}$$
$$\Gamma \vdash_\Sigma M : A \qquad \text{Object } M \text{ has type } A$$
$$\Gamma \vdash_\Sigma \theta : \Delta \qquad \text{Substitution } \theta \text{ matches context } \Delta$$

Since all judgments are standard we only show the last one for typing substitutions which is perhaps less widely known. We write $M[\theta]$ and $A[\theta]$ for the application of a substitution.

$$\frac{}{\Gamma \vdash \cdot : \cdot} \qquad \frac{\Gamma \vdash \theta : \Delta \qquad \Gamma \vdash M : A[\theta]}{\Gamma \vdash (\theta, M/x) : (\Delta, x{:}A)}$$

So a substitution $\Gamma \vdash \theta : \Delta$ maps a term defined over a context Δ to a term over a context Γ. We write $\theta_1 \circ \theta_2$ for composition of substitutions, so that $M[\theta_1][\theta_2] = M[\theta_1 \circ \theta_2]$, and write id_Γ for the identity substitution $\Gamma \vdash \text{id}_\Gamma : \Gamma$.

As a running example we use natural numbers defined in terms of zero (z) and successor (s), together with relations for inequality (le) and addition (plus).[1] The corresponding signature is given in Figure 1. Note that free variables in a declaration are implicitly universally quantified in that declaration; the Twelf implementation will reconstruct these quantifiers and the types of the free variables [15].

```
nat : type.
z  : nat.
s  : nat → nat.
le : nat → nat → type.
le_refl : le X X.
le_s : le X Y → le X (s Y).
plus : nat → nat → nat → type.
plus_z : plus z X X.
plus_s : plus X₁ X₂ Y → plus (s X₁) X₂ (s Y).
```

Fig. 1. Natural numbers with ordering and addition

3   Uniqueness Mode Checking

Logical frameworks that support higher-order abstract syntax, such as LF or hereditary Harrop formulas, are based on a simply typed or dependently typed

---

[1] This running example does not illustrate the higher-order nature of our analysis, but unfortunately space constraints do not permit us to include larger and more realistic examples. However, we have executed the uniqueness checker against higher-order examples drawn from [3, 4].

λ-calculus. Function spaces in such a calculus are purposely impoverished in order to support the use of meta-language functions to represent object language abstractions and hypothetical proofs: too many such functions would invalidate the judgments-as-types or judgments-as-propositions methodology. In particular, these frameworks prohibit function definitions by cases or by primitive recursion. Adding such functions appears to require modal types or an explicit stratification of the type theory [5, 23, 20, 21]; related approaches are still a subject of current research (see, for example, [25, 22]).

The traditional and practically tested approach is to represent more complex functions as either type families or relations, depending on whether the framework is a type theory or a logic.[2] In many cases relational representations of functions are sufficient, but there are also many instances where meta-reasoning requires us to know that relations do indeed represent (possibly partial) functions. We can encode this property by defining explicit equality relations. For example, if we need to know that the relation plus is actually a function of its first two arguments, we can define

```
eq  : nat  →  nat  →  type.
refl  : eq X X.
```

We then have to prove: "If plus X_1 X_2 Y and plus X_1 X_2 Y' then eq Y Y'."

There are two difficulties with this approach: the first is simply that equality predicates need to be threaded through many judgments, and various rather trivial and tedious properties need to be proved about them. The second is that this methodology interferes with dependent typing because the equality between Y and Y' in the example above cannot be exploited by type-checking, since eq is just a user-declared relation.

As uses of the meta-reasoning capabilities of the logical framework become increasingly complex [3, 4], intrinsic support for recognizing and exploiting relations that are indeed functions is becoming more and more important. There are two distinct, interconnected problems to be solved. The first is to verify that particular relations are partial functions. The second is to exploit this information to verify that the same or other relations are total.

In this section we address the former: how can we automatically verify that particular relations are partial functions of some of their inputs. This is a stricter version of *mode checking* familiar from logic programming. There, we designate some arguments to a relation as inputs and others as outputs. The property we verify with mode checking is that if the inputs are given as ground terms, and proof search succeeds, then the outputs will also be ground terms [18]. The sharpened version requires in addition that if proof search succeeds, then some designated outputs are uniquely determined. We refer to this process as *uniqueness mode checking*.

---

[2] Even though we are working in the LF type theory, we will use the terms *type family*, *relation*, and *predicate* interchangeably, expressing the intended meaning of the type families under consideration.

In our applications we actually need to exploit a slightly stronger property: if the designated input arguments to a relation are given as ground terms, then designated output arguments must be ground and uniquely determined, *independent of the proof search strategy*. In other words, our analysis must be based on a non-deterministically complete proof search strategy, rather than depth-first logic program execution (which is incomplete).

We use terminology from logic programming in the description of our algorithm below.

For the sake of simplicity we restrict the relations for which we verify uniqueness to consist of Horn clauses, which means the relations we analyze are inductively defined. However, the domains of quantification in the clauses are still arbitrary LF terms, which may be dependently typed and of arbitrary order.

In our syntax for the Horn fragment, we refer to a constant declaration that is to be analyzed as a *clause*. We group dependently occurring arguments into a quantifier prefix $\Pi\Gamma$ and the non-dependent arguments into a conjunction of *subgoals* G. We call the atomic type Q the *head* of a clause $c : \Pi\Gamma. G \to Q$. We sometimes refer to a term with free variables that are subject to unification as a *pattern*. All constructors for type families a appearing at the head of an atomic goal in a program must also be part of the program and satisfy the Horn clause restrictions.

$$
\begin{array}{lll}
\textit{Atomic Goals } Q & ::= & a\ M_1 \ldots M_n \\
\textit{Goals} & G & ::= Q \mid G_1 \wedge G_2 \mid \top \\
\textit{Clauses} & D & ::= c : \Pi\Gamma.\ G \to Q \\
\textit{Programs} & \mathcal{P} & ::= D_1, \ldots, D_n
\end{array}
$$

In the implementation, we do not make this restriction and instead analyze arbitrary LF signatures, enriched with *world declarations* [19]. A description and correctness proof of this extension is the subject of current research and beyond the scope of this paper.

Mode declarations. In order to verify mode properties of relations, we specify each argument of a relation to be either an input (+), an output (-), a unique output (-1), or unmoded (*). Intuitively, the declarations are tied to a non-deterministic proof search semantics and express:

> If all input (+) arguments to a predicate are ground when it is invoked, and search succeeds, then all output arguments are ground (-). Moreover, in all successful proofs, corresponding unique outputs (-1) must not only be ground, but equal. Unmoded arguments remain unconstrained.

Mode information for a type family a is reflected in the functions $\text{ins}(a)$, $\text{outs}(a)$, and $\text{uouts}(a)$, returning the sets of indices for the input arguments, output arguments, and unique output arguments respectively.

In our example, the following declarations would be correct:

```
%mode le +X -Y.
%mode plus +X1 +X2 -1Y.
```

The first one expresses that if a goal of the form le M Y for a ground term M succeeds, then Y must also be ground. The second one expresses that every successful search for a proof of plus M_1 M_2 Y with ground M_1 and M_2 yields the same term N for Y. In other words, plus represents a partial function from its first two arguments to its third argument. The second declaration yields ins(plus) = $\{1, 2\}$, outs(plus) = $\{\,\}$, and uouts(plus) = $\{3\}$.

Our algorithm for uniqueness mode checking verifies two properties: disjointness of input arguments and uniqueness of output arguments.

Disjointness of inputs. For a given relation with some uniqueness modes on its output arguments, we verify that no two clause heads unify on their input arguments. This entails that any goal with ground input arguments unifies with no more than one clause head. As an example, consider the relation plus from Figure 1 with mode plus +X1 +X2 -1Y. Uniqueness mode checking verifies that plus z X _ and plus (s X_1) X_2 _ do not have a unifier. This is easy because z and s in the first argument clash. We use the algorithm in [6] which will always terminate, but may sometimes generate constraints that cannot be solved. In that case, uniqueness mode checking will fail.

Strictness. Because we can make the assumption that input arguments are ground, what is most relevant to our analysis is not full unification, but higher-order dependently typed matching. Schürmann [19] has shown that each variable in a higher-order matching problem that has at least one strict occurrence has a unique, ground solution. An occurrence of a variable is *strict* if it is applied to distinct bound variables and it is not in an argument to another unification variable (see [14] for a more formal definition).

Strictness is central in our analysis to conclude that if matching a pattern against a ground term succeeds, variables with at least one strict occurrence in the pattern are guaranteed to be ground. In our specific situation, we actually employ unification of two types $a\,M_1 \ldots M_n \doteq a\,N_1 \ldots N_n$ where certain subproblems (for example, $M_i \doteq N_i$ for $i \in$ ins(a)) are known to be matching problems.

Checking uniqueness of outputs. Uniqueness of outputs is verified by an abstract non-deterministic logic programming interpreter with left-to-right subgoal selection[3]. The domain used is the space of abstract substitutions with elements *unknown* (u), *ground* (g), and *unique* (q) for each variable x where u carries no information and q the most information. Note that in order for a variable to be unique (q) it must also be ground. Variables of unknown status (u) may become known as ground (g) or unique (q) during analysis in the following situations:

– An unknown variable that occurs in a strict position in an input argument of the clause head becomes known to be unique.

---

[3] Left-to-right subgoal selection is convenient for this abstract interpretation, but not critical for its soundness.

$\Psi \vdash Q^{+1} > \Psi'$	all strict variables in inputs of Q are q in Ψ'
$\Psi \vdash Q^- > \Psi'$	all strict variables in outputs of Q are at least g in Ψ'
$\Psi \vdash Q^{-1} > \Psi'$	all strict variables in unique outputs of Q are q in Ψ'
$\Psi \vdash Q^{+1}$	if all variables in inputs of Q are q
$\Psi \vdash Q^+$	if all variables in inputs of Q are at least g
$\Psi \vdash Q^{-1}$	if all variables in unique outputs of Q are q
$\Psi \vdash Q^-$	if all variables in outputs of Q are at least g

Fig. 2. Judgments on abstract substitutions

- An unknown variable becomes known to be ground if it occurs in a strict position in the output of a subgoal all of whose inputs are known to be ground or unique.
- An unknown or ground variable becomes known to be unique if it occurs in a strict position in a unique output of a subgoal all of whose inputs are known to be unique.

We next describe in detail the uniqueness mode checking for the Horn clause fragment of LF. The checker relies on two sets of judgments on *abstract substitutions*, which provide reliable, though approximate, information about the actual substitution at any point during search for a proof of a goal. The corresponding non-deterministic search strategy is explained in Section 4.

$$\begin{array}{ll} \text{\textit{Abstract objects}} & \mu ::= \mathsf{u} \mid \mathsf{g} \mid \mathsf{q} \\ \text{\textit{Abstract substitutions}} \ \Psi ::= \cdot \mid \Psi, \mu/x \end{array}$$

The first set of judgments have the form $\Psi \vdash Q^m > \Psi'$ where Ψ is an abstract substitution with known information, Q is an atomic predicate $a\,M_1 \ldots M_n$, m indicates which arguments to a are analyzed, and Ψ' is the result of the analysis of Q. Both Ψ and Ψ' will be defined on the free variables in Q. Moreover, Ψ' will always contain the same or more information than Ψ.

The second set of judgments $\Psi \vdash Q^m$ hold if Q satisfies a property specified by m given the information in Ψ. Again, if $\Gamma \vdash Q : \text{type}$, then Ψ will be defined on the variables in Γ. The various forms of these judgments are given in Figure 2.

The judgments on abstract substitutions are employed by the uniqueness mode checker, which is itself based on two judgments: $\vdash c : \Pi\Gamma.G \to P$ for checking clauses in the program, and $\Psi \vdash G > \Psi'$ for analyzing goals G, where Ψ' may contain more information than Ψ and both Ψ and Ψ' are defined on the free variables of G.

The mode checker is defined by the inference rules of Figure 3. We view these rules as an algorithm for mode checking by assuming Ψ and G to be given, and constructing Ψ' such that $\Psi \vdash G > \Psi'$, searching for derivations of the premises from first to last. We write $\Psi(\Gamma)$ for the abstract context corresponding to the (concrete) context Γ, where each variable is marked as unknown (u).

Definition 1 (Mode correct programs). *Given a program $\mathcal{P}$, we write $\mathcal{P}(a)$ for the set of clauses in $\mathcal{P}$ with a as head. We say $\mathcal{P}$ is mode-correct if*

$$\frac{\begin{array}{l} \Psi(\Gamma) \vdash P^{+1} > \Psi_1 \\ \Psi_1 \vdash G > \Psi_2 \\ \Psi_2 \vdash P^- \\ \Psi_2 \vdash P^{-1} \end{array}}{\vdash c : \Pi\Gamma.G \to P} \qquad \frac{\begin{array}{l} \Psi_0 \vdash Q^{+1} \\ \Psi_0 \vdash Q^- > \Psi_1 \\ \Psi_1 \vdash Q^{-1} > \Psi_2 \end{array}}{\Psi_0 \vdash Q > \Psi_2} \qquad \frac{\begin{array}{l} \Psi_0 \vdash Q^+ \\ \Psi_0 \vdash Q^- > \Psi_1 \end{array}}{\Psi_0 \vdash Q > \Psi_1}$$

$$\frac{\begin{array}{l} \Psi_0 \vdash G_1 > \Psi_1 \\ \Psi_1 \vdash G_2 > \Psi_2 \end{array}}{\Psi_0 \vdash G_1 \wedge G_2 > \Psi_2} \qquad \frac{}{\Psi_0 \vdash \mathsf{T} > \Psi_0}$$

Fig. 3. Uniqueness mode checking

1. *For every type family a in $\mathcal{P}$, if a is declared to have unique outputs, then for any two distinct $c_1 : \Pi\Gamma_1.G_1 \to Q_1$ and $c_2 : \Pi\Gamma_2.G_2 \to Q_2$ in $\mathcal{P}(a)$, Q_1 and Q_2 are not unifiable on their inputs.*
2. *For every constant c declared in $\mathcal{P}$, we have $\vdash c : \Pi\Gamma.G \to P$*

Part (2) of the definition requires each predicate to have a mode declaration, but we may default this to consider all arguments unmoded ($*$) if none is given.

As an example, consider once again the plus predicate from Figure 1 with mode plus +X1 +X2 -1Y. We have to check clauses plus_z and plus_s. We present the derivations in linear style, eliding arguments to predicates that are ignored in any particular judgments.

$$\frac{\begin{array}{l} u/X \vdash (\text{plus z } X \ \_)^{+1} > q/X \\ q/X \vdash \mathsf{T} > q/X \\ q/X \vdash (\text{plus } \_\ \_\ \_)^- \\ q/X \vdash (\text{plus } \_\ \_\ X)^{-1} \end{array}}{\vdash \text{plus\_z} : \Pi X{:}\text{nat}. \ \mathsf{T} \to \text{plus z } X \ X}$$

$$\frac{\begin{array}{l} u/X_1, u/X_2, u/Y \vdash (\text{plus } (\text{s } X_1) \ X_2 \ \_)^{+1} > q/X_1, q/X_2, u/Y \\ q/X_1, q/X_2, u/Y \vdash (\text{plus } X_1 \ X_2 \ \_)^{+1} \\ q/X_1, q/X_2, u/Y \vdash (\text{plus } \_\ \_\ \_)^- > q/X_1, q/X_2, u/Y \\ q/X_1, q/X_2, u/Y \vdash (\text{plus } \_\ \_\ Y)^{-1} > q/X_1, q/X_2, q/Y \\ q/X_1, q/X_2, u/Y \vdash \text{plus } X_1 \ X_2 \ Y > q/X_1, q/X_2, q/Y \\ q/X_1, q/X_2, q/Y \vdash (\text{plus } \_\ \_\ \_)^- \\ q/X_1, q/X_2, q/Y \vdash (\text{plus } \_\ \_\ (\text{s } Y))^{-1} \end{array}}{\vdash \text{plus\_s} : \Pi X_1{:}\text{nat}. \ \Pi X_2{:}\text{nat}. \ \Pi Y{:}\text{nat}. \ \text{plus } X_1 \ X_2 \ Y \to \text{plus } (\text{s } X_1) \ X_2 \ (\text{s } Y).}$$

4   Correctness of Uniqueness Mode Checking

We next define a non-deterministic operational semantics for the Horn fragment and show that uniqueness mode checking approximates it. The judgment has the form $\theta \models G > \theta'$, where θ and θ' are substitutions for the free variables in goal G. We think of θ and goal G as given and construct a derivation and substitution θ'.

The semantics is given by the system of Figure 4. In the first rule, σ and θ_1 represent substitutions that unify P and $Q[\theta_0]$. The fact that these substitutions may not be computable, or that they may not be most general, does not concern us here, since uniqueness mode checking guarantees that *any* unifier must ground all variables in Γ that have a strict occurrence in the input arguments of P, provided the input arguments of $Q[\theta_0]$ are ground.

$$\frac{\Pi\Gamma.G \to P \in \mathcal{P} \qquad P[\sigma] = Q[\theta_0][\theta_1] \qquad \sigma \models G > \theta_2}{\theta_0 \models Q > \theta_0 \circ \theta_1 \circ \theta_2}$$

$$\frac{\theta_0 \models G_1 > \theta_1 \qquad \theta_1 \models G_2 > \theta_2}{\theta_0 \models G_1 \wedge G_2 > \theta_2} \qquad \frac{}{\theta_0 \models \mathsf{T} > \theta_0}$$

Fig. 4. Operational semantics

Definition 2 (Approximation). *We define when an abstract substitution approximates a set of substitutions as follows: Given an abstract substitution $\Psi : \Gamma$ and a set Θ of substitutions $\Gamma_i' \vdash \theta_i : \Gamma$, we say Ψ approximates Θ ($\Psi \prec \Theta$) if for every x in the domain of Ψ*

1. *if $\Psi(x) = \mathsf{g}$ then for all $\theta_i \in \Theta$, $\theta_i(x)$ is ground, and*
2. *if $\Psi(x) = \mathsf{q}$ then for some ground term M and all $\theta_i \in \Theta$, $\theta_i(x) = M$.*

Lemma 1 (Soundness of uniqueness mode checking). *Let $\mathcal{P}$ be a mode-correct program, G a goal, $\Psi : \Gamma$ an abstract substitution such that $\Psi \vdash G > \Psi'$, and Θ a set of substitutions. If $\Psi \prec \Theta$ then $\Psi' \prec \{\rho \mid \theta \models G > \rho, \theta \in \Theta\}$.*

Proof. We let D be the set of all derivations of $\theta \models G > \rho$ for all $\theta \in \Theta$. We show by induction on pairs (d, d') of derivations in D, where d derives $\theta \models G > \rho$ and d' derives $\theta' \models G > \rho'$, that if $\Psi \prec \{\theta, \theta'\}$ then $\Psi' \prec \{\rho, \rho'\}$. Since d, d' are arbitrary the lemma follows for the whole set.

The only nontrivial case is that of an atomic goal Q where the mode checking derivation for Q has the form

$$\frac{\begin{array}{l} \Psi_0 \vdash Q^{+1} \\ \Psi_0 \vdash Q^- > \Psi_1 \\ \Psi_1 \vdash Q^{-1} > \Psi_2 \end{array}}{\Psi_0 \vdash Q > \Psi_2} \qquad \begin{array}{l} \text{(input variables of } Q \text{ must be mapped to } \mathsf{q}) \\ \text{(output variables of } Q \text{ are mapped to } \mathsf{g}) \\ \text{(unique output variables of } Q \text{ are mapped to } \mathsf{q}) \end{array}$$

The two derivations d and d' have the form

$$\frac{\begin{array}{l} \Pi\Gamma.G \to P \in \mathcal{P} \\ P[\sigma] = Q[\theta_0][\theta_1] \\ \sigma \models G > \theta_2 \end{array}}{\theta_0 \models Q > \theta_0 \circ \theta_1 \circ \theta_2} \qquad \frac{\begin{array}{l} \Pi\Gamma.G' \to P' \in \mathcal{P} \\ P'[\sigma'] = Q[\theta_0'][\theta_1'] \\ \sigma' \models G' > \theta_2' \end{array}}{\theta_0' \models Q > \theta_0' \circ \theta_1' \circ \theta_2'}$$

Write θ_{out} for $\theta_0 \circ \theta_1 \circ \theta_2$ and θ_{out}' for $\theta_0' \circ \theta_1' \circ \theta_2'$.

It is easy to see, for each input variable x of Q, that $\theta_{out}(x) = \theta_{out}'(x) = \theta_0(x) = \theta_0'(x)$, so the approximation relation is satisfied for the input variables of Q.

For the output variables, there are two subcases: either there is uniqueness information for the type family of Q, so that only one clause head can match Q, or there is no uniqueness information.

For the first subcase $P = P'$ and $G = G'$. We use the mode correctness of the program to obtain the subgoal mode check $\Psi_1' \vdash G > \Psi_2'$, where Ψ_2' enforces the mode annotations for the input and output variables of P. $\Psi_1' \prec \{\sigma, \sigma'\}$, so by induction $\Psi_2' \prec \{\theta_2, \theta_2'\}$. Then θ_{out} and θ_{out}' satisfy the mode annotations for the output variables of Q, as required.

For the second subcase the reasoning is similar, but there are no output uniqueness requirements and more than one clause head can match Q.   □

Lemma 2 (Completeness of non-deterministic search). *Given $\Delta \vdash Q :$ type. If Q contains only ground terms in its input positions, and there is a substitution θ and term M such that $\cdot \vdash M : Q[\theta]$, then $\mathrm{id}_\Delta \models Q > \theta'$ and there is a substitution θ'' such that $\theta = \theta' \circ \theta''$.*

Proof. The proof is standard, using induction on the structure of M, exploiting the non-deterministic nature of the operational semantics to guess the right clauses and unifying substitutions.   □

5   Coverage

Coverage checking is the problem of deciding whether any closed term of a given type is an instance of at least one of a given set of patterns. Our work on exploiting uniqueness information in coverage checking is motivated by its application to proof assistants and proof checkers, where it can be used to check that all possible cases in the definition of a function or relation are covered. The coverage problem and an approximation algorithm for coverage checking in LF are described in [24], extending prior work by Coquand [2] and McBride [11].

More precisely, a coverage problem is given by a coverage goal and a set of patterns. In our setting it is sufficient to consider coverage goals that are types with free variables $\Delta \vdash A :$ type; it is straightforward to translate general coverage goals to this form.

Definition 3 (Immediate Coverage). *We say a coverage goal* $\Delta \vdash A :$ type *is* immediately covered *by a collection of patterns* $\Delta_i \vdash A_i :$ type *if there is an* i *and a substitution* $\Delta \vdash \sigma_i : \Delta_i$ *such that* $\Delta \vdash A \equiv A_i[\sigma_i] :$ type.

Coverage requires immediate coverage of every ground instance of a goal.

Definition 4 (Coverage). *We say* $\Delta \vdash A :$ type *is* covered *by a collection of patterns* $\Delta_i \vdash A_i :$ type *if every ground instance* $\cdot \vdash A[\tau] :$ type *for* $\cdot \vdash \tau : \Delta$ *is immediately covered by the collection* $\Delta_i \vdash A_i :$ type.

As an example, consider again the plus predicate from Figure 1. We have already shown that the output of plus, if it exists, is unique. In order to show that plus is a total function of its first two arguments, we need to show that it always terminates (which is easy—see [18, 16]), and that the inputs cover all cases. For the latter requirement, we transform the signature into coverage patterns by eliding the outputs:

X:nat $\vdash$ plus z X _.
X_1:nat, X_2:nat $\vdash$ plus (s X_1) X_2 _.

The coverage goal:

Y_1:nat, Y_2:nat $\vdash$ plus Y_1 Y_2 _.

In this example, the goal is covered by the two patterns since every ground instance of the goal plus M_1 M_2 _ will be an instance of one of the two patterns. However, the goal is not immediately covered because Y_1 clashes with z in the first pattern and s in the second.

When a goal $\Delta \vdash A :$ type is not immediately covered by any pattern, the algorithm makes use of an operation called *splitting*, which produces a set of new coverage goals by partially instantiating free variables in Δ. Each of the resulting goals is covered if and only if the original goal is covered. Intuitively, splitting works by selecting a variable u in Δ, and instantiating it to all possible top-level structures based on its type.

In the example, the clashes of Y_1 with z and s suggest splitting of Y_1, which yields two new coverage goals

Y:nat $\vdash$ plus z Y _.
Y_1:nat, Y_2:nat $\vdash$ plus (s Y_1) Y_2 _.

These are immediately covered by the first and second pattern, respectively, but in general many splitting operations may be necessary.

The process of repeated splitting of variables in goals that are not yet covered immediately will eventually terminate according to the algorithm in [24], namely when the failed attempts to immediately cover a goal no longer suggest any promising candidates for splitting. Unfortunately, this algorithm is by necessity incomplete, since coverage is in general an undecidable property. Sometimes, this is due to a variable $x{:}B$ in a coverage goal which has no ground instances, in which case the goal is vacuously covered. Sometimes, however, the coverage

preserv : plus X_1 X_3 Y $\rightarrow$ plus X_2 X_3 Y$'$ $\rightarrow$ le X_1 X_2 $\rightarrow$ le Y Y$'$ $\rightarrow$ type.
preserv_refl : preserv S_1 S_2 le_refl le_refl.
preserv_s : preserv S_1 S_2 L L$'$ $\rightarrow$ preserv S_1 (plus_s S_2) (le_s L) (le_s L$'$).

Fig. 5. Addition preserves ordering

checker reaches a situation where several terms must be equal in order to obtain immediate coverage. It is in these situations that uniqueness information can help, as we explain in the next section.

6   Uniqueness in Coverage

We begin with an example that demonstrates failure of coverage due to the absence of uniqueness information.

Given type families for natural numbers, addition, and ordering, a proof that addition of equals preserves ordering can be encoded as the relation preserv in Figure 5. Note that, as before, free variables are implicitly quantified on each clause. Moreover, arguments to type families whose quantifiers were omitted earlier (as, for example, ΠX:nat in the clause le_refl : leXX) are also omitted, and determined by type reconstruction as in the Twelf implementation [15].

In order to verify that preserv constitutes a meta-theoretic proof, we need to verify that for all inputs S_1 : plus X_1 X_3 Y, S_2 : plus X_2 X_3 Y$'$, and L : le X_1 X_2 there exists an output L$'$: le Y Y$'$ which witnesses that $x_1 + x_3 \leq x_2 + x_3$ if $x_1 \leq x_2$.

The initial coverage goal has the form

X_1:nat, X_2:nat, X_3:nat, Y:nat, Y$'$:nat,
        S_1:plus X_1 X_3 Y, S_2:plus X_2 X_3 Y$'$, L:le X_1 X_2 $\vdash$ preserv S_1 S_2 L _.

This fails, and after one step of splitting on the variable L we obtain two cases, the second of which is seen to be covered by the preserv_s clause after one further splitting step, while the first has the form

X_1:nat, X_3:nat, Y:nat, Y$'$:nat, S_1:plus X_1 X_3 Y, S_2:plus X_1 X_3 Y$'$.
        $\vdash$ preserv S_1 S_2 le_refl _.

The clause preserv_refl does not immediately cover this case, because the types of the two variable S_1 and S_2 in this clause are the same, namely plus X_1 X_3 Y. This is because the use of reflexivity for inequality in the third and fourth arguments of the clause requires $X_1 = X_2$ and $Y = Y'$. Our extended coverage checker will allow us to show automatically that this case is covered by exploiting the uniqueness information for plus.

We first define the situations in which uniqueness information may potentially be helpful, depending on the outcome of a unification problem. We then show how to exploit the result of unification to specialize a coverage goal.

Definition 5 (Specializing a coverage goal). *Given a mode-correct program* $\mathcal{P}$ *containing a type family* a *with unique outputs, and a coverage goal* $\Delta \vdash A :$ type, *uniqueness specialization for* a *may be applicable if*

1. Δ *contains distinct assumptions* $x_1 : a\ M_1 \ldots M_n$ *and* $x_2 : a\ N_1 \ldots N_n$, *and*
2. *for all* $i \in ins(a)$, $M_i = N_i$, *and*
3. *for some* $k \in uouts(a)$, $M_k \neq N_k$.

To specialize the goal, attempt simultaneous higher-order unification of M_k *with* N_k *for all* $k \in uouts(a)$. *If a most general pattern unifier (mgu) for this problem exists, write it as* $\Delta' \vdash \sigma : \Delta$, *and generate a new specialized goal* $\Delta' \vdash A[\sigma] :$ type.

There are three possible outcomes of the given higher-order unification problem, with the algorithm in [6]: (1) it may yield an mgu, in which case the specialized coverage goal is equivalent to the original one but has fewer variables, (2) it may fail, in which case the original goal is vacuously covered (that is, it has no ground instances), or (3) the algorithm may report remaining constraints, in which case this specialization is not applicable. Assertions (1) and (2) are corollaries of the next two lemmas.

Lemma 3. *If uniqueness information for a type family* a *is potentially applicable to a coverage goal* $g = \Delta \vdash A :$ type, *but no unifier exists, then there are no ground instances of* g *(and thus* g *is vacuously covered by any set of patterns).*

Proof. Assume we had a substitution $\cdot \vdash \theta : \Delta$ (so that $A[\theta]$ is ground). Using the notation from Definition 5, we have $M_i = N_i$ for all $i \in ins(a)$ and therefore $M_i[\theta] = N_i[\theta]$. By Lemma 2, we have $\cdot \models (a\ M_1 \ldots M_n)[\theta] > \theta_1$ and $\cdot \models (a\ N_1 \ldots N_n)[\theta] > \theta_2$. Since the empty abstract substitution approximates the empty substitution, we know by Lemma 1 that for all $k \in uouts(a)$, $M_k[\theta] = N_k[\theta]$. But this is impossible since for at least one $k \in uouts(a)$, M_k and N_k were non-unifiable. $\square$

Lemma 4. *Let* $g = \Delta \vdash A :$ type *be a coverage goal, and* $\mathcal{P}$ *a mode-correct program with uniqueness information for* a *potentially applicable to* g. *If an mgu* $\Delta' \vdash \sigma : \Delta$ *exists and leads to coverage goal* $\Delta' \vdash A[\sigma] :$ type, *then every ground instance* $A[\theta]$ *of* A *is equal to a ground instance of* $A[\sigma]$.

Proof. As in the proof of the preceding lemma, assume $\cdot \vdash \theta : \Delta$ (so that $A[\theta]$ is ground). Again we have $M_i = N_i$ for all $i \in ins(a)$ and therefore $M_i[\theta] = N_i[\theta]$. By Lemma 2, we have $\cdot \models (a\ M_1 \ldots M_n)[\theta] > \theta_1$ and $\cdot \models (a\ N_1 \ldots N_n)[\theta] > \theta_2$ for some θ_1 and θ_2. From Lemma 1 we now know that for all $k \in uouts(a)$, $M_k[\theta] = N_k[\theta]$. But, by assumption, σ is a most general simultaneous unifier of $M_k \doteq N_k$ for all $k \in uouts(a)$. Hence $\theta = \sigma \circ \theta'$ for some θ' and $A[\theta] = A[\sigma \circ \theta'] = (A[\sigma])[\theta']$. $\square$

We return to the coverage checking problem for the type family of Figure 5. As observed above, without uniqueness information for plus it cannot be seen that all cases are covered. The failed coverage goal is

X_1:nat, X_3:nat, Y:nat, Y′:nat, S_1:plus X_1 X_3 Y, S_2:plus X_1 X_3 Y′.
        ⊢ preserv S_1 S_2 le_refl _.

Exploiting uniqueness information for plus, we have the unification problem $Y \doteq Y'$, with mgu Y/Y', yielding the new goal

X_1:nat, X_3:nat, Y:nat, S_1:plus X_1 X_3 Y, S_2:plus X_1 X_3 Y.
        ⊢ preserv S_1 S_2 le_refl _.

Since S_1 and S_2 have the same type, the new goal is immediately covered by the clause preserv_refl, completing the check of the original coverage goal.

7   Conclusion

We have described an algorithm for verifying uniqueness of specified output arguments of a relation, given specified input arguments. We have also shown how to exploit this information in coverage checking, which, together with termination checking, can guarantee the existence of output arguments when given some inputs. We can therefore also verify unique existence, by separately verifying existence and uniqueness. While our algorithms can easily be seen to terminate, they are by necessity incomplete, since both uniqueness and coverage with respect to ground terms are undecidable in our setting of LF.

The uniqueness mode checker of Section 3 has been fully implemented as described. In fact, it allows arbitrary signatures, rather than just Horn clauses at the top level, although our critical correctness proof for Lemma 1 has not yet been extended to the more general case. We expect to employ a combination of the ideas from [18] and [19] to extend the current proof. In practice, we have found the behavior of the uniqueness checker to be predictable and the error messages upon failure to be generally helpful.

We are considering three further extensions to the uniqueness mode checker, each of which is relatively straightforward from the theoretical side. The first is to generalize left-to-right subgoal selection to be instead non-deterministic. This would allow verification of uniqueness for more signatures that were not intended to be executed with Twelf's operational semantics. The second would be to check that proof terms (and not just output arguments) will be ground or ground and unique. That would enable additional goal specialization in coverage checking. The third is to integrate the idea of *factoring* [17] in which overlapping clauses are permitted as long as they can be seen to be (always!) disjoint on the result of some subgoal.

In terms of implementation, we have not yet extended the coverage checker implementation in Twelf to take advantage of uniqueness information. Since specialization always reduces the complexity of the coverage goal when applicable, we propose an eager strategy, comparing inputs of type families having some unique outputs whenever possible. Since terms in the context tend to be rather small, we do not expect this to have any significant impact on overall performance.

Finally, we would like to redo the theory of foundational proof-carrying code [3, 4] taking advantage of uniqueness modes to obtain a concrete measure of the improvements in proof size in a large-scale example. We expect that most uses of explicit equality predicates and the associated proofs of functionality can be eliminated in favor of uniqueness mode checking and extended coverage checking. As a small proof of concept, we have successfully uniqueness-checked four type families in the theory, amounting to about 150 lines of Twelf code in which the use of functional arguments is pervasive. Combined with coverage checking, these checks might eliminate perhaps 250 lines of proof.

8   Acknowledgements

We thank the anonymous referees for several helpful suggestions.

References

1. T. Coquand. An algorithm for testing conversion in type theory. In G. Huet and G. Plotkin, editors, *Logical Frameworks*, pages 255–279. Cambridge University Press, 1991.
2. T. Coquand. Pattern matching with dependent types. In *Proceedings of the Workshop on Types for Proofs and Programs*, pages 71–83, Båstad, Sweden, 1992.
3. K. Crary. Toward a foundational typed assembly language. In G. Morrisett, editor, *Proceedings of the 30th Annual Symposium on Principles of Programming Languages*, pages 198–212, New Orleans, Louisiana, Jan. 2003. ACM Press.
4. K. Crary and S. Sarkar. A metalogical approach to foundational certified code. Technical Report CMU-CS-03-108, Carnegie Mellon University, Jan. 2003.
5. J. Despeyroux and P. Leleu. A modal lambda calculus with iteration and case constructs. In T. Altenkirch, W. Naraschewski, and B. Reus, editors, *Types for Proofs and Programs*, pages 47–61, Kloster Irsee, Germany, Mar. 1998. Springer-Verlag LNCS 1657.
6. G. Dowek, T. Hardin, C. Kirchner, and F. Pfenning. Unification via explicit substitutions: The case of higher-order patterns. In M. Maher, editor, *Proceedings of the Joint International Conference and Symposium on Logic Programming*, pages 259–273, Bonn, Germany, Sept. 1996. MIT Press.
7. R. Harper, F. Honsell, and G. Plotkin. A framework for defining logics. *Journal of the Association for Computing Machinery*, 40(1):143–184, Jan. 1993.
8. R. Harper and F. Pfenning. On equivalence and canonical forms in the LF type theory. *Transactions on Computational Logic*, 2003. To appear. Preliminary version available as Technical Report CMU-CS-00-148.
9. M. Hofmann. *Extensional Concepts in Intensional Type Theory*. PhD thesis, Department of Computer Science, University of Edinburgh, July 1995. Available as Technical Report CST-117-95.
10. M. Hofmann and T. Streicher. The groupoid model refutes uniqueness of identity proofs. In *Proceedings of the 9th Annual Symposium on Logic in Computer Science (LICS'94)*, pages 208–212, Paris, France, 1994. IEEE Computer Society Press.
11. C. McBride. *Dependently Typed Functional Programs and their Proofs*. PhD thesis, University of Edinburgh, 1999. Available as Technical Report ECS-LFCS-00-419.

12. F. Pfenning. Structural cut elimination I. intuitionistic and classical logic. *Information and Computation*, 157(1/2):84–141, Mar. 2000.
13. F. Pfenning. Logical frameworks. In A. Robinson and A. Voronkov, editors, *Handbook of Automated Reasoning*, chapter 17, pages 1063–1147. Elsevier Science and MIT Press, 2001.
14. F. Pfenning and C. Schürmann. Algorithms for equality and unification in the presence of notational definitions. In T. Altenkirch, W. Naraschewski, and B. Reus, editors, *Types for Proofs and Programs*, pages 179–193, Kloster Irsee, Germany, Mar. 1998. Springer-Verlag LNCS 1657.
15. F. Pfenning and C. Schürmann. System description: Twelf — a meta-logical framework for deductive systems. In H. Ganzinger, editor, *Proceedings of the 16th International Conference on Automated Deduction (CADE-16)*, pages 202–206, Trento, Italy, July 1999. Springer-Verlag LNAI 1632.
16. B. Pientka. Termination and reduction checking for higher-order logic programs. In *First International Joint Conference on Automated Reasoning (IJCAR)*, pages 401–415, Siena, Italy, 2001. Springer Verlag, LNCS 2083.
17. A. Poswolsky and C. Schürmann. Factoring pure logic programs. Draft manuscript, Nov. 2003.
18. E. Rohwedder and F. Pfenning. Mode and termination checking for higher-order logic programs. In H. R. Nielson, editor, *Proceedings of the European Symposium on Programming*, pages 296–310, Linköping, Sweden, Apr. 1996. Springer-Verlag LNCS 1058.
19. C. Schürmann. *Automating the Meta Theory of Deductive Systems*. PhD thesis, Department of Computer Science, Carnegie Mellon University, Aug. 2000. Available as Technical Report CMU-CS-00-146.
20. C. Schürmann. Recursion for higher-order encodings. In L. Fribourg, editor, *Proceedings of the Conference on Computer Science Logic (CSL 2001)*, pages 585–599, Paris, France, August 2001. Springer Verlag LNCS 2142.
21. C. Schürmann. A type-theoretic approach to induction with higher-order encodings. In *Proceedings of the Conference on Logic for Programming, Artificial Intelligence and Reasoning(LPAR 2001)*, pages 266–281, Havana, Cuba, 2001. Springer Verlag LNAI 2250.
22. C. Schürmann. Delphin – toward functional programming with logical frameworks. Technical Report TR #1272, Yale University, Department of Computer Science, 2004.
23. C. Schürmann, J. Despeyroux, and F. Pfenning. Primitive recursion for higher-order abstract syntax. *Theoretical Computer Science*, 266:1–57, 2001.
24. C. Schürmann and F. Pfenning. A coverage checking algorithm for LF. In D. Basin and B. Wolff, editors, *Proceedings of the 16th International Conference on Theorem Proving in Higher Order Logics (TPHOLs 2003)*, pages 120–135, Rome, Italy, Sept. 2003. Springer-Verlag LNCS 2758.
25. G. Washburn and S. Weirich. Boxes go bananas: Encoding higher-order abstract syntax with parametric polymorphism. In *Proceedings of the Eighth International Conference on Functional Programming*, pages 249–262, Uppsala, Sweden, Aug. 2003. ACM Press.

A Program Logic for Resource Verification

David Aspinall[1], Lennart Beringer[1], Martin Hofmann[2],
Hans-Wolfgang Loidl[2], and Alberto Momigliano[1]

[1] Laboratory for Foundations of Computer Science,
School of Informatics, University of Edinburgh,
Edinburgh EH9 3JZ, Scotland
{da,lenb,amomigl1}@inf.ed.ac.uk
[2] Institut für Informatik, Ludwig-Maximilians Universität,
D-80538 München, Germany
{mhofmann,hwloidl}@informatik.uni-muenchen.de

Abstract. We present a program logic for reasoning about resource consumption of programs written in Grail, an abstract fragment of the Java Virtual Machine Language. Serving as the target logic of a certifying compiler, the logic exploits Grail's dual nature of combining a functional interpretation with object-oriented features and a cost model for the JVM. We present the resource-aware operational semantics of Grail, the program logic, and prove soundness and completeness. All of the work described has been formalised in the theorem prover Isabelle/HOL, which provides us with an implementation of the logic as well as confidence in the results. We conclude with examples of using the logic for proving resource bounds on code resulting from compiling high-level functional programs.

1 Introduction

For the effective use of mobile code, resource consumption is of great concern. A user who downloads an application program onto his mobile phone wants to know that the memory requirement of executing the program does not exceed the memory space available on the phone. Likewise, concerns occur in Grid computing where service providers want to know that user programs adhere to negotiated resource policies and users want to be sure that their program will not be terminated abruptly by the scheduler due to violations of some resource constraints.

The Mobile Resource Guarantees (MRG) project [27] is developing Proof-Carrying Code (PCC) technology [23] to endow mobile code with *certificates* of bounded resource consumption. Certificates in the PCC sense contain proof-theoretic evidence. A service provider can check a certificate to see that a given resource policy will be adhered to before admitting the code to run. The feasibility of the PCC approach relies on the observation that, while it may be difficult to produce a formal proof of a certain program property, it should be easy to check such a proof. Furthermore, resource properties are in many cases easier to verify than general correctness properties.

Following the PCC paradigm the code producer uses a combination of program annotations and analysis to construct a machine proof that a resource policy is met. The proof is expressed in a specialized program logic for the language in which the

K. Slind et al. (Eds.): TPHOLs 2004, LNCS 3223, pp. 34–49, 2004.

code is transmitted. In the MRG project, this target language is Grail [4], an abstract representation of (a subset of) the Java Virtual Machine Language (JVML). Certificate generation is performed by a certifying compiler, e.g. [7], which transforms programs written in MRG's high-level functional language Camelot into Grail [17]. Certificates are based on Camelot-level type systems for reasoning about resource consumption of functional programs [3, 11, 12]. For example, the Camelot program

```
let rev l acc = match l with Nil@d -> acc
                           | Cons(h,t)@d -> rev t (Cons(h,acc)@d)
```

for reversing a list does not consume heap space. In the match statement, the annotation @ names the heap cell inhabited by the value, so that it can be reused when constructing new list nodes in the body. Restrictions on the usage of such annotations are subject of the type system [3, 11] and we have an automatic inference of such annotations for Camelot [12]. Indeed, we will prove later that the Grail code emitted for rev by our compiler does not allocate memory.

Contributions: We introduce a resource-aware program logic for Grail in which the certificates are expressed (Sections 2 and 3). The presentation of the logic follows the approach of the Vienna Development Method (VDM), a variation of Hoare-style program logic where assertions may refer to initial as well as to final states [14]. In our case, pre- and post-conditions are combined into single assertions ranging over pre-and post-heap, the environment in which the Grail expression is evaluated, the result value, and a component for the consumption of temporal and spatial resources. We discuss the meta-theoretic properties of soundness and (relative) completeness of the logic with respect to the functional operational semantics of Grail, based on a full formalisation in the theorem prover Isabelle/HOL. Since the program logic and its implementation are part of the trusted code base of the PCC infrastructure, it is essential for the overall security of the system to have such results available. Our formalisation builds upon previous work on embedding program logics in theorem provers, in particular that of Kleymann [15] and Nipkow [24] (see Section 5 for details). In contrast to that, our logic features a semantics that combines object-oriented aspects with a functional-style big-step evaluation relation, and includes a treatment of resource consumption that is related to a cost model for the execution of Grail on a virtual machine platform. The logic is tailored so that it can be proven sound and complete while at the same time it can be refined to be used for PCC-oriented program verification. This has influenced the departure from the more traditional Hoare format, where the need of auxiliary variables to propagate intermediate results from pre- to post-assertions is a serious issue w.r.t. automation. As a main technical result, we give a novel treatment of rules for mutually recursive procedures and adaptation that do not need separate judgements or a very complex variation of the consequence rule, but are elegantly proven admissible. Our focus on using Grail as an intermediate language, namely as the target of Camelot compilation, also motivates the decision not to provide a full treatment of object-oriented features such as inheritance and overriding. The expressiveness of our logic is demonstrated by verifying in Isabelle/HOL some resource properties of heap-manipulating Grail programs that were obtained by compiling Camelot programs (Section 4).

2   Grail

The Grail language [4] was designed as a compromise between raw bytecode and low-level functional languages, and serves as the target of the Camelot compilation. While the object and method structure of bytecode is retained, each method body consists of a set of mutually tail-recursive first-order functions. The syntax comprises instructions for object creation and manipulation, method invocation and primitive operations such as integer arithmetic, as well as let-bindings to combine program fragments. In the context of the Camelot compiler, static methods are of particular interest. Using a whole-program compilation approach, all datatypes are implemented by a single Grail class, the so-called "diamond" class [11], and functions over these datatypes result in distinct static methods operating on objects of this class [17]. The main characteristic of Grail is its dual identity: its (impure) call-by-value functional semantics is shown to coincide with an imperative interpretation of the expansion of Grail programs into the Java Virtual Machine Language, provided that some mild syntactic conditions are met. In particular, these require that actual arguments in function calls coincide syntactically with the formal parameters of the function definitions. This allows function calls to be interpreted as immediate jump instructions since register shuffling at basic block boundaries is performed by the calling code rather than being built into the function application rule. Consequently, the consumption of resources at virtual machine level may be expressed in a functional semantics for Grail: the expansion into JVML does not require register allocation or the insertion of gluing code.

We give an operational semantics and a program logic for a functional interpretation of Grail, where it is assumed (though not explicitly enforced) that expressions are in Administrative-Normal-Form, that is all intermediate values are explicitly named.

Syntax. The syntax of Grail expressions makes use of mutually disjoint sets of integers, $\mathcal{M}$ of method names, $\mathcal{C}$ of class names, $\mathcal{F}$ of function names (i.e. labels of basic blocks), $\mathcal{T}$ of (virtual or static) field names and $\mathcal{X}$ of variables, ranged over by i, m, c, f, t, and x, respectively. We also introduce *self* as a reserved variable. In the following grammar, *op* denotes a primitive operation of type $\mathcal{V} \Rightarrow \mathcal{V} \Rightarrow \mathcal{V}$ such as an arithmetic operation or a comparison operator. Here $\mathcal{V}$ is the semantic category of values (ranged over by v), comprising integers, references r, and the special symbol $\bot$, which stands for the absence of a value. Boolean values are represented as integers. Heap references are either null or of the form Ref l where l is a location (represented by a natural number). Formal parameters of method invocations may be integer or object variables. Actual arguments are sequences of variable names or immediate values – complex expressions which may occur as arguments in Camelot functions are eliminated during the compilation process.

$a \in args ::= \text{var } x \mid \text{null} \mid i$

$e \in expr ::= \text{null} \mid \text{int } i \mid \text{var } x \mid \text{prim } op\; x\; x \mid \text{new } c\; \overline{[t_i := x_i]} \mid x.t \mid x.t := x \mid c \diamond t := x \mid$
$\qquad\qquad c \diamond t \mid \text{let } x = e \text{ in } e \mid e;e \mid \text{if } x \text{ then } e \text{ else } e \mid \text{call } f \mid x \cdot m(\overline{a}) \mid c \diamond m(\overline{a})$

Expressions represent basic blocks and are built from operators, constants, and previously computed values (names). Expressions such as $x.t := y$ (putfield) correspond to primitive sequences of bytecode instructions that may, as a side effect, alter the heap or frame stack. Similarly, $c \diamond t$ and $c \diamond t := y$ denote static field lookup and assignment, which are needed in Camelot's memory management. The binding $\text{let } x = e_1 \text{ in } e_2$ is used if the evaluation of e_1 returns an integer or reference value on top of the JVM stack while $e_1; e_2$ represents purely sequential composition, used for example if e_1 is a field update $x.t := y$. Object creation includes the initialisation of the object fields according to the argument list: the content of variable x_i is stored in field t_i. Function calls (call) follow the Grail calling convention (i.e. correspond to immediate jumps) and do not carry arguments. The instructions $x \cdot m(\overline{a})$ and $c \diamond m(\overline{a})$ represent virtual (instance) and static method invocation. Although a formal type and class system may be imposed on Grail programs, our program logic abstracts from these restrictions; heap and class file environment are total functions on field and method names, respectively.

We assume that all method declarations employ distinct names for identifying inner basic blocks. A program is represented by a table FT mapping each function identifier to a list of (distinct) variables (the formal parameters) and an expression, and a table MT associating the formal method parameters (again a list of distinct variables) and the initial basic block to class names and method identifiers.

Dynamic Semantics. The machine model is based on semantic domains $\mathcal{H}$ of heaps, $\mathcal{E}$ of environments (maps from variables to values) and $\mathcal{R}$ of resource components. A heap h maps locations to objects, where an object comprises a class name and a mapping of field names to values. In our formalisation, we follow an approach inspired by Burstall, where the heap is split into several components: a total function from field names to locations to values, and a partial function from locations to class names. In addition, we also introduce a total map for modelling static (reference) fields, mapping class names and field names to references.

Variables which are local to a method invocation are kept in an environment E that corresponds to the local store of the JVM. Environments are represented as total functions, with the silent assumption that well-defined method bodies only access variables which have previously been assigned a value. We use $E\langle x \rangle$ to denote the lookup operation and $E\langle x := v \rangle$ to denote an update. Since the operational semantics uses environments to represent the local store of method frames, no explicit frame stack is needed. The height of the stack is mentioned as part of the resource component.

Resource consumption is modelled by resource tuples $p \in \mathcal{R}$, where

$$p = \langle clock \quad callc \quad invkc \quad invkdpth \rangle.$$

The four components range over $\mathbb{N}$ and represent the following costs. The *clock* represents a global abstract instruction counter. The *callc* and *invkc* components are more refined, i.e. they count the number of function calls (jump instructions) and method invocations. We can easily count other types of instructions, but we chose these initially as interesting cases: for example they may be used to formally verify Grail-level optimisations such as the replacement of method (tail) recursion by function recursion. Finally, *invkdpth* models the maximal invocation depth, i.e. the maximal height of the frame stack throughout an execution. From this, the maximal frame stack height may be approximated by considering the maximal size of single frames. The size of the heap is not monitored explicitly in the resource components, since it can be deduced from the representation of the object heap as $|dom(h)|$.

The operational semantics and the program logic make use of two operators on resources, $p \oplus q$ and $p \smile q$. In the first three components, both operators perform pointwise addition, as all instruction counts behave additionally during program composition. In the fourth component, the operator $\oplus$ again adds the respective components of p and q, while $\smile$ takes their maximum. By employing $\smile$ in the rules for let-bindings we can thus model the release of frame stacks after the execution of method invocations.

The semantics is a big-step evaluation relation based on the functional interpretation of Grail, with judgements of the form

$$E \vdash h, e \Downarrow (h', v, p).$$

Such a statement reads "in variable environment E and initial heap h, code e evaluates to the value v, yielding the heap h' and consuming p resources."

$$\frac{}{E \vdash h, \texttt{null} \Downarrow (h, \texttt{null}, \langle 1\,0\,0\,0 \rangle)} \text{ (NULL)} \qquad \frac{}{E \vdash h, \texttt{int } i \Downarrow (h, i, \langle 1\,0\,0\,0 \rangle)} \text{ (INT)}$$

$$\frac{}{E \vdash h, \texttt{var } x \Downarrow (h, E\langle x \rangle, \langle 1\,0\,0\,0 \rangle)} \text{ (VAR)}$$

$$\frac{}{E \vdash h, \texttt{prim } op\ x\ y \Downarrow (h, op\ (E\langle x \rangle)\ (E\langle y \rangle), \langle 3\,0\,0\,0 \rangle)} \text{ (PRIM)}$$

$$\frac{E\langle x \rangle = \text{Ref } l}{E \vdash h, x.t \Downarrow (h, h(l).t, \langle 2\,0\,0\,0 \rangle)} \text{ (GETF)} \qquad \frac{E\langle x \rangle = \text{Ref } l}{E \vdash h, x.t := y \Downarrow (h[l.t \mapsto E\langle y \rangle], \bot, \langle 3\,0\,0\,0 \rangle)} \text{ (PUTF)}$$

$$\frac{}{E \vdash h, c \diamond t \Downarrow (h, h(c).t, \langle 2\,0\,0\,0 \rangle)} \text{ (GFST)} \qquad \frac{}{E \vdash h, c \diamond t := y \Downarrow (h[c.t \mapsto E\langle y \rangle], \bot, \langle 3\,0\,0\,0 \rangle)} \text{ (PFST)}$$

$$\frac{l = freshloc(h)}{E \vdash h, \texttt{new } c\ [\overline{t_i := x_i}] \Downarrow (h[l \mapsto (c, \{t_i := E\langle x_i \rangle\})], \text{Ref } l, \langle (n+1)\,0\,0\,0 \rangle)} \text{ (NEW)}$$

$$\frac{E\langle x \rangle = \text{true} \quad E \vdash h, e_1 \Downarrow (h_1, v, p)}{E \vdash h, \texttt{if } x \texttt{ then } e_1 \texttt{ else } e_2 \Downarrow (h_1, v, \langle 2\,0\,0\,0 \rangle \oplus p)} \text{ (IFTRUE)}$$

$$\frac{E\langle x \rangle = \text{false} \quad E \vdash h, e_2 \Downarrow (h_1, v, p)}{E \vdash h, \texttt{if } x \texttt{ then } e_1 \texttt{ else } e_2 \Downarrow (h_1, v, \langle 2\,0\,0\,0 \rangle \oplus p)} \text{ (IFFALSE)}$$

$$\frac{E \vdash h, e_1 \Downarrow (h_1, w, p) \quad w \neq \bot \quad E\langle x := w \rangle \vdash h_1, e_2 \Downarrow (h_2, v, q)}{E \vdash h, \texttt{let } x = e_1 \texttt{ in } e_2 \Downarrow (h_2, v, \langle 1\,0\,0\,0 \rangle \oplus (p \smile q))} \text{ (LET)}$$

$$\frac{E \vdash h, e_1 \Downarrow (h_1, \bot, p) \quad E \vdash h_1, e_2 \Downarrow (h_2, v, q)}{E \vdash h, e_1; e_2 \Downarrow (h_2, v, p \smile q)} \text{ (COMP)}$$

$$\frac{E \vdash h, snd(FT\ f) \Downarrow (h_1, v, p)}{E \vdash h, \texttt{call } f \Downarrow (h_1, v, \langle 1\,1\,0\,0 \rangle \oplus p)} \text{ (CALL)}$$

$$\frac{(newframe\ \texttt{null}\ fst(MT\ c\ m)\ \overline{a}\ E) \vdash h, snd(MT\ c\ m) \Downarrow (h_1, v, p)}{E \vdash h, c \diamond m(\overline{a}) \Downarrow (h_1, v, \langle (2 + |\overline{a}|)\,0\,1\,1 \rangle \oplus p)} \text{ (SINV)}$$

$$\frac{classOf\ E\ h\ x\ c \quad (newframe\ E\langle x\rangle\ fst(MT\ c\ m)\ \overline{a}\ E) \vdash h, snd(MT\ c\ m) \Downarrow (h_1, v, p)}{E \vdash h, x \cdot m(\overline{a}) \Downarrow (h_1, v, \langle (4+ |\overline{a}|)\ 0\ 1\ 1\rangle \oplus p)}$$

(VINV)

In rule GETF, the notation $h(l).t$ represents the value of field t in the object at heap location l, while in rule PUTF the notation $h[l.t \mapsto v]$ denotes the corresponding update operation. Similarly for static fields. In rule NEW, the function *freshloc*(h) returns a fresh location outside the domain of h, and $h[l \mapsto (c, \{\overline{t_i := E\langle x_i\rangle}\})]$ represents the heap that agrees with h on all locations different from l and maps l to an object of class c, with field entries $t_i := E\langle x_i\rangle$. In the rules CALL, SINV and VINV the lookup functions *FT* and *MT* are used to obtain function and method bodies from names. These are here implemented as static tables, though they could be used to model a class hierarchy. In particular *MT* has type $C \Rightarrow \mathcal{M} \Rightarrow (X\ list \times expr)$, where the parameter passing in method invocations is modelled by accessing the parameter values from the caller's environment. Each method invocation allocates a new frame on the frame stack, where the function *newframe* creates the appropriate environment, given a reference to the invoking object, the formal parameters and the actual arguments. The environment contains bindings for the self object and the method parameters. If we invoke a static method we set the self variable to null, otherwise to the current object.

The resource tuples in the operational semantics abstractly characterise resource consumption in an unspecified virtual machine; because resources are treated separately, these values could be changed for particular virtual machines. The temporal costs associated to basic instructions reflect the number of bytecode instructions to which the expression expands. For example, the PUTF operation involves two instructions for pushing the object pointer $E\langle x\rangle$ and the new content $E\langle y\rangle$ onto the operand stack, plus one additional instruction for performing the actual field modification. In rule NEW we charge a single clock tick for object creation, and n for field initialisation. The costs for primitive operations may be generalised to a table lookup. In the rules for conditionals, we charge for pushing the value $E\langle x\rangle$ onto the stack, with an additional clock tick for evaluating the branch condition and performing the appropriate jump. In rule CALL, the Grail functional call convention explains why we treat the call as a jump, continuing with the execution of function body. We charge for one anonymous instruction, and also explicitly for the execution of a jump. In rule SINV, the body of method is executed in an environment which represents a fresh frame. The instruction counter is incremented by 2 for pushing and popping the frame and $|\overline{a}|$ for evaluating the arguments. In addition, both the invocation counter and the invocation depth are incremented by one — the usage of $\oplus$ ensures that the depth correctly represents the nesting depth of frames. Finally, in rule VINV, the predicate *classOf E h x c* first retrieves the dynamic class name c associated to the object pointed to by x. Then, the method body associated to m and c is executed in a fresh environment which contains the reference to $E\langle x\rangle$ in variable *self* and the formal parameters as above. The costs charged arise again by considering the evaluation of $E\langle x\rangle$ and the method arguments, and the pushing and popping of the frame, but we also charge one clock tick for the indirection needed to retrieve the correct method body from the class file.

3 Program Logic

The program logic targets the partial correctness of resource bounds such as heap allocation and combines aspects of VDM-style verification [14] and Abadi-Leino's logic for object calculi [1]. Sequents are of the form $\Gamma \triangleright e : P$ and relate a Grail expression $e \in expr$ to a specification $P \in \mathcal{A}$ in a context $\Gamma \in \mathcal{G}$ (see definition below). We abbreviate $\emptyset \triangleright e : P$ to $\triangleright e : P$. We follow the *extensional* approach to the representation of assertions [15], where specifications are predicates (in the meta-logic) over semantic components and can refer to the initial and final heaps of a program expression, the initial environment, the resources consumed and the result value: $\mathcal{A} \equiv \mathcal{E} \to \mathcal{H} \to \mathcal{H} \to \mathcal{V} \to \mathcal{R} \to \mathcal{B}$, where $\mathcal{B}$ is the set of booleans. Satisfaction of a specification P by program e is denoted by $\models e : P$. We interpret a judgement $\models e : \lambda E h h' v p. P E h h' v p$ to mean that whenever the execution of e for initial heap h and environment E terminates and delivers final heap h', result v and resources p, P is satisfied, that is that $E \vdash h, e \Downarrow (h', v, p)$ implies $P E h h' v p$.

Similar to assertions in VDM logics, our specifications relate pre- and post-states without auxiliary variables. For example, programs that do not allocate heap space satisfy the assertion $|dom(h)| = |dom(h')|$.

Rules: In the program logic, contexts Γ manage assumptions when dealing with (mutually) recursive or externally defined methods. They consist of pairs of expressions and specifications: $\mathcal{G} \equiv expr \times \mathcal{A}$. In addition to rules for each form of program expression there are two logical rules, VAX and VCONSEQ.

$$\frac{(e,P) \in \Gamma}{\Gamma \triangleright e : P} \text{ (VAX)} \qquad \frac{\Gamma \triangleright e : P \quad \forall E h h' v p. P E h h' v p \longrightarrow Q E h h' v p}{\Gamma \triangleright e : Q} \text{ (VCONSEQ)}$$

$$\frac{}{\Gamma \triangleright \mathtt{null} : \lambda E h h' v p. h' = h \wedge v = \mathtt{null} \wedge p = \langle 1\,0\,0\,0 \rangle} \text{ (VNULL)}$$

$$\frac{}{\Gamma \triangleright \mathtt{int}\, i : \lambda E h h' v p. h' = h \wedge v = i \wedge p = \langle 1\,0\,0\,0 \rangle} \text{ (VINT)}$$

$$\frac{}{\Gamma \triangleright \mathtt{var}\, x : \lambda E h h' v p. h' = h \wedge v = E\langle x \rangle \wedge p = \langle 1\,0\,0\,0 \rangle} \text{ (VVAR)}$$

$$\frac{}{\Gamma \triangleright \mathtt{prim}\, op\, x\, y : \lambda E h h' v p.\, v = op\, E\langle x \rangle\, E\langle y \rangle \ \wedge h' = h \wedge p = \langle 3\,0\,0\,0 \rangle} \text{ (VPRIM)}$$

$$\frac{}{\Gamma \triangleright x.t : \lambda E h h' v p. \exists l.\, E\langle x \rangle = \mathsf{Ref}\, l \wedge h' = h \ \wedge v = h'(l).t \ \wedge p = \langle 2\,0\,0\,0 \rangle} \text{ (VGETF)}$$

$$\frac{}{\Gamma \triangleright x.t{:=}y : \lambda E h h' v p. \exists l.\, E\langle x \rangle = \mathsf{Ref}\, l \wedge p = \langle 3\,0\,0\,0 \rangle \ \wedge \ h' = h[l.t \mapsto E\langle y \rangle] \ \wedge v = \bot} \text{ (VPUTF)}$$

$$\frac{}{\Gamma \triangleright c \diamond t : \lambda E h h' v p. h' = h \ \wedge v = h(c).t \ \wedge p = \langle 2\,0\,0\,0 \rangle} \text{ (VGETST)}$$

$$\frac{}{\Gamma \triangleright c \diamond t{:=}y : \lambda E h h' v p. h' = h[c.t \mapsto E\langle y \rangle] \ \wedge v = \bot \wedge p = \langle 3\,0\,0\,0 \rangle} \text{ (VPUTST)}$$

$$\frac{}{\Gamma \triangleright \text{new } c\ \overline{[t_i := x_i]} : \lambda E\, hh'\, v\, p.\, \exists l.\ l = freshloc(h) \land p = \langle (n+1)\ 0\ 0\ 0 \rangle \land} \quad \text{(VNEW)}$$
$$h' = h[l \mapsto (c, \{\overline{t_i := E\langle x_i \rangle}\})] \land v = \text{Ref } l$$

$$\frac{\Gamma \triangleright e_1 : P_1 \quad \Gamma \triangleright e_2 : P_2}{\Gamma \triangleright \text{if } x \text{ then } e_1 \text{ else } e_2 : \lambda E\, hh'\, v\, p.\, \exists p'.\ p = p' \oplus \langle 2\ 0\ 0\ 0 \rangle \land} \quad \text{(VIF)}$$
$$(E\langle x \rangle = \text{true} \longrightarrow P_1\, E\, hh'\, v\, p') \land$$
$$(E\langle x \rangle = \text{false} \longrightarrow P_2\, E\, hh'\, v\, p') \land$$
$$(E\langle x \rangle = \text{true} \lor E\langle x \rangle = \text{false})$$

$$\frac{\Gamma \triangleright e_1 : P_1 \quad \Gamma \triangleright e_2 : P_2}{\Gamma \triangleright \text{let } x = e_1 \text{ in } e_2 : \lambda E\, hh'\, v\, p.\, \exists\ p_1\ p_2\ h_1\ w.\ (P_1\, E\, hh_1\, w\, p_1) \land w \neq \bot \land} \quad \text{(VLET)}$$
$$(P_2\, (E\langle x := w \rangle)\, h_1\, h'\, v\, p_2) \land$$
$$p = \langle 1\ 0\ 0\ 0 \rangle \oplus (p_1 \smile p_2)$$

$$\frac{\Gamma \triangleright e_1 : P_1 \quad \Gamma \triangleright e_2 : P_2}{\Gamma \triangleright e_1 ; e_2 : \lambda E\, hh'\, v\, p.\, \exists\ p_1\ p_2\ h_1.\ P_1\, E\, hh_1\, \bot\, p_1 \land} \quad \text{(VCOMP)}$$
$$P_2\, E\, h_1\, h'\, v\, p_2 \land p = p_1 \smile p_2$$

$$\frac{\Gamma \cup \{(\text{call } f, P)\} \triangleright snd(FT\, f) : \lambda E\, hh'\, v\, p.\, P\, E\, hh'\, v\, \langle 1\ 1\ 0\ 0 \rangle \oplus p}{\Gamma \triangleright \text{call } f : P} \quad \text{(VCALL)}$$

$$\frac{\Gamma \cup \{(c \diamond m(\overline{a}), P)\} \triangleright snd(MT\, c\, m) : \lambda E\, hh'\, v\, p.\, \forall\ E'.\ E = (newframe\ \text{null}\ fst(MT\, c\, m)\ \overline{a}\ E')}{\Gamma \triangleright c \diamond m(\overline{a}) : P} \quad$$
$$\longrightarrow P\, E'\, hh'\, v\, \langle (2 + |\overline{a}|)\ 0\ 1\ 1 \rangle \oplus p$$

(VSINV)

$$\frac{\Gamma \cup \{x \cdot m(\overline{a}), P)\} \triangleright}{\Gamma \triangleright x \cdot m(\overline{a}) : P}$$
$$snd(MT\, c\, m) : \lambda\, E\, h\, h'\, v\, p.\, \forall\, E'.\, (classOf\, E\, h\, x\, c \land$$
$$E = (newframe\, (E'\langle x \rangle)\, fst(MT\, c\, m)\ \overline{a}\ E'))$$
$$\longrightarrow (E', h, h', v, \langle (4 + |\overline{a}|)\ 0\ 1\ 1 \rangle \oplus p) \in P$$

(VVINV)

The axiom rule VAX allows one to use specifications found in the context. The VCON-SEQ consequence rule derives an assertion Q that follows from another assertion P. The leaf rules (VNULL to VNEW) directly model the corresponding rules in the operational semantics, with constants for the resource tuples. The VIF rule uses the appropriate assertion based on the boolean value in the variable x. Since the evaluation of the branch condition does not modify the heap we only existentially quantify over the resource tuple p'. In contrast, rule VLET existentially quantifies over the result value w, the heap h_1 resulting from evaluating e_1, and the resources from e_1 and e_2. Apart from the absence of environment update, rule VCOMP is similar to VLET. By relating pre and post conditions in a single assertion we avoid the complications associated to the usual VDM rules for sequencing [14]. However, this makes reasoning about *total* correctness more difficult. The rules for recursive functions and methods involve the context and generalize Hoare's original rule for parameterless recursive procedures. They require one to prove that the function or method body satisfies the required specification (with an updated resource component) under the additional assumption that the assertion holds for further calls or invocations.

Admissible Rules: A context weakening rule is easily seen to be admissible. We can also prove the following cut rule by induction on derivations of $\{(e',P)\} \cup \Delta \rhd e : Q$,

$$\frac{\{(e',P)\} \cup \Delta \rhd e : Q \qquad \Gamma \rhd e' : P \qquad \Gamma \subseteq \Delta}{\Delta \rhd e : Q} \quad \text{(CUT)}$$

One of the contributions of this paper lies in an innovative approach to mutually recursive procedures and adaptation. In fact, rules VCALL, VSINV and VVINV already cover the case of mutual recursion. So we do not need a separate derivation system for judgements with *sets* of assertions and related set introduction and elimination rules, as for example Nipkow does [24], nor do we need to modify the consequence rule to take care of adaptation. The treatment is based on specification tables for functions and methods. A function specification table *FST* maps each function identifier to an assertion, a virtual method specification table *vMST* maps triples consisting of variable names, method names and (actual) argument lists to assertions, and a static method specification table *sMST* maps triples consisting of class names, method names and (actual) argument lists to assertions. Since the types allow us to disambiguate between the three tables, we use the notation *ST* to refer to their union.

A context Γ is *good* with respect to the specification tables, notation $good_{ST}(\Gamma)$, if all entries $(e,P) \in \Gamma$ satisfy

$$(\exists f. \, e = \mathtt{call}\, f \,\wedge\, P = FST\, f \,\wedge\, \Gamma \rhd snd(FT\, f) : Q_0(f)) \,\vee$$
$$(\exists c\, m\, \overline{a}. \, e = c \diamond m(\overline{a}) \,\wedge\, P = ST\, c\, m\, \overline{a} \,\wedge\, \forall \overline{b}. \Gamma \rhd snd(MT\, c\, m) : Q_1(c,m,\overline{b})) \,\vee$$
$$(\exists x\, m\, \overline{a}. \, e = x \cdot m(\overline{a}) \,\wedge\, P = ST\, x\, m\, \overline{a} \,\wedge\, \forall y\, \overline{b}\, c. \, \Gamma \rhd snd(MT\, c\, m) : Q_2(c,m,\overline{b},y))$$

where

$$Q_0(f) \equiv \lambda E h h' v p. (FST\, f) \, E\, h\, h'\, v\, (\langle 1\, 1\, 0\, 0 \rangle \oplus p)$$
$$Q_1(c,m,\overline{b}) \equiv \lambda E h h' v p. \forall E'. \, E = (newframe\; \mathtt{null}\, fst(MT\, c\, m)\, \overline{b}\, E')$$
$$\longrightarrow ST\, c\, m\, \overline{b}\, E'\, h\, h'\, v\, (\langle (2 + |\overline{b}|)\, 0\, 1\, 1 \rangle \oplus p)$$
$$Q_2(c,m,\overline{b},y) \equiv \lambda E h h' v p. \forall E'. \, (classOf\; E'\, h\, y\, c \,\wedge$$
$$E = (newframe\; (E'\langle y \rangle)\, fst(MT\, c\, m)\, \overline{b}\, E'))$$
$$\longrightarrow ST\, y\, m\, \overline{b}\, E'\, h\, h'\, v\, (\langle (4 + |\overline{b}|)\, 0\, 1\, 1 \rangle \oplus p).$$

Using the cut rule, we can prove that *good* contexts are subset-closed.

Lemma 1. $good_{ST}(\Gamma) \longrightarrow good_{ST}(\Gamma - \{(e,P)\})$.

By combining this lemma with another application of CUT, one can prove by induction on the size of Γ the following rule for mutually recursive function calls or method invocations, for the *empty* context,

$$\frac{\Gamma \, finite \quad good_{ST}(\Gamma) \quad (e,P) \in \Gamma}{\rhd e : P} \quad \text{(MUTREC)}$$

A variant of Lemma 1 also plays an important part in the proof of our adaptation rule. Parameter adaptation is notoriously problematic and has often been coupled with rules of consequence, resulting in fairly complicated rules [15, 24, 25]. Instead, building on the notion of *good*, we can prove (via cut and weakening) the following lemma, which allows one to change the actual parameters from $\overline{b}$ to $\overline{a}$.

Lemma 2. $(good_{ST}(\Gamma) \wedge (c \diamond m(\overline{b}), ST \ c \ m \ \overline{b}) \in \Gamma) \longrightarrow$
$$\Gamma - \{(c \diamond m(\overline{b}), ST \ c \ m \ \overline{b})\} \triangleright c \diamond m(\overline{a}) : ST \ c \ m \ \overline{a}$$

The predicate *good* ensures, that for every pair method invocation/specification over given actual arguments, the context proves that the method body satisfies the same specification over any other arguments, provided the former is updated to reflect the new environment with the appropriate binding for the formal parameters. Since we want to prove specifications in the empty context, the lemma allows one to shrink the context.

From that, adaptation in the empty context follows:

$$\frac{\Gamma \, finite \quad good_{ST}(\Gamma) \quad (c \diamond m(\overline{b}), ST \ c \ m \ \overline{b}) \in \Gamma}{\triangleright c \diamond m(\overline{a}) : ST \ c \ m \ \overline{a}} \tag{ADAPTS}$$

We shall see this rule in action in Section 4. Both, Lemma 2 and rule ADAPTS, have counterparts for virtual methods.

Soundness. We first define the *validity* of an assertion for a given program expression in a given context. In order to deal with soundness of function calls and method invocations we additionally parameterise the operational semantics by a natural number acting as the height of the evaluation [10, 15, 24].

Definition 1. *(Validity) Specification P is valid for e, written* $\models_n e : P$, *if*

$$(m \leq n \ \wedge E \vdash h, e \Downarrow_m (h', v, p)) \longrightarrow P E h h' v p.$$

We define $\models e : P$ as $\forall n. \models_n e : P$. Note that the counter n restricts the set of pre- and post-states for which P has to be fulfilled. It is easy to show that this bound, occurring negatively in the validity formula, can be weakened, i.e. $(m < n \wedge \models_n e : P) \longrightarrow \models_m e : P$. Validity is generalised to contexts as follows:

Definition 2. *(Context Validity) Context Γ is valid, written* $\models_n \Gamma$, *if* $\models_n e : P$ *holds for all* $(e, P) \in \Gamma$. *Assertion P is valid for e in context Γ, denoted* $\Gamma \models_n e : P$, *if* $\models_n \Gamma$ *implies* $\models_n e : P$.

The soundness theorem follows from a stronger result expressing the soundness property for contextual, relativised validity.

Theorem 1. *(Soundness)* $\Gamma \triangleright e : P \longrightarrow \forall n. \Gamma \models_n e : P$.

Completeness. The program logic may be proven complete relative to the ambient logic (here HOL) using the notion of *strongest specifications*, similar to *most general triples* in Hoare-style verification.

Definition 3. *(Strongest Specification) The strongest specification of expression e is*

$$SSpec(e) = \lambda E \ h \ h' \ v \ p. \ E \vdash h, e \Downarrow (h', v, p).$$

It is not difficult to prove that strongest specifications are valid, i.e. $\models e : SSpec(e)$, and further that they are stronger than any other valid specification, that is ($\models e : P \wedge SSpec(e)\ E\ h\ h'\ v\ p$) $\longrightarrow P\ E\ h\ h'\ v\ p$.

The overall proof idea of completeness follows [10, 24]: we first prove a lemma that allows one to relate *any* expression e to $SSpec(e)$ in a context Γ, provided that Γ in turn relates each function or method call to its strongest specification.

Lemma 3. $\begin{pmatrix} \forall\,f.\ \Gamma \triangleright \mathtt{call}\,f : SSpec(\mathtt{call}\,f)\ \wedge \\ \forall\,c\,m\,\overline{a}.\ \Gamma \triangleright c \diamond m(\overline{a}) : SSpec(c \diamond m(\overline{a}))\ \wedge \\ \forall\,x\,m\,\overline{a}.\ \Gamma \triangleright x \cdot m(\overline{a}) : SSpec(x \cdot m(\overline{a})) \end{pmatrix} \longrightarrow \Gamma \triangleright e : SSpec(e)$

The proof of this lemma proceeds by induction on the structure of e. Next, we define a specific context, $\widehat{\Gamma}$, containing exactly the strongest specifications for all function calls and method invocations.

$$\widehat{\Gamma} \equiv \{(e, P) \mid P = SSpec(e)\ \wedge\ \begin{pmatrix} (\exists f.\ e = \mathtt{call}\,f) \vee (\exists\,c\,m\,\overline{a}.\ e = c \diamond m(\overline{a})) \vee \\ (\exists\,x\,m\,\overline{a}.\ e = x \cdot m(\overline{a})) \end{pmatrix}\}.$$

We also define specification tables that associate the strongest assertions to all calls and invocations:

$$\widehat{ST} \equiv (\lambda f.\ SSpec(\mathtt{call}\,f)) \cup (\lambda\,c\,m\,\overline{a}.\ SSpec(c \diamond m(\overline{a}))) \cup (\lambda\,x\,m\,\overline{a}.\ SSpec(x \cdot m(\overline{a}))).$$

Next, we show that $\widehat{\Gamma}$ is *good* with respect to these tables:

Lemma 4. $good_{\widehat{ST}}(\widehat{\Gamma})$.

On the other hand, combining a variant of rule CUT and MUTREC with Lemma 3 yields

Lemma 5. *If $good_{ST}(\widehat{\Gamma})$ and $\widehat{\Gamma}$ finite, then $\triangleright e : SSpec(e)$ holds for all e,*

for arbitrary specification tables ST. Finally, combining Lemmas 4 and 5 and rule VCONSEQ yields

Theorem 2. *(Completeness) If $\widehat{\Gamma}$ finite and $\models e : P$ then $\triangleright e : P$.*

The finiteness condition merely represents a constraint on the syntactic categories of function and method names. It is fulfilled for any concrete program.

4 Examples

In this section we give examples of proving resource properties of Grail programs working on integer lists. We first discuss how lists are modelled in our formalisation and then consider in-place list reversal and doubling elements in a list as example programs. The Grail code in this section corresponds to the Isabelle-output of the Camelot compiler.

During the compilation, heap-allocated data structures arise from algebraic datatypes in Camelot. Values of the type `ilist = Nil | Cons of int * ilist` are represented as a linked list of objects of the diamond class. Each node contains fields HD, TL and TAG, where TAG indicates the constructor (`Nil` or `Cons`) used to create the cell. Since our verification targets the consumption of resources rather than full correctness we use a representation predicate that ensures that a portion of the heap represents a list structure without considering the data contained in individual cells. The predicate takes the form $h, l \models_X n$, to be read as "starting at location l the sub-heap of h given by the set X of locations contains a list of length n". It is defined inductively, using the additional notation $class_h(l)$ to refer to the class of the object located at l in heap h.

$$(class_h(l) = \mathsf{ILIST} \wedge h(l).\mathsf{TAG} = 0) \longrightarrow h, l \models_{\{l\}} 0$$

$$\left(\begin{array}{l} class_h(l) = \mathsf{ILIST} \wedge h(l).\mathsf{TAG} = 1 \wedge \\ h(l).\mathsf{TL} = \mathsf{Ref}\, r \wedge l \notin X \wedge h, r \models_X n \end{array} \right) \longrightarrow h, l \models_{X \cup \{l\}} n + 1$$

Similar predicates have been used by Reynolds in separation logic [26]. Notice that in the second case the reference l has to be distinct from all previously used locations X.

In-place reversal: Returning to our motivating example from the introduction, the following Grail code is produced for the method *rev* in class ILIST with formal parameters $[l, acc]$:

```
let tag=l.TAG in   let b=prim iszero tag tag in
if b then var acc
    else let h=l.HD in  let t=l.TL in  let one=int 1 in
              l.TAG:=one;l.HD:=h;l.TL:=acc;ILIST ◇ rev([t,l])
```

We constrain the specification tables to contain the entry

$$ST\ \mathsf{ILIST}\ rev\ z\ E\ h\ h'\ v\ p =$$
$$\forall\, n\, a\, X\, m\, b\, Y.\ \left(\begin{array}{l} (eval\ E\ z = [\mathsf{Ref}\, a, \mathsf{Ref}\, b] \wedge h, a \models_X n \wedge h, b \models_Y m \wedge X \cap Y = \emptyset) \\ \longrightarrow |dom(h)| = |dom(h')| \wedge p = \langle (29n + 13)\ 0\ (n+1)\ (n+1) \rangle \end{array} \right)$$

If the first method argument points initially to a list of length n, and the second argument points to some other (disjoint) list, any terminating execution of *rev* returns a heap of the same size as the initial heap, and the number of instructions and function calls (jump instructions) depend linearly on n. The function *eval* implements the evaluation of methods arguments and is part of the *newframe* construction. We aim to prove the property

$$\triangleright \mathsf{ILIST} \diamond rev([x, y]) : ST\ \mathsf{ILIST}\ rev\ [x, y] \tag{1}$$

which states that an invocation of *rev* with (arbitrary) arguments x and y satisfies its specification. The generic structure of a proof of such a resource predicate first applies the rule ADAPTS. The required context Γ contains one entry for each method invocation that occurs in the method body, pairing each such call with its specification:

$$\Gamma \equiv \{ (\mathsf{ILIST} \diamond rev([t, l]), ST\ \mathsf{ILIST}\ rev\ [t, l]) \}.$$

As the main lemma we then prove that Γ is *good* with respect to the specification tables:

$$good_{ST}(\Gamma).$$

The proof of this statement proceeds by first applying the VDM rules VSINV and VCON-SEQ, and then the other syntax-directed rules according to the program text, closing the recursion by an invocation of VAX. This first phase can be seen as a classical VCG over the program logic rules. Two side conditions remain, requiring us to show that both branches satisfy the specification — the verification condition of the recursion case amounts to a loop invariant. Both side conditions can be discharged by unfolding the definition of $h, l \models_x n$ and instantiating some quantifiers.

Where do the polynomials in the specification come from? Currently, we have left those values indeterminate and have them generated during a proof. In a later phase of the project, the Camelot compiler will generate certificates for such resource properties based on high-level program analysis similar to [12]'s type system for heap space consumption. The syntactic form of *rev* would allow a tail-call optimisation, where the recursive method invocation is transformed into a recursive function call satisfying the Grail calling convention.

Doubling a list: Consider the following code for doubling the elements of a list.

```
let double l = match l with
                    Nil@d -> Nil@d
                  | Cons(h,t)@d -> Cons(h,Cons(h,double t)@d)
```

Remember the usage of @ indicates that heap cells which are freed during a match may be reused later — but only once [11] — so the outer application of Cons will require the allocation of fresh memory. Since the recursion occurs in non-tail position, it cannot be replaced by a simple function recursion and the resulting Grail code contains a static method ILIST $\diamond$ *double*(*l*) with body

$$
\begin{aligned}
&\text{let } x = l.\text{TAG in} \quad \text{let } b = \text{prim } iszero \; x \; x \text{ in} \\
&\text{if } b \text{ then let } zero = \text{int } 0 \text{ in} \quad l.\text{TAG}:=zero;\text{var } l \\
&\quad\quad \text{else let } x = l.\text{HD in} \quad \text{let } t = l.\text{TL in} \quad \text{let } y = \text{var } l \text{ in} \\
&\quad\quad\quad \text{let } z = \text{ILIST} \diamond double([t]) \text{ in} \quad \text{let } one = \text{int } 1 \text{ in} \\
&\quad\quad\quad y.\text{TAG}:=one;y.\text{HD}:=x;y.\text{TL}:=z;\text{let } l = \text{var } y \text{ in} \\
&\quad\quad\quad \text{new ILIST } [(\text{TAG}, one), (\text{HD}, x), (\text{TL}, l)]
\end{aligned}
$$

The specification has the same general structure as before, but now asserts that the heap grows by n many objects, that no function calls occur, and that both the number and the nesting depth of method invocations are linear in n.

$$
ST \text{ ILIST } double \; z \; E \; h \; h' \; v \; p = \forall \, n \, a \, X. \left(
\begin{array}{l}
(eval \, E \, z \, = \, [\text{Ref } a] \, \wedge \, h, a \models_x n) \\
\longrightarrow \, |dom(h')| = |dom(h)| + n \wedge \\
p = \langle (35n + 18) \; 0 \; (n+1) \; (n+1) \rangle
\end{array}
\right)
$$

We prove the following resource property for an arbitrary x:

$$
\triangleright \text{ ILIST} \diamond double([x]) : ST \text{ ILIST } double \; [x]
$$

The proof has the same overall structure as the previous one, where the auxiliary lemma now reads

$$
good_{ST}(\{ \, (\text{ILIST} \diamond double([t])), ST \text{ ILIST } double \; [t] \, \}) .
$$

5   Related Work

Most closely related to our work on the meta-theoretical side are Nipkow's implementation of Hoare logic in Isabelle/HOL [24], the Java-light logic by von Oheimb [29], Kleymann's thesis [15], and Hofmann's [10] work on completeness of program logics. The logic by Nipkow in [24] is for a while-language with parameterless functions, with proofs of soundness and completeness. Several techniques we use in our treatment are inspired by this work, such as modelling of the heap via mini-heaps. However, we have made progress on the treatment of mutual recursion and adaptation. Several options for formalising either VDM or Hoare-style program logics have been explored by Kleymann [15]. In particular this work demonstrates how to formalise an adaptation rule that permits to modify auxiliary variables. The techniques used in our completeness proof are based on those by one of the authors in [10].

The program logic for Java-light by von Oheimb [29] is encoded in Isabelle/HOL and proven sound and complete. It covers more object-oriented features, but works on a higher level than our logic for a bytecode language and does not cover resources. Moreover, it is hardly suitable for concrete program verification.

With respect to other relevant program logics, de Boer [8] presents a sound and complete Hoare-style logic for an sequential object-oriented language with inheritance and subtyping. In contrast to our approach, the proof system employs a specific assertion language for object structures, whose WP calculus is heavily based on syntactical substitutions. Recently a tool supporting the verification of annotated programs (flowcharts) yielding verification conditions to be solved in HOL has been produced [5]. This also extends to multi-threaded Java [2].

Abadi and Leino combine a program logic for an object-oriented language with a type system [1, 16]. The language supports sub-classing and recursive object types and attaches specifications as well as types to expressions. In contrast to our logics, it uses a global store model, with the possibility of storing pointers to arbitrary methods in objects. As a result of this design decision this logic is incomplete. An implementation of this logic and a verification condition generator are described in [28].

Several projects aim at developing program logics for subsets of Java, mainly as tools for program development. Müller and Poetzsch-Heffter present a sound Hoare-style logic for a Java subset [22]. Their language covers class and interface types with subtyping and inheritance, as well as dynamic and static binding, and aliasing via object references, see also the Jive tool [20]. As part of the LOOP project, Huisman and Jacobs [13] present an extension of a Hoare logic that includes means for reasoning about abrupt termination and side-effects, encoded in the PVS theorem prover. Krakatoa [18] is a tool for verifying JML-annotated Java programs that acts as front-end to the Why system [9], using Coq to model the semantics and conduct the proofs. Why produces proof-obligations for programs in imperative-functional style via an interpretation in a type theory of effects and monads. Similarly, the target of the JACK environment [6] are verification conditions for the B system from JML annotations, though much effort is invested in making the system usable by Java programmers. We also mention [19], which embeds a Hoare logic in HOL, following previous work by Mike Gordon, to reason about pointer programs in a simple while-language. As an example, the authors provide an interactive proof in ISAR of the correctness of the Schorr-Waite algorithm.

Finally, [21] proves properties of the JVM in ACL2 directly from invariants and the operational semantics, that is without resorting to a VCG.

6 Conclusions

This paper has presented a resource-aware program logic for Grail, together with proofs of soundness and completeness. Our logic is unique in combining reasoning about resources for a general object-oriented language with completeness results for this logic. Grail is an abstraction over the JVM bytecode language which can be given a semi-functional semantics. We have developed admissible rules to work with mutually recursive methods, including parameter adaptation. While the logic already covers dynamic method invocation, we left a formalisation of the class hierarchy for future research. The logic has been encoded in the Isabelle/HOL theorem prover, and the formalisation of the soudness and completeness proofs provide additional confidence in the results. We demonstrated the usability of the logic by giving some examples, where we proved concrete resource bounds on space and time. These example programs have been generated by the Camelot compiler, indicating that the logic is sufficiently expressive to serve as the target logic in our proof-carrying-code infrastructure. In order to mechanise the verification of concrete programs, we are currently defining more specialised logics for various resources. These logics are defined in terms of the logic presented in this paper and thus inherit crucial properties such as soundness.

Acknowledgements

This research was supported by the MRG project (IST-2001-33149) which is funded by the EC under the FET proactive initiative on Global Computing. We would like to thank all the MRG members as well as Tobias Nipkow and his group for discussions about formalising program logics.

References

1. M. Abadi and R. Leino. A Logic of Object-Oriented Programs. In *TAPSOFT '97: Theory and Practice of Software Development*, volume 1214 of *LNCS*, pages 682–696. Springer, 1997.
2. E. Abraham-Mumm, F. S. de Boer, W. P. de Roever, , and M. Steffen. A tool-supported proof system for mutlithreaded Java. In F. de Boer, M. Bonsangue, S. Graf, and W.-P. de Roever, editors, *FMCO 2002: Formal Methods for Component Objects, Proceedings*, LNCS. Springer, 2003.
3. D. Aspinall and M. Hofmann. Another Type System for In-Place Update. In *ESOP'02 – European Symposium on Programming*, volume 2305 of *LNCS*, pages 36–52. Springer, 2002.
4. L. Beringer, K. MacKenzie, and I. Stark. Grail: a Functional Form for Imperative Mobile Code. *Electronic Notes in Theoretical Computer Science*, 85(1), 2003.
5. F. d. Boer and C. Pierik. Computer-aided specification and verification of annotated object-oriented programs. In B. Jacobs and A. Rensink, editors, *FMOODS 2002*, volume 209 of *IFIP Conference Proceedings*, pages 163–177. Kluwer, 2002.

6. L. Burdy and A. Requet. Jack: Java applet correctness kit. In *4th Gemplus Developer Conference,*, 2002.
7. C. Colby, P. Lee, G. Necula, F. Blau, M. Plesko, and K. Cline. A Certifying Compiler for Java. In *PLDI'00 – Conference on Programming Language Design and Implementation*, pages 95–107. ACM Press, 2000.
8. F. de Boer. A WP-calculus for OO. In *Foundations of Software Science and Computation Structures*, volume 1578 of *LNCS*, pages 135–149. Springer, 1999.
9. J.-C. Filliâtre. Why: a multi-language multi-prover verification tool. Research Report 1366, LRI, Université Paris Sud, Mar. 2003. http://www.lri.fr/ filliatr/ftp/publis/why-tool.ps.gz.
10. M. Hofmann. Semantik und Verifikation. Lecture Notes, WS 97/98 1998. TU Darmstadt.
11. M. Hofmann. A Type System for Bounded Space and Functional In-place Update. *Nordic Journal of Computing*, 7(4):258–289, 2000.
12. M. Hofmann and S. Jost. Static Prediction of Heap Space Usage for First-Order Functional Programs. In *POPL'03 – Symposium on Principles of Programming Languages*, pages 185–197, New Orleans, LA, USA, Jan. 2003. ACM Press.
13. M. Huisman and B. Jacobs. Java Program Verfication via a Hoare Logic with Abrupt Termination. In *FASE'00 – Fundamental Approaches to Software Engineering*, volume 1783 of *LNCS*, pages 284–303. Springer, 2000.
14. C. Jones. *Systematic Software Development Using VDM*. Prentice Hall, 1990.
15. T. Kleymann. *Hoare Logic and VDM: Machine-Checked Soundness and Completeness Proofs*. PhD thesis, LFCS, University of Edinburgh, 1999.
16. R. Leino. Recursive Object Types in a Logic of Object-oriented Programs. *Nordic Journal of Computing*, 5(4):330–360, 1998.
17. K. MacKenzie and N. Wolverson. Camelot and Grail: Compiling a Resource-aware Functional Language for the Java Virtual Machine. In *TFP'03, Symposium on Trends in Functional Languages*, Edinburgh, Sep. 11–12, 2003.
18. C. Marche, C. Paulin-Mohring, and X. Urbain. The KRAKATOA tool for certification of JAVA/JAVACARD programs annotated in JML. *Journal of Logic and Algebraic Programming*, 58:89, January 2004.
19. F. Mehta and T. Nipkow. Proving pointer programs in higher-order logic. In F. Baader, editor, *Automated Deduction – CADE-19*, volume 2741 of *LNCS*, pages 121–135. Springer, 2003.
20. J. Meyer, P. Müller, and A. Poetzsch-Heffter. The JIVE system–implementation description. Available from www.informatik.fernuni-hagen.de/pi5/publications.html, 2000.
21. J. S. Moore. Proving theorems about Java and the JVM with ACL2. *NATO Science Series Sub Series III Computer and Systems Sciences*, 191:227–290, 2003.
22. P. Müller and A. Poetzsch-Heffter. A Programming Logic for Sequential Java. In *ESOP'99 – European Symposium on Programming*, volume 1576 of *LNCS*, pages 162–176, 1999.
23. G. Necula. Proof-carrying Code. In *POPL'97 – Symposium on Principles of Programming Languages*, pages 106–116, Paris, France, January 15–17, 1997. ACM Press.
24. T. Nipkow. Hoare Logics for Recursive Procedures and Unbounded Nondeterminism. In *Computer Science Logic (CSL 2002)*, volume 2471 of *LNCS*, pages 103–119. Springer, 2002.
25. C. Pierik and F. d. Boer. A rule of adaptation for OO. Technical Report UU-CS-2003-032, Utrecht University, 2004.
26. J. Reynolds. Separation Logic: A Logic for Shared Mutable Data Structures. In *LICS'02 – Symposium on Logic in Computer Science*, Copenhagen, Denmark, July 22–25, 2002.
27. D. Sannella and M. Hofmann. Mobile Resource Guarantees. EU OpenFET Project, 2002. http://www.dcs.ed.ac.uk/home/mrg/.
28. F. Tang. *Towards feasible, machine assisted verification of object-oriented programs*. PhD thesis, School of Informatics, University of Edinburgh, 2002.
29. D. von Oheimb. Hoare logic for Java in Isabelle/HOL. *Concurrency and Computation: Practice and Experience*, 13(13):1173–1214, 2001.

Proof Reuse with Extended Inductive Types

Olivier Boite

Institut d'Informatique d'Entreprise, Laboratoire CEDRIC,
18 allée Jean Rostand F-91025 Evry, France
boite@iie.cnam.fr

Abstract. Proof assistants based on type theory such as COQ or LEGO, put emphasis on inductive specifications and proofs by featuring expressive inductive types. It is frequent to modify an existing specification or proof by adding or modifying constructors in inductive types. In the context of language design, adding constructors is a common practice to make progress step-by-step. In this article, we propose a mechanism to extend and parameter inductive types, and a proof reuse mechanism founded on proof terms reuse.

1 Motivations

Using a theorem prover to specify and prove properties increases the confidence we can have in proofs. It often happens that we write specifications and prove theorems, then modify specifications and check if theorems are still valid. Since proving is time and effort consuming, reusing existing specifications and proofs can be very useful. However, this problem is difficult and a lot of works concern proof reuse.

Proof assistants based on type theory such as COQ or LEGO, put emphasis on inductive specifications and proofs by featuring expressive inductive types. Extending an inductive type by adding cases in the specifications is a frequent practice. But, in this case all the proofs must be replayed and updated. Usually one will reuse the previous proofs with the *cut and paste* facilities of his/her favorite editor. Adding constructors step-by-step allows to reuse or adapt existing specifications and proofs, to save time. In the context of language semantics, this kind of approach is frequently adopted: as in [Pie00], we are often interested in verifying if a semantic property remains valid even if new constructions are imported. A famous example is a property related to type systems and evaluation, that is the well-known subject reduction theorem (SRT): the execution of a well-typed program, will never meet a type error. In pen and paper proofs of SRT, we can admit that a proof is similar to the previous one for the common cases. We often read: "the proof is similar to Damas Milner's". Many embeddings have been performed in theorem provers [NOP00,Dub00,Sym99,Van97]. Nevertheless in machine assisted proofs, no tool exists and the reuse is simply done by *cut and paste* of the proof script, checking where modifications are necessary.

To formalize and prove a property, we first need to give specifications with abstract types, inductive types, functions and predicates. Then, before proving

K. Slind et al. (Eds.): TPHOLs 2004, LNCS 3223, pp. 50–65, 2004.
© Springer-Verlag Berlin Heidelberg 2004

a complex theorem we can prove preliminary but simple lemmas, or use a proof library. This collection of definitions and proofs is called a formal development. Our mechanism relies on the dependencies introduced between the components of a formal development. Indeed, when we add constructors in an inductive type (such as the abstract syntax of expressions, or the type system), all lemmas proved by induction or case analysis need to be proved again. The new proofs contain the old unchanged cases and new cases, corresponding to the supplementary constructors. So, the script of the previous version of the lemma can be reused, it only needs to be completed for the new cases.

The COQ system [Bar03] is a theorem prover based on the Calculus of Constructions, a typed λ-calculus. C. Paulin [PM96] extended this theory to the Calculus of Inductive Construction (CIC), where inductive types are native objects in the system. An inductive definition is specified by its name, its type, and the names and the types of the constructors.

The reuse we address here is restricted to reuse proofs after extension of inductive types or after adding parameters. When we add one or more constructors in an inductive definition, other constructors are unchanged. However, when a parameter is added, the existing constructors need to be updated by a dummy parameter. The modifications in inductive types we describe, are on top of the CIC, our purpose is not to provide a new calculus incorporating extension of inductive types. We adopt a simple and pragmatic approach: we propose a syntactic construction to extend and parameter an inductive type, and a proof reuse mechanism illustrated on top of COQ. Reusing proof can be realized in different ways: reusing scripts or reusing proof terms. We discuss briefly the first approach. The paper focuses on the second approach, which is definitly more powerful.

The paper is organised as follows. In section 2, we present some related work. In section 3, an example illustrates a scenario of extension and reuse. Section 4, presents a first attempt that relies on proof scripts. Then, in section 5 we describe a calculus of dependencies and the consequences on proofs. In section 6, we present the extension and parameterisation of inductive types, and our approach of formal reuse based on proof terms. In the last section, we formalize our approach.

2   Related Work

In this section we survey works that deal with adding constructors in an inductive type or more generally with reusing proofs. We also address the embedding of language semantics in proof checkers, because we focus on that application domain.

Extending an inductive type I in J with new constructors establishes a subtyping relation because all the elements defined with the constructors of I can also be defined with the constructors of J. E. Poll [Pol97] formalizes a notion of subtyping by adding constructors in an inductive type. However he focuses on programs and consequences on proofs are not explored. G. Barthe [BR00] proves Constructor Subtyping is well-behaved, but there is no corresponding implementation.

When a type I is a subtype of J and $\Gamma \vdash x : I$ is valid, we would like $\Gamma \vdash x : J$ to be valid too. A coercive subtyping consists in giving rules and a mechanism to allow such derivations. The tool PLASTIC [Cal00] implements coercive subtyping [Luo96]. The COQ system also incorporates a mechanism of implicit coercion. When defining a coercion from I to J, the user can transparently use objects of type I when a type J is expected. Adding constructors looks like adding methods in object oriented programming languages. We could expect to have an analogy with inheritance. However E. Poll showed in [Pol97] these two notions of adding are dual: adding a constructor in an inductive type produces a supertype, whereas adding a method produces a subtype. The comparison stops here, and our proof reuse will not use coercive subtyping.

Work on proof reuse exist in the domain of type isomorphisms [Mag03,BP01]. But, in our context the extended types are no longer isomorphic to the initial ones and we cannot explore this way.

With the tool TinkerType [LP99] developed by B. Pierce and M. Levin we can construct type systems by assembling a choice of typing rules among hundred ones. The system checks the consistency and produces a type checker. Unfortunately this framework does not provide any proof capacity.

S. Gay [Gay01] proposes a framework to formalize π- calculus type systems - calculus of mobile processes - in Isabelle/HOL. In this framework the formalization of type soundness proof, a general theory on type environments and the use of a meta-language facilitate the reuse for variations on type systems. However this reuse is finally done by hand.

The toolset Jakarta [BDHdS01] allows to reason about the JavaCard platform. [BC02] proposes to generate an elimination principle from a recursive function, to automatize reasoning about executable specifications. The technic used in this work is close to our's: we both implement a tactic that transforms λ-terms and generates proof obligations.

Tools exist to help in machine assisted semantics or more generally in formal proof, but, as far as we know, in the context of automated proofs no tool provides extension of inductive types with the feature of formal proof reuse.

3   A First Example

We describe here an example to illustrate the user's point of view of our proof reuse. The example presented here is very simple by lack of place. Its purpose is to illustrated how reusing a formal development with some new tactics incorporated in COQ (v7.4). We first define the type of very simple expressions built from natural numbers and additions:

```
Inductive expr : Set :=
    C : nat → expr | Add : expr → expr → expr.
```

The predicate (eval e n) claims the expression e is evaluated in n (plus is the function implementing addition between natural numbers).

```
Inductive eval : expr → nat → Prop :=
   evalC : ∀n:nat (eval (C n) n)
 | evalAdd : ∀e1,e2:expr ∀n1,n2:nat
               (eval e1 n1) → (eval e1 n2) →
               (eval (Add e1 e2) (plus n1 n2)).
```

Then we prove by induction on the first hypothesis that `eval` is deterministic.

```
Lemma eval_det : ∀e:expr, ∀n,m:nat (eval e n) → (eval e m) → n=m.
```

Now, we add variables in our language, so we need to define a new type for these expressions. We provide the command `Extend .. as .. with ..`, to generate this new type. We first introduce the abstract type `var` of variables.

```
Parameter var : Set.
Extend expr as expr2 with Var : var → expr2.
```

This last command generates the following definition, where old constructors are renamed by fresh identifiers.

```
Inductive expr2  : Set :=
     C0 : nat→expr2
   | Add0 : expr2→expr2→expr2
   | Var : var→expr2.
```

The type `expr2` is now available, together with the corresponding elimination principles generated by CoQ.

Before proving the determinism of the new language, we need to extend `eval` since it is used by the lemma. The evaluation requires now an environment represented as a function from identifier to natural numbers. So, we extend `eval` and we parameter with an environment `rho`.

```
Definition  env := (var → nat).
Parameter eval as eval2 with rho:env
 and extend with evalVar: (v:var)(eval2 rho (Var v) (rho v)).
```

This is equivalent to the following definition

```
Inductive eval2 [rho:env] : expr2→nat→Prop :=
     evalC0 : ∀n:nat (eval2 rho (C0 n) n)
   | evalAdd0 : ∀e1,e2:expr2, ∀r1,r2:nat
                  (eval2 rho e1 r1) →(eval2 rho e1 r2)
                  →(eval2 rho (Add0 e1 e2) (plus r1 r2))
   | evalVar : ∀v:var (eval2 rho (Var v) (rho v))
```

The type `eval2` is now parametered by `rho`, and occurences of `eval2` is the type of constructors have to be parametered by `rho` too. Now, the new lemma can be proved by using our tactic `Reuse`.

```
Lemma eval_det2 : ∀rho:env  ∀e:expr2 ∀n,m:nat (eval2 rho e n) →
                  (eval2 rho e m) → n=m.
Intro rho.
Reuse eval_det.
```

One subgoal is generated, for the variable case of the induction. We solve it with usual tactics.

```
rho : env
v : var
==============================
Vm:nat (eval2 rho (Var v) m)→(rho v)=m
```

```
Intros m Heval; Inversion Heval; Trivial.
```

4 Script Reuse

We describe here a first and naïve implementation of proof reuse based on tactic-style proof construction.

In the CoQ system, as in many other proof assistants LEGO [LP92], HOL [GM93], NuPRL [CAB+86], the standard way of building a proof consists in an interactive goal-directed process: the proof is obtained by successive refinements described by tactics. A tactic is applied to the current goal to split it in one or more subgoals, usually simpler to prove. A tactic may be a basic tactic (such as Intro or Case), or a composite one. Different combinators are provided, such as tacticals (for instance ; or orelse) or user-defined tactics implemented in the language Ltac [Del00] or decision procedures (for instance Omega).

The more basic method to reuse proof is to reuse the script of the old proof to construct automatically an incomplete proof. In the previous example, if we replay the script of eval_det to prove eval_det2, it remains a subgoal that corresponds to the new case.

From the user's point of view, a proof is just a list of tactics. Although a script is linear, it hides a tree structure called a tactic tree. A tactic tree is a tree of sequents - a goal and a context - where each node has associated with it a status, close or open, and the tactic which refines the node in its children. When the status of a node is *close*, the subtrees of the node are the result of the application of the *tactic* on the node. When the status is *open* the list of subtrees is empty as no tactic has been applied yet.

The tactic tree in CoQ is internally maintained until the proof is completed. In our context of extending and reusing, we do not throw it away: we keep and save it as an annotated script, where an annotation is the path in the tactic tree, of the tactic application.

We assume that a property L is conservative towards the extension of the type I. So, the set of the nodes in the tactic tree of the complete proof of L before extension of I, constitute a tactic tree of an incomplete proof of L after the extension of I:

- the new tactic tree contains all the paths contained in the old tactic tree
- for all common paths, the context, the goal and the tactic in the node of the old tactic tree are the same in the new one modulo renaming of extended lemmas and functions

Indeed, when a tactic related to an inductive definition I, such as Case, Induction, is applied to a goal, the generated subgoals are presented in the same order as the constructors in the definition of I. When we extend the type I by adding m new constructors, these new constructors are added *at the end* of the new inductive type. This is crucial to keep the same paths, when we construct the new tactic tree. The only difference in the new tactic tree is that some nodes have supplementary children whose status is *open*. These new subgoals are not proved, and the user must complete them by giving tactics.

This script approach allows a mechanized and sure *cut and paste* facility. It is a very simple way of reusing proofs, easy to implement and portable to any tactics oriented proof assistant. We have implemented it for COQ.

However this approach suffers from some drawbacks. The first one is that the script of the old version of the proof must be played and annotated with paths. Then, the whole of the proof script is played again to build the new incomplete proof, consequently it may be time consuming in large developments.

A second drawback concerns the extension of functions defined by case analysis on an extended type. The success of the reuse lies on the hypothesis that the function has been extended in a conservative way. This method cannot easily check this requirement.

Another drawback is that we have to preprocess the tactic tree before annotating it. Indeed, a composite tactic may use the tactical ";" that allows to factorize some tactics. In Induction x; Apply H the tactic Apply H is applied to all subgoals generated by Induction x. When the type of x is extended, it may happen that Apply H does not apply on the new branches. The solution is to transform all composite tactics into simple ones. An algorithm can be found in [Pon99].

Finally, with this approach, we can extend a type but cannot parameter it, or consider other modifications. To remedy these drawbacks, we propose another approach which operates directly on the λ-terms representing proofs, called proof terms in the following.

5   Dependencies

When we want to reuse proofs after modifications of types among specifications in a formal development, some of the proofs in the development may not be concerned by the modified types. In that case, they do not need to be modified. This section describes a mechanism to compute dependencies between lemmas, functions and types. Dependencies are the underpinning of our reuse approach based on proof terms.

5.1   Computing Dependencies

The COQ system has the particularity to construct a proof term (a λ-term of the CIC) from a complete proof script, or from a definition. COQ type-checks it and stores it in its environment. A λ-term may contain free identifiers representing previously defined objects, for example functions, intermediate lemmas, or elimination principles, stored in the environment.

Definition 1. *If L_1 and L_2 are two identifiers denoting definitions, lemmas, functions, or types, a dependency between L_1 and L_2 exists when L_1 is a free identifier occuring in the λ-term associated with L_2.*

As in [PBR98], we compute the dependencies of a lemma L by looking for free identifiers in the λ-term associated to the proof of L. A dependency graph represents all the dependencies between the objects of a development. Such a graph contributes to the documentation of the proof development and is useful to support proof extension and maintenance.

5.2   Transparent and Opaque Dependencies

A dependency graph can be considered as a proof plan. Since the extensions we could perform are supposed to be conservative, the graph is expected to remain identical after extension. The graph shows the dependencies between objects stored in the database, and we want to detect which nodes - which proofs - are unchanged and which ones need to be modified after an extension. So, for all lemmas that are not linked in the graph to one of the extended types, we know their proof will not need to be completed.

Nevertheless, if a lemma L is linked to an extended type I, it is possible that the proof of L does not need modifications. Indeed, if the proof of L only uses the type of I, and eventually other lemmas, the fact that I has now more constructors doesn't matter. So, the basic notion of dependency becomes too weak. We will now distinguish transparent dependencies and opaque dependencies.

Definition 2. *An object L has a transparent dependency with an inductive type I, if L has a dependency with an induction principle of I, or if a case analysis on type I is performed in the λ-term representing L.*

Definition 3. *An object L has an opaque dependency with an inductive type I, if its dependency with I is not transparent.*

5.3   Consequences on Proofs

When we extend one or more types, we compute the dependency graph of the formal development, and we distinguish transparent and opaque dependencies.

For all lemmas L of this graph, if L has a transparent dependency with an extended inductive type, we know the proof will have to be completed, when we will use our reuse method. This one generates only the subgoals corresponding to the new cases of the extended inductive type. Then the user completes the proof by providing the tactics to fill the holes. For other lemmas, the proof will remain exactly the same, it will be completely automatic as there is no hole to be filled.

The figure 1 represents the generated graph, for the example of section 3, where eval_det has a transparent dependency with the extended types expr and eval. Dotted arrows stand for transparent dependencies, and painted gray nodes show objects concerned by an extension.

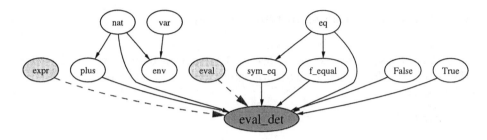

Fig. 1. A dependency graph

The proof term of a lemma L may contain free identifiers that are dependencies in the generated graph. The dependencies can be lemmas or functions and have to be updated before proving L.

6   To Extend, Parameter and Reuse

In this section, we first give the syntax of the commands to extend and parameter an inductive type. Then we describe the reuse approach based on proof terms.

6.1   Extension of an Inductive Definition

We propose the following syntax to extend an inductive type:

```
Extend I as J with c1 : u1 | ... | cm : um.              (with m⩾0)
```

An object of type J can be built from the constructors of I or the new ones: c1,...,cm. This syntactic construction is compiled into a COQ inductive type. As COQ does not allow overloading, we have to rename the constructors of I. We give here the scheme of the compilation. Let I be defined by:

```
Inductive I [list of parameters] : T :=
  d1 : t1 | ... | dn : tn.
```

The clause:

```
Extend I as J with c1 : u1 | ... | cm : um.
```

is compiled into

```
Inductive J [list of parameters] : T :=
   d1' : t1[I := J] | ... | dn' : tn[I := J]
 | c1  : u1 | ... | cm : um.
```

The substitution $[I := J]$ replaces the free occurrences of I in the type t1,...,tn by J. The constructors di of I are renamed by fresh names di' to ensure their uniqueness. Elimination principles on J are automatically generated by CoQ.

6.2   Parameterisation of an Inductive Type

An inductive type I can have one or more parameters p:P. In this case, in the type of the constructors, all occurences of I are parametered by p. We give here the syntax to add supplementary parameters to a type I when we extend it. Let I be the type:

```
Inductive I [k1:h1;...;kl:hl] : T :=
  d1 : t1 | ... | dn : tn.
```

The following command

```
Parameter I as J with p1:t1;...; pq:tq
  and extend with c1 : u1 | ... | cm : um.
```

is compiled into

```
Inductive J [k1:h1;...;kl:hl ; p1:t1;...;pq:tq] : T :=
  d1': t1[(I  k1..kl) := (J  k1..kl  p1..pq)]  |  ...
| dn': tn[(I  k1..kl) := (J  k1..kl  p1..pq)]
| c1 : u1 | ... | cm : um.
```

The substitutions $[(I\ k1..kl) := (J\ k1..kl\ p1..pq)]$ in the types ti, rename occurences of I in J and complete the list of parameters of J. Once again, elimination principles on J are generated by CoQ.

6.3   Reusing Proofs

We present here the approach based on proof terms reuse after extension of inductive types in the CoQ proof assistant, for conservative problems. Conservative means that when we extend types, the lemmas are still true for these new types.

In section 5, we explained that the extension of an inductive type I has consequences on all dependencies of I. In particular, proofs by induction on I need to be completed. The important contribution of our method is to automatically reuse old proofs. Our approach is very simple and consists in extending λ-terms, by adding holes to be filled later.

Within CoQ system, instead of giving tactics to build a proof, the user can also directly provide a proof term. This proof term can be a complete one or an incomplete one, using the tactic *Refine* implemented by JC Filliâtre [Bar03]. An incomplete term is a term containing metavariables. This tactic takes a proof term as argument, with metavariables representing holes in the proof. Then CoQ generates as many subgoals as holes in the proof term.

The principle of our **Reuse <lemma>** command is to reuse the old proof term of **<lemma>** by completing the pattern-matching of case analysis (which has to be exhaustive), and adding holes for the new constructors. If we have parametered a type I, we add dummy parameters everywhere I is applied. We also update the names of the extended types, the constructors, and the recursors associated with the extended types. Then we provide this term as a proof term with a patch of the tactic *Refine* (patched by the author).

We also provide a command **Reuse <lemma> as <lemma'>**. The system first creates the new lemma **<lemma'>** and starts the proof by using the previous reuse method. The difference with **Reuse <lemma>** is that the user does not need to express the new lemma, it is automatically generated from **<lemma>** by applying substitutions of all updated types.

The system allows to extend one or more inductive types (as shown in the initial example **expr, eval**), but also allows to extend a type in different ways.

6.4   Extension of Functions

Functions defined by fixpoint or case analysis use an exhaustive pattern matching. So, if this pattern matching relies on an extended type I, the function has to be extended. This is detected in the dependency graph because such a function has a transparent dependency on I. For example, imagine an inductive type I with two constructors **c1** and **c2** whose respective types are I and $I \rightarrow I$, and a function $f : I \rightarrow t$ defined by:

```
λx:I. Cases x of  c1   => e1
                | c2 y => Cases y of c1   => e2
                                   | c2 z => e3
                         end
       end
```

Now, we extend I in J with a constructor c3 of type $I \rightarrow I$. The following command:

```
Complete f as f'.
```

updates in the λ-term of f, the names, and complete the pattern-matching on x by adding metavariables, denoted in COQ **?n**.

The resulting λ-term of $f' : J \rightarrow t$ is as follows:

```
λx:J. Cases x of   c1'   => e1
                 | c2' y => Cases y of c1' => e2
                                     | c2' z => e3
                                     | c3 u => ?1
                           end
                 | c3 v => ?2
       end
```

To define the extended function, we refine the extended λ-term, as we did for proofs. The COQ system generates subgoals corresponding to the metavariables.

To help the user, we generate from the incomplete λ-term, equations giving the shape of each matching clause. For the previous example, the equations would be

```
(f' (c2' (c3 u)))=
(f' (c3 v))=
```

This computation requires a tree traversal in the incomplete λ-term.

7   Correctness of the Proof Term Approach

We deal here with metavariables in λ-terms to represent incomplete proofs. Then we formalize our modifications to reuse proof terms.

7.1   Metavariables

To represent incomplete proofs in λ-calculus, we use metavariables for holes in the proof term, as in ALF [Mag94]. Substitution of usual variables cannot refine metavariables. We need a λ-calculus with metavariables and a mechanism of *instanciation*. We use here the notations introduced by C. Muñoz, and the main property of [Muñ96].

Definition 4. *A refinement or an instanciation of a λ-term Λ replaces a meta-variable X in Λ, by a term t without renaming any bound variables. We denote it by $\Lambda\{X \mapsto t\}$*

To each metavariable X, we associate its type T_X, the context Γ_X where X has been defined and the implicit typing rule $\dfrac{}{\Gamma_X \vdash X : T_X}$ $(Meta_X)$

Definition 5. *A signature Σ is a list of metavariable declarations $\Gamma_X \vdash X : T_X$*

To type a λ-term Λ with metavariables, we need the typing context Γ for variables, but we also need the signature Σ for metavariables of Λ. This is denoted by judgments $\Sigma \triangleright \Gamma \vdash M : A$, where $\triangleright$ separates the signature Σ from the typing context Γ.

Proposition 1. *Type preservation by refinement*
If $\Sigma \triangleright \Gamma_X \vdash t : T_X$ and $\Sigma, (\Gamma_X \vdash X : T_X) \triangleright \Gamma \vdash \Lambda : \phi$, then $\Sigma \triangleright \Gamma \vdash \Lambda\{X \mapsto t\} : \phi$.

In other words, a typing judgment obtained by refinement of a valid typing judgment is valid.

The COQ system provides a metavariable construction and a mechanism of instanciation, weaker than those of C. Muñoz, but sufficient to represent incomplete proofs.

$$
\begin{array}{ll}
T := s & \text{sort (Set, Prop, Type)} \\
\quad x, y, f, i... & \text{identifier} \\
\quad \varPi x : T.T & \text{dependent product} \\
\quad \lambda x : T.T & \text{abstraction} \\
\quad T\,\overline{T} & \text{application} \\
\quad let\ x = T\ in\ T & \text{local definition} \\
\quad Ind(i : T)[\overline{x : T}]\{\overline{T}\} & \text{inductive type of name } i \\
\quad Constr(n, i) & n\text{th constructor of } i \\
\quad Case\ T \Rightarrow \overline{T}\ end & \text{case analysis of } T \\
\quad Fix\ f : T.T & \text{fixpoint construction}
\end{array}
$$

Fig. 2. Simplified definition of terms of CCI

7.2   Correctness of the Reuse Method

We outline here a formalization of the modifications of λ-terms, to be reused after an extension. Then we formalize the correctness of our reuse method.

A definition of the λ-terms of the CCI can be found in [Wer94,PM96]. We give in figure 2 a simplified definition, where $\overline{T}$ (or $\overline{x : T}$) stands for a list of terms T (or a list of pair $x : T$).

The application $N\,\overline{M}$ where $\overline{M}$ is the list $M_1..M_q$, is equivalent to the successive applications $(((((NM_1)M_2)..M_q)$. The construction $Ind(i : T)[p_1 : T_1...p_n : T_n]\{N_1...N_k\}$ is the inductive type of name i, of type T, which has k constructors of type $N_1...N_k$, and where the parameters $p_1 : T_1...p_n : T_n$ are explicitly given. The keyword Fix in $Fix\ f : T.N$ binds the function f in the body N. In $Case\ e \Rightarrow \overline{N}$, the cases are examined in the same order as the constructors of the inductive type of e. The terms in the list $\overline{N}$ take as many arguments as the corresponding constructor.

Let I be $Ind(I : t)[\overline{q : T_q}]\{\overline{T}\}$. We extend I in J with list of fresh parameters $\overline{p}$ (to avoid renaming) of type $\overline{T_p}$, and new constructors of type $\overline{K}$. We define the operation of extension $[\![.]\!]$ by: $[\![A]\!]$ is the λ-term A where application of I are completed by the list of dummy parameters $\overline{p}$, where occurrences of the inductive type I are substituted by J, and where constructors of I are replaced by corresponding constructors of J. As in case analysis pattern-matching on constructors is exhaustive, we complete pattern-matching on expressions of type J by adding the new constructors of J, associated with metavariables as corresponding expressions. An identifier x (of type τ) depending on I (functions, lemmas ...) is replaced by the identifier x' (of type $[\![\tau]\!]$), supposed to be in the environment. The constants I_ind, I_rec, I_rect are also replaced by J_ind, J_rec, J_rect whose lists of arguments are completed by metavariables. We assume, as it is in practice, inductive principles are totally applied. Their arguments are spit up as follows: $I\_ind\ (\overline{q} + P + \overline{N} + \overline{M})$, where $\overline{q}$ are the parameters of I, P is the property on which the induction principle is applied, $\overline{N}$ correspond to the proofs of P for the constructors of I, and $\overline{M}$ are quantifications over arguments of P.

A formal definition of $[\![.]\!]$ is given in figure 3. The transformation is implicitly parameterized by I, J and $\overline{p}$. The symbol $+$ is used to concatenate lists. In $[\![\overline{N}]\!]$,

$$\llbracket s \rrbracket = s$$
$$\llbracket x \rrbracket = x' \text{ if } x \text{ depends on } I \text{ and is updated in } x'$$
$$= x \quad \text{otherwise}$$
$$\llbracket \Pi x : M.N \rrbracket = \Pi x : \llbracket M \rrbracket.\llbracket N \rrbracket$$
$$\llbracket \lambda x : M.N \rrbracket = \lambda x : \llbracket M \rrbracket.\llbracket N \rrbracket$$
$$\llbracket I \ (\overline{q} + \overline{N}) \rrbracket = J \ (\overline{q} + \overline{p} + \llbracket \overline{N} \rrbracket)$$
$$\llbracket I\_ind \ (\overline{q} + P + \overline{N} + \overline{M}) \rrbracket = J\_ind \ (\overline{q} + \overline{p} + \llbracket P \rrbracket + \llbracket \overline{N} \rrbracket + \overline{X} + \llbracket \overline{M} \rrbracket)$$
$$\llbracket I\_rec \ (\overline{q} + P + \overline{N} + \overline{M}) \rrbracket = J\_rec \ (\overline{q} + \overline{p} + \llbracket P \rrbracket + \llbracket \overline{N} \rrbracket + \overline{X} + \llbracket \overline{M} \rrbracket)$$
$$\llbracket I\_rect \ (\overline{q} + P + \overline{N} + \overline{M}) \rrbracket = J\_rect \ (\overline{q} + \overline{p} + \llbracket P \rrbracket + \llbracket \overline{N} \rrbracket + \overline{X} + \llbracket \overline{M} \rrbracket)$$
$$\llbracket M \ \overline{N} \rrbracket = \llbracket M \rrbracket \ \llbracket \overline{N} \rrbracket \quad \text{if } M \neq I\_ind, I\_rec, I\_rect$$
$$\llbracket let \ x = c \ in \ d \rrbracket = let \ x = \llbracket c \rrbracket \ in \ \llbracket d \rrbracket$$
$$\llbracket Ind(I : t)\overline{[q : T_q]}\{\overline{T}\} \rrbracket = Ind(J : \llbracket t \rrbracket)\overline{[q : \llbracket T_q \rrbracket]} + \overline{p : T_p}\{\llbracket \overline{T} \rrbracket + \overline{K}\}$$
$$\llbracket Ind(i : t)\overline{[q : T_q]}\{\overline{T}\} \rrbracket = Ind(i : \llbracket t \rrbracket)\overline{[q : \llbracket T_q \rrbracket]}\{\llbracket \overline{T} \rrbracket\} \qquad \text{if } i \neq I$$
$$\llbracket Constr(n, I) \rrbracket = Constr(n, J)$$
$$\llbracket Constr(n, i) \rrbracket = Constr(n, i) \qquad \text{if } i \neq I$$
$$\llbracket Case \ M \Rightarrow \overline{N} \ end \rrbracket = Case \ \llbracket M \rrbracket \Rightarrow (\llbracket \overline{N} \rrbracket + \overline{X}) \ end \quad \text{if } M : I$$
$$= Case \ \llbracket M \rrbracket \Rightarrow \llbracket \overline{N} \rrbracket \ end \qquad \text{otherwise}$$
$$\llbracket Fix \ f : t.M \rrbracket = Fix \ f : \llbracket t \rrbracket.\llbracket M \rrbracket$$

Fig. 3. Definition of $\llbracket . \rrbracket$ when I is extended in J

$\llbracket . \rrbracket$ is mapped to all elements of $\overline{N}$. We note $\overline{X}$ the list of metavariables, whose length is those of $\overline{K}$, introduced for new constructors of J. When a metavariable is added, the signature Σ is implicitly enriched with the typing rule of the metavariable.

Proposition 2.
If $\Gamma \vdash \Lambda : \phi$ and if I is extended in J and parametered by $\overline{p}$ of type $\overline{T_p}$, then
$\Sigma \triangleright \Gamma, \Gamma_1, (\overline{p : T_p}) \vdash \llbracket \Lambda \rrbracket : \llbracket \phi \rrbracket$
where Γ_1 contains all the updated constants that depended on I, and where Σ is the signature of the metavariables introduced by $\llbracket . \rrbracket$

When we want to prove $\llbracket \phi \rrbracket$, we assume we have defined all needed dependencies, with the help of the dependency graph, so that Γ_1 contains all the updated constants that depended on I. We also add in typing context the types of parameters $\overline{p : T_p}$. We can establish that $\Sigma \triangleright \Gamma, \Gamma_1, (\overline{p : T_p}) \vdash \llbracket \Lambda \rrbracket : \llbracket \phi \rrbracket$ by a structural induction on Λ and applying rules of figure 3.

The lemma we want to prove after an extension is $(\overline{p : T_p})\llbracket \phi \rrbracket$. The proof term we produce is $\lambda \overline{p : T_p}.\llbracket \Lambda \rrbracket$, then the user refines metavariables. The following proposition expresses the produced term has the type of the lemma to prove.

Proposition 3. *Our reuse method is correct:*
If $\Gamma \vdash \Lambda : \phi$, if I is extended in J and parametered by $\overline{p}$ of type $\overline{T_p}$, then
$\Gamma, \Gamma_1 \vdash \lambda \overline{p : T_p}.\llbracket \Lambda \rrbracket \{X_i \mapsto t_i\} : (\overline{p : T_p})\llbracket \phi \rrbracket$
where Γ_1 contains all the updated constants that depended on I, where X_i are the metavariables introduced by $\llbracket \Lambda \rrbracket$, and where t_i are terms whose type is those of X_i in the signature.

The context Γ_1 is supposed produced before trying to extend Λ with $[\![.]\!]$. The terms t_i are constructed by the user when tactics are given to solve goals produced from metavariables. As $\Gamma \vdash \Lambda : \phi$, we get $\Sigma \triangleright \Gamma, \Gamma_1, \overline{(p : T_p)} \vdash [\![\Lambda]\!] : [\![\phi]\!]$ by proposition 2. By applying the typing rule of the CCI for λ-abstraction, we obtain: $\Sigma \triangleright \Gamma, \Gamma_1 \vdash \lambda \overline{p : T_p}.[\![\Lambda]\!] : \overline{(p : T_p)}[\![\phi]\!]$. The system instanciates the metavariables X_i, typed in Σ, from user's tactics, so $\Gamma, \Gamma_1 \vdash \lambda \overline{p : T_p}.[\![\Lambda]\!] \{X_i \mapsto t_i\} : \overline{(p : T_p)}[\![\phi]\!]$ follows from proposition 1. □

If the property we try to prove with our reuse method is not conservative, the user will not be able to discharge the generated subgoals. For instance, suppose a lemma is proved with an empty inductive type. When we extend this empty type, the generated subgoals will be false and the user will not be able to finish the proof.

8   Conclusion

We have described a formal approach for reusing proofs after extension of inductive types. A prototype written for COQ 7.4 is available.

To extend a specification, we only propose here to add constructors in some inductive types, or add parameters. Nevertheless this kind of extension is limited, and we may need to change a definition to incorporate a new notion in the specifications. A good example of such an extension concerns the incorporation of mutable values in a functional kernel of a programming language. As we have to take into account the store, the reduction relation has more parameters, the type environment is redefined, and some lemmas are redefined. However the global structure of the type soundness proof remains. In [BD01], we have exposed the problem of redefinition when we want to reuse. Reusing a proof at script level is definitely no more possible.

Our purpose is to allow proof reusing in semantics language properties, when we enrich the language with modifications more general than simply adding constructors or parameters. Simple modifications can be modifying type of existing constructors, or the type of an inductive type, by adding premises.

In prospect, for this kind of modifications, we imagine to reuse parts of the proof term, but the modifications in this one reach another level of complexity, and the user will have to produce more informations.

Acknowledgments

The author is grateful to his supervisor Catherine Dubois for various discussions, comments, suggestions and reviews of this paper. Thanks to David Delahaye, Olivier Pons and Véronique Viguié Donzeau Gouge for the ideas and discussions we had with them. We also thank Yves Bertot and anonymous referees for their constructive remarks on a preliminary version of this paper.

References

[Bar03]   B. Barras et al. *The Coq Proof Assistant, Reference Manual (v7.4)*. INRIA Rocquencourt, 2003.

[BC02]   G. Barthe and P. Courtieu. Efficient reasoning about executable specifications in coq. In C. Muñoz and S. Tahar, editors, *Proceedings of TPHOL'02*, volume 2410 of *LNCS*, pages 31–46. Springer-Verlag, 2002.

[BD01]   O. Boite and C. Dubois. Proving Type Soundness of a Simply Typed ML-like Language with References. In R. Boulton and P. Jackson, editors, *Supplemental Proceedings of TPHOL'01, Informatics Research Report EDI-INF-RR-0046 of University of Edinburgh*, pages 69–84, 2001.

[BDHdS01]   G. Barthe, G. Dufay, M. Huisman, and S. Melo de Sousa. Jakarta: a toolset for reasoning about javacard. In I. Attali and T. Jensen, editors, *Proceedings of SMART'01*, volume 2140 of *LNCS*, pages 2–18, 2001.

[BP01]   G. Barthe and O. Pons. Type Isomorphisms and Proof Reuse in Dependent Type Theory. In F. Honsell and M. Miculan, editors, *Proceedings of FOSSACS'01*, volume 2030 of *LNCS*, pages 57–71. Springer-Verlag, 2001.

[BR00]   G. Barthe and F. van Raamsdonk. Constructor Subtyping in the Calculus of Inductive Constructions. In J. Tuyrin, editor, *Proceedings of FOSSACS'00*, volume 1784 of *LNCS*, pages 17–34. Springer-Verlag, 2000.

[CAB+86]   R. L. Constable, Stuart F. Allen, H. M. Bromley, W. R. Cleaveland, J. F. Cremer, R. W. Harper, Douglas J. Howe, T. B. Knoblock, N. P. Mendler, P. Panangaden, James T. Sasaki, and Scott F. Smith. *Implementing Mathematics with the Nuprl Development System*. Prentice-Hall, NJ, 1986.

[Cal00]   P. Callaghan. Coherence checking of coercions in plastic. In *Workshop on Subtyping and Dependent Types in Programming*, Ponte de Lima, July 2000.

[Del00]   D. Delahaye. A Tactic Language for the System Coq. In *Proceedings of Logic for Programming and Automated Reasoning (LPAR), Reunion Island*, volume 1955 of *LNCS*, pages 85–95. Springer-Verlag, 2000.

[Dub00]   C. Dubois. Proving ML Type Soundness Within Coq. In *Proceedings of TPHOL'00*, volume 1869 of *LNCS*, pages 126–144, Portland, Oregon, USA, 2000. Springer-Verlag.

[Gay01]   S. J. Gay. A Framework for the Formalisation of Pi Calculus Type Systems. In R.J. Boulton and P.B. Jackson, editors, *14th International Conference, TPHOL'01*, volume 2152 of *LNCS*, pages 217–232, Edinburgh, Scotland, UK, September 2001. Springer-Verlag.

[GM93]   M. J. C. Gordon and T. F. Melham, editors. *Introduction to HOL A theorem proving environment for higher order logic*. Cambridge University Press, 1993.

[LP92]   Z. Luo and R. Pollack. LEGO proof development system: User's manual. Technical Report ECS-LFCS-92-211, LFCS, The King's Buildings, Edinburgh EH9 3JZ, 1992.

[LP99]   M. Y. Levin and B. C. Pierce. Tinkertype: A language for playing with formal systems. Technical Report MS-CIS-99-19, Dept of CIS, University of Pennsylvania, July 1999.

[Luo96]   Z. Luo. Coercive subtyping in type theory. In *CSL*, pages 276–296, 1996.

[Mag94]   L. Magnusson. *The Implementation of ALF—a Proof Editor Based on Martin-Löf's Monomorphic Type Theory with Explicit Substitution*. PhD thesis, Chalmers University of Technology - Göteborg University, 1994.

[Mag03]   N. Magaud. Changing data representation within the coq system. In *Proceedings of TPHOL'03*, volume 2758 of *LNCS*, pages 87–102, Roma, Italy, September 2003. Springer-Verlag.

[Muñ96]   C. Muñoz. Proof representation in type theory: State of the art. In *Proc. XXII Latinamerican Conference of Informatics CLEI Panel 96*, Santafé de Bogotá, Colombia, June 1996.

[NOP00]   T. Nipkow, D. von Oheimb, and C. Pusch. Java: Embedding a Programming Language in a Theorem Prover. *In F.L. Bauer and R. Steinbruggen, editors, Foundations of Secure Computation. IOS Press*, 2000.

[PBR98]   O. Pons, Y. Bertot, and L. Rideau. Notions of dependency in proof assistants. In *Electronic Proceedings of User Interfaces for Theorem Provers*, Sophia-Antipolis, France, 1998.

[Pie00]   B. C. Pierce. *Types and Programming Languages*. MIT Press, 2000.

[PM96]   C. Paulin-Mohring. *Définitions Inductives en Théorie des Types d'Ordre Supérieur*. Habilitation à diriger les recherches, Université Lyon I, December 1996.

[Pol97]   E. Poll. Subtyping and Inheritance for Inductive Types. *In Proceedings of TYPES'97 Workshop on Subtyping, inheritance and modular development of proofs*, September 1997.

[Pon99]   O. Pons. *Conception et réalisation d'outils d'aide au développement de grosses théories dans les systèmes de preuves interactifs*. PhD thesis, Conservatoire National des Arts et Métiers, 1999.

[Sym99]   D. Syme. Proving Java Type Sound. In *In Jim Alves-Foss, editor, Formal Syntax and Semantics of Java.*, volume 1523 of *LNCS*. Springer-Verlag, 1999.

[Van97]   M. VanInwegen. Towards Type Preservation in Core SML. *Technical report, Cambridge University*, 1997.

[Wer94]   B. Werner. *Une théorie des constructions inductives*. PhD thesis, Université Paris 7, 1994.

Hierarchical Reflection

Luís Cruz-Filipe[1,2] and Freek Wiedijk[1]

[1] NIII, Radboud University of Nijmegen
{lcf,freek}@cs.kun.nl
[2] Center for Logic and Computation, Lisboa

Abstract. The technique of reflection is a way to automate proof construction in type theoretical proof assistants. Reflection is based on the definition of a type of syntactic expressions that gets interpreted in the domain of discourse. By allowing the interpretation function to be partial or even a relation one gets a more general method known as "partial reflection". In this paper we show how one can take advantage of the partiality of the interpretation to uniformly define a family of tactics for equational reasoning that will work in different algebraic structures. The tactics then follow the hierarchy of those algebraic structures in a natural way.

1 Introduction

1.1 Problem

Computers have made formalization of mathematical proof practical. They help getting formalizations correct by verifying all the details, but they also make it easier to formalize mathematics by automatically generating parts of the proofs.

One way to automate proving is the technique called *reflection*. With reflection one describes the desired automation *inside* the logic of the theorem prover, by formalizing relevant meta-theory. Reflection is a common approach for proof automation in type theoretical systems like NuPRL and Coq, as described for example in [1] and [10] respectively. Another name for reflection is "the two-level approach".

In Nijmegen we formalized the Fundamental Theorems of Algebra and Calculus in Coq, and then extended these formalizations into a structured library of mathematics named the C-CoRN library [3, 5]. For this library we defined a reflection tactic called rational that automatically establishes equalities of rational expressions in a field by bringing both to the same side of the equal sign and then multiplying everything out. With this tactic, equalities like

$$\frac{1}{x} + \frac{1}{y} = \frac{x+y}{xy}$$

can be automatically proved without any human help.

The rational tactic only works for expressions in a field, but using the same idea one can define analogous tactics for expressions in a ring or a group. The

K. Slind et al. (Eds.): TPHOLs 2004, LNCS 3223, pp. 66–81, 2004.

trivial way to define these is to duplicate the definition of the rational tactic and modify it for these simpler algebraic structures by removing references to division or multiplication. This was actually done to implement a ring version of rational.

However this is not efficient, as it means duplication of the full code of the tactic. In particular the *normalization function* that describes the simplification of expressions, which is quite complicated, has to be defined multiple times. But looking at the normalization function for field expressions, it is clear that it contains the normalization function for rings. In this paper we study a way to *integrate* these tactics for different algebraic structures.

1.2 Approach

In the C-CoRN library algebraic structures like fields, rings and groups are organized into an *Algebraic Hierarchy*. The definition of a field reuses the definition of a ring, and the definition of a ring reuses the definition of a group. This hierarchy means that the theory about these structures is maximally reusable. Lemmas about groups are automatically also applicable to rings and fields, and lemmas about rings also apply to fields.

At the same time, a tactic for proving equalities in arbitrary fields was developed using a partial interpretation relation, as described in [10]. In this paper we show how we can take advantage of this partial interpretation relation to reuse the same tactic for simpler structures. As it turns out, the simplification of expressions done in a field can be directly applied to rings and groups as well. This is quite surprising: the normal forms of expressions that get simplified in this theory will contain functions like multiplication and division, operations that do not make sense in a group.

1.3 Related Work

In the C-CoRN setoid framework, rational is the equivalent of the standard Coq tactic field for Leibniz equality (see [7] and [4, Chapter 8.11]). Both tactics were developed at about the same time. The field tactic is a generalization of the Coq ring tactic [4, Chapter 19], so with the field and ring tactics the duplication of effort that we try to eliminate is also present. Also the ring tactic applies to rings as well as to semirings (to be able to use it with the natural numbers), so there is also this kind of duplication within the ring tactic itself.

Reflection has also been widely used in the NuPRL system as described originally in [1]. More recently, [12] introduces other techniques that allow code reuse for tactics in MetaPRL, although the ideas therein are different from ours. Since the library of this system also includes an algebraic hierarchy built using subtyping (see [15]), it seems reasonable to expect that the work we describe could be easily adapted to that framework.

1.4 Contribution

We show that it is possible to have one unified mechanism for simplification of expressions in different algebraic structures like fields, rings and groups. We also show that it is not necessary to have different normalization functions for these expressions, but that it is possible to decide equalities on all levels with only one normalization function. Presently, both the ring and the field versions of the tactic are used extensively throughout C-CoRN (a total of more than 1.500 times).

Another extension which we present is the addition of uninterpreted function symbols. With it we can now automatically prove goals of the form $|t_1| = |t_2|$, which earlier had to be manually simplified to $t_1 = t_2$.

The whole tactic is about 100kb of code, divided between the ML implementation (17kb), the normalization function (14kb) and the interpretation relation and correctness (23kb for groups, 25kb for rings and 29kb for fields); in Section 6 we discuss why the correctness has to be proved anew for each structure.

We compared the speed of our tactic with that of ring and field, and also with a similar tactic for the HOL Light system [11]. All these tactics have a comparable speed: our tactic is a bit faster than ring, but slower than field.

1.5   Outline

In Section 2 we summarize the methods of reflection and partial reflection. In Section 3 we describe in detail the normalization function of the rational tactic. Section 4 is a small detour where we generalize the same method to add uninterpreted function symbols to the expressions that rational understands. In Section 5 we show how to do reflection in an algebraic hierarchy in a hierarchical way. Finally in Section 6 we present a possibility to have even tighter integration in a hierarchical reflection tactic, which unfortunately turns out to require the so-called K axiom [14].

2   Reflection and Partial Reflection

In this section we will briefly summarize [10]. That paper describes a generalization of the technique of *reflection* there called *partial reflection*. One can give a general account of reflection in terms of decision procedures, but here we will only present the more specific method of reflection with a normalization function, which is used to do equational reasoning.

In the normal, "total", kind of reflection one defines a type E of *syntactic expressions* for the domain A that one is reasoning about, together with an *interpretation function*

$$\llbracket - \rrbracket_\rho : E \to A$$

which assigns to a syntactic expression e an interpretation $\llbracket e \rrbracket_\rho$. In this, ρ is a *valuation* that maps the variables in the syntactic expressions to values in A. The type E is an inductive type, and therefore it is possible to recursively define a *normalization function* $\mathcal{N}$ on the type of syntactic expressions *inside* the type theory (this is not possible for A; so the reason for introducing the type E is to be able to define this $\mathcal{N}$).

$$\mathcal{N} : E \to E$$

One then proves the correctness lemma stating that the normalization function conserves the interpretation.

$$[\![e]\!]_\rho =_A [\![\mathcal{N}(e)]\!]_\rho$$

Then, to reason about the domain A that $[\![-]\!]$ maps to, one first constructs a valuation ρ and syntactic expressions in E which map under $[\![-]\!]_\rho$ to the terms that one want to reason about, and then one uses the lemma to do the equational reasoning.

For instance, suppose that one wants to prove $a =_A b$. One finds e, f and ρ with $[\![e]\!]_\rho = a$ and $[\![f]\!]_\rho = b$. Now if $\mathcal{N}(e) = \mathcal{N}(f)$ then we get $a = [\![e]\!]_\rho =_A [\![\mathcal{N}(e)]\!]_\rho = [\![\mathcal{N}(f)]\!]_\rho =_A [\![f]\!]_\rho = b$. (Clearly this uses the correctness lemma twice, see Figure 1.) Note that the operation of finding an expression in E that corresponds to a given expression in A (dotted arrows) is not definable in the type theory, and needs to be implemented *outside* of it. In a system like Coq it will be implemented in ML or in the tactic language $\mathcal{L}_{\text{tac}}$ described in [6] and [4, Chapter 9].

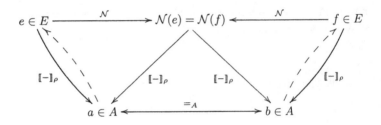

Fig. 1. Proving equalities

Things get more interesting when the syntactic expressions in E contain *partial* operations, like division. In that case the interpretation $[\![e]\!]_\rho$ will not always be defined. To address this we generalized the method of reflection to *partial reflection*. The naive way to do this is to define a predicate

$$wf_\rho : E \to \mathsf{Prop}$$

that tells whether an expression is *well-formed*. Then the interpretation function takes another argument of type $wf_\rho(e)$.

$$[\![-]\!]_\rho : \Pi_{e:E}.\, wf_\rho(e) \to F$$

The problem with this approach is that the definition of wf needs the interpretation function $[\![-]\!]$. Therefore the inductive definition of wf and the recursive definition of $[\![-]\!]$ need to be given simultaneously. This is called an *inductive-recursive definition*. Inductive-recursive definitions are not supported by the Coq system, and for a good reason: induction-recursion makes a system significantly stronger. In set theory it corresponds to the existence of a Mahlo cardinal [8].

The solution from [10] for doing partial reflection without induction-recursion is to replace the interpretation function with an inductively defined *interpretation relation*.

$$\mathbb{I}_\rho \subseteq E \times A$$

The relation $[\![e]\!]_\rho = a$ now becomes $e \; \mathbb{I}_\rho \, a$. It means that the syntactic expression e is interpreted under the valuation ρ by the object a. The lemmas that one then proves are the following.

$$e \; \mathbb{I}_\rho \, a \wedge e \; \mathbb{I}_\rho \, b \;\Rightarrow\; a =_A b$$

$$e \; \mathbb{I}_\rho \, a \;\Rightarrow\; \mathcal{N}(e) \; \mathbb{I}_\rho \, a$$

The first lemma states that the interpretation relation is *functional*, and the second lemma is again the correctness of the normalization function. Note that it is not an equivalence but just an implication. This is the only direction that is needed. In fact, in our application the equivalence does not hold[1].

For each syntactic expression e that one constructs for an object a, one also needs to find an inhabitant of the statement $e \; \mathbb{I}_\rho \, a$. In [10] types $\bar{E}_\rho(a)$ of *proof loaded syntactic expressions* are introduced to make this easier. These types correspond to the expressions that evaluate to a. They are mapped to the normal syntactic expressions by a forgetful function

$$|-| : \bar{E}_\rho(a) \to E$$

and they satisfy the property that for all $\bar{e}$ in the type $\bar{E}_\rho(a)$

$$|\bar{e}| \; \mathbb{I}_\rho \, a.$$

In this paper we will not go further into this, although everything that we do also works in the presence of these proof loaded syntactic expressions.

3   Normalization Function

We will now describe how we defined the normalization function for our main example of *rational expressions*. Here the type E of syntactic expressions is given by the following grammar.

$$E ::= \mathbb{Z} \mid \mathbb{V} \mid E + E \mid E \cdot E \mid E/E$$

In this $\mathbb{Z}$ are the integers, and $\mathbb{V}$ is a countable set of *variable names* (in the Coq formalization we use a copy of the natural numbers for this). Variables will be denoted by x, y, z, integers by i, j, k. The elements of this type E are just *syntactic* objects, so they are different kind of objects from the *values* of these expressions in specific fields. Note that in these expressions it is possible to divide by zero: $0/0$ is one of the terms in this type.

---

[1] A simple example is $e = 1/(1/0)$, which does not relate to any a. Its normal form is $0/1$, which interprets to 0.

Other algebraic operations are defined as an abbreviation from operations that occur in the type. For instance, subtraction is defined by

$$e - f \equiv e + f \cdot (-1)$$

We now will describe how we define the normalization function $\mathcal{N}(e)$ that maps an element of E to a normal form. As an example, the normal form of $\frac{1}{x-y} + \frac{1}{x+y}$ is

$$\mathcal{N}\left(\frac{1}{x-y} + \frac{1}{x+y}\right) = \frac{x \cdot 2 + 0}{x \cdot x \cdot 1 + y \cdot y \cdot (-1) + 0}.$$

This last expression is the "standard form" of the way one would normally write this term, which is

$$\frac{2x}{x^2 - y^2}.$$

From this example it should be clear how the normalization function works: it multiplies everything out until there is just a quotient of two polynomials left. These polynomials are then in turn written in a "standard form". The expressions in normal form are given by the following grammar.

$$F ::= P/P$$
$$P ::= M + P \mid \mathbb{Z}$$
$$M ::= \mathbb{V} \cdot M \mid \mathbb{Z}$$

In this grammar F represents a fraction of two polynomials, P are the polynomials and M are the monomials. One should think of P as a "list of monomials" (where $+$ is the "cons" and the integers take the place of the "nil") and of M as a "list of variables" (where $\cdot$ is the "cons" and again the integers take the place of the "nil").

On the one hand we want the normalization function to terminate, but on the other hand we want the set of normal forms to be as small as possible. We achieve this by requiring the polynomials and monomials to be *sorted*; furthermore, no two monomials in a polynomial can have exactly the same set of variables. Thus normal forms for polynomials will be unique.

For this we have an ordering of the variable names. So the "list" that is a monomial has to be sorted according to this order on $\mathbb{V}$, and the "list" that is a polynomial also has to be sorted, according to the corresponding lexicographic ordering on the monomials. If an element of P or M is sorted like this, and monomials with the same set of variables have been collected together, we say it is *in normal form*.

Now to define $\mathcal{N}$ we have to "program" the multiplying out of E expressions together with the sorting of monomials and polynomials, and collecting factors and terms. This is done simultaneously: instead of first multiplying out the expressions and then sorting them to gather common terms, we combine these two things.

We recursively define the following functions (using the `Fixpoint` operation of Coq).

$$
\begin{aligned}
- \cdot_{MZ} - &: M \times \mathbb{Z} \to M \\
- \cdot_{MV} - &: M \times \mathbb{V} \to M \\
- \cdot_{MM} - &: M \times M \to M \\
- +_{MM} - &: M \times M \to M \\
- +_{PM} - &: P \times M \to P \\
- +_{PP} - &: P \times P \to P \\
- \cdot_{PM} - &: P \times M \to P \\
- \cdot_{PP} - &: P \times P \to P \\
- +_{FF} - &: F \times F \to F \\
- \cdot_{FF} - &: F \times F \to F \\
- /_{FF} - &: F \times F \to F
\end{aligned}
$$

(Actually, these functions all have type

$$E \times E \to E$$

as we do not have separate types for F, P and M. However, the idea is that they only will be called with arguments that are of the appropriate shape and in normal form. In that case the functions will return the appropriate normal form. In the other case they will return any term that is equal to the sum or product of the arguments – generally we just use the sum or product of the arguments.)

For example, the multiplication function $\cdot_{MM}$ looks like

$$
e \cdot_{MM} f := \begin{cases} f \cdot_{MZ} i & \text{if } e = i \in \mathbb{Z} \\ (e_2 \cdot_{MM} f) \cdot_{MV} e_1 & \text{if } e = e_1 \cdot e_2 \\ e \cdot f & \text{otherwise} \end{cases}
$$

and the addition function $+_{PM}$ is[2]

$$
e +_{PM} f := \begin{cases} i +_{MM} j & \text{if } e = i \in \mathbb{Z},\, f = j \in \mathbb{Z} \\ f + i & \text{if } e = i \in \mathbb{Z} \\ e_1 + (e_2 +_{PM} i) & \text{if } e = e_1 + e_2,\, f = i \in \mathbb{Z} \\ e_2 +_{PM} (e_1 +_{MM} f) & \text{if } e = e_1 + e_2,\, e_1 = f \\ e_1 + (e_2 +_{PM} f) & \text{if } e = e_1 + e_2,\, e_1 <_{\text{lex}} f \\ f + e & \text{if } e = e_1 + e_2,\, e_1 >_{\text{lex}} f \\ e + f & \text{otherwise} \end{cases}
$$

where the lexicographic ordering $<_{\text{lex}}$ is used to guarantee that the monomials in the result are ordered.

Finally we used these functions to recursively "program" the normalization function. For instance the case where the argument is a division is defined like

$$\mathcal{N}(e/f) := N(e) /_{FF} N(f).$$

---

[2] In the fourth case, the equality $e_1 = f$ is equality *as lists*, meaning that they might differ in the integer coefficient at the end.

The base case (when e is a variable) looks like

$$\mathcal{N}(v) := \frac{v \cdot 1 + 0}{1}.$$

To prove that $a = b$, then, one builds the expression corresponding to $a - b$ and checks that this normalizes to an expression of the form $0/e$. (This turns out to be stronger than building expressions e and f interpreting to a and b and verifying that $\mathcal{N}(e) = \mathcal{N}(f)$, since normal forms are in general not unique.)

4   Uninterpreted Function Symbols

When one starts working with the tactic defined as above, one quickly finds out that there are situations in which it fails because two terms which are easily seen to be equal generate two expressions whose difference fails to normalize to 0. A simple example arises is when function symbols are used; for example, trying to prove that

$$f(a + b) = f(b + a)$$

will fail because $f(a + b)$ will be syntactically represented as a variable x and $f(b + a)$ as a (different) variable y, and the difference between these expressions normalizes to

$$\frac{x \cdot 1 + y \cdot (-1) + 0}{1},$$

which is not zero.

In this section we describe how the syntactic type E and the normalization function $\mathcal{N}$ can be extended to recognize and deal with function symbols. The actual implementation includes unary and binary total functions, as well as unary partial functions (these are binary functions whose second argument is a proof)[3]. We will discuss the case for unary total functions in detail; binary and partial functions are treated in an analogous way.

Function symbols are treated much in the same way as variables; thus, we extend the type E of syntactic expressions with a new countable set of *function variable names* $\mathbb{V}_1$, which is implemented (again) as the natural numbers. The index 1 stands for the arity of the function; the original set of variables is now denoted by $\mathbb{V}_0$. Function variables will be denoted u, v.

$$E ::= \mathbb{Z} \mid \mathbb{V}_0 \mid \mathbb{V}_1(E) \mid E + E \mid E \cdot E \mid E/E$$

Intuitively, the normalization function should also normalize the arguments of function variables. The grammar for normal forms becomes the following.

$$F ::= P/P$$
$$P ::= M + P \mid \mathbb{Z}$$
$$M ::= \mathbb{V}_0 \cdot M \mid \mathbb{V}_1(F) \cdot M \mid \mathbb{Z}$$

---

[3] Other possibilities, such as ternary functions or binary partial functions, were not considered because this work was done in the setting of the C-CoRN library, where these are the types of functions which are used in practice.

But now a problem arises: the extra condition that both polynomials and monomials correspond to sorted lists requires ordering not only variables in V_0, but
also expressions of the form $V_1(F)$. The simplest way to do this is by defining
an ordering on the whole set E of expressions.

This is achieved by ordering first the sets V_0 and V_1 themselves. Then, expressions are recursively sorted by first looking at their outermost operator

$$x <_E i <_E e + f <_E e \cdot f <_E e/f <_E v(e)$$

and then sorting expressions with the same operator using a lexicographic ordering. For example, if $x <_{V_0} y$ and $u <_{V_1} v$, then

$$x <_E y <_E 2 <_E 34 <_E x/4 <_E u(x+3) <_E u(2 \cdot y) <_E v(x+3).$$

With this different ordering, the same normalization function as before can be
used with only trivial changes. In particular, the definitions of the functions $\cdot_{MM}$
and $+_{PM}$ remain unchanged. Only at the very last step does one have to add a
rule saying that

$$\mathcal{N}(v(e)) := \frac{v(\mathcal{N}(e)) \cdot 1 + 0}{1}.$$

Notice the similarity with the rule for the normal form of variables.

The next step is to change the interpretation relation. Instead of the valuation
ρ, we now need two valuations

$$\rho_0 : V_0 \to A$$
$$\rho_1 : V_1 \to (A \to A)$$

and the inductive definition of the interpretation relation is extended with the
expected constructor for interpreting expressions of the form $v(e)$.

As before, one can again prove the two lemmas

$$e \llbracket_{\rho_0,\rho_1} a \wedge e \llbracket_{\rho_0,\rho_1} b \Rightarrow a =_A b$$

$$e \llbracket_{\rho_0,\rho_1} a \Rightarrow \mathcal{N}(e) \llbracket_{\rho_0,\rho_1} a$$

Our original equality $f(a+b) = f(b+a)$ can now easily be solved: $f(a+b)$
can be more faithfully represented by the expression $v(x+y)$, where $\rho_1(v) = f$,
$\rho_0(x) = a$ and $\rho_0(y) = b$; the syntactic representation of $f(b+a)$ becomes
$v(y+x)$; and each of these normalizes to

$$\frac{v\left(\frac{x \cdot 1 + y \cdot 1 + 0}{1}\right) \cdot 1 + 0}{1},$$

so that their difference normalizes to 0 as was intended.

Adding binary functions simply requires a new sort V_2 of binary function
symbols and extend the type of expressions to allow for the like of $v(e, f)$; the
normalization function and the interpretation relation can easily be adapted, the
latter requiring yet another valuation

$$\rho_2 : V_2 \to (A \times A \to A).$$

Partial functions are added likewise, using a sort V_χ for partial function symbols and a valuation

$$\rho_\chi : \mathbb{V}_\chi \to (A \not\to A).$$

As was already the case with division, one can write down expressions like $v(e)$ even when $\rho_\chi(v)$ is not defined at the interpretation of e; the definition of $[\![$$\cdot$$]\!]_{\rho_0,\rho_1,\rho_\chi,\rho_2}$ ensures that only correctly applied partial functions will be interpreted.

5   Hierarchical Reflection

The normalization procedure described in Section 3 was used to define a tactic which would prove algebraic equalities in an arbitrary field in the context of the Algebraic Hierarchy of [9].

In this hierarchy, fields are formalized as rings with an extra operation (division) which satisfies some properties; rings, in turn, are themselves Abelian groups where a multiplication is defined also satisfying some axioms. The question then arises of whether it is possible to generalize this mechanism to the different structures of this Algebraic Hierarchy. This would mean having three "growing" types of syntactic expressions E_G, E_R and E_F (where the indices stand for groups, rings and fields respectively) together with interpretation relations[4].

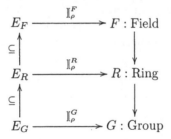

However one can do better. The algorithm in the normalization function works outwards; it first pushes all the divisions to the outside, and then proceeds to normalize the resulting polynomials. In other words, it first deals with the field-specific part of the expression, and then proceeds working within a ring. This suggests that the same normalization function could be reused to define a decision procedure for equality of algebraic expressions within a ring, thus allowing E_F and E_R to be unified.

Better yet, looking at the functions operating on the polynomials one also quickly realizes that these will never introduce products of variables unless they are already implicitly in the expression (in other words, a new product expression can arise e.g. from distributing a sum over an existing product, but if the

---

[4] For simplicity we focus on the setting where function symbols are absent; the more general situation is analogous.

original expression contains no products then neither will its normal form). So our previous picture can be simplified to this one.

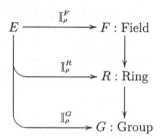

The key idea is to use the partiality of the interpretation relation to be able to map E into a ring R or a group G. In the first case, expressions of the form e/f will not be interpreted; in the latter, neither these nor expressions of the form $e \cdot f$ relate to any element of the group.

There is one problem, however. Suppose x is a variable with $\rho(x) = a$; then $a + a$ is represented by $x + x$, but

$$\mathcal{N}(x + x) = \frac{x \cdot 2 + 0}{1} \; \mathbb{I}_\rho^G \; a + a$$

does not hold.

In order to make sense of the normal forms defined earlier, one needs to interpret the special cases $e/1$ in groups and rings, as well as $e \cdot f$ with $f = i \in \mathbb{Z}$ in groups (assuming, of course, that e can be interpreted).

The following table summarizes what each of the interpretation relations can interpret.

	$\mathbb{I}_\rho^G$	$\mathbb{I}_\rho^R$	$\mathbb{I}_\rho^F$
$v \in V$	yes	yes	yes
$i \in \mathbb{Z}$	if $i = 0$	yes	yes
$e + f$	yes	yes	yes
$e \cdot f$	if $f \in \mathbb{Z}$	yes	yes
e/f	if $f = 1$	if $f = 1$	if $f \neq 0$

In the last three cases the additional requirement that e and f can be interpreted is implicit.

Once again, one has to prove the lemmas

$$e \; \mathbb{I}_\rho^G \; a \wedge e \; \mathbb{I}_\rho^G \; b \;\Rightarrow\; a =_A b$$

$$e \; \mathbb{I}_\rho^G \; a \;\Rightarrow\; \mathcal{N}(e) \; \mathbb{I}_\rho^G \; a$$

and analogous for $\mathbb{I}_\rho^R$ and $\mathbb{I}_\rho^F$.

In these lemmas, one needs to use the knowledge that the auxiliary functions will only be applied to the "right" arguments to be able to finish the proofs.

This is trickier to do for groups than for rings and fields. For example, while correctness of $\cdot_{MM}$ w.r.t. $[\![_\rho^F$ is unproblematic, as it states that

$$e \; [\![_\rho^F \; a \; \wedge \; f \; [\![_\rho^F \; b \; \Rightarrow \; e \cdot_{MM} f \; [\![_\rho^F \; a \cdot b,$$

the analogue of this statement for $[\![_\rho^G$ cannot be written down, as $a \cdot b$ has no meaning in a group. However, by definition of $[\![_\rho^F$, this is equivalent to the following.

$$e \cdot f \; [\![_\rho^F \; a \cdot b \; \Rightarrow \; e \cdot_{MM} f \; [\![_\rho^F \; a \cdot b$$

Now this second version does possess an analogue for $[\![_\rho^G$, by replacing the expression $a \cdot b$ with a variable.

$$e \cdot f \; [\![_\rho^G \; c \; \Rightarrow \; e \cdot_{MM} f \; [\![_\rho^G \; c.$$

This is still not provable, because $\cdot_{MM}$ can swap the order of its arguments. The correct version is

$$e \cdot f \; [\![_\rho^G \; c \; \vee \; f \cdot e \; [\![_\rho^G \; c \; \Rightarrow \; e \cdot_{MM} f \; [\![_\rho^G \; c;$$

the condition of this statement reflects the fact that the normalization function will only require computing $e \cdot_{MM} f$ whenever either e or f is an integer.

The implementation of the tactic for the hierarchical case now becomes slightly more sophisticated than the non-hierarchical one. When given a goal $a =_A b$ it builds the syntactic representation of a and b as before; and then looks at the type of A to decide whether it corresponds to a group, a ring or a field. Using this information the tactic can then call the lemma stating correctness of $\mathcal{N}$ w.r.t. the appropriate interpretation relation.

Optimization

As was mentioned in Section 3, normal forms for polynomials are unique, contrarily to what happens with field expressions in general. This suggests that, when A is a group or a ring, the decision procedure for $a =_A b$ can be simplified by building expressions e and f interpreting respectively to a and b and comparing their normal forms. Clearly, this is at most as time-consuming as the previous version, since computing $\mathcal{N}(e - f)$ requires first computing $\mathcal{N}(e)$ and $\mathcal{N}(f)$.

Also, since the normalization function was not defined at once, but resorting to the auxiliary functions earlier presented, it is possible to avoid using divisions altogether when working in rings and groups by defining directly $\mathcal{N}'$ by e.g.

$$\mathcal{N}'(e + f) = \mathcal{N}'(e) +_{PP} \mathcal{N}(f)';$$

the base case now looks like

$$\mathcal{N}'(v) = v \cdot 1 + 0.$$

Notice that although we now have two different normalization functions we still avoid duplication of the code, since they are both defined in terms of the same auxiliary functions and these are where the real work is done.

6 Tighter Integration

In the previous section we managed to avoid having different syntactic expressions for the different kinds of algebraic structures. We unified the types of syntactic expressions into one type E.

However we still have different interpretation relations $[\![_\rho^F$, $[\![_\rho^R$ and $[\![_\rho^G$. We will now analyze the possibility of unifying those relations into one interpretation relation $[\![_\rho^S$. This turns out to be possible, but when one tries to prove the relevant lemmas for it one runs into problems: to get the proofs finished one needs to assume an axiom (in the type theory of Coq).

Every field, ring or group has an underlying carrier. We will write $\hat{A}$ for the carrier of an algebraic structure A. We now define an interpretation relation $[\![_\rho^S$ from the type of syntactic expressions E to an *arbitrary* set[5] S, where that set is a parameter of the inductive definition. This inductive definition quantifies over *different* kinds of algebraic structures in the clauses for the different algebraic operations. For instance the inductive clause for addition quantifies over groups.

$$\Pi_{G:\mathrm{Group}}\Pi_{e,f:E}\Pi_{a,b,c:\hat{G}}\,(a +_G b =_G c) \to (e\ [\![_\rho^{\hat{G}}\ a) \to (f\ [\![_\rho^{\hat{G}}\ b) \to (e + f\ [\![_\rho^{\hat{G}}\ c)$$

With this definition the diagram becomes the following.

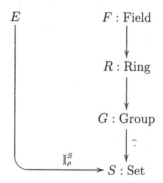

This gives a nice unification of the interpretation relations. However, when one tries to prove the relevant lemmas for it in Coq, the obvious way does not work. To prove e.g.

$$e\ [\![_\rho^S\ a \wedge e\ [\![_\rho^S\ b \Rightarrow a =_A b$$

one needs to use inversion with respect to the inductive definition of $[\![_\rho^S$ to get the possible ways that $e\ [\![_\rho^S\ a$ can be obtained; but the inversion tactic of Coq then only produces an equality between dependent pairs where what one needs is equality between the second components of those pairs. In Coq this is not derivable without the so-called K axiom, which states uniqueness of equality proofs [13].

---

[5] In the formalization we actually have *setoids* instead of sets, but that does not make a difference.

```
forall (A:Set) (x:A) (p:(x=x)), p = refl_equal A x
```

We did not want to assume an axiom to be able to have our tactic prove equalities in algebraic structures that are clearly provable without this axiom. For this reason we did not fully implement this more integrated version of hierarchical reflection.

7   Conclusion

7.1   Discussion

We have shown how the rational tactic (first described in [10]), which is used to prove equalities of expressions in arbitrary fields, can be generalized in two distinct directions.

First, we showed in Section 4 how this tactic could be extended so that it would also look at the arguments of functions; the same mechanism can be applied not only to unary total functions, as explained, but also to binary (or n-ary) functions, as well as to partial functions as defined in the C-CoRN library [3].

In Section 5 we discussed how the same syntactic type E and normalization function $\mathcal{N}$ could be reused to define similar tactics that will prove equalities in arbitrary rings or commutative groups. The work described here has been successfully implemented in Coq, and is intensively used throughout the whole C-CoRN library.

Further extensions of this tactic are possible; in particular, the same approach easily yields a tactic that will work in commutative monoids (e.g. the natural numbers with addition). For simplicity, and since this adds nothing to this presentation, this situation was left out of this paper.

Extending the same mechanism to non-commutative structures was not considered. The normalization function intensively uses commutativity of both addition and multiplication, so it cannot be reused for structures that do not satisfy these; and the purpose of this work was to reuse as much of the code needed for rational as possible.

The correctness of the normalization function w.r.t. the interpretation relation had to be proved three times, one for each type of structure. In Section 6 we showed one possible way of overcoming this, which unfortunately failed because proving correctness of the tactic would then require assuming an axiom which is not needed to prove the actual equalities that the tactic is meant to solve. It would be interesting to know whether this approach can be made to work without needing the K axiom. Though this axiom is required to prove these lemmas using inversion, there might be an alternative way to prove them that avoids this problem.

A different approach to the same problem would be to use the constructor subtyping of [2]. This would allow one to define e.g. the interpretation relation for rings $[\![\cdot]\!]_\rho^R$ by adding one constructor to that for groups $[\![\cdot]\!]_\rho^G$; proving the relevant lemmas for the broader relation would then only require proving the new case in all the inductive proofs instead of duplicating the whole code.

Another advantage of this solution, when compared to the one explored in Section 6, would be that the tactic could be programmed and used for e.g. groups before rings and fields were even defined. It would also be more easily extendable to other structures. Unfortunately, constructor subtyping for Coq is at the moment only a theoretical possibility which has not been implemented.

Acknowledgments

The first author was partially supported by FCT and FEDER under POCTI, namely through grant SFRH / BD / 4926 / 2001 and CLC project FibLog FEDER POCTI / 2001 / MAT / 37239.

References

1. Stuart F. Allen, Robert L. Constable, Douglas J. Howe, and William Aitken. The Semantics of Reflected Proof. In *Proceedings of the 5th Symposium on Logic in Computer Science*, pages 95–197, Philadelphia, Pennsylvania, June 1990. IEEE, IEEE Computer Society Press.
2. Gilles Barthe and Femke van Raamsdonk. Constructor subtyping in the Calculus of Inductive Constructions. In Jerzy Tiuryn, editor, *Proceedings 3rd Int. Conf. on Foundations of Software Science and Computation Structures, FoSSaCS'2000, Berlin, Germany, 25 March – 2 Apr 2000*, volume 1784, pages 17–34, Berlin, 2000. Springer-Verlag.
3. Constructive Coq Repository at Nijmegen. http://c-corn.cs.kun.nl/.
4. The Coq Development Team. *The Coq Proof Assistant Reference Manual*, April 2004. Version 8.0.
5. L. Cruz-Filipe, H. Geuvers, and F. Wiedijk. C-CoRN: the Constructive Coq Repository at Nijmegen. To appear.
6. David Delahaye. A Tactic Language for the System Coq. In Michel Parigot and Andrei Voronkov, editors, *Proceedings of Logic for Programming and Automated Reasoning (LPAR), Reunion Island*, volume 1955 of *LNCS*, pages 85–95. Springer-Verlag, 2000.
7. David Delahaye and Micaela Mayero. Field: une procédure de décision pour les nombres réels en Coq. *Journées Francophones des Langages Applicatifs*, January 2001.
8. Peter Dybjer and Anton Setzer. Induction-recursion and initial algebras. *Annals of Pure and Applied Logic*, 124:1–47, 2003.
9. H. Geuvers, R. Pollack, F. Wiedijk, and J. Zwanenburg. The Algebraic Hierarchy of the FTA Project. *Journal of Symbolic Computation, Special Issue on the Integration of Automated Reasoning and Computer Algebra Systems*, pages 271–286, 2002.
10. H. Geuvers, F. Wiedijk, and J. Zwanenburg. Equational Reasoning via Partial Reflection. In M. Aagaard and J. Harrison, editors, *Theorem Proving in Higher Order Logics, 13th International Conference, TPHOLs 2000*, volume 1869 of *LNCS*, pages 162–178, Berlin, Heidelberg, New York, 2000. Springer Verlag.

11. John Harrison. *The HOL Light manual (1.1)*, 2000. http://www.cl.cam.ac.uk/users/jrh/hol-light/manual-1.1.ps.gz.

12. Jason Hickey, Aleksey Nogin, Robert L. Constable, Brian E. Aydemir, Eli Barzilay, Yegor Bryukhov, Richard Eaton, Adam Granicz, Alexei Kopylov, Christoph Kreitz, Vladimir N. Krupski, Lori Lorigo, Stephan Schmitt, Carl Witty, and Xin Yu. MetaPRL – A Modular Logical Environment. In David Basin and Burkhart Wolff, editors, *Proceedings of the 16th International Conference on Theorem Proving in Higher Order Logics (TPHOLs 2003)*, volume 2758 of *LNCS*, pages 287–303. Springer-Verlag, 2003.

13. Martin Hoffman and Thomas Streicher. The Groupoid Interpretation of Type Theory. In Giovanni Sambin and Jan Smith, editors, *Proceedings of the meeting of Twenty-five years of constructive type theory, Venice*. Oxford University Press, 1996.

14. Thomas Streicher. *Semantical Investigations into Intensional Type Theory*. LMU München, 1993. Habilitationsschrift.

15. Xin Yu, Aleksey Nogin, Alexei Kopylov, and Jason Hickey. Formalizing Abstract Algebra in Type Theory with Dependent Records. In David Basin and Burkhart Wolff, editors, *16th International Conference on Theorem Proving in Higher Order Logics (TPHOLs 2003)*. *Emerging Trends Proceedings*, pages 13–27. Universität Freiburg, 2003.

Correct Embedded Computing Futures

Al Davis

School of Computing
University of Utah

Abstract. Embedded computing systems have always been significantly more diverse than their mainstream microprocessor counterparts, but they have also been relatively more simple to design and validate. Given the current global fascination with ubiquitous information and communication services in a highly mobile world, simplicity is rapidly disappearing. Advanced perception systems such as speech and visual feature and gesture recognizers, 3G and 4G cellular telephony algorithms can not currently be done in real time on performance microprocessors let alone at a power budget commensurate with mobile embedded devices. This talk will describe an architectural approach to embedded systems which outperforms performance microprocessors while consuming less power than current embedded systems for the above applications. This approach will be used as a way to highlight new issues of correctness in embedded systems. Namely correctness applies to functional, energy consumption, and real time processing constraints. Given that these issues become even more critical as technology scales makes life even more complex. In order to deal with these hard problems, system architects are creating new system models where the application, operating system, and hardware interact in new ways to collaboratively manage the computational rates and energy consumption. This new system model generates a new set of validation problems that will become critical roadblocks to progress in advanced embedded systems of the future. The talk will conclude with a description of validation challenge problems inspired by the new system model.

K. Slind et al. (Eds.): TPHOLs 2004, LNCS 3223, p. 82, 2004.
© Springer-Verlag Berlin Heidelberg 2004

Higher Order Rippling in IsaPlanner

Lucas Dixon and Jacques Fleuriot

School of Informatics, University of Edinburgh,
Appleton Tower, Crighton Street, Edinburgh, EH8 9LE, UK
{lucas.dixon,jacques.fleuriot}@ed.ac.uk

Abstract. We present an account of rippling with proof critics suitable
for use in higher order logic in Isabelle/IsaPlanner. We treat issues not
previously examined, in particular regarding the existence of multiple
annotations during rippling. This results in an efficient mechanism for
rippling that can conjecture and prove needed lemmas automatically as
well as present the resulting proof plans as Isar style proof scripts.

1   Introduction

Rippling [5] is a rewriting technique that employs a difference removal heuristic to guide the search for proof. Typically, it is used to rewrite the step case
in a proof by induction until the inductive hypothesis can be applied. Within
the context of proof planning [4], this technique has been used in a variety
of domains including the automation of hardware verification [6], higher order
program synthesis [13], and more recently to automate proofs in nonstandard
analysis [14].

In this paper we describe a higher order version of rippling which has been
implemented for the Isabelle proof assistant [15] using the IsaPlanner proof
planner [9]. We believe this is the first time that rippling with a proof critics
mechanism has been implemented outside the Clam family of proof planners.
Our account bears similarity to that presented by Smaill and Green [19], but
uses a different mechanism for annotating differences more closely related to
rippling in first order domains. It also exposes and treats a number of issues
not previously examined regarding situations where multiple embeddings and
annotations are possible. This leads to an efficient implementation of rippling.

This work is also of particular interest to Isabelle users as it provides improved
automation and means of conjecturing and proving needed lemmas, as well as
automatically generating Isar proofs scripts [20].

The structure of the paper is as follows: in the next section, we give a brief
introduction to IsaPlanner. In Sections 3 and 4, we introduce static rippling
and dynamic rippling. In Section 5, we describe the version of rippling implemented in IsaPlanner and then outline, in Section 6, a technique that combines
rippling with induction, and some proof critics. We present an example application in the domain of ordinal arithmetic in Section 7, and some further results
in Section 8. Finally, Sections 9 and 10 describe related work and present our
conclusions and future work.

K. Slind et al. (Eds.): TPHOLs 2004, LNCS 3223, pp. 83–98, 2004.

2 IsaPlanner

IsaPlanner[1] is a generic framework for proof planning in the interactive theorem prover Isabelle. It facilitates the encoding of reasoning techniques, which can be used to conjecture and prove theorems automatically. A salient characteristic of IsaPlanner is its derivation of fully formal proofs, expressed in readable Isar style proof scripts as part of the proof planning process.

Proof planning in Isabelle/IsaPlanner is split into a series of *reasoning states* which capture 'snapshots' of the planning process. Each reasoning state contains the current partial proof plan, the next reasoning technique to be applied, and any appropriate contextual information. Reasoning techniques are encoded as functions from a reasoning state to a sequence of reasoning states, where each state in the resulting sequence represents a possible way in which the technique can be applied. This encoding of techniques allows the reasoning process to be decomposed into steps which are evaluated in a 'lazy' fashion.

The contextual information captures any knowledge that might be applicable to the current proof process and can be modified during proof planning. Contextual information also facilitates the design and definition of reasoning techniques by providing a data structure to hold knowledge derived during proof planning. Examples of such information include a conjecture database, annotations for rippling, and a high level description of the proof planning process.

Proof planning is performed by searching through the possible ways a reasoning technique can be applied. It terminates when a desired reasoning state is found, or when the search space is exhausted. Search mechanisms such as Depth First, Iterative Deepening, Breadth First and Best First have been implemented in IsaPlanner. Moreover, search strategies can be attached to a technique and used locally within its application. This allows us to take advantage of the heuristic measure given by rippling to choose the 'most promising' future state by using best first search, for example.

3 An Introduction to Rippling

While there are many variations of rippling [5], the central principle is to remove the differences between all or part of a goal and some defined *skeleton* constructed from the inductive hypothesis or, in some cases, from another assumption or theorem. Through the removal of this difference, the assumption or theorem that was employed to construct the skeleton can then be used to solve the goal in a process termed *fertilisation*. Thus rippling gives a direction to the rewriting process.

The difference removal is facilitated by specialised annotations on the goal known as *wave fronts, wave holes*, and *sinks*. More specifically, wave fronts indicate difference between the skeleton and the goal while wave holes identify subterms inside the wave fronts that are similar to parts of the goal. Sinks,

---

[1] http://isaplanner.sourceforge.net/

for their part, indicate *positions* in the skeleton that correspond to universally quantified variables and towards which wave fronts can be moved before being eventually discarded. Fertilisation is possible when the wave fronts have been removed from a subterm matching the skeleton, or placed in sinks appropriately. Thus, there are two directions rippling can pursue:

rippling-out: tries to remove the differences, or move them to the top of the term tree, thereby allowing fertilisation in a subterm.

rippling-in: tries to move the differences into sinks, as discussed above.

As an example consider the skeleton $\forall b.\ a+b = b+a$, then the term $Suc(a)+b = Suc(b+a)$ can be annotated as: $\boxed{Suc(\underline{a})}^{\uparrow} + \lfloor b \rfloor = \boxed{Suc(\underline{\lfloor b \rfloor + a})}^{\downarrow}$. The boxes indicate the wave fronts, and the underlined subterms are the wave holes. The up and down arrows indicate rippling outward and inward respectively, and the annotations $\lfloor b \rfloor$ indicate that b is at the location of a sink.

To provide rippling with a direction and to ensure its termination, a measure is used that decreases each time the goal is rewritten. The measure is a pair of lists of natural numbers that indicates the number of wave fronts (outward and inward) at each depth in the skeleton term. The outward list is obtained by counting the number of outward wave fronts from leaf to root and the inward list by tallying the inward ones from root to leaf. For example, the term tree for the annotation shown earlier is as follows:

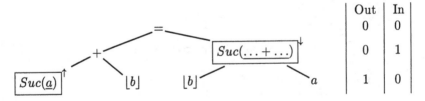

which results in the measure $([1,0,0],[0,1,0])$. Such measures are compared lexicographical as if they were a single list starting with the outward elements. This provides a mechanism that allows wave fronts to move from *out* to *in* but not visa-versa.

3.1 Static Rippling

We will refer to the rippling mechanism described by Bundy et al. [5], as *static rippling*. In this, measure decreasing annotated rewrite rules, called *wave rules*, are generated from axioms and theorems before rippling is performed. These wave rules are then applied *blindly* to rewrite the goal. If, at some point in the proof, no wave rules apply and the goal cannot be fertilised, then the goal is said to be *blocked*. This typically indicates that some backtracking is required, or that a lemma is needed.

In static rippling, annotations are expressed at the object level by inserting object level function symbols (identity functions) for wave fronts and wave holes.

For example, the function symbols wfout, wfin and wh may be used to represent outward wave fronts, inward wave fronts and wave holes respectively. The annotated term $p(\boxed{g(\underline{c})}^{\uparrow})$, for instance, can be represented using p(wfout(g(wh(c)))). Many wave rules can be created from a single theorem - in general, an exponential number on the size of the term. However, once wave rules are generated, fast rule selection can be performed by using discrimination nets [7], for example.

We now present a simple example of static rippling that considers the step case in an inductive proof of the commutativity of addition $(a + b = b + a)$ in Peano arithmetic. We will use the following wave rules:

$$\boxed{Suc(\underline{X})}^{\uparrow} + Y \Rightarrow \boxed{Suc(\underline{X + Y})}^{\uparrow} \tag{1}$$

$$X + \boxed{Suc(\underline{Y})}^{\uparrow} \Rightarrow \boxed{Suc(\underline{X + Y})}^{\uparrow} \tag{2}$$

A rippling proof of the step case uses the inductive hypothesis as the skeleton with which to annotate the goal:

$$\boxed{Suc(\underline{a})}^{\uparrow} + \lfloor b \rfloor = \lfloor b \rfloor + \boxed{Suc(\underline{a})}^{\uparrow}$$

$\downarrow$ Ripple using wave rule: 1

$$\boxed{Suc(a + \lfloor b \rfloor)}^{\uparrow} = \lfloor b \rfloor + \boxed{Suc(\underline{a})}^{\uparrow}$$

$\downarrow$ Ripple using wave rule: 2

$$\boxed{Suc(a + \lfloor b \rfloor)}^{\uparrow} = \boxed{Suc(\lfloor b \rfloor + a)}^{\uparrow}$$

$\downarrow$ Fertilise using the inductive hypothesis.

$$Suc(b + a) = Suc(b + a)$$

This shows how rippling can be used to guide a proof by induction. A formal account for static rippling in first order logic has been developed by Basin and Walsh [1]. They observe that if the normal notion of substitution is used, then it is possible for rewriting to produce strange annotations that do not correspond to the initial skeleton. The resulting effect is that rippling may no longer terminate but, even if it does so successfully, due to the changed skeleton, fertilisation may not be possible.

For an example of incorrect annotation consider the following:

1. A wave rule: $g(\boxed{f(\underline{X}, c)}^{\uparrow}) \Rightarrow \boxed{h(X, \underline{g(X)})}^{\uparrow}$

2. A goal, $g(\boxed{f(k(\boxed{g(\underline{z})}^{\uparrow}), c))}^{\uparrow})$ which has the skeleton $g(k(z)))$

3. The goal rewrites to $\boxed{h(k(\boxed{g(z)}^{\uparrow}), g(k(\boxed{g(z)}^{\uparrow})))}^{\uparrow}$, which does not even have a well defined skeleton.

To avoid these problems, Basin and Walsh provide and use a modified notion of substitution for their calculus of rippling. If such an approach were taken when working in a theorem prover such as Isabelle or HOL, where any extra-logical work must be verified within the logical kernel, then rippling steps would have to be repeated by the theorem prover once rippling is successful.

4   Dynamic Rippling with Embedding

An alternative approach to annotations for rippling is taken by Smaill and Green [19], and used to automate proofs in the domain of ordinal arithmetic by Dennis and Smaill [8]. Their approach avoids the need for a modified notion of substitution by recomputing the possible annotations each time a rule is applied. We call this *dynamic rippling*. The key feature of dynamic rippling is that the annotations are stored separately from the goal and are recomputed each time the goal is rewritten.

The central motivation for dynamic rippling, as noted by Smaill and Green, arises from problems with object level annotations when working in the lambda calculus. In particular:

- object level annotations are not stable over beta reduction. In particular, if the wave fronts are expressed at the object level, then it is not possible to use pre-annotated rules as they may not be skeleton preserving after beta reduction.
- in a context with meta variables, incorrect annotations can accidentally be introduced by unification.

In the setting of the lambda calculus, it is not clear how beta reduction could be redefined to get the desired properties for rippling. Furthermore, we are interested in a generic approach to rippling that can be used across logics without redefining substitution.

4.1   Embeddings for Annotating Difference

Smaill and Green use embedding trees to represent the difference annotations used in rippling [19]. However, their work leaves a number of open questions regarding what direction to give wave fronts in an embedding, and what to do when the skeleton can be embedded into the goal in more than one way.

Additionally, we observe that the embedding of a bound variable is not restricted by its associated quantifier. For example, an embedding is possible from the term $\forall x.\exists y.P(x,y)$ into $\forall a.\exists b.\forall c.P(a,c)$, where the y is existentially quantified in the skeleton, but embedded into c which is universally quantified. We believe that this is due to the lack of a well defined relationship between the annotations for difference and the underlying semantics. However, in practice this is rarely an issue and we have not found any domains where this causes a problem.

Nonetheless, if rippling is to be used in a domain with many different quantifiers then it may be worthwhile to impose further restrictions on embeddings. For example, by requiring, for each quantified variable being embedded, that the quantifier in the skeleton and the goal should be identical, or that the quantifier in the skeleton should embed into the quantifier in the goal. Such constraints would prune the search space and bring a closer semantic relationship between the embedding of bound variables and their quantifiers.

5   Rippling in IsaPlanner

We now describe our version of rippling and its treatment of multiple annotations. We use dynamic rippling which avoids redefinition of substitution and is suitable for use in higher order logics. Before rippling starts, theorems and axioms are added to a *wave rule set* which will be used during the process. We do not use all theorems and axioms during rippling for reasons described in Section 5.2.

Given a wave rule set, our version of rippling is composed of three parts:

1. **Setup:** Rippling is given a skeleton with which to create an initial list of possible annotations. We use the contextual information of ISAPLANNER to store the annotations for rippling and keep track of the associated goal. This information also facilitates the later development of proof planning critics that can use the annotations to patch failed proof attempts, as described in the work of Ireland and Bundy [12].
2. **Ripple Steps:** Theorems in the wave rule set are used to perform a single step of rewriting on the goal. Note that the order in which the rules are applied is irrelevant as the rewriting process is guided by the rippling measure. After each successful rule application, the goal is beta-reduced and a new set of annotations is created. If this set is empty then the rewrite is considered to be an invalid ripple step and another rule is tried.
3. **Fertilisation:** When no more rules apply, rippling has either completed successfully, allowing fertilisation, or failed. Upon failure, our version of rippling either applies a proof critic, discussed in Section 6.1, or backtracks and tries rippling with different wave rules.

We note that in general, the open problems with dynamic rippling arise because there are many ways to embed a skeleton in a goal and, for each embedding, there are a number of ways in which it can be annotated. Thus each goal is associated with a set of annotations, rather than a single annotation, as was the case in static rippling. Further problems arise when rippling inward, computing the measure, and when deciding which rules to use for rippling. In the following subsections we describe how our version of dynamic rippling addresses these issues.

5.1   Depth for Measures and Inward Rippling

To avoid a large number of possible annotations, inward wave fronts are typically restricted to being placed above a subterm that contains a sink. However, in higher order abstract syntax (HOAS) the idea of 'above' or 'below' is not immediately obvious as function symbols are leaf nodes in the term tree. We address this by defining a suitable notion of depth which removes the need for product types as used by Smaill and Green [19]. An advantage of our approach is that users are free to use a curried representation with a notion of measure similar to that used in first order static rippling.

The central idea is to treat depth in the following way: If x has depth d in the term u, then x has depth d in $\lambda y.u$ and $app(u, v)$ (the HOAS application of u to v), and in $app(v, u)$, x has depth $d + 1$. This 'uncurries' the syntax in the way we would expect: no height ordering is given to different curried arguments of a function. For example, the term $Suc(a) + b$, expressed in the HOAS as $app(app(+, app(Suc, a)), b)$, gives a depth of 0 to $+$, 1 to Suc and b, and 2 to a. In contrast, the usual notion of depth in HOAS is 1 for b, 2 for $+$, and 3 for Suc and a.

5.2   Selection of the Wave Rule Set

It is often cited as one of the advantages of rippling that the annotation process provides a means of ensuring termination and that therefore all resulting rules can be added to the set of wave rules. In static rippling, only measure decreasing wave rules are created. This avoids rewrites which have no valid annotation such as $x \Rightarrow 0 + x$.

However, recall that in dynamic rippling, theorems are used to rewrite the goal and then the possible annotations are checked in order to avoid goals where the measure does not decrease. Unfortunately, this approach can causes rules that are not beneficial but frequently applicable, such as $x \Rightarrow 0 + x$, to slow down search.

To avoid this, we filter the possible ways a theorem can be used to write a goal, removing those with a left hand side that is identical to a subterm of the right, such as $x \Rightarrow x + 0$. We also remove any rewrites that would introduce a new variable, such as $1 \Rightarrow x^0$. While this solution does not correspond exactly to the first order case, it works well in practice.

5.3   A Richer Representation of Annotations

Smaill and Green represent annotations using embeddings. However, this does not correspond directly to the first order account of rippling annotations given by Basin and Walsh. In particular, annotations such as $f(\boxed{g(\underline{x})}^{\downarrow})^{\uparrow}$ cannot be expressed with their embedding representation.

In order to maintain a flexible and efficient mechanism for annotated terms, we use a different representation (shown in Fig 1) that holds more information

$$aterm = aAbs(type, aterm, annot)$$
$$| \ aApp(aterm, aterm, annot)$$
$$| \ aConst(Const, annot)$$
$$| \ aVar(Var, annot)$$
$$| \ aBound(Bound, annot)$$

Fig. 1. A datatype to express annotated terms (*aterm*). The types: *annot* expresses an annotation, which is typically either *in*, *out* or *none*; *type* is the type of a bound variable; *Const* is a constant, *Var* is a variable, and *Bound* is a bound variable using de Bruijn indices.

than the embedding trees used by Smaill and Green[2]. This allows multiple adjacent wave fronts with different orientations. Using our annotations, the above example would then be expressed as

aApp(aConst(f,out),(aApp(aConst(g,in),aVar(x,none),in)),out).

The extra information held in this representation provides an easy way to experiment with different measures and mechanisms for annotation. Additionally, combined with the depth mechanism described in the previous section, our version of annotated terms produces the measures similar to first order rippling even when working with curried style functions.

5.4 Choices in the Direction of Wave Fronts

Whether using Smaill and Green's embedding mechanism or our annotated terms, one still has to worry about the direction of wave fronts. Initially, they are always outward but after applying a rule there is a choice of direction for each wave front.

For example, returning to the proof the commutativity of addition, the initial annotated goal is $\boxed{Suc(\underline{a})}^{\uparrow} + \lfloor b \rfloor = \lfloor b \rfloor + \boxed{Suc(\underline{a})}^{\uparrow}$, but after applying the theorem $Suc(x) + y = Suc(x + y)$ from left to right, there are two possible ways the new goal can be annotated:

$$\boxed{Suc(a + \lfloor b \rfloor)}^{\uparrow} = \lfloor b \rfloor + \boxed{Suc(\underline{a})}^{\uparrow} \tag{3}$$

$$\boxed{Suc(a + \lfloor b \rfloor)}^{\downarrow} = \lfloor b \rfloor + \boxed{Suc(\underline{a})}^{\uparrow} \tag{4}$$

---

[2] Note that IsaPlanner uses a more efficient but more complex datatype that maintains the same information as the one presented here.

Note that the static account of rippling only allows inward wave fronts where there is a sink below the wave front (in the term structure). Without this restriction, as needed by some of the proof critics in $\lambda Clam$, there are many more possible annotations.

We observe that in order to manage the multitude of annotations, only a single measure needs to be stored. We call this the *threshold* measure. Initially, this is the highest measure in the ordering. After a rule is applied, the new annotations are analysed to yield the highest measure lower than the current threshold. This becomes the new threshold. If no such measure can be found then search backtracks over the rules application. This strategy ensures that all possible rippling solutions are in the search space.

5.5   Managing Multiple Annotations

While only a single measure is needed to represent all annotations, we observe that the mere existence of multiple annotations for a goal can result in rippling applying unnecessary proof steps. For example, when trying to prove $a + 0 = a$ in Peano arithmetic, we arrive at an annotated step case of $\boxed{Suc(\underline{a})}^{\uparrow} + 0 = \boxed{Suc(\underline{a})}^{\uparrow}$, which we will rewrite with the theorem $Suc(X) + Y = Suc(X + Y)$, named add_Suc:

$$\boxed{Suc(\underline{a})}^{\uparrow} + 0 = \boxed{Suc(\underline{a})}^{\uparrow} \quad Measure : ([1,1,0],[0,0,0])$$

$$\Big\downarrow \text{ Ripple using add\_Suc from left to right}$$

$$\boxed{Suc(\underline{a} + 0)}^{\uparrow} = \boxed{Suc(\underline{a})}^{\uparrow} \quad Measure : ([0,2,0],[0,0,0])$$

$$\Big\downarrow \text{ Ripple using add\_Suc from right to left}$$

$$\boxed{Suc(\underline{a})}^{\downarrow} + 0 = \boxed{Suc(\underline{a})}^{\uparrow} \quad Measure : ([0,1,0],[0,0,1])$$

$$\Big\downarrow \text{ Ripple using add\_Suc from left to right}$$

$$\boxed{Suc(\underline{a} + 0)}^{\downarrow} = \boxed{Suc(\underline{a})}^{\downarrow} \quad Measure : ([0,0,0],[0,2,0])$$

$$\Big\downarrow \text{ Fertilise using the inductive hypothesis.}$$

$$Suc(a) = Suc(a)$$

This redundancy in rewriting steps is an important inefficiency for a number of reasons: the search space will be larger, the proofs found will be less readable, the proofs may be more brittle (have unnecessary dependencies), and when being used for program synthesis [13], for example, inefficient programs may be created.

While the number of redundant proof steps is smaller if inward wave fronts are restricted to occurring above a sink, the problem still manifests itself when there are multiple sinks and wave fronts.

In the following section, we describe a general inefficiency with rippling, and then present a solution that prunes the search space and thereby addresses the problem described in this section and the more general inefficiency.

5.6   Avoiding Redundant Search in Rippling

A simple observation which can be made during rippling is that it is often possible to ripple many different parts of a goal independently, and thus it is of no help to backtrack and try a different order. For example, in the proof of the commutativity of addition presented earlier, either the right hand side or the left hand side can be rippled out first.

In ISAPLANNER, the goal terms during rippling are cached (without annotation), so that the same rippling state is not examined more than once. This removes symmetry in the search space, and thus provides an efficiency improvement. By using this mechanism to keep the shortest possible proof (in terms of ripple steps) we also significantly reduce the problems with redundant steps in rippling. This mechanism is provided by a generic search space caching in ISAPLANNER.

5.7   Implementation Details

Rippling is encoded in ISAPLANNER in two parts: a module, called the *ripple state*, that holds annotations associated with a goal, and the *rippling technique* which is defined in terms of the ripple state module. The notion of embedding is defined in a generic way in terms of Isabelle's HOAS. Embeddings are used by the ripple state and transformed into a set of possible annotations. The ripple state module has two main functions: firstly, to set up a new state from a goal and skeleton that has an initial set of annotations, and secondly, to update a state given a new goal.

The abstract interface for a ripple state allows us to use different annotation mechanisms without changing any of the code for the rippling technique. To implement a new form of rippling, only a new implementation of the ripple state module needs be created. Furthermore, ISAPLANNER supports multiple versions of rippling simultaneously. This provides us with a framework to test and easily create variations of the technique.

ISAPLANNER provides an interactive interface that can be used to trace through the proof planning attempt. We remark that this was particularly useful for debugging the rippling technique as well as understanding the rippling proofs.

A feature of using ISAPLANNER is that it allows encoded techniques to automatically generate readable, executable proof scripts of the Isabelle/Isar style.

This is particularly beneficial when lemmas are speculated and proved as it provides a form of automatic theory formation. For an example of a generated proof script see Section 7.

6 A Technique Combining Induction and Rippling

As mentioned earlier, the most common use of rippling is to guide inductive proof. Moreover, rippling is particularly suited to the application of proof critics as the annotations provide additional information that can be used when searching for a way to patch a failed proof attempt. Indeed, we found that a combination of induction with rippling, Ireland's lemma calculation critic [12], and Boyer-Moore style generalisation [3] provides a powerful tool for automation. The technique starts an inductive proof and uses rippling to solve the step case(s). When rippling becomes blocked, the lemma speculation and generalisation critics are applied. The base cases are tackled using Isabelle's simplification tactic which is also combined with the lemma speculation and generalisation critics.

The induction technique selects and applies an induction scheme based on the inductively defined variables in the goal. Although there are various ways to select the variable for induction, such as ripple analysis [17], we found that search backtracks quickly enough for the choice of variable to be largely insignificant in the domains we examined. This is partially due to the caching mechanism that allow proof planning to use a significant portion of the failed proof attempt. For example, when proving $i^{(j+k)} = i^j \cdot i^k$ in Peano arithmetic, wrongly trying induction on i results in the proof of 3 of the 4 needed lemmas, and the only additional lemma to prove is the trivial theorem $x + 0 = x$.

This technique combining induction and rippling is similar to that used by Dennis and Smaill [8] in $\lambda Clam$. The main differences are within rippling, where we use a different mechanism for annotation, and provide a number of efficiency measures. Additionally, we make use of Isabelle's induction and simplification tactics as well as provide some further optimisation to lemma speculation as described below. In Section 8, we briefly compare our implementation with that in $\lambda Clam$.

6.1 Efficient Lemma Conjecturing and Proof

We have attached a lemma speculation and generalisation critic to rippling and incorporated the following efficiency measures into the speculation and proof of lemmas:

- if a conjecture is proved to be false, then the search space of possible alternative proofs should be pruned. Additionally, the search space of any conjecture of which the false one is an instance should also be pruned. At present our rippling technique does not use any sophisticated means of detecting false conjectures, although we intend to make use of Isabelle's refutation and counter example finding tools in future work.

- if the search space for the proof of a conjecture is exhausted, then it seems reasonable (and is useful in practice) to avoid making the same conjecture at a later point in proof planning.
- when a lemma is successfully proved, but later the proof of the main goal fails, it will not help to find alternative proofs for the lemma. This suggests that when a lemma is proved, the search space for other proofs of the lemma (or an instance of it) should be pruned.

These are available in a generic form in ISAPLANNER and can be used in any technique that speculates and tries to prove lemmas. We remark that using a global cache of proved lemmas is difficult in systems such as $\lambda Clam$ where backtracking removes derived information.

7   A Brief Case Study in Ordinal Arithmetic

We now briefly describe a formalisation in Isabelle/ISAPLANNER of ordinal arithmetic similar to that developed in $\lambda Clam$ by Dennis and Smaill [8]. Ordinal notation is defined using the following datatype:

$$ordinal = 0 \mid Suc \; of \; ordinal \mid Lim \; (nat \to ordinal)$$

A feature of Isabelle is that the transfinite induction scheme for the ordinal notation is automatically generated by the datatype package [18]. The induction scheme is then automatically used by the induction technique in ISAPLANNER.

The arithmetic operations on ordinals are defined using Isabelle's primitive recursive package. For example, addition is defined as follows:

```
primrec
  ord_add_0   : "(x + 0) = (x :: Ord)"
  ord_add_Suc : "x + (Suc y) = Suc (x + y)"
  ord_add_Lim : "x + (Lim f) = Lim (λn. x + (f n))"
```

The other arithmetic operations are defined and named similarly. Using these definitions, the induction and rippling technique is able to derive and produce automatically Isabelle/Isar proof scripts for all the theorems proved in the work of Dennis and Smaill. The theorem that takes longest to prove is the following:

```
theorem "x ^ (y * z) = (x ^ y) ^ z"
proof (induct "z")
  show "x ^ (y * 0) = (x ^ y) ^ 0" by (simp)
next
  fix Ord :: "Ord"
  assume ind_hyp1: "x ^ (y * Ord) = (x ^ y) ^ Ord"
  have "x ^ (y * Ord + y) = x ^ (y * Ord) * x ^ y" by (rule auto_lemma_0)
  hence "x ^ (y * Ord + y) = (x ^ y) ^ Ord * x ^ y" by (rwstep sym[OF ind_hyp1])
  hence "x ^ (y * Ord + y) = (x ^ y) ^ Suc Ord" by (rwstep ord_exp_Suc)
  thus "x ^ (y * Suc Ord) = (x ^ y) ^ Suc Ord" by (rwstep ord_mul_Suc)
next
```

```
fix f :: "nat => Ord"
assume ind_hyp1: "!!xa. x ^ (y * f xa) = (x ^ y) ^ f xa"
have "Lim (λn. (x ^ y) ^ f n) = Lim (λn. (x ^ y) ^ f n)" by (simp)
hence "Lim (λn. x ^ (y * f n)) = Lim (λn. (x ^ y) ^ f n)" by (rwstep ind_hyp1)
hence "Lim (λn. x ^ (y * f n)) = (x ^ y) ^ Lim f" by (rwstep ord_exp_Lim)
hence "x ^ Lim (λn. y * f n) = (x ^ y) ^ Lim f" by (rwstep ord_exp_Lim)
thus "x ^ (y * Lim f) = (x ^ y) ^ Lim f" by (rwstep ord_mul_Lim)
qed
```

where ord_exp_Suc, ord_exp_Lim, ord_mul_Suc and ord_mul_Lim are the names of the defining equations in the recursive definitions for exponentation and multiplication. Also note that the following needed lemmas are all automatically conjectured and proved:

```
lemma auto_lemma_5: "g0 + (g2 + g1) = g0 + g2 + g1"
lemma auto_lemma_4: "g1 * g2 + g1 * g0 = g1 * (g2 + g0)"
lemma auto_lemma_3: "g1 * g0 * x = g1 * (g0 * x)"
lemma auto_lemma_1: "g1 = 0 + g1"
lemma auto_lemma_0: "x ^ (g0 + y) = x ^ g0 * x ^ y"
```

As a final remark, note that in the automatically generated Isar script above, the tactic **rwstep** simply applies a single step of rewriting with the given theorem.

8 Results

We have applied our technique with depth first search to over 300 problems in a mixture of first and higher domains, including a theory of lists, Peano arithmetic, and ordinal arithmetic. A table highlighting some of the results is given in Fig 2.

To distinguish the automation provided by the rippling technique from that gained by working in the richly developed theories of Isabelle, the tests were carried out in a formalisation without any auxiliary lemmas. All needed lemmas were automatically conjectured and proved. To get an idea of the improved automation, we note that none of the theorems shown in Figure 2 are provable using Isabelle's existing automatic tactics, even after the manual application of induction.

As a comparison with $\lambda Clam$ we observe that:

- $\lambda Clam$ has specialised methods for various domains, such as non-standard analysis [14], which provide it with the ability to prove some theorems not provable by IsaPLANNER's default rippling machinary.
- IsaPLANNER makes use of Isabelle's configurable tactics such as the simplifier which is user configurable and can be used to provide conditional rewriting for the base cases of inductive proofs. This can provide IsaPLANNER with automation not possible in $\lambda Clam$.
- IsaPLANNER executes the proof plan, ensuring soundness of the result, where $\lambda Clam$ is currently not interfaced to an object level theorem prover.

Domain	Theorem	Time (in seconds)	Lemmas Proved
Properties of Lists	$length\ l = length(rev\ l)$	0.2	1
	$length(xs\ @\ ys) = length(xs)\ +\ length(ys)$	0.3	1
	$rev(map\ f\ xs) = map\ f\ rev(xs)$	0.3	1
	$rev(rev(xs)) = xs$	1.0	1
Peano Arithmetic	$a \cdot b = b \cdot a$	0.1	3
	$(a \cdot b) \cdot c = a \cdot (b \cdot c)$	1.6	8
	$a^{(b+c)} = (a^b) \cdot (a^c)$	2.0	11
	$a \cdot (b \cdot c) = b \cdot (a \cdot c)$	2.5	15
Ordinal Arithmetic	$x \cdot (y + z) = (x \cdot y) + (x \cdot z)$	0.8	1
	$(a \cdot b) \cdot c = a \cdot (b \cdot c)$	1.0	2
	$x^{(y+z)} = x^y \cdot x^z$	1.6	4
	$x^{(y \cdot z)} = (x^y)^z$	2.0	5

Fig. 2. Some results using the induction and rippling technique in IsaPlanner showing the theorem proved, the time taken, and number of lemmas conjectured and proved automatically. The timings were obtained from a 2GHz Intel PC with 512MB of RAM, and using Isabelle2004 with PolyML.

- Higher order rippling in IsaPlanner is appears to be exponentially faster than in λ *Clam*. Simple theorems are solved in almost equivalent time but those with more complex proofs involving lemmas are significantly quicker to plan *and* prove in IsaPlanner. For example, the ordinal theorem $x^{(y \cdot z)} = (x^y)^z$ takes over five minutes in λ *Clam* compared to 2 seconds in IsaPlanner. We believe that this is largely due to the efficiency measures described in this paper.
- The resulting proof plans from IsaPlanner are readable and clear whereas those produced by λ *Clam* are difficult to read. For example, at present the proof plan generated by λ *Clam* for the associativity of addition in Peano arithmetic is 12 pages long (without any line breaks). The proof script generated by IsaPlanner is one page long and in the Isar style.
- Upon failure to prove a theorem, λ *Clam* does not give any helpful results, whereas IsaPlanner is able to provide the user with proofs for useful auxiliary lemmas. For example, upon trying to prove $x^{(y \cdot z)} = (x^y)^z$ in Peano arithmetic, IsaPlanner conjectures and proves 13 lemmas, including the associativity and distributivity rules for multiplication.

We remark that many of the automatically conjectured and proved lemmas can be obtained by simplification from previously generated ones. This shows a certain amount of redundancy in the generated lemmas. In future work, we intend to prune these and identify those which are of obvious use to the simplifier. Future work will also include support for working with theorems that do not contain equalities.

9 Related Work

Boulton and Slind [2] developed an interface between Clam and HOL. Unlike our approach which tries to take advantage of the tactics in Isabelle, their interface did not use the tactics developed in HOL as part of proof planning. Additionally, problems were limited to being first order, whereas our approach is able to derive proof plans for higher order theorems.

A general notion of annotated rewriting has been developed by Hutter [10] and extended to the setting of a higher order logic by Hutter and Kohlhase [11]. They develop a novel calculus which contains annotations. This is a mixture between dynamic and static rippling as after each rewrite skeleton preservation still needs to be checked, but the wave rules can be generated beforehand.

A proof method that combines logical proof search and static rippling has been implemented for the NuPrl system by Pietntka and Kreitz [16]. Their implementation is as a tactic without proof critics and focuses on the incremental instantiation of meta variables. They employ a different measure based on the sum of the distances between wave fronts and sinks.

10 Conclusions & Further Work

We have presented an account of rippling, based on the dynamic style described by Smaill and Green and extended it to use annotations that bear a closer similarity to the account of static rippling within first order domains. Additionally, we have exposed and treated important issues that affect the size of the search space. This has lead to an efficient version of rippling.

We have implemented our version of rippling in ISAPLANNER for use in the higher order logic of Isabelle. This provides a framework for comparing and experimenting with extensions to rippling, such as the addition of proof critics and the use of modified measures. We believe that this is an important step in the development of a unified view of this proof planning technique.

Our version of rippling, combined with induction, lemma speculation, and generalisation gives improved automation in Isabelle, can generate Isar proof scripts and is able to conjecture and prove needed lemmas. This work also serves as a test-bed for the ISAPLANNER framework and facilitates the application of proof planning techniques to interactive higher order theorem proving.

There are many ways in which this work can be extended. It would be interesting to experiment with various mechanisms for annotation and develop a complete picture of the effect of the design choices for dynamic rippling. This would work towards a complete and formal account of dynamic rippling for a higher order setting. In terms of proof automation, there are many proof critics that could be added to our implementation and compared. This would provide further automation and test the flexibility of our framework. It would also be interesting to compare rippling with the existing simplification package in Isabelle. Additionally, we would like to examine the automation that rippling can provide to the various large 'real world' theory developments in Isabelle.

Acknowledgments

This research was funded by the EPSRC grant *A Generic Approach to Proof Planning* - GR/N37314/01. The authors would also like to thank the anonymous referees for their constructive and helpful feedback.

References

1. D. Basin and T. Walsh. A calculus for and termination of rippling. *JAR*, 16(1-2):147–180, 1996.
2. R. Boulton, K. Slind, A. Bundy, and M. Gordon. An interface between CLAM and HOL. In *TPHOLs'98*, volume 1479 of *LNAI*, pages 87–104, 1998.
3. R. S. Boyer and J. S. Moore. *A Computational Logic Handbook, (Perspectives in Computing, Vol 23)*. Academic Press Inc, 1988.
4. A. Bundy. Proof planning. In B. Drabble, editor, *AIPS'96*, pages 261–267, 1996.
5. A. Bundy, A. Stevens, F. van Harmelen, A. Ireland, and A. Smaill. Rippling: A heuristic for guiding inductive proofs. *Artificial Intelligence*, 62:185–253, 1993.
6. F. Cantu, A. Bundy, A. Smaill, and D. Basin. Experiments in automating hardware verification using inductive proof planning. In *FMCAD'96*, volume 1166 of *LNCS*, pages 94–108, 1996.
7. E. Charniak, C. Riesbeck, D. McDermott, and J. Meehan. *Artificial Intelligence Programming*. Lawrence Erlbaum Associates, 1980.
8. L. A. Dennis and A. Smaill. Ordinal arithmetic: A case study for rippling in a higher order domain. In *TPHOLs'01*, volume 2152 of *LNCS*, pages 185–200, 2001.
9. L. Dixon and J. D. Fleuriot. IsaPlanner: A prototype proof planner in Isabelle. In *Proceedings of CADE'03*, LNCS, pages 279–283, 2003.
10. D. Hutter. Annotated reasoning. *Annals of Mathematics and Artificial Intelligence*, 29(1-4):183–222, 2000.
11. D. Hutter and M. Kohlhase. A colored version of the lambda-calculus. In *CADE'97*, volume 1249 of *LNCS*, pages 291–305, 1997.
12. A. Ireland and A. Bundy. Productive use of failure in inductive proof. *Journal of Automated Reasoning*, 16(1–2):79–111, 1996.
13. D. Lacey, J. D. C. Richardson, and A. Smaill. Logic program synthesis in a higher order setting. In *Computational Logic*, volume 1861 of *LNCS*, pages 87–100, 2000.
14. E. Maclean, J. Fleuriot, and A. Smaill. Proof-planning non-standard analysis. In *The 7th International Symposium on AI and Mathematics*, 2002.
15. L. C. Paulson. *Isabelle: A generic theorem prover*. Springer-Verlag, 1994.
16. B. Pientka and C. Kreitz. Automating inductive specification proofs in NuPRL. *Fundamenta Mathematicae*, 34:1–20, 1998.
17. J. Richardson and A. Bundy. Proof planning methods as schemas. *J. Symbolic Computation*, 11:1–000, 1999.
18. K. Slind. Derivation and use of induction schemes in higher-order logic. In *TPHOLs'97*, volume 1275 of *LNCS*, pages 275–290, 1997.
19. A. Smaill and I. Green. Higher-order annotated terms for proof search. In *TPHOLs'96*, pages 399–413, 1996.
20. M. Wenzel. Isar - a generic interpretative approach to readable formal proof documents. In *TPHOLs'99*, volume 1690 of *LNCS*, pages 167–184, 1999.

A Mechanical Proof of the Cook-Levin Theorem

Ruben Gamboa and John Cowles

University of Wyoming
Department of Computer Science
Laramie, WY 82071

Abstract. As is the case with many theorems in complexity theory, typical proofs of the celebrated Cook-Levin theorem showing the NP-completeness of satisfiability are based on a clever construction. The Cook-Levin theorem is proved by carefully translating a possible computation of a Turing machine into a boolean expression. As the boolean expression is built, it is "obvious" that it can be satisfied if and only if the computation corresponds to a valid and accepting computation of the Turing machine. The details of the argument that the translation works as advertised are usually glossed over; it is the translation itself that is discussed. In this paper, we present a formal proof of the correctness of the translation. The proof is verified with the theorem prover ACL2.

1 Introduction

This paper presents a mechanical proof of the Cook-Levin theorem. A number of reasons led us to this investigation. The Cook-Levin theorem is the central theorem in NP-completeness theory, as it was the first to demonstrate the existence of an NP-complete problem, namely satisfiability [3, 7]. Moreover, having taught several undergraduate and introductory graduate courses on the theory of computer science, one of the authors has always been uncomfortable with the format of most proofs in the field. Many such proofs hinge on an algorithm that translates an instance of a problem from one domain to another. The transformation can be quite intricate, but seldom is its correctness actually proved. More often the correctness of the transformation is left as being obvious. Since the correctness proof is almost certainly tedious, we see it as an opportunity for formal approaches to proof. Other efforts have used the Boyer-Moore theorem prover to prove similar results, such as [1, 2, 8, 9].

We chose to use the theorem prover ACL2 for our formalization. ACL2 is a theorem prover over a first-order logic of total functions, with minimal support for quantifiers. The logic of ACL2 is based on the applicative subset of Common Lisp. Its basic structure and inference mechanisms are taken from its predecessor, the Boyer-Moore theorem prover. In fact, ACL2 arose out of a desire to enhance the Boyer-Moore prover to make it more suitable for industrial use, and in that respect it has succeeded marvelously. For example, it has been used to verify aspects of the floating-point units of microprocessors at AMD and IBM, and it

K. Slind et al. (Eds.): TPHOLs 2004, LNCS 3223, pp. 99–116, 2004.
© Springer-Verlag Berlin Heidelberg 2004

is also in use in the simulation and verification of microprocessors at Rockwell-Collins. ACL2 has also been used in many other verification projects, ranging from the algebra of polynomials to properties of the Java virtual machine [5, 6].

This paper does not assume familiarity with ACL2. However, we will use regular ACL2 syntax to introduce ACL2 definitions and theorems. We assume, therefore, that the reader is comfortable with Lisp notation.

The remainder of the paper is organized as follows. In Sect. 2 we present an informal proof of the Cook-Levin theorem, such as the one found in many introductory texts. We formalize this proof in Sect. 3. The formalization in ACL2 will follow the constructive parts of the informal proof quite closely. In Sect. 4 we present some final thoughts and some directions for further research.

2   An Informal Proof

We assume the reader is familiar with Turing machines and the NP-completeness of satisfiability. In this section we present an informal proof of this fact, merely to fix the terminology and lay the foundation for the formal proof to come later. Our exposition follows [4] quite closely. There are other proofs of the Cook-Levin theorem, some more recent and easier to follow. We chose this particular exposition because we considered it to be the most amenable to mechanization.

Informally, a Turing machine consists of a single tape that is divided into an infinite number of cells. The tape has a leftmost cell but no rightmost cell. The machine has a read/write head that can process a single cell at a time. The head can also move to the left or the right one step at a time. The behavior of the machine is governed by a finite control, with transitions based on its current state and the tape symbol being scanned. More formally a Turing machine $M = (Q, \Sigma, \delta, q_0, q_f)$ where Q is a finite set of states including q_0 and q_f, Σ is the finite alphabet of the tape not including the special blank symbol B, and δ is a relation mapping a state and a symbol into a possible move. The states q_0 and q_f are called the initial and accepting states of M, respectively.

The Cook-Levin theorem shows the relationship between Turing machines and satisfiability:

Theorem 1 (Cook, Levin). *Let M be a Turing Machine that is guaranteed to halt on an arbitrary input x after $p(n)$ steps, where p is a (fixed) polynomial and n is the length of x. $L(M)$, the set of strings x accepted by M, is polynomially reducible to satisfiability.*

Consider the behavior of machine M on input x. Initially, the tape contains the input x followed by blanks, the head is scanning the first symbol of x, and the machine M is in its initial state q_0. The machine goes through a sequence of steps, each of which is characterized by the contents of the tape, the position of the head, and the internal state of the machine. After at most $p(n)$ steps, the machine halts. If it halts while in state q_f the machine accepts input x, and otherwise it rejects x.

So a computation of the machine can be formalized as the sequence of steps $S_0, S_1, \ldots, S_{p(n)}$, where S_0 corresponds to the initial configuration of the machine with input x, and each S_{i+1} follows from S_i according to the rules of the machine M. As a matter of convenience, if the machine halts before $p(n)$ steps, we let the last step repeat so that we always end up with $p(n) + 1$ steps.

The step S_i can be represented by its tape, the location of the head, and the internal state of the machine M. It is also helpful to store explicitly the move taken by M from state S_i to S_{i+1}. The tape can hold at most $p(n)$ characters, because it takes at least one step to write a character. We may assume that all tapes have exactly $p(n)$ characters, simply by padding the tapes with blanks on the right. Thus the tapes in the computation can be represented by the two-dimensional array $T(i, j)$ where $i \in [0, p(n)]$ is the step of the computation and $j \in [1, p(n)]$ is the position of the character in the tape. We will use the notation $T(i, *)$ to refer to all the cells in a single step of the computation.

To complete the representation of a computation, we need only represent the position of the head and the machine state at each step of the computation, as well as the moves taken between steps of the computation. A convenient way to do this is to encode this information in the array T. The value of $T(i, j)$ is normally a symbol in the tape. But if the head is at position j at step S_i, then $T(i, j)$ is the composite symbol $\langle c, q, m \rangle$, where c is the character in position j of the tape, q is the state of the machine at step S_i, and m is the move taken by the Turing machine from step S_i to step S_{i+1}.

The transformation to satisfiability is carried out using this data structure. It is clear that the value of $T(i, j)$ is in $\Gamma = \Sigma \cup \{B\} \cup (\Sigma \cup \{B\}) \times Q \times img(\delta)$. For each $i \in [0, p(n)]$, $j \in [1, p(n)]$, and $X \in \Gamma$ we define the proposition $C_{i,j,X}$ with informal meaning $T(i, j) = X$. The expression E_x over these variables is the conjunction of the following four subexpressions:

- The truth assignment really does represent a unique array $T(i, j)$. That is, for each i and j precisely one of the $C_{i,j,X}$ is true.
- The values in $T(0, *)$ correspond to the initial configuration of the machine with x in the input tape.
- The machine is in its final accepting state q_f in $T(p(n), *)$.
- For each $i \in [1, p(n)]$, the configuration represented by $T(i, *)$ follows from the configuration at $T(i - 1, *)$.

Taken together, these expressions are satisfiable if and only if there is some valid computation of M that starts with the input x and ends in an accepting state.

3   A Formal Proof

3.1   The Turing Machine Models

As there are many variants of Turing machines, it is important to specify precisely which variant we are using. Our Turing machines have a semi-infinite tape that is allowed to grow without bounds but only to the right. The input is placed at the beginning of this tape. The machine has a single initial and a final state. Once the machine enters the final state, it is constrained to stay there.

We encode a specific Turing machine in a data structure that contains the machine's alphabet, its set of states, the initial and final states, and the transitions specifying how the machine changes state. The transitions are encoded as a list mapping state/symbol pairs into a list of possible moves. We use the functions ndtm-alphabet, ndtm-states, ndtm-initial, ndtm-final, and ndtm-transition to select individual components from a Turing machine.

A configuration stores the information about a single step in the computation: The current contents of the tape, the position of the read/write head, and the current internal state of the machine. To make traversals of the tape easier, we split the tape into two halves. The right half of the tape begins with the symbol currently being scanned by the head; its remaining elements contain all the symbols to the right of the head in increasing order. The left half of the tape contains all the symbols to the left of the head in *reverse* order. The functions config-lhs, config-rhs, and config-state will be used to access the members of this structure.

The basic mechanics of the Turing machine are modeled by the function ndtm-step, which takes in a Turing machine and a configuration and returns all the possible configurations that may follow it:

```
(defun ndtm-step (machine config)
  (let ((moves (ndtm-moves (config-state config)
                           (first (config-rhs config))
                           (ndtm-transition machine)))))
    (ndtm-step-with-move-list config moves)))
```

The function ndtm-moves returns all the valid transitions that the Turing machine can make when it is at the given state and looking at the given symbol on the tape. The function ndtm-step-with-move-list applies the selected moves to the configuration, returning a list containing all the resulting configurations.

We can not allow a machine to move the read/write head to the left when it is in the first cell position. This is enforced in the function ndtm-step-with-move (called by ndtm-step-with-move-list). When the head attempts to move past the beginning of the tape, we leave the head scanning the first cell of the tape.

We use a breadth-first strategy to model the non-determinism of the Turing machine. Using this search strategy allows us to decouple the search from the acceptance check. The function ndtm-step-n returns all the possible configurations that can occur after stepping through an initial configuration n times. We test acceptance with the function ndtm-accept which takes a list of configurations and checks to see if any of them are in the accepting state. The function ndtm-accepts-p takes a machine, input, and number of steps, and returns true if the machine accepts the given input in that number of steps.

We place some restrictions on the Turing machines: We insist that once a machine enters its final state it should stay there; we require that a machine have *some* transition for every possible combination of internal state and tape symbol read; and we require some syntactic conditions, such as the initial and final states being listed in the possible states, and that each transition write a valid character in the tape and move to a valid state. These properties are encapsulated in the predicate `valid-machine`. We chose to write this as restrictions on the possible Turing machines, rather than to enforce them in the function `ndtm-step`, to simplify the Turing machine model.

The functions `ndtm-step-n` and `ndtm-accept` faithfully model traditional Turing machines. But the proof of the Cook-Levin theorem makes use of computations, i.e., paths through the tree explored by `ndtm-step-n`. In contrast these functions only store the frontier of the tree, since Turing machines do not keep a "memory" of their previous states. To bridge this gap, we introduced another model of Turing machines, one based on computations instead of configurations.

A computation consists of a sequence of configurations and the Turing machine transitions or moves that link them together. Consider the sequence S_1, S_2, ..., S_n of configurations, and further let m_i be the move that transforms S_{i-1} into S_i. Then we represent this with the list ($(S_n \ . \ m_n)$ $(S_{n-1} \ . \ m_{n-1})$ ...(S_1, nil)). Notice that the list contains the last (or current) configuration in the front, making it easier to extend recursively.

The functions `ndtm-comp-step-n` and `ndtm-comp-accept` are direct analogs of `ndtm-step-n` and `ndtm-accept`. In particular, we use the exact same search strategy in the `ndtm-comp-*` functions as we do in the `ndtm-*` functions. This simplifies the proof of the equivalence between the two Turing machine models.

3.2 The Model of Satisfiability

Boolean expressions are considerably simpler than Turing machines. We must make clear that by "boolean expression" we mean any expression made up of propositional variables and the connectives "and," "or," and "not." In particular, we do not restrict ourselves to clausal representation.

What we need to model boolean expressions is an interpreter that can input arbitrary expression trees over `and`, `or`, and `not` as well as a list associating variables with values, and return the value of the expression. We defined the interpreter `booleval` that fits this description. For example, the expression

```
(booleval '(and (or p q) (not r)) '((r . nil) (p . t) (q . t)))
```

returns true, i.e., `t`. In addition, we proved a number of simple theorems about `booleval`, such as the following:

```
(defthm booleval-and
  (implies (equal (first x) 'and)
           (equal (booleval x a)
                  (and (booleval (second x) a)
                       (booleval (third x) a)))))
```

For the remainder of the proof, the actual definition of `booleval` was irrelevant and in fact disabled. Only properties such as the above were used in the proof.

3.3 The Translation

In this section, we describe the formal translation from a Turing machine instance into satisfiability. Rather than presenting the complete translation, we will focus only on the functions that will be needed in the formal proofs to follow.

Recall that the boolean expression E_x consists of the conjunction of four parts, with rough semantics equal to "the assignment consistently represents an array," "the first configuration is the initial configuration for the input," "the final configuration is an accepting configuration," and "successive configurations follow each other legally, according to the rules of the machine." Formally we build this expression as follows:

```
(defun ndtm2sat (machine input nsteps ncells)
  (let ((alphabet (ndtm2sat-alphabet machine)))
    (fold-and (is-a-2d-array 1 nsteps ncells alphabet)
              (first-string-is-input ncells input machine)
              (last-string-accepts nsteps ncells machine)
              (valid-computation nsteps ncells machine)))))
```

The function `ndtm2sat-alphabet` builds the alphabet of the array $T(i, j)$. This includes not just the alphabet of the Turing machine, but also all the composite symbols $\langle x, q, \delta \rangle$ encoding a tape symbol, a state, and a legal move. Note: The function `fold-and` returns an expression corresponding to the conjunction of its arguments.

We will now consider each subexpression, starting with `is-a-2d-array`. This function loops over all steps making sure each one is a valid string:

```
(defun is-a-2d-array (step nsteps ncells alphabet)
  (declare (xargs :measure (nfix (1+ (- nsteps step)))))
  (if (or (not (integerp nsteps)) (not (integerp step))
          (> step nsteps))
      t
    (list 'and
          (is-a-string step 1 ncells alphabet)
          (is-a-2d-array (1+ step) nsteps ncells alphabet))))
```

The `:measure` is used to justify the termination of this function. All ACL2 functions are total, so ACL2 tries to prove a function terminates before accepting it. When the termination argument is non-obvious, it is necessary to provide an explicit `:measure` that ACL2 can use in the termination proof.

The definition of `is-a-string` is just like that of `is-a-2d-array`, except that it iterates over the function `is-a-character`, which returns a boolean expression that is sasisfiable precisely when there is exactly one character at position $T(i, j)$:

```
(defun is-a-character (step cell alphabet)
  (list 'and
        (is-one-of-the-characters step cell alphabet)
        (is-not-two-characters step cell alphabet)))
```

Checking that the symbol is one of the characters is straightforward. We need only iterate over the `alphabet` and take the disjunction of all terms (`prop step cell X`) where X is one of the members of `alphabet`. Similarly, to make sure there are not two different characters at this position, we consider each member of `alphabet` against each of the *remaining* elements of `alphabet`:

```
(defun is-not-2nd-character (step cell char alphabet)
  (if (endp alphabet)
      t
    (list 'and
          (list 'not
                (list 'and
                      (prop step cell char)
                      (prop step cell (first alphabet))))
          (is-not-2nd-character step cell char (rest alphabet))))))

(defun is-not-two-characters (step cell alphabet)
  (if (or (endp alphabet) (endp (rest alphabet)))
      t
    (list 'and
          (is-not-2nd-character step cell (first alphabet)
                                (rest alphabet))
          (is-not-two-characters step cell (rest alphabet)))))
```

A similar story explains first-string-is-input. We already know what the input should be, so we need only check that the appropriate propositions are true. The function string-holds-values performs such a check. Given a step, a beginning and end tape position, and a list, it creates a conjunction specifying that the tape holds the characters in the given list. The only complication is that the first character is actually a composite symbol, so we do not know exactly which proposition will be true. This forces us to iterate over all legal moves when the machine is in its initial state and scanning the first character of the input.

The function last-string-accepts is also quite simple. It iterates over all the cells in a given step, checking to see if that cell is one of the elements of the final alphabet.

Not surprisingly, valid-computation is the hardest part of the translation. The function iterates over successive steps checking that the second follows from the first. We do this by looping over each of the cells in the second tape, making sure that it is correct. The difficulty lies with validating a single cell.

We use the function valid-cell to perform this check. A minor difficulty has to do with boundary conditions. The cell $T(i, j)$ depends on the values of $T(i-1, j-1)$, $T(i-1, j)$, and $T(i+1, j)$, which we call the neighbors of $T(i, j)$. But when the cell j is at the beginning or end of the tape, we must drop the neighbors that lie outside the edges. This also prevents the read/write head from scanning past the left edge of the tape. So valid-cell performs a case split to check the position of the cell. We will avoid this complication in this presentation, since it only splits the proof into four very similar cases.

For a cell in the "middle" of the tape, there are four ways in which $T(i, j)$ can follow from $T(i-1, *)$. First, it is possible that $T(i-1, j-1)$ is a composite symbol corresponding to a move of the read/write head towards the right, in which case $T(i, j)$ will become a composite symbol. A similar story holds if $T(i-1, j+1)$ represents a move to the left. When $T(i-1, j)$ is composite, then

$T(i,j)$ will change as the machine will write a (possibly new) symbol on cell j. In all other cases, $T(i,j)$ will retain the old value of $T(i-1,j)$.

The functions valid-moves-left, -right, -middle, and -rest check for these cases. The first three functions scan the valid composite symbols to find the ones that may affect the symbol $T(i,j)$. These functions return two values. The first value is the boolean expression that will be true if and only if $T(i-1,j')$ is a composite symbol resulting in $T(i,j)$. The second value is a list of the composite symbols examined. This list is needed by valid-moves-rest, so it can perform the "else" case. To make this clear, consider the definition of valid-moves-left:

```
(defun valid-moves-left (prevstep curstep curcell machine)
  (let* ((alphabet (cons nil (ndtm-alphabet machine)))
         (composites (strip-right
                       (composite-symbols
                        alphabet (ndtm-states machine)
                        (ndtm-transition machine)))))
    (cons (make-valid-moves prevstep (1- curcell)
                            curstep curcell
                            composites alphabet machine)
          (prop-list prevstep (1- curcell) composites))))
```

This function handles the case where $T(i-1,j-1)$ is a composite affecting $T(i,j)$. The alphabet consists of the alphabet of the Turing machine and the designated blank symbol, which is represented by nil. The auxiliary function strip-right returns all the relevant moves, i.e., those that move to the right. The function prop-list stores the propositions representing the fact that $T(i-1,j-1)$ is a relevant composite symbol. The function make-valid-moves loops over the relevant composite symbols in $T(i-1,j-1)$ and possible tape symbols in $T(i,j)$ and calls make-valid-move to generate the given constraint. The definition of make-valid-move is given below:

```
(defun make-valid-move (prevstep prevcell curstep curcell
                        composite symbol machine)
  (let* ((newstate (move-nextstate (symb-move composite)))
         (moves (ndtm-moves newstate symbol
                            (ndtm-transition machine))))
    (list 'and
          (prop prevstep prevcell composite)
          (prop prevstep curcell symbol)
          (make-valid-move-list curstep curcell
                                newstate symbol moves))))
```

This function depends on make-valid-move-list which loops over the given moves and generates the appropriate composite symbol:

```
(defun make-valid-move-list (curstep curcell state symbol moves)
  (if (endp moves)
      nil
```

```
(list 'or
      (prop curstep curcell (symb symbol state (first moves)))
      (make-valid-move-list curstep curcell state
                            symbol (rest moves)))))
```

The function `valid-moves-right` is completely symmetrical; in fact, it uses many of the same auxiliary functions. The function `valid-moves-middle` is also very similar, but it is slightly more complicated because it takes into account the new symbol written by the machine. That leaves `valid-moves-rest` which handles the else case. That is, if a given cell is not affected by a neighboring composite symbol, then it retains its previous value:

```
(defun valid-moves-rest (prevstep curstep curcell machine cases)
  (list 'and
        (list 'not (fold-or cases))
        (remains-unchanged prevstep curstep curcell
                           (cons nil (ndtm-alphabet machine)))))
```

The list `cases` contains all of the propositions encoding neighboring composite symbols. This is compiled from the second value of the other `valid-moves-*` functions. The function `remains-unchanged` iterates over the given alphabet making sure that $T(i-1,j) = T(i,j)$ and is a member of the alphabet.

Note in particular that `remains-unchanged` is called only for characters that are part of the real alphabet of the tape, i.e., the machine alphabet and the special blank character. No composite symbols are ever passed through this function, since the composite symbols always change according to the rules of the `valid-moves-*` functions.

All of these constraints come together in `valid-cell`, which ties these functions while taking care of the special cases. The following excerpt will suffice to show how this function operates:

```
(defun valid-cell (prevstep curstep curcell ncells machine)
  (if (> curcell 1)
      (if (< curcell ncells)
          (let ((left (valid-moves-left prevstep curstep
                                        curcell machine))
                (middle (valid-moves-middle prevstep curstep
                                            curcell machine))
                (right (valid-moves-right prevstep curstep
                                          curcell machine)))
            (fold-or (first left) (first middle) (first right)
                     (valid-moves-rest
                      prevstep curstep curcell machine
                      (append (rest left) (rest middle)
                              (rest right)))))
          ...)
```

3.4   Case I: The Turing Machine Accepts

In this section we will show that the boolean expression generated in Sect. 3.3
is satisfied when the Turing machine accepts the input. The expression consists
of the conjunction of four main subexpressions which we can consider in turn.

Before delving into the details, it is worth a moment to look at the basic
structure of the proofs. Suppose we have a valid computation of the machine
accepting x. We want to show that a term (booleval expr alist) is true,
where expr is E_x and alist is a truth assignment generated from the accepting
computation. The expr is constructed by piecing together a large number of
local terms. For example, the subexpression for valid-cell will only examine
propositions that correspond to neighboring cells. The alist is also constructed
in this manner. We will process the computation and translate pieces of it into
truth assignments which are then joined together. So the essence of the proof
will be to dive into both expr and alist, such that we can show a particular
subexpression expr1 is true under the truth assignment alist1. Then we will
"lift" this result to the complete truth assignment, so that expr1 is satisfied by
alist. Finally, we put together all the subexpressions to complete the proof.

We begin our study of the proof with the extraction of a truth assignment
from a computation. A computation is a list of configurations and the moves that
link them together, and a configuration consists of a tape and a state. The most
basic extraction function, therefore, converts a tape into a truth assignment:

```
(defun convert-tape-to-assignment (tape step cell ncells)
  (declare (xargs :measure (nfix (1+ (- ncells cell)))))
  (if (or (not (integerp ncells)) (not (integerp cell))
          (> cell ncells))
      nil
    (cons (cons (prop step cell (first tape)) t)
          (convert-tape-to-assignment (rest tape) step (1+ cell)
                                       ncells))))
```

This is the only place where we will assign a value to a proposition; notice
in particular that the only propositions assigned are given a true value. The
following routine is used to extract an assignment from a configuration:

```
(defun convert-config-move-to-assignment (config move step ncells)
  (convert-tape-to-assignment
   (append (reverse (config-lhs config))
           (cons (symb (first (config-rhs config))
                       (config-state config)
                       move)
                 (rest (config-rhs config))))
   step 1 ncells))
```

To finish the conversion of a computation to a truth assignment, it is only necessary to step over all the configurations in the computation and append the

resulting assignments. However, there is a slight complication. The computations associate a configuration with the move that results in that configuration, while the composite symbols associate a state and symbol with the move that is possible *from* that configuration. So we must stagger the moves as we process them. In addition, we must explicitly find a possible (e.g., the first) move extending the last configuration, since this is needed to form the composite symbol but it is not present in the computation.

Now that the truth assignment is constructed, let us consider the proof that it represents a 2D array. We break the boolean expression down into its smallest terms and find the corresponding local section of the truth assignment. Recall how is-a-2d-array is defined in terms of is-a-string, all the way down to is-one-of-the-characters. So we begin by considering the latter function:

```
(defthm tape-to-assignment-is-one-of-the-characters-aux
  (implies (member symbol alphabet)
           (booleval (is-one-of-the-characters step cell alphabet)
                     (cons (cons (prop step cell symbol) t)
                           alist)))))
```

As the theorem shows, the simplest truth assignment that makes this expression true is one that begins with a boolean proposition corresponding to this particular cell. As it turns out, the function convert-tape-to-assignment has just this property, so it is easy to show the following:

```
(defthm tape-to-assignment-is-one-of-the-characters
  (implies (and (member (first tape) alphabet)
                (integerp ncells) (integerp cell)
                (<= cell ncells))
           (booleval (is-one-of-the-characters step cell alphabet)
                     (convert-tape-to-assignment tape step cell
                                                 ncells)))))
```

The satisfiability of is-not-two-characters is easy to establish in the same way. So now we are ready to lift the result higher in the truth assignment.

But this is not as simple as it would appear at first. The problem is that the instance of convert-tape-to-assignment used in the theorem above hardcodes the value of cell. We need to generalize this theorem to allow other cell values, such as the ones in the call from convert-config-move-to-assignment. This assignment has some values in front of, not just behind, the one we need.

This is not straightforward. It is possible that one of the assignments in front gives a different value to a proposition. Even if the assignments are disjoint; i.e., if they assign values to different propositions, it is possible for the combination to provide unexpected results. The reason for this is that booleval implicitly assigns a value of false to any proposition that is not explicitly assigned, which is a valuable property of booleval because it allows truth assignments to be built incrementally. Compatibility of truth assignments depends not only on the assignments themselves, but on the variables used in the term being evaluated.

To continue the proof, therefore, we have to consider the propositions that are assigned values by a truth assignment, as well as the propositions used in an expression. We defined the functions `assigned-vars` and `vars-in-term` for this purpose. Typical theorems about these include the following:

```
(defthm vars-in-term-one-of-the-characters
  (implies (member prop (vars-in-term
                          (is-one-of-the-characters step cell
                                                    alphabet)))
           (and (equal (prop-step prop) step)
                (equal (prop-cell prop) cell))))

(defthm assigned-vars-convert-tape-to-assignment
  (implies (member prop (assigned-vars
                          (convert-tape-to-assignment
                           tape step cell ncells)))
           (and (equal (prop-step prop) step)
                (<= cell (prop-cell prop))
                (<= (prop-cell prop) ncells))))
```

Now it is possible to lift the theorem to bigger truth assignments. We only need lemmas specifying how `booleval` composes the truth assignment. The following lemma is the one we need for this specific case:

```
(defthm booleval-append-alist-left
  (implies (and (not (intersectp-equal (vars-in-term x)
                                       (assigned-vars a)))
                (alistp a))
           (equal (booleval x (append a b))
                  (booleval x b))))
```

This suffices to lift the theorem so that we know the truth assignment generated by `convert-config-move-to-assignment` satisfies `is-a-string`:

```
(defthm move-to-assignment-is-a-string
  (implies (and (no-duplicates alphabet)
                (subsetp (config-lhs config) alphabet)
                (subsetp (config-rhs config) alphabet)
                (member (symb (first (config-rhs config))
                              (config-state config)
                              move)
                        alphabet)
                (member nil alphabet)
                (not (zp ncells)))
           (booleval (is-a-string step 1 ncells alphabet)
                     (convert-config-move-to-assignment
                      config move step ncells))))
```

Notice the requirements that the move appear in the alphabet, and that the tape is a subset of the alphabet. This is needed because `is-a-string` tests not only that the truth assignment is a consistent representation of a string, but also that the string is over a particular alphabet.

To complete the satisfiability of `is-a-string`, we need to apply the theorem `move-to-assignment-is-a-string` to all the configurations in the computation. In particular, we need to show that the hypothesis of this lemma will be satisfied by all the configurations in the computation. But this follows when the initial tape uses symbols only from the alphabet, since subsequent tapes will also satisfy the requirement as long as the transitions in the machine are valid. So we have completed the proof of the satisfiability of `is-a-2d-array`.

The proof of the other three major subexpressions follows the same pattern. The proofs of `first-string-is-input` and `last-string-accepts` do not bring anything new to the table, so we will omit them. It is only worth noting that the proof of `last-string-accepts` depends on the fact that the last configuration has a composite symbol. In particular, the left tape is not allowed to grow by more than the number of steps, which is straightforward to show.

That leaves the proof that the assignment satisfies `valid-computation`. Our plan is to split the tape into three parts. In the middle are the cells around the read/write head, which could possibly be affected by a move. The remaining cells are considered to be either to the left or to the right.

So our first task is to see what happens to a character that is (far enough) to the left of the head. Consider what happens to the actual tape. Suppose `config1` and `config2` are valid configurations. We explore every possible way in which `config2` can follow `config1`. The following theorem is representative:

```
(defthm cdr-lhs-tape-does-not-change-left-move-possible
  (implies (and (equal (move-direction move) 'left)
                (consp (config-lhs config1))
                (valid-step machine config1 move config2))
           (equal (rest (config-lhs config1))
                  (config-lhs config2))))
```

Using this lemma, it is possible to show that if a cell has a given value and the cell is (far enough) to the left of the read/write head, the cell has the same value at the next iteration. Since propositions explicitly in the truth assignments are assigned true, truth is equivalent to membership in the assignment. This results in the following theorem, which is representative of the various cases to consider:

```
(defthm early-cell-in-convert-config-left-move-possible
  (implies (and (consp (config-lhs config1))
                (not (zp ncells))
                (<= (len (config-lhs config1)) ncells)
                (member prop (assigned-vars
                              (convert-config-move-to-assignment
                                config1 move step ncells)))
                (< (prop-cell prop) (len (config-lhs config1)))
```

```
                   (equal (move-direction move) 'left)
                   (valid-step machine config1 move config2))
         (member (prop (1+ step) (prop-cell prop)
                       (prop-char prop))
               (assigned-vars
                (convert-config-move-to-assignment
                 config2 move2 (1+ step) ncells)))))
```

Naturally, the next step is to lift this result to the larger truth assignments.

Theorems such as the one above show precisely what happens to all the cells in a tape, except for two cells around the read/write head, the one which the head is scanning and the one to which the head will move. We have to handle these cases separately. Although these results are more interesting, in the sense that this is where the machine is performing some action, they are easier to prove than the ones above because we know precisely which cells are involved. That means we can prove an exact theorem, such as the following:

```
(defthm middle-cell-in-convert-config-move-left-move-possible-1
  (implies (and (consp computation)
                (consp (rest computation))
                (equal (first (first computation)) config2)
                (equal (rest (first computation)) move)
                (equal (first (first (rest computation))) config1)
                (consp (config-lhs config1))
                (not (zp ncells))
                (<= (len (config-lhs config1)) ncells)
                (equal step (len computation))
                (equal (move-direction move) 'left)
                (valid-computation machine computation))
           (and (member (prop (1- step)
                              (len (config-lhs config1))
                              (first (config-lhs config1)))
                        (assigned-vars
                         (convert-config-move-to-assignment
                          config1 move (1- step) ncells)))
                (member (prop step
                              (len (config-lhs config1))
                              (symb (first (config-lhs config1))
                                    (config-state config2)
                                    prevmove))
                        (assigned-vars
                         (convert-config-move-to-assignment
                          config2 prevmove step ncells))))))
```

This theorem covers the cell position to which the head moves. A similar theorem takes care of the cell position originally containing the read/write head.

These lemmas are almost ready to be stitched together into the final theorem. The missing piece is the fact that the "else" case in the definition of valid-cell, which allows a cell in the tape that is away from the head to retain its value, requires the cell not to have a relevant neighbor. So we must prove that when a cell is (far enough) away from the head, the cells around it are not composite.

Combining all the theorems proved so far shows that valid-computation is satisfied by the generated truth assignment. Then combining that with the other parts of the condition, we get the final result:

```
(defthm valid-transformation-computation-best
  (implies (and (integerp n) (< 1 n)
                (valid-machine machine)
                (alphabet-symbol-list-p (ndtm-alphabet machine))
                (no-duplicates (ndtm2sat-alphabet machine))
                (ndtm-accepts-p machine input (1- n))
                (subsetp input (ndtm-alphabet machine)))
           (booleval (ndtm2sat machine input n n)
                     (convert-computation-to-assignment
                      machine
                      (accepting-witness machine input (1- n))
                      n))))
```

Note: The function accepting-witness searches for a valid, accepting computation.

3.5   Case II: The Expression Is Satisfiable

In this section we explore the other half of the proof. We wish to show that when the expression E_x is satisfiable, the input x is accepted by the machine. To do this, we will extract a computation from a truth assignment that satisfies E_x by looking at all the propositional formulas $C_{i,j,X}$ for each i and j, and selecting the one X that makes it true. So the most fundamental function is extract-char-alist, which finds the X that makes $C_{i,j,X}$ true:

```
(defun extract-char-alist (step cell alphabet alist)
  (if (endp alphabet)
      nil
    (if (booleval (prop step cell (first alphabet)) alist)
        (first alphabet)
      (extract-char-alist step cell (rest alphabet) alist))))
```

Notice that we must know the relevant alphabet a priori.

With this function we can define extract-lhs-tape and extract-rhs-tape, which extract the left and right halves of the tape, respectively. It is only necessary to know where to split the tape. We do this by iterating over all the cells in the tape until we find a composite cell. We wrote different functions for the left and right halves of the tape since the former is stored in reversed order. Once these functions are defined, it is a simple matter to write `extract-config`, which extracts a configuration, and use that to define `extract-computation` which extracts the candidate valid, accepting computation.

At this point, we have a situation similar to the one we faced in trying to prove E_x is satisfiable if there is a valid computation. It would appear that the remaining part of the proof is as difficult as what has gone before, since in both cases we are considering an expression of the form (`booleval expr alist`). But there is a key difference. Previously, we had a valid computation and we used that to extract an `alist`. The extraction process was localized, so it was necessary to dig into portions of the `alist` to find the part that made a particular expression true. But in this case, the `alist` is known a priori, so we need only split `expr` into its subexpressions, leaving the `alist` unchanged.

The key point is that we break up the structure of `expr`, not of `alist`. Since the function `booleval` is defined precisely in this way, this leads to much simpler lemmas, without worrying about issues such as inconsistent truth assignments. This came as a very pleasant discovery for us. We noticed that the proof in this direction was much easier partly because so much more of the proof was discovered automatically by ACL2. It was in trying to understand why we were so lucky that we discovered the delicious asymmetry of `booleval`. Since the proof is much more mechanical in this direction, we will only present an outline.

Notice that the function `extract-computation` is guaranteed to extract only one computation. However, it is possible that more computations can be extracted from the truth assignment. Of course this is not the case, and at first we thought there was no real need to prove this, but it turns out that this uniqueness property is crucial in the other proofs. Many times it will not be enough to know that $C_{i,j,X}$ is true; we must also know that $C_{i,j,Y}$ is false for all $Y \neq X$.

As before, the strategy is to isolate what happens around the read/write head. This corresponds to the composite symbol, so it is necessary to know that there is only one composite symbol at any step in the truth assignment. We do this by counting the number of composite symbols in a given step. If we know that this number is equal to 1 and we find a composite symbol at some cell, then we are guaranteed that none of the symbols in other cells are composite.

Next we show that if a cell changes from one step to the next, then one of its neighbors must be a composite symbol. Moreover, the composite symbol is restricted based on its relationship to the cell that changed. For example, if $T(i,j) \neq T(i-1,j)$ and $T(i-1,j-1)$ is a composite, then it must be a composite symbol corresponding to a right move of the tape.

To complete the proof we observe that every step in the computation has exactly one composite symbol. It is easy to show that if one configuration has only one composite symbol, the next one can have at most one such symbol, and if a configuration has no composite symbols neither does the next. Since the initial and final configurations have one composite symbol, so must all the other ones in the computation, and this is the one found when we split the left and right tapes in the transformation.

Essentially the proof is now complete. The cells that are sufficiently to the left of *the* composite symbol in a step are unchanged, as are the ones that are sufficiently to the right. The behavior of the cells immediately around the composite symbol is also known. This is enough to show that two successive configurations extracted from the truth assignment legally follow according to the rules of the Turing machine.

The only remaining complication is that the computation that is extracted is not the computation that `ndtm-comp-step-n` will enumerate. But the only difference is that the extracted computations pads the right tape with blanks to make $p(n)$ cells. It is easy to show that such starting configurations are equivalent, in the sense that if one of them ends in an accepting state so does the other.

3.6   Timing Analysis

Thus far we have ignored the issue of timing. But it is an important aspect of the Cook-Levin theorem that the transformation take only polynomial time, so we would like to address this as well.

Unlike higher-order theorem provers, ACL2 does not provide any introspection mechanisms that can be used for cost measurement. It does provide a mechanism for defining an interpreter over certain functions, but this interpreter is unsuitable for measuring costs, since it uses the functions directly to evaluate results without opening up their definitions.

Curiously, ACL2's prececessor, the Boyer-Moore theorem prover, did have a facility that would be useful in this context. In that theorem prover, every function definition extended a set of built-in interpreters, including `v&c$` which computed the value and the cost of an expression.

Without such an interpreter, however, we are forced to proceed differently. What we did was to define a `cost-*` version of each function used in the translation. This function returns a pair, the first element being the normal value of the function, and the second a measure of the cost used to compute this value. For each such function, we also proved two theorems about it. The first states that the `cost-*` function accurately computes the function it emulates. The second gives an upper bound for the cost.

4   Conclusions

In this paper we described a formal proof in ACL2 of the Cook-Levin theorem. The formal proof fills in the gaps typically left by higher-level proofs. In particular, we showed that the transformation mapping instances of Turing machines to satisfiability really does work.

We attempted to use this proof while teaching a one-hour graduate course introducing students to ACL2. The format of the course requires each student to make a presentation during at least one class period. One of the challenges in teaching a course like this is keeping students interested in each other's presentations. By having each student make a small contribution to a larger research project, we hoped to establish a continuity between the presentations that would involve them throughout the semester. Unfortunately this did not work as planned. The students did gain experience with ACL2, and some of them are becaming proficient in it, but they found the Cook-Levin theorem too difficult to formalize. Not having had a course that covered this theorem in detail, many found even the informal proof too difficult to follow.

This is a shame because the proof does follow many classic patterns of formal proofs: It builds a formal model of the entities involved, namely Turing machines and boolean expressions; it constructs mappings between them; and it shows that the mappings are connected in important ways. Moreover, in doing the proof we discovered that the asymmetry in the definition of `booleval` led to one half of the proof being much easier than the other. This is a beautiful example of the deep connection between recursion and induction. One direction is easier because its natural induction scheme mirrors the recursive structure of the function, making everything work smoothly.

The major weakness in the formalization lies in the analysis of the time complexity of the translation. It is an important aspect of the proof that the translation can be performed in polynomial time. But this is not the sort of reasoning that comes naturally in ACL2. Currently we are investigating a way to extend ACL2 to introduce interpreters that can compute the cost of evaluating an expression as well as its value. There are some very interesting challenges, such as the termination proof for the interpreter.

References

1. R. S. Boyer and J Moore. A mechanical proof of the turing completeness of pure Lisp. In W. W. Bledsoe and D. W. Loveland, editors, *Automated Theorem Proving: After 25 Years*. American Mathematical Society, 1984.
2. R. S. Boyer and J Moore. A mechanical proof of the unsolvability of the halting problem. *Journal of the ACM*, 1984.
3. S. Cook. The complexity of theorem proving procedures. In *Proceedings of the 3rd ACM Symposium on Theory of Computing*, 1971.
4. J. Hopcroft and J. Ullman. *Introduction to Automata Theory, Languages, and Computation*. Addison Wesley, 1979.
5. M. Kaufmann, P. Manolios, and J S. Moore. *Computer Aided Reasoning: An Approach*. Kluwer Academic Publishers, 2000.
6. M. Kaufmann and J S. Moore. The ACL2 home page. http://www.cs.utexas.edu/users/moore/acl2/acl2-doc.html.
7. L. A. Levin. Universal sorting problems. *Problemi Peredachi Informatsii*, 1973.
8. N. Shankar. *Proof Checking Metamathematics*. PhD thesis, University of Texas, 1984.
9. N. Shankar. Towards mechanical metamathematics. *Journal of Automated Reasoning*, 1985.

Formalizing the Proof of the Kepler Conjecture

Thomas Hales

Department of Mathematics
University of Pittsburgh

Abstract. The Kepler Conjecture states that the densest packing of spheres in three dimensions is the familiar cannonball arrangement. Although this statement has been regarded as obvious by chemists, a rigorous mathematical proof of this fact was not obtained until 1998.

The mathematical proof of the Kepler Conjecture runs 300 pages, and relies on extensive computer calculations. The refereeing process involved more than 12 referees over a five year period. This talk will describe the top-level structure of the proof of this theorem. The proof involves methods of linear and non-linear optimization, and arguments from graph theory and discrete geometry. In view of the complexity of the proof and the difficulties that were encountered in refereeing the proof, it seems desirable to have a formal proof of this theorem. This talk will give details about what would be involved in giving a formal proof of this result.

K. Slind et al. (Eds.): TPHOLs 2004, LNCS 3223, p. 117, 2004.
© Springer-Verlag Berlin Heidelberg 2004

Interfacing Hoare Logic and Type Systems for Foundational Proof-Carrying Code⋆

Nadeem Abdul Hamid and Zhong Shao

Department of Computer Science, Yale University
New Haven, CT 06520-8285, USA
{hamid,shao}@cs.yale.edu

Abstract. In this paper, we introduce a Foundational Proof-Carrying Code (FPCC) framework for constructing certified code packages from typed assembly language that will interface with a similarly certified runtime system. Our framework permits the typed assembly language to have a "foreign function" interface, in which stubs, initially provided when the program is being written, are eventually compiled and linked to code that may have been written in a language with a different type system, or even certified directly in the FPCC logic using a proof assistant. We have increased the potential scalability and flexibility of our FPCC system by providing a way to integrate programs compiled from different source type systems. In the process, we are explicitly manipulating the interface between Hoare logic and a syntactic type system.

1 Introduction

Proof-Carrying Code (PCC) [16, 17] is a framework for generating executable machine code along with a machine-checkable proof that the code satisfies a given safety policy. The initial PCC systems specified the safety policy using a logic extended with many (source) language-specific rules. While allowing implementation of a scalable system [18, 7], this approach to PCC suffers from too large of a trusted computing base (TCB). It is still difficult to trust that the components of this system – the verification-condition generator, the proof-checker, and even the logical axioms and typing rules – are free from error.

The development of another family of PCC implementations, known as Foundational Proof-Carrying Code (FPCC) [4, 3], was intended to reduce the TCB to a minimum by expressing and proving safety using only a foundational mathematical logic without additional language-specific axioms or typing rules. The trusted components in such a system are mostly reduced to a much simpler logic and the proof-checker for it.

Both these approaches to PCC have one feature in common, which is that they have focused on a single source language (*e.g.* Java or ML) and compile (type-correct) programs from that language into machine code with a safety proof. However, the runtime systems of these frameworks still include components that are not addressed in

---

⋆ This research is based on work supported in part by DARPA OASIS grant F30602-99-1-0519, NSF grant CCR-9901011, NSF ITR grant CCR-0081590, and NSF grant CCR-0208618. Any opinions, findings, and conclusions contained in this document are those of the authors and do not reflect the views of these agencies.

K. Slind et al. (Eds.): TPHOLs 2004, LNCS 3223, pp. 118–135, 2004.

the safety proof [3, 10] and that are written in a lower-level language (like C): memory management libraries, garbage collection, debuggers, marshallers, *etc.* The issue of producing a safety proof for code that is compiled and linked together from two or more different source languages was not addressed.

In this paper, we introduce an FPCC framework for constructing certified machine code packages from typed assembly language (TAL) that will interface with a similarly certified runtime system. Our framework permits the typed assembly language to have a "foreign function" interface in which stubs, initially provided when the program is being written, are eventually compiled and linked to code that may have been written in a language with a different type system, or even certified directly in the FPCC logic using a proof assistant. To our knowledge, this is the first account of combining such certification proofs from languages at different levels of abstraction. While type systems such as TAL facilitate reasoning about many programs, they are not sufficient for certifying the most low-level system libraries. Hoare logic-style reasoning, on the other hand, can handle low-level details very well but cannot account for embedded code pointers in data structures, a feature common to higher-order and object-oriented programming. We outline for the first time a way to allow both methods of verification to interact, gaining the advantages of both and circumventing their shortcomings.

Experience has shown that foundational proofs are much harder to construct than those in a logic extended with type-specific axioms. The earliest FPCC systems built proofs by constructing sophisticated semantic models of types in order to reason about safety at the machine level. That is, the final safety proof incorporated no concept of source level types – each type in the source language would be interpreted as a predicate on the machine state and the typing rules of the language would turn into lemmas which must prove properties about the interaction of these predicates. While it seems that this method of FPCC would already be amenable to achieving the goals outlined in the previous paragraph, the situation is complicated by the complexity of the semantic models [11, 5, 1] that were required to support a realistic type system. Nonetheless, the overall framework of this paper may work equally well with the semantic approach.

In this paper, we adopt the "syntactic" approach to FPCC, introduced in [14, 13] and further applied to a more realistic source type system by [9, 10]. In this framework, the machine level proofs do indeed incorporate and use the syntactic encoding of elements of the source type system to derive safety. Previous presentations of the syntactic approach involve a monolithic translation from type-correct source programs to a package of certified machine code. In this paper, we refine the approach by inserting a generic layer of reasoning above the machine code which can *(1)* be a target for the compilation of typed assembly languages, *(2)* certify low-level runtime system components using assertions as in Hoare logic, and *(3)* "glue" together these pieces by reasoning about the compatibility of the interfaces specified by the various types of source code.

A simple diagram of our framework is given in Figure 1. Source programs are written in a typed high-level language and then passed through a certifying compiler to produce machine code along with a proof of safety. The source level type system may provide a set of functionality that is accessed through a library interface. At the machine level, there is an actual library code implementation that should satisfy that interface. The non-trivial problem is how to design the framework such that not only will the two

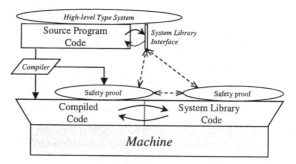

Fig. 1. FPCC certified runtime framework.

pieces of machine code link together to run, but that the safety proofs originating from two different sources are also able to "link" together, consistent with the high-level interface specification, to produce a unified safety proof for the entire set of code.

Notice that the interaction between program and library is two-way: either piece of code may make direct or indirect function calls and returns to the other. Ideally, we want to be able to certify the library code with no knowledge of the source language and type system that will be interacting with it. At the same time we would like to support first-class code pointers at all levels of the code. Methods for handling code pointers properly have been one of the main challenges of FPCC and are one of the differentiating factors between semantic and syntactic FPCC approaches. For the framework in this paper, we have factored out most of the code pointer reasoning that is needed when certifying library code so that the proofs thereof can be relatively straightforward.

In the following sections, after defining our machine and logic, we present the layer of reasoning which will serve as the common interface for code compiled from different sources. Then we present a typical typed assembly language, extended with library interfaces and external call facilities. We finally show how to compile this language to the target machine, expanding external function stubs, and linking in the runtime library, at the same time producing the proof of safety of the complete package. We conclude with a brief discussion of implementation in the Coq proof assistant and future and related work.

2   A Machine and Logic for Certified Code

In this section, we present our machine on which programs will run and the logic that we use to reason about safety of the code being run. We use an idealized machine for purposes of presentation in this paper although implementation upon the IA-32 (Intel x86 architecture) is in progress. A "real" machine introduces many engineering details (*e.g.* fixed-size integers, addressing modes, memory model, variable length instructions and relative addressing) which we would rather avoid while presenting our central contributions along the subject of this paper.

2.1   The Machine

The hardware components of our idealized machine are a memory, register file, and a special register containing the current program counter (*pc*). These are defined to be

$$Word \ni w, i, pc ::= 0 \mid 1 \mid \ldots$$

$$Regt \ni r \qquad ::= \mathsf{r0} \mid \mathsf{r1} \mid \ldots \mid \mathsf{r15}$$

$$Cmd \ni c \qquad ::= \mathsf{add}\, r_d, r_s, r_t \mid \mathsf{addi}\, r_d, r_s, i \mid \mathsf{mov}\, r_d, r_s \mid \mathsf{movi}\, r_d, i$$
$$\mid \mathsf{bgt}\, r_s, r_t, w \mid \mathsf{bgti}\, r_s, i, w \mid \mathsf{ld}\, r_d, r_s(i) \mid \mathsf{st}\, r_d(i), r_s$$
$$\mid \mathsf{jd}\, w \mid \mathsf{jmp}\, r \mid \mathsf{illegal}$$

$$\mathbb{M} \in Mem = Word \to Word$$

$$\mathbb{R} \in RFile = Regt \to Word$$

$$\mathbb{S} \in State = Mem \times RFile \times Word$$

Fig. 2. Machine state: memory, registers, and instructions (commands).

if $\mathsf{Dc}(\mathbb{M}(pc)) =$	then $\mathsf{Step}(\mathbb{M}, \mathbb{R}, pc) =$
$\mathsf{add}\, r_d, r_s, r_t$	$(\mathbb{M}, \mathbb{R}\{r_d \mapsto \mathbb{R}(r_s) + \mathbb{R}(r_t)\}, pc+1)$
$\mathsf{addi}\, r_d, r_s, i$	$(\mathbb{M}, \mathbb{R}\{r_d \mapsto \mathbb{R}(r_s) + i\}, pc+1)$
$\mathsf{mov}\, r_d, r_s$	$(\mathbb{M}, \mathbb{R}\{r_d \mapsto r_s\}, pc+1)$
$\mathsf{movi}\, r_d, i$	$(\mathbb{M}, \mathbb{R}\{r_d \mapsto i\}, pc+1)$
$\mathsf{ld}\, r_d, r_s(i)$	$(\mathbb{M}, \mathbb{R}\{r_d \mapsto \mathbb{M}(\mathbb{R}(r_s) + i)\}, pc+1)$
$\mathsf{st}\, r_d(i), r_s$	$(\mathbb{M}\{\mathbb{R}(r_d) + i \mapsto \mathbb{R}(r_s)\}, \mathbb{R}, pc+1)$
$\mathsf{bgt}\, r_s, r_t, w$	$(\mathbb{M}, \mathbb{R}, pc+1)$ when $\mathbb{R}(r_s) \le \mathbb{R}(r_t)$ *and* $(\mathbb{M}, \mathbb{R}, w)$ when $\mathbb{R}(r_s) > \mathbb{R}(r_t)$
$\mathsf{bgti}\, r_s, i, w$	$(\mathbb{M}, \mathbb{R}, pc+1)$ when $\mathbb{R}(r_s) \le i$ *and* $(\mathbb{M}, \mathbb{R}, w)$ when $\mathbb{R}(r_s) > i$
$\mathsf{jd}\, w$	$(\mathbb{M}, \mathbb{R}, w)$
$\mathsf{jmp}\, r$	$(\mathbb{M}, \mathbb{R}, \mathbb{R}(r))$
$\mathsf{illegal}$	$(\mathbb{M}, \mathbb{R}, pc)$

Fig. 3. Machine semantics.

the machine state, as shown in Figure 2. We use a 16-register word-addressed machine with an unbounded memory of unlimited-size words. We also define a decoding function Dc which decodes integer words into a structured representation of instructions ("commands"), also shown in Figure 2. The machine is thus equipped with a Step function that describes the (deterministic) transition from one machine state to the next, depending on the instruction at the current pc.

The operational semantics of the machine is given in Figure 3. The instructions' effects are quite intuitive. The first half involve arithmetic and data movement in registers. The ld and st load and store data from/to memory. These are followed by the conditional and unconditional branch instructions. An $\mathsf{illegal}$ (non-decodable) instruction puts the machine in an infinite loop.

2.2 The Logic

In order to produce FPCC packages, we need a logic in which we can express (encode) the operational semantics of the machine as well as define the concept and criteria of safety. A code producer must then provide a code executable (initial machine state) along with a proof that the initial state and all future transitions therefrom satisfy the safety condition.

The foundational logic we use is the calculus of inductive constructions (CiC) [24, 20]. CiC is an extension of the calculus of constructions (CC) [8], which is a higher-order typed lambda calculus. Due to limited space we forgo a discussion of CiC here and refer the reader unfamiliar with the system to the cited references.

CiC has been shown to be strongly normalizing [25], hence the corresponding logic is consistent. It is supported by the Coq proof assistant [24], which we use to implement a prototype system of the results presented in this paper.

2.3   Defining Safety and Generating Proofs

The safety condition is a predicate expressing the fact that code will not "go wrong." We say that a machine state $\mathbb{S}$ is safe if every state it can ever reach satisfies the safety policy SP:

$$\mathsf{Safe}\,(\mathbb{S}, \mathsf{SP}) = \Pi n : \mathsf{Nat}.\ \mathsf{SP}\,(\mathsf{Step}^n\,(\mathbb{S}))$$

A typical safety policy may require such things as the program counter must point to a valid instruction address in the code area and that any writes (reads) to (from) memory must be from a properly accessible area of the data space. For the purposes of presentation in this paper, we will be using a very simple safety policy, requiring only that the machine is always at a valid instruction:

$$\mathsf{BasicSP}\,(\mathbb{M}, \mathbb{R}, pc) = \mathsf{Dc}\,(\mathbb{M}(pc)) \neq \texttt{illegal} \wedge \mathsf{InCodeArea}(\mathbb{M}, pc)$$

We can easily define access controls on memory reads and writes by including another predicate in the safety policy, $\mathsf{SafeRdWr}(\mathbb{M}, \mathbb{R}, pc)$. By reasoning over the number of steps of computation more complex safety policies including temporal constraints can potentially be expressed. However, we will not be dealing with such policies here.

The FPCC code producer has to provide an encoding[1] of the initial state $\mathbb{S}_0$ along with a proof A that this state satisfies the safety condition BasicSP, specified by the code consumer. The final FPCC package is thus a pair:

$$F = (\mathbb{S}_0 : \textit{State},\ A : \mathsf{Safe}\,(\mathbb{S}_0, \mathsf{BasicSP})).$$

3   A Language for Certified Machine Code (CAP)

We know now what type of proof we are looking for; the hard part is to generate that proof of safety. Previous approaches for FPCC [4, 2, 5, 14] have achieved this by constructing an induction hypothesis, also known as the global invariant, which can be proven (*e.g.* by induction) to hold for all states reachable from the initial state and is strong enough to imply the safety condition. The nature of the invariant has ranged from a semantic model of types at the machine level (Appel *et al.* [4, 2, 5, 23]) to a purely syntactic well-formedness property [14, 13] based on a type-correct source program in a typed assembly language.

---

[1] We must trust that our encoding of the machine and its operational semantics, and the definition of safety, are correct. Along with the logic itself and the proof-checker implementation thereof, these make up most of our software trusted computing base (TCB).

What we have developed in this paper refines these previous approaches. We will still be presenting a typed assembly language in Section 4, in which most source programs are written. However, we introduce another layer between the source type system and the "raw" encoding of the target machine in the FPCC logic. This is a "type system" or "specification system" that is defined upon the machine encoding, allowing us to reason about its state using assertions that essentially capture Hoare logic-style reasoning. Such a layer allows more generality for reasoning than a fixed type system, yet at the same time is more structured than reasoning directly in the logic about the machine encoding.

Our language is called CAP and it uses the same machine syntax as presented in Figure 2. The syntax of the additional assertion layer is given below:

$$P, Q, R \in Pred \quad = State \rightarrow Prop$$

$$\Phi \in CdSpec = Word \rightharpoonup (Word \times Pred)$$

$$CmdList \ni \mathbb{C} ::= \emptyset \mid c :: \mathbb{C}$$

$$WordList \ni \mathbb{W} ::= \emptyset \mid w :: \mathbb{W}$$

The name CAP is derived from its being a "Certified Assembly Programming" language. An initial version was introduced in [27] and used to certify a dynamic storage allocation library. The version we have used for this paper introduces some minor improvements such as a unified data and code memory, assertions on the whole machine state, and support for user-specifiable safety policies (Section 3.3).

Assertions (P,Q,R) are predicates on the machine state and the code specification (Φ) is a partial function mapping memory addresses to a pair of an integer and a predicate. The integer gives the length of the command sequence at that address and the predicate is the precondition for the block of code. (The function of this is to allow us to specify the addresses of valid code areas of memory based on Φ.)

The operational semantics of the language has already been presented in Section 2.1. We now introduce CAP inference rules followed by some important safety theorems.

3.1 Inference Rules

CAP adds a layer of inference rules ("typing rules") allowing us to prove specification judgments of the forms:

$$\Phi \vdash \{P\} \mathbb{C} \quad \textit{well-formed command sequence}$$

$$\vdash M : \Phi \quad \textit{well-formed code specification}$$

$$\vdash (M, \mathbb{R}, pc) \textit{ well-formed machine state}$$

The inference rules for these judgments are shown in Figure 4. The rules for well-formed command sequences essentially require that if the given precondition P is satisfied in the current state, there must be some postcondition Q, which is the precondition of the remaining sequence of commands, that holds on the state after executing one step. The rules directly refer to the **Step** function of the machine; control flow instructions additionally use the code specification environment Φ in order to allow for the certification of mutually dependent code blocks.

$$\frac{c \in \{\text{add}, \text{addi}, \text{mov}, \text{movi}, \text{1d}\} \quad \forall \mathbb{S}.(P(\mathbb{S}) \wedge \text{curcmd}(\mathbb{S}) = c) \rightarrow Q(\text{Step}(\mathbb{S}))) \qquad \Phi \vdash \{Q\} \, \mathbb{C}}{\Phi \vdash \{P\} \, c :: \mathbb{C}} \text{(CAP-PURE)}$$

$$\frac{\forall \mathbb{S}.(P(\mathbb{S}) \wedge \text{curcmd}(\mathbb{S}) = \text{st} \, r_d(i), r_s) \rightarrow \begin{array}{l} Q(\text{Step}(\mathbb{S})) \\ \wedge \neg \text{InCodeArea}(\Phi, \mathbb{S}.\mathbb{R}(r_d) + i)) \end{array} \qquad \Phi \vdash \{Q\} \, \mathbb{C}}{\Phi \vdash \{P\} \, \text{st} \, r_d(i), r_s :: \mathbb{C}} \text{(CAP-ST)}$$

$$\frac{\begin{array}{l} \forall \mathbb{S}.(P(\mathbb{S}) \wedge \text{curcmd}(\mathbb{S}) = \text{bgt} \, r_s, r_t, w) \\ \rightarrow (\mathbb{S}.\mathbb{R}(r_s) \leq \mathbb{S}.\mathbb{R}(r_t) \rightarrow Q(\text{Step}(\mathbb{S}))) \wedge (\mathbb{S}.\mathbb{R}(r_s) > \mathbb{S}.\mathbb{R}(r_t) \rightarrow Q'(\text{Step}(\mathbb{S}))) \\ \Phi \vdash \{Q\} \, \mathbb{C} \hfill where \; \Phi(w) = (n, Q') \end{array}}{\Phi \vdash \{P\} \, \text{bgt} \, r_s, r_t, w :: \mathbb{C}} \text{(CAP-BGT)}$$

$$\frac{\forall \mathbb{S}.(P(\mathbb{S}) \wedge \text{curcmd}(\mathbb{S}) = \text{jd} \, w) \rightarrow Q'(\text{Step}(\mathbb{S})) \qquad where \; \Phi(w) = (n, Q')}{\Phi \vdash \{P\} \, \text{jd} \, w :: \emptyset} \text{(CAP-JD)}$$

$$\frac{\forall \mathbb{S}.(P(\mathbb{S}) \wedge \text{curcmd}(\mathbb{S}) = \text{jmp} \, r) \rightarrow Q'(\text{Step}(\mathbb{S}))) \quad where \; \Phi(\mathbb{S}.\mathbb{R}(r)) = (n, Q')}{\Phi \vdash \{P\} \, \text{jmp} \, r :: \emptyset} \text{(CAP-JMP)}$$

$$\frac{\begin{array}{l} \text{Flatten}(\mathbb{W}, \mathbb{M}, f) \qquad \Phi \vdash \{P\} \, (\text{Map}(\text{Dc}, \mathbb{W})) \\ for \; all \; f \; where \; \Phi(f) = (\text{length}(\mathbb{W}), P) \end{array}}{\vdash \mathbb{M} : \Phi} \text{(CAP-CDSPEC)}$$

$$\frac{\begin{array}{ll} \vdash \mathbb{M} : \Phi & \Phi \vdash \{P\} \, (\text{Map}(\text{Dc}, \mathbb{W})) \\ \text{Flatten}(\mathbb{W}, \mathbb{M}, pc) & \text{InCodeArea}(\Phi, pc) \qquad P(\mathbb{M}, \mathbb{R}, pc) \end{array}}{\vdash (\mathbb{M}, \mathbb{R}, pc)} \text{(CAP-STATE)}$$

Fig. 4. CAP inference rules.

We group as "pure" commands all those which do *not* involve control flow and do not change the memory (*i.e.* everything other than branches, jumps, and st). The st command requires an additional proof that the address being stored to is not in the code area (*i.e.* we do not permit self-modifying code). curcmd($\mathbb{S}$) is defined as:

$$\text{curcmd}(\mathbb{M}, \mathbb{R}, pc) = \text{Dc}(\mathbb{M}(pc))$$

The InCodeArea predicate in the rules uses the code addresses and sequence lengths in Φ to determine whether a given address lies within the code area. The (CAP-CDSPEC) rule ensures that the addresses and sequence lengths specified in Φ are consistent with the code actually in memory.

The Flatten predicate is defined as:

$$\text{Flatten}(\emptyset, \mathbb{M}, f) = \text{True}$$
$$\text{Flatten}(w :: \mathbb{W}, \mathbb{M}, f) = \mathbb{M}(f) = w \wedge \text{Flatten}(\mathbb{W}, \mathbb{M}, f+1)$$

3.2   Safety Properties

The machine will execute continuously, even if an illegal instruction is encountered. Given a well-formed CAP state, however, we can prove that it satisfies our basic safety policy, and that executing the machine one step will result again in a good CAP state.

Theorem 1 (Safety Policy and Preservation).
For some state $\mathbb{S}$*, if* $\vdash \mathbb{S}$ *then (1)* BasicSP($\mathbb{S}$) *and (2)* $\vdash \text{Step}^n(\mathbb{S})$ *for all* n.

For the purposes of FPCC, we are interested in obtaining safety proofs in the context of our policy as described in Section 2.3. From Theorem 1 we can easily derive:

Theorem 2 (CAP Safety). *For any* $\mathbb{S}$, *if* $\vdash \mathbb{S}$ *then* $\mathsf{Safe}(\mathbb{S}, \mathsf{BasicSP})$.

Thus, to produce an FPCC package we just need to prove that the initial machine state is well-formed with respect to the CAP inference rules. This provides a structured method for constructing FPCC packages in our logic. However, programming and reasoning in CAP is still much too low-level for the practical programmer. We thus need to provide a method for compiling programs from a higher-level language and type system to CAP. The main purpose of programming directly in CAP will then be to "glue" code together from different source languages and to certify particularly low-level libraries such as memory management. In the next few sections, we present a "conventional" typed assembly language and show how to compile it to CAP.

3.3 Advanced Safety Policies

In the theorems above, and for the rest of this paper, we are only interested in proving safety according to our basic safety policy. For handling more general safety policies using CAP, we can extend our CAP inference rules by parameterizing them with a "global safety predicate" SP: $\Phi \vdash_{\mathsf{SP}} \{P\} \mathbb{C}$, $\vdash_{\mathsf{SP}} \mathbb{M} : \Phi$, and $\vdash_{\mathsf{SP}} (\mathbb{M}, \mathbb{R}, pc)$.

The inference rule for each command in this extended system requires an additional premise that the precondition for the command implies the global safety predicate. Then, using a generalized version of Theorem 1, we can establish that:

Theorem 3. *For any* $\mathbb{S}$ *and* SP, *if* $\vdash_{\mathsf{SP}} \mathbb{S}$ *then* $\mathsf{Safe}(\mathbb{S}, \lambda \mathbb{S}' : State.\ \mathsf{SP}(\mathbb{S}') \wedge \mathsf{BasicSP}(\mathbb{S}'))$.

Threading an arbitrary SP through the typing rules is a novel feature not found in the initial version of CAP [27]. In that case, there was no way to specify that an arbitrary safety policy beyond BasicSP (which essentially provides type safety) must hold at every step of execution.

4   Extensible Typed Assembly Language with Runtime System

In this section, we introduce an extensible typed assembly language (XTAL) based on that of Morrisett *et al.* [15]. After presenting the full syntax of XTAL, we give here only a brief overview of its static and dynamic semantics, due to space constraints of this paper. A more complete definition of the language can be found in the Coq implementation itself or the technical report [12].

4.1   Syntax

To simplify the presentation, we will use a much scaled down version of typed assembly language (see Figure 5)–its types involve only integers, pairs, and integer arrays. (We have extended our prototype implementation to include existential, recursive, and polymorphic code types.) The code type $\forall[\Gamma]$ describes a code pointer that expects a register file satisfying Γ. The register file type assigns types to the word values in each register and the heap type keeps track of the heap values in the data heap. We have

(type)	τ	$::= \mathsf{int} \mid \mathsf{array} \mid \tau_0 \times \tau_1 \mid \forall[\Gamma]$
(reg file type)	Γ	$::= \{r_0 : \tau_0, \ldots, r_n : \tau_n\}$
(heap type)	Ψ	$::= \{l_0 : \tau_0, \ldots, l_n : \tau_n\}$
(label)	l	$::= 0 \mid 1 \mid \ldots$
(register)	r	$::= \mathsf{r0} \mid \mathsf{r1} \mid \ldots \mid \mathsf{r7}$
(word val)	v	$::= l \mid i$
(code heap val)	$\overline{h}$	$::= \mathsf{code}\,[\Gamma].I \mid \mathsf{stub}\,[\Gamma].\emptyset$
(heap val)	h	$::= [i_0, \ldots, i_n] \mid \langle v_0, v_1 \rangle$
(instr)	ι	$::= \mathsf{add}\,r_d, r_s, r_t \mid \mathsf{movi}\,r_d, i \mid \mathsf{movl}\,r_d, l \mid \mathsf{ld}\,r_d, r_s(i)$
		$\mid \mathsf{st}\,r_d(i), r_s \mid \mathsf{bgt}\,r_s, r_t, l \mid \mathsf{bgti}\,r_s, i, l \mid \mathsf{newpair}\,r_d[\tau_0, \tau_1]$
(instr seq)	I	$::= \iota; I \mid \mathsf{jd}\,l \mid \mathsf{jmp}\,r$
(code heap)	$\mathcal{C}$	$::= \{l_0 \mapsto \overline{h}_0, \ldots, l_n \mapsto \overline{h}_n\}$
(data heap)	H	$::= \{l_0 \mapsto h_0, \ldots, l_n \mapsto h_n\}$
(reg file)	R	$::= \{r_0 \mapsto v_0, \ldots, r_n \mapsto v_n\}$
(program)	$\mathcal{P}$	$::= (\mathcal{C}, H, R, I)$

Fig. 5. XTAL syntax.

separated the code and data heaps at this level of abstraction because the code heap will remain the same throughout the execution of a program.

Unlike many conventional TALs, our language supports "stub values" in its code heap. These are placeholders for code that will be linked in later from another source (outside the XTAL system). Primitive "macro" instructions that might be built into other TALs, such as array creation and access operations, can be provided as an external library with interface specified as XTAL types. We have also included a typical macro instruction for allocating pairs (newpair) in the language. When polymorphic types are added to the language, this macro instruction could potentially be provided through the external code interface; however, in general, providing built-in primitives can allow for a richer specification of the interface (see the typing rule for newpair below).

The abstract state of an XTAL program is composed of code and data heaps, a register file, and current instruction sequence. Labels are simply integers and the domains of the code and data heaps are to be disjoint. Besides the newpair operation, the arithmetic, memory access, and control flow instructions of XTAL correspond directly to those of the machine defined in 2.1. The movl instruction is constrained to refer only to code heap labels. Note that programs are written in continuation passing style; thus every code block ends with some form of jump to another location in the code heap.

4.2 Static and Dynamic Semantics

The dynamic (operational) semantics of the XTAL abstract machine is defined by a set of rules of the form $\mathcal{P} \mapsto \mathcal{P}'$. This evaluation relation is entirely standard (see [15, 13]) except that the case when jumping to a stub value in the code heap is not handled. The complete rules are omitted here.

Judgment	Meaning
$\vdash \Gamma_0 \subseteq \Gamma_1$	Γ_0 is a register file subtype of Γ_1
$\vdash (\mathcal{C}, H, R, I)$	$(\mathcal{C}, H, R, I)$ is a well-formed program
$\vdash \mathcal{C}$	$\mathcal{C}$ is a well-formed code heap
$\vdash H : \Psi$	H is a well-formed data heap of type Ψ
$\mathcal{C}; \Psi \vdash R : \Gamma$	R is a well-formed reg. file of type Γ
$\mathcal{C} \vdash \overline{h}$ cdval	$\overline{h}$ is a well-formed code heap value
$\Psi \vdash h : \tau$ hval	h is a well-formed data heap value of type τ
$\Psi; \vdash v : \tau$	v is a well-formed word value of type τ
$\mathcal{C}; \Gamma \vdash I$	I is a well-formed instruction sequence

Fig. 6. Static judgments.

For the static semantics, we define a set of judgments as illustrated in Figure 6. Only a few of the critical XTAL typing rules are presented here. The top-level typing rule for XTAL programs requires well-formedness of the code and data heaps, register file, and current instruction sequence, and that I is somewhere in the code heap:

$$\frac{\vdash \mathcal{C} \qquad \vdash H : \Psi \qquad \mathcal{C}; \Psi \vdash R : \Gamma \qquad \mathcal{C}; \Gamma \vdash I}{\vdash (\mathcal{C}, H, R, I)} \text{ (PROG)}$$
$$\exists l \in Dom(\mathcal{C}). \mathcal{C}(l) = \text{code } [\Gamma'].I' \text{ and } I \subseteq_{tail} I'$$

Heap and register file typing depends on the well-formedness of the elements in each. Stub values are simply assumed to have the specified code type. From the instruction typing rules, we show below the rules for newpair, jd, and jmp. The newpair instruction expects initialization values for the newly allocated space in registers r0 and r1 and a pointer to the new pair is put in r_d.

$$\frac{\mathcal{C}; \Gamma \vdash I}{\mathcal{C} \vdash \text{code } [\Gamma].I \text{ cdval}} \text{ (CODE)} \qquad \frac{}{\mathcal{C} \vdash \text{stub } [\Gamma].\emptyset \text{ cdval}} \text{ (STUB)}$$

$$\frac{\Gamma(r0) = \tau_0 \qquad \Gamma(r1) = \tau_1 \qquad \mathcal{C}; \Gamma\{r_d : \tau_0 \times \tau_1\} \vdash I}{\mathcal{C}; \Gamma \vdash \text{newpair } r_d[\tau_0, \tau_1]; I} \text{ (IS-NEWPAIR)}$$

$$\frac{\text{typeof}(\mathcal{C}(l)) = \forall[\Gamma'] \qquad \vdash \Gamma \subseteq \Gamma'}{\mathcal{C}; \Gamma \vdash \text{jd } l} \text{ (IS-JD)} \qquad \frac{\Gamma(r) = \forall[\Gamma'] \qquad \vdash \Gamma \subseteq \Gamma'}{\mathcal{C}; \Gamma \vdash \text{jmp } r} \text{ (IS-JMP)}$$

Although the details of the type system are certainly important, the key thing to be understood here is just that we are able to encode the syntactic judgment forms of XTAL in our logic and prove soundness in Wright-Felleisen style [26]. We will then refer to these judgments in CAP assertions during the process of proving machine code safety.

4.3 External Code Stub Interfaces

XTAL can pass around pointers to arrays in its data heap but has no built-in operations for allocating, accessing, or modifying arrays. We provide these through code stubs:

$$\text{newarray} \mapsto \text{stub } [\{ \text{ r0}:\text{int, r1}:\text{int, r7}:(\forall[\{r0:\text{array}\}]) \}].\emptyset$$
$$\text{arrayget} \mapsto \text{stub } [\{ \text{ r0}:\text{array, r1}:\text{int, r7}:(\forall[\{r0:\text{int}\}]) \}].\emptyset$$
$$\text{arrayset} \mapsto \text{stub } [\{ \text{ r0}:\text{array, r1}:\text{int, r2}:\text{int, r7}:(\forall[\{r0:\text{array}\}]) \}].\emptyset$$

newarray expects a length and initial value as arguments, allocates and initializes a new array accordingly, and then jumps to the code pointer in r7. The accessor operations similarly expect an array and index arguments and will return to the continuation pointer in r7 when they have performed the operation. As is usually the case when dealing with external libraries, the interfaces (code types) defined above do not provide a complete specification of the operations (such as bounds-checking issues). Section 5.3 discusses how we deal with this in the context of the safety of XTAL programs and the final executable machine code.

4.4   Soundness

As usual, we need to show that our XTAL type system is sound with respect to the operational semantics of the abstract machine. This can be done using the standard progress and preservation lemmas. However, in the presence of code stubs, the complete semantics of a program is undefined, so at this level of abstraction we can only assume that those typing rules are sound. In the next section, when compiling XTAL programs to the real machine and linking in code for these libraries and stubs, we will need to prove at that point that the linked code is sound with respect to the XTAL typing rules. Let us define the state when the current XTAL program is jumping to external code:

Definition 1 (External call state). *We define the current instruction of a program,* $(\mathcal{C}, H, R, I)$, *to be an* external call *if* $I \in \{$jd l, jmp r, bgt..., bgti...$\}$ *and* $\mathcal{C}(l) =$ stub $[\Gamma].\emptyset$ *or* $\mathcal{C}(R(r)) =$ stub $[\Gamma].\emptyset$, *as appropriate.*

Theorem 4 (XTAL Progress). *If* $\vdash \mathcal{P}$ *and the current instruction of* $\mathcal{P}$ *is not an external call then there exists* $\mathcal{P}'$ *such that* $\mathcal{P} \mapsto \mathcal{P}'$.

Theorem 5 (XTAL Preservation). *If* $\vdash \mathcal{P}$ *and* $\mathcal{P} \mapsto \mathcal{P}'$ *then* $\vdash \mathcal{P}'$.

These theorems are proven by induction on the well-formed instruction premise $(\mathcal{C}; \Gamma \vdash I)$ of the top level typing rule ($\vdash \mathcal{P}$). Of course the proof of these must be done entirely in the FPCC logic in which the XTAL language is encoded.

In our previous work [14, 13], we demonstrated how to get from these proofs of soundness directly to the FPCC safety proof. However, now we have an extra level to go through (the CAP system) in which we will also be linking external code to XTAL programs, and we must ensure safety of the complete package at the end.

5   Compilation and Linking

In this section we first define how abstract XTAL programs will be translated to, and laid out in, the real machine state (the runtime memory layout). We also define the necessary library routines as CAP code (the runtime system). Then, after compiling and linking an XTAL program to CAP, we must show how to maintain the well-formedness of that CAP state so that we can apply Theorem 2 to obtain the final FPCC proof of safety.

5.1   The Runtime System

In our simple runtime system, memory is divided into three sections – a static data area (used for global constants and library data structures), a read-only code area (which might be further divided into subareas for external ($\mathcal{E}$) and program code), and the dynamic heap area, which can grow indefinitely in our idealized machine. We use a data allocation framework where a heap limit, stored in a fixed allocation pointer register[2], designates a finite portion of the dynamic heap area as having been allocated for use. (Our safety policy could use this to specify "readable" and "writeable" memory.)

5.2 Translating XTAL Programs to CAP

We now outline how to construct (compile) an initial CAP machine state from an XTAL program. Given an initial XTAL program, we need the following (partial) functions or mappings to produce the CAP state:

- $\mathcal{A}_C$: *label* $\rightharpoonup$ *Word* – a layout mapping from XTAL code heap labels to CAP machine addresses.
- $\mathcal{A}_D$: *label* $\rightharpoonup$ *Word* – a layout mapping from XTAL data heap labels to CAP machine addresses. Both the domain and range of the two layout functions should be disjoint. We use $\mathcal{A}$ without any subscript to indicate the union of the two: $\mathcal{A} = \mathcal{A}_C \cup \mathcal{A}_D$.
- $\mathcal{E}$: *Word* $\rightharpoonup$ *CmdList* $\times$ *Pred* – the external (from XTAL's point of view) code blocks and their CAP preconditions for well-formedness. Proving that these blocks are well-formed according to the preconditions will be a proof obligation when verifying the safety of the complete CAP state. The range of $\mathcal{A}_C$ may overlap with the domain of $\mathcal{E}$ – these addresses are the implementation of XTAL code stubs.

With these elements, the translation from XTAL programs to CAP is quite straightforward. As in [14], we can describe the translation by a set of relations and associated inference rules. Because of limited space, we only show here the top-level rule:

$$\frac{\begin{array}{c} \mathcal{A} \vdash (\mathcal{C}, H) \Rightarrow \mathbb{M} \quad \mathcal{A} \vdash R \Rightarrow \mathbb{R} \quad \mathcal{A}_C \vdash I \Rightarrow \mathbb{C} \quad \mathsf{Flatten}(\mathbb{C}, \mathbb{M}, pc) \\ \exists l.\, \mathcal{C}(l) = \mathsf{code}\,[\Gamma].I' \ \wedge \ I \subseteq_{tail} I' \ \wedge \ pc = \mathcal{A}_C(l) + |I'| - |I| \\ \forall w \in Dom(\mathcal{E}).\, \mathsf{Flatten}(\mathsf{Fst}(\mathcal{E}(w)), \mathbb{M}, w) \end{array}}{\mathcal{E}; \mathcal{A} \vdash (\mathcal{C}, H, R, I) \Rightarrow (\mathbb{M}, \mathbb{R}, pc)} \ \text{(TR-PROG)}$$

Register files and word values translate fairly directly between XTAL and the machine. XTAL labels are translated to machine addresses using the $\mathcal{A}$ functions. Every heap value in the code and data heaps must correspond to an appropriately translated sequence of words in memory. All XTAL instructions translate directly to a single machine command except newpair which translates to a series of commands that adjust the allocation pointer to make space for a new pair and then copy the initial values from r0 and r1 into the new space. We ignore the stubs in the XTAL code heap translation because they are handled in the top-level translation rule shown above (when $\mathcal{E}$ is Flatten'ed).

5.3 Generating the CAP Proofs

In this section we proceed in a top-down manner by first stating the main theorem we wish to establish. The theorem says that for a given runtime system, any well-typed

---

[2] XTAL source programs use fewer registers than the actual machine provides.

XTAL program that compiles and links to the runtime will result in an initial machine state that is well-formed according to the CAP typing rules. Applying Theorem 2, we would then be able to produce an FPCC package certifying the safety of the initial machine state.

Theorem 6 (XTAL-CAP Safety Theorem). *For some specified external code environment* $\mathcal{E}$, *and for all* $\mathcal{P}$ *and* $\mathcal{A}$, *if* $\vdash \mathcal{P}$ *(in XTAL) and* $\mathcal{E}; \mathcal{A} \vdash \mathcal{P} \Rightarrow \mathbb{S}$, *then* $\vdash \mathbb{S}$ *(in CAP).*

To prove that the CAP state is well-formed (using the (CAP-STATE) rule, Figure 4), we need a code heap specification, Φ, and a top-level precondition, P, for the current program counter. The code specification is generated as follows: $\Phi = \mathsf{CpGen}(\mathcal{E}, \mathcal{A}_C, \mathcal{C})$, where

$$\mathsf{CpGen}(\mathcal{E}, \mathcal{A}_C, \mathcal{C})(w)$$
$$= \begin{cases} \mathsf{CpInv}(\mathcal{A}_C, \mathcal{C}, \Gamma) & \text{if } w \notin Dom(\mathcal{E}) \text{ and } \exists l. \mathcal{A}_C(l) = w \wedge \mathcal{C}(l) = (\mathsf{code} \ [\Gamma].I) \\ \mathsf{Snd}(\mathcal{E}(w)) & \text{if } w \in Dom(\mathcal{E}) \end{cases}$$

That is, for external code blocks, the precondition comes directly from $\mathcal{E}$, while for code blocks that have been compiled from XTAL, the CAP preconditions are constructed by the following definition:

$$\mathsf{CpInv}(\mathcal{A}_C, \mathcal{C}, \Gamma) = \lambda \mathbb{S}. \exists \mathcal{A}_D, \Psi, H, R. (\vdash \mathcal{C}) \wedge (\vdash H : \Psi) \wedge (\mathcal{C}; \Psi \vdash R : \Gamma)$$
$$\wedge (\mathcal{A} \vdash (\mathcal{C}, H) \Rightarrow \mathbb{S}.\mathbb{M}) \wedge (\mathcal{A} \vdash R \Rightarrow \mathbb{S}.\mathbb{R})$$

For any given program, the code heap and layout ($\mathcal{C}$ and $\mathcal{A}_C$) must be unchanged, therefore they are global parameters of these predicate generators. CpInv captures the fact that at a particular machine state there is a well-typed XTAL memory and register file that syntactically corresponds to it. We only need to specify the register file type as an argument to CpInv because the typing rules for the well-formed register file and heap will imply all the necessary restrictions on the data heap structure. One of the main insights of this work is the definition of CpInv, which allows us to both establish a syntactic invariant on CAP machine states as well as define the interface between XTAL and library code at the CAP level. CpInv is based on a similar idea as the global invariant defined in [14] but instead of a generic, monolithic safety proof using the syntactic encoding of the type system, CpInv makes clear what the program-specific preconditions are for each command (instruction) and allows for easy manipulation and reasoning thereupon, as well as interaction with other type system-based invariants.

Returning to the proof of Theorem 6, if we define the top-level precondition of the (CAP-STATE) rule to be $\mathsf{CpInv}(\mathcal{A}_C, \mathcal{C}, \Gamma)$, then it is trivially satisfied on the initial state $\mathbb{S}$ by the premises of the theorem. We now have to show well-formedness of the code at the current program counter, $\Phi \vdash \{P\} \mathbb{C}$, and, in fact, proofs of the same judgment form must be provided for each of the code blocks in the heap, according to the (CAP-CDSPEC) rule. The correctness of the CAP code memory is shown by the theorem:

Theorem 7 (XTAL-CAP Code Heap Safety). *For a specified* $\mathcal{E}$, *and for any XTAL program state* $(\mathcal{C}, H, R, I)$, *register file type* Γ, *layout functions* $\mathcal{A}$, *and machine state* $(\mathbb{M}, \mathbb{R}, pc)$, *such that* $\vdash (\mathcal{C}, H, R, I)$ *and* $\mathcal{E}; \mathcal{A} \vdash (\mathcal{C}, H, R, I) \Rightarrow (\mathbb{M}, \mathbb{R}, pc)$, *if* $\Phi = \mathsf{CpGen}(\mathcal{E}, \mathcal{A}_C, \mathcal{C})$, *then* $\vdash \mathbb{M} : \Phi$.

This depends in turn on the proof that each well-typed XTAL instruction sequence translated to machine commands will be well-formed in CAP under CpInv:

Theorem 8 (XTAL-CAP Instruction Safety). *For a specified $\mathcal{E}$, and for all $\mathcal{A}_C$, $\mathcal{C}$, I, Γ, and $\mathbb{C}$ (where $\Phi = \mathsf{CpGen}(\mathcal{E}, \mathcal{A}_C, \mathcal{C})$), if $\mathcal{C}; \Gamma \vdash I$ and $\mathcal{A}_C \vdash I \Rightarrow \mathbb{C}$, then $\Phi \vdash \{\mathsf{CpInv}(\mathcal{A}_C, \mathcal{C}, \Gamma)\} \mathbb{C}$.*

Due to space constraints, we omit details of the proof of this theorem except to mention that it is proved by induction on I. In cases where the current instruction directly maps to a machine command (*i.e.*, other than newpair), the postcondition (Q in the CAP rules) is generated by applying CpInv to the updated XTAL register file type. We use the XTAL safety theorems (4 and 5) here to show that Q holds after one step of execution. In the case of the expanded commands of newpair, we must construct the intermediate postconditions by hand and then show that CpInv is re-established on the state after the sequence of expanded commands has been completed. In the case when jumping to external code, we use the result of Proof Obligation 10 below.

Finally, establishing the theorems above depends on satisfying some proof obligations with respect to the external library code and its interfaces as specified at the XTAL level. First, we must show that the external library code is well-formed according to its supplied preconditions:

Proof Obligation 9 (External Code Safety) *For a given $\mathcal{E}$, if $\Phi = \mathsf{CpGen}(\mathcal{E}, \mathcal{A}_C, \mathcal{C})$ for any $\mathcal{A}_C$ and $\mathcal{C}$, then $\Phi \vdash \{\mathsf{Snd}(\mathcal{E}(w))\} \, \mathsf{Fst}(\mathcal{E}(w))$, for all $w \in Dom(\mathcal{E})$.*

For now, we assume that the proofs of this lemma are constructed "by hand" using the rules for well-formedness of CAP commands.

Secondly, when linking the external code with a particular XTAL program, where certain labels of the XTAL code heap are mapped to external code addresses, we have to show that the typing environment that would hold at any XTAL program that is jumping to that label implies the actual precondition of that external code:

Proof Obligation 10 (Interface Correctness) *For a given $\mathcal{E}$, $\mathcal{A}_C$, and $\mathcal{C}$, and for all l such that $\mathcal{C}(l) = \mathsf{stub}\,[\Gamma].\emptyset$ and $\mathcal{A}_C(l) = w$, if $\mathsf{CpInv}(\mathcal{A}_C, \mathcal{C}, \Gamma)(\mathbb{S})$ then $\mathsf{Snd}(\mathcal{E}(w))(\mathbb{S})$.*

These properties must be proved for each instantiation of the runtime system $\mathcal{E}$. With them, the proofs of Theorems 8, 7, and, finally, 6 can be completed.

5.4 arrayget Example

As a concrete example of the process discussed in the foregoing subsection, let us consider arrayget. The XTAL type interface is defined in Section 4.3. An implementation of this function could be:

$$\mathbb{C}_{aget} = [\mathsf{ld}\ r8, r0(0);\ \mathsf{addi}\ r1, r1, 1;\ \mathsf{bgt}\ r1, r8, \mathsf{bnderr};\ \mathsf{add}\ r0, r0, r1;\ \mathsf{ld}\ r0, r0(0);\ \mathsf{jmp}\ r7]$$

The runtime representation of an array in memory is a length field followed by the actual array of data. We assume that there is some exception handling routine for out-of-bounds accesses with a trivial precondition defined by $\mathcal{E}(\mathsf{bnderr}) = (\mathbb{C}_{bnderr}, Q_{bnderr})$.

Before describing the CAP assertions for the safety of $\mathbb{C}_{aget}$, notice that the code returns indirectly to an XTAL function pointer. Similarly, the arrayget address can be passed around in XTAL programs as a first-class code pointer. While the syntactic type system handles these code pointers quite easily using the relevant XTAL types, dealing with code pointers in a Hoare logic-based setup like CAP requires a little bit of machinery.

We can thus proceed to directly define the precondition of $\mathbb{C}_{aget}$ as,

$$Q_{aget} = \mathsf{CpInv}(\mathcal{A}_C, \mathcal{C}, \{\, \mathsf{r0}:\mathsf{array},\ \mathsf{r1}:\mathsf{int},\ \mathsf{r7}:(\forall[\{\mathsf{r0}:\mathsf{int}\}])\,\})$$

for some $\mathcal{A}_C$ and $\mathcal{C}$. Then we certify the library code in CAP by providing a derivation of $(\Phi \vdash \{Q_{aget}\}\,\mathbb{C}_{aget})$. We do this by applying the appropriate rules from Figure 4 to track the changes that are made to the state with each command. When we reach the final jump to r7, we can then show that $\mathsf{CpInv}(\mathcal{A}_C, \mathcal{C}, \{\mathsf{r0}:\mathsf{int}\})$ holds, which must be the precondition specified for the return code pointer by $\Phi(\mathbb{S}.\mathbb{R}(\mathsf{r7}))$ (see the definition of Φ in the beginning of Section 5.3). The problem with this method of certifying arrayget, however, is that we have explicitly included details about the source language type system in its preconditions. In order to make the proof more generic, while at the same time be able to leverage the syntactic type system for certifying code pointers, we follow a similar approach as in [27]: First, we define generic predicates for the pre- and postconditions, abstracting over an arbitrary external predicate, P_{aget}. The actual requirements of the arrayget code are minimal (for example, that the memory area of the array is readable according to the safety policy). The post-condition predicate relates the state of the machine upon exiting the code block to the initial entry state:

$$\mathsf{Pre} = \lambda P_{aget}.\lambda\mathbb{S}.\ P_{aget}(\mathbb{S}) \wedge \mathsf{SafeToRead}(\mathbb{S}.\mathbb{M},\ \mathbb{S}.\mathbb{R}(\mathsf{r0}),\ \mathbb{S}.\mathbb{R}(\mathsf{r1})+1)$$
$$\mathsf{Post} = \lambda(\mathbb{M},\mathbb{R},pc).\ \lambda(\mathbb{M}',\mathbb{R}',pc').\ \mathbb{M}' = \mathbb{M} \wedge pc' = \mathbb{S}.\mathbb{R}(\mathsf{r7})$$
$$\wedge\ \mathbb{R}'(\mathsf{r0}) = \mathbb{M}(\mathbb{R}(\mathsf{r0})+\mathbb{R}(\mathsf{r1})+1) \wedge \ldots$$

Now we certify the arrayget code block, quantifying over all P_{aget} and complete code specifications Φ, but imposing some appropriate restrictions on them:

$$\forall\Phi, P_{aget}.\ \Phi(\mathsf{bnderr}) = Q_{bnderr} \wedge (\forall\mathbb{S}, \mathbb{S}'.\mathsf{Pre}(P_{aget})(\mathbb{S}) \wedge \mathsf{Post}(\mathbb{S})(\mathbb{S}')$$
$$\to \Phi(\mathbb{S}.\mathbb{R}(\mathsf{r7}))(\mathbb{S}'))$$
$$\to \Phi \vdash \{\mathsf{Pre}(P_{aget})\}\,\mathbb{C}_{aget}$$

Thus, under the assumption that the Pre predicate holds, we can again apply the inference rules for CAP commands to show the well-formedness of the $\mathbb{C}_{aget}$ code. When we reach the final jump, we show that the Post predicate holds and then use that fact with the premise of the formula above to show that it is safe to jump to the return code pointer.

The arrayget code can thus be certified independent of any type system, by introducing the quantified P_{aget} predicate. Now, when we want to use this as an external function for XTAL programs, we instantiate P_{aget} with Q_{aget} above. We have to prove the premise of the formula above, $(\forall\mathbb{S}, \mathbb{S}'.\mathsf{Pre}(Q_{aget})(\mathbb{S}) \wedge \mathsf{Post}(\mathbb{S})(\mathbb{S}') \to \Phi(\mathbb{S}.\mathbb{R}(\mathsf{r7}))(\mathbb{S}'))$. Proving this is not difficult, because we use properties of the XTAL type system to show that from a state satisfying the precondition–*i.e.* there is a well-formed XTAL program whose register file satisfies the arrayget type interface– the changes described by the Post predicate will result in a state to which there does correspond another well-formed

XTAL program, one where the register r0 is updated with the appropriate element of the array. Then we can let $\mathcal{E}(\mathsf{arrayget}) = (\mathbb{C}_{aget}, \mathsf{Pre}(Q_{aget}))$ and we have satisfied Proof Obligation 9. Proof Obligation 10 follows almost directly given our definition of Q_{aget}.

In summary, we have shown how to certify runtime library code independent of a source language. In order to handle code pointers, we simply assume their safety as a premise; then, when using the library with a particular source language type system, we instantiate with a syntactic well-formedness predicate in the form of CpInv and use the facilities of the type system for checking code pointers to prove the safety of indirect jumps.

6   Implementation and Future Work

We have a prototype implementation of the system presented in this paper, developed using the Coq proof assistant. Due to space constraints, we have left out its details here. As mentioned earlier in the paper, our eventual goal is to build an FPCC system for real IA-32 (Intel x86) machines. We have already applied the CAP type system to that architecture and will now need to develop a more realistic version of XTAL. Additionally, our experience with the Coq proof assistant leads us to believe that there should be more development on enhancing the automation of the proof tactics, because many parts of the proofs needed for this paper are not hard or complex, but tedious to do given the rather simplistic tactics supplied with the base Coq system.

In this paper, we have implicitly assumed that the CAP machine code is generated from one of two sources: *(a)* XTAL source code, or *(b)* code written directly in CAP. However, more generally, our intention is to support code from multiple source type systems. In this case, the definition of CpGen (Section 5.3) would utilitize code precondition invariant generators (CpInv) from the multiple type systems. The general form of each CpInv would be the same, although, of course, the particular typing environments and judgments would be different for each system. Then we would have a series of theorems like those in Section 5.3, specialized for each CpInv. Proof Obligation 10 would also be generalized as necessary, requiring proofs that the interfaces between the various type systems are compatible. Of course there will be some amount of engineering required to get such a system up and running, but we believe that there is true potential for building a realistic, scalable FPCC framework along these lines.

7   Related Work and Conclusion

In the context of the original PCC systems cited in the Introduction, there has been recent work to improve their flexibility and reliability by removing type-system specific components from the framework [19]. These systems have the advantage of working, production-quality implementations but it is still unclear whether they can approach the trustworthiness goals of FPCC.

We also mentioned the first approaches to generating FPCC, which utilized semantic models of the source type system, and their resulting complexities. Attempting to address and hide the complexity of the semantic soundness proofs, Juan Chen *et al.* [6] have developed LTAL, a low-level typed assembly language which is used to compile core ML to FPCC. LTAL is based in turn upon an abstraction layer, TML (typed machine language) [22], which is an even lower-level intermediate language. Complex parts of the semantic proofs, such as the indexed model of recursive types and stratified model of mutable fields, are hidden in the soundness proof of TML and as long as a typed assembly language can be compiled to TML, one need not worry about the semantic models. All the same, LTAL and TML are only assembly language type systems, albeit at a much lower level that XTAL. They do not provide CAP's generality of reasoning nor can their type systems be used to certify their own runtime system components. It should be clearly noted that the ideas presented in this paper are not restricted to use with a syntactic FPCC approach, as we have pursued. Integrating LTAL or TML with the CAP framework of this paper to certify their runtime system components seems feasible as well.

Along the syntactic approach to FPCC, Crary [9, 10] applied our methods [14, 13] to a realistic typed assembly language initially targeted to the Intel x86. He even went on to specify invariants about the garbage collector interface, but beyond the interface the implementation is still uncertified. In his work he uses the metalogical framework of Twelf [21] instead of the CiC-based Coq that we have been using.

In conclusion, there is much ongoing development of PCC technology for producing certified machine code from high-level source languages. Concurrently, there is exciting work on certifying garbage collectors and other low-level system libraries. However, integrating the high and low-level proofs of safety has not yet received much attention. The ideas presented in this paper represent a viable approach to dealing with the issue of interfacing and integrating safety proofs of machine code from multiple sources in a fully certified framework.

Acknowledgments

We would like to thank the anonymous referees for their comments on an earlier version of this paper.

References

1. A. Ahmed, A. W. Appel, , and R. Virga. A stratified semantics of general references embeddable in higher-order logic. In *Proc. 17th Annual IEEE Symposium on Logic in Computer Science*, pages 75–86, June 2002.
2. A. J. Ahmed. Mutable fields in a semantic model of types. Talk presented at 2000 PCC Workshop, June 2000.
3. A. W. Appel. Foundational proof-carrying code. In *Proc. 16th Annual IEEE Symposium on Logic in Computer Science*, pages 247–258, June 2001.
4. A. W. Appel and A. P. Felty. A semantic model of types and machine instructions for proof-carrying code. In *Proc. 27th ACM Symp. on Principles of Prog. Lang.*, pages 243–253. ACM Press, 2000.
5. A. W. Appel and D. McAllester. An indexed model of recursive types for foundational proof-carrying code. *ACM Trans. on Programming Languages and Systems*, 23(5):657–683, Sept. 2001.
6. J. Chen, D. Wu, A. W. Appel, and H. Fang. A provably sound tal for back-end optimization. In *Proc. 2003 ACM Conf. on Prog. Lang. Design and Impl.*, pages 208–219, New York, 2003. ACM Press.

7. C. Colby, P. Lee, G. Necula, F. Blau, M. Plesko, and K. Cline. A certifying compiler for Java. In *Proc. 2000 ACM Conf. on Prog. Lang. Design and Impl.*, pages 95–107, New York, 2000. ACM Press.

8. T. Coquand and G. Huet. The calculus of constructions. *Information and Computation*, 76:95–120, 1988.

9. K. Crary. Towards a foundational typed assembly language. In *Proc. 30th ACM Symp. on Principles of Prog. Lang.*, pages 198 – 212. ACM Press, Jan. 2003.

10. K. Crary and S. Sarkar. A metalogical approach to foundational certified code. Technical Report CMU-CS-03-108, Carnegie Mellon University, Jan. 2003.

11. A. Felty. Semantic models of types and machine instructions for proof-carrying code. Talk presented at 2000 PCC Workshop, June 2000.

12. N. A. Hamid and Z. Shao. Coq code for interfacing hoare logic and type systems for fpcc. Available at flint.cs.yale.edu/flint/publications, May 2004.

13. N. A. Hamid, Z. Shao, V. Trifonov, S. Monnier, and Z. Ni. A syntactic approach to foundational proof carrying-code. *Journal of Automated Reasoning, Special issue on Proof-Carrying Code*, page (to appear).

14. N. A. Hamid, Z. Shao, V. Trifonov, S. Monnier, and Z. Ni. A syntactic approach to foundational proof carrying-code. In *Proc. 17th Annual IEEE Symposium on Logic in Computer Science*, pages 89–100, June 2002.

15. G. Morrisett, D. Walker, K. Crary, and N. Glew. From System F to typed assembly language. In *Proc. 25th ACM Symp. on Principles of Prog. Lang.*, pages 85–97. ACM Press, Jan. 1998.

16. G. Necula. Proof-carrying code. In *Proc. 24th ACM Symp. on Principles of Prog. Lang.*, pages 106–119, New York, Jan. 1997. ACM Press.

17. G. Necula. *Compiling with Proofs*. PhD thesis, School of Computer Science, Carnegie Mellon Univ., Sept. 1998.

18. G. Necula and P. Lee. Safe kernel extensions without run-time checking. In *Proc. 2nd USENIX Symp. on Operating System Design and Impl.*, pages 229–243, 1996.

19. G. C. Necula and R. R. Schneck. A sound framework for untrusted verification-condition generators. In *Proc. 18th Annual IEEE Symposium on Logic in Computer Science*, pages 248–260, June 2003.

20. C. Paulin-Mohring. Inductive definitions in the system Coq—rules and properties. In M. Bezem and J. Groote, editors, *Proc. TLCA*, volume 664 of *LNCS*. Springer-Verlag, 1993.

21. F. Pfenning and C. Schürmann. System description: Twelf - a meta-logical framework for deductive systems. In *Proc. 16th International Conference on Automated Deduction*, volume 1632 of *LNCS*, pages 202–206. Springer-Verlag, July 1999.

22. K. N. Swadi and A. W. Appel. Typed machine language and its semantics. Unpublished manuscript available at www.cs.princeton.edu/~appel/papers, July 2001.

23. G. Tan, A. W. Appel, K. N. Swadi, and D. Wu. Construction of a semantic model for a typed assembly language. In *5th International Conference on Verification, Model Checking, and Abstract Interpretation (VMCAI '04)*, page (to appear), Jan. 2004.

24. The Coq Development Team. The Coq proof assistant reference manual. The Coq release v7.1, Oct. 2001.

25. B. Werner. *Une Théorie des Constructions Inductives*. PhD thesis, A L'Université Paris 7, Paris, France, 1994.

26. A. K. Wright and M. Felleisen. A syntactic approach to type soundness. *Information and Computation*, 115(1):38–94, 1994.

27. D. Yu, N. A. Hamid, and Z. Shao. Building certified libraries for PCC: Dynamic storage allocation. In *Proc. 2003 European Symposium on Programming (ESOP'03)*, April 2003.

Extensible Hierarchical Tactic Construction in a Logical Framework*

Jason Hickey and Aleksey Nogin

Department of Computer Science, California Institute of Technology
M/C 256-80, Pasadena, CA 91125
{jyh,nogin}@cs.caltech.edu

Abstract. Theorem provers for higher-order logics often use *tactics* to implement automated proof search. Often some basic tactics are designed to behave very differently in different contexts. Even in a prover that only supports a fixed base logic, such tactics may need to be updated dynamically as new definitions and theorems are added. In a logical framework with multiple (perhaps conflicting) logics, this has the added complexity that definitions and theorems should only be used for automation only in the logic in which they are defined or proved.

This paper describes a very general and flexible mechanism for extensible hierarchical tactic maintenance in a logical framework. We also explain how this reflective mechanism can be implemented efficiently while requiring little effort from its users.

The approaches presented in this paper form the core of the tactic construction methodology in the MetaPRL theorem prover, where they have been developed and successfully used for several years.

1 Introduction

Several provers [1, 2, 4–6, 9, 10, 18] use higher-order logics for reasoning because the expressivity of the logics permits concise problem descriptions, and because meta-principles that characterize entire classes of problems can be proved and re-used on multiple problem instances. In these provers, proof automation is coded in a *meta-language* (often a variant of ML) as *tactics*.

It can be very useful for some basic tactics to be designed and/or expected to behave very differently in different contexts. One of the best examples of such a tactic is the *decomposition tactic* [14, Section 3.3] present in the NuPRL [1, 4] and MetaPRL [9, 13] theorem provers. When applied to the conclusion of a goal sequent, it will try to decompose the conclusion into simpler ones, normally by using an appropriate introduction rule. When applied to a hypothesis, the decomposition tactic would try to break the hypothesis into simpler ones, usually by applying an appropriate elimination rule.

---

* This work was supported in part by the DoD Multidisciplinary University Research Initiative (MURI) program administered by the Office of Naval Research (ONR) under Grant N00014-01-1-0765, the Defense Advanced Research Projects Agency (DARPA), the United States Air Force, the Lee Center, and by NSF Grant CCR 0204193.

K. Slind et al. (Eds.): TPHOLs 2004, LNCS 3223, pp. 136–151, 2004.
© Springer-Verlag Berlin Heidelberg 2004

Table 1. Decomposition Tactic Examples

	Goal sequent	$\implies$	Desired subgoals
Conclusion decomposition	$\cdots \vdash A \wedge B$	$\implies$	$\cdots \vdash A$ and $\cdots \vdash B$
Hypothesis decomposition	$\cdots ; A \wedge B; \cdots \vdash \cdots$	$\implies$	$\cdots ; A; B; \cdots \vdash \cdots$

Example 1. The desired behavior for the decomposition tactic on $\wedge$-terms is shown in Table 1.

Whenever a theory is extended with a new operator, the decomposition tactic needs to be updated in order for it to know how to decompose this new operator. More generally, whenever a new rule (including possibly a new axiom, a new definition, a new derived rule or a new theorem) is added to a system, it is often desirable to update some tactic (or possibly several tactics) so that it makes use of the newly added rule. For example, if a $\wedge$ introduction rule is added to the system, the decomposition tactic would be updated with the information that if the conclusion is a $\wedge$-term, then the new introduction rule should be used.

There are a number of problems associated with such tactic updates. A very important requirement is that performing these tactic updates must be easy and not require much effort from end-users. Our experience with NuPRL and Meta-PRL theorem provers strongly suggests that the true power of the updatable tactics only becomes apparent when updates are performed to account for *almost all* the new theorems and definitions added to the system. On the other hand, when updates require too much effort, many users forgo maintaining the general tactics, reverting instead to using various ad-hoc workarounds and using the tactics updated to handle only the core theory.

Another class of problems are those of scoping. The updates must be managed in an extensible manner – when a tactic is updated to take into account a new theorem, all new proofs should be done using the updated tactic, but the earlier proofs might need to still use the previous version in order not to break. If a theorem prover allows defining and working in different logical theories, then the tactic update mechanism needs to make sure that the updated tactic will only attempt to use a theorem when performing proof search in the appropriate theory. And if the prover supports inheritance between logical theories, then the updates mechanism needs to be compositional – if a theory is composed of several subtheories (each potentially including its own theorems), then the tactic updates from each of the subtheories need to be composed together.

Once the tactics updates mechanism becomes simple enough to be used for almost all new definitions, lemmas and theorems, efficiency becomes a big concern. If each new update slows the tactic down (for example, by forcing it to try more branches in its proof search), then this approach to maintaining tactics would not scale. At a minimum, the updates related to, for example, a new definition should not have significant impact on the performance of the tactic when proving theorems that do not make any use of the new definition (even when that definition is in scope).

In the MetaPRL theorem prover [9, 13] we have implemented a number of very general mechanisms that provide automatic scoping management for tactic updates, efficient data structures for making sure that new data does not have a significant impact on performance, and a way for the system to come up with proper tactic updates automatically requiring only very small hints from the user. In Sections 3, 4 and 5 we describe these mechanisms and explain how they help in addressing all of the issues outlined above. In Section 6 we show how some of the most commonly used MetaPRL tactics are implemented using these general mechanisms.

2   MetaPRL

In order to better understand this paper, it is helpful to know the basic structure of the MetaPRL theorem prover.

The core of the prover is its *logical engine* written in OCaml [15, 20]. MetaPRL *theories* are implemented as OCaml modules, with each theory having a separate interface and implementation files containing both logical contents (definitions, axioms, theorems, *etc*) as well as the traditional ML contents (including tactics). The logical theories are organized into an inheritance hierarchy [9, Section 5.1], where large logical theories are constructed by inheriting from a number of smaller ones. The MetaPRL *frontend* is a CamlP4-based preprocessor that is capable of turning the mixture of MetaPRL content and ML code into plain ML code and passing it to OCaml compiler. Finally, MetaPRL has a user interface that includes a *proof editor*.

3   Resources

We implement the process of maintaining context-sensitive tactics is automated through a mechanism called *resources*. A resource is essentially a collection of *scoped* pieces of data.

Example 2. The decomposition tactic of Example 1 could be implemented using a combination of two resources – a resource collecting information on introduction rules ("intro resource") and one collecting information on elimination rules ("elim resource"). For each of the two resources, the data points that would be passed to the resource manager for collection will each consist of a pattern (e.g. $A \wedge B$) paired with the corresponding tactic (e.g. a tactic that would apply a $\wedge$ introduction rule).

The MetaPRL resource interface provides a scoping mechanism based on the inheritance hierarchy of logical theories. Resources are managed on a per-theorem granularity – when working on a particular proof, the resource state reflects everything collected from the current theory up to the theorem being proved, as well as everything inherited from the theories that are ancestors of the current one in the logical hierarchy, given in the appropriate order.

Our implementation of the resource mechanism has two layers. The lower layer is invisible to the user – its functions are not supposed to be called directly by MetaPRL users; instead the appropriate calls will be inserted by the MetaPRL frontend.

Internal Interface. The interface contains the following:

```
type bookmark
type ('input, 'intermediate, 'output) description =
 { empty: 'intermediate;
   add: 'intermediate -> 'input -> 'intermediate;
   retrieve: 'intermediate -> 'output }

val create: string -> ('input, 'intermediate, 'output) resource ->
   bookmark -> 'output

val improve : string -> Obj.t -> unit
val bookmark : string -> unit
val extends_theory : string -> unit
val close_theory : string -> unit

val find : string * string -> bookmark
```

The create function takes a name of the resource and a function for turning a list of collected data points (in the order that is consistent with the order in which they were added to the appropriate theories and the inheritance hierarchy order) of the 'input type into an appropriate result of the 'output type (usually tactic, int -> tactic, or similar) and returns a lookup function that given a theorem bookmark will give the value of that resource at that bookmark.

The lookup function is lazy and it caches both the 'intermediate and the 'output results. For example, if bookmark B extends from a bookmark A and the lookup is called on bookmark B, then the lookup system will use the add function to fold all the relevant data into the empty value and will memoize the 'intermediate values for all the bookmarks it encounters above B in the inheritance hierarchy (including A and B itself). Next it calls the retrieve function to get the final data for the bookmark B, memoizes and returns the resulting data. Next time the lookup is called on bookmark B, it will simply return the memoized 'output data. Next time the lookup function is called on the bookmark A, it will only call the retrieve on the memoized 'intermediate value (and memoize the resulting 'output value as well)[1]. Finally, next time the lookup function is called on another descendant of A, the lookup function will retrieve the 'intermediate value for A and then add the remaining data to it.

The improve function adds a new data entry to the named resource. Note that the Obj.t here signifies a shortcut across the type system – the MetaPRL frontend will add a coercion from the actual input type into an Obj.t and will also add a type constraint on the expression being coerced to make sure that this mechanism is still type safe.

The bookmark function adds the named bookmark to all resources (the name here is usually a name of a theorem); extends_theory tells the resource manager

---

[1] In case there were no new data added between A and B, then the 'output value for B will be simply reused for A.

that the current theory inherits from another one (and that it needs to inherit the data for all resources); close_theory tells the resource manager that it has received all the resource data for the named theory and that all the recent bookmark and extends_theory calls belong to the given theory.

Finally, find finds the bookmark for a given theorem in a given theory.

External Interface. The next layer is essentially a user interface layer and it consists of statements that would be recognized by the MetaPRL frontend in MetaPRL theories. First, in the theory interface files we allow declarations of the form

resource (*input*, *output*) *name*

where resource is a MetaPRL keyword, *input* and *output* are the ML types describing the data inputs that the resource is going to get and the resulting output type, and *name* is, unsurprisingly, the name of the resource (must be globally unique).

Whenever a resource is declared in a theory interface, the corresponding implementation file must define the resource using the

let (*input*, *output*) resource *name* = *expr*

construct, where *expr* is an ML expression on an appropriate description type. When a resource is defined, the MetaPRL frontend will create a function get_*name*_resource of the type bookmark -> *output*.

All tactics in MetaPRL have access to the "proof obligation" object, which includes the bookmark corresponding to the scope of the current proof. By applying the appropriate get_*name*_resource function to the current bookmark, the tactic can get access to the appropriate value of any resource. This mechanism is purely functional – there is no imperative "context switch" when switching from one proof to another; instead tactics in each proof have immediate access to the *local value* of each resource's 'output data.

Example 3. Once the intro and elim resources (with the tactic and int -> tactic output types respectively) of Example 2 are defined (Section 6.4 will describe the implementation in detail), the decomposition tactic could be implemented as simple as

```
let dT p n =
   let bookmark = get_bookmark p in
   if n = 0 then
      get_intro_resource bookmark
   else
      get_elim_resource bookmark n
```

where p is the proof obligation argument and n is the index of the hypothesis to decompose (index 0 stand for the conclusion).

To add data to a resource, a MetaPRL user only has to write (and as we will see in Section 4 even that is usually automated away):

let resource *name* += *expr*

where *expr* has the appropriate *input* type, and the MetaPRL frontend will translate it into an appropriate `improve` call.

The scoping management of the resource data is fully handled by the frontend itself, without requiring any resource-specific input from the user. Whenever a logical theory is specified as inheriting another logical theory (using the `extends Theory_name` statement), the frontend will include the appropriate `extends_theory` call. Whenever a new theorem is added to a theory, the frontend will insert a call to `bookmark`. Finally, at the end of each theory, the frontend will insert a call to `close_theory`.

4   Reflective Resource Annotations

Even in the presence of the hierarchical resource mechanism of Section 3, writing the appropriate `let resource +=` code every time new definitions and theorems are added takes some expertise and could be somewhat time consuming. On the other hand, it also turns out that most such resource updates are rather uniform and most of the needed information is already present in the system. If the rules are expressed using a well-defined logical meta-language (such as the sequent schemas language [16] used by MetaPRL), then we can use the *text* of the rules as a source of information.

Example 4. Suppose a new introduction rule is added to the system and the user wants to add it to the `intro` resource. Using the mechanism given in the previous Section, this might look as[2]:

$$\text{rule xyz1:} \quad \frac{\cdots}{\Gamma \vdash \text{xyz}\{a;b;c\}}$$

`let resource intro += (xyz{`$a;b;c$`}, xyz1)`

In the above example it is clear that the resource improvement line is pretty redundant[3] – it does not contain anything that can not be deduced from the rule itself. If the system would be given access both to the *text* of the rule and the primitive tactic for *applying* the rule[4], it will have most (if not all) of the information on how to update the decomposition tactic! By examining the text of the rule it can see what kind of term is being introduced and create an appropriate pattern for inclusion into the resource and it is clear which tactic should be added to the `intro` resource – the primitive tactic that would apply the newly added rule.

By giving tactics access to the text of the rules we make the system a bit more reflective – it becomes capable of using not only the *meaning* of the rules in its proof search, but their *syntax* as well.

---

[2] For clarity, we are using the pretty-printed syntax of MetaPRL terms here in place of their ASCII representations.

[3] The redundancy is not very big here, of course, but in more complicated examples it can get quite big.

[4] In the MetaPRL system, all the rules (including derived rules and theorems) are compiled to a *rewriting engine bytecode*, so a tactic for applying a primitive rule does not have direct access to the text of the rule it is applying.

From the MetaPRL user's perspective this mechanism has a form of *resource annotations*. When adding a new rule, a user only has to annotate it with the names of resources that need to be automatically improved. Users can also pass some optional arguments to the automatic procedure in order to modify its behavior. As a result, when a new logical object (definition, axiom, theorem, derived rule, *etc.*) is added to a MetaPRL theory, the user can usually update all relevant proof search automation by typing only a few extra symbols.

Example 5. Using the resource annotations mechanism, the code of the Example 4 above would take the form

$$\text{rule xyz1 \{| intro [] |\}: } \frac{\cdots}{\Gamma \vdash \text{xyz}\{a; b; c\}}$$

where the annotation "`{| intro [] |}`" specifies that the new rule has to be added to the `intro` resource.

Example 6. The resource annotation for the $\wedge$ elimination rule in MetaPRL would be written as `{| elim [ThinOption thinT] |}` which specifies that the `elim` resource should be improved with an entry for the $\wedge$ term and that by default it should use the `thinT` tactic to thin out (weaken) the original $\wedge$ hypothesis after applying the elimination rule.

5   Term Table

One of the most frequent uses of resources is to construct tactics for term rewriting or rule application based on the collection of rewrites and rules in the logic. For example, as discussed the `dT` tactic selects an inference rule based on the term to be decomposed. Abstractly, the `dT` tactic defines a (perhaps large) set of rules indexed by a set of terms.

In a very naive implementation, given a term to decompose, the prover would apply each of the rules it knows about in order until one of them succeeds. This would of course be very inefficient, taking time linear in the number of rules in the logic. There are many other kinds of operations that have the same kind of behavior, including syntax-directed proof search, term evaluation, and display of terms [8] based on their syntax.

Abstractly stated, the problem is this: given a set S of (*pattern, value*) pairs, and a term t, find a matching pattern and return the corresponding value. In case there are several matches, it is useful to have a choice between several strategies:

- return the most recently added value corresponding to the "most specific" match, or
- return the list of all the values corresponding to the "most specific" match (most recently added first), or
- return the list of all values corresponding to the matching patterns, the ones corresponding to "more specific" matches first.

Note that when values are collected through the resources mechanism, the "most resent" means the "closest to the leaves of the inheritance hierarchy". In other words we want to get the value from the most specialized subtheory first, because this allows specialized theories to shadow the values defined in the more generic "core" theories.

We call this data structure a *term table* and we construct it by collecting patterns *in an incremental manner* into a discrimination tree [3, 7]. Since the patterns we use are higher-order, we simplify them before we add them to the discrimination tree (thus allowing false positive matches). The original higher-order patterns are compiled into the bytecode programs for the MetaPRL rewriting engine [12], which can be used to test the matches found by the discrimination tree, killing off the false positives.

We begin the description with some definitions.

5.1 Second-Order Patterns

MetaPRL represents syntax using the *term schemas* [16]. Each term schema is either an object (first-order) variable v, a second-order meta-variable ν or it has an *operator* that represents the "name" of the term drawn from a countable set, and a set of subterms that may contain bindings of various arities. The second-order variables are used to specify term patterns and substitution for rewriting [16].

The following table gives a few examples of term syntax, and their conventional notation. The `lambda` term contains a binding occurrence: the variable x is bound in the subterm b.

Displayed form	Term
$\lambda x.b$	`lambda{ x. b }`
$f(a)$	`apply { f; a }`
$x + y$	`sum{ x; y }`

Second-order variables are used to specify term patterns and substitution for rewriting. A second-order variable pattern has the form $\nu[v_1; \cdots ; v_n]$, which represents an arbitrary term that may have free variables $v_1, \ldots, v_n$. The corresponding substitution has the form $\nu[t_1; \cdots ; t_n]$, which specifies the simultaneous, capture-avoiding substitution of terms $t_1, \ldots, t_n$ for $v_1, \ldots, v_n$ in the term matched by ν.

Example 7. Below are a few examples illustrating our second-order pattern language. For the precise definition of the language, see [16].

  - Pattern $\nu + \nu$ matches the term $1 + 1$, but does not match the term $1 + 2$.
  - The term $\lambda x.x + 1$ is matched by the pattern $\lambda x.\nu[x]$, but not by the pattern $\lambda x.\nu$.
  - Pattern $\lambda x.\nu[x] + \nu[1]$ matches terms $\lambda y.y + 1$ and $\lambda z.2 * z + 2 * 1$.

5.2 Simplified Patterns

Before a second-order pattern is added to a discrimination tree, we simplify it by replacing all second-order variable instances with a "wildcard" pattern and by re-interpreting first-order variables as matching an arbitrary first-order variable. The language of *simplified patters* is the following:

$$
\begin{aligned}
p &::= \_ &&\text{the wildcard pattern} \\
&\mid \; operator(\overline{p}_1, \ldots, \overline{p}_n) &&\text{a pattern with } n \text{ subterms} \\
&\mid \; v &&\text{stands for an arbitrary first-order variable} \\
\overline{p} &::= (i, p) &&i \text{ stands for the number of binding occurrences}
\end{aligned}
$$

A matching relation can be defined on term patterns $t \simeq p$ as follows. First any term t matches the wildcard pattern $t \simeq \_$. For the inductive case, the term $t = operator(\overline{t}_1, \ldots, \overline{t}_n)$ matches the pattern $p = operator(\overline{p}_1, \ldots, \overline{p}_n)$ iff $\overline{t}_j \simeq \overline{p}_j$ for all $j \in \{1, \ldots, n\}$. A subterm $v_1, \ldots, v_m.t$ matches a subpattern (m, p) iff $t \simeq p$.

In many cases when the term table is constructed, a term will match several patterns. In general, the table should return the most *specific* match. Any non-wildcard pattern is considered more specific than the wildcard one and two patterns with the same top-level operator and arities are compared according to the lexicographical order of the lists of their immediate subpatterns.

5.3 Implementation

The term tables are implemented by collecting the simplified patterns into discrimination trees. Each pattern in the tree is associated with the corresponding value, as well as with the rewriting engine bytecode that could be used to check whether a potential match is a faithful second-order match. When adding a new pattern to a tree, we make sure that the order of the entries in the tree is consistent with the "more specific" relation.

As described in the beginning of this Section, our term table implementation provides a choice of several lookup functions. In addition to choosing between returning just the most specific match and returning all matches, the caller also gets to choose whether to check potential matches with the rewriting engine (which is slower, but more accurate) or not (which is faster, but may return false positives).

In order to take advantage of the caching features of the resources mechanism, the interface for building term tables is incremental – it allows extending the tables functionally by adding one pattern at a time. In order to make the interface easier to use, we provide a function that returns an appropriate resource `description` (see Section 3) where the `'intermediate` type is a term table and only the `retrieve` field needs to be provided by the user.

6   Resource-Driven Tactics in MetaPRL

The resource mechanisms described in the previous sections are a big part of all the most commonly used tactics in MetaPRL. In this Section we will describe some of the most heavily used MetaPRL resources. The goal of this chapter, however, is not to describe some particular MetaPRL tactics, but to give an impression of the wide range of tactics that the resource mechanisms could be used to implement.

Those who are interested in full details of a particular tactic implementation may find additional information in [11].

6.1   The "n-th Hypothesis" Tactic

The "*conclusion immediately follows from the n-th hypothesis*" tactic ("nthHypT") is probably the simplest resource-based tactic in MetaPRL. It is designed to prove sequents like $\Gamma; T; \Delta \vdash T$, $\Gamma; x : T; \Delta[x] \vdash T$ Type, and $\Gamma; x : Void; \Delta[x] \vdash C[x]$, where the conclusion of the sequent immediately follows from a hypothesis.

The nthHypT is implemented via a term table resource that maps terms to int -> tactic. The input to the nth_hyp resource is a term containing both the hypothesis and the conclusion packed together and the output is the corresponding tactic that is supposed to be able to prove in full any goals of that form. As in Example 3, the code of the tactic itself takes just a few lines:

```
let nthHypT p n =
    let t = make_pair_term (get_nth_hyp p n) (get_concl p) in
        lookup (get_nth_hyp_resource p) t n
```

where p is the current proof obligation and n is the hypothesis number (same as in Example 3).

MetaPRL also implements the annotations for this resource – whenever a rule is annotated with {| nth_hyp |}, MetaPRL would check whether the annotated rule has the correct form and if so, if will pair its hypothesis with its conclusion and add the corresponding entry to the nth_hyp resource.

6.2   The Auto Tactic

In addition to the decomposition tactic we have already mentioned, the generic proof search automation tactics are among the most often used in MetaPRL. We have two such tactics. The autoT tactic attempts to prove a goal "automatically," and the trivialT tactic proves goals that are "trivial." The resource mechanism allowed us to provide a *generic* implementation of these two tactics. In fact, the implementation turns out to be surprisingly simple – all of the work in automatic proving is implemented by the resource mechanism and in descendant theories.

The auto resource builds collections of tactics specified by a data structure with the following type:

```
type auto_info =
    { auto_name : string;
      auto_tac : tactic;
      auto_prec : auto_prec;
      auto_type : auto_type;
    }
```

```
and auto_type =
   AutoTrivial
 | AutoNormal
 | AutoComplete
```

The auto_name is the name used to describe the entry (for debugging purposes). The auto_tac is the actual tactic to try. auto_prec is used to divide the
entries into precedence levels; tactics with higher precedence are applied first.

Finally, auto_type specifies how autoT and trivialT will use each particular
entry. AutoTrivial entries are the only ones used by trivialT; autoT attempts
using them before any other entries. AutoComplete will be used by autoT after
all AutoTrivial and AutoNormal entries are exhausted; it will consider an application of an AutoComplete entry to be successful only if it would be able to
completely prove all subgoals generated by it.

The onSomeHypT nthHypT ("try finding a hypothesis nthHypT would apply
to" – see Section 6.1) is an important part of the trivialT tactic and dT 0 –
the intro part of the decomposition tactic – is an important part of the autoT
tactic. As we will see in Section 6.4, parts of dT 0 are added to the AutoNormal
level of autoT and the rest – at the AutoComplete level.

6.3   Type Inference

Another very interesting example of a resource-driven approach in MetaPRL is
type inference. There are several factors that make it stand out. First, the type
inference resource is used to create a recursive function, with each data item
responsible for a specific recursive case. Second, the output type of the type
inference resource is not a tactic, but rather a helper function that can be used
in various other tactics.

The type inference resource is complicated (unfortunately), so we will start
by presenting a very simplified version of the resource. Suppose, the pair operator
and the Cartesian product type is added to a logic and we want to augment the
type inference resource. In first approximation, this would look something like

```
let typeinf_pair infer t =
   let a, b = destruct_pair_term t in
      construct_product_term (infer a) (infer b)

let resource typeinf += (⟨a, b⟩, typeinf_pair)
```

where the infer argument to the typeinf_pair function is the type inference
function *itself*, allowing for the recursive call. The typeinf resource would be
implemented as a term lookup table (see Section 5) and will therefore have the
input type term and the output type inference_fun -> inference_fun, where
inference_fun is defined as term -> term.

Once the table resource is defined, the actual type inference function can be
defined simply as follows:

```
let infer_type p =
  let table = get_typeinf_resource p in
  let rec infer t = lookup table t infer t in
    infer
```

where p is the current proof obligation (same as in Example 3). Above, lookup table t returns the appropriate inference_fun -> inference_fun function which, given the infer itself returns the inference_fun function which is then used to infer the type of the term t.

MetaPRL currently has two different implementations of a type inference algorithm. Both implementations are similar to the simplified one outlined above, except the inference_fun type would be more complicated.

The first implementation is used *as a heuristic* for inferring a type of expressions in a Martin-Löf style type theory. There the type is defined as

```
type typeinf_fun =
  ty_var_set -> var_env -> eqnlist -> opt_eqns -> var_env -> term
    -> eqnlist * opt_eqns * var_env * term
```

An inference function takes as arguments: a set of variables that should be treated as constants when we use unification, a mapping from variable names to the types these variables were declared with, a list of equations we have on our type variables, a list of optional equations (that could be used when there is not enough information in the main equations, but do not have to be satisfied), a list of default values for type variables (that can be used when the equations do not provide enough information), and a term whose type we want to infer. It returns the updated equations, the updated optional equations, the updated defaults and the type (possibly containing new variables). The corresponding infer_type would call the infer function and then use unification to get the final answer.

The second implementation is used for inferring a type of expressions in an ML-like language with a decidable type inference algorithm and it is a little simpler than the type theory one, but is still pretty complicated.

In future we are hoping to add resource annotation (at least some partial one) support to the type inference resources, however it is not obvious whether we would be able to find a sufficiently general (yet simple) way of implementing the annotations. For now the type inference resources have to be maintained by manually adding entries to it, which is pretty complicated (even the authors of these resources have to look up the inference_fun type definitions once in a while to remind themselves of the exact structure of the resource) Because of such complexity this solution is not yet fully satisfactory.

6.4 Decomposition Tactic

As we have mentioned in Examples 1, 3 and 5, in MetaPRL the decomposition tactic ("dT") is implemented using two resources. The intro resource is used to collect introduction rules; and the elim resource is used to collect elimination rules. The components of both resources take a term that describes the shape of the goals to which they apply, and a tactic to use when goals of that form are recognized. The elim resource takes a tactic of type int -> tactic (the tactic takes the number of the hypothesis to which it applies), and the intro resource takes a tactic of type tactic.

The resources also allow resource annotations in rule definitions. Typically, the annotation is added to explicit introduction or elimination rules, like the following:

$$\text{rule and\_intro \{| intro [] |\}:} \quad \frac{\Gamma \vdash A \qquad \Gamma \vdash B}{\Gamma \vdash A \wedge B}$$

Once this rule is defined, an application of the tactic dT 0 to a conjunction will result in an application of the and_intro rule.

The intro resource annotations take a list of optional arguments of the following type:

```
type intro_option =
    SelectOption of int
  | IntroArgsOption of (proof_obl -> term -> term) * term option
  | AutoMustComplete
  | CondMustComplete of proof_obl -> bool
```

The SelectOption is used for rules that require a selection argument. For instance, the disjunction introduction rule has two forms for the left and right-hand forms.

$$\text{rule or\_intro\_left \{| intro [SelectOption 1] |\}:} \quad \frac{\Gamma \vdash A}{\Gamma \vdash A \vee B}$$

$$\text{rule or\_intro\_right \{| intro [SelectOption 2] |\}:} \quad \frac{\Gamma \vdash B}{\Gamma \vdash A \vee B}$$

These options require selT arguments: the left rule is applied with selT 1 (dT 0) and the right rule is applied with selT 2 (dT 0).

The IntroArgsOption is used to *infer* arguments to the rule. A typical usage would have the form

$$\text{rule apply\_type \{| intro [intro\_typeinf } a \text{] |\} } A :$$
$$\frac{\Gamma \vdash f \in (A \rightarrow B) \qquad \Gamma \vdash a \in A}{\Gamma \vdash (f\,a) \in B}$$

where intro_typeinf is an appropriate IntroArgsOption option that uses the type inference resource (Section 6.3). Once such rule is added to the system, whenever a proof obligation has the form $\cdots \vdash (f\,a) \in B$, dT 0 would attempt to infer the type of the corresponding a and use such type as an argument to the apply_type rule.

The AutoMustComplete option can be used to indicate that the autoT tactic (see Section 6.2) should not use this rule unless it is capable of finishing the proof on its own. This option is used to mark irreversible rules that may take a provable goal and produce potentially unprovable subgoals. The CondMustComplete option is a conditional version of `AutoMustComplete`; it is used to pass in a predicate controlling when to activate the `AutoMustComplete`.

The `elim` resource options are defined with the following type:

```
type elim_option =
    ThinOption of (int -> tactic)
  | ElimArgsOption of (proof_obl -> term -> term list) * term option
```

The `ElimArgsOption` provides the tactic with a way to find correct rule arguments in the same way as the `IntroArgsOption` does it in the `intro` case. The `ThinOption` is an argument that provides an optional tactic to "thin" the hypothesis after application of the elimination rule.

The `dT` resources are implemented as term tables that store the term descriptions and tactics for "decomposition" reasoning. The `dT` tactic selects the most appropriate rule for a given goal and applies it. The (`dT 0`) tactic is added to the `auto` resource by default.

6.5   Term Reduction and Simplification Tactic

The resource mechanisms are also widely used in MetaPRL *rewriting* tactics. The best example of such a tactic is the `reduceC` reduction and simplification tactic, which reduces a term by applying standard reductions. For example, the type theory defines several standard reductions, some of which are listed below. When a term is reduced, the `reduceC` tactic applies these rewrites to its subterms in outermost order.

```
rewrite beta {| reduce |}:  (λv.ν₁[v]) ν₂ ⟷ ν₁[ν₂]
rewrite pair {| reduce |}:
```
$$\textbf{rewrite beta } \{|\text{ reduce }|\}\colon\ (\lambda v.\nu_1[v])\ \nu_2 \longleftrightarrow \nu_1[\nu_2]$$
$$\textbf{rewrite pair } \{|\text{ reduce }|\}\colon$$
$$(\textbf{match }(\nu_1,\nu_2)\ \textbf{with }(u,v)\rightarrow \nu_3[u,v]) \longleftrightarrow \nu_3[\nu_1,\nu_2]$$

The `reduce` resource is implemented as a term table that, given a term, returns a rewrite tactic to be applied to that term. The `reduceC` rewrite tactic is then constructed in two phases: the `reduceTopC` tactic applies the appropriate rewrite to a term without examining subterms, and the `reduceC` is constructed from tacticals (rewrite tacticals are also called conversionals), as follows.

```
let reduceC = repeatC (higherC reduceTopC)
```

The `higherC` conversional searches for the outermost subterms where a rewrite applies, and the `repeatC` conversional applies the rewrite repeatedly until no more progress can be made.

7   Conclusions and Related Work

The discrimination trees and other term-indexed data structures are a standard technique in a large number of theorem provers. The main novelties of our term tables approach is in the integration with the rest of the resources mechanism and in usage of the rewriting engine to perform matching against second-order patterns.

A number of provers include some term-indexed and/or context-sensitive and/or updatable tactics. Examples include the decomposition and Auto tactics in NuPRL [14], *simplification tactics* in Isabelle [17], *table tactics* in the Ergo theorem prover [19]. Our goal however was to provide a *generic* mechanism that allows for easy creation of new scoped updatable tactics and, even more importantly, provides a very simple mechanism for updating all these tactics is a *consistent* fashion.

While initially the mechanisms presented in this paper were only meant to simplify the implementation of a few specific tactics (mainly the decomposition tactic), the simplicity and easy-of-use of this approach gradually turned it into the core mechanism for implementing and maintaining tactics in the MetaPRL theorem prover.

Acknowledgments

We are very grateful to Carl Witty, Alexei Kopylov and anonymous reviewers for extremely valuable discussions and feedback.

References

1. Stuart Allen, Robert Constable, Richard Eaton, Christoph Kreitz, and Lori Lorigo. The NuPRL open logical environment. In David McAllester, editor, *Proceedings of the 17ᵗʰ International Conference on Automated Deduction*, volume 1831 of *Lecture Notes in Artificial Intelligence*, pages 170–176. Springer Verlag, 2000.
2. Bruno Barras, Samuel Boutin, Cristina Cornes, Judicaël Courant, Jean-Christophe Filliâtre, Eduardo Giménez, Hugo Herbelin, Gérard-Mohring, Amokrane Saïbi, and Benjamin Werner. *The Coq Proof Assistant Reference Manual*. INRIA-Rocquencourt, CNRS and ENS Lyon, 1996.
3. Jim Christian. Flatterms, discrimination nets, and fast term rewriting. *Journal of Automated Reasoning*, 10(1):95–113, February 1993.
4. Robert L. Constable, Stuart F. Allen, H. M. Bromley, W. R. Cleaveland, J. F. Cremer, R. W. Harper, Douglas J. Howe, T. B. Knoblock, N. P. Mendler, P. Panangaden, James T. Sasaki, and Scott F. Smith. *Implementing Mathematics with the NuPRL Proof Development System*. Prentice-Hall, NJ, 1986.
5. Judy Crow, Sam Owre, John Rushby, Natarajan Shankar, and Mandayam Srivas. A tutorial introduction to PVS. In *WIFT '95: Workshop on Industrial-Strength Formal Specification Techniques*, April 1995. http://www.csl.sri.com/sri-csl-fm.html.
6. Michael Gordon and Tom Melham. *Introduction to HOL: A Theorem Proving Environment for Higher-Order Logic*. Cambridge University Press, Cambridge, 1993.
7. Peter Graf. *Term Indexing*, volume 1053 of *Lecture Notes in Artificial Intelligence*. Springer, 1995.
8. Jason Hickey and Aleksey Nogin. Extensible pretty-printer specifications. In preparation.
9. Jason Hickey, Aleksey Nogin, Robert L. Constable, Brian E. Aydemir, Eli Barzilay, Yegor Bryukhov, Richard Eaton, Adam Granicz, Alexei Kopylov, Christoph Kreitz, Vladimir N. Krupski, Lori Lorigo, Stephan Schmitt, Carl Witty, and Xin Yu. MetaPRL – A modular logical environment. In David Basin and Burkhart Wolff, editors, *Proceedings of the 16ᵗʰ International Conference on Theorem Proving in Higher Order Logics (TPHOLs 2003)*, volume 2758 of *Lecture Notes in Computer Science*, pages 287–303. Springer-Verlag, 2003.

10. Jason J. Hickey. NuPRL-Light: An implementation framework for higher-order logics. In William McCune, editor, *Proceedings of the 14th International Conference on Automated Deduction*, volume 1249 of *Lecture Notes in Artificial Intelligence*, pages 395–399. Springer, July 13–17 1997. An extended version of the paper can be found at http://www.cs.caltech.edu/~jyh/papers/cade14_nl/default.html.

11. Jason J. Hickey, Brian Aydemir, Yegor Bryukhov, Alexei Kopylov, Aleksey Nogin, and Xin Yu. A listing of MetaPRL theories. http://metaprl.org/theories.pdf.

12. Jason J. Hickey and Aleksey Nogin. Fast tactic-based theorem proving. In J. Harrison and M. Aagaard, editors, *Theorem Proving in Higher Order Logics: 13th International Conference, TPHOLs 2000*, volume 1869 of *Lecture Notes in Computer Science*, pages 252–266. Springer-Verlag, 2000.

13. Jason J. Hickey, Aleksey Nogin, Alexei Kopylov, et al. MetaPRL home page. http://metaprl.org/.

14. Paul B. Jackson. *Enhancing the NuPRL Proof Development System and Applying it to Computational Abstract Algebra*. PhD thesis, Cornell University, Ithaca, NY, January 1995.

15. Xavier Leroy. *The Objective Caml system release 1.07*. INRIA, France, May 1997.

16. Aleksey Nogin and Jason Hickey. Sequent schema for derived rules. In Victor A. Carreño, Cézar A. Muñoz, and Sophiène Tahar, editors, *Proceedings of the 15th International Conference on Theorem Proving in Higher Order Logics (TPHOLs 2002)*, volume 2410 of *Lecture Notes in Computer Science*, pages 281–297. Springer-Verlag, 2002.

17. L. Paulson and T. Nipkow. Isabelle tutorial and user's manual. Technical report, University of Cambridge Computing Laboratory, 1990.

18. Lawrence C. Paulson. *Isabelle: A Generic Theorem Prover*, volume 828 of *Lecture Notes in Computer Science*. Springer-Verlag, New York, 1994.

19. Mark Utting, Peter Robinson, and Ray Nickson. Ergo 6: A generic proof engine that uses Prolog proof technology. *Journal of Computation and Mathematics*, 5:194–219, 2002.

20. Pierre Weis and Xavier Leroy. *Le langage Caml*. Dunod, Paris, 2nd edition, 1999. In French.

Theorem Reuse by Proof Term Transformation

Einar Broch Johnsen[1] and Christoph Lüth[2]

[1] Department of Informatics, University of Oslo, Norway
`einarj@ifi.uio.no`
[2] FB 3 – Mathematics and Computer Science, Universität Bremen, Germany
`cxl@informatik.uni-bremen.de`

Abstract. Proof reuse addresses the issue of how proofs of theorems in a specific setting can be used to prove other theorems in different settings. This paper proposes an approach where theorems are generalised by *abstracting* their proofs from the original setting. The approach is based on a representation of proofs as logical framework proof terms, using the theorem prover Isabelle. The logical framework allows type-specific inference rules to be handled uniformly in the abstraction process and the prover's automated proof tactics may be used freely. This way, established results become more generally applicable; for example, theorems about a data type can be reapplied to other types. The paper also considers how to reapply such abstracted theorems, and suggests an approach based on mappings between operations and types, and on systematically exploiting the dependencies between theorems.

1 Introduction

Formal proof and development requires considerable effort, which can be reduced through reuse of established results. Often, a new datatype or theory resembles a previously developed one and there is considerable gain if theorems can carry over from one type to another. Previous work in this area addresses reuse by proof or tactic modification in response to changes in the proof goal such as modifying the constructors of a datatype, or unfortunate variable instantiations during a proof search [6, 7, 14, 22, 26]. In contrast, type-theoretic approaches [12, 13, 20] investigate the generalisation and modification of proofs by transforming the associated proof terms in the context of constructive type theory. This paper proposes a method for abstracting previously established theorems by proof transformations in a logical framework with proof terms. Logical frameworks are particularly well-suited for this approach, because inference rules are represented as formulae in the formalism; the choice of object logic becomes independent of the meta-logic in which the proof terms live.

The method we propose has been implemented in Isabelle [16], using the proof terms recently added by Berghofer and Nipkow [4]. Isabelle offers a wide range of powerful tactics and libraries, and we can work in any of the logics encoded into Isabelle, such as classical higher-order logic (HOL), Zermelo-Fraenkel set theory (ZF), and various modal logics [17]. However, the approach should be applicable to any logical framework style theorem prover.

K. Slind et al. (Eds.): TPHOLs 2004, LNCS 3223, pp. 152–167, 2004.
© Springer-Verlag Berlin Heidelberg 2004

The paper is organised as follows. Sect. 2 presents the different proof transformations of the abstraction method and Sect. 3 discusses how the transformations are implemented as functions on Isabelle's proof terms. Sect. 4 considers how to reuse abstracted theorems in a different setting, and demonstrates our approach in practice. Sect. 5 considers related work and we conclude in Sect. 6.

2   Generalising Theorems by Proof Transformation

This section proposes a method for abstracting theorems in logical frameworks by means of proof transformations, in order to derive generally applicable inference rules from specific theorems. A logical framework [8,19] is a meta-level inference system which can be used to specify other, object-level, deductive systems. Well-known examples of implementations of logical frameworks are Elf [18], λProlog [15], and Isabelle [17]. The work presented uses Isabelle, the meta-logic of which is intuitionistic higher-order logic extended with Hindley-Milner polymorphism and type classes.

In the logical framework, the formulae of an object logic is represented by higher-order abstract syntax and object logic derivability by a predicate on the terms of the meta-logic: Meta-level implication $\Longrightarrow$ reflects object level derivability. Object logics are represented by axioms encoding the axioms and inference rules of the object logic. The meta-logic is typed, with a special type *prop* of logical formulae (propositions); object logics extend the type system. The meta-level quantifier $\bigwedge$ can range over terms of any type, including *prop*. The logical framework allows us to prove theorems directly in the meta-logic. The correctness of all instantiations of a meta-logic theorem, or *schema*, follows from the correctness of the representation of the rules of the object logic. Theorems established in the meta-logic are derived inference rules of the object logic. Hence, new object logic inference rules can be derived within the logical language.

For the presentation of the abstraction method, we consider a proof π of a theorem ϕ, consisting of a series of inference steps in the meta-logic. The proposed generalisation process will transform π in a stepwise manner into a proof of a schematic theorem which may be instantiated in any other setting, i.e. a derived inference rule of the logic. The process consists of three phases:

1. making assumptions explicit;
2. abstracting function symbols;
3. abstracting type constants.

Each step in this process results in a proof of a theorem, obtained by transforming the proof of the theorem from the previous step. In order to replace function symbols by variables, all relevant information about these symbols, such as defining axioms, must be made explicit. In order to replace a type constant by a type variable, function symbols of this type must have been replaced by variables. Hence, each phase of the transformation assumes that the necessary steps of the previous phases have already occurred. The final step results in a proof π' from which we derive a schematic theorem $\psi \Longrightarrow \phi'$, where ϕ' is a modification of the initial formula ϕ. In such theorems, the formulae of ψ are called *applicability conditions* as they identify theorems that are needed to successfully apply the derived rule. A necessary precondition for the second abstraction step is that the logical framework allows for higher-order variables, and for the third step that the logical framework allows for type variables.

It is in principle possible to abstract over all theorems, function symbols, and types occurring in a proof. However, such theorems are hard to use; for applicability, it is essential to strike a balance between abstracting too much and too little. Some tactics guiding the application of abstracted theorems are considered in Sect. 4.

2.1   Making Proof Assumptions Explicit

In tactical theorem provers such as Isabelle, the use of auxiliary theorems in a proof may be hidden to the user, due to the automated proof techniques. These contextual dependencies of a theorem can be made explicit by inspecting its proof term. In a natural deduction proof, auxiliary theorems can be introduced as leaf nodes in open branches of the proof tree.

Given an open branch with a leaf node theorem in the proof, we can close the branch by the implication introduction rule, thus transforming the conclusion of the proof. By closing all open branches in this manner, every auxiliary theorem used in the proof becomes visible in the root formula of the proof. To illustrate this process, let us reconsider the proof π of theorem ϕ. At the leaf node of an open branch π_i in the proof we find a theorem, say $\psi_i(x_1^i, \ldots, x_{k_i}^i)$. We close the branch π_i by applying $\Longrightarrow$-introduction at the root of the proof, which leads to a proof of a formula $\forall x_1^i, \ldots, x_{k_i}^i \ \psi_i(x_1^i, \ldots, x_{k_i}^i) \Longrightarrow \phi$, where ψ_i has been transformed into a closed formula ψ_i' by quantifying over free variables, to respect variable scoping. The transformation of a branch is illustrated in Figure 1. This process is repeated for every branch in π with a relevant theorem in its leaf node. If we need to make j theorems explicit, we thereby derive a proof π' of the formula $(\psi_1' \wedge \ldots \wedge \psi_j') \Longrightarrow \phi$.

Generally, we may assume that a leaf node theorem is stronger than necessary for the specific proof. Therefore, it is possible to modify the applicability conditions of the derived theorem in order to make these easier to prove in a new setting. For example, if ψ_i is simplified by an elimination rule in the branch, we may (repeatedly) cut off the branch above the weaker theorem before closing the branch. Proofs in higher-order natural deduction can be converted into a normal form where all elimination rules appear above the introduction rules in each branch of the proof [21]. With this procedure, proofs on normal form result in the weakest possible applicability conditions, but proofs on normal form are not required for the abstraction process and proof normalisation is therefore not considered in this paper. Furthermore, if ψ_i is the leaf node theorem of an open branch in the proof π and all leaf node theorems in open branches in the proof of ψ_i are included among the leaf node theorems of other open branches of π, expanding π with the proof of ψ_i at appropriate leaf nodes before the proof transformation will remove superfluous applicability conditions from the derived

Fig. 1. The transformation and closure of a branch in the proof, binding the free variable x of the leaf node formula.

theorem. The usefulness of these improvements depends on the form of the proof and may cause considerable growth in the size of the proof term. An alternative is to consider the dependency graph between theorems (see Sect. 4.4). Our present approach is to transform the proof as it is given.

2.2   Abstracting Function Symbols

The next phase of the transformation process consists of replacing function symbols by variables. When all implicit assumptions concerning a function symbol F have been made explicit, as in the transformed theorem above, all relevant information about this function symbol is contained within the new theorem. The function symbol has become an *eigenvariable* because the proof of the theorem is independent of the context with regard to this function symbol. Such function symbols can be replaced by variables throughout the proof. Let $\phi[x/t]$ and $\pi[x/t]$ denote substitution, replacing t by x in a formula ϕ or proof π, renaming bound variables as needed to avoid variable capture.

A central idea in logical framework encodings is to represent object logic variables by meta-logic variables [19], which are placeholders for meta-logic terms. Hereafter, all free variables will be meta-variables and the abstraction process replaces function symbols by meta-variables. If the function symbol F is of type τ and a is a meta-variable of this type, the theorem $(\psi'_1 \wedge \ldots \wedge \psi'_i) \implies \phi$ may be further transformed into

$$(\psi'_1[a/F] \wedge \ldots \wedge \psi'_i[a/F]) \implies \phi[a/F], \tag{1}$$

by transforming the proof π' into a new proof $\pi'[a/F]$.

2.3   Abstracting Types

When all function symbols depending on a given type have been replaced by term variables, the name of the type is arbitrary. In fact, we can now replace such type constants by free type variables. The higher-order resolution mechanism of the theorem prover will then instantiate type variables as well as term variables when we attempt to apply the derived inference rule to a proof goal. However, the formal languages used by theorem provers have structured types which may give rise to type-specific inference rules. When these occur in the proofs, they must also be made explicit for type abstraction to work. This is illustrated by the following example.

2.4 Example

We assume as object logic a higher-order equational logic, with axioms including symmetry (sym), reflexivity ($refl$), etc. In this object logic, consider a theory including the standard operations 0, S, $+$, and axioms defining addition and induction on the type N of natural numbers:

$$ax1 \equiv x + 0 = x \qquad ax2 \equiv x + Sy = S(x + y)$$
$$ind \equiv [\![p(0); \bigwedge t.p(t) \Longrightarrow p(St)]\!] \Longrightarrow p(x).$$

A proof of $x + 0 = 0 + x$ in this theory is as follows, slightly edited for brevity:

$$(2)$$

Applying the first step of the abstraction method, all theorems from the theory become assumptions, which results in a proof of the following theorem:

$$[\![[\![p(0); \bigwedge t.p(t) \Longrightarrow p(St)]\!] \Longrightarrow p(x); x + 0 = x; x + Sy = S(x + y))]\!]$$
$$\Longrightarrow x + 0 = 0 + x$$

In the second and third step of the process, we first replace 0, S, and $+$ by the meta-variables a, b, and c, respectively. When this is done, we can replace the type constant N with a free type variable α, resulting in a proof of the theorem

$$[\![[\![p(a); \bigwedge t.p(t) \Longrightarrow p(b(t))]\!] \Longrightarrow p(x); c(x, a) = x; c(x, b(y)) = b(c(x, y))]\!]$$
$$\Longrightarrow c(x, a) = c(a, x),$$

which can be applied as an inference rule to a formula of any type. In order to discharge the applicability conditions of the inference rule, the formula representing the induction rule must be a theorem for the new type.

3 Implementation of the Abstraction Techniques

Under the Curry-Howard isomorphism, proofs correspond to terms in a typed λ-calculus. We have implemented the abstraction processes from Sect. 2 in the theorem prover Isabelle, which records proofs as meta-logic proof terms. The user can use all of Isabelle's automatic and semi-automatic proof infrastructure and Isabelle automatically constructs the corresponding meta-logic proof term [4]. Given a proof term, a theorem may be derived by replaying the meta-logic inference rules. We use this facility to derive new theorems: Given a theorem to abstract, we obtain its proof term, perform appropriate transformations on the proof term and replay the derived proof term to obtain a generalised theorem. Hence, the correctness of the derived theorem is guaranteed by the Isabelle's replay facility for proof terms. The implementation of abstraction functions does not impose any restrictions on the proof or the theorem: The abstraction process can be applied to any theorem, including those from Isabelle's standard libraries.

3.1   Proof Terms

This section introduces Isabelle's proof terms, which may be presented as

$$p ::= h \mid c_{[\tau_n/\alpha_n]} \mid \lambda h : \phi.p \mid \lambda x :: \tau.p \mid p \cdot p \mid p\, t \tag{3}$$

where h, c, x, t, ϕ, α, and τ denote proof variables, proof constants, term variables, terms of arbitrary type, propositions, type variables, and types, respectively. The language defined by (3) allows for abstraction over term and proof variables, and application of proofs and terms to proofs, corresponding to the introduction and elimination of $\bigwedge$ and $\Longrightarrow$. Proof terms live in an environment which maps proof variables to terms representing propositions and term variables to their type. Proof constants correspond to axioms or already proved theorems. For more details and formal definitions, including the definition of provability in this setting, see [4].

Proof terms can be illustrated by the example of Proof (2). We identify theorem names with proof constants: $ax1$, $ax2$, $refl$, etc. The leftmost branch of the proof consists of the axiom $refl \equiv x = x$, with x instantiated by 0. This is reflected by the proof term

$$\pi_1 = refl\ 0.$$

The middle branch introduces a meta-implication in the proof term

$$\pi_2 = (\lambda H : (\bigwedge x : N.x + 0 = 0 + x).\ \psi),$$

where ψ represents the body of the proof term (omitted here). The proof variable H represents an arbitrary proof of the proposition $\bigwedge x : N.x + 0 = 0 + x$ and is introduced by proof term λ-abstraction. We can refer to a proof of this proposition in the proof term ψ by the proof variable H. The whole proof term for (2) becomes

$$\pi = ind\,(\lambda u.\,u + 0 = 0 + u)\,x \cdot \pi_1 \cdot \pi_2.$$

The premises π_1 and π_2, which correspond to the base case and the induction step, are applied to the induction rule ind, reflecting elimination of meta-implication. In contrast to proof level λ-abstraction, term level λ-abstraction allows the higher-order variable p in ind to be instantiated with $\lambda u.\,u + 0 = 0 + u$.

3.2   Implementing Abstraction by Proof Term Transformations

The abstractions presented in Sect. 2 are implemented as functions which take theorems to theorems by transforming proof terms.

In proof terms, assumptions are represented by proof constants corresponding to previously proved theorems. For example, the proof term π above contains proof constants $ax1$, $ax2$ and ind, which can now be lifted to applicability conditions as described in Sect. 2.1. This is done by adding a proof term λ-abstraction outside the proof term and replacing occurrences of the theorem inside the proof term with an appropriate variable. After abstraction over $ax1$ and $ax2$ (omitting the lengthy but similar abstraction over ind), we obtain the proof term

$$\phi = \lambda H : (\bigwedge x\,y : N.x + Sy = S(x+y)).\lambda H' : (\bigwedge x : N.x + 0 = x).\pi[ax1/H', ax2/H]$$

which can be replayed to yield the following theorem:

$$[\![\forall x, y \cdot x + Sy = S(x+y); \forall x \cdot x + 0 = x]\!] \implies x + 0 = 0 + x$$

Internally, deBruijn indices are used for bound variables, which explains the occurrence of H' in the second proof term. This gives a first simple version of the theorem abstraction function: traverse the proof tree, replace all nodes referring to the theorem we want to abstract over with the appropriate deBruijn index, and add a λ-abstraction in front of the proof term.

When we use a theorem in a proof, both schematic and type variables are instantiated. If we make the theorem an applicability condition we need to quantify over both the schematic and type variables, hence the meta-quantification in H and H' above. However, abstraction over type variables is not possible in the Hindley-Milner type system of Isabelle's meta-logic, where type variables are always implicitly quantified at the outermost level. Instead, distinct assumptions must be provided for each type instance. For example, a proof of the theorem

$$map\,(f \cdot g)\,x = map\,f\,(map\,g\,x), \tag{4}$$

contains three different type instances of the definition of map for non-empty lists $map\,f\,(Cons\,x\,y) = Cons\,(f\,x)\,(map\,f\,y)$.

At the implementation level, abstracting operations (Sect. 2.2) and types (Sect. 2.3) is more straightforward. Traversing the proof term we replace operations and types by schematic and type variables, respectively. When abstracting over polymorphic operations, we need distinct variables for each type instance of the operation symbol, similar to the theorems above. If we consider map in Theorem (4), we need to abstract over each of the three type instances separately, resulting in three different function variables.

3.3   Abstraction over Theories

The previously defined *elementary abstraction functions* operate on single theorems, operations, and types. For a more high-level approach, *abstraction tactics* may be defined, which combine series of elementary abstraction steps.

An example of such a tactic is *abstraction over theories*. A theory in Isabelle can be thought of as a signature defining type constructors and operations, and a collection of theorems. Theories are organised hierarchically, so all theorems established in ancestor theories remain valid.

The tactic abstracts a theorem which belongs to a theory T_1 into an ancestor theory T_2. It collects all theorems, operations, and types from the proof term which do not occur in T_2, and applies elementary tactics recursively to abstract over each, starting with theorems and continuing with function symbols and types. Finally, the derived proof term is replayed in the ancestor theory, thus establishing the validity of the abstracted theorem in the theory T_2 [1].

Abstraction over all theorems, function symbols, and types will generally lead to theorems which are hard to reuse. In the next section, we will consider tactics which aid in the abstraction and reuse of abstracted theorems.

4   Reapplying Abstracted Theorems

This section considers different examples of abstraction, and scenarios to reapply abstracted theorems. As part of our experimentation with the abstraction method, we have generalised approximately 200 theorems from Isabelle's libraries, and reapplied these. A systematic approach to reapplication is suggested in order to facilitate reuse of sets of theorems.

4.1   Simple Abstraction and Reuse

A simple example of abstraction and reuse is to derive a theorem about natural numbers by abstraction from the theorem $\texttt{append\_Nil2} \equiv x \, @ \, [\,] = x$ about lists. Applying the abstraction tactic $\texttt{abs\_to\_thy}$ described in Sect. 3.3, we derive a theorem independent of the theory of lists:

$$
\begin{aligned}
&[\![\forall P \, l. \, [\![P \, nil \, ; \, \forall a \, l. \, P \, l \Longrightarrow P \, (cons \, a \, l)]\!] \Longrightarrow P \, l; \\
&\quad \forall y. \, app \, nil \, y = y \, ; \\
&\quad \forall u \, x \, y. \, app \, (cons \, u \, x) \, y = cons \, u \, (app \, x \, y)]\!] \\
&\qquad \Longrightarrow app \, x \, nil = x
\end{aligned}
\tag{5}
$$

The abstraction process introduces new names for the constant $[\,]$ and the infix operator $@$, favouring lexically suitable variable names.

We can now use this theorem to show that $x + 0 = x$. We proceed in two stages: we first instantiate the variables nil with 0, app with $+$ and $cons$ with $\lambda x.Suc$ (note we need the vacuous argument x here). This yields

$$
\begin{aligned}
&[\![\forall P \, l. \, [\![P \, 0; \, \forall a \, l. \, P \, l \Longrightarrow P \, (Suc \, l)]\!] \Longrightarrow P \, l; \\
&\quad \forall y. \, y + 0 = y; \\
&\quad \forall u \, x \, y. \, Suc \, x + y = Suc(x + y) \,]\!] \Longrightarrow x + 0 = x.
\end{aligned}
$$

---

[1] Due to Isabelle's typeclasses an operation which is defined in T may not occur in the signature of T directly; in this case, the user has to explicitly give the operation.

The premises correspond to well-known theorems about natural numbers (induction and the definition of $+$). Resolving with these, we obtain the theorem $x + 0 = x$. Apart from the small simplification step required by moving from a parametric to a non-parametric type, this process can be completely automated.

4.2   Change of Data Representation

A more challenging situation occurs when we want to implement a datatype by another one. For example, suppose we implement the unary representation of natural numbers by a binary representation, which may be given as follows:

datatype bNat =   datatype Pos =
    Zero   One
  | PBin Pos | Bit Pos bool

The standard functions on *Nat* may be defined by means of bit operations in the binary number representation. We first define the successor functions *bSucc* on *bNat* and *pSucc* on *Pos* by primitive recursion. The latter is defined as

$$pSucc\ One = Bit\ One\ False$$
$$pSucc\ (Bit\ x\ b) = if\ b\ then\ Bit\ (pSucc\ x)\ False$$
$$else\ Bit\ x\ True$$

Subsequently, we define binary addition *bPlus* by primitive recursion by

$$bPlus\ Zero\ x = x$$
$$bPlus\ (Pbin\ x)\ y = (case\ y\ of\ Zero \Rightarrow Pbin\ x$$
$$| Pbin\ y \Rightarrow Pbin\ (pPlus\ x\ y))$$

For *Pos*, we get:

$$pPlus\ One\ y = pSucc\ y$$
$$pPlus\ (Bit\ x\ b1)\ y =$$
$$(case\ y\ of\ One \Rightarrow pSucc\ (Bit\ x\ b1)$$
$$| (Bit\ z\ b2) \Rightarrow Bit\ (pPlus\ x\ (if\ (b1\ \&\ b2)\ then\ pSucc\ z$$
$$else\ z))$$
$$(b1 \neq b2)$$

We show how to prove $bPlus\ x\ Zero = x$ by reusing the abstracted form (5) of theorem `append_Nil2` (*xs @ Nil = xs*). We instantiate, this time *nil* with *Zero*, *app* with *bPlus* and *cons* with $\lambda x.bSucc$, and obtain the theorem

$$[\![\forall P\ l.[\![P\ Zero; \forall a\ l.\ P\ l \Longrightarrow P\ (bSucc\ l)]\!] \Longrightarrow P\ l;$$
$$\forall x.\ bPlus\ Zero\ x = x;$$
$$\forall u\ x\ y.\ (bSucc\ x)\ y = bSucc\ (bPlus\ x\ y)]\!] \Longrightarrow bPlus\ x\ Zero = x \qquad (6)$$

The first premise corresponds to the induction scheme, and the second and third premises correspond to the primitive recursive definition of addition on natural numbers. The induction principle on *Pos* is given by the structure of the datatype, not by natural induction. For the first premise, we therefore need to show that the usual natural induction rule can be derived for *bNat*. This is done by first establishing an isomorphism between Nat and bNat, i.e. two functions $n2b$: nat $\longrightarrow$ bNat and $b2n$: bNat $\longrightarrow$ nat which are shown to be mutually inverse. The second premise is given by the definition of *bPlus*. The third premise can be proved through case analysis on x and y.

We next show how to prove *bPlus x (bSucc y) = bSucc (bPlus x y)* by reusing the proof of $\forall m\ n.\ m + Suc\ n = Suc\ (m + n)$ from the theory of natural numbers. The abstraction tactic gives us the theorem:

$$\llbracket \forall P\ n.\ \llbracket P\ zero;\ \forall n.\ P\ n \Longrightarrow P\ (suc\ n) \rrbracket \Longrightarrow P\ n;$$
$$\forall n.\ plus\ zero\ n = n;$$
$$\forall u\ n.\ plus\ (suc\ u)\ n = suc\ (plus\ u\ n) \rrbracket$$
$$\Longrightarrow plus\ m\ (suc\ n) = suc\ (plus\ m\ n)$$

Instantiation (*zero* with *Zero*, *plus* with *bPlus*, *suc* with *bSucc*) yields a theorem with three premises, which are identical to the premises of (5), except that there are no vacuous quantified variables in the first and third premise. Hence, resolution with the theorems needed above directly proves the goal.

4.3   Moving Theorems Along Signature Morphisms

In the previous examples, the process of moving theorems from the theory Nat to bNat is quite mechanical: take a theorem from Nat, abstract all operations and types from Nat, then instantiate the resulting variables with the corresponding operations from bNat. In general, we can move theorems from a source theory to a target theory if there is a suitable mapping of types and operations between the theories. Such mappings between types and operations are known as *signature morphisms*.

A *signature* $\Sigma = \langle T, \Omega \rangle$ is given by *type constructors* T, with *arity ar$_T$* : $T \to \mathbb{N}$, and *operations* Ω, with arity $ar_\Omega : \Omega \to T^*$. T^* is the set of all well-formed types built from the type constructors and a (finitely countable) set of type variables. A signature morphism is a map between type constructors and operations preserving the arities of the type constructors, and the domain and range of the operations. Formally, given two signatures $\Sigma_1 = \langle T_1, \Omega_1 \rangle$ and $\Sigma_2 = \langle T_2, \Omega_2 \rangle$, a *signature morphism* $\sigma : \Sigma_1 \to \Sigma_2$ is given by a map $\sigma_T : T_1 \to T_2$ on type constructors and a map $\sigma_\Omega : \Omega_1 \to \Omega_2$ on operation symbols, such that

$$\forall \tau \in T_1.\ ar_{T_1}(\tau) = ar_{T_2}(\sigma_T(\tau)) \tag{7}$$
$$\forall \omega \in \Omega_1.\ \overline{\sigma}_T(\omega) = \sigma_\Omega(\omega) \tag{8}$$

where $\overline{\sigma}_T : T_1^* \to T_2^*$ is the unique extension of σ_T to all well-formed types. A *partial* signature morphism is given by partial maps $\sigma_T : T_1 \rightharpoonup T_2$ and $\sigma_\Omega : \Omega_1 \rightharpoonup \Omega_2$ such that all type constructors appearing in the source of any operation in the domain of σ_Ω are in the domain of σ_T.

Let Thy$_1$ and Thy$_2$ be Isabelle theories with signatures $\Sigma(\text{Thy}_1)$ and $\Sigma(\text{Thy}_2)$, and let $\sigma : \Sigma(\text{Thy}_1) \to \Sigma(\text{Thy}_2)$ be a signature morphism. Any proof term from

Thy_1 can be translated into a proof term in Thy_2 if the proof does not contain references to theorems from Thy_1. This gives us a canonical way of moving theorems from Thy_1 to Thy_2: first abstract all theorems from Thy_1 occuring in the proof of the theorem, then replace type constructors τ with $\sigma_T(\tau)$, and all operation symbols ω with $\sigma_\Omega(\omega)$, and replay the proof. Conditions (7) and (8) ensure that the translated proof term is well-typed.

In order to extend the implementation of the theorem reuse method with mappings of this kind, we define an abstract ML type `sig_morph` for partial signature morphisms. Signature morphisms are obtained using a constructor which checks the conditions (7) and (8) above, when given source and target signatures and the function graphs. We can apply the signature morphism in order to map types and terms from the source into the target signature. The invariants of the signature morphisms make sure that a translated term typechecks if the original term did. Given this type, we can define an abstraction tactic

```
val abs_translate : sig_morph-> thm-> thm
```

which moves a theorem along a signature morphism. Applying this abstraction tactic to our example, we can move any theorem from `Nat` to `bNat`, such as the theorems `add_0_right`, `add_Suc_right` (see Sect 4.2), and `add_commute`:

$$[\![\ \forall P\ n.\ [\![\ P\ Zero;\ \forall n.\ P\ n \Longrightarrow P\ (bSucc\ n)\ ]\!] \Longrightarrow P\ n;$$
$$\forall n.\ bPlus\ Zero\ n = n;\ \forall m.\ bPlus\ m\ Zero = m;$$
$$\forall u\ n.\ bPlus\ (bSucc\ u)\ n = bSucc\ (bPlus\ u\ n);$$
$$\forall m\ n.\ bPlus\ m\ (bSucc\ n) = bSucc\ (bPlus\ m\ n)\ ]\!]$$
$$\Longrightarrow bPlus\ m\ n = bPlus\ n\ m$$

In the translated theorems, the applicability conditions correspond to theorems that were used in the proof of the source theorems. This suggests that we can partially automate discharge of the applicability conditions when moving several theorems from a source theory to a target theory by considering the order in which the theorems are established in the source theory.

4.4   Analysing Theorem Dependencies

This section considers how to reduce proof work when moving theorems between theories. In the previous examples, we have seen that it was necessary to prove certain applicability conditions in the derived theorems. Some applicability conditions occur in several theorems (e.g. the induction rule above) and a derived theorem may occur as an applicability condition in another. Proof of applicability conditions may be considerably simplified by analysis of the source theory prior to theorem reuse.

In the example of `Nat` and `bNat`, successor and addition for `bNat` were defined in terms of bit operations. This resulted in applicability conditions to ensure that the definition of addition in `Nat` was valid in `bNat`. In general, we would like to identify an appropriate, small set of theorems that need manual proof in a target theory in order to move a larger selection of theorems from the source theory to the target theory automatically. We shall call such a set of theorems an *axiomatic base*. Finding an axiomatic base is a process which is hard to automate; for the Nat example above, the axiomatic base is the Peano axioms and the definition of addition. We will below give an algorithm which checks if a given set of theorems form an axiomatic base, and if so provides an abstraction tactic to move across theorems automatically. Isabelle's visualisation tool for the dependency graph may help determine an appropriate axiomatic base.

We say that a theorem φ *depends on* another theorem ψ, written $\psi \longrightarrow \varphi$, if ψ occurs as a leaf node in the proof of φ. The *premises* $prem(\varphi)$ of a theorem φ is the set of all theorems on which the theorem depends, i.e. $prem(\varphi) = \{\psi \mid \psi \longrightarrow \varphi\}$. This allows the construction of a *dependency graph* for a theory, in which the nodes are theorems of the theory, and the (unlabelled) edges are $\psi \longrightarrow \phi$ for theorems ψ and ϕ. The dependency graph of the source theory helps to identify an appropriate axiomatic base.

Given a set Φ of theorems, let $pre(\Phi)$ denote the *preconditions* of Φ, i.e. the set of all theorems needed to derive the theorems in Φ. This set can be obtained from the dependency graph by a simple depth- or breadth-first search:

$$pre(\Phi) = \Phi \cup pre(\{\psi \mid \psi \longrightarrow \varphi \text{ for } \varphi \in \Phi\}).$$

A theorem φ is *directly derivable* from a set Ψ of theorems, written $\Psi \vdash \varphi$, if all its premises (in the theory) are contained in Ψ:

$$\Psi \vdash \varphi \Leftrightarrow prem(\varphi) \subseteq \Psi.$$

This means that if we have translated all theorems in Ψ, we can establish the translation of φ by replaying its translated proof term. The set of theorems *derivable* by proof replay from a set of theorems Φ is the closure under derivability:

$$der(\Phi) = \Phi \cup der(\{\psi \mid \Phi \vdash \psi\}).$$

Given a source theory with a set Φ of theorems and an axiomatic base B, a target theory, and a partial signature morphism between the theories, we can systematically abstract all theorems in the set

$$A \stackrel{def}{=} pre(\Phi) \setminus pre(B)$$

and instantiate according to the signature morphism, deriving theorems in the target theory. A necessary condition for the success of this translation is that $A \subseteq der(B)$, i.e. the axiomatic base is strong enough to derive the theorems in Φ. In order to move theorems to another theory, the theorems of the axiomatic base, translated according to the signature morphism, must be proved in the target theory. In the example of Sect. 4.2, if Φ includes add_commute, the axiomatic base will typically include the Peano axioms for addition, but need not include add_0_right, which is derivable from these axioms. If the theorems of Φ are translated in the order of dependency, such that the premises $prem(\varphi)$ are moved before φ for all $\varphi \in A$, the applicability conditions of the derived theorems in the target theory can be discharged automatically.

Our implementation provides a module which implements the necessary graph algorithms. For simplicity and speed, we refer to theorems by their name throughout. In particular, the function

```
val saturate : DG -> string list-> string list
                        -> (string* string list) list
```

will, given a dependency graph, an axiomatic base and a list of theorems, provide a list of pairs of theorems and the names of their premises in order of dependency. This list can be given to the abstraction tactic which moves across the theorems.

5   Related Work

The problem of proof reuse has been addressed previously. Some approaches apply branches or fragments from old proofs when solving new problems: Melis and Whittle [14] study reasoning by analogy, a technique for reusing problem solving experience by proof planning; Giunchiglia, Villefiorita, and Walsh [7] study abstraction techniques, where a problem is translated into a related abstract problem which should be easier to prove as irrelevant details are ignored; and Walther and Kolbe, in their PLAGIATOR system [26], suggest proof reuse in first-order equational theories by so-called proof catches, a subset of the leaf nodes in a proof tree, similar to our applicability conditions.

The KIV system reuses proof fragments to reprove old theorems after modifications to an initial program [22]. The approach exploits a correspondence between positions in a program text and in the proofs, so that subtrees of the original proof tree can be moved to new positions. This depends on the underlying proof rules, so the approach is targeted towards syntax-driven proof methods typical of program verification. A more semantic approach are development graphs as implemented in MAYA [3], where a specification is represented by a development graph, a richer version of the dependency graphs from Sect. 4.4.

In a logical framework setting, Felty and Howe [6] describe a generic approach to generalisation and reuse of tactic proofs. In their work, a proof is a nested series of proof steps which may have open branches. Reuse is achieved by replacing the substitutions of a proof with substitutions derived from a different proof goal by means of higher-order resolution. This opens for an elegant way to reuse steps from abortive proof attempts for e.g. unfortunate variable instantiations, which can to some extent be mimicked by considering different unifiers for our derived inference rules. In contrast to the cited works, our approach allows a generalisation over types as well as function symbols. In particular, proof reuse as in the examples of Sect. 4 is not feasible in the cited approaches.

Proof reuse and generalisation of theorems have been studied in the Coq system. Proofs in Coq resemble proof terms in Isabelle, but in a richer type theory. Pons, Magaud and Bertot [13, 20] consider transformation of proofs, similar to ours, replacing operation symbols and types by variables, and Magaud and Bertot [13] consider change of data representation in this setting, studying in particular the same example as in Sect. 4.2 (in fact, our example was inspired by this work), extended further to type-specific inference rules in [12]. The richer type theory used by Coq makes proof term manipulation more involved than in the logical framework setting of our approach. For reuse, proofs have to be massaged into a particular form, and e.g. induction and case distinction have to be given special treatment. There are particular methods which either generalise theorems [13, 20], or handle change of data type representations [12, 13]. In our approach induction and case distinction are represented as meta-logic axioms, which allows a uniform treatment of these situations by appropriate abstraction tactics. For example, the dependency analysis (Sect. 4.4) is built on top of the more elementary abstraction and reuse tactics. Further, theorems abstracted with our method may be instantiated several times in different settings, thus allowing multiple reuse.

Dependency graphs and similar structures have been considered in systems such as KIV or Maya [3]. Isabelle can visualise the dependency graph, but not in an interactive way. More interesting here is the work by Bertot, Pons and Pottier [5], who implemented an interactive visualisation of the dependency graph, allowing manipulations such as removing and grouping of edges and labels. An interactive tool in this vein would greatly aid the user in establishing an axiomatic base.

6   Conclusion and Future Work

This paper demonstrates how theorems can be generalised from a given setting and reapplied in another, exploiting the possibilities offered by proof terms in logical framework style theorem provers. This approach combines proof term manipulation as known from type theory with the flexibility and power of logical frameworks. The combination is particularly well suited for changing data representations because object logic inference rules and theorems may be given a uniform treatment in both the abstraction and reuse process. Consequently, the transformation method may be applied to any theorem in a direct way, allowing multiple reuse of the abstracted theorem in different settings.

The considered strategies for reuse point in interesting directions. Signature morphisms are used as a structuring mechanism in algebraic specification languages such as CASL [2], and for structured development in e.g. Maya [3] or Specware [23, 25]. The proposed analysis of theorem dependencies is promising, and should be supported by a (probably graphical) tool, which would allow the user to interactively determine an axiomatic base for the theory, assisted by appropriate heuristics.

In addition to theorem reuse as discussed in this paper, the proposed method may have applications in formal program development. In this field, several approaches have been suggested based on specialised transformation rules [23, 24] or deriving rules from theorems [1, 11]. However a coherent framework is lacking, allowing users to systematically generalise existing developments to a widely applicable set of transformation rules. The proposed abstraction method may be of use here. A small demonstration of this application, deriving transformation rules from correctness proofs of data refinements, may be found in [10].

The suggested proof term transformations and reuse strategies have been implemented in Isabelle 2003[2]. The implementation comprises only about one thousand lines of ML code, with the abstraction tactics accounting for roughly 40%, dependency analysis and signature morphisms about 30%, and auxiliaries and utilities the rest. The compactness of the code suggests that the framework of meta-logic proof terms provided by Isabelle is well-suited for this kind of transformations. At a technical level, there are several ways of improving the proposed abstraction method. An interesting improvement is to incorporate the technique of coloured terms [9], which would allow several variables to replace the same function symbol during abstraction.

Acknowledgements

Part of this work was done while the first author was affiliated with the University of Bremen. The work was supported by the DFG under grant LU 707-1. We are grateful to Till Mossakowski and Burkhart Wolff for interesting discussions on the subject of abstraction in Isabelle, to Erwin R. Catesbeiana for pointing out potential pitfalls, and to Stefan Berghofer for explaining some technicalities of Isabelle's proof terms to us.

References

1. P. Anderson and D. Basin. Program development schemata as derived rules. *Journal of Symbolic Computation*, 30(1):5–36, July 2000.
2. E. Astesiano, M. Bidoit, H. Kirchner, B. Krieg-Brückner, P. D. Mosses, D. Sannella, and A. Tarlecki. CASL: The Common Algebraic Specification Language. *Theoretical Computer Science*, 286(2):153–196, 2002.
3. S. Autexier, D. Hutter, T. Mossakowski, and A. Schairer. The development graph manager MAYA. In H. Kirchner and C. Ringeissen, editors, *Proc. 9th Int. Conf. Algebraic Methodology and Software Technology (AMAST'02)*, LNCS 2422, p. 495–501. Springer, 2002.
4. S. Berghofer and T. Nipkow. Proof terms for simply typed higher order logic. In J. Harrison and M. Aagaard, editors, *13th Intl. Conf. on Theorem Proving in Higher Order Logics (TPHOLs'00)*, LNCS 1869, p. 38–52. Springer, 2000.
5. Y. Bertot, O. Pons, and L. Rideau. Notions of dependency in proof assistants. In *User Interfaces in Theorem Provers*, Eindhoven Univ. of Technology, 1998.
6. A. Felty and D. Howe. Generalization and reuse of tactic proofs. In F. Pfenning, editor, *5th Intl. Conf. on Logic Programming and Automated Reasoning (LPAR'94)*, LNCS 822, pages 1–15. Springer, July 1994.
7. F. Giunchiglia, A. Villafiorita, and T. Walsh. Theories of abstraction. *AI Communications*, 10(3-4):167–176, 1997.
8. R. Harper, F. Honsell, and G. Plotkin. A framework for defining logics. *Journal of the ACM*, 40(1):143–184, Jan. 1993.

---

[2] The source code and examples of this paper may be downloaded from
http://www.informatik.uni-bremen.de/~cxl/sources/tphols04.tar.gz

9. D. Hutter and M. Kohlhase. Managing structural information by higher-order colored unification. *Journal of Automated Reasoning*, 25:123–164, 2000.

10. E. B. Johnsen and C. Lüth. Abstracting refinements for transformation. *Nordic Journal of Computing*, 10(4):313–336, 2003.

11. C. Lüth and B. Wolff. TAS – a generic window inference system. In J. Harrison and M. Aagaard, editors, *13th Intl. Conf. Theorem Proving in Higher Order Logics (TPHOLs'00)*, volume LNCS 1869, p. 405–422. Springer, 2000.

12. N. Magaud. Changing data representation within the Coq system. In *16th Intl. Conf. Theorem Proving in Higher Order Logics (TPHOLs'03)*, LNCS 2758, p. 87–102. Springer, 2003.

13. N. Magaud and Y. Bertot. Changing data structures in type theory: A study of natural numbers. In P. Callaghan, Z. Luo, J. McKinna, and R. Pollack, editors, *Types for Proofs and Programs, Intl. Workshop (TYPES 2000)*, LNCS 2277, p. 181–196. Springer, 2002.

14. E. Melis and J. Whittle. Analogy in inductive theorem proving. *Journal of Automated Reasoning*, 22(2):117–147, 1999.

15. D. Miller, G. Nadathur, F. Pfenning, and A. Scedrov. Uniform proofs as a foundation for logic programming. *Annals of Pure and Applied Logic*, 51:125–157, 1991.

16. T. Nipkow, L. C. Paulson, and M. Wenzel. *Isabelle/HOL – A Proof Assistant for Higher-Order Logic*, LNCS 2283. Springer, 2002.

17. L. C. Paulson. Isabelle: The next 700 theorem provers. In P. Odifreddi, editor, *Logic and Computer Science*, p. 361–386. Academic Press, 1990.

18. F. Pfenning. Logic programming in the LF logical framework. In G. Huet and G. Plotkin, editors, *Logical Frameworks*, p. 149–181. Cambridge Univ. Press, 1991.

19. F. Pfenning. Logical frameworks. In A. Robinson and A. Voronkov, editors, *Handbook of Automated Reasoning*, p. 1063–1147. Elsevier Science Publishers, 2001.

20. O. Pons. Generalization in type theory based proof assistants. In P. Callaghan, Z. Luo, J. McKinna, and R. Pollack, editors, *Types for Proofs and Programs, Intl. Workshop (TYPES 2000)*, LNCS 2277, p. 217– 232. Springer, 2002.

21. D. Prawitz. Ideas and results in proof theory. In J. E. Fenstad, editor, *Proceedings of the Second Scandinavian Logic Symposium, Studies in Logic and the Foundations of Mathematics* 63, p. 235–307. North-Holland, Amsterdam, 1971.

22. W. Reif and K. Stenzel. Reuse of proofs in software verification. In R. K. Shyamasundar, editor, *Proc. Foundations of Software Technology and Theoretical Computer Science*, LNCS 761, p. 284–293. Springer, 1993.

23. D. Smith. Constructing specification morphisms. *Journal of Symbolic Computation*, 15:571– 606, 1993.

24. D. R. Smith and M. R. Lowry. Algorithm theories and design tactics. *Science of Computer Programming*, 14:305– 321, 1990.

25. Y. V. Srinivas and R. Jullig. Specware: Formal support for composing software. In *Proc. Conf. Mathematics of Program Construction*, LNCS 947. Springer, 1995.

26. C. Walther and T. Kolbe. Proving theorems by reuse. *Artificial Intelligence*, 116(1–2):17–66, 2000.

Proving Compatibility Using Refinement

Michael Jones*, Aaron Benson**, and Dan Delorey

Department of Computer Science
Brigham Young University
Provo, Utah, USA
jones@cs.byu.edu, pierce@cs.byu.edu, agb23@wsu.edu

Abstract. Previously, we have found that incremental refinement, using the event based B method, supports the effective management of proof complexity when verifying properties of IO protocols, such as PCI. In the context of IO protocols, another important verification task is to show that a new protocol can be made compatible with an existing protocol. In this article, we report on our efforts to show that RapidIO, a new IO standard, can be made compatible with the transaction ordering property expected by PCI, a legacy standard. This is done by creating a refinement sequence for RapidIO as a branch in our previously completed PCI refinement chain. We found that incremental refinement simplifies specification reuse and allows a precise statement of compatibility. Ongoing work seeks to identify proof engineering methods to increase proof reuse for compatibility proofs.

1 Introduction

The introduction of a new IO standard, such as RapidIO, requires a great deal of design and verification effort to maintain adequate compatibility with legacy standards while improving performance. In this paper, we report on our efforts to show compatibility between RapidIO [Rap01] and PCI [PCI95] using incremental refinement from a common specification. This work builds on our previous efforts to refine PCI from a specification of its transaction ordering property [WJM+02].

In simplest terms, refinement is a way of showing that a machine implements a specification. Compatibility is the problem of showing that *two* machines satisfy the same specification. One way to show compatibility is to create a branch in the refinement chain. Incremental refinement supports such an approach by enforcing a rigid theory structure in which it is easy to identify where to create the branch. The resulting proof shows precisely at what level of abstraction and for which properties two machines are compatible. Both of these results would be more difficult to obtain in a general purpose theorem prover – without using

---

* Supported by a grant from the Intel corporation.
** Now affiliated with the Department of Agricultural and Resource Economics at Washington State University, Pullman, Washington, USA.

K. Slind et al. (Eds.): TPHOLs 2004, LNCS 3223, pp. 168–183, 2004.
© Springer-Verlag Berlin Heidelberg 2004

the same theory structure. Since refinement tools already support such a theory structure, they are a natural choice for showing compatibility.

The primary purpose of this work was to investigate the suitability of using the B method [Abr96] (as implemented in AtelierB [Cle02]) to show compatibility between the PCI and RapidIO protocols for the PCI transaction ordering property. We reused a refinement chain showing that PCI implements the property and created a new chain for RapidIO. The RapidIO chain includes 4 new abstract machines and required completing 952 non-obvious proof obligations. Of which, about 700 simply required the correct invocation of AtelierB decision procedures. The sequence of RapidIO models identifies the subset of RapidIO network topologies and message types for which RapidIO can be used to implement PCI transaction ordering.

While one case study does not a methodology make, we found that incremental refinement is an excellent method for reusing formal specifications when showing compatibility between IO standards. Specifically, we found that refinement imposes a useful structure on the refinement proofs and refinement supports precise statements about the level of abstraction at which compatibility is proven. More generally, refinement can be useful when several implementations must be shown to satisfy the same complex specification. This problem frequently arises in industrial microprocessor and system on a chip design.

We had hoped to get more proof reuse in addition to specification reuse. However, the structure of the first refinement chain dictated that the RapidIO chain should begin at a rather high level of abstraction. Since most of the hard proof work appeared lower in the chain, we obtained little proof reuse.

The next section explains event based refinement in the B method. Section 3 describes the problem of showing PCI/RapidIO compatibility in detail and introduces the approach we took to making a subset of RapidIO compatible using an adaptor. Section 4 describes a solution to the compatibility problem and the models and proofs used in the formalization of the solution are presented in Section 5. We discuss proof metrics and make a comparison with higher-order logic theorem proving in Section 6. We offer conclusions and future work in Section 7.

2   Event Based Refinement and AtelierB

The goal in the event based B method is to show that successively more complex concrete systems refine an abstract system. We do this incrementally to distribute the difficulty of the entire sequence. In this approach, a *system* consists of state variables, invariants and events. The invariants describe properties that must be true of the state variables and the events describe transitions between values of state variables.

In particular, an event has the form

$$\text{any } x \text{ where } P(x, v) \text{ then } v := E(x, v) \tag{1}$$

for local state x and global state v. The predicate P is called the *guard* and the relation E is the *update* relation. For this event, the global state v is updated to

$E(x, v)$ if there exists an x such that $P(x, v)$ holds. The event in Equation 1 is said to *refined by* an event

$$\text{any } y \text{ where } Q(y, w) \text{ then } w := F(y, w)$$

if the following proof obligation can be discharged:

$$I(v) \wedge J(v, w) \wedge Q(y, w) \Rightarrow \exists x. P(x, v) \wedge J(E(x, v), F(y, w))$$

for invariant I and gluing invariant J.

In every system there is a special event called the *skip* event. The skip event has no guard and does not change any state variables. An event refines the *skip* event if it also does not change any state variables. An event that refines the *skip* event is called a *silent* event.

Given two systems, A and C, the abstract system A is refined by a more concrete system C, $C \sqsubseteq_S A$, if the following three conditions are satisfied:

- Correctness. Every event in C refines either an event in A or the *skip* event in A. Otherwise, an event in C could perform a behavior not duplicated by A.
- Progress. A non-silent event in C is always eventually enabled. Otherwise, C might continuously perform silent events and appear to do nothing relative to the behavior of A.
- Relative deadlock freedom. At least one guard in C is satisfied whenever at least one guard in A is satisfied. Otherwise, C would introduce more deadlocks than A.

AtelierB is an implementation of the B method. AtelierB consists of three main parts: a specification language, a proof obligation generator and an interactive proof assistant. The specification language encodes first order logic extended with set theory. While the specification language is not based on higher-order logic *per se*, it is capable of expressing similar higher-order concepts using quantification over the subsets of a set [ACL02]. The proof assistant includes a "predicate prover" (PP) which is a decision procedure for the predicate calculus. A more detailed discussion of the predicate prover and the similarities between AtelierB and HOL proof assistants can be found in [AC03].

Given an abstract system and a machine, the AtelierB proof tool generates the proof obligations required to show correctness for *only* the correctness part of system refinement. The progress condition can be met using a measure function in silent events of the concrete machine. The relative deadlock freedom condition can be met by proving that the conjunction of the guards in the abstract matching imply the conjunction of the guards in the concrete machine under the gluing invariant. In this case study, we have only proved the correctness condition for every refinement step.

3   PCI/RapidIO Compatibility Problem

Figure 1 shows the system that can be constructed after completing a compatibility proof. Since RapidIO maintains the p/c property, a set of PCI terminals

Fig. 1. Connecting PCI devices across a RapidIO network while preserving PCI transaction ordering properties.

can use a RapidIO network (possibly through an adaptor, as described shortly) to communicate while preserving PCI translation ordering. The motivation for the solving the compatibility problem is to show that PCI devices can be connected across a RapidIO network while maintaining PCI transaction ordering. This is not possible for arbitrary RapidIO networks because RapidIO includes behaviors that violate PCI transaction ordering. More precisely, the problem is to show *how certain* RapidIO networks can be used to connect PCI devices (through an adaptor) while preserving PCI transaction ordering. Transaction ordering for PCI devices is defined by the producer/consumer (p/c) property.

The relationship needed to implement the system shown in Figure 1 can be stated more precisely in terms of system refinement. The definition is somewhat idealized to precisely capture the our notion of compatibility. The idealization presupposes the existence of concrete formal models that define each protocol. Since both protocols are defined with English prose, no such model exists for either protocol. We use $\mathcal{PCI}$ and $\mathcal{RIO}$ to denote the mathematically definitions of PCI and RapidIO. For the p/c property, we say that $\mathcal{RIO}$ with adaptor $\mathcal{A}$ is compatible with $\mathcal{PCI}$ for p/c at level M iff:

$$\begin{array}{c} \mathcal{PCI} \sqsubseteq_S \\ \mathcal{RIO} \cup \mathcal{A} \sqsubseteq_S \end{array} M \sqsubseteq_S p/c$$

We have proven this property for models of PCI and RapidIO that are more abstract than $\mathcal{PCI}$ and $\mathcal{RIO}$, but concrete enough to include a significant amount of detail. Since the actual descriptions of RapidIO and PCI consist of imprecise English prose and figures, completing refinement down to $\mathcal{RIO}$ and $\mathcal{PCI}$ is not possible.

The remaining parts of this section describe the PCI and RapidIO protocols and describe several reasons why the protocols are incompatible.

3.1   PCI

The PCI standard defines two kinds of messages: posted and delayed. Posted messages are unacknowledged writes that may not be dropped during transit. Delayed messages are acknowledged reads or writes that may be dropped during transit before they are committed. A delayed transaction is committed when an attempt has been made to send it across an electrical bus. Messages are sent and received by agents and stored in intermediate bridges. A bridge sits between two electrical busses and contains two queues, one facing either bus. Messages may pass each other in queues under the condition that no message may pass a posted message. The passing rules are designed to avoid deadlock while preserving end-to-end message ordering rules.

The end-to-end message ordering rules are stated in terms of a distributed p/c property in Appendix A of the PCI specification. The p/c property states that:

1. if an agent, the producer, issues a write to a data address followed by a write to a flag address, where the flag and data addresses may be located at different agents, and
2. another agent, the consumer, issues a read to the flag address, and
3. the consumer issues a read to the data address after receiving the results of the flag read, and
4. the producer's flag write had arrived before the consumer's flag read, then
5. the consumer's data read always returns the value written by the producer, assuming no other values were written to the data address in the interim.

This property is particularly interesting for two reasons. First, the producer's writes and the consumer's reads can be in transit in the network at the same time and may pass each other in accordance with the passing rules. Second, the published PCI standard was intended to satisfy this property, but does not. Our previous refinement case study demonstrated that a corrected version of the PCI standard does satisfy this property [WJM$^+$02].

3.2   RapidIO

The RapidIO standard defines a high-speed serial interconnect designed to replace slower bus-based interconnects such as PCI. RapidIO messages consist of requests and replies. RapidIO networks consist of agents connected by a network of switches. RapidIO switches contain four queues and may be arranged in any topology. Messages must be routed through the switches in a way that avoids cyclic topology based deadlocks.

Both requests and replies are issued within a priority flow. A priority flow is defined by the priority, source and destination of a message. Switches maintain message ordering within a priority flow but not between priority flows. There are four priority classes in RapidIO. Requests are issued in the lowest three classes while replies may be issued in any class. A reply to a request at level i may be issued at the next highest level $i+1$ to prevent deadlock. RapidIO switches may not drop messages but endpoints may ignore messages and issue retry requests. Retry requests are returned to the sender and cause the sender to resend the discarded message.

3.3   Why They Don't Work Together

Because RapidIO passing rules and topologies are more relaxed than PCI, the two protocols are not immediately compatible. There are seven specific problems we identified in our efforts to make them compatible.

1. RapidIO uses switches instead of a single shared bridge as in PCI. This allows messages to take separate paths to a common destination.
2. RapidIO switches cannot know what types of messages are being sent, but PCI bridges have to so that they can control message reordering. This means that the RapidIO switches cannot be in control of message ordering based on message type.
3. RapidIO uses priority classes to enforce message ordering. This could allow p/c dataread messages to pass datawrite messages if they are not sent with the correct priority.
4. Messages are ordered in transaction flows (flows originated at the same source). This allows dataread to pass datawrite because they originate at different sources.
5. Priority is only used to order messages that enter a RapidIO switch at a common port and at targeted to a common destination port. This could allow the dataread to pass the datawrite even if they are sent at the same priority but enter a switch at different ports.
6. Retries in RapidIO propagate back to the originating device because switches do not store retry information. PCI devices do not retry messages because PCI bridges handle retrying packets.
7. When a message is retried in RapidIO, all further messages are silently discarded as it is assumed that the sending device will resend the retried message and all subsequent messages until it gets back to the point at which it received the retried message.

Since it is evident that RapidIO and PCI are not completely compatible, the central challenge in showing their compatibility is showing which RapidIO networks and messages can be used to satisfy PCI ordering rules.

4   Solving the Compatibility Problem

There are two requirements a RapidIO network must meet in order to guarantee the message ordering necessary to maintain the p/c property. The first is that the datawrite, flagwrite and dataread messages all be sent with the same priority. The second is that there must be at least two consecutive switches that the datawrite, flagwrite and dataread messages pass through on the way to the flag and data devices; and that the datawrite and the flagwrite are mutually constrained from the producer to the second common switch. By mutually constrained, we mean that the path they take to the second common switch must be the same. The path itself is unconstrained.

These requirements, along with the message ordering rules of RapidIO, guarantee the message ordering behavior needed to ensure the p/c property. Forcing the dataread to pass through the same two consecutive switches as the datawrite causes the RapidIO switch ordering rules to take effect. RapidIO guarantees consistent path selection from any switch to a single destination. The dataread and the datawrite are both destined for the data device, so from that second common switch they are guaranteed to follow the same path.

From the second common switch to the data device, the datawrite and the dataread will always enter the switches at the same port and leave the switches at the same port. If they have the same priority then the dataread cannot pass the datawrite as long as the dataread enters the second common switch behind the datawrite. The flagwrite cannot pass the datawrite before the second common switch because they are mutually constrained up to the second common switch and they are required to be sent at the same priority. The dataread cannot pass the flagwrite because it cannot be sent until the flagread has completed. Other cases are unimportant because the p/c property is only required when the flagread does not pass the flagwrite.

Unfortunately, the constraints discussed so far do not solve the problem caused by the different retry mechanisms in PCI and RapidIO. We solve this problem using a PCI to RapidIO adapter. An adapter is required anyway to translate the messages between the two protocols. We add additional functionality to the adapter to facilitate retries and still maintain the p/c property.

We do not explicitly identify the implementation specific details of the adapter. We only identify general characteristics the adapter must have. First, at the sending end, the adapter must have a method of queuing sent messages until they have posted at their destination so that the adapter can retry the packets if necessary. Second, the adapter must guarantee that the messages are delivered to the PCI device in the order that they were received at the adapter. Third, if the adapter retries a write, it must at least block all reads to that address, possibly by queuing those reads or by retrying those reads, until it receives and accepts the retried write. A strength of refinement is that we can use an abstract description of an adapter in the proof. Any implementation that refines this model will preserve correctness.

5   Models and Proofs

The goal of our research is to show that compatibility between IO standards can be demonstrated by using incremental refinement from a common specification. We examined the PCI models previously used in [WJM+02], and determined that the best point at which to make the break in the refinement chain was after the third PCI model. The first three PCI models describe a subset of RapidIO behavior, but the fourth PCI model introduces PCI-specific topology and bridge behavior, making it unsuitable as an abstract description of RapidIO. Once the decision was made to branch our refinement after the third PCI model, we were presented with the question of exactly how to model RapidIO. The first three PCI models will be described here in order to provide background for understanding the RapidIO models, which will be discussed in more detail in following sections.

5.1   Abstraction of the Producer/Consumer Property

The first model abstracts the p/c property and introduces the basic variables used in the refinement. A set, $DATA$, is created, as well as two constants, AD

and *VAL*, which are defined to be subsets of *data*, where $AD \cap VAL = \emptyset$. The variables introduced in the model are *prod* and *cons*, which are defined as partial functions from *AD* to *VAL*; (e.g. $prod \in AD \nrightarrow VAL$) The invariant of the model requires that $cons \subseteq prod$. There are only two events in the first model, *produce* and *consume*. They are defined as follows:

> $produce =$ **any** *ad, data* **where**
> > $ad \in AD \ \wedge \ ad \notin \mathrm{DOM}(prod) \ \wedge \ data \in VAL$
>
> **then**
> > $prod := prod \cup \{ad \mapsto data\}$
>
> **end;**

> $consume =$ **any** *ad* **where**
> > $ad \in AD \ \wedge \ ad \in \mathrm{DOM}(prod) \ \wedge \ ad \notin \mathrm{DOM}(cons)$
>
> **then**
> > $cons := cons \cup \{ad \mapsto prod(ad)\}$
>
> **end;**

This model is easily understood and describes correct p/c behavior. The *produce* event takes an address to which data has not been written, and assigns some data to it. The *consume* event then takes any address which has had data written to it, and adds that address to the set of addresses that have been read. This prevents a Consumer device from reading the data until the Producer device has written that data.

5.2   Adding the Flag and Data Devices

The second PCI model adds variables and events to describe the Flag and Data devices. In this model, the Producer, Consumer, data device and flag device agents are distributed but communication is "magic" in the sense that exact mechanism for communication is not specified. The new variables are *mem* and *flag*, which are defined as partial functions from *AD* to *VAL*. In addition to the requirement of the first model, the invariant states:

$$cons \subseteq flag \subseteq mem \subseteq prod$$

So, data can only be consumed if it has been produced, written to memory and had a flag set.

There are two new events added to this model, which refine the silent, or skip, events of the first PCI model. These events send information between devices. The *datawrite* event takes messages that have been produced (where $\{ad \mapsto VAL\} \in prod$), and adds them into a set called *mem*. The second new event, *flagwrite*, takes messages which are in the *mem* set and adds them to a set, *flag*. While the *produce* event remains unchanged in this model, the *consume* event is changed to require that $ad \in \mathrm{DOM}(flag)$ in its guard, but is otherwise the same.

5.3   Message Transactions

In the next model, actual message transactions are described. The primary details added in this model are split reads in which the sending of a read message and the return of the data are separated. Six new sets are used, dw for $datawrite$ transactions, dr for $dataread$ transactions, cdr for $dataread\ completion$ messages, fw for $flagwrite$ messages, fr for $flagread$ messages, and cfr for $flagread\ completion$ messages. Each of these new sets is defined as a subset of the addresses set (e.g. $dw \subseteq AD$). So, if an address is in one of the preceding sets, it can be easily determined which message has been written for that specific address. For example, if an address is in the dr set, then the $dataread$ message has been received by the Data device for that address, and if the same address is not in the cdr set, then the $dataread\ completion$ message has not yet been received by the Consumer device.

The following statements are added to the invariant:

$$dw = \text{DOM}(mem) \; \wedge \; fw = \text{DOM}(flag) \; \wedge \; fr \subseteq fw \wedge \; cfr \subseteq \; fr \cap dw \; \wedge$$
$$dr \subseteq dw \; \wedge \; dr \subseteq cfr \; \wedge \; cdr \subseteq dr \; \wedge \; \text{DOM}(cons) \subseteq cdr$$

The p/c property in this particular model is expressed as: $fr \subseteq fw \; \wedge \; dr \subseteq dw$, meaning that the flag for a specific address can only be read if the flag has been written, and that the data for a specific address can only be read if the data has been written for that address.

The new events are $flagread$, $compflagread$, $dataread$, and $compdataread$. The guard of the $consume$ event is changed to require that $ad \in cdr$, and the $flagwrite$ and $datawrite$ events add the address to their respective sets. Specifically, the line $dw := dw \cup \{ad\}$ is added to the substitution of $datawrite$ and the line $fw := fw \cup \{ad\}$ is added to the substitution of $flagwrite$. The new events are:

$flagread = $ **any** ad **where**
$\qquad ad \in AD \; \wedge ad \notin fr \; \wedge ad \in fw$
$\quad$ **then**
$\qquad fr := fr \cup \{ad\}$
$\quad$ **end;**

$compflagread = $ **any** ad **where**
$\qquad ad \in AD \; \wedge \; ad \notin cfr \; \wedge \; ad \in fr$
$\quad$ **then**
$\qquad cfr := cfr \cup \{ad\}$
$\quad$ **end;**

$dataread = $ **any** ad **where**
$\qquad ad \in AD \; \wedge \; ad \in cfr \; \wedge \; ad \notin dr$
$\quad$ **then**
$\qquad cdr := cdr \cup \{ad\}$
$\quad$ **end;**

$compdataread = $ **any** ad **where**
$\qquad ad \in AD \; \wedge \; ad \in dr \; \wedge \; ad \notin cdr$
$\quad$ **then**
$\qquad cdr := cdr \cup \{ad\}$
$\quad$ **end;**

5.4   Modeling RapidIO Switches and Topology

The introduction of PCI-specific topology constraints and bridge behavior in the fourth PCImodel required the branch to the RapidIO refinement chain to be made after the third PCI model. It seemed natural, therefore, to include the necessary RapidIO topology constraints in our first RapidIO model.

As explained in previous sections, we modeled RapidIO topology by including two switches. Because the ordering rules within the RapidIO switches are based on ports within the switch, each switch is sufficiently represented by sets for its input and output ports. The behavior inside a switch is omitted in this model, but added later.

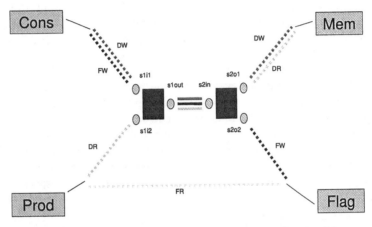

Fig. 2. Each device is eventually connected to the two switches in this manner. The dotted lines represent paths of switch sequences.

The first switch has two input ports and one output port. The second switch has one input port (connected to the first switch's output port) and two output ports. Each input and output port of each switch are described using a different function. The connections between switch ports and the names of the corresponding port functions are shown in Figure 2. The function, *s1i1* represents the first input port of the first switch, *s1out* represents the output port of the first switch, *s2in* represents the input port of the second switch, and *s2o1* represents the first output port of the second switch. Our additional p/c topology constraints require that the Producer device connect to the RapidIO network through *s1i2*, that the Consumer device connect through *s1i1*, and the Data and Flag devices through *s2o1* and *s2o2*, respectively.

We define a set of states:

$$STATES = \{CDR, FW, DR, DW, FR, CFR\}$$

where each element of $STATES$ is an element of the $DATA$ set (e.g. $CDR \in DATA$), and each element of $STATES$ is distinct.

Each switch function is defined as a partial injection from the natural numbers to addresses paired with data (e.g. $s1i1 \in \mathbb{N} \rightarrowtail AD \times STATES$). A counter for each switch (for example, $cs1in$ and $cs1out$ are the counters for messages entering and exiting the first switch) is assigned to each message when the message passes through the port, and the counter is incremented after the message passes through. The port function maps the counter to the message. The counters are used to determine the order in which messages have entered the switch.

Informally the *datawrite* event takes an address which has not been written, and adds it to the $s1i1$ set paired with its associated DW data as the image of the counter. The event also adds the address to the set dw, and increments the input counter of the first switch. The $DWout1$ event takes an address-DW pair which has been put into the $s1i1$ set, but is not in $s1out$, and adds it to the $s1out$, $s2in$ and $dw1$ sets, while incrementing the output counter of the first switch and the input counter of the second switch. The $DWout2$ event takes an address-DW pair which is in the $s2in$ set, but not yet in the $s2o1$ set, adds it to the $s2o1$ and the $dw2$ sets, and increments the output counter of the second switch.

The following sequence of events describe how a *datawrite* message moves through the system. First, a new address ad is selected which has not been used previously. A new address is unused if there are no datawrite messages with that address in the memory, mem, or the input of switch one, $s1i1$. Having chosen such an address, a message is created which pairs the address with the value produced for that address $prod(ad)$. The address value pair is given a timestamp $cs1in$. The timestamp marks the order in which messages arrived at a given switch.

> $datawrite = \textbf{any } ad \textbf{ where}$
> > $ad \in AD \;\wedge\; ad \in \text{DOM}(prod) \;\wedge\; ad \notin \text{DOM}(mem) \;\wedge$
> > $(ad \mapsto DW) \notin \text{RAN}(s1i1) \;\wedge\; ad \notin dw \;\wedge$
> > $cs1in \notin \text{DOM}(s1i1)$
>
> $\textbf{then}$
> > $mem := mem \cup \{ad \mapsto prod(ad)\} \;\|$
> > $s1i1 := s1i1 \cup \{cs1in \mapsto (ad \mapsto DW)\} \;\|$
> > $dw := dw \cup \{ad\} \;\|$
> > $cs1in := cs1in{+}1$
>
> $\textbf{end};$

Next, the $DWout1$ event describes the movement of a *datawrite* message from the output of switch 1, $s1out$, to the input of switch 2, $s2in$. The third conjunct in the precondition ensures that more messages have arrived at switch 1 than have been output by switch 1. While this property is intuitively obvious, it ensures that switch 1 does not forward messages before receiving them. The remaining conjuncts ensure that the message is not forwarded more than once. If the guard is satisfied, $DWout1$ moves the message into the output of switch 1 and into the input of switch 2. Timestamps are incremented and associated with the message in each port.

$DWout1 = $ **any** ad **where**

$ad \in AD \ \wedge \ ad \in \text{DOM}(prod) \ \wedge \ cs1out < cs1in \ \wedge$
$cs1out \notin \text{DOM}(s1out) \ \wedge \ cs2in \notin \text{DOM}(s2in) \ \wedge$
$(ad \mapsto DW) \in \text{RAN}(s1i1) \ \wedge \ (ad \mapsto DW) \notin \text{RAN}(s1out) \ \wedge$
$ad \in dw \ \wedge \ ad \notin dw1 \ \wedge$

then

$dw1 := dw1 \cup \{ad\} \ \|$
$s1out := s1out \cup \{cs1out \mapsto (ad \mapsto DW)\} \ \|$
$cs1out := cs1out+1 \ \|$
$s1ing := s1in \cup \{cs2in \mapsto (ad \mapsto DW)\} \ \|$
$cs2in := cs2in+1$

end;

Finally, the $DWout2$ event moves the message from the output port of switch 2 to the input port of the data device memory device, $dw2$. The guard and action of this event are similar to the guard on the $DWout1$ event shown above

$DWout2 = $ **any** ad **where**

$ad \in AD \wedge ad \in \text{DOM}(prod) \wedge (ad \mapsto DW) \in \text{RAN}(s2in) \ \wedge$
$(ad \mapsto DW) \notin \text{RAN}(s2o1) \ \wedge \ cs2out \notin \text{DOM}(s2o1)$
$ad \in dw1 \ \wedge \ ad \notin dw2 \ \wedge \ cs2out < cs2in \ \wedge$

then

$cs2out := cs2out+1 \ \|$
$s2o1 := s2o1 \cup \{cs2out \mapsto (ad \mapsto DW)\} \ \|$
$dw2 := dw2 \cup \{ad\}$

end;

The *dataread* and *flagwrite* messages are modeled similarly, except that the *dataread* address-DR pair is initially added to the *s1i2* set, and the *flagwrite* address-FW pair is finally added to the *s2o2* set. Each message passes through both switches, except for the *flagread* messages, which are not required to pass through the switches to maintain p/c.

The guard of *compdataread* is modified to require that $ad \in dr2$. This guarantees that the *dataread* message has passed through the second switch before the completion can be sent and received by the Consumer device.

Since the *flagread* messages are not required to pass through the switches to guarantee the p/c property, the behavior of the *flagread* messages maintain the same level of abstraction that they have in the third PCI model through the rest of the refinement.

The invariant requires *datawrite* and *flagwrite* messages to have passed through an input port before they pass through an output port. The invariant also states that a *flagwrite* message cannot enter the second switch before its corresponding *datawrite* message.

5.5   Priority and Reordering

The second RapidIO refinement models priority, and allows the switches to reorder messages based on priority, as described in Section 3.2. An event assigns each message a priority of either 0, 1, or 2, by assigning the message to a function which maps address and message pairs to the set $\{0,1,2\}$. The function will never assign an address and message pair to 3, as 3 is reserved in the RapidIO specification for message retries.

The events that model messages leaving switches (DWout1, DWout2, FWout1, etc) are guarded by statements like the following, (from the guard of the DWout1 event):

$$DWout1 = \mathbf{ANY}\, ad\ \mathbf{where}$$
$$\forall\, (msg).(msg \in AD \times DATA \wedge msg \in ran(s1i1) \wedge$$
$$msg \notin ran(s1out) \wedge msg \notin ran(s2in) \wedge$$
$$s1i1^{-1}(msg) < s1i1^{-1}(ad \mapsto DW))$$
$$\Rightarrow$$
$$prior(msg) < prior(ad \mapsto DW)$$

(other conditions omitted for clarity)

then
$$dw1 := dw1 \cup \{ad\}\ \|$$
$$s1out := s1out \cup \{cs1out \mapsto (ad \mapsto DW)\}\ \|$$
$$cs1out := cs1out{+}1\ \|$$
$$s1ing := s1in \cup \{cs2in \mapsto (ad \mapsto DW)\}\ \|$$
$$cs2in := cs2in{+}1$$
end;

This particular statement requires that there be no other message with higher priority waiting in the queue before a *datawrite* message can be passed on into the next queue. This allows messages with higher priority to bypass messages with lower priority. If the guard is satisfied, the event moves the message as before.

5.6   Interfacing PCI Devices Across a RapidIO Network

The final step in our refinement was to model the way in which our PCI-to-RapidIO adapters would work in the event of a retry being issued for a *datawrite* message. In PCI, if a message cannot reach a device, the bridge will resend the message until the device is able to accept it. In RapidIO if a device cannot accept a message, it drops the packet, and sends a retry message to the device where the message originated. The danger of this characteristic of the RapidIO specification, with respect to the p/c property, is that, if a *datawrite* message is dropped, then there is no guarantee that the corresponding *dataread* message will not be accepted by the data device before the retried *datawrite* message. Our solution is to create a set which holds all *datawrite* and *dataread* messages between the second switch and the data device. The *dataread* message is not passed from this intermediate set, and into the data device, before its corresponding *datawrite* message. In the event of a retry, the *datawrite* message waits in the adapter set, until it completes, and then the *dataread* message is free to pass through to the data device.

The new sets are *ad1, ad2, retries, resent, dw3* and *dr3*. The adapters are represented by *ad1* and *ad2, retries* is the set of all addresses for which *datawrite* messages have been retried, and *resent* is the set of all addresses for which the retried messages have been successfully resent. The sets *dw3* and *dr3* are the sets of all addresses for which *datawrite* and *dataread* messages have passed through the adapter. Four events (*DWout3, DRout3, retry,* and *resend*) are added to this model.

Note that the *flagwrite* messages are not modeled to pass through the adapter. This is because a retry on a *flagwrite* message will not violate the p/c property. The p/c property is only guaranteed if the Consumer device is able to read the flag set by the Producer.

The *DWout2* and *DRout2* events are changed to add the address-data pair to the *ad2* set, in addition to the substitutions of the previous model. The *DWout3* event adds a message to the *dw3* set, and is guarded by the statement,

> $DWout3 = $ **ANY***ad* **where**
> $\qquad \neg(ad \in retries \wedge ad \notin resent)$
> (other conditions omitted for clarity)
> **then**
> $\qquad dw3 := dw3 \cup \{ad\}$
> **end;**

which means that if a message has been retried, then it must have been successfully resent before the adapter can send it to the Data device. The *DRout3* adds a message to the *dr3* set only if $ad \in dw3$, or if the corresponding *data write* message has been successfully received by the Data device.

The other two new events are *retry* and *reset.* The *retry* event takes an address which is in the *ad2* set as an address-DW pair, and adds the address to the *retries* set. The *resend* event takes an arbitrary address (using the choice operator) from the *retries* set and adds it to the *resent* set. Since the actual mechanism of resending messages does not affect the p/c property, our *resend* event does not necessitate any refinement. Invariants describing the *retries* and *resent* sets are added to this model.

6   Proof Metrics and Comparison

The refinement of RapidIO from the transaction ordering property was completed by two researchers over a five month period. The proof involved a total of 6133 obvious (solved by AtelierB's predicate prover) and 952 non-obvious (required interactive proof) proof obligations. Of these proof obligations, only 736 obvious and 59 non-obvious proof obligations were reused without modifications from the previous PCI proof. In this project, proving refinement for each increasingly concrete models uniformly required discharging more proof obligations. More than half of the non-obvious obligations were discharged using AtelierB's automated decision procedures based predicate calculus. A decision procedures based on counter logic with uninterpreted functions (CLU) may have solved more proof obligations [BLS02]. CLU is particularly well-suited for this problem domain because models of queues and buffers often include simple arithmetic to denote message ordering.

The five months included time for both researchers to learn to use AtelierB. The forced structure of event based modeling and incremental refinement required the researchers to engineer their models and proofs to simplify proof obligations and break complex refinements into simpler steps. In contrast, three expert users failed to complete a similar proof for PCI using a higher-order logic theorem prover after a combined 18 months of effort [MHJG00].

Although the general purpose higher-order logic theorem prover did provide a superior interactive proof environment due to better decision procedure support and tactical programming support, it did not provide the same rigid structure in which to engineer models to manage complexity.. Instead, the refinement was done in one step and the resulting proofs were extremely difficult. Of course, the construction of a theory of event-based refinement in a general purpose higher-order logic theorem prover would combine the rigid proof structure with decision procedures and tactical programming support. We did not find any compelling reason to favor set-based (as in AtelierB) or type-based specification languages (as in an HOL tool). Both were adequate for this problem.

7 Conclusion

When describing the results of a formal verification project, it is important to precisely state what was proved, at what level of abstraction and using which proof technique[1]. Using refinement to show compatibility allows a precise statement of what was proved and a well-defined level of abstraction at which it was proved. More specifically, the statement of compatibility is the behavior of the most abstract common ancestor and the level of abstraction is least abstract common successor.

In this case study, the statement of compatibility is the first abstract model in which the producer creates unique data values and the consumer reads them. The level of abstraction is the third model in which the producer writes the data to a data location, sets a flag at a third location and the consumer reads the flag then reads the data.

Our use of refinement to show compatibility is similar to Mery and Cansell's use of refinement to study feature interaction [CM01]. When studying feature interaction, the refinement chain is split into two branches, called horizontal and vertical refinement, but is rejoined at the next concrete level. When showing compatibility, we also split the refinement into two branches, one for each protocol, but do not rejoin them at the next concrete level. This is because we do not allow both protocols to have arbitrary interactions in the same system. Our lowest level RapidIO does allow PCI devices to be connected at the periphery of the network, but does not allow a heterogeneous network of PCI and RapidIO interconnects.

---

[1] A point clearly articulated by Cohn [Coh89] in the context of hardware verification, but which applies more generally.

We had hoped to reuse more proofs between the two refinement sequences. Instead, non-compatible details used early in the PCI refinement chain prevented their reuse in the RapidIO refinement chain. One possible method of increasing proof re-use would be to explore methods of pushing complexity to the earlier models of the first refinement. If the preliminary models of the original refinement chain were complex enough to require more difficult proofs, then the refinement of the second system would share those difficult proofs, and reduce total effort involved in the process. The difficulty will be to balance complexity with a level of abstraction that describes both specifications.

References

[Abr96]   Jean-Raymond Abrial. *The B Book - Assigning Programs to Meanings.* Cambridge University Press, 1996.

[AC03]   J-R. Abrial and D. Cansell. Clink'n Prove: Interactive proofs within set theory. In David A. Basin and Burkhart Wolff, editors, *Theorem Proving in Higher Order Logics*, volume 2758 of *Lecture Notes in Computer Science*, pages 1–24. Springer, 2003.

[ACL02]   J-R. Abrial, D. Cansell, and G. Laffitte. "Higher-order" mathematics in B. In D. Bert, J. P. Bowen, M. C. Henson, and K. Robinson, editors, *The Second International Z and B Conference*, number 2272 in LNCS, pages 370–393, Grenoble, France, January 2002. Springer.

[BLS02]   R. Bryant, S. K. Lahiri, and S. A. Seshia. Modeling and verifying systems using a logic of counter arithmetic with lambda expressions and uninterpreted functions. In E. Brinksma and K.G. Larsen, editors, *Computer Aided Verification (CAV'02)*, number 2404 in LNCS, pages 78–92. Springer, 2002.

[Cle02]   Aix-en-Provence (F) ClearSy. Atelier B, 2002. Version 3.5.

[CM01]   Dominique Cansell and Dominique Mery. *Language Constructs for Describing Features*, chapter Abstraction and refinement of features, pages 65–84. Springer-Verlag, 2001.

[Coh89]   Avra Cohn. The notion of proof in hardware verification. *Journal of Automated Reasoning*, 5(2):127–139, 1989.

[MHJG00]   A. Mokkedem, R. Hosabettu, M. D. Jones, and G. Gopalakrishnan. Formalization and proof of a solution to the PCI 2.1 bus transaction ordering problem. *Formal Methods in Systems Design*, 16(1):93–119, January 2000.

[PCI95]   PCISIG. PCI Special Interest Group–PCI Local Bus Specification, Revision 2.1, June 1995.

[Rap01]   RapidIO Trade Association. RapidIO interconnect specification, revision 1.1,3/2001, 2001.

[WJM+02]   A. Weinzoepflen, M. Jones, D. Mery, D. Cansell, and G. Gopalakrishnan. Incremental construction of a proof the producer/consumer property for the PCI protocol. In D. Bert, J. P. Bowen, M. C. Henson, and K. Robinson, editors, *The Second International Z and B Conference*, number 2272 in LNCS, pages 22–42, Grenoble, France, January 2002. Springer.

Java Program Verification via a JVM Deep Embedding in ACL2

Hanbing Liu and J. Strother Moore

Department of Computer Science
University of Texas at Austin
Austin, Texas, 78712-1188, USA

Abstract. In this paper, we show that one can "deep-embed" the Java bytecode language, a fairly complicated language with a rich semantics, into the first order logic of ACL2 by modeling a realistic JVM. We show that with proper support from a semi-automatic theorem prover in that logic, one can reason about the correctness of Java programs. This reasoning can be done in a direct and intuitive way without incurring the extra burden that has often been associated with hand proofs, or proofs that make use of less automated proof assistance. We present proofs for two simple Java programs as a showcase.

1 Introduction

In order to reason about software/hardware artifacts mathematically, we need to represent the artifacts as mathematical objects. We often formalize them by assigning a precise semantics to the underlying language constructs or hardware primitives.

In cases where there exists an axiomatic semantics for the language, we can reason about the artifact directly using axioms and specialized derivation rules. A typical example is Hoare logic [7].

However, such an approach makes it hard to use existing general purpose theorem provers such as ACL2 [13] and PVS [3], because for each different logical system, a new computer aided reasoning engine must be constructed. Constructing a specialized theorem prover comparable to current mature general purpose ones is often time consuming and error prone. Generic theorem proving environments such as Isabelle [18] prove to be useful in this setting, because Isabelle can be configured to function as a specialized theorem prover for different formalisms. Alternatively, if we can embed the language into the formalism of a powerful general purpose theorem prover, we can use that theorem prover for program verification projects. We think that this approach is also practical.

There are two common choices for formalizing a program artifact in the logic of a theorem prover. In a "shallow embedding" one describes a process by which a conjecture about a given program may be converted to an "equivalent" formula. Neither the programs (the original forms in the old syntax) nor the process are defined within the logic – they are meta-level entities. In a "deep embedding",

K. Slind et al. (Eds.): TPHOLs 2004, LNCS 3223, pp. 184–200, 2004.

programs and their environments are logical objects that are related by functions and relations formally defined within the logic. Usually, the syntax of the original programs is preserved. The semantics of the basic language constructs are formalized instead of the semantics of specific programs.

Each approach has its pros and cons. Shallow embedding requires less logical infrastructure and often produces simpler conjectures to prove. Deep embedding, however, allows one to reason formally not just about a given program but about relations between programs and properties of the semantics itself. For example, deep embedding a program with a semantics for the underlying programming language allow the user to reason about properties shared by a set of programs. Deep embedding also allows the user to derive new proof rules as theorems. However, much logical manipulation must occur to wade through the details of the semantics. Automation is highly desirable and brings new capabilities, such as simulation, symbolic evaluation, and other analysis tools.

It is this paper's thesis that Java program verification via a deep embedding of the JVM into the logic of ACL2 is a viable approach. In fact, we believe that with the proper support from a powerful semi-automatic theorem prover, the deep embedding approach is better than the shallow embedding approach in the sense that it brings more assurance of the verification result without incurring much extra burden.

In section 2, we present our deep embedding of a full featured JVM into ACL2. The executability of ACL2 models allows one to use such a complete deep embedding as a JVM simulator. In the section 3, we present correctness proofs for two simple Java programs to demonstrate the approach and illustrate some useful techniques in handling a deep embedding. In section 4, we review other work and comment on the proof effort required by our method and explain briefly the limitations of our work. We summarize and conclude in section 5.

2   Deep Embedding a JVM in ACL2

We wrote a precise model of the JVM in ACL2 to formally capture the meaning of Java bytecode programs. The JVM model is based on the JVM specification. We follow the KVM, a C implementation of the JVM, as a reference model in our "implementation"[1].

ACL2 is an applicative (side-effect free) subset of Common Lisp. Our JVM model can be executed as a Lisp program. It is implemented with around ten thousand lines of Lisp (ACL2) in about 25 modules. It implements most features of a JVM such as dynamic class loading, thread synchronization via monitors, together with 21 out of the 41 native methods defined in Java 2 Microedition's CLDC library [22]. The features that are missing are the "reflection" capability in the full JVM, user defined class loaders, floating point arithmetic, and native methods related to some I/O operations.

Realistic Java programs can execute on the model. We expect to run a suitable subset of some conformance test suite at some point. The details of the

---

[1] In the process, we discovered several implementation errors in the KVM. Some were already known to Sun. Some are forwarded to the KVM development team.

model are described in the paper [12], which we presented in the workshop of *Interpreter, Virtual Machine and Emulator 2003*, affiliated with PLDI[2].

2.1   Motivation to Embed a JVM

We are interested in applying theorem proving techniques to software verifications projects. In particular, we are interested in reasoning about the properties of the Java virtual machine and Java software executing on the JVM.

This is one of the reasons that we decided to deep-embed the Java bytecode language via a JVM model. The other reason is that we feel more confident in our ability to formalize the semantics of the bytecode language of the Java Virtual Machine than our ability to correctly assign meanings to specific Java programs or the Java programming language.

Like most imperative programming languages, the semantics of Java are hard to formalize directly. The object oriented features such as method overriding, dynamic method resolution, access permissions, and constructs such as inner classes present significant challenges.

As expressed in our position paper [11], the JVM bytecode is simpler and more precisely defined than Java. We therefore define the semantics of the bytecode language with an operational JVM interpreter. We reason about Java programs by reasoning about the corresponding bytecode program via javac on the JVM model. This approach was demonstrated by Yu [1] using the predecessor of ACL2, Nqthm to reason about C via gcc and a model of the Motorola 68020.

Because the model is formally defined in the logic, we can also reason about it independent of the consideration of any particular program. This allows us to derive new proof rules from the semantics, as well as to explore the implications of semantics, i.e. properties of the JVM itself. Both activities increase our understanding of and confidence in the semantics; and both activities are supported by machine-checked reasoning rather than informal reasoning. Finally, the bytecode analyzed is more closely related to what is actually executed than the original Java. In summary, we regard deep embedding as offering higher assurance than shallow embedding.

2.2   The JVM Model in ACL2

The completeness of our JVM embedding determines the range of Java programs that we can reason about as well as the relevance of our formal statements about the Java programs. Our model is fairly complete – it is a realistic JVM simulator that executes most Java programs that do not use I/O nor floating point operations.

Since ACL2 is applicative, we have to model the JVM state explicitly. All aspects of the machine state are encoded explicitly in one logical object denoted by a term. A JVM state in this model is a seven-tuple consisting of a global

---

[2] A revised version was accepted for publication in a special issue of the journal "Science of Computer Programming" for IVME'03.

program counter, a current thread register, a heap, a thread table, an internal class table that records the runtime representations of the loaded classes, an environment that represents the source from which classes are to be loaded, and a fatal error flag used by the interpreter to indicate an unrecoverable error.

The thread table is a table containing one entry per thread. Each entry has a slot for a saved copy of the global program counter, which points to the next instruction to be executed the next time this thread is scheduled. Among other things, the entry also records the method invocation stack (or "call stack") of the thread. The call stack is a stack of frames. Each frame specifies the method being executed, a return pc, a list of local variables, an operand stack, and possibly a reference to a Java object on which this invocation is synchronized.

The heap is a map from addresses to instance objects. The internal class table is a map from class names to descriptions of various aspects of each class, including its direct superclass, implemented interfaces, fields, methods, access flags, and the byte code for each method.

All of this state information is represented as a single Lisp object composed of lists, symbols, strings, and numbers. Operations on state components, including determination of the next instruction, object creation, and method resolution, are all defined as Lisp functions on these Lisp objects.

As a concrete example of how a piece of state is represented, the following entry is taken from an actual thread table when we used our model to execute a multi-threaded program for computing factorial. A semicolon (;) begins a comment extending to the end of the line.

```
(THREAD 0                      ; thread id is 0
  (SAVED-PC .   0)             ; slot for saved pc
  (CALL-STACK
   (FRAME (RETURN_PC .   7) ; pc to return to
          (OPERAND-STACK)    ; empty operand stack
          (LOCALS 104)
          (METHOD-PTR "FactHelper" "<init>" ...)
          (SYNC-OBJ-REF .  -1))
   (FRAME (RETURN_PC .  18)
          ...
          (METHOD-PTR "FactHelper" "compute"...)
          (SYNC-OBJ-REF .  -1))
   ...)
  (STATUS THREAD_ACTIVE)       ; thread state
  (MONITOR .  -1)              ; lock
  (MDEPTH .  0)                ; entering count
  (THREAD-OBJ .  55))          ; object rep in heap
```

Each thread table entry has slots for recording a thread id, a pc, a call stack, a thread state, a reference to the monitor, the number of times the thread has entered the monitor, and a reference to the Java object representing the thread in the heap.

The semantics of the JVM instructions are modeled operationally as state transition functions. Here is the state transition function for the IDIV instruction.

```
(defun execute-IDIV (inst s)
  (let ((v2 (topStack s))
        (v1 (secondStack s)))
    (if (equal v2 0)
        (raise-exception "java.lang.ArithmeticException" s)
      (advance-pc
        (pushStack (int-fix (truncate v1 v2))
                   (popStack (popStack s)))))))
```

Here, inst is understood to be a parsed IDIV instruction. Advance-pc is a Lisp macro to advance the global program counter by the size of the instruction. PushStack pushes a value on the operand stack of the *current frame* (the top call frame of the current thread) and returns the resulting state. When the item on the top of the operand stack of the current frame is zero, the output of execute-IDIV is a state obtained from s by raising an exception of type java.lang.ArithmeticException. If the top item is not zero, the resulting state is obtained by changing the operand stack in the current frame and advancing the program counter. The operand stack is changed by pushing a certain value (described below) onto the result of popping two items off the initial operand stack. The value pushed is the twos-complement integer represented by the low-order 32-bits of the integer quotient of the second item on the initial operand stack divided by the first item on it. In ACL2, the function truncate returns an integer quotient rounded toward 0.

The top level interpreter loop is modeled as following:

```
(defun run (sched s)
  (if (endp sched) s          ; end of schedule
    (let ((nid (car sched)) ; else
          (cid (current-thread s)))
      (if (equal cid nid)
          (run (cdr sched) (step s)) ; execute one step
        (run (cdr sched)
          (loadExecutionEnvironment
            nid                ; proper thread context switch
            (storeExecutionEnvironment s)))))))
```

Our JVM model takes a "schedule" (a list of thread ids) and a state as the input and repeatedly executes the next instruction from the thread as indicated in the schedule, until the schedule is exhausted.

The scheduling policy is thus left unspecified. Any schedule can be simulated. However to use the model as an execution engine without providing a schedule list explicitly, we have implemented some simple scheduling policies. One of them is a not-very-realistic round-robin scheduling algorithm, which does a rescheduling after executing each bytecode instruction.

Before concluding this section, we observe that the defun of run (and of each of the other functions shown above) can be thought of in either of two ways. First, it defines a side-effect free Lisp program which can be executed on concrete data. Second, it introduces a new logical definitional equation which can be used to prove theorems about the newly defined function symbol. Preserving the view that we are "merely" defining an executable model often provides valuable clarity. Executing the model often provides assistance in the search for true statements about programs and in the search for proofs. In some sense, the "embedding" is so direct that it is transparent, i.e. we are reasoning about the JVM directly.

3   Java Program Verification

With our choice of a deep embedding of the Java bytecode language, reasoning about any Java bytecode program implies that we need to deal with the complexity of the JVM in addition to the program itself. The task seems to be formidable. This additional complexity is considered one of the major drawbacks of the deep embedding approach.

We acknowledge that deep embedding adds extra complexity in the verification of programs. But if one can accomplish the program verification task at this level, we believe that additional confidence is gained.

The central remaining question is whether one can reduce the "extra" complexity to an acceptable level. It is our experience with the JVM and ACL2 that one can achieve this reduction by configuring the rewriting engine of ACL2 using lemma libraries. Such configuration needs to be done only once for a class of programs.

In this section, we present proofs of two simple programs to show how we manage the complexity in ACL2. We show the proof for the first program in some detail and refer readers to the actual proof scripts for comments and other details in the supporting material [6].

3.1   ADD1 Program

The first program is trivial.

```
public class First {
    public static void main(String[] args) {
        int i=1;
        int j=i+1;
        i=j;
        return;}}
```

The main method is straight line code that only modifies the operand stack and local variables in the current call frame, i.e. the top most activation record from the call stack of the current thread. With this example, we illustrate how we can reason about programs and segments of programs which only manipulate the current call frame.

Our tool *jvm2acl2* transforms the First.class into the following format, which directly corresponds to the class file format [23].

```
'(class "First"                  ; class name is First
        "java.lang.Object"       ; Superclass is java.lang.Object
        ....
        (fields)                 ; list of field definitions
        (methods                 ; list of method definitions
            (method "<init>"
                ....)
            (method "main"       ; method name.
                (parameters (array (class "java.lang.String")))
                (returntype void)
                (accessflags *class* *public* *static* )
                (code
                    (max_stack 2) ...
                    (parsedcode
                        (0 (iconst_1)) ;; *Note: (0 (iload_2))
                        (1 (istore_1))
                        (2 (iload_1))
                        (3 (iconst_1))
                        (4 (iadd))
                        (5 (istore_2))
                        (6 (iload_2))
                        (7 (istore_1))
                        (8 (return))
                        (endofcode 9))
                    (Exceptions )
                    (StackMap )))))
        ....)
```

This logical constant represents the First.class file. A list of such class constants together with the JVM interpreter gives the semantics of the original Java program. For this program, the semantics of the main method only depends on the JVM interpreter and this particular class itself; for more complicated programs, the meaning of a user-defined class often depends on other classes.

To make the example slightly more interesting, we change by hand the first instruction, (0 (iconst_1)), to (0 (iload_2))[3]. We prove that by starting in a state where the pc is 0 and executing 7 steps according to a round robin scheduling algorithm, we produce a state in which the value in the second slot of the locals is increased by one from its original value. We describe what is essential to configure ACL2 in deriving this.

---

[3] In fact, this makes the class file fail to pass bytecode verification. Here we are trying to make the proof a little bit more interesting by proving an assertion in form of $\forall i, P(i)$.

The first step is to identify the appropriate abstractions of JVM executions and formalize those concepts properly. For example, consider the intuitive understanding of what the "next instruction" is. In our JVM model, such a concept is complex because the state is complex. The next instruction of a given state is the instruction that resides at a certain offset within the bytecode of the current method, where the offset is given as the value of the pc field of the state; and the current method is identified by consulting the current class table using the method identifier in the activation record of the current thread. One must also consider special conditions, such as when the current thread does not exist or has been stopped by another thread. Such complexity is reduced by defining a named function of state, `next-inst`, and using it consistently within the model so that the above details are not exposed. We regard this as just good modeling practice. We typically configure ACL2 so as not to expand the definitions of these abstractions ("disabling" the associated rules in ACL2's database). We will rely only on a set of properties of these operations on "states of interest", which we prove before we disable the definition.

The reason that the intuitive informal notion of "next instruction" appears simpler is probably because the user evaluates it only on symbolic states for which `next-inst` returns constants. That is, when considering the verification of a particular program in thread 0 informally, we do not contemplate whether there can be a context switch to a thread, or whether the current activation record corresponds to the program of interest.

In the second step, we formalize the concepts that capture the identified domain, i.e. "states of interest". We prove that in the identified domain, complicated primitive operations have the simple behavior as expected. To formalize this we introduce an equivalence relation on states, `equiv-state`, that means, roughly, "the states are executing the same program." We are more precise below. ACL2's rewrite engine can use arbitrary equivalences and congruence lemmas (which establish that certain functions cannot distinguish "equivalent" input) to descend through the subterms of a term and replace occurrences of target terms by equivalent terms.

To cause the next instruction concept to expand only on the states of interest we prove the following lemma and then disable the definition of `next-inst`

```
(defthm equiv-state-init-state-next-inst
  (implies (equiv-state s (init-state))
           (equal (next-inst s)
                  (inst-by-offset (pc s) (theMethod)))))
```

The theorem asserts that for any state running the program of interest (that in the constant (`init-state`)), the next instruction can be computed by looking at a certain offset of the program of interest. This is a trivial theorem to prove. On states equivalent to (`init-state`) the body of `next-inst` can be reduced to a constant, namely, the next instruction. Thus, by proving this lemma and disabling `next-inst`, ACL2 will reduce (`next-inst s`) to a constant instruction if s is running the program of interest, but will not change the `next-inst` term otherwise.

In order to use the just established theorem to rewrite (next-inst s) into a simpler form, where s is a (round-robin-run s n) term, we need to reason about the run function th a round robin scheduler. In particular, we need to prove that there is no context switch as the program steps from one instruction to the next. To prove there is no context switch, we proved three types of theorems around the equivalence relation that we identified:

- A congruence on the equivalence relation equiv-state, which asserts that the round robin scheduler always picks the same thread if two states are equiv-state.

```
(defthm round-robin-schedule-equal-in-equiv-state
   (implies (equiv-state s s-equiv)
            (equal (round-robin-schedule s-equiv)
                   (round-robin-schedule s))))
 :rule-classes :congruence)
```

- A theorem that states the properties of the initial state. In this case, the round robin scheduler picks the thread 0 to execute in the initial state.

```
(defthm round-robin-schedule-init-state
   (equal (round-robin-schedule (init-state)) 0))
```

- Theorems that state equivalence is preserved by executing each primitive, e.g., pushStack.

```
(defthm pushStack-preserves-equiv-state
   (equiv-state (pushStack v s) s))
```

Having so configured ACL2 by proving these lemmas, JVM execution of straight line code can be expanded into a composition of primitives by ACL2 automatically. For example,

```
(defthm round-robin-run-expansion-example
   (implies (and (equiv-state  s1 (init-state))
                 (equal (pc s1) 2))
            (equiv-state (round-robin-run s1 4)
                         (init-state))))
```

is proved automatically. The theorem prover expands the (round-robin-run s1 4) symbolically step by step using the rewrite rules derived from the proven theorems.

In this example, starting from pc equals 2, (round-robin-run s 4) executes (iload_1)), (iconst_1), (iadd), and (istore_2) in sequence. Because every instruction is one byte. Executing 4 instructions shall result in a term of the following form, where pc is 6.

```
(state-set-pc 6                            ;#
  (popStack                                ;#
    (state-set-local 2 (topStack ..)       ;# cf. ISTORE_2
      (state-set-pc 5                       ;*
        (pushStack                          ;*
          (int-fix (binary-+ ...)) ;*
            (popStack (popStack   ;* cf. IADD
              (state-set-pc 4 ....)))))))))
                                           ;% cf. ICONST_1
                                           ;$     ILOAD_1
```

Compare this expected form to one of the intermediate goals generated by ACL2:

```
Subgoal 1'5'
(IMPLIES
 (AND (EQUIV-STATE S1 (INIT-STATE))
      (EQUAL (PC S1) 2)  ; pc = 2 in starting state
      (EQUAL 0 (CURRENT-THREAD S1)))
 (EQUIV-STATE
  (POPSTACK                                ;*
   (POPSTACK                               ;* cf. partial IADD
    (STATE-SET-PC                          ;%
     4                                     ;%
     (PUSHSTACK 1                          ;% cf. ICONST_1
      (STATE-SET-PC 3                      ;$
       (PUSHSTACK (LOCAL-AT 1 (LOCALS (CURRENT-FRAME S1)))
                  S1))))))                 ;$ cf. ILOAD_1
  (INIT-STATE))).
```

In Subgoal 1'5', ACL2 has reduced

```
(equiv-state (state-set-pc 6 (popStack (state-set-local 2 ...)))
             (init-state))
```

into

```
(equiv-state (popStack (popStack (state-set-pc 4 ...)))
             (init-state))
```

after "peeling off" some outer primitives such as (state-set-pc 6 ...).

This shows that reasoning about (next-inst s) is entirely automatic. The theorem prover "knows" enough to determine the next instruction and then to execute it as a symbolic execution engine. A formula involving the round-robin-run is thus reduced to a composition of primitives, such a pushStack, popStack, state-set-pc. The structure of the composition of primitives can be traced back to the instructions in the original bytecode sequence.

The third configuration step is to arrange for the theorem prover to reason about compositions of different primitives. This is closely related to the second step – identifying conditions under which the primitives behave according to our intuitions.

For example, we have an understanding of the effects of the push and pop operations on a stack. The following should obviously be true.

$$\text{(popStack (pushStack v s))} = \text{s}$$

However the above is not so obvious in a Java program without some implicit hypothesis. PushStack pushes a value onto the operand stack of the topmost call frame of the current thread. For the above to be true, we need to explicitly show (or configure the theorem prover to automatically recognize), no other part of the state is changed. The similar problem manifests itself in other places such as showing that setting the program counter does not affect the operand stack. This is the pattern called the "frame" problem in AI research. To describe the effect of an operation, we not only need to be explicit about what is changed, but also be explicit about what does not change.

Our current solution is built around equivalences and associated congruence rules. We identify what is not changing and introduce an equivalence that groups the states that share the unchanged part. We prove that primitive operations preserve those equivalences. We prove other properties of those equivalences in the form of congruence rules.

In this ADD1 program proof, we recognize that the program is straight line code that only modifies the operand stack and the locals. We defined the state equivalence to capture the following: if the only difference between two states are the operand stack and locals of their respective current frame, they are equivalent.

This strategy has worked well. However we can foresee limitations in our approach. When dealing with more complicated operations such as the ones that manipulate the heap, we may face the need to define a hierarchy of equivalence relations to characterize differences between different operations.

The following is the final theorem we proved about the ADD1 program[4]. The current proof script in ACL2 is about 2000 lines with over 140 user typed lemmas[5].

```
(defthm first-is-correct
  (let ((old (local-at 2 s1)))
  (implies (and (equiv-state s1 (init-state))
                (current-thread-exists? s1)
                (wff-state-regular s1)
                (wff-thread-table-regular (thread-table s1))
                (wff-call-frame-regular (current-frame s1))
                (unique-id-thread-table (thread-table s1))
                (equal (pc s1) 0)
                (integerp old))
           (equal (local-at 2 (round-robin-run s1 7))
                  (int-fix (+ 1 old)))))))
```

---

[4] ACL2 has implicit universal quantifiers over all free variables appearing in a formula.

[5] This proof script represents a first cut at the problem. It can be improved. The proof is available as part of the supporting material [6].

The apparent complexity in the statement is partly inherent in the JVM specification. Others result from our particular choice in implementation. Almost all efforts in this proof are devoted for defining a proper domain and configuring our theorem prover to reason about interactions between primitives in that domain.

One can argue that we could have saved effort by reasoning about this program at a higher level. We agree with this view. However, the effort expended to configure ACL2 to reason about this simple program does not have to be repeated. We have developed an ACL2 "book" (a file containing definitions and lemmas) that codifies the necessary "concepts" and "knowledge", and configures ACL2 to reason about straight-line programs automatically. We thus have high confidence in our semantics and can reason about it without difficulty. In fact, we have proved properties of a different piece of straight line program that computes (int-fix (+ 4 (* 2 old))), with 100 lines[6].

3.2   Recursive Factorial Program

In this section, we briefly discuss our experience with a second proof effort that reuses the definitions and lemmas developed in the ADD1 program proof. The program computes the factorial of its input, or, to be more precise, it computes the signed integer representation of the low order 32-bits of the mathematical factorial.

The program of interest is as follows

```
(class "Second"
    ....
  (method "fact"
      (parameters int)
      (returntype int)
      ....
      (code
          ....
          (parsedcode
          (0 (iload_0))
          (1 (ifgt 6))   ;;to TAG_0
          (4 (iconst_1))
          (5 (ireturn))
          (6 (iload_0)) ;;at TAG_0
          (7 (iload_0))
          (8 (iconst_1))
          (9 (isub))
          (10 (invokestatic (methodCP "fact" "Second" (int) int)))
          (13 (imul))
          (14 (ireturn))
          ....))))
```

---

[6] Details are available from the supporting materials.

This program is still very simple conceptually but much more complicated than the ADD1 program. We proved the following theorem

```
(defthm second-is-correct
  (implies (and (poised-for-execute-fact s)
                (wff-state-regular s)
                (wff-thread-table-regular (thread-table s))
                (no-fatal-error? s)
                (integerp n)
                (<= 0 n)
                (intp n)
                (equal n (topStack s)))
           (equal (simple-run s (fact-clock n))
                  (state-set-pc (+ 3 (pc s))
                                (pushStack (int-fix (fact n))
                                           (popStack s)))))))
```

The theorem may be read as follows. Let s be a state poised to invoke our fact method, i.e., whose next instruction is an invokestatic of fact. Suppose the state is in some suitable sense well-formed, that n is a nonnegative 32-bit integer and that n is on top of the stack. Run s a certain number of steps, namely (fact-clock n). The result is a state that could be alternately obtained by incrementing the pc of s by 3 (the number of bytes in the invokestatic instruction), popping the stack (to remove n), and pushing the int representation of (fact n). Here fact is defined in the logic as the standard mathematical factorial.

What is new in the program is that it involves the method invocation that changes the call stack of the current thread.

What may at first be surprising is that the second proof is much shorter than the proof about the ADD1 program. One reason is because in the first proof we reasoned about a round robin scheduler. However, the more essential reason is that we reused our results from the first proof about straight line code.

To explain, it is necessary to describe how ACL2 works. ACL2 is a semi-automatic theorem prover. The user submits definitions, and formulas that are asserted to be theorems. The system attempts to establish the legality of each definition and the validity of each alleged theorem. When a formula is proven to be a theorem it is converted into a rule and stored in the database. In most cases, a rewrite rule is generated. By submitting an appropriate sequence of lemmas the user can configure ACL2 to prove theorems with certain strategies. The sequence of interactions is called a session. The file containing the definitions and lemmas is called a "book." Subsequent sessions may begin by including books taken "from the shelf." The ACL2 distribution contains many standard books on arithmetic, sets, vectors, floating point, etc. Using the ADD1 program as a "challenge" problem, we created a book that codifies how to reason about straight-line programs that modify only the operand stack and locals.

To prove fact correct we start with the basic ADD1 book (or just continue the ADD1 session) and follow the same strategy. We introduce the abstraction of `pushFrame`, `popFrame`; we introduce a new state equivalence that captures what does not change during a call stack manipulation; and we prove theorems to guide ACL2 reasoning about compositions of operand stack primitives with call stack primitives.

The surprise in this proof effort is that the semantics of invoking a method in JVM (and Java) is rather rich. It involves dynamic class resolution, which in turn relies on primitives that load a class. Moreover, loading a class is related to creating objects dynamically in the heap. Thread synchronization and class initialization are also involved. We spend a major part of our efforts in reasoning about those primitives. In the final theorem, we assume **s** is a state in which the class is already loaded by asserting the starting state is "equivalent" to some constant state where the "Second" class is loaded. More details and some explanations are available in the supporting material [6] for this paper.

4   Review and Related Work

The challenge in using a deep embedding of a realistic programming language like JVM bytecode is managing the complexity at proof-time. We presented two proofs to show that the apparent complexity involved in the deep embedding can be alleviated by introducing the necessary abstractions and proving properties of those primitives in an identified domain.

Identifying the appropriate abstractions is relatively simple. Most work involves correctly identifying the domain where the primitives behave according to the intuition of the user. Another major effort is establishing properties of the abstract primitives and configuring the theorem proving engine to use them (typically, but not exclusively) as rewrite rules.

The main limitation of the current work is that we have not yet developed a good and concise set of primitives and their properties. Even though the proof of the `ADD1` program is automatic, it is quite long. On the other hand, our experience with the factorial program proof shows that even with the non-optimized set of lemmas, one can still benefit from the support of the computer aided reasoning tool. In developing the lemmas for the factorial program proof we do not have to think about how to reason about straight-line code – a problem solved once and for all in the `ADD1` proof. In the factorial proof we focus on the primitives that manipulate the call stack.

We have not explored proofs about more complicated JVM operations in our model, such as allocation of new objects in the heap or synchronization using monitors. Programs using such primitives have been verified with ACL2 using a simpler JVM model that does not include our modeling of dynamic class loading and exceptions [16].

The sample proofs presented here are proofs for complete correctness. The lemma library about primitives can be reused for proving partial correctness of Java programs. In his CHARME 2003 paper [15], Moore shows that Floyd-Hoare style assertion based program proofs can be constructed directly from the formal operational semantics with little extra logical overhead, i.e. with no need to write a verification condition generator or other meta-logical tools. To make effective use of the operational semantics in place of a conventional verification condition generator, ACL2 needs to be configured to simplify the compositions of JVM primitives. Thus the present work may be viewed as a follow-up to Moore's work on Floyd-Hoare style proofs for bytecode programs on a very complete JVM model.

In addition to using our model to verify properties of bytecode programs, we are using it to explore the correctness of the JVM bytecode verifier. In our approach, defining a realistic JVM is one of the necessary steps in that effort. This is an additional justification for the choice of a deep embedding: it allows us to state and prove "meta-level" properties. For existing works on formalizing bytecode verification, the special issue on Java bytecode verification from the Journal of Automated Reasoning is a good reference [17].

The collection of "Formal syntax and semantics of Java" edited by Alves-Foss contains many early works in formalizing the Java programming language [4]. The Java Language Specification [10] provides the informal specification. Although we feel it is hard to formalize a complex language by designing an axiomatic semantics, the LOOP project [21] has formalized the semantics of Java and a Java annotation language JML based on *coalgebra*. They are also deriving proof rules in the style of Hoare logic for embedding Java into PVS [8].

To us, a more feasible method is to give Java an operational semantics. In [9], Attali et.al. present an operational semantics for Java using the structural operational semantics approach [19]. We think that our operational semantics given by state transformation appeals to human intuition better than the operational semantics based on structural transformation. This in turn makes it easier to validate the formal semantics against informal specifications and benchmark implementations. In addition, we feel that a structural operational semantics would be awkward to support in ACL2.

Börger et. al use abstract state machines for modeling the dynamic semantics of Java [20]. This work seems close to our work at the JVM level. The work by T. Nipkow, et. al., on μJava [24] and the Bali project[5] embeds a subset of Java and the Java bytecode language into the theorem prover Isabelle/HOL to reason about the type safety of those languages. Recently, J. Meseguer's group in UIUC has used the rewriting logic and engine Maude [2] to formalize the semantics of Java and the JVM [14].

In contrast to the above efforts, our work presented in this paper is focused on modeling an executable JVM and reasoning about Java program via the direct and intuitive state transformation semantics of its corresponding bytecode program on the JVM model.

5   Conclusion

To use a general purpose theorem prover in formal program verification the semantics of a program to be verified must be expressed in the language of the theorem prover's logic.

In this paper, we show that one can deeply embed the Java bytecode language, a fairly complicated language with rich semantics, into the first order logic of ACL2 by modeling a realistic JVM. We reason "about Java programs" by compiling them with Sun's javac and then reasoning about the bytecode.

We claim that this is a viable approach in doing Java program verification. One of the obvious advantages of deep embedding is that its operational nature makes the semantics correspond closely to informal descriptions in the JVM specification and with benchmark implementations, increasing one's confidence in the model. The behavior of programs under the model and properties of the model are then derived by the theorem proving engine, increasing one's confidence that the reasoning is sound.

The central question is whether we can effectively deal with the complexity introduced by this approach. We show that with the support of a user guided, semi-automatic computer proof assistant, the user can reason about programs at a fairly intuitive level. In a system like ACL2 the necessary support can be arranged by defining appropriate abstractions and proving lemmas about them for automatic use by the system. We demonstrate this by covering two concrete proofs, with the later one reusing the results of the first one as a lemma library.

We feel the limitation of the current work is that our lemma libraries for reasoning about Java programs are still unoptimized and only cover selected JVM primitives. Our current focus has been in formalizing the correctness of the Java bytecode verifier. We are looking forward to extending our work to provide a full-fledged Java verification system.

Acknowledgement

Authors would like to thank our reviewers for their valuable advices. We would also like to thank our group members in Austin Serita Van Groningen, Robert Krug and Omar El-Domeiri, for their efforts in "debugging" the paper with us.

References

1. R. S. Boyer and Y. Yu. Automated proofs of object code for a widely used microprocessor. *Journal of the ACM*, 43(1):166–192, January 1996.
2. M. Clavel, F. Durán, S. Eker, P. Lincoln, N. Martí-Oliet, J. Meseguer, and J. Quesada. *A Maude Tutorial*. SRI International, 2000.
3. J. Crow, S. Owre, J. Rushby, N. Shankar, and M. Srivas. A tutorial introduction to PVS. In *Workshop on Industrial-Strength Formal Specification Techniques*, Boca Raton, FL, April 1995.
4. J. Alves Foss, editor. *Formal Syntax and Semantics of Java*, volume 1523 of *LNCS*. Springer-Verlag, 1999.
5. G. Klein, T. Nipkow, D. von Oheimb, C. Pusch, and L. P. Nieto. Project Bali. Available from http://isabelle.in.tum.de/bali/, May 2004.
6. H. Liu and J S. Moore. Supplement: proof scripts, etc. http://coldice.csres.utexas.edu/~hbl/tphol2004/, Feb 2004.

7. C. A. R. Hoare. An axiomatic basis for computer programming. *Commun. ACM*, 12(10):576–580, 1969.
8. Marieke Huisman and Bart Jacobs. Java program verification via a Hoare logic with abrupt termination. *Lecture Notes in Computer Science*, 1783:284+, 2000.
9. I. Attali, D. Caromel, and M. Russo. A formal executable semantics for java. In *Proceedings of Formal Underpinnings of Java Workshop, OOPSLA'98*, 1998.
10. J. Gosling, B. Joy, G. L. Steele Jr., and G. Bracha. *The Java Language Specification*. Addison-Wesley Publisher, second edition, 2000.
11. J S. Moore, R. Krug, H. Liu, and G. Porter. Formal models of Java at the JVM level: A survey from the ACL2 perspective. In *Workshop on Formal Techniques for Java Programs, ECOOP 2001*. 2001.
12. H. Liu and J S. Moore. Executable JVM model for analytical reasoning: a study. In *Proceedings of the 2003 workshop on Interpreters, Virtual Machines and Emulators*, pages 15–23. ACM Press, 2003.
13. M. Kaufmann, P. Manolios, and J S. Moore. *Computer-aided Reasoning: An approach*. Kluwer Academic Publishers, 2000.
14. J. Meseguer. Rewriting logic based semantics and analysis of concurrent programs. Talk at UT-Austin, Feb 2004.
15. J S. Moore. Inductive assertions and operational semantics. In *the 12th Advanced Research Working Conference on Correct Hardware Design and Verification Methods (CHARME 2003)*, volume 2860 of *LNCS*, October 2003.
16. J S. Moore. Proving theorems about Java and the JVM with ACL2. In M. Broy and M. Pizka, editors, *Models, Algebras and Logic of Engineering Software*, pages 227–290. IOS Press, Amsterdam, 2003.
   http://www.cs.utexas.edu/users/moore/publications/marktoberdorf-03.
17. T. Nipkow, editor. *Java Bytecode Verification*, volume 30(3-4), 2003.
18. L. C. Paulson. *Isabelle: a generic theorem prover*. Springer-Verlag, 1994.
19. G. Plotkin. A structural approach to operational semantics. Technical report, University of Aarhus, Denmark, 1981.
20. R. F. Stärk, J. Schmid, and E. Börger. *Java and the Java Virtual Machine: Definition, Verification, Validation*. Springer, 2001.
21. University of Nijmegen Security of System Group. LOOP project. http://www.cs.kun.nl/~bart/LOOP/.
22. Connected Limited Device Configuration (CLDC) Specification 1.1. http://jcp.org/en/jsr/detail?id=139.
23. T. Lindholm and F. Yellin. *The Java Virtual Machine Specification*. Addison-Wesley Publisher, second edition, 1999.
24. T. Nipkow, D. Oheimb, and C. Pusch. μJava: Embedding a programming language in a theorem prover. In F. L. Bauer and R. Steinbrüggen, editors, *Foundations of Secure Computation*, volume 175 of *NATO Science Series F: Computer and Systems Sciences*, 2000.

Reasoning About CBV Functional Programs in Isabelle/HOL[*]

John Longley and Randy Pollack

Edinburgh University, UK
{jrl,rap}@inf.ed.ac.uk

1 Introduction

We consider the old problem of proving that a computer program meets some specification. By proving, we mean machine checked proof in some formal logic. The programming language we choose to work with is a call by value functional language, essentially the functional core of Standard ML (SML). In future work we hope to add exceptions, then references and I/O to the language.

The full SML language has a formal definition in terms of a big-step operational semantics [MTHM97]. While such a definition may support formal reasoning about meta-theoretical properties of the language, it is too low-level for convenient reasoning about programs [Sym94,GV94]. Our approach stands in an alternative tradition of high-level, axiomatic *program logics* [GMW79,Pau87], and allows programmers to reason relatively directly at a level they are familiar with. In these respects, our work has roots in the logic of the LAMBDA 3.2 theorem prover and the ideas of Fourman and Phoa [PF92].

In contrast to some approaches, where the programming language is embedded in a first order logic [Tho95,HT95,Stä03], we have chosen to use higher order logic (HOL) as a meta language in order to have a rich set-theoretic language for writing program specifications. For example, we will discuss a program for sorting lists. The specification involves mathematical definitions of being an ordered list and being a permutation of another list, which are expressed in HOL using inductively defined relations.

A key feature of our approach is that the meaning of the logic can be explained in terms of purely operational concepts, such as syntactic definability and observational equivalence. Thus the logic will be intelligible to SML programmers. On the other hand, the *soundness* of our logic with respect to this interpretation can be justified by a denotational semantics; indeed, in designing our logic we have relied on well-understood denotational models for guidance.

It is clear that non-trivial proofs about programs require powerful proof automation facilities combined with flexible user interaction. The Isabelle/HOL system [NPW02] provides a ready made proof environment with these features. Using a higher order abstract syntax (HOAS) presentation in Isabelle/HOL,

---

[*] Research supported by EPSRC grant GR/N64571: "A proof system for correct program development".

K. Slind et al. (Eds.): TPHOLs 2004, LNCS 3223, pp. 201–216, 2004.

we have done pragmatic experiments without developing syntactical and logical foundations from scratch. However, we have not found it possible to give a completely faithful encoding of our logic in Isabelle/HOL (see sections 2.1 and 3.3), so our work should be regarded as an experimental prototype rather than a finished tool for reasoning about programs. We have in mind an approach that would fix these problems (section 3.3), but building a system that implements this approach is left as a possibility for future work.

The Isabelle/HOL/Isar source files of our work are available from URL http://homepages.inf.ed.ac.uk/rap/mlProgLog.tgz.

Related Work. In addition to related work mentioned above, our work is very close in spirit to Extended ML [KST97,KS98]. That work takes specification and reasoning about official SML programs much further than we do, including SML program modules, and deep study of modularity for specifications. However, our approach differs from that of Extended ML in its use of insights from denotational semantics, which has enabled us to design a clean and soundly-based logic, without the explosion in complexity that beset the Extended ML project.

A foundational development of domain theory, also in Isabelle/HOL, is described in [MNvOS99]. This work is not an operational program logic, but provides a HOL type of continuous functions, and the tools to reason about them. It also goes further in uniform definition of datatypes than we have yet. However, the need to reason foundationally limits its pragmatic convenience. Furthermore, we believe our presentation, based on a logically fully abstract model (section 3.2), can be soundly extended to prove more observational equivalences than the system of [MNvOS99].

An embedding of the Ocaml language into Nuprl Type theory is reported in [Kre04]. Since Nuprl is extensional, fixpoints can be directly represented using the Y combinator. However, these fixpoints can only be typed in a total setting, so this approach cannot reason about non-terminating functions, but only about functions total on a specified domain. E.g. our proof (section 5.1) that removing all zeros from a stream of naturals returns a stream without any zeros cannot be developed in the Nuprl approach.

Structure of the Paper. In section 2 we present the syntax of the core programming language, and axioms of our logic for this core. In section 3 we explain the operational interpretation we have in mind for the logic, and outline the denotational semantics that underpins and justifies it. In section 4 we add datatypes for natural numbers and polymorphic lists to our language, and describe some case studies in reasoning about programs on these datatypes. In fact, reasoning about programs on these well-founded datatypes is not so different from reasoniong in logics of total functions, like HOL iteself. Thus in section 5 we consider the recursive datatype of streams, and set a problem for ourselves that cannot be treated in a coinductive system of total functions. Indeed, we need one more general axiom to reason about recursive datatypes. The example of streams points the way towards a uniform treatment of all positive recursive datatypes.

2 The Core Language

2.1 Syntax of the Programming Language

See figure 1. There is a typeclass, SML, to contain programming language types, and a subclass, SMLeq, for SML equality types. Types in other typeclasses retain their purely logical meaning in HOL. Variables in typeclass SML range over syntactic programs.

We use a higher order syntax embedding of the programming language into Isabelle/HOL: an ML function type constructor, -> (which applies only to SML types, and will be axiomatized as strict), is distinguished from the logical HOL function type, => (which applies to all HOL types, and is non-strict, even on SML types). As usual, there are constants

```
lam :: "('a => 'b) => 'a->'b"          (binder "fn " 30)
APP :: "['a->'b,'a] => 'b"             (infixl "$" 55)
```

relating object and meta function types. In these declarations, 'a and 'b are inferred to be in typeclass SML, and $ is infix application for SML functions. Isabelle binder syntax allows to write fn x. F x for lam F, where F has HOL functional type. We have polymorphic constants Fix (a fixpoint operator) and bot (a non-terminating program), which are definable in official SML.

UNIT, BOOL, ** (product) and ++ (sum) types are given atomically, with their constructors (e.g. tt and ff) and destructors (e.g. BCASE). From the declared type of BCASE you can see that it is non-strict in its branches, which is correct for an SML case statement.

Using Isabelle syntax translations, we can improve our syntax somewhat (see bottom of figure 1), but Isabelle parsing is so complex that we prefer not to steer too close to the wind with overloading and syntax translations.

Isabelle/HOL typechecking over typeclass SML serves to typecheck programs. This is very convenient for both developing and using our tool, but not quite faithful to the SML definition, as HOL polymorphism is not the same as SML polymorphism. For example, ML *let polymorphism* is not captured in our encoding. Different representations are possible, with explicit typing judgements, that would overcome this problem, but these are significantly more complicated.

2.2 Logic for the Core Programming Language

HOL equality over types in the SML typeclass represents observational equivalence in the SML semantics, i.e. indistinguishability in any context. Equal programs may be intensionally different. For example, a naive Fibonacci program is equal to an efficient one, although they have different complexities. This is part of our approach: prove contextual properties of a simple, but inefficient program, prove that an efficient program is equal to the simple one, and conclude that the efficient program has the same contextual properties.

In figure 2 we define a judgement of definedness (i.e. termination), dfd, and syntax udfd for its negation. The defined constant mlIter will be explained below.

```
classes
  SML < type          --{* a class of programming language types *}
  SMLeq < SML         --{* a subclass for equality types        *}

defaultsort SML

typedecl  UNIT
typedecl  BOOL
typedecl  ('a,'b) "->"      (infixr 80)  --{* functions *}
typedecl  ('a,'b) "++"      (infixr 85)  --{* sums *}
typedecl  ('a,'b) "**"      (infixr 90)  --{* products *}

arities
  UNIT :: SMLeq
  BOOL :: SMLeq
  "->" :: (SML,SML)SML
  "++" :: (SML,SML)SML
  "++" :: (SMLeq,SMLeq)SMLeq
  "**" :: (SML,SML)SML
  "**" :: (SMLeq,SMLeq)SMLeq

consts     --{* bottom, unit and bool *}
  bot   :: "'a::SML"                              --{* polymorphic bottom *}
  UN    :: UNIT                    ("<>")
  tt    :: BOOL
  ff    :: BOOL
  EQ    :: "('a::SMLeq) -> 'a -> BOOL"
  BCASE :: "['a,'a] => (BOOL ->'a)"                    --{* non-strict *}
consts  --{* product: one constructor *}
  PAIR  :: "'a -> 'b -> 'a ** 'b"
  PCASE :: "('a -> 'b -> 'c) => ('a ** 'b -> 'c)"     --{* non-strict *}
consts  --{* sum: two constructors *}
  inl     :: "'a -> 'a ++ 'b"
  inr     :: "'b -> 'a ++ 'b"
  SumCASE :: "['a->'c, 'b->'c] => ('a ++ 'b -> 'c)"  --{* non-strict *}
consts  --{* functions and recursion *}
  lam   :: "('a => 'b) => 'a->'b"            (binder "fn " 30)
  APP   :: "['a->'b,'a] => 'b"               (infixl "$" 55)
  Fix   :: "(('a->'b) -> 'a->'b) -> 'a->'b"

syntax  --{* some syntactic sugar *}
  IF    :: "[BOOL, 'a, 'a] => 'a"
  "[,]" :: "'a => 'b => 'a ** 'b"            (infixr 30)
  "[=]" :: "[('a::SMLeq), 'a] => BOOL"       (infixl 34)
translations
  "IF b x y" == "(BCASE x y) $ b"  --{* x and y are non-strict *}
  "x[,]y" == "PAIR $ x $ y"          --{* pairing strict in both args *}
  "x[=]y" == "EQ $ x $ y"            --{* EQ strict in both args *}
```

Fig. 1. Language

```
constdefs     --{* definedness defined in terms of bot *}
  dfd :: "'a => bool"
  "dfd x == x ~= bot"
translations
  "udfd x" == "~ dfd x"


--{* we will use HOL naturals to talk about least fixed point *}
consts        --{* usual iteration on HOL naturals *}
  iter :: "nat => ('a::type) => ('a => 'a) => 'a"
constdefs     --{* special iterator for use in Fix_min axiom *}
  mlIter :: "nat => ('a->'b) => (('a->'b) -> 'a->'b) => 'a ->'b"
  "mlIter n b F == iter n b (%h. fn x. F $ h $ x)"
```

Fig. 2. Logical preliminaries

Axioms for the core are given in figure 3. (One more general axiom will be introduced in section 5.1.) Application is strict (see axiom beta_rule); any expression lam F is defined. There is an extensionality rule, fn_ext, for SML functions. Eta follows from extensionality.

Unlike [Stä03], we do not use a notion of *value* in formulating our axioms, but the notion, dfd, of definedness, since observational equivalence (equality in the logic) preserves definedness, but not "valueness".

UNIT, BOOL, ** and ++ types are treated as if inductively defined. Their constructors and destructors are dfd, and their computation rules are axiomatized (e.g. if_true and if_false). As mentioned, the CASE constants are non-strict in their branches: when applied to a value, only the chosen branch is evaluated. Each of the type (constructors) UNIT, BOOL, ** and ++ also have an induction principle.

Least fixpoint axiom. We want an axiom to say that Fix is the *least fixpoint* operator. First, assuming F is defined, from axiom Fix_rule we have

$$\text{Fix \$ F = fn x. F \$ (Fix \$ F) \$ x.}$$

Informally, Fix \$ F should be the "limit" of approximations

$$h_0 = \bot$$
$$h_{n+1} = \text{fn x. F \$ } h_n \text{ \$ x}$$

Rewriting this using iter, the iteration constant over HOL naturals (figure 2), we have

$$h_n = \text{iter } n \perp (\%h. \text{ fn x. F \$ h \$ x).}$$

Abstracting this equation by n, F, and $\perp$[1], we get the definition of mlIter in figure 2.

To state that Fix \$ F is the least fixpoint of F we say that if Fix \$ F is defined in any context C::('a->'b)=>'c, then some finite unfolding, h_n, is already defined in that context:

---

[1] For technical reasons it is convenient to parameterise mlIter by the base case.

```
axioms
        --{* application *}
  bot_ap[simp]:   "udfd f ==> udfd (f $ x)"
  ap_bot[simp]:   "udfd x ==> udfd (f $ x)"          --{* strict *}

        --{* function types *}
  beta_rule[simp]: "dfd x ==> (lam F) $ x = F x"   --{* call-by-value *}
  fn_ext:   "[| dfd f; dfd g; !!x. dfd x ==> (f$x) = (g$x) |] ==> f = g"
  fn_dfd[simp]:     "dfd (lam F)"

        --{* least fixpoints *}
  Fix_rule: "Fix = (fn F x. F $ (Fix $ F) $ x)"
  Fix_min:  "[| dfd F; dfd (C (Fix $ F)) |] ==>
                          EX k. dfd (C (mlIter k bot F))"

        --{* UNIT type *}
  unit_Induct     : "[| P <>; dfd x |] ==> P x"
  unit_dfd [simp]: "dfd <>"

        --{* BOOL type *}
  dfd_BCASE[simp]:  "dfd (BCASE f g)"
  boolInduct:       "[| P tt; P ff; dfd x |] ==> P x"
  if_true [simp]:   "IF tt x y = x"
  if_false [simp]:  "IF ff x y = y"
  eq_dfd [simp]:    "[| dfd x; dfd y |] ==> dfd (x [=] y)"
  eq_reflection:    "((x [=] y) = tt)  =  (dfd x & x = y)"

        --{* product types *}
  dfd_PCASE[simp]: "dfd (PCASE f)"
  pair_induct: "[|!!x y. [|dfd x; dfd y |]==> P(x[,]y); dfd z |]==> P z"
  pair_dfd[simp]:  "[| dfd x; dfd y |] ==> dfd (x[,]y)"
  split[simp]:      "PCASE c $ (x[,]y) = c $ x $ y"

        --{* sum types *}
  dfd_SumCASE[simp]: "dfd (SumCASE f g)"
  dfd_inl[simp]:        "dfd inl"
  dfd_inr[simp]:        "dfd inr"
  SumCASE_inl[simp]: "SumCASE f g $ (inl $ x) = f $ x"
  SumCASE_inr[simp]: "SumCASE f g $ (inr $ y) = g $ y"
  Sum_induct:          "[| !!x. dfd x ==> P (inl $ x);
                          !!y. dfd y ==> P (inr $ y); dfd z |] ==> P z"
```

Fig. 3. Core language axioms

$$\text{dfd (C (Fix \$ F))} \Longrightarrow \exists n.\ \text{dfd (C } h_n).$$

Using `mlIter` for h_n in this equation, we get the axiom `Fix_min` of figure 3.

The notion of a function being total in one argument is defined:

```
tot1 :: "('a -> 'b) => bool"
"tot1 f == ALL x. dfd x --> dfd (f $ x)"
```

This is used in examples below.

2.3   Observational Order

We define *observational order, observational equivalence* (syntax x <o= y and x =o= y resp.) and *observational limit.*

```
obsLeq :: "'a => 'a => bool"          (infixl "<o=" 18)
"a <o= b == ALL (C::'a => UNIT). dfd (C a) --> dfd (C b)"
obsEq :: "'a => 'a => bool"           (infixl "=o=" 18)
"a =o= b == (a <o= b) & (b <o= a)"
obsLim :: "'a => (nat => 'a) => bool"
"obsLim y x ==
    ALL (C::'a => UNIT). dfd (C y) = (EX (n::nat). dfd (C (x n)))"
```

<o= is in fact a partial order, preserved by every context. bot is the <o=-least element of every SML type. It is worth noting that the following are equivalent

- a =o= b
- ALL (C::'a => UNIT). C a = C b
- ALL (C::'a => UNIT). dfd (C a) = dfd (C b)
- EX x. obsLim a x & obsLim b x

The lemma we need for later proofs is:

```
Fix_lim_iter: "dfd F ==> obsLim (Fix $ F) (%n. mlIter n bot F)"
```

saying that Fix $ F is the observational limit of finite iterations of F.

3   Interpretations of Our Logic

We outline two kinds of semantic interpretations for our logic: one in terms of purely operational concepts, and one in terms of a denotational model for the programming language. The former is what we expect the programmer to have in mind, while the latter is used to justify the soundness of our logic, and also to inspire the design of the logic in the first place. The agreement between these two interpretations is a property known as *logical full abstraction* [LP97].

The language presented in section 2 is intended to provide an extensible core for more realistic programming languages, so we formulate our interpretations in a general setting. To begin with, let us merely assume that we have

- A programming language $\mathcal{L}$ consisting of types of typeclass SML, and of terms of such types, extending the language defined by figure 1.
- An intended operational semantics for $\mathcal{L}$. It suffices to give a relation $M \Downarrow v$ between closed monomorphic terms M of $\mathcal{L}$ and certain "observable values" v, whose precise nature we need not specify[2].
- A logical language $K(\mathcal{L})$, whose formulae are constructed from terms of $\mathcal{L}$ by means of the usual logical operators =, /\, \/, ~, ALL, EX.

In the logic presented in Section 2, there are many formulae not in $K(\mathcal{L})$, since for instance we may mix types of $\mathcal{L}$ with HOL types such as nat. However, in order to give the idea behind the operational interpretation, it is simplest to concentrate on $K(\mathcal{L})$.

3.1   Operational Interpretation

We now give a simple way of reading formulae of $K(\mathcal{L})$ in terms of operational concepts, by defining what it means for a formula to be *operationally true*. For closed monomorphic formulae P (i.e. those containing no free term or type variables), operational truth is defined by structural induction:

- A formula M=N is operationally true if M and N are observationally equivalent: i.e., for all contexts $C(-)$ of $\mathcal{L}$ and all observable values v we have

$$C(M) \Downarrow v \quad \text{iff} \quad C(N) \Downarrow v \tag{1}$$

The programming intuition is that M may be replaced by N in any larger program without affecting the result[3].
- A formula P/\Q is operationally true if both P and Q are operationally true; similarly for \/ and ~. Thus, the propositional connectives have their familiar classical reading.
- A formula ALL$(x::t)$.P is operationally true if, for all closed terms $M::t$ of $\mathcal{L}$, the formula $P[M/x]$ is operationally true. Similarly for EX. The important point is that variables range over syntactically definable programs, rather than elements of some independent mathematical structure.

If two terms are observationally equivalent, they will satisfy exactly the same predicates; i.e. substitutivity of equality is sound for this interpretation. Thus, the above is the usual classical interpretation of first order logic (with a separate ground sort for each type), where a type t is interpreted as the set of closed monomorphic terms of type t modulo observational equivalence.

---

[2] Typically the observable values would be printable values of ground types such as integers and booleans, plus a dummy value used to indicate termination for programs of higher type.

[3] For how this relates to the formal definition of observational equivalence given in section 2, see section 5.1 below.

We now extend our interpretation to open and polymorphic formulae:

- An open monomorphic formula P (with free variables $x_1, \ldots, x_n$) is operationally true if all of its closed instances $P[M_1/x_1, \ldots, M_n/x_n]$ are operationally true, where the M_i are closed terms of appropriate types.
- A polymorphic formula P (with type variables $\alpha_1, \ldots, \alpha_m$) is operationally true if all its monomorphic instances $P[t_1/\alpha_1, \ldots, t_m/\alpha_m]$ are operationally true, where the t_i are monomorphic types of $\mathcal{L}$.

Is it convincing, on purely operational grounds, that the axioms of figure 3 are operationally true? In principle this might depend on the language $\mathcal{L}$, but in fact most of our axioms have been formulated to be true for a wide range of languages, even including non-functional fragments of SML.

Glossing over details, the only axioms that raise interesting questions are `fn_ext` and `Fix_min`. The axiom `fn_ext` (function extensionality) is the only one of our axioms that is specific to functional languages, and corresponds to what is known as the *context lemma*: if two programs are applicatively equivalent then they are observationally equivalent. The idea behind axiom `Fix_min` is that any "experiment" `C` which yields a value when performed on a term `Fix $ F` can only unroll the recursion operator a finite number of times, so that the same experiment must succeed when performed on `mlIter k bot F` for some k.

`Fix_min` plays more or less the same role as the familiar *Scott induction* principle in program logics such as LCF [Sco93]. We prefer the `Fix_min` axiom partly because it avoids the reference to inclusive predicates, and partly because it is not dependent on an order relation $\sqsubseteq$ in the style of domain theory. If we introduced such a relation as primitive, we would be obliged to axiomatize it, which is problematic since the appropriate order relation may vary from one language $\mathcal{L}$ to another[4].

3.2   Denotational Interpretation

Whilst our axioms can (with hindsight) be justified on purely operational grounds, it is better to achieve this by showing that they hold in some denotational model which agrees with our operational one in a suitable sense. The use of a denotational semantics has several advantages. Firstly, our understanding of the model can be used to suggest what the axioms ought to be in the first place. Secondly, the verifications that the axioms hold in the model tend to involve more abstract reasoning than the corresponding operational verifications, and to be more easily transferable from one language to another. Thirdly, a denotational semantics can be used to show soundness (and hence consistency) for the whole logic, not just the fragment $K(\mathcal{L})$, whereas it is unclear how the operational interpretation could be extended to cover types such as UNIT->nat.

Without going into technical details, the model we have in mind is a *presheaf category* $[\mathcal{C}^{op}, \mathbf{Set}]$, where $\mathcal{C}$ is some denotational model of $\mathcal{L}$. Types of our logic

---

[4] There are even "functional" languages for which the order relation is not defined extensionally, see e.g. [Lon99].

will be interpreted by objects X in the presheaf category, and closed terms by morphisms $1 \to X$. We then interpret our logic in the ordinary classical way over the homsets $\mathrm{Hom}(1, X)$.

The category $[\mathcal{C}^{\mathrm{op}}, \mathbf{Set}]$ has two important full subcategories, corresponding to $\mathbf{Set}$ and to $\mathcal{C}$ itself. We use objects of $\mathbf{Set}$ to interpret pure HOL types such as nat or nat->nat, and objects of $\mathcal{C}$ to interpret SML types. Thus, $[\mathcal{C}^{\mathrm{op}}, \mathbf{Set}]$ offers a model in which the ordinary mathematical universe of sets lives side-by-side with the computational universe of SML types and programs.

Moreover, we can choose the category $\mathcal{C}$ to be a model of $\mathcal{L}$ that is both *fully abstract* (observationally equivalent programs have the same denotation) and *universal* (every element of the relevant object is the denotation of some program). From these facts it is not hard to see that, when restricted to $K(\mathcal{L})$, our interpretation agrees precisely with the operational one given earlier. This goodness-of-fit property is known as *logical full abstraction*.

In future work we will extend our logic to deal with some non-functional fragments of SML including exceptions, references and I/O. An overview of the denotational ideas underpinning our approach is given in [Lon03].

3.3   Some Serious Problems

An attempt to give a denotational semantics in this way for the whole of our logic, as currently formalized, shows up two significant problems. These arise from certain features of Isabelle/HOL: firstly, the definite description operator (written THE) is available for all types, and secondly, the mathematical set bool of booleans also does duty as the type of propositions. Consider the following "programs":

```
UNIT_swap :: "UNIT -> UNIT"
"UNIT_swap == fn x. (THE y. ~y=x)"

UNIT_swap' :: "UNIT -> UNIT"
"UNIT_swap' == fn x. If (x=bot) <> bot"
```

Each of these terms claims to be a function that swaps bot and <>. However, this function cannot be definable in SML (with it, one could solve the halting problem), violating our operational requirement that terms of an SML type are SML definable. In fact, one can derive a contradiction using the term UNIT_swap and the axiom Fix_rule, since UNIT_swap clearly does not have a fixed point.

The definite description operator is pragmatically essential in pure HOL, and useful in specifications of programs, but its use must be controlled, as the above example shows. Also, the two roles of bool must be separated out. Our proposed solution to these problems (which can be justified by our denotational semantics) is as follows. First, we introduce a typeclass mathtype for "pure mathematical types", a subclass of type analogous to SML and corresponding denotationally to $\mathbf{Set}$. We then insist that free variables in the body of a definite description are restricted to be of class mathtype. We also distinguish appropriately between the mathematical type bool of booleans and a type prop of propositions (not itself

```
typedecl  NAT
arities   NAT :: SMLeq
consts        --{* datatype of natural numbers *}
  ZZ    :: NAT
  SS    :: "NAT -> NAT"
  NCASE :: "'a => (NAT -> 'a) => (NAT -> 'a)" --{* case is non-strict *}
axioms        --{* nat as a datatype *}
  ZZ_dfd [simp]:    "dfd ZZ"
  SS_tot1 [simp]:   "tot1 SS"
  dfd_NCASE [simp]: "dfd (NCASE f g)"
  nat_Induct:
      "[| P ZZ; !!y. [| dfd y; P y |] ==> P (SS $ y); dfd x |] ==> P x"
  NCASE_ZZ [simp]:  "NCASE ZZ x y = x"
  NCASE_SS [simp]:  "NCASE (SS $ n) x y = (y $ n)"
```

Fig. 4. A datatype of natural numbers

a mathtype). Finally, we also restrict the HOL function extensionality rule to functions whose domain is a mathtype (though we do not know whether our logic is consistent without this last restriction.) Unfortunately, this proposal cannot be implemented without significant re-engineering of Isabelle/HOL, or building our own system from scratch. However, we are confident that all the proofs we have done would go through in such a system.

4   Inductive Datatypes

In section 5 we indicate, using the example of streams, how all positive recursive datatypes can be uniformly constructed from the types of their constructors. In this section we simply axiomatize inductively defined (well founded) datatypes NAT and LIST as examples, to show we can reason about them straightforwardly.

Modulo a good deal of detailed work, reasoning about total programs over well founded datatypes is not so different than reasoning about systems of total functions, such as type theory or HOL itself. For example, uniform iteration and recursion functions are defined (primitive recursion over NAT, fold over LIST, ...), and their properties proved. These can be used to define other programs whose totality (on defined inputs) follows easily.

4.1   Natural Numbers

The formalization of NAT is shown in figure 4. There are constants for the constructors ZZ and SS, and for the eliminator NCASE. These are axiomatized to be dfd and tot1. There are axioms for the computation of NCASE. Only the induction axiom, nat_Induct, while natural, needs serious semantic justification.

By primitive recursion over HOL natural numbers (nat) there is an injection from nat onto the defined NATs. By this means we can convert many properties of NAT into properties of nat, which may be automatically proved by Isabelle's tactics.

By HOL inductive definition we define order relations on NAT, e.g. the less-than relation (syntax x[<]y).

```
inductive NATLT intros
NATLT_Z: "dfd x ==> ZZ [<] SS $ x"
NATLT_S: "m [<] n ==> SS $ m [<]  SS $ n"
```

For specification, this relation is more convenient than the BOOLean valued program that computes less-than. Complete induction can be derived, and from this a least number principle and well founded induction for NAT-valued measures. As an example, we have defined a naive Fibonacci program, and a fast Fibonacci program, and proved they are equal. The naive Fibonacci program is easily seen to satisfy the Fibonacci recursion equations, hence so does the fast Fibonacci program. Moreover, every program satisfying the Fibonacci recursion equations is equal to the the naive Fibonacci program.

4.2   Lists

Polymorphic LIST is axiomatised analagously with NAT. We use infix [::] for CONS; the list eliminator is LCASE. Basic functions like map, append, flatten and reverse are easily defined from the uniform fold operator. Their correctness follows from showing they have the expected recursion equations, usually by a few steps of computation. Many basic properties follow by easy induction: map distributes over composition, append is associative, reverse is involutive, ... We give an efficient reverse program, and show it is equal to naive reverse.

After defining a length function, we derive a length induction principle for lists from the wellfounded measure induction over NAT (section 4.1). With this we prove a more challenging example: theorem 16 from Paulson's textbook [Pau91]

```
aop $ y $ (foldleft $ aop $ e $ xs) = foldleft $ aop $ y $ xs
```

where aop is associative and e, a right identity of aop, is dfd.

Sorting. The examples mentioned above are trivial in one sense: correctness is expressed in terms of some recursion equations. Our stated reason for axiomatising ML in HOL, instead of FOL, is to have a richer language for program specifications. The specification for sorting involves abstract properties *ordered* and *permutation*. For example, *permutation* (syntax xs ~ ys) is given as a HOL inductive definition:

```
consts perm :: "('a LIST * 'a LIST) set"
inductive perm    intros
perm_trn:  "[| xs ~ ys; ys ~ zs |] ==> xs ~ zs"
perm_NIL:  "NIL ~ NIL"
perm_CONS: "[| dfd x; xs ~ ys |] ==> x[::]xs ~ x[::]ys"
perm_hd:"[|dfd x; dfd y; dfd zs |]==> x[::]y[::]zs ~ y[::]x[::]zs"
```

We give a program for insertion sort (figure 5), and prove it is correct. The sort program itself is a polymorphic function taking in a BOOLean valued order

```
insrt :: "('a -> 'a -> BOOL) -> 'a -> 'a LIST -> 'a LIST"
"insrt == fn le x. Fix $ (fn f. LCASE (unl x)
                                (fn y ys. IF (le $ x $ y)
                                             (x[::](y[::]ys))
                                             (y[::](f $ ys))))"
isort :: "('a -> 'a -> BOOL) -> 'a LIST -> 'a LIST"
"isort == fn le. Fix $
   (fn f xs. LCASE NIL (fn y ys. insrt $ le $ y $ (f $ ys)) $ xs)"
```

Fig. 5. Insertion sort program

```
pre_rmZZs :: "(NAT SEQ -> NAT SEQ) -> NAT SEQ -> NAT SEQ"
"pre_rmZZs == fn F. SCASE (fn p.
             IF (Fst$p [=] ZZ)
             (F $ (Snd$p $ <>))
             (Fst$p[:::](fn z. F $ (Snd$p $ <>))))"
rmZZs :: "NAT SEQ -> NAT SEQ"
"rmZZs == Fix $ pre_rmZZs"
```

Fig. 6. A function to remove all zeros from a NAT SEQ

function, le, and a list, and returning a sorted list. We use an Isabelle *locale* to specify the properties the order function must have, and prove in that locale that isort returns an ordered permutation of the input list. Thus for any instantiation of that locale (e.g. with the order function LE over NAT) isort is a correct sort program.

5 Recursive Datatypes: Streams

The examples in preceding sections, over inductive datatypes, could be carried out in logics of total functions. In this section we address an example that cannot be treated in logics of totality. Consider the type of polymorphic streams (SEQ for *sequence*), that would be defined in SML by:

```
datatype 'a SEQ = SCONS of 'a * (unit -> 'a SEQ)
```

We represent this datatype using the well known characterization that ('a SEQ, SCONS) is the initial algebra of the functor ST X = 'a ** (UNIT->X). As an example over SEQ, consider the function, rmZZs, that recurses through a NAT SEQ removing all the zeros (figure 6). A datatype analogous to SEQ is definable using coinduction in HOL, Coq, and Nuprl, but the function rmZZs could only be definable in a complex way, with a restricted domain.

Streams are formalised (figure 7) with two constants and three axioms. The constructor, SCONS (infix [:::]) is dfd and tot1. The other constant, Psi, canonically completes the initial algebra property. This is expressed by axiom seq_init, which states that if g::ST('b)->'b is dfd, then Psi $ g is the unique dfd function f making the diagram commute:

```
typedecl   'a SEQ
arities    SEQ :: (SML)SML    --{* no SMLeq arity *}


--{* covariant functor characterises 'a Seq" *}
types ('a, 'b) ST = "'a ** (UNIT -> 'b)"   --{* object part of functor *}
constdefs                                  --{* arrow part of functor *}
  ST :: "('c->'d) -> ('a,'c)ST -> ('a,'d)ST"
  "ST == fn f. PCASE (fn (a::'a) (h::UNIT->'c). (a [,] (f oo h)))"
consts  --{* sequences (lazy lists) *}
  SCONS :: "('a,'a SEQ)ST -> 'a SEQ"        --{* constructor *}
  Psi :: "(('a,'b)ST -> 'b) -> 'a SEQ -> 'b"
constdefs     --{* the initial algebra property *}
  SEQ_Init_sq :: "(('a,'b)ST -> 'b) => ('a SEQ -> 'b) => bool"
  "SEQ_Init_sq g f == (dfd f) & ((f oo SCONS) = (g oo (ST $ f)))"
axioms --{* stream as a datatype *}
  dfd_SCONS[simp]:   "dfd SCONS"
  tot1_SCONS[simp]:  "tot1 SCONS"
  seq_init:          "dfd g ==> SEQ_Init_sq g f = (f = Psi $ g)"
```

Syntax note: oo is program composition, i.e. f oo g = fn x. f $ (g $ x).

Fig. 7. Streams as an initial algebra

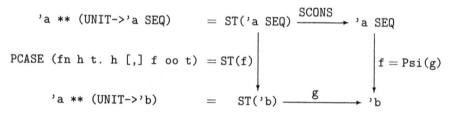

From this we define the categorical destructor

```
  SDESTR :: "'a SEQ -> ('a ** (UNIT->'a SEQ))"
  "SDESTR == Psi $ (ST $ SCONS)"
```

and prove that SCONS and SDESTR are inverse isomorphisms. The SML case eliminator for streams is defined, and its computation rule proved:

```
  SCASE :: "('b -> (UNIT -> 'b SEQ) -> 'a) => ('b SEQ -> 'a)"
  "SCASE f == PCASE f oo SDESTR"
lemma SCASE_SCONS: "SCASE y $ (a[:::]as) = y $ a $ as"
```

Examples. Now we can define many standard functions on streams, and prove their usual properties: head and tail (shd, stl), nth element from a stream (snth), take or drop n elements from the front of a stream (sTAKE, sdrop). For example:

```
sdrop $ n $ (stl $ xs $ <>) = stl $ (sdrop $ n $ xs) $ <>
snth $ n $ s = shd $ (sdrop $ n $ s)
```

Interesting from a semantic viewpoint, we show that every stream is the observational limit of its initial segments

```
lemma s_lim_sTAKEs: "obsLim s (%n. sTAKE n $ s)"
```

However, we do not yet seem able to prove *stream extensionality*

```
(ALL n. snth $ n $ s = snth $ n $ t) ==> s = t
```

which is operationally true. Stream extensionality is equivalent to a characterization proposed in [Pit94]. Finally, we cannot prove that (ST, SDESTR) is a final coalgebra. Thus, another axiom seems needed.

5.1 Another General Axiom

Our final general axiom reflects that x =o= y means x and y are indistinguishable in any context.

```
axioms    obs_eq: "x =o= y ==> x = y"
```

This can be seen as saying that Leibniz equality (e.g. observational equivalence) implies extensional equality. By a fact from section 2.3, this is equivalent to uniqueness of observational limits

```
obsLim a x ==> obsLim b x ==> a = b
```

From this second formulation it is clear that stream extensionality follows from s_lim_sTAKEs. Furthermore, from stream extensionality we conjecture we can prove that that (ST, SDESTR) is a final coalgebra.

Using stream extensionality, we have proved that the program rmZZs returns a sequence with no zeros!

6 Conclusion

Reasoning about programs is hard. Our high level, operationally inspired logic doesn't remove the need to reason about the details of a program. However Isabelle's automation proved very useful for routine details, such as the frequent need for case distinction between dfd and udfd arguments in our CBV language. There is plenty of scope for special purpose tactics to address other routine tasks. We found the use of HOL, with its inductive definition of properties, to be much better than first order (i.e. equational) specification, and were also able to convert some questions about SML datatypes into questions about HOL types that are easily solved in Isabelle/HOL.

References

[GMW79]   Michael Gordon, Robin Milner, and Christopher Wadsworth. *Edinburgh LCF: A Mechanized Logic of Computation*, volume 78 of *LNCS*. Springer-Verlag, 1979.

[GV94]   E. Gunter and M. VanInwegen. HOL-ML. In J. Joyce and C. Seger, editors, *Higher Order Logic Theorem Proving and Its Applications*, volume 780 of *LNCS*. Springer-Verlag, 1994.

[HT95]   Steve Hill and Simon Thompson. Miranda in Isabelle. In Lawrence Paulson, editor, *Proceedings of the first Isabelle Users Workshop*, number 397 in University of Cambridge Computer Laboratory Tech. Report Series, 1995.

[Kre04]   Christoph Kreitz. Building reliable, high-performance networks with the nuprl proof development system. *J. Funct. Prog.*, 14(1), January 1004.

[KS98]   S. Kahrs and D. Sannella. Reflections on the design of a specification language. In *Proc. Intl. Colloq. on Fundamental Approaches to Software Engineering. ETAPS'98*, volume 1382 of *LNCS*. Springer-Verlag, 1998.

[KST97]   Stefan Kahrs, Donald Sannella, and Andrzej Tarlecki. The definition of Extended ML: A gentle introduction. *Theoretical Comp. Sci.*, 173, 1997.

[Lon99]   J.R. Longley. When is a functional program not a functional program? In *Proc. 4th International Conference on Functional Programming, Paris*, pages 1–7. ACM Press, 1999.

[Lon03]   John Longley. Universal types and what they are good for. In GQ Zhang, J. Lawson, Y.M. Liu, and M.K. Luo, editors, *Domain Theory, Logic and Computation, Proc. 2nd Inter. Symp. on Domain Theory*. Kluwer, 2003.

[LP97]   J. Longley and G. Plotkin. Logical full abstraction and PCF. In J. Ginzburg, editor, *Tbilisi Symposium on Language, Logic and Computation*. SiLLI/CSLI, 1997.

[MNvOS99] Olaf Müller, Tobias Nipkow, David von Oheimb, and Oscar Slotosch. HOLCF = HOL + LCF. *J. Funct. Prog.*, 9:191–223, 1999.

[MTHM97] R. Milner, M. Tofte, R. Harper, and D. MacQueen. *The Definition of Standard ML (Revised)*. MIT Press, 1997.

[NPW02]   Tobias Nipkow, Lawrence C. Paulson, and Markus Wenzel. *Isabelle/HOL – A Proof Assistant for Higher-Order Logic*, volume 2283 of *LNCS*. Springer, 2002.

[Pau87]   L. Paulson. *Logic and Computation: Interactive Proof with Cambridge LCF*. Camb. Univ. Press, 1987.

[Pau91]   L. Paulson. *ML for the Working Programmer*. Camb. Univ. Press, 1991.

[PF92]   W. Phoa and M. Fourman. A proposed categorical semantics for pure ML. In W. Kuich, editor, *Proceedings on Automata, Languages and Programming (ICALP '92)*, volume 623 of *LNCS*. Springer-Verlag, 1992.

[Pit94]   A. M. Pitts. A co-induction principle for recursively defined domains. *Theoretical Computer Science*, 124:195–219, 1994.

[Sco93]   D.S. Scott. A type-theoretical alternative to ISWIM, CUCH, OWHY. *Theoretical Computer Science*, 121:411–440, 1993.

[Stä03]   R. F. Stärk. Axioms for strict and lazy functional programs. *Annals of Pure and Applied Logic*, 2003. To appear.

[Sym94]   D. Syme. Reasoning with the formal definition of Standard ML in HOL. *Lecture Notes in Computer Science*, 780:43–58, 1994.

[Tho95]   Simon Thompson. A Logic for Miranda, Revisited. *Formal Aspects of Computing*, 7, 1995.

Proof Pearl:
From Concrete to Functional Unparsing

Jean-François Monin

VERIMAG – Centre Equation 2 avenue de Vignate, F-38610 Gières, France
jean-francois.monin@imag.fr
http://www-verimag.imag.fr/~monin/

Abstract. We provide a proof that the elegant trick of Olivier Danvy for expressing printf-like functions without dependent types is correct, where formats are encoded by functional expressions in continuation-passing style. Our proof is formalized in the Calculus of Inductive Constructions. We stress a methodological point: when one proves equalities between functions, a common temptation is to introduce a comprehension axiom and then to prove that the considered functions are extensionally equal. Rather than weakening the result (and adding an axiom), we prefer to strenghten the inductive argumentation in order to stick to the intensional equality.

1 Introduction

In [1], Olivier Danvy proposes an elegant trick for expressing printf-like functions and procedures in the ML type system. His idea is to replace the concrete version of the first argument, on which the number and the type of remaining arguments depend, with a higher-order function. In order to avoid questions related to side-effects, let us consider the *sprintf* function, which builds a string from its arguments. The first argument of *sprintf* is a *format*, which specifies the number and the type of the remaining arguments. In practice, notably in the C language, the format is often a string, where occurrences of %d (respectively, of %s, etc.) specify that an integer (respectively, a string, etc.) should be inserted there. For instance, in ML syntax,

$$\textit{sprintf} \text{ "The \%s is \%d \%s." "distance" 10 "meters"} \tag{1}$$

would return the string `"The distance is 10 meters."`.

It is more convenient, at least for reasoning purposes, to represent formats using a concrete type such as lists of an appropriate type of directives. For example, the first argument of (1) could be represented by

$$[\textit{Lit}(\text{"The "}); \textit{String}; \textit{Lit}(\text{" is "}); \textit{Int}; \textit{String}; \textit{Lit}(\text{"."})]. \tag{2}$$

In a language where dependent types are allowed, it is then a simple exercise to program the desired behavior. In the case of ML, Danvy proposes to represent the format by a functional expression:

$$\textit{lit} \text{ "The " } \circ \textit{str} \circ \textit{lit} \text{ " is " } \circ \textit{sint} \circ \textit{str} \circ \textit{lit} \text{ "."}, \tag{3}$$

K. Slind et al. (Eds.): TPHOLs 2004, LNCS 3223, pp. 217–224, 2004.

where $\circ$ is the sequential composition of functions, and the functions such as int and string take a continuation on strings, a string, an argument of the appropriate type and return a continuation on strings. More specifically, str is defined by $\lambda k\, a\, s.\, k(a\hat{\,}s))$, where $\hat{\,}$ is string catenation and $sint$ is defined by $\lambda k\, a\, n.\, k(a\hat{\,}\, string\_of\_int\, n))$. The definition of lit is $\lambda s\, k\, a.\, k(a\hat{\,}s))$. Reducing these definitions in (3) yields

$$\lambda k\, a\, s_1\, n\, s_2.\, k\, (a\hat{\,}\, \text{"The "}\hat{\,}\, s_1\hat{\,}\, \text{" is "}\hat{\,}\, string\_of\_int\, n\hat{\,}\, s_2\hat{\,}\, \text{"."}) \quad (4)$$

and we see that applying the following continuation-based version of $sprintf$ to a functional format does the job.

$$sprintfk := \lambda f.\, f\, (\lambda s.\, s)\, \text{""} \quad (5)$$

An interesting feature of functional formats is that they are more general than concrete formats given by either a string as in (1), or a list as in (2): concrete formats are bound to a fixed number of data types, whereas functional formats are extensible – they can handle any data type X, provided we are given a function from X to $string$.

If we look at types, we remark that str has the type $(string \to \beta) \to string \to string \to \beta$, $sint$ has the type $(string \to \alpha) \to string \to int \to \alpha$, hence $str \circ sint$ has the type $(string \to \alpha) \to string \to string \to int \to \alpha$. In general, the type of a functional format has the form $(string \to \alpha) \to string \to X_1 \to \cdots \to X_n \to \alpha$. If two formats f_1 and f_2 are respectively of type

$$(string \to \beta) \to string \to X_1 \to \cdots \to X_n \to \beta \quad (6)$$

and

$$(string \to \alpha) \to string \to X_{n+1} \to \cdots \to X_{n+p} \to \alpha, \quad (7)$$

their composition $f_1 \circ f_2$ is of type

$$(string \to \alpha) \to string \to X_1 \to \cdots \to X_n \to X_{n+1} \to \cdots \to X_{n+p} \to \alpha \quad (8)$$

while the type inference mechanism yields

$$\beta = X_{n+1} \to \cdots \to X_{n+p} \to \alpha. \quad (9)$$

We provide here a formal proof that Danvy's functional formats are correct representations of usual concrete formats. More precisely, for any concrete format ϕ, we inductively define its functional representation $kformat\, \phi$ and we prove that $sprintf$ applied to ϕ yields the same function as $sprintfk$ applied to $kformat\, \phi$ – these functions are even convertible.

As the result relates dependent types with polymorphic types, we need a logic where these two features are present. Our formalization is carried out in the Calculus of Inductive Constructions [2]. Two proof techniques are illustrated: making the statement of an inductive property on functions more intensional, rather than reasoning on extensional equality; and using type transformers to recover what is performed by type inference in (9). A complete Coq script (V8.0) is available on the web page of the author.

2 Type Theory and Notation

The fragment of the Calculus of Inductive Constructions to be used here includes a hierarchy of values and types. On the first level we have basic inductive and functional values such as 0 and $\lambda x : nat.\ x$. They inhabit types such as nat or $nat \to nat$, which are themselves values at the second level and have the type Set. In the sequel α, β, γ, δ range over such types. Polymorphic types are obtained using explicit universal quantification, e.g. $\forall \alpha\ \alpha \to \alpha$. We can also construct type transformers such as $\lambda \alpha.\ nat \to \alpha$, of type $Set \to Set$. The type of Set and of $Set \to Set$ is called $Type$. Types can depend on values of any level.

Functions are defined using the following syntax:

Definition $function\_name\ arg_1 \ldots arg_n : type\_of\_the\_result := body.$

where $type\_of\_the\_result$ depends on $arg_i, i \in 1 \ldots n$. In the case of a recursive definition, Definition is replaced with Fixpoint.

We suppose that we are given a type $string$ (in Set), endowed with a binary operation $\_\hat{\ }\_$ (catenation) and the empty string denoted by $""$. We don't need an algebraic law for catenation.

3 Concrete Formats

Our definitions will be illustrated on a format specified by $"foo\ \%s\ bar\ \%i"$ in C language notation. Assuming two strings foo and bar, the structured concrete representation that we will use is:

$$\text{Definition } example := Lit\ foo\ (Str\ (Lit\ bar\ (Int\ Stop))) \tag{10}$$

where Str and Int are respectively of type $string \to format \to format$ and $int \to format \to format$; $format$ is a dedicated inductive type defined below.

For the sake of generality (functional formats can handle arbitrary printable data) we first introduce a structure for printable data, composed of a carrier X and of a function r_X which appends a printed representation of a value of type X to the right of a given string. This is equivalent to providing a function for converting an inhabitant of X to a string, but turns out to be much more handy.

Record $Printable : Type := mkpr\ \{X : Set;\ r\_X : string \to X \to string\}.$

In Coq, a record is just a tuple and fields are represented by projections. For our example, we suppose that we are given a type int for integers and a corresponding function r_int. Then we can define $pint$ as $mkpr\ int\ r\_int$, and we have $X\ pint = int$ and $r\_X\ pint = rint$. We use the notation $"a\ \hat{p}\ x\ "$ for $r\_X P\ a\ x$, where P is a $Printable$, a is a string and x is an XP.

The type of concrete formats is given by:

Type $format := Stop \mid Data$ of $Printable \times format \mid Lit$ of $string \times format.$

In our example, Int is defined as $Data\ pint$. Note that from printable integers, it is easy to add printable lists of integers and so on.

In the sequel, ϕ ranges over $format$ and P ranges over $Printable$.

4   A First Translation

In this section, we work with a monomorphic version of Danvy's functional formats. This it is not satisfactory, but the proof technique that we want to use is simple to explain. Polymorphic functional formats will be considered in section 5.

The type associated to a format is:

Fixpoint $type\_of\_fmt\ \phi : Set :=$
  match ϕ with
  | $Stop \Rightarrow string$
  | $Data\ P\ \phi \Rightarrow XP \rightarrow type\_of\_fmt\ \phi$
  | $Lit\ s\ \phi \Rightarrow type\_of\_fmt\ \phi$
  end.

For example, $type\_of\_fmt\ example$ reduces to $string \rightarrow int \rightarrow string$.

4.1   Basic Version of *sprintf* with Dependent Types

We start with a loop which prints on the right of an additional argument.

Fixpoint $r\_sprintf\ \phi : string \rightarrow type\_of\_fmt\ \phi\ :=$
  match ϕ with
  | $Stop \Rightarrow \lambda a.\ a$
  | $Data\ P\ \phi \Rightarrow \lambda a\,x.\ r\_sprintf\ \phi\ (a\ \hat{p}\ x)$
  | $Lit\ s\ \phi \Rightarrow \lambda a.\ r\_sprintf\ \phi\ (a\char`^ s)$
  end.

The desired function provides the empty string "" as the initial accumulator to the previous function.

Definition $sprintf\ \phi := r\_sprintf\ \phi$ "".

4.2   Monomorphic Functional Formats

The following type of Danvy's *sprintfk* is allowed in the Damas-Milner type system, it can then be used in languages of the ML and Haskell family. Though there is no restriction over α, the only form α can take is ($type\_of\_fmt\ \phi$) for some format ϕ. However, the point is that ϕ itself is no longer an argument of *sprintfk*.

Definition *sprintfk*: $\forall \alpha\ ((string \rightarrow string) \rightarrow string \rightarrow \alpha) \rightarrow \alpha := \lambda f.\ f\,(\lambda s.\ s)$ "".

Functional formats are constructed using primitive formats such as *lit*, *str*, *sint*, etc. The two latter are themselves special cases of our *kdata*, which is not admitted in ML, in contrast with *str*, *sint*, etc. However we keep *kdata* here for the sake of generality in the reasoning. In ML examples, we use only instances of *kdata*.

Definition $kid : (string \rightarrow string) \rightarrow string \rightarrow string := \lambda k\,a.\ k\,a.$

Definition $kdata\ P : \forall \alpha\ (string \rightarrow \alpha) \rightarrow string \rightarrow XP \rightarrow \alpha :=$
  $\lambda \alpha.\ \lambda k.\ \lambda a\,x.\ k\,(a\,\hat{p}\,x).$

Definition $lit\ (x{:}string) : \forall \alpha\ (string \rightarrow \alpha) \rightarrow string \rightarrow \alpha := \lambda \alpha.\ \lambda k\,a.\ k\,(a\char`^ x).$

4.3   Translation

Here is the general construction of functional formats from concrete formats.

Fixpoint *kformat* ϕ : $(string \to string) \to string \to type\_of\_fmt\,\phi$:=
  match ϕ with
  | *Stop* $\Rightarrow$ *kid*
  | *Data P* ϕ $\Rightarrow$ $(kdata\,P\;(type\_of\_fmt\;\phi)) \circ (kformat\;\phi)$
  | *Lit x* ϕ $\Rightarrow$ $(lit\,x\;(type\_of\_fmt\;\phi)) \circ (kformat\;\phi)$
  end.

For example, *kformat example* is convertible with
  $(lit\,foo\;(string \to int \to string)) \circ$
  $(str\;(int \to string)) \circ (lit\,bar\;(int \to string)) \circ (sint\;string)$.

4.4   Correctness of *sprintfk* w.r.t. *sprintf*

A brutal attempt to prove that $(sprintf\;\phi) = (sprintfk\;(kformat\;\phi))$ holds for all ϕ fails, because the accumulator changes at each recursive call (an induction on ϕ would lead us to to prove something on $""$ ^ s while the induction hypothesis is on $""$). The usual trick is then to replace $""$ with a variable (let us call it a) which is in the scope of the induction. We first unfold *sprintf* and *sprintfk* in order to work with *r_sprintf* and *kformat*. Then, if we try to prove

$$\forall a\; r\_sprintf\,\phi\;a \; = \; kformat\;\phi\;(\lambda s.\,s)\;a \tag{11}$$

by induction on ϕ, we face another problem: how to prove

$$\lambda x.\;r\_sprintf\,\phi\;(a\;\hat{p}\;x) \; = \; \lambda x.\;kformat\,\phi\;string\;(\lambda s.\,s)\;(a\;\hat{p}\;x)$$

from the induction hypothesis (11)? This is a typical case where extensionality makes life easier. Adding the following axiom would allow us to finish the proof in a trivial way.

Axiom *extensionality*:
  $\forall \alpha\,\beta,\;\forall f g : \alpha \to \beta,\;(\forall x{:}\alpha,\;f\,x = g\,x) \to (\lambda x.\,f\,x) = (\lambda x.\,g\,x)$.

But this workaround is not satisfactory. In order to prove the desired (intensional) equality, without any additional axiom, we work with a *still more intensional* statement:

$$\lambda a.\;r\_sprintf\,\phi\;a \; = \; \lambda a.\;kformat\,\phi\;(\lambda s.\,s)\;a \tag{12}$$

or even a η-reduced version of the latter:

$$r\_sprintf\,\phi \; = \; kformat\,\phi\;(\lambda s.\,s). \tag{13}$$

The proof is very short. The key is to observe that $\lambda a\,x.\;k\,(a\;\hat{p}\;x) = kdata\,P\,\alpha\,k$, and similarly for *lit*. We can then rewrite *r_sprintf* as follows:

Fixpoint $r\_sprintf1$ ϕ : $string \to type\_of\_fmt$ ϕ :=
  match ϕ with
  | $Stop \Rightarrow \lambda a.\ a$
  | $Data\ P\ \phi \Rightarrow kdata\ P\ (type\_of\_fmt\ \phi)\ (r\_sprintf1\ \phi)$
  | $Lit\ s\ \phi \Rightarrow lit\ s\ (type\_of\_fmt\ \phi)\ (r\_sprintf1\ \phi)$
  end.

The following lemma is easily proved by induction on ϕ:

$$\forall \phi\ \ r\_sprintf1\ \phi = kformat\ \phi\ (\lambda s.\ s). \tag{14}$$

Unfolding definitions and converting $r\_sprintf$ to $r\_sprintf1$ provides the desired corollary.

Theorem $sprintf\_sprintfk$: $\ \forall \phi\ sprintf\ \phi = sprintfk\ (kformat\ \phi)$.

5   Typing Formats with Type Transformers

The previous typing of $kformat$ is unfair. If ϕ is a given closed format, the expression $kformat$ ϕ has a closed type as well. A limitation of this typing is that it prevents formats to be sequentially composed. For example,

$$(kformat\ (Lit\ foo\ (Str\ Stop)))\ \circ\ (kformat\ (Lit\ bar\ (Int\ Stop))) \tag{15}$$

is ill-typed. In order to recover plain Danvy's functional formats, which do not suffer from such limitations, we use type transformers. In some sense, the latter implement the type inference mechanism of the ML type system. In our example, the type transformer to be considered maps a type α to $string \to int \to \alpha$.

Definition $idt := \lambda\alpha.\ \alpha$.
Definition $datat\ P := \lambda\alpha.\ (X P \to \alpha)$.
Fixpoint $type\_transf\_of\_fmt$ ϕ : $Set \to Set$:=
  match ϕ with
  | $Stop \Rightarrow idt$
  | $Data\ P\ \phi \Rightarrow (datat\ P)\ \circ\ (type\_transf\_of\_fmt\ \phi)$
  | $Lit\ s\ \phi \Rightarrow type\_transf\_of\_fmt\ \phi$
  end.

The new typing of $r\_sprintf$ is as follows.

Fixpoint $r\_sprintf$ ϕ : $string \to type\_transf\_of\_fmt$ ϕ $string$:=
  match ϕ with
  | $Stop \Rightarrow \lambda a.\ a$
  | $Data\ P\ \phi \Rightarrow \lambda a\ x.\ r\_sprintf\ \phi\ (a\ \hat{p}\ x)$
  | $Lit\ s\ \phi \Rightarrow \lambda a.\ r\_sprintf\ \phi\ (a\,\hat{}\,s)$
  end.

Definition $sprintf$ $\phi := r\_sprintf$ ϕ "".

5.1   Polymorphic Functional Formats

In this version, the type given to a functional format takes the form $kt\ tf$, where tf is a type transformer.

Definition $kt\ (tf\colon Set \to Set) := \forall \alpha\ (string \to \alpha) \to string \to tf\ \alpha.$

Accordingly, the new typings of kid, $kdata$ and lit are:

Definition $kid : kt\ idt := \lambda \alpha.\ \lambda k\ a.\ k\ a.$

Definition $kdata\ P : kt\ (\lambda \alpha.\ X\,P \to \alpha) := \lambda \alpha.\ \lambda k\colon string \to \alpha.\ \lambda a\, x.\ k\,(a\,\hat{p}\,x).$

Definition $lit\ x : kt\ idt := \lambda \alpha.\ \lambda k\ a.\ k\,(a\,\hat{\ }\,x).$

Observe that, in this version, no additional argument is needed in lit and $kdata$ (or its instances such as $sint$).

The counterpart of type unification shown in equations (6) to (9) of the introduction is performed in the following version of function composition.

Definition $u\_seq\ (tg, tf\colon Set \to Set) : kt\ tg \to kt\ tf \to kt\ (tg \circ tf) :=$
$\quad \lambda g f.\ \lambda \alpha.\ \lambda k.\ g\,(tf\,\alpha)\,(f\,\alpha\ k).$

We use the infix notation $\odot$ for u_seq.

5.2   Translation

Definition $sprintfk\ (tf\colon Set \to Set) : kt\ tf \to tf\ string := \lambda f.\ f\ string\,(\lambda s.\ s)\ ""$.

Fixpoint $kformat\ \phi : kt\ (type\_transf\_of\_fmt\ \phi) :=$
$\quad$ match ϕ with
$\quad \mid Stop \Rightarrow kid$
$\quad \mid Data\ P\ \phi \Rightarrow (kdata\ P) \odot (kformat\ \phi)$
$\quad \mid Lit\ x\ \phi \Rightarrow (lit\ x) \odot (kformat\ \phi)$
$\quad$ end.

As desired, formats can be composed. For example, $kformat\ example$ is convertible with $(kformat\ (Lit\ foo\ (Str\ Stop))) \odot (kformat\ (Lit\ bar\ (Int\ Stop)))$. A format can even be composed with itself, as in

let $kex = kformat\ example$ in $kex \odot kex$.

5.3   Correctness of *sprintfk* w.r.t. *sprintf*

The proof is along the same lines as before. In the induction steps, we have to recognize a higher-order pattern involving another kind of function composition, which is defined by $f \circ_2 g := \lambda x\, y.\ f\,(g\,x\,y)$.

The two key remarks are:

$$\forall P\quad kdata\ P = \lambda \alpha.\ \lambda k\colon string \to \alpha.\ k \circ_2 (r\_X\ P) \tag{16}$$

and

$$\forall tf\colon Set \to Set\ \forall f\colon kt\ tf\ \forall P\ (kdata\ P) \odot f = \lambda \alpha.\ \lambda k.\ (f\ \alpha\ k) \circ_2 (r\_X\ P) \tag{17}$$

where $=$ stands for convertibility. We can inline these identities in order to get versions of $r\_sprintf$ and $kformat$ which are convertible with the original ones.

Fixpoint $r\_sprintf1$ ϕ : $string \to type\_transf\_of\_fmt$ ϕ $string$:=
   match ϕ with
   | $Stop \Rightarrow \lambda a.\ a$
   | $Data\,P\,\phi \Rightarrow (r\_sprintf1\,\phi) \circ_2 (r\_X\,P)$
   | $Lit\,s\,\phi \Rightarrow (r\_sprintf1\,\phi) \circ (\lambda a.\ a\hat{\ }s)$
   end.

Fixpoint $kformat1$ ϕ: $kt\ (type\_transf\_of\_fmt\ \phi)$:=
   match ϕ with
   | $Stop \Rightarrow kid$
   | $Data\,P\,\phi \Rightarrow \lambda\alpha.\ \lambda k.\ (kformat1\ \phi\,\alpha\,k) \circ_2 (r\_X\,P)$
   | $Lit\,x\,\phi \Rightarrow \lambda\alpha.\ \lambda k.\ (kformat1\ \phi\,\alpha\,k) \circ (\lambda a.\ a\hat{\ }x)$
   end.

Using them, we can prove that:

$$\forall\phi\ \ r\_sprintf\,\phi\ =\ kformat\ \phi\ string\ (\lambda s.\ s) \tag{18}$$

by a straightforward induction over ϕ, and we get the desired theorem in the same way as in section 4.

Theorem $sprintf\_sprintfk$: $\forall\phi\ sprintf\,\phi = sprintfk\,(kformat\ \phi)$.

Acknowledgement

The work reported here was started during a stay at SRI, thanks to an invitation of N. Shankar and J. Rushby. The first draft of this paper was written in a undisclosable amount of time using the coqdoc tool of J.-C. Filliâtre. I also wish to thank anonymous referees for their constructive comments.

References

1. Olivier Danvy. Functional Unparsing. *Journal of Functional Programming*, 8(6):621–625, 1998.
2. The Coq Development Team, LogiCal Project, V8.0. The Coq Proof Assistant Reference Manual. Technical report, INRIA, 2004.

A Decision Procedure for Geometry in Coq

Julien Narboux

LIX, École Polytechnique*
Julien.Narboux@inria.fr

Abstract. We present in this paper the development of a *decision procedure* for affine plane geometry in the Coq proof assistant. Among the existing decision methods, we have chosen to implement one based on the *area method* developed by Chou, Gao and Zhang, which provides *short* and *"readable"* proofs for geometry theorems. The idea of the method is to express the goal to be proved using three geometric quantities and eliminate points in the reverse order of their construction thanks to some *elimination lemmas*.

1 Introduction

Geometry is one of the most successful areas of automated theorem proving. Many difficult theorems can be proved by computer programs using synthetic and algebraic methods. A decision procedure using quantifier elimination was first introduced by A. Tarski [15]. His method was further improved by Collins' cylindrical decomposition algorithm [4]. Among the efficient methods we can cite also the algebraic method of Wu which succeeded in finding the proofs of hundreds of geometry theorems [3, 18] and later the method of Chou, Gao, Zhang which produces short and readable proofs [2] (they are readable in the sense that one can understand these proofs without difficulty as they manipulate small terms.)

Recently, developments have also been produced towards the formalization of elementary geometry in proof assistants: Hilbert's *Grundlagen* [10] have been formalized in Isabelle/Isar by Laura Meikle and Jacques Fleuriot [14], and by Christophe Dehlinger in the Coq system [5]. Gilles Kahn has formalized Jan von Plato's constructive geometry in the Coq system [12, 17]. Frédérique Guilhot has done a large development in Coq dealing with French high school geometry [7].

We believe that automated theorem proving and interactive proof development are complementary to formal proof generation. Proof assistants can deal with a very large span of theorems, but they need automation to ease the development. The goal of this work is to bring the level of automation provided by the method of Chou, Gao and Zhang to the Coq proof assistant [13]. This is done by implementing the decision procedure as a Coq tactic. A tactic is a program which expresses the sequence of the basic logical steps needed to formally prove a theorem.

---

* Projet LogiCal, Pôle Commun de Recherche en Informatique, plateau de Saclay, École Polytechnique, CNRS, INRIA Futurs, Université Paris Sud.

K. Slind et al. (Eds.): TPHOLs 2004, LNCS 3223, pp. 225–240, 2004.

Formalizing a decision procedure within Coq, has not only the advantage of simplifying the tedious task of proving geometry theorems but also allows us to combine the geometrical proofs provided by the tactic with arbitrary complicated proofs developed interactively using the full strength of the underlying logic of the theorem prover. For instance, theorems involving induction over the number of points in the figure can be formalized in Coq. This approach has also the advantage of providing a higher level of reliability than *ad hoc* geometry theorem provers because the proofs generated by our tactic are double checked by the Coq internal proof-checker.

The issues related to the treatment of nondegeneracy conditions are crucial; this is emphasized in our formalization.

This paper is arranged as follows: we will first give an overview of the decision method, and then we will explain how it has been implemented in the Coq proof assistant.

2   The Chou, Gao and Zhang Decision Procedure

Chou, Gao and Zhang's decision procedure is the mechanization of the *area method*. It is a mix of algebraic and synthetic methods. The idea of the method is to express the goal in a constructive way and treat the points in the reverse order of their construction. The treatment of each point consists in eliminating every occurrence of the point in the goal. This can be done thanks to the *elimination lemmas*.

To be in the language of the procedure, the goal to be proved must verify two conditions: first the theorem has to be stated as a sequence of constructions (constructing points as intersections of lines or on the parallel to a line passing through a point, *etc.*)[1]. Second, the goal must be expressed as an arithmetic expression using only three geometric quantities: the ratio of two oriented distances $(\frac{\overline{AB}}{\overline{CD}})$ with AB parallel to CD, the signed area of a triangle (S_{ABC}) and the Pythagoras difference (the difference between the sum of the squares of two sides of a triangle and the square of the other side $P_{ABC} = \overline{AB}^2 + \overline{BC}^2 - \overline{AC}^2)$[2]. These three geometric quantities are sufficient to deal with a large part of plane geometry as shown in Table 1 on page 228. They verify elementary properties such as $S_{AAB} = 0$, $S_{ABC} = -S_{BAC}$ and $S_{ABC} = S_{BCA}$. That will be made explicit in Sect. 3. For the time being only the first two geometric quantities are formalized in our development in Coq, it means that we can only deal with affine plane geometry. The formulas treated by our tactic are those of the form:

$$\forall A_1, \ldots A_n : Point, \ C_i(A_o, \ldots, A_p) \to \ldots \to C_j(A_q, \ldots, A_r) \to R = 0$$

---

[1] Note that it is subject to conditions (that may not be decidable) and that constructive in this context does not mean the same as constructible with ruler and compass (this will be detailed later in Sect. 3.1). Note also that different constructions can lead to slightly different nondegeneracy conditions and so slightly different theorems.

[2] Note that $P_{ABC} = -2(\overrightarrow{AB}.\overrightarrow{BC})$ and $4S_{ABC}^2 = (\overrightarrow{AB} \wedge \overrightarrow{BC})^2$ where . is dot product and $\wedge$ is vector cross product.

where R is an arithmetical expression containing signed areas and ratios and C_i are predicates expressing the sequence of constructions. For each constructed point there is some C_i stating how it has been constructed. Note that the dependency graph of the constructions must be cycle free.

To eliminate a point from the goal we need to apply one of the elimination lemmas shown on Table 2 on page 229. This table can be read as follows: To eliminate a point Y, choose the line corresponding to the way Y has been constructed, and apply the formula given in the column corresponding to the geometric quantity in which Y is used. The lemmas rewrite any geometric quantity containing an occurrence of a point Y (S_{ABY} or $\frac{\overline{AY}}{\overline{CD}}$ for any A,B,C and D such that $AY \parallel CD$.) into an expression with no occurrence of Y [3]. There is one lemma for each combination of construction and geometric quantity. As far as geometry of incidence is concerned, we have five ways to construct a point and two geometric quantities; this provides ten elimination lemmas. Note that there are more constructions than needed (some constructions can be expressed using others). This is used to simplify the statement of the theorems and shorten the proofs by providing specific elimination lemmas for non primitive constructions. The constructions involving a quantity λ can be used to build a point at some fixed distance (if λ is instantiated) or at any distance (if λ is kept as a variable). These last constructions are used to build what are called "semi-fixed points".

When all the constructed points have disappeared from the goal, the result is an arithmetic expression containing geometric quantities using only free points (free points are those that can be freely moved in the plane, those whose position can be arbitrarily chosen while drawing the figure). At this step these geometric quantities use only free points but are not necessarily independent. In case these geometric quantities are not independent we decompose them using three non collinear points (that can be seen as a base). This will be detailed in Sect. 3. If all the geometric quantities are independent, the goal can be seen as an equation between two polynomials, which can be easily decided.

The steps of the method can be summarized using this informal description:

- express the goal in a *constructive* way (as a sequence of basic constructions) using only the three geometric quantities;
- remove bound points from the goal using the *elimination lemmas*;
- change the goal into an expression containing only *independent* geometric quantities;
- *decide* if the resulting equality is universally true or not.

2.1 Example

Let's consider the midpoint theorem as an example:

---

[3] Note that every occurrence of Y is removed only if the points present in the geometric quantity containing Y (A,B,C and D) are different from Y, this problem is treated in the implementation.

Table 1. Expressing some common geometric notions using $\mathcal{S}$, ratios and $\mathcal{P}$

Geometric notions	Formalization
A, B and C are collinear	$\mathcal{S}_{ABC} = 0$
$AB \parallel CD$	$\mathcal{S}_{ABC} = \mathcal{S}_{ABD}$
I is the midpoint of AB	$\frac{\overline{AB}}{\overline{AI}} = 2 \wedge \mathcal{S}_{ABI} = 0$
$AB \perp BC$	$\mathcal{P}_{ABC} = 0$
$AB \perp CD$	$\mathcal{P}_{ACD} = \mathcal{P}_{BCD}$
$A = B$	$\mathcal{P}_{ABA} = 0$

Example 1 (Midpoint theorem). Let ABC be a triangle, and let A' and B' be the midpoints of BC and AC respectively. Then the line $A'B'$ is parallel to the base AB.

Proof (using the method). We first translate the goal $(A'B' \parallel AB)$ into its equivalent using the signed area:

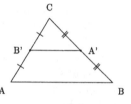

$$\mathcal{S}_{A'B'A} = \mathcal{S}_{A'B'B}$$

Then we eliminate compound points from the goal starting by the last point in the order of their construction. The geometric quantities containing an occurrence of B' are $\mathcal{S}_{A'B'B}$ and $\mathcal{S}_{A'B'A}$, B' has been constructed using the first construction on Table 2 with $\lambda = \frac{1}{2}$:

$$\mathcal{S}_{A'B'A} = \mathcal{S}_{AA'B'} = \frac{1}{2}\mathcal{S}_{AA'A} + \frac{1}{2}\mathcal{S}_{AA'C} = \frac{1}{2}\mathcal{S}_{AA'C}$$

and

$$\mathcal{S}_{A'B'B} = \mathcal{S}_{BA'B'} = \frac{1}{2}\mathcal{S}_{BA'A} + \frac{1}{2}\mathcal{S}_{BA'C}$$

The new goal is

$$\mathcal{S}_{AA'C} = \mathcal{S}_{BA'A} + \mathcal{S}_{BA'C}$$

Now we eliminate A' using:

$$\mathcal{S}_{CAA'} = \frac{1}{2}\mathcal{S}_{CAB} + \frac{1}{2}\mathcal{S}_{CAC} = \frac{1}{2}\mathcal{S}_{CAB}$$

$$\mathcal{S}_{ABA'} = \frac{1}{2}\mathcal{S}_{ABB} + \frac{1}{2}\mathcal{S}_{ABC} = \frac{1}{2}\mathcal{S}_{ABC}$$

$$\mathcal{S}_{CBA'} = \frac{1}{2}\mathcal{S}_{CBB} + \frac{1}{2}\mathcal{S}_{CBC} = 0$$

The new goal is:

$$\frac{1}{2}\mathcal{S}_{CAB} = \frac{1}{2}\mathcal{S}_{ABC}$$

The proof is completed as $\mathcal{S}_{CAB} = \mathcal{S}_{ABC}$.

Table 2. Elimination lemmas

Construction	Description (Nondegeneracy condition)	Elimination formulas	
		$S_{ABY} =$	If $AY \parallel CD$ then $\overline{\dfrac{AY}{CD}} =$
$P \quad Y \quad Q$	Take Y on line PQ such that $\dfrac{\overline{PY}}{\overline{PQ}} = \lambda$. ($P \neq Q$)	$\lambda S_{ABQ} + (1-\lambda)S_{ABP}$	$\begin{cases} \dfrac{\frac{\overline{AP}}{\overline{PQ}} + \lambda}{\frac{\overline{CD}}{\overline{PQ}}} & \text{if } A \in PQ \\[2mm] \dfrac{S_{APQ}}{S_{CPDQ}} & \text{otherwise}^a. \end{cases}$
$U,\ Y,\ P,\ Q,\ V$	Take Y at the intersection of PQ and UV. ($PQ \nparallel UV$)	$\dfrac{S_{PUV}S_{ABQ} + S_{QVU}S_{ABP}}{S_{PUQV}}$	$\begin{cases} \dfrac{S_{AUV}}{S_{CUDV}} & \text{if } A \notin UV \\[2mm] \dfrac{S_{APQ}}{S_{CPDQ}} & \text{otherwise}. \end{cases}$
$R,\ Y,\ P,\ Q$	Take Y on the parallel to PQ passing through R such that $\dfrac{\overline{RY}}{\overline{PQ}} = \lambda$. ($P \neq Q$)	$S_{ABR} + \lambda S_{APBQ}$	$\begin{cases} \dfrac{\frac{\overline{AR}}{\overline{PQ}} + \lambda}{\frac{\overline{CD}}{\overline{PQ}}} & \text{if } A \in RY \\[2mm] \dfrac{S_{APRQ}}{S_{CPDQ}} & \text{otherwise}. \end{cases}$
$R,\ Y,\ U,\ P,\ Q,\ V$	Take Y at the intersection of UV and the parallel to PQ passing through R. ($PQ \nparallel UV$)	$\dfrac{S_{PUQR}S_{ABV} - S_{PVQR}S_{ABU}}{S_{PUQV}}$	$\begin{cases} \dfrac{S_{AUV}}{S_{CUDV}} & \text{if } A \notin UV \\[2mm] \dfrac{S_{APRQ}}{S_{CPDQ}} & \text{otherwise}. \end{cases}$
$Q,\ W,\ Y,\ R,\ P,\ U,\ V$	Take Y at the intersection of the parallel to PQ passing through R and the parallel to UV passing through W. ($PQ \nparallel UV$)	$\dfrac{S_{PWQR}}{S_{PUQV}} S_{AUBV} + S_{ABW}$	$\begin{cases} \dfrac{S_{APRQ}}{S_{CPDQ}} & \text{if } AY \nparallel PQ \\[2mm] \dfrac{S_{AUWV}}{S_{CUDV}} & \text{otherwise}. \end{cases}$

^{a} S_{ABCD} is a notation for $S_{ABC} + S_{ACD}$.

3   Implementation in Coq

The formalization of the procedure consists in choosing an axiomatic, proving the propositions needed by the tactic and writing the tactic itself. These three steps are described in this section, but to ease the development, in our implementation we have intermixed the proofs of the propositions and the tactics. Our tactic is decomposed into sub-tactics performing the following tasks (we will give their precise description later):

- initialization;
- simplification;
- unification;
- elimination;
- conclusion.

The simplification and unification tactics are used to prove some propositions needed by the other sub-tactics.

Our tactic is mainly implemented using the Ltac language included in the Coq system. This language provides primitives to describe Coq tactics within Coq itself (without using Ocaml, the implementation language of Coq). But some of our sub-tactics are implemented using the reflection method [11, 9, 1]. This method consists of reflecting a subset of the Coq language (here the arithmetical expressions build on the geometric quantities) into an object of the Coq language itself (in our case an inductive type denoting arithmetical expressions). This means that the computation performed by the traditional tactic in some metalanguage (Ltac or Ocaml) is here done using the internal reduction of Coq. The reflexive tactic is composed of:

- a small piece of Ltac (or Ocaml) to reflect the object language into the metalanguage,
- a Coq term which solves the problem expressed in the metalanguage,
- a Coq term which reflects the metalanguage into the object language,
- and the proof of the validity of the transformation performed by this term.

This method has the advantage of producing more efficient tactics and shorter proofs because the application of the tactic is just one computation step (using the conversion rule of the calculus of inductive constructions).

We have used the reflection method to implement the simplification and unification tactics. We have not chosen to use the reflection method for the whole tactic for two reasons:

1. We believe that the proof process would not be much faster and the generated proof would be comparable in size. Indeed the proofs generated by our tactic are roughly a sequence of the few applications of the elimination lemmas.
2. Expressing the tactic as a Coq term, and proving the validity of this transformation would have been cumbersome. We make heavy use of the high level primitives provided by the Ltac language such as matching the context for terms or sub-terms, clearing hypotheses *etc*. All this machinery and the proof of its validity would have to be developed within Coq to use the reflection method on the whole tactic.

3.1   The Axiomatic

There are many axiomatics for elementary geometry. The best known are the axiomatics of Euclid, Tarski and Hilbert [6, 16, 10]. The axiomatic used to formalize this decision method in Coq is inspired by the axiomatic of Chou, Gao and Zhang and is given in Table 3 on the following page. We could define this axiomatic as an undirected, semi-analytic, axiomatic with points as primitive objects. We mean by these adjectives that:

- This axiomatic has the property of being unordered, this simplifies the treatment of a lot of cases but it has the drawback that one cannot express the *Between* predicate which can be found in Tarski[4].
- This axiomatic contains the axioms of a field. This means that there is some notion of numbers, but it is still coordinate free.
- This axiomatic has the characteristic of being based on points: lines are not primitive objects as in Hilbert's axiomatic for example which contains not only *Points* but also *Lines* as primitive objects. This means that we can not quantify over the set of lines, *etc.*

The first axiom is the fact that we have a set of points.

We assume that we have a field of characteristic different from two. The axioms of a field are standard and hence omitted. The fact that the characteristic is different from two is used first to simplify the axiomatic (because $2 \neq 0 \land S_{ABC} = -S_{BAC} \rightarrow S_{AAC} = 0$) and second to allow the construction of the midpoint[5] of a segment without explicitly stating that two is different from zero.

We assume that we have one binary function $(\overline{AB})$ and one ternary (S_{ABC}) from points to our field (F). The first depicts the signed distance between A and B, the second represents the signed area of the triangle A,B,C.

The axioms of dimension express that all points are in the same plane and not all points are collinear.

The axioms of construction express that we can build a point on a line determined by two points A and B at some given distance. The given distance is not necessarily a "constructive distance" so the notion of theorems stated constructively is not the same as the notion of constructible with ruler and compass. The constructed point is unique if A is different from B.

The axiom of proportions is central and gives a relation between oriented distances and signed areas.

Our axiomatic differs in some points with the axiomatic of Chou, Gao and Zhang.

---

[4] This issue can be addressed using an ordered field. In this case we can express the *Between* predicate and we could generalize the procedure to allow the treatment of a goal which is an inequality. But the procedure could still not deal with inequalities in the hypotheses.

[5] The midpoint is given such attention because it is used to prove the validity of constructions involving parallel lines.

Table 3. The axiomatic

Points Point : Set

Field $\quad\begin{array}{l} F \text{ is a field} \\ 2 \neq 0 \end{array}$

Signed distance $\quad\begin{array}{l} \overline{\cdot} : \text{Point} \to \text{Point} \to F \\ \overline{AB} = 0 \iff A = B \end{array}$

Signed area $\quad\begin{array}{l} \mathcal{S} : \text{Point} \to \text{Point} \to \text{Point} \to F \\ \mathcal{S}_{ABC} = \mathcal{S}_{CAB} \\ \mathcal{S}_{ABC} = -\mathcal{S}_{BAC} \end{array}$

Chasles'axiom $\mathcal{S}_{ABC} = 0 \to \overline{AB} + \overline{BC} = \overline{AC}$

Dimension $\quad\begin{array}{l} \exists A, B, C : \text{Point}, \mathcal{S}_{ABC} \neq 0 \\ \mathcal{S}_{ABC} = \mathcal{S}_{DBC} + \mathcal{S}_{ADC} + \mathcal{S}_{ABD} \end{array}$

Construction $\quad\begin{array}{l} \forall r : F \; \exists P : \text{Point}, \mathcal{S}_{ABP} = 0 \wedge \overline{AP} = r\overline{AB} \\ A \neq B \; \begin{array}{l} \wedge \; \mathcal{S}_{ABP} = 0 \wedge \overline{AP} = r\overline{AB} \\ \wedge \; \mathcal{S}_{ABP'} = 0 \wedge \overline{AP'} = r\overline{AB} \end{array} \to P = P' \end{array}$

Proportions $A \neq C \to \mathcal{S}_{PAC} \neq 0 \to \mathcal{S}_{ABC} = 0 \to \dfrac{\overline{AB}}{\overline{AC}} = \dfrac{\mathcal{S}_{PAB}}{\mathcal{S}_{PAC}}$

First we do not assume that we have a notion of collinearity, this notion is defined using the signed area. In [2] the notion of collinearity of three points A, B and C is used to express some axioms and then proved to be equivalent to $\mathcal{S}_{ABC} = 0$.

Second we can divide arbitrary distances, whereas Chou's axiomatic restricts to ratios of oriented distances $\frac{\overline{AB}}{\overline{CD}}$ where the lines AB and CD are parallel. The coherence is preserved because the oriented distance can be interpreted by the standard analytic model. The fact that we can divide arbitrary distances means that to give an interpretation to the distance function we have to give an orientation to the lines of our plane.

But the decision procedure requires explicitly that for every ratio of oriented distances $\frac{\overline{AB}}{\overline{CD}}$, AB is parallel to CD. Our lemmas used in the procedure state explicitly that the lines are parallel. This means that in our formalization one can write the ratio of two arbitrary distances but it cannot be dealt with by the decision procedure. This choice of formalization implies that the decision procedure is not complete (the goals which are not in the language of the tactic will be rejected).

This formalization is more convenient because it is more general and it allows to use an "ordinary" field, and use the standard tactic dealing with fields provided by Coq. Otherwise we would have had to give some axioms and prove some properties concerning the link between the ratio function and products, sums, *etc.* It also allows us to manipulate ratios of distances which are supported by parallel lines without *explicitly* stating that these lines are parallel. This is useful sometimes. For example with the same assumptions as in the midpoint theorem, if we want to state that $\frac{\overline{A'B'}}{\overline{AB}} = \frac{1}{2}$ we do not want to add an assumption stating that $A'B' \parallel AB$ because it is a *consequence* of other assumptions. As a result of this choice, two invariants must be kept along the proof:

1. for each denominator of a fraction there is a proof in the context that it is different from zero
2. for each ratio of oriented distances $\frac{\overline{AB}}{\overline{CD}}$ there is a proof in the context that AB is parallel to CD

3.2 Propositions Needed by the Tactic

Here is a quick overview of the propositions that have been proven using the Coq system for this development:

Basic propositions are used to rewrite geometric quantities, *etc.* these are the very basic propositions used by unification and simplification tactics, they come very early in order to take advantage of the unification and simplification tactics as soon as possible.

Lemmas are used in the whole development.

Construction lemmas are used to prove that each construction shown on Table 2 is a consequence of the axiom of construction.

Constructed points elimination lemmas are used to eliminate fixed points and preserve our invariants.

Free points lemmas are used to express geometric quantities using independent variables.

3.3 The Tactic Itself

We give in this section a detailed description of the sub-tactics we use.

Initialization Tactic

1. The initialization tactic (called **geoinit**) checks that the goal is compatible with the decision procedure. (This includes verification that the invariants are initially true.)
2. It unfolds all the definitions which are not treated directly by the decision procedure. (for example midpoint is expanded as a ratio of distances, and a statement expressing the collinearity)
3. It introduces all the hypotheses in the context.
4. It decomposes the logical part of the goal if needed. (split the conjunctions and decompose the compound constructions)

Example 2. The midpoint theorem is stated using our language [8] in the syntax of Coq V8.0 as follows:

```
Theorem midpoint_A :
 forall A B C A' B' : Point, midpoint A' B C -> midpoint B' A C ->
 parallel A' B' A B.
geoInit.
1 subgoal
  A : Point
  B : Point
  C : Point
  A' : Point
  B' : Point
  H : on_line_d A' B C (1 / 2)
  HO : on_line_d B' A C (1 / 2)
  ==============================
  S A' A B' + S A' B' B = 0
```

on_line_d A' B C (1/2) states that A' is on line BC and $\frac{\overline{BA'}}{\overline{BC}} = \frac{1}{2}$.

Simplification tactics. The simplification tactic (basic_simpl) performs basic simplifications in the hypotheses *and* the goal. Note that we need to perform exactly the same simplifications in the goal and hypotheses in order to preserve our invariants. For instance if the denominator of a fraction is simplified, the same simplification must be applied to the proof that this denominator is non-zero otherwise we lose the invariant that we have a proof that every term which syntactically occurs in the denominator of a fraction is non-zero.

Basic simplifications consist in:

- removing degenerated directed distances or signed areas (*e.g.* $\frac{\overline{AA}}{\overline{AB}}$, S_{AAB}...)
- rewriting $-(-x)$ into x
- rewriting -0 into 0
- rewriting $0 * x$ and $x * 0$ into 0
- rewriting $1 * x$ and $x * 1$ into x
- rewriting $x + 0$ and $0 + x$ into x

This tactic is necessary to keep the goal as small as possible. Not simplifying the goal at each step would lead to huge terms. Examples show that the computation becomes intractable without simplification.

Unification tactics. (unify_signed_areas,unify_signed_distances)

There are two unification tactics, one for each geometric quantity. The unification tactics change the goal and hypotheses in order to unify the geometric quantities. For instance if both $\overline{AB}$ and $\overline{BA}$ are used in the context or in the goal, $\overline{AB}$ is changed into $-\overline{BA}$[6].

---

[6] The choice to rewrite $\overline{AB}$ or $\overline{BA}$ is arbitrarily made by the tactic.

This has two purposes:

1. It can speed up some steps, because any rewrite of one of these quantities will be done only once.
2. It is necessary that geometric quantities which are equals have the same form. Indeed the last step of the procedure is a call to the Coq standard `field`[7] tactic on an arithmetic expression containing independent geometric quantities, and `field` would consider $\overline{AB}$ and $\overline{BA}$ as different variables (because `field` doesn't know anything about the oriented distance function).

Example 3. In this context:

```
H9 : S C A B <> 0
H8 : S B A C <> 0
H1 : S A B C <> 0
==============================
S P B C / S A B C + S P A C / S B A C + S P A B / S C A B = 1
```

the tactic `unify_signed_areas` changes the goal into:

```
H8 : - S A B C <> 0
H1 : S A B C <> 0
==============================
S P B C / S A B C + S P A C / - S A B C + S P A B / S A B C = 1
```

Elimination tactic. This tactic (called `eliminate_all`) first searches the context for a point which is not used to build another point (a leaf in the dependency graph). Then for each occurrence of the point in the goal, it applies the right lemma from Table 2 by finding in the context how the point has been constructed and which geometric quantity it appears in. Finally it removes the hypotheses stating how the point has been constructed from the context.

Note that some lemmas have a side condition to their application, in this case a recursive call on the whole tactic is done. If the condition is true then the lemma is applied, in the other case we need to do a step of classical reasoning: we reason by cases on the side condition. The formalization in Coq emphasizes the use of this classical reasoning step. As noted before, the elimination lemmas given in Table 2 on page 229, do eliminate an occurrence of a point Y only if Y appears only one time in the geometric quantity (A,B,C and D must be different from Y). If Y appears twice in S, this is not a problem because then the geometric quantity is zero, and so already eliminated by the simplification phase. But if Y appears twice in a ratio (for instance in $\frac{\overline{AY}}{\overline{BY}}$) this is a special case which needs to be treated apart. This is done in the implementation.

---

[7] `field` is a reflexive tactic included in the distribution of Coq. It decides equality on any field defined by the user.

Example 4.   In this context:

```
1 subgoal
A : Point
B : Point
C : Point
A' : Point
B' : Point
H : on_line_d A' B C (1 / 2)
HO : on_line_d B' A C (1 / 2)
==============================
S A' A B' + S B A' B' = 0
```

the tactic `eliminate B'` changes the goal into:

```
1 subgoal
A : Point
B : Point
C : Point
A' : Point
B' : Point
H : on_line_d A' B C (1 / 2)
==============================
1 / 2 * S A' A C + (1 - 1 / 2) * S A' A A +
(1 / 2 * S B A' C + (1 - 1 / 2) * S B A' A) = 0
```

Free point elimination tactic. This tactic supposes that the goal is an expression using geometric quantities involving only free points (every constructed point has already been eliminated by the elimination tactic). The role of this tactic is to change the goal into an expression involving only independent variables. Geometric quantities involving free points are not necessarily independent, they are bound by the following relation:

$$\mathcal{S}_{ABC} = \mathcal{S}_{DBC} + \mathcal{S}_{ADC} + \mathcal{S}_{ABD}$$

But geometric quantities involving free points can be transformed into a bunch of independent variables by expressing them with respect to a base. For that purpose we choose three arbitrary non collinear points O, U and V and we use the following lemma to rewrite geometric quantities containing more than one point which is different from the base points:

$$\mathcal{S}_{OUV} \neq 0 \rightarrow \mathcal{S}_{ABC} = \begin{vmatrix} \mathcal{S}_{OUA} & \mathcal{S}_{OVA} & 1 \\ \mathcal{S}_{OUB} & \mathcal{S}_{OVB} & 1 \\ \mathcal{S}_{OUC} & \mathcal{S}_{OVC} & 1 \end{vmatrix}$$

If there are three points in the context which are known to be not collinear, we use them as the base O, U, V. Otherwise we build three non collinear points thanks to the dimension axiom.

Conclusion tactic. When this tactic is called, the goal is an expression of independent variables. If the rational equality is universally true, the theorem is proved. Otherwise there is some mapping from the variables to the field which make the equality false, and this provides a counter-example to the goal. To check if the equality is universally true, this last tactic applies the standard Coq tactic `field` to solve the goal and then solves the generated subgoals (stating that the denominators are different from zero) using the hypotheses and/or decomposing them using the fact that $x \neq 0 \wedge y \neq 0 \rightarrow x * y \neq 0$. As the `field` tactic does not provide counter-examples, our tactic is not able to give counter-examples either. This is just a technical limitation. This tactic is small enough to be fully explained:

```
Ltac field_and_conclude :=
    abstract(field; repeat (assumption || apply nonzeromult); geometry).
```

This tactic does a call to `field`[8], and tries to apply one of the assumptions to the generated subgoals. If it fails, it decomposes the product in the goal and solves the subgoals using `geometry`. This last tactic is able to solve common goals such as $\overline{AB} \neq 0$ when the fact that A is different from B is one of the hypotheses. The `abstract` tactic is here for technical reasons: this Coq tactic speeds up the typing process by creating a lemma.

3.4   A Full Example

Example 5. In this section we give a detailed description of how the tactic works on the first example by decomposing the procedure into small steps[9].

```
forall A B C A' B' : Point, midpoint A' B C -> midpoint B' A C ->
parallel A' B' A B.
```

At this step it would be enough to type `autogeom` to solve the goal using our decision procedure, but for this presentation we mimic the behavior of the decision procedure using the sub-tactics described in the previous sections. We give the name of the sub-tactics on the left, and Coq output on the right[10]:

```
geoInit.                H : on_line_d A' B C (1 / 2)

                        H0 : on_line_d B' A C (1 / 2)

                        ==============================

                        S A' A B' + S A' B' B = 0
```

---

[8] The tactic `field` from Coq version 8.0 is very slow at solving some goals, the reason is that the `field` tactic is based on another simplification tactic called `ring` that is very slow at computing with constants on abstract domains such as our field of measures. We incidentally had to reimplement a version of `ring` that computes using binary numbers in order to be able to compute efficiently the last phase of our decision procedure for geometry.

[9] These steps are not exactly the same steps as those executed by our automatic procedure (the automatic procedure may treat the points in another order, and perform more simplification and unification steps).

[10] For this presentation the fact that A, B, C, D and E are of type `point` has been removed from the context.

```
eliminate B'.          H : on_line_d A' B C (1 / 2)
                       ==============================

                       1 / 2 * S A' A C + (1 - 1 / 2) * S A' A A +
                       (1 / 2 * S B A' C + (1 - 1 / 2) * S B A' A) = 0


basic_simpl.           H : on_line_d A' B C (1 / 2)
                       ==============================

                       1 / 2 * S A' A C + (1 / 2 * S B A' C + 1 / 2 * S B A' A) = 0


eliminate A'.          ==============================

                       1 / 2 * (1 / 2 * S A C C + (1 - 1 / 2) * S A C B) +
                       (1 / 2 * (1 / 2 * S C B C + (1 - 1 / 2) * S C B B) +
                        1 / 2 * (1 / 2 * S A B C + (1 - 1 / 2) * S A B B)) = 0


basic_simpl.           ==============================

                       1 / 2 * (1 / 2 * S A C B) + 1 / 2 * (1 / 2 * S A B C) = 0


unify_signed_areas.    ==============================

                       1 / 2 * (1 / 2 * S A C B) + 1 / 2 * (1 / 2 * - S A C B) = 0


field_and_conclude.    Proof completed.
```

4 Future Work

This development can be extended in two directions: treat more geometrical
notions and adapt this work to other axiomatic systems or formal developments.
The first direction is straightforward and consists in extending the approach
presented in this paper to deal with circles, perpendiculars, vectors, complex
numbers and spatial geometry as shown in the book of Chou, Gao and Zhang.
To achieve this goal, our tactic can easily be adapted, we only need to prove
the construction and elimination lemmas corresponding to the new geometric
quantities (for example the pythagoras difference) and update the unification
and simplification tactics.

The second direction consists in building bridges to other formalizations of
geometry (using different axiomatics). Preliminary work has been done towards
the integration of our tactic with Frédérique Guilhot's Coq development dealing
with high school geometry. This integration would open the door to pedagogi-
cal applications. Involving a student in the process of formally proving a basic
geometry theorem is not an unreachable goal if he is saved from the burden of
solving some technical goals thanks to our automatic tactic (for instance goals
dealing with nondegeneracy conditions). We have initiated a discussion in order
to define a common language for stating formal geometry theorems [8]. Although
the logic used to formalize elementary geometry is very simple, the problem of
defining a common language is not trivial. Indeed, different axiomatics can lead
to different yet natural definitions for the same informal object. For instance the

common notion of collinearity in a vector-based approach (A, B, C are collinear if $\exists k, \overrightarrow{AB} = k.\overrightarrow{AC}$) is different from the notion of collinearity in our development.

5 Conclusion

We have shown in this paper how automatic theorem proving can be combined with interactive proof development in the framework of the Coq proof assistant. Our implementation gives an example of how the tactic language of Coq (Ltac) and the reflection mechanism can be jointly used to build a somewhat short development of a tactic (6500 lines) without sacrificing the efficiency (our implementation within Coq is slower than the original but 20 examples including the well-known theorems of Ceva, Menelaus, Pascal and Desargues are proved in a couple of minutes). This formalization at the same time emphasizes the role of nondegeneracy conditions and provides a way to get rid of them. Our formalization also clarifies the usage of classical reasoning.

Availability. This development is available at:
http://www.lix.polytechnique.fr/~jnarboux/ChouGaoZhang/index.html

Acknowledgements

I want to thank Hugo Herbelin for his help during the elaboration of this work.

References

1. S. Boutin. Using reflection to build efficient and certified decision procedures. In M. Abadi and T. Ito, editors, *Proceedings of TACS'97*, volume 1281 of *LNCS*. Springer-Verlag, 1997.
2. S.C. Chou, X.S. Gao, and J.Z. Zhang. *Machine Proofs in Geometry*. World Scientific, Singapore, 1994.
3. Shang-Ching Chou. *Mechanical Geometry Theorem Proving*. D. Reidel Publishing Company, 1988.
4. G. E. Collins. Quantifier elimination for real closed fields by cylindrical algebraic decomposition. In *Lecture Notes In Computer Science*, volume 33, pages 134–183. Springer-Verlag, 1975.
5. Christophe Dehlinger, Jean-François Dufourd, and Pascal Schreck. Higher-order intuitionistic formalization and proofs in Hilbert's elementary geometry. In *Automated Deduction in Geometry*, pages 306–324, 2000.
6. Euclide. *Les éléments*. Presses Universitaires de France, 1998. Traduit par Bernard Vitrac.
7. Frédérique Guilhot. Formalisation en coq d'un cours de géométrie pour le lycée. In *Journées Francophones des Langages Applicatifs*, Janvier 2004.
8. Frédérique Guilhot and Julien Narboux. Toward a "common" language for formally stating elementary geometry theorems. Draft.

9. J. Harrison. Meta theory and reflection in theorem proving:a survey and critique. Technical Report CRC-053, SRI International Cambridge Computer Science Research Center, 1995.

10. David Hilbert. *Les fondements de la géométrie*. Dunod, Paris, Jacques Gabay edition, 1971. Edition critique avec introduction et compléments préparée par Paul Rossier.

11. D. Howe. Computation meta theory in nuprl. In E. Lusk and R. Overbeek, editors, *The Proceedings of the Ninth International Conference of Automated Deduction*, volume 310, pages 238–257. Springer-Verlag, 1988.

12. Gilles Kahn. Constructive geometry according to Jan von Plato. Coq contribution. Coq V5.10.

13. The Coq development team. *The Coq proof assistant reference manual*. LogiCal Project, 2004. Version 8.0.

14. Laura I. Meikle and Jacques D. Fleuriot. Formalizing Hilbert's grundlagen in isabelle/isar. In *Theorem Proving in Higher Order Logics*, pages 319–334, 2003.

15. A. Tarski. *A decision method for elementary algebra and geometry*. University of California Press, 1951.

16. A. Tarski. What is elementary geometry? In P. Suppes L. Henkin and A. Tarski, editors, *The axiomatic Method, with special reference to Geometry and Physics*, pages 16–29, Amsterdam, 1959. North-Holland.

17. Jan von Plato. The axioms of constructive geometry. In *Annals of Pure and Applied Logic*, volume 76, pages 169–200, 1995.

18. Wen-Tsün Wu. On the decision problem and the mechanization of theorem proving in elementary geometry. In *Scientia Sinica*, volume 21, pages 157–179. 1978.

Recursive Function Definition for Types with Binders

Michael Norrish

Canberra Research Laboratory, National ICT Australia
Research School of Information Science and Engineering,
Australian National University,
Acton 0200, Australia
Michael.Norrish@nicta.com.au

Abstract. This work describes the proof and uses of a theorem allowing definition of recursive functions over the type of λ-calculus terms, where terms with bound variables are identified up to α-equivalence. The theorem embodies what is effectively a principle of primitive recursion, and the analogues of this theorem for other types with binders are clear. The theorem's side-conditions require that the putative definition be well-behaved with respect to fresh name generation and name permutation. A number of examples over the type of λ-calculus terms illustrate the use of the new principle.

1 Introduction

Theorem-proving tools have long supported the definition of (potentially recursive) algebraic or inductive types. Not only do the tools prove the existence of such types, and establish them within the logical environment, but they also provide methods for defining new functions over those types. Typically this is done by proving and using the new type's recursion theorem.

For example, a definition of a type of lists would assert that the new type had two constructors: nil and cons, and that the cons constructor took two arguments, an element of the parameter type α, and another list. The recursion theorem proved to accompany this type would state:

$$\forall n\, c.\ \exists h.$$
$$h(\mathsf{nil}) = n\ \wedge$$
$$\forall a\, t.\ h(\mathsf{cons}(a,t)) = c(a,t,h(t))$$

This theorem states that given any n, specifying the value of the function-to-be when applied to empty lists, and given any c, specifying what should happen when the function is applied to a "cons-cell", there exists a function h that exhibits the desired behaviour. The cons behaviour, c, may refer to the component parts of the list, a and t, as well as the result of h's action on t.

For example, the existence of the map function can be demonstrated by instantiating the recursion theorem so that n is $\lambda f.\ \mathsf{nil}$, and c is $\lambda(a,t,r)f.\ \mathsf{cons}(f(a),r(f))$. Note how map's additional parameter has been accommodated by making the range of the function h itself a function-space.

K. Slind et al. (Eds.): TPHOLs 2004, LNCS 3223, pp. 241–256, 2004.

In the friendlier world that users expect to inhabit, the user provides a definition for map that looks like

$$\text{map } f \text{ nil} = \text{nil}$$
$$\text{map } f \, (\text{cons}(h,t)) = \text{cons}(f(h), \text{map } f \, t)$$

It is then the responsibility of the tool implementation to recognise that this is a primitive recursion over a list, to instantiate the recursion theorem appropriately, and to manipulate the resulting theorem so that it again looks like what the user specified. If, for example, the tool instantiates the theorem as above, it proves the existence of a map function with its parameters in the wrong order; a little more work is required to demonstrate the existence of the function that takes its function parameter first.

Finally, note that when a multi-parameter function's other arguments do not change in the recursive call (as happens with map, but not, for example, with foldl), it is also possible to instantiate the theorem differently, but to the same ultimate effect. In the case of map, n would be set to nil, and c to $\lambda(a, t, r). \, \text{cons}(f(a), r)$. The resulting instantiation of the recursion theorem would have f free. This could be generalised, giving:

$$\forall f. \, \exists h.$$
$$h(\text{nil}) = \text{nil} \, \wedge$$
$$\forall a \, t. \, h(\text{cons}(a,t)) = \text{cons}(f(a), h(t))$$

An appeal to the Axiom of Choice[1] (skolemisation) then moves the variable h out over the universally quantified f, demonstrating the existence of an h taking two parameters. This trick is not necessary with primitive recursive functions over normal inductive types, but it will be useful in some of the examples below.

This much is well-understood technology. Unfortunately, there is no comparable, simple story to be told about the type of λ-calculus terms where bound variables are identified up to α-equivalence (or indeed, any type featuring α-equivalence). Section 7 discusses other approaches to this problem. Presented here is a new approach, based on two significant sources: Gordon and Melham's characterisation of α-equivalent λ-calculus terms [5], and the Gabbay-Pitts idea of name (or atom) permutation as the basis for syntax with binding [4].

Gordon and Melham's work is a significant starting point because it defines a type in HOL (classical simple type theory) exactly corresponding to the type of (untyped) λ-calculus terms, augmented with a "constant" constructor allowing the injection of any other arbitrary type into the terms. It corresponds to a type that one might declare in SML as

```
datatype 'a term = CON of 'a
                 | VAR of string
                 | APP of 'a term * 'a term
                 | LAM of string * 'a term
```

except that the bodies of abstractions (under the LAM constructor) are identified up to α-equivalence.

---

[1] The recursion theorem can be strengthened so that $\exists h$ turns into $\exists ! h$. Moving this out past universal quantifiers is then only an appeal to the Axiom of Definite Choice.

Accompanying this type are the core theorems and constants that identify it as an implementation of the λ-calculus. There is a substitution function, a function for calculating free variables, and various theorems that describe how these functions behave. There are two further important facts about the Gordon-Melham work:

- Despite their potentially misleading title, "Five axioms of alpha conversion", Gordon and Melham did not assert any new HOL axioms. Their type is constructed entirely definitionally, on top of a model of de Bruijn terms.
- Their theory of terms is first-order. By α-equivalence, the following equation holds

$$\text{LAM } v \ (\text{VAR } v) = \text{LAM } u \ (\text{VAR } u)$$

but LAM is not a binder at the logical level, and there are no function spaces used. The Gordon-Melham theory is not one of higher-order abstract syntax, and there are no exotic terms.

Using the CON constructor, it is straightforward to construct new types with binders on top of the basic Gordon-Melham terms. In earlier work [7], I implemented the types Λ' and Λ'^* from Barendregt [2], and proved finiteness of developments and the standardisation theorem. That work demonstrated that the Gordon-Melham theory is a viable basis for theorem-proving with binders.

Nonetheless, in this earlier work, I had to manually define the new types, and almost all of the various functions over them. This sort of work is painful and a significant obstacle for many users. The current work describes technology for solving one of these two important problems, that of function definition. The other problem, that of defining new types, is another significant project in its own right.

My second inspiration, Gabbay's and Pitts's ideas about permutation as a basis for syntax with binders, is itself an independent approach to the problem of recursive function definition. It is discussed in this role in Section 7. My work attempts to take the permutation idea and move it into a setting where some of its fundamental assumptions no longer apply. This is valuable because permutations exhibit properties, even in HOL's classical simple type theory, that make them much easier to work with than substitutions.

The rest of this paper is arranged as follows: Section 2 provides a series of motivating examples, designed to illustrate a range of different problems in function definition. Section 3 is a discussion of how the Gordon-Melham recursion principle can be slightly adjusted, enabling the definition of a size function. Section 4 describes how a permutation or swap function can be defined using the same principle. Section 5 then presents the derivation of the final recursion principle. Section 6 describes how the principle forms the basis for an automatic tool for performing function definition, and how it copes with the examples of Section 2. I discuss related work in Section 7, and conclude in Section 8.

2   Motivating Examples

The following functions, with their increasing complexity, provide a test for any principle of function definition. They are presented here in the form in which users would want to write them, mimicking how one might write them in a functional language with pattern-matching.

Each of the given functions respects the α-equivalence relation. A clause of the form

$$f(\text{LAM } v\ t) = E$$

has equal values E for every possible renaming of the bound variable v (possibly subject to side-conditions on the equation, see below). If $f(\text{LAM } v\ t)$ were E, but $f(\text{LAM } u\ (t[v \mapsto u]))$ were E', and these expressions had different values, then this would be a contradiction: the two input terms are equal, so their f-values must be equal too. This work's new recursion principle embodies restrictions which ensures that the new functions are well-behaved in this respect.

Case analysis: The `is_app` function distinguishes constructors without looking at their arguments.

```
is_app (CON k)   = F        is_app (VAR s)   = F
is_app (APP t u) = T        is_app (LAM v t) = F
```

Examining constructor arguments: The `rator` function pulls apart an application term and returns the first argument. On other types of term, its value is unspecified.

```
rator (APP t u) = t
```

There is a sister function, `rand` which returns the other argument of an APP.

Simple recursion: The `size` function returns a numeric measurement of the size of a term.

```
size (CON k)   = 1
size (VAR s)   = 1
size (APP t u) = 1 + size t + size u
size (LAM v t) = 1 + size t
```

Recursion mentioning a bound variable: The `enf` function is true of a term if it is in η-normal form. (The FV function returns the set of a term's free variables.)

```
enf (CON k)   = T
enf (VAR s)   = T
enf (APP t u) = enf t ∧ enf u
enf (LAM v t) = enf t ∧
                (is_app t ∧ rand t = VAR v ⇒
                  v ∈ FV (rator t))
```

Simple recursion (terms as range type): The (admittedly artificial) `stripc` function replaces all CON terms with $(\lambda x.x)$.

```
stripc (CON k)   = LAM "x" (VAR "x")
stripc (VAR s)   = VAR s
stripc (APP t u) = APP (stripc t) (stripc u)
stripc (LAM v t) = LAM v (stripc t)
```

Recursion with an additional parameter: Given the ternary type of possible directions to follow when passing through a term ($\{Lt, Rt, In\}$), corresponding to the two sub-terms of an APP constructor and the body of an abstraction, return the set of paths (lists of directions) to the occurrences of the given free variable in a term.

```
v_posns v (VAR s)   = if s = v then {[]} else ∅
v_posns v (CON k)   = ∅
v_posns v (APP t u) = (IMAGE (CONS Lt) (v_posns v t))
                             ∪
                      (IMAGE (CONS Rt) (v_posns v u))

v ≠ x ⇒
    v_posns v (LAM x t) = IMAGE (CONS In) (v_posns v t)
```

The IMAGE (CONS x) construction above takes a set and adds x to the front of all its elements (which are all lists). After this definition is made, it is easy to prove (by induction) that

$$v \notin \mathrm{FV}(t) \quad \Rightarrow \quad \text{v\_posns } v\, t = \emptyset$$

Another useful LAM clause immediately follows:

```
v_posns v (LAM v t) = ∅
```

One advantage of the new recursion principle is that it automatically derives the side-condition attached to the LAM-clause above, necessary to make it valid.

Recursion with varying parameters (terms as range): A variant of the substitution function, which substitutes a term for a variable, but further adjusts the term being substituted by wrapping it in one application of the variable "f" per binder traversed.

```
sub' M v (VAR s)   = if v = s then M else VAR s
sub' M v (CON k)   = CON k
sub' M v (APP t u) = APP (sub' M v t) (sub' M v u)

v ≠ x ∧ "f" ≠ x ∧ x ∉ FV (M) ⇒
    sub' M v (LAM x t) =
        LAM x (sub' (APP (VAR "f") M) v t)
```

Again, the preconditions on the LAM-clause in this example ensure that the function respects α-equivalence. This function can be given another clause for the LAM constructor in the same way as for v_posns above, giving

```
sub' M v (LAM v t) = LAM v t
```

Even with this addition, the equations may not seem to provide a complete specification of the behaviour of the function. What, for example, is the behaviour if the bound variable is "f"? In fact, the function is well-defined, but its value may need to be calculated by first α-converting an abstraction to use a new bound variable. That this is always possible is guaranteed by the new recursion principle: it requires that there be only finitely many names to which a bound variable can not be renamed. Here, the unavailable names are v, "f" and the nmaes in FV(M).

3 The Recursion Principle: First Steps

One of the Gordon-Melham theorems characterising the type of λ-calculus terms is the following principle of recursion (where $t[v \mapsto u]$ is a capture-avoiding substitution of a term u for a variable v throughout term t):

$$\forall con\ var\ app\ lam.$$
$$\exists hom.$$
$$(\forall k.\ hom(\text{CON}\,k) = con(k)) \land$$
$$(\forall s.\ hom(\text{VAR}\,s) = var(s)) \land \tag{1}$$
$$(\forall t\ u.\ hom(\text{APP}\,t\,u) = app\ (hom\ t)\ (hom\ u)\ t\ u) \land$$
$$(\forall v\ t.\ hom(\text{LAM}\,v\,t) =$$
$$lam\ (\lambda y.\ hom(t[v \mapsto \text{VAR}(y)]))\ (\lambda y.\ t[v \mapsto \text{VAR}(y)]))$$

This differs from the usual form of a recursion theorem in the clause for LAM. The *lam* function is not passed the result of a recursive call, but a function instead. This function takes a string, substitutes it for the bound variable through the body, and returns the result of the recursive function applied to this. Similarly, rather than getting access to the body of the abstraction directly, *lam* only gets to see it hidden behind another function that performs a substitution.

The last of the Gordon-Melham "axioms" states the existence of a function ABS such that

$$\text{LAM}\,v\,t\ =\ \text{ABS}(\lambda y.\ t[v \mapsto \text{VAR}(y)]) \tag{2}$$

Now instantiate *lam* of (1) with

$$\lambda f\ g.\ \text{let}\ z = \text{NEW}(\text{FV}(\text{ABS}(g)) \cup X)\ \text{in}\ lam'\ (f\ z)\ z\ (g\ z)$$

The NEW function takes a finite set of strings, and returns a string not in that set.

Using (2), the last clause of the recursion theorem becomes

$$\forall v\ t.\ hom(\text{LAM}\,v\,t) =$$
$$\text{let}\ z = \text{NEW}(\text{FV}(\text{LAM}\,v\,t) \cup X)\ \text{in} \tag{3}$$
$$lam'\ (hom(t[v \mapsto \text{VAR}(z)]))\ z\ (t[v \mapsto \text{VAR}(z)])$$

This introduces two new free variables into the theorem: *lam'*, which now gets direct access to the result of a recursion, a bound variable and a term body; and X, an additional set of variables that is to be avoided in the choice of z.

This is a generalisation of the technique that Gordon and Melham use in [5] to define their Lgh ("length") function (similar to size in Section 2 above). The extra X parameter will be vital in defining permutation in Section 4 below. It is also important to have access to the new name z, which stands in for a bound variable that has been renamed to be fresh. Though the new recursion theorem has made the types involved in the LAM clause slightly more palatable, the recursive call in the LAM clause is still over a term that has had a substitution applied to it.

In the case of size (as done in [5]), it is possible to separately prove by induction that size is invariant under variable renamings, that $size(t[v \mapsto \text{VAR}(y)]) = size(t)$. This simplifies the LAM-clause so that the reference to the fresh z can disappear. This trick is not strong enough in general. It doesn't work for the `stripc` example function, as it is not the case that $\text{stripc}(t[v \mapsto \text{VAR}(y)]) = \text{stripc}(t)$. Still, the `size` function is needed to perform induction on the size of terms, and so this first attempt at a definitional principle is used to define the `size` constant. This preliminary principle also helps with the definition of `swap` (see below), before being discarded.

4   Permutation in HOL

Next, the system must be extended with definitions of name permutation for all of the relevant types[2]. Because variables in the λ-calculus terms are of type string, names are taken to be strings. The basic action of permutation on strings is simple to define:

$$\text{swapstr } x\, y\, s \quad \hat{=} \quad \text{if } x = s \text{ then } y \text{ else (if } y = s \text{ then } x \text{ else } s)$$

Defining a swap function over terms requires the use of the new version of the LAM-clause (3) and the original principle (1), with the following instantiations[3]

$$
\begin{array}{rcl}
var & \mapsto & \lambda s.\ \text{VAR}(\text{swapstr } x\, y\, s) \\
con & \mapsto & \text{CON} \\
app & \mapsto & \lambda rt\, ru\, t\, u.\ \text{APP } rt\, ru \\
X & \mapsto & \{x, y\} \\
lam' & \mapsto & \lambda rt\, v\, t.\ \text{LAM } v\, rt
\end{array}
$$

After generalising over x and y, and then applying the Axiom of Choice (skolemising), this results in the following theorem:

$$
\begin{aligned}
&\exists \text{swap}.\ \forall x\, y. \\
&\quad (\forall s.\ \text{swap } x\, y\ (\text{VAR } s) = \text{VAR}(\text{swapstr } x\, y\, s)) \wedge \\
&\quad (\forall k.\ \text{swap } x\, y\ (\text{CON } k) = \text{CON } k) \wedge \\
&\quad (\forall t\, u.\ \text{swap } x\, y\ (\text{APP } t\, u) = \text{APP } (\text{swap } x\, y\, t)\ (\text{swap } x\, y\, u)) \wedge \qquad (4) \\
&\quad (\forall v\, t.\ \text{swap } x\, y\ (\text{LAM } v\, t) = \\
&\qquad\qquad \text{let } z = \text{NEW}(\text{FV}(\text{LAM } v\, t) \cup \{x, y\}) \text{ in} \\
&\qquad\qquad \text{LAM } z\ (\text{swap } x\, y\ (t[v \mapsto \text{VAR}(z)])))
\end{aligned}
$$

This suffices as a definition for a new constant `swap`, but the LAM-clause is unacceptable as it stands. It needs to be shown that

$$\text{swap } x\, y\ (\text{LAM } v\, t) \;=\; \text{LAM } (\text{swapstr } x\, y\, v)\ (\text{swap } x\, y\, t)$$

This can be done by first showing that `swap` distributes over substitutions of variables for variables:

$$
\begin{aligned}
&\text{swap } x\, y\ (t[u \mapsto \text{VAR}(v)]) = \\
&\quad (\text{swap } x\, y\, t)[\text{swapstr } x\, y\, u \mapsto \text{VAR}(\text{swapstr } x\, y\, v)]
\end{aligned}
\qquad (5)
$$

---

[2] Gabbay and Pitts use the notation $(x\, y) \cdot t$ to mean the permutation of x and y in t, where x and y are names and t is generally of any type. In what follows, I use a wordier, but more explicit, notation, where each swapping function is given a different name depending on the type of the third argument.

[3] The rt and ru names are chosen because these parameters correspond to the results of recursive calls on t and u parameters respectively.

Glossing over some of the details, this theorem suffices because it allows the swap and the substitution to move past each other in the LAM-clause of (4), and for the LAM z (...) there to be recognised as equal (through α-equivalence) to LAM ($\texttt{swapstr } x \, y \, v$) (...).

The proof of (5) is by induction on the size of t.

The next important property of swap is that it can be used instead of substitution when a fresh variable is being substituted for another:

$$v \notin \text{FV}(t) \quad \Rightarrow \quad t[u \mapsto \text{VAR}(v)] = \texttt{swap } u \, v \, t \tag{6}$$

This means that α-equivalence can be expressed using swap:

$$v \notin \text{FV}(t) \quad \Rightarrow \quad \text{LAM } u \, t = \text{LAM } v \, (\texttt{swap } u \, v \, t)$$

This much confirms that the Gordon-Melham λ-calculus terms can be equipped with a permutation action that behaves as the Gabbay-Pitts theory requires.

5   A New Recursion Principle

The aim of this work is the proof of a recursion principle with a LAM clause that looks, as much as possible, like

$$\forall v \, t. \, hom(\text{LAM } v \, t) = lam' \, (hom(t)) \, v \, t \tag{7}$$

How does one start with (3), that is:

$$\forall v \, t. \, hom(\text{LAM } v \, t) =$$
$$\text{let } z = \text{NEW}(\text{FV}(\text{LAM } v \, t) \cup X) \text{ in}$$
$$lam' \, (hom(t[v \mapsto \text{VAR}(z)])) \, z \, (t[v \mapsto \text{VAR}(z)])$$

and derive (7)? And what extra side-conditions need to be added to make the transformation valid?

A simple examination of the two formulas suggests that the desired strategy would be to pull out the substitutions so that there was just one, at the top-level underneath the let, and to then have that substitution "evaporate" somehow. The essence of the principle-to-come is the side-condition that allows this.

The first observation is that permutations move around terms much more readily than substitutions. Secondly, the freshness of z (it is the result of a call to NEW) and (6) mean that the substitutions in (3) can be replaced by permutations, giving

$$\forall v \, t. \, hom(\text{LAM } v \, t) =$$
$$\text{let } z = \text{NEW}(\text{FV}(\text{LAM } v \, t) \cup X) \text{ in}$$
$$lam' \, (hom(\texttt{swap } z \, v \, t)) \, (\texttt{swapstr } z \, v \, v) \, (\texttt{swap } z \, v \, t)$$

To move the swap terms upwards, one would clearly need that

$$hom(\texttt{swap } x \, y \, t) = \texttt{swap } x \, y \, (hom(t)) \tag{8}$$

and that

$$lam' \, (\texttt{swap } x \, y \, t_1) \, (\texttt{swapstr } x \, y \, s) \, (\texttt{swap } x \, y \, t_2) = \texttt{swap } x \, y \, (lam' \, t_1 \, s \, t_2)$$

The final stage is getting the swap x y to "evaporate". The obvious property to appeal to is

$$x \notin \mathrm{FV}(t) \wedge y \notin \mathrm{FV}(t) \Rightarrow \mathrm{swap}\ x\ y\ t = t \tag{9}$$

Note the abuse of notation in this discussion of strategy: the two swap functions in (8) have different types. On the left, swap swaps strings in a λ-calculus term; on the right, swap is swapping strings in the result type. There are also two different swaps in the formula stating the desired commutativity of *lam'*. Finally, the swap in (9) is also over the result type. The final theorem has a side-condition requiring that the result type has swap and FV functions that behave appropriately. This notion of appropriateness is encoded in the swapping predicate, which specifies the properties that a permutation action and an accompanying free-variable function must satisfy:

$$
\begin{aligned}
&\text{swapping } sw\ fv \equiv \\
&\quad (\forall x\,z.\ sw\ x\ x\ z = z) \wedge \\
&\quad (\forall x\,y\,z.\ sw\ x\ y\ (sw\ x\ y\ z) = z) \wedge \\
&\quad (\forall x\,y\,z.\ x \notin fv(z) \wedge y \notin fv(z) \Rightarrow sw\ x\ y\ z = z) \wedge \\
&\quad (\forall x\,y\,z\,s.\ s \in fv(sw\ x\ y\ z) \equiv (\text{swapstr } x\ y\ s) \in fv(z))
\end{aligned}
\tag{10}
$$

The final recursion principle is presented in Figure 1. The rest of this section explains some of its details, and comments on its proof.

5.1 Parameters

In the presence of additional parameters, satisfying (8) becomes more difficult. This is clear with the example function sub′ (and normal substitution as well). If *hom* is taken to be sub′ M v, then (8) is not true. The action of the permutations must be allowed to affect the parameters. In the case of sub′, the appropriate theorem is actually

$$
\begin{aligned}
&x \neq \texttt{"f"} \wedge y \neq \texttt{"f"} \quad \Rightarrow \\
&\quad \mathrm{swap}\ x\ y\ (\mathrm{sub'}\ M\ v\ t) = \mathrm{sub'}\ (\mathrm{swap}\ x\ y\ M)\ (\mathrm{swapstr}\ x\ y\ v)\ (\mathrm{swap}\ x\ y\ t)
\end{aligned}
$$

In general, not only does the result type of the desired function need swap and FV functions, but so too do any parameters. The final recursion principle explicitly acknowledges one unspecified parameter type, and both the final *hom* function, as well as the *con*, *var*, *app* and *lam* values all now take an additional parameter[4].

It is easy to specify a permutation action for a function type, if one has permutation actions for its domain and range types. This is done below in the definition of swapfn. Given this, one might wonder why the final recursion principle needs its explicit treatment of parameters: is it possible instead to simply require that the range of the new function support a permutation action, and expect the use of swapfn to specify this when there are extra parameters? Unfortunately, this is *not* possible: the problem does not arise in the requirement that the new function respect permutations, but rather in the requirement that it not generate too many fresh names (see the second block of antecedents in Figure 1).

---

[4] One parameter is sufficient: additional curried parameters can be dealt with by first showing the existence of an isomorphic uncurried, or tupled, version of the function. The no parameter case is obtained by letting the parameter type be the singleton type one, also known as unit.

swapping rswap rFV ∧ swapping pswap pFV ∧
FINITE X ∧ ($\forall p$. FINITE (pFV p)) ∧

($\forall k\ p$. rFV (con $k\ p$) $\subseteq X\ \cup$ pFV p) ∧
($\forall s\ p$. rFV (var $s\ p$) $\subseteq \{s\}\ \cup$ pFV $p\ \cup X$) ∧
($\forall t'\ u'\ t\ u\ p$.
    ($\forall p$. rFV ($t'\ p$) $\subseteq$ FV $t\ \cup$ pFV $p\ \cup X$) ∧
    ($\forall p$. rFV ($u'\ p$) $\subseteq$ FV $u\ \cup$ pFV $p\ \cup X$) $\Rightarrow$
    rFV (app $t'\ u'\ t\ u\ p$) $\subseteq$ FV (APP $t\ u$) $\cup$ pFV $p\ \cup X$) ∧
($\forall t'\ v\ t\ p$.
    ($\forall p$. rFV ($t'\ p$) $\subseteq$ FV $t\ \cup$ pFV $p\ \cup X$) $\Rightarrow$
    rFV (lam $t'\ v\ t\ p$) $\subseteq$ FV (LAM $v\ t$) $\cup$ pFV $p\ \cup X$) ∧

($\forall k\ x\ y\ p$.
    $x \notin X\ \wedge\ y \notin X \Rightarrow$
    (rswap $x\ y$ (con $k\ p$) = con k (pswap $x\ y\ p$))) ∧
($\forall s\ x\ y\ p$.
    $x \notin X\ \wedge\ y \notin X \Rightarrow$
    (rswap $x\ y$ (var $s\ p$) = var (swapstr $x\ y\ s$) (pswap $x\ y\ p$))) ∧
($\forall t\ t'\ u\ u'\ x\ y\ p$.
    $x \notin X\ \wedge\ y \notin X \Rightarrow$
    (rswap $x\ y$ (app $t'\ u'\ t\ u\ p$) =
     app (swapfn pswap rswap $x\ y\ t'$) (swapfn pswap rswap $x\ y\ u'$)
     (swap $x\ y\ t$) (swap $x\ y\ u$) (pswap $x\ y\ p$))) ∧
($\forall t'\ t\ x\ y\ v\ p$.
    $x \notin X\ \wedge\ y \notin X \Rightarrow$
    (rswap $x\ y$ (lam $t'\ v\ t\ p$) =
     lam (swapfn pswap rswap $x\ y\ t'$) (swapstr $x\ y\ v$) (swap $x\ y\ t$)
     (pswap $x\ y\ p$))) $\Rightarrow$

$\exists hom$.
    ($\forall k\ p$.   hom (CON k) p = con $k\ p$) ∧
    ($\forall s\ p$.   hom (VAR s) p = var $s\ p$) ∧
    ($\forall t\ u\ p$. hom (APP $t\ u$) p = app (hom t) (hom u) $t\ u\ p$) ∧
    ($\forall v\ t\ p$.
     $v \notin X\ \cup$ pFV $p \Rightarrow$
       (hom (LAM $v\ t$) p = lam (hom t) $v\ t\ p$)) ∧

    ($\forall t\ p\ x\ y$.
     $x \notin X\ \wedge\ y \notin X \Rightarrow$
     (hom (swap $x\ y\ t$) p = rswap $x\ y$ (hom t (pswap $x\ y\ p$)))) ∧
    ($\forall t\ p$. rFV (hom $t\ p$) $\subseteq$ FV $t\ \cup$ pFV $p\ \cup X$)

Fig. 1. The recursion principle for λ-calculus terms. The second block of antecedents requires that the function not create too many fresh names. The third block requires that the function respect permutation. The second block of properties in the conclusion state that these properties *do* hold for the resulting hom function. For the definition of swapping, see (10).

Consider defining the substitution function, where the free names of the additional parameters may appear in the result. Without using the parameter information, it is impossible to provide a free variable function (rFV in Figure 1) for the result-type (a function-space) that will satisfy the new principle's antecedents. Such an rFV must simultaneously return small enough sets of names to satisfy the second block of antecedents, and also have an accompanying permutation action, rswap. This permutation action must satisfy the requirements embodied in swapping and the third block of antecedents. For example, the "null" instantiation, taking rFV to always return the empty set, in turn requires rswap to be the identity function (because of the third conjunct of swapping's definition (10)), and thus fails to satisfy

$$\text{rswap } x \, y \, (var \, s) = var \, (\text{swapstr } x \, y \, s)$$

where
$$var = \lambda s \, v \, M. \text{ if } s = v \text{ then } M \text{ else } (\text{VAR } s)$$

5.2   Proving the Theorem

To begin the derivation of the final recursion principle, it is necessary to return to (1) and instantiate *lam* with

$$\lambda f \, g \, p. \text{ let } z = \text{NEW}(\text{FV}(\text{ABS}(g)) \cup \text{pFV}(p) \cup X) \text{ in } lam' \, (f \, z) \, z \, (g \, z) \, p$$

As before, $\text{ABS}(g)$ is equal to the original term, so that z is now fresh with respect to it as well as the parameter. The set of strings to avoid for p's sake is given by the pFV function. The finite set X is used to avoid those free names that are somehow implicit in the function itself. Such a name is the "f" present in the definition of the sub' example.

When the substitutions of (1) are replaced with permutations, the LAM-clause becomes

$$\forall v \, t \, p. \, hom \, (\text{LAM } v \, t) \, p =$$
$$\text{let } z = \text{NEW}(\text{FV}(\text{LAM } v \, t) \cup \text{pFV}(p) \cup X) \text{ in}$$
$$lam' \, (hom(\text{swap } z \, v \, t)) \, (\text{swapstr } z \, v \, v) \, (\text{swap } z \, v \, t) \, p$$

The strategy sketched at the beginning of this section is still the right way to proceed, even after the complication of parameters has been introduced. Its first stage is to move permutations upwards in the above clause, appealing to commutativity results. The third block of antecedents in the final principle allow this to occur. This block also features the use of swapfn, which defines permutation on a function space, given permutation actions for the domain and range type. Its definition is

$$\text{swapfn } dsw \, rsw \, x \, y \, f = \lambda z. \, rsw \, x \, y \, (f \, (dsw \, x \, y \, z))$$

Use of swapfn is required because the result type of *hom* is a function space, so that in expressions such as *app* $(hom(t)) \, (hom(u)) \, t \, u \, p$, the first two arguments to *app* are functions.

The final part of the strategy is to appeal to (9). The strategy is to have the swap terms in

$$\text{let } z = \text{NEW}(\text{FV}(\text{LAM } v \ t) \cup \text{pFV}(p) \cup X) \text{ in}$$
$$\text{rswap } z \ v \ (lam' \ (hom(t))) \ v \ t \ (\text{pswap } z \ v \ p))$$

"evaporate". The variable v is the original bound variable of the abstraction, and the condition on the equation being derived requires it to not be present in the free variables of p. Variable z shares this property by construction, so ($\text{pswap } z \ v \ p$) can be replaced by p. The $\text{rswap } z \ v$ term can only be eliminated if the side-conditions in the theorem ensure that hom, and thus all of the helper functions, do not generate too many new names in the result. This is guaranteed by the second block of antecedents in the recursion principle.

The proof consists of showing that the hom known to exist from the original principle has the properties specified in the final recursion principle. It begins by showing that the new function doesn't produce too many free variables, i.e., that the theorem's conclusion's very last conjunct holds. This proof is by induction, using the original Gordon-Melham induction principle. Next, the commutativity result is shown (the second to last conjunct). This is done by an induction on the size of the term. Finally, both of these results are used according to the strategy described above, to prove the nice form of the LAM-clause.

The course of the proof of the final recursion principle also reveals exactly what properties are needed of the swap and FV functions in the theorem's two other types (parameter and range). These properties are defined by the predicate swapping (10) that appears in the final recursion principle.

6   Application and Implementation

The final recursion principle allows the definition of all of the functions given in Section 2. Further, I have implemented a tool to automatically attempt those definitions where there is just one parameter. This means that definitions for all the examples except v_posns and sub' can be made entirely automatically. The tool does not cope with parameterised definitions because I have yet to implement the (rather uninteresting) logic that would translate something like $f \ x \ t \ z$ into $f \ t \ (x,z)$, and back again, as required. Currently, my code also always instantiates the X parameter with the empty set.

The implemented code includes a rudimentary database of types, which is used to provide appropriate permutation and swapping information about result types. The function definition tool can therefore instantiate all of the recursion principle without user intervention. For the simple examples, such as size, and even enf, the result type is one that doesn't support a swapping action. It is easy to see that the null-swap, ($\lambda x \ y \ z. \ z$) and the everywhere-empty free variable function ($\lambda x. \ \emptyset$) satisfy the requirements of swapping in (10). Such an instantiation also leads to immediate simplifications in the final recursion principle itself. For example, the second block of antecedents completely disappears.

After instantiation, the tool must try to discharge the side conditions. Clearly, arbitrary definition attempts might produce side-conditions that no automatic tool could be expected to discharge. At the moment, however, all of the one-parameter cases (those given above, and also all those that arose in my formalisation of the standardisation theorem) are handled by the tool with little more than a call to the standard simplifier, appropriately augmented with relevant rewrite theorems.

While the code can not yet cope with functions of more than one parameter, it is not difficult to instantiate the final recursion principle by hand. For sub', the instantiation of the helper functions is as follows (where I have arbitrarily decided that the parameter type pairs the string and the term in that order):

$$
\begin{aligned}
var &\mapsto \lambda s\ (v,M).\ \text{if } s = v \text{ then } M \text{ else } \text{VAR}(s) \\
con &\mapsto \lambda k\ p.\ \text{CON}(k) \\
app &\mapsto \lambda rt\ ru\ t\ u\ p.\ \text{APP}\ (rt\ p)\ (ru\ p) \\
lam &\mapsto \lambda rt\ u\ t\ (v,M).\ \text{LAM}\ u\ (rt\ (v,\ \text{APP}\ (\text{VAR}("f"))\ M))
\end{aligned}
$$

These instantiations require no creative thought to calculate, and it is clear that an automatic tool to do this work would be straightforward to implement.

Similarly, the existing database, mapping types to likely swapping and free variable functions, makes it clear what the instantiations for the following variables should be:

$$
\begin{aligned}
\text{rswap} &\mapsto \text{swap} \\
\text{rFV} &\mapsto \text{FV} \\
\text{pswap} &\mapsto \lambda x\ y.\ (\text{swapstr}\ x\ y \times \text{swap}\ x\ y) \\
\text{pFV} &\mapsto \lambda(v,M).\ \{v\} \cup \text{FV}(M)
\end{aligned}
$$

Finally, sub' requires X to be $\{"f"\}$ [5].

The instantiation for sub' above creates quite a complicated instance of the final recursion principle. Nonetheless, the derived side-conditions are easy to eliminate.

The definition of functions such as $rator$, where values for whole classes of argument are left unspecified, brings up one last wrinkle. The database storing information about each type should record a value in each type that has no free names (if possible: the type $string$ has no such value). This value can then be provided as the result value for the omitted constructors. If this can't be done then the X parameter will need to be instantiated to cover the extra free names present in whatever value was chosen to be the value in the unspecified cases. This is something to avoid if possible, because it results in the commutativity result in the conclusion of the recursion principle retaining its annoying side-conditions.

7   Related Work

There are three pieces of work closely similar to the topic of this paper. All explicitly concern themselves with the specification of a recursion (or "iteration") principle for types with binders and α-equivalence, and all three apply the developed theory in a mechanised setting. Two are the inspiration for my own work: Gordon and Melham [5],

---

[5] A general rule for the calculation of X might be to include in X any names mentioned explicitly in a proposed definition. This question probably doesn't warrant much investigation, as functions like sub', with their own free names, seem unlikely to arise in practice.

and the Gabbay-Pitts theory of Fraenkel-Mostowski sets, particularly §10.3 of Gabbay's PhD thesis [3]. The third is work by Ambler, Crole and Momigliano in [1].

Clearly, this work would have been impossible without the underlying Gordon-Melham characterisation of λ-calculus terms up to α-equivalence. My claim is that, complicated side-conditions notwithstanding, the final recursion principle in Figure 1 is an improvement on the original Gordon-Melham principle (1). This is because the new principle has a conclusion that allows functions to be defined in a way that much more closely approximates familiar and traditional principles of primitive recursion.

Inasmuch as the new principle embodies restrictions imported from the theory of FM-sets, it can not define all of those functions definable with the original principle. For example, neither principle will support the definition of a function with clause

$$f\ (\text{LAM}\ v\ t) = t$$

because this is unsound. But it is not difficult to use (1) to define a function with clause

$$f\ (\text{LAM}\ v\ t) = t[v \mapsto \text{NEW}(\text{FV}(\text{LAM}\ v\ t))]$$

This returns the body of the abstraction with an arbitrary, fresh name substituted through for the bound variable. Appealing as it does to the Axiom of Choice, in a way that would allow the enumeration of all names, this function is impossible to define in the Fraenkel-Mostowski theory, and also impossible to define using Figure 1's recursion principle.

My work has been greatly inspired by the theory of permutations developed by Gabbay and Pitts. It might be characterised as an attempt to bring the nice features of this FM-theory into the world of classical higher-order logic. In this "HOL world", one need not give up the Axiom of Choice. Nor need one assert that the set of names is infinite, but that its subsets are all either finite or have finite complements. Instead those axioms of the FM-theory that are absolutely necessary for function definition in the primitive recursive style are imported as side-conditions. These side-conditions are easily discharged for definitions that are well-behaved; seemingly the vast majority. For those definitions that are not so well behaved, the HOL resident can always resort to (1); in the world of FM-sets, these definitions remain inadmissible. The only significant loss in the classical setting would appear to be the Иquantifier, or at least its nice properties, such as $(\text{И}x.\neg P) \equiv \neg(\text{И}x.P)$.

Another possible advantage of the approach described here is that the user is able to choose the instantiations for pswap and rswap on a case-by-case basis. If, for example, a function used strings in a way unconnected with their role as names, one wouldn't provide swapstr as the permutation function, but rather the null swapping function ($\lambda x\ y\ z.\ z$). This freedom may or may not be significant in practice. A related idea, though one that also loses this flexibility, might be to use Isabelle/HOL's axiomatic type classes to automatically associate types with appropriate permutation and free-name functions, thereby allowing the swapping side conditions in the recursion principle to disappear.

Finally, recent work by Ambler, Crole and Momigliano [1] presents a recursion principle for a (weak) higher-order abstract syntax view of the untyped λ-calculus (in classical Isabelle/HOL). This work gets around some of the typical problems associated with higher-order abstract syntax by working with terms-in-infinite-contexts, thereby providing a type of terms Λ where the function space $(var \rightarrow \Lambda)$ is isomorphic to the original type Λ. This is achieved by making Λ itself a function space: $(var^{\infty} \rightarrow \Lambda_0)$, for an underlying algebraic type Λ_0. Ambler *et al.* then define an inductive relation prop that isolates the "proper" or non-exotic values of Λ. In order to retain the use of meta-level functions in the object syntax, the proper terms are not used as the basis for the definition of a new type. So, while Λ still includes exotic terms, prop allows them to be identified.

The recursion combinator is a perfect instance of primitive recursion in its behaviour under the abstraction binder, but the extra infinite context parameters add complexity. When passing under a binder in the definition of substitution, for example, variable indices need to be incremented in both the term being substituted and the body being substituted into. This is rather reminiscent of the de Bruijn implementation of substitution.

The work by Ambler *et al.* is the first to prove a recursion principle for function definition over (weak) higher-order abstract syntax. Their paper provides pointers to a number of other HOAS approaches to the problem. Work by Schürmann, Despeyroux, and Pfenning [8], and by Washburn and Weirich [9], exemplifies one such approach. In this work, sophisticated type systems (modal λ-calculus, and first-class parametric polymorphism respectively) prevent the untrammeled use of function-spaces, thereby avoiding exotic terms while allowing iteration over these structures. Meta-theoretic reasoning about such embedded systems (e.g., proving results akin to the standardisation theorem for the untyped λ-calculus) remains a challenging area for future research.

8   Conclusion

I have presented a new recursion principle for the type of λ-terms that allows the ready definition of recursive functions over these terms. It has been proved in HOL, and motivates a definitional technique that looks as much as possible like primitive recursion. The validity of recursions that pass under binders is ensured by appeal to side-conditions that embody restrictions based on the ideas of Gabbay's and Pitts's Fraenkel-Mostowski set theory.

I have further implemented a small HOL library that allows users to write definitions in the obvious "pattern-matching" style, and which automatically discharges the FM-related side conditions. This is done with the help of a small database mapping types to information about how they support permutation and the notion of free names.

The theorem and the library have been tested on the definitions made in the course of an earlier project mechanising a substantial piece of λ-calculus theory. A sample of representative functions (all of which the theorem handles) is presented in Section 2 above.

Versions of the recursion principle for other types with binders are easy to state: in the antecedents, they simply require that all the functions standing in for the constructors of the new type (the equivalents of *var*, *con*, *app* and *lam* in Figure 1) not generate too many fresh names, and that they and permutations commute. In the conclusion of these theorems, the equations for constructors that are binders acquire side conditions stating that the recursive characterisation is invalid for finitely many choices of bound variable name. Automating the *proof* of such theorems is the key task in being able to define new types with binders automatically.

Future work. In the short term, I hope to soon extend the implementation of the library to support the definition of functions with more than one parameter. This is not conceptually difficult: the work required is simply that of implementing transformations such as moving from tupled to curried arguments, and switching parameter orders.

A recursion principle that supported the definition of well-founded functions would also be very useful. This would allow definitions that recursed at arbitrary depths under binders. HOL's existing implementation of definition by well-founded recursion requires that constructors be injective, something not true of binders.

A more significant project is the development of theory and code to support the establishment of new types with binders. It is not difficult to establish new types by hand, and it is also clear what the recursion principle for new types should be. The challenge will be establishing types automatically, including the proof of their recursion principles.

Availability. All of the theory and code described in this paper will be available as part of the next distribution of the HOL system.

References

1. Simon J. Ambler, Roy L. Crole, and Alberto Momigliano. A definitional approach to primitive recursion over higher order abstract syntax. In Honsell et al. [6]. Available at http://doi.acm.org/10.1145/976571.976572.
2. H. P. Barendregt. *The Lambda Calculus: its Syntax and Semantics*, volume 103 of *Studies in Logic and the Foundations of Mathematics*. Elsevier, Amsterdam, revised edition, 1984.
3. M. J. Gabbay. *A Theory of Inductive Definitions with Alpha-Equivalence*. PhD thesis, University of Cambridge, 2001.
4. M. J. Gabbay and A. M. Pitts. A new approach to abstract syntax involving binders. In *14th Annual Symposium on Logic in Computer Science*, pages 214–224. IEEE Computer Society Press, Washington, 1999.
5. A. D. Gordon and T. Melham. Five axioms of alpha conversion. In J. von Wright, J. Grundy, and J. Harrison, editors, *Theorem Proving in Higher Order Logics: 9th International Conference, TPHOLs'96*, volume 1125 of *Lecture Notes in Computer Science*, pages 173–190. Springer-Verlag, 1996.
6. Furio Honsell, Marino Miculan, and Alberto Momigliano, editors. *Merlin 2003, Proceedings of the Second ACM SIGPLAN Workshop on Mechanized Reasoning about Languages with Variable Binding*. ACM Digital Library, 2003.
7. Michael Norrish. Mechanising Hankin and Barendregt using the Gordon-Melham axioms. In Honsell et al. [6]. Available at http://doi.acm.org/10.1145/976571.976577.
8. Carsten Schürmann, Joëlle Despeyroux, and Frank Pfenning. Primitive recursion for higher-order abstract syntax. *Theoretical Computer Science*, 266(1–2):1–57, September 2001.
9. Geoffrey Washburn and Stephanie Weirich. Boxes go bananas: Encoding higher-order abstract syntax with parametric polymophism. In *ICFP'03: Proceedings of the Eighth ACM SIGPLAN International Conference on Functional Programming*, pages 249–262. ACM Press, 2003.

Abstractions for Fault-Tolerant Distributed System Verification

Lee Pike[1], Jeffrey Maddalon[1], Paul Miner[1], and Alfons Geser[2]

[1] Formal Methods Group
NASA Langley Research Center
M/S 130, Hampton, VA 23681-2199
{lee.s.pike,j.m.maddalon,paul.s.miner}@nasa.gov
[2] National Institute of Aerospace
144 Research Drive, Hampton, VA 23666
geser@nianet.org

Abstract. Four kinds of abstraction for the design and analysis of fault–tolerant distributed systems are discussed. These abstractions concern system messages, faults, fault–masking voting, and communication. The abstractions are formalized in higher–order logic, and are intended to facilitate specifying and verifying such systems in higher–order theorem–provers.

1 Introduction

In recent years, we have seen tremendous growth in the development of embedded computer systems with critical safety requirements [10, 12], and there is no expectation that this trend will abate. For instance, steer-by-wire systems are currently being pursued [11]. To withstand faulty behavior, safety-critical systems have traditionally employed analog backup systems in case the digital system fails; however, many new "by-wire" systems have no analog backup. Instead, they rely on integrated digital fault-tolerance.

Due to their complexity and safety-critical uses, fault-tolerant embedded systems require the greatest assurance of design correctness. One means by which a design can be shown correct is formal methods. Formal methods are especially warranted if we recall that published and peer-reviewed informal proofs-of-correctness of seemingly simple fault-tolerant algorithms have been incorrect [16]. Here, we focus on formal methods involving higher-order theorem-provers.

Although many fault-tolerant distributed systems and algorithms have been specified and verified, the abstractions used have often been ad-hoc and system-specific. Developing appropriate abstractions is often the most difficult and time-consuming part of formal methods [26]. We present these abstractions to systematize and facilitate the practice of abstraction.

The abstractions presented are in the spirit of abstractions of digital hardware developed by Thomas Melham [19, 18]. They are intended to make specifications and their proofs of correctness less tedious [14], less error-prone, and more uniform. Although the abstractions we describe are quite general, we intend for them to be accessible to the working verification engineer.

K. Slind et al. (Eds.): TPHOLs 2004, LNCS 3223, pp. 257–270, 2004.
© Springer-Verlag Berlin Heidelberg 2004

These abstractions are the outcome of the on-going project, "Scalable Processor-Independent Design for Electromagnetic Resilience" (SPIDER), at NASA's Langley Research Center and at the National Institute of Aerospace [29]. SPIDER is the basis of an FAA study exploring the use of formal methods, especially theorem-proving, in avionics certification. One of the project goals is to specify and verify the Reliable Optical Bus (ROBUS), a state-of-the-art fault-tolerant communications bus [28, 21]. The abstractions have proved useful in this project, and in fact are the basis of a generalized fault-tolerant library of PVS theories mentioned in Sect. 8.

The structure of our paper is as follows. We discuss fault-tolerant distributed systems in Sect. 2. Section 3 gives an overview of the four abstractions presented in this paper. Sections 4 through 7 explain these abstractions. Each section presents an abstraction, and then the abstraction is formalized in higher-order logic. We provide some concluding remarks and point toward future work in the final section.

2   Fault–Tolerant Distributed Systems

Introductory material on the foundations of distributed systems and algorithms can be found in Lynch [17]. Some examples of systems that have fault-tolerant distributed implementations are databases, operating systems, communication busses, file systems, and server groups [3, 28, 2].

A *distributed system* is modeled as a graph with directed edges. Vertices are called *processes*. Directed edges are called *communication channels* (or simply *channels*). If channel c points from process p to process p', then p can send messages over c to p', and p' can receive messages over c from p. In this context, p is the *sending process* (or *sender*) and p' is the *receiving process* (or *receiver*). Channels may point from a process to itself. In addition to sending and receiving messages, processes may perform local computation.

A *fault-tolerant* system is one that continues to provide the required functionality in the presense of faults. One way to implement a fault-tolerant system is to use a distributed collection of processes such that a fault that affects one process will not adversely affect the whole system's functionality. This type of system is referred to as a *fault-tolerant distributed system*.

3   Four Kinds of Abstraction

We introduce four fundamental abstractions in the domain of fault-tolerant distributed systems. *Message Abstractions* address the correctness of individual messages sent and received. *Fault Abstractions* address the kinds of faults possible as well as their effects in the system. *Fault-Masking Abstractions* address the kinds of local computations processes make to mask faults. Finally, *Communication Abstractions* address the kinds of data communicated and the properties required for communication to succeed in the presence of faults.

Our formal expressions are stated in the language of higher-order functions: variables can range over functions, and functions can take other functions as arguments. Furthermore, we use uninterpreted functions (i.e., functions with no defining body) that act as constants when applied to their arguments. Curried functions and lambda abstraction are also used. For a brief overview of higher-order logic from a practitioner's perspective, see, for example, Melham [19] or the PVS language reference [9]. A small datatype, fully explained in Sect. 4, is also used.

The abstractions have been formalized in the Prototype Verification System (PVS), a popular interactive industrial-strength theorem proving system [22, 8]. They are available at NASA [24].

4 Abstracting Messages

4.1 Abstraction

Messages communicated in a distributed system are abstracted according to their correctness. We distinguish between *benign messages* and *accepted messages*. The former are messages that a non-faulty receiving process recognizes as incorrect; the latter are messages that a non-faulty receiving process does not recognize as incorrect. Note that an accepted message may be incorrect: the receiving process just does not *detect* that the message is incorrect.

Benign messages abstract various sorts of misbehavior. A message that is sufficiently garbled during transmission may be caught by an error-checking code [7] and deemed benign. Benign messages also abstract the absence of a message: a receiver expecting a message but detecting the absence of one takes this to be the 'reception' of a benign message. In synchronized systems with global communication schedules, they abstract messages sent and received at unscheduled times.

4.2 Formalization

Let the set MSG be a set of messages of a given type. MSG is the base set of elements over which the datatype is defined. The set of all possible datatype elements is denoted by $ABSTRACT\_MSG[MSG]$.

The datatype has two constructors, $accepted\_msg$ and $benign\_msg$. The former takes an element $m \in MSG$ and creates the datatype element $accepted\_msg[m]$. The constructor also has an associated extractor $value$ such that

$$value(accepted\_msg[m]) = m .$$

The other constructor, $benign\_msg$, is a constant datatype element; it is a constructor with no arguments. All benign messages are abstracted as a single message; thus, the abstracted incorrect message cannot be recovered. Finally, we define two recognizers, $accepted\_msg$? and $benign\_msg$? with the following definitions. Let $a \in ABSTRACT\_MSG[MSG]$.

$$accepted\_msg?(a) \overset{\mathrm{df}}{=} \exists m.\, m \in MSG \wedge a = accepted\_msg[m] ,$$

and
$$benign\_msg?(a) \overset{\mathrm{df}}{=} a = benign\_msg \ .$$
We summarize this datatype in Fig. 1. Let $m \in MSG$.

Constructors	Extractors	Recognizers
$accepted\_msg[m]$	$value$	$accepted\_msg?$
$benign\_msg$	none	$benign\_msg?$

Fig. 1. Abstract Messages Datatype

5   Abstracting Faults

There are two closely related abstractions with respect to faults. The first abstraction, *error types*, partitions the possible locations of faults. The second abstraction, *fault types*, partitions faults according to the manifestation of the errors caused by the faults[1].

5.1   Abstracting Error Types

Picking the right level of abstraction and the right components to which faults should be attributed is a modeling issue that has been handled in many different ways. We think this is a particularly good example of the extent to which modeling choices can affect specification and proof efficacy.

Both processes and channels can suffer faults [17], but reasoning about process and channel faults together is tedious. Fortunately, such reasoning is redundant – channel faults can be abstracted as process faults. A channel between a sending process and a receiving process can be abstracted as being an extension either of the sender or of the receiver. For instance, a lossy channel abstracted as an extension of the sender is modeled as a process failing to send messages.

Even if we abstract all faults to ones affecting processes and not channels, we are left with the task of abstracting how the functionality of a process – sending, receiving, or computing – is degraded. One possibility is to consider a process as an indivisible unit so that a fault affecting one of its functions is abstracted as affecting its other functions, too. Another possibility is to abstract all faults to ones affecting a process' ability to send and receive messages as in [27, 23]. Finally, models implicit in [5, 16] abstract process faults as being ones affecting *only* a process' ability to send messages. So even if a fault affects a process' ability to receive messages or compute, the fault is abstractly propagated to a fault affecting the process' ability to send messages.

All three models above are *conservative*, i.e., the abstraction of a fault is at least as severe as the fault. This is certainly true of the first model in which the

---

[1] An *error* is "that part of the system state which is *liable to lead to subsequent failure*," while a *fault* is "the *adjudged or hypothesized cause* of an error" [15].

whole process is considered to be degraded by any fault, and it is true for the second model, too. Even though it is assumed that a process can always compute correctly, its computed values are inconsequential if it can neither receive nor send correct values. As for the third model, the same reasoning applies – even if a faulty process can receive messages *and* compute correctly, it cannot send its computations to other processes.

The model we choose is one in which all faults are abstracted to be ones degrading send functionality, and in which channels are abstracted as belonging to the sending process. There are two principal advantages to this model, both of which lead to simpler specifications and proofs. First, the model allows us to disregard faults when reasoning about the ability of processes to receive and compute messages. Second, whether a message is successfully communicated is determined solely by a process' send functionality; the faultiness of receivers need not be considered.

5.2   Abstracting Fault Types

Faults result from innumerable occurrences including physical damage, electromagnetic interference, and "slightly-out-of-spec" communication [4]. We collect these fault occurrences into *fault types* according to their effects in the system.

We adopt the *hybrid fault model* of Thambidurai and Park [30]. A process is called *benign*, or *manifest*, if it sends only benign messages, as described in Sect. 4. A process is called *symmetric* if it sends every receiver the same message, but these messages may be incorrect. A process is called *asymmetric*, or *Byzantine* [13], if it sends different messages to different receivers. All non-faulty processes are also said to be *good*.

Other fault models exist that provide more or less detail than the hybrid fault model above. The least detailed fault model is to assume the worst case scenario, that all faults are asymmetric. The fault model developed by Azadmanesh and Kieckhafer [1] is an example of a more refined model. All such fault models are consistent with the other abstractions in this paper.

5.3   Formalization

We begin by formalizing fault types. Let S and R be sets of processes sending and receiving messages, respectively, in a round of communication. Let *asym*, *sym*, *ben*, and *good* be constants representing the fault types asymmetric, symmetric, benign, and good, respectively.

As mentioned, we abstract all faults to ones that affect a process' ability to send messages. To model this formally, we construct a function modeling a process sending a message to a receiver. The range of the function is the set of abstract messages, elements of the datatype defined in Sect. 4. As explained, MSG is a set of messages, and $ABSTRACT\_MSG[MSG]$ is the set of datatype elements parameterized by MSG. Let $s \in S$ and $r \in R$ be a sending and receiving process, respectively. Let msg_map be a function from senders to the message they intend to send, and let $sender\_status$ be a function mapping senders to their fault partition. The function outputs the abstract message received by r from s.

$$
send(msg\_map, sender\_status, s, r) \overset{\mathrm{df}}{=}
$$
$$
\begin{cases}
accepted\_msg[msg\_map(s)] & : & sender\_status(s) = good \\
benign\_msg & : & sender\_status(s) = ben \\
sym\_msg(msg\_map(s), s) & : & sender\_status(s) = sym \\
asym\_msg(msg\_map(s), s, r) & : & sender\_status(s) = asym \ .
\end{cases}
$$

If s is good, then r receives an accepted abstract message, defined in Sect. 4, from s. If s is benign, then r receives a benign message. In the last two cases – in which s suffers a symmetric or asymmetric fault – uninterpreted functions are returned. Applied to their arguments, sym_msg and $asym\_msg$ are uninterpreted constants of the abstract message datatype defined in Sect. 4. The function $asym\_msg$ models a process suffering an asymmetric fault by taking the receiver as an argument: for receivers r and r', $asym\_msg(msg\_map(s), s, r)$ is not necessarily equal to $asym\_msg(msg\_map(s), s, r')$. On the other hand, the function sym_msg does not take a receiver as an argument, so all receivers receive the same arbitrary abstract message from a particular sender.

6 Abstracting Fault-Masking

6.1 Abstraction

Some of the information a process receives in a distributed system may be incorrect due to the existence of faults as described in Sect. 5. A process must have a means to mask incorrect information generated by faulty processes. Two of the most well-known are (variants of) a majority vote or a middle-value selection, as defined in the following paragraph. These functions are similar enough to abstract them as a single fault-masking function.

A majority vote returns the majority value of some multiset (i.e., a set in which repetition of values is allowed), and a default value if no majority exists. A middle-value selection takes the middle value of a linearly-ordered multiset if the cardinality of the multiset is odd. If the cardinality is an even integer n, then the natural choices are to compute one of (1) the value at index $\lfloor n/2 \rfloor$, (2) the value at index $\lceil n/2 \rceil$, or (3) the average of the two values from (1) and (2). Of course, these options may yield different values; in fact, (3) may yield a value not present in the multiset.

For example, for the multiset $\{1, 1, 2, 2, 2, 2\}$, the majority value is 2, and the middle-value selection is also 2 for any of the three ways to compute the middle-value selection. For any multiset that can be linearly-ordered, if a majority value exists, then the majority value is equal to the middle-value selection (for any of the three ways to compute it mentioned above).

The benefit of this abstraction is that we can define a single fault-masking function (we call it a *fault-masking vote*) that can be implemented as either a majority vote or a middle-value selection (provided the data over which the function is applied is linearly-ordered).

This allows us to model what are usually considered to be quite distinct fault-tolerant distributed algorithms uniformly. Concretely, this abstraction, coupled with the other abstractions described in this paper, allow certain clock synchronization algorithms (which usually depend on a middle-value selection) and algorithms in the spirit of an Oral Messages algorithm [13, 16] (which usually depend on a majority vote) to share the same underlying models [20].

6.2   Formalization

The formalization we describe models a majority vote and a middle-value selection over a multiset. A small lemma stating their equivalence follows. Definitions of standard and minor functions are omitted.

Based on the NASA Langley Research Center PVS *Bags* Library [6], a multiset is formalized as a function from values to the natural numbers that determines how many times a value appears in the multiset (values not present are mapped to 0). Thus, let V be a nonempty finite set of values[2], and let $ms : V \rightarrow \mathbb{N}$ be a multiset.

To define a majority vote, we define the cardinality of a multiset ms to be the summation of value-instances in it:

$$|ms| \stackrel{\mathrm{df}}{=} \sum_{v \in V} ms(v) \,.$$

The function maj_set takes a multiset ms and returns the set of majority values in it.

$$maj\_set(ms) \stackrel{\mathrm{df}}{=} \{v \mid 2 \times ms(v) > |ms|\} \,.$$

This set is empty if no majority value exists, or it is a singleton set. Thus, we define $majority$ to be a function returning the special constant $no\_majority$ if no majority value exists and the single majority value otherwise.

$$majority(ms) \stackrel{\mathrm{df}}{=} \begin{cases} no\_majority & : \quad maj\_set(ms) = \emptyset \\ \epsilon(maj\_set(ms)) & : \quad \text{otherwise} \,. \end{cases}$$

The function ϵ is the choice operator that takes a set and returns an arbitrary value in the set if the set is nonempty. Otherwise, an arbitrary value of the same type as the elements in the set is returned [19].

Now we formalize a middle-value selection. Let V have the linear order $\preceq$ defined on it. The function mid_val_set takes a multiset and returns the set of values at index $\lceil n/2 \rceil$ when the values are ordered from least to greatest (we arbitrarily choose this implementation). The set is always a singleton set.

$$mid\_val\_set(ms) \stackrel{\mathrm{df}}{=}$$
$$\left\{ v \,\middle|\, \begin{array}{l} 2 \times |lower\_filter(ms, v)| > |ms| \,\wedge \\ 2 \times |upper\_filter(ms, v)| \geq |ms| \end{array} \right\} \,.$$

---

[2] If V is finite, then multisets are finite. Fault-masking votes can only be taken over finite multisets.

The function *lower_filter* filters out all of the values of *ms* that are less than or equal to *v*, and *upper_filter* filters out the values greater than or equal to *v*. The function *lower_filter* is defined as follows:

$$lower\_filter(ms, v) \stackrel{\text{df}}{=} \lambda i. \begin{cases} ms(i) & : & i \preceq v \\ 0 & : & \text{otherwise} . \end{cases}$$

Similarly,

$$upper\_filter(ms, v) \stackrel{\text{df}}{=} \lambda i. \begin{cases} ms(i) & : & v \preceq i \\ 0 & : & \text{otherwise} . \end{cases}$$

The relation *mid_val_set(ms)* is guaranteed to be a singleton set, so using the function ϵ mentioned above, we can define *middle_value* to return the middle value of a multiset:

$$middle\_value(ms) \stackrel{\text{df}}{=} \epsilon(mid\_val\_set(ms)) .$$

The following theorem results.

Theorem 1 (Middle Value Is Majority). *majority(ms)* $\neq$ *no_majority implies middle_value(ms) = majority(ms)*.

7   Abstracting Communication

We identify two abstractions with respect to communication. First, we abstract the kinds of data communicated. Second, we identify the fundamental conditions that must hold for communication to succeed.

7.1   Abstracting Kinds of Communication

Some kinds of information can be modelled by real valued, uniformly continuous functions. Intuitively, a function is uniformly continuous if small changes in its argument produce small changes in its result; see e.g., Rosenlicht [25]. For example, the values of analog clocks and of thermometers vary with time, and the rate of change is bounded. In a distributed system, a process may *sample* such a function, i.e., determine an approximation of the function's value for a given input. We call such functions *inexact functions* and the communication of their values *inexact communication*. We call discrete functions, such as an array sorting algorithm, *exact functions* and communication involving them *exact communication*.

7.2   Abstracting Communication Conditions

Communication in a fault-tolerant distributed system is successful if *validity* and *agreement* hold. For exact communication, their general forms are:

Exact Validity: A good receiver's fault-masking vote is equal to the value of the function good processes compute.

Exact Agreement: All good processes have equal fault-masking votes.

For inexact communication we have similar conditions:

Inexact Validity: A good receiver's fault-masking vote is bounded above and below by the samples from good processes, up to a small error margin.

Inexact Agreement: All good processes differ in their fault-masking votes by at most a small margin of error.

A validity property can thus be understood as an agreement between senders and receivers, whereas an agreement property is an agreement between the receivers. For lack of space, we limit our presentation to guaranteeing validity. Agreement is treated similarly, and complete PVS formalizations and proofs for both are located at NASA [24].

We distinguish between a *functional model* and a *relational model* of communication. In the former, communication is modeled computationally (e.g., using functions like *send* from Sect. 5). In the latter more abstract model, conditions on communication are stated such that if they hold, communication succeeds. This section presents a relational model of communication.

We specifically present conditions that guarantee validity holds after a single *broadcast communication round* in which each process in a set of senders sends messages to each process in a set of receivers (a degenerate case is when these are singleton sets modeling point-to-point communication between a single sender and receiver). A functional model of a specific communication protocol can be shown to satisfy these conditions through step-wise refinement.

First we describe how a single round of exact communication satisfies exact validity, provided that the three conditions *Majority Good, Exact Function*, and *Function Agreement* hold. The three conditions state, respectively, that the majority of the values over which a vote is taken come from good senders, that good senders compute functions exactly (i.e., there is no approximation in sampling an exact function), and that every good sender computes the same function.

For a single round of inexact communication, we have inexact validity if the two conditions *Majority Good* and *Inexact Function* hold. *Majority Good* is the same as above. The *Inexact Function* condition bounds the variance allowed between the sample of an inexact function computed by a good process for a given input and the actual value of the function for that input. That is, let ε_l and ε_u be small positive constants representing the lower and upper variation, respectively, allowed between an inexact function f and potential samples of it as depicted in Fig. 2. The sample computed by a good process is bounded by $f - \varepsilon_l$ and $f + \varepsilon_u$. We do not present an analog to the Function Agreement condition in the inexact case since processes often compute and vote over slightly different functions. For example, each process might possess a distinct local sensor that it samples. It is assumed, however, that the functions are related, e.g., each sensor measures the same aspect of the environment.

Clock synchronization [17] is an important case of inexact communication. Clocks distributed in the system need to be synchronized in order to avoid drifting too far apart. In this case, sampling a local clock yields an approximation of time.

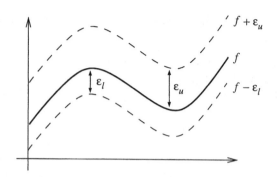

Fig. 2. The *Inexact Function* Condition for Inexact Communication

7.3   Formalization for Exact Communication

First we present the model of a round of exact communication. For a single round of communication, let S be the set of senders sending in that round. Let *good_senders* $\subseteq S$ be a subset of senders that are good. This set can change as processes become faulty and are repaired, so we treat it as a variable rather than a constant. For an arbitrary receiver[3], let *eligible_senders* $\subseteq S$ be the set of senders trusted by the receiver (we assume that receivers trust all good senders). Then the condition *Majority Good* is defined

$$majority\_good(good\_senders, eligible\_senders) \overset{\text{df}}{=}$$
$$2 \times |good\_senders| > |eligible\_senders| \wedge$$
$$good\_senders \subseteq eligible\_senders .$$

This stipulates that a majority of the senders in *eligible_senders* are in *good_senders*.

Next we describe the values sent and received. Let MSG be the range of the function computed – these are the messages communicated. The variable *ideal* : $S \rightarrow MSG$ maps a sender to the exact value of a function to be computed by the sender, for a given input. This frees us from representing the particular function computed. Similarly, *actual* : $S \rightarrow MSG$ maps a sender to the value that sender actually computes for the same function and input. Good senders compute exact functions exactly:

$$exact\_function(good\_senders, ideal, actual) \overset{\text{df}}{=}$$
$$\forall s. \, s \in good\_senders \implies ideal(s) = actual(s) .$$

Function Agreement states that the functions computed by any two good senders is the same (i.e., they send the same messages).

$$function\_agreement(good\_senders, ideal) \overset{\text{df}}{=}$$
$$\forall s_1, s_2. \, s_1 \in good\_senders \wedge s_2 \in good\_senders \implies ideal(s_1) = ideal(s_2) .$$

---

[3] The receiver can be *any* receiver, good or faulty. The abstractions described in Sect. 5 allow us to ignore the fault status of receivers in formal analysis.

Before stating the validity result, we must take care of a technical detail with respect to forming the multiset of messages over which a receiver takes a fault-masking vote. For an arbitrary receiver, let the function $make\_bag$ take as arguments a nonempty set $eligible\_senders$ and a function mapping senders to the message the receiver gets. It returns a multiset of received messages from senders in $eligible\_senders$.

$$make\_bag(eligible\_senders, actual) \stackrel{\mathrm{df}}{=}$$
$$\lambda v. \left| \{s \mid s \in eligible\_senders \wedge actual(s) = v\} \right| .$$

For exact messages, validity is the proposition that for any good sender, the exact value of the function it is to compute is the value computed by the receiver's fault-masking vote. This proposition is defined as follows:

$$exact\_validity(eligible\_senders, good\_senders, ideal, actual) \stackrel{\mathrm{df}}{=}$$
$$\forall s. s \in good\_senders \implies$$
$$ideal(s) = majority(make\_bag(eligible\_senders, actual)) .$$

We use $majority$ for the fault-masking vote, but middle-value selection is acceptable given Thm. 1. Using $majority$, the Exact Validity Theorem reads:

Theorem 2 (Exact Validity).
   $majority\_good(good\_senders, eligible\_senders)$ and
   $exact\_function(good\_senders, ideal, actual))$ and
   $function\_agreement(good\_senders, ideal)$
implies that
   $exact\_validity(eligible\_senders, good\_senders, ideal, actual) .$

7.4   Formalization for Inexact Communication

Next we model a round of inexact communication. The *Majority Good* condition is formalized the same as for exact communication. To define *Inexact Function*, we now assume that the elements of MSG have at least the structure of an additive group linearly ordered by $\preceq$. *Inexact Function* is defined as the conjunction of two conditions, *Lower Function Error* and *Upper Function Error*. These two conditions specify, respectively, the maximal negative and positive error between the exact value of an inexact function and a good sender's approximation of the inexact function, for a given input.

$$lower\_function\_error(good\_senders, ideal, actual) \stackrel{\mathrm{df}}{=}$$
$$\forall s. s \in good\_senders \implies ideal(s) - \varepsilon_l \preceq actual(s) ;$$
$$upper\_function\_error(good\_senders, ideal, actual) \stackrel{\mathrm{df}}{=}$$
$$\forall s. s \in good\_senders \implies actual(s) \preceq ideal(s) + \varepsilon_u ;$$

$$inexact\_function(good\_senders, ideal, actual) \overset{\mathrm{df}}{=}$$
$$lower\_function\_error(good\_senders, ideal, actual) \wedge$$
$$upper\_function\_error(good\_senders, ideal, actual) \,.$$

For inexact communication, validity is the proposition that for a fixed receiver, the value determined by a fault-masking vote is bounded both above and below by the messages received from good senders, modulo error values ε_l and ε_u. Note that each sender may be computing a different inexact function, so the vote window depends on both the functions computed as well as the errors in approximating them. This is illustrated in Fig. 3, where s_1 and s_2 are good senders.

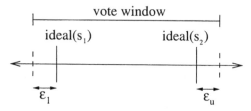

Fig. 3. Inexact Validity

$$inexact\_validity(eligible\_senders, good\_senders, ideal, actual) \overset{\mathrm{df}}{=}$$
$$\exists s_1. \, s_1 \in good\_senders \wedge$$
$$ideal(s_1) - \varepsilon_l \preceq middle\_value(make\_bag(eligible\_senders, actual)) \wedge$$
$$\exists s_2. \, s_2 \in good\_senders \wedge$$
$$middle\_value(make\_bag(eligible\_senders, actual)) \preceq ideal(s_2) + \varepsilon_u \,.$$

The Inexact Validity Theorem then reads:

Theorem 3 (Inexact Validity).
$$majority\_good(good\_senders, eligible\_senders) \; and$$
$$inexact\_function(good\_senders, ideal, actual)$$
implies that
$$inexact\_validity(eligible\_senders, good\_senders, ideal, actual) \,.$$

8   Conclusion

This paper presents, in the language of higher-order logic, four kinds of abstractions for fault-tolerant distributed systems. These abstractions pertain to messages, faults, fault-masking, and communication. We believe that they abstract a wide-variety of fault-tolerant distributed systems.

Other useful abstractions have been developed, too. For example, Rushby demonstrates how to derive a time-triggered system from the specification of the system as a (synchronous) functional program [27]. This work has been used in the specification and verification of the Time-Triggered Architecture [23]. With respect to these works, the abstractions we give systematize specification and verification at the level of the functional programs.

Our abstractions have proved their merit in an industrial-scale formal specification and verification project. We are sure that similar projects will profit. We are developing a distributed fault-tolerance library as part of the SPIDER project. It is designed to be a generic library of PVS theories that may be used in the specification and verification of a wide variety of fault-tolerant distributed systems. The abstractions described in this paper form the backbone of the library.

Acknowledgments

We would like to thank Victor Carreño and Kristen Rozier as well as our anonymous referees for helpful comments.

References

1. Mohammad H. Azadmanesh and Roger M. Kieckhafer. Exploiting omissive faults in synchronous approximate agreement. *IEEE Transactions on Computers*, 49(10):1031–1042, 2000.
2. Miguel Castro and Barbara Liskov. Practical Byzantine fault tolerance. In *ACM Proceedings: Operating Systems Design and Implementation (OSDI)*, pages 173–186, February 1999.
3. Flaviu Cristian. Understanding fault-tolerant distributed systems. *Communications of the ACM*, 34(2), February 1991.
4. Kevin Driscoll, Brendan Hall, Håkan Sivencrona, and Phil Zumsteg. Byzantine fault tolerance, from theory to reality. In G. Goos, J. Hartmanis, and J. van Leeuwen, editors, *Computer Safety, Reliability, and Security*, Lecture Notes in Computer Science, pages 235–248. The 22nd International Conference on Computer Safety, Reliability and Security SAFECOMP, Springer-Verlag Heidelberg, September 2003.
5. Alfons Geser and Paul Miner. A formal correctness proof of the SPIDER diagnosis protocol. Technical Report 2002-211736, NASA Langley Research Center, Hampton, Virginia, August 2002. Technical Report contains the Track B proceedings from Theorem Proving in Higher Order Logics (TPHOLSs).
6. NASA LaRC Formal Methods Group. NASA Langley PVS libraries. Available at `http://shemesh.larc.nasa.gov/fm/ftp/larc/PVS-library/pvslib.html`.
7. Gerard J. Holzmann. *Design and Validation of Computer Protocols*. Prentice Hall, 1991.
8. SRI International. PVS homepage. Available at `http://pvs.csl.sri.com/`.
9. SRI International. PVS language reference, version 2.4. Available at `http://pvs.csl.sri.com/manuals.html`, December 2001.
10. Steven D. Johnson. Formal methods in embedded design. *Computer*, pages 104–106, Novemeber 2003.

11. Philip Koopman, editor. *Critical Embedded Automotive Networks*, volume 22-4 of *IEEE Micro*. IEEE Computer Society, July/August 2002.
12. Hermann Kopetz. *Real-Time Systems*. Kluwer Academic Publishers, 1997.
13. Lamport, Shostak, and Pease. The Byzantine generals problem. *ACM Transactions on Programming Languages and Systems*, 4:382–401, July 1982.
14. Leslie Lamport. Composition: A way to make proofs harder. *Lecture Notes in Computer Science*, 1536:402–423, 1998.
15. Jean-Claude Laprie. Dependability – its attributes, impairments and means. In B. Randell, J.-C. Laprie, H. Kopetz, and B. Littlewood, editors, *Predictability Dependable Computing Systems*, ESPRIT Basic Research Series, pages 3–24. Springer, 1995.
16. Patrick Lincoln and John Rushby. The formal verification of an algorithm for interactive consistency under a hybrid fault model. In Costas Courcoubetis, editor, *Computer-Aided Verification, CAV '93*, volume 697 of *Lecture Notes in Computer Science*, pages 292–304, Elounda, Greece, June/July 1993. Springer-Verlag.
17. Nancy A. Lynch. *Distributed Algorithms*. Morgan Kaufmann, 1996.
18. Thomas F. Melham. Abstraction mechanisms for hardware verification. In G. Birtwistle and P.A. Subrahmanyam, editors, *VLSI Specification, Verification, and Synthesis*, pages 129–157, Boston, 1988. Kluwer Academic Publishers.
19. Thomas F. Melham. *Higher Order Logic and Hardware Verification*. Cambridge Tracts in Theoretical Computer Science. Cambridge University Press, 1993.
20. Paul Miner, Alfons Geser, Lee Pike, and Jeffrey Maddalon. A unified fault-tolerance protocol. In preparation. Available at http://shemesh.larc.nasa.gov/fm/spider/spider_pubs.html, April 2004.
21. Paul S. Miner, Mahyar Malekpour, and Wilfredo Torres-Pomales. Conceptual design of a Reliable Optical BUS (ROBUS). In *21st AIAA/IEEE Digital Avionics Systems Conference DASC*, Irvine, CA, October 2002.
22. Sam Owre, John Rushby, Natarajan Shankar, and Friedrich von Henke. Formal verification for fault-tolerant architectures: Prolegomena to the design of PVS. *IEEE Transactions on Software Engineering*, 21(2):107–125, February 1995.
23. Holger Pfeifer. *Formal Analysis of Fault-Tolerant Algorithms in the Time-Triggered Architecture*. PhD thesis, Universität Ulm, 2003. Available at http://www.informatik.uni-ulm.de/ki/Papers/pfeifer-phd.html.
24. Lee Pike, Jeffrey Maddalon, Paul Miner, and Alfons Geser. PVS specifications and proofs for fault-tolerant distributed system verification. Available at http://shemesh.larc.nasa.gov/fm/spider/tphols2004/pvs.html, 2004.
25. Maxwell Rosenlicht. *Introduction to Analysis*. Dover Publications, Inc., 1968.
26. John Rushby. Formal methods and digital systems validation for airborne systems. Technical Report CR–4551, NASA, December 1993.
27. John Rushby. Systematic formal verification for fault-tolerant time-triggered algorithms. *IEEE Transactions on Software Engineering*, 25(5):651–660, September/October 1999.
28. John Rushby. A comparison of bus architectures for safety-critical embedded systems. Technical report, Computer Science Laboratory, SRI International, Menlo Park, CA, September 2001. Available at http://www.csl.sri.com/~rushby/abstracts/buscompare.
29. SPIDER homepage, NASA Langley Research Center, Formal Methods Team. Available at http://shemesh.larc.nasa.gov/fm/spider/.
30. Philip Thambidurai and You-Keun Park. Interactive consistency with multiple failure modes. In *7th Reliable Distributed Systems Symposium*, pages 93–100, October 1988.

Formalizing Integration Theory
with an Application to Probabilistic Algorithms

Stefan Richter

LuFG Theoretische Informatik, RWTH Aachen,
Ahornstraße 55, 52056 Aachen, Germany
richter@informatik.rwth-aachen.de

Abstract. Inter alia, Lebesgue-style integration plays a major role in advanced probability. We formalize a significant part of its theory in Higher Order Logic using Isabelle/Isar. This involves concepts of elementary measure theory, real-valued random variables as Borel-measurable functions, and a stepwise inductive definition of the integral itself. Building on previous work about formal verification of probabilistic algorithms, we exhibit an example application in this domain; another primitive for randomized functional programming is developed to this end.

1 Prologue

> Verifying more examples of probabilistic algorithms will inevitably necessitate more formalization; in particular we already can see that a theory of expectation will be required to prove the correctness of probabilistic quicksort. If we can continue our policy of formalizing standard theorems of mathematics to aid verifications, then this will provide long-term benefits to many users of the HOL theorem prover.   *Joe Hurd*

This quote from the Future Work section of Joe Hurd's PhD thesis "Formal Verification of Probabilistic Algorithms" [7, p. 131] served as a starting point for the work subsumed in here. Integration translates to expectation in probability theory. The concept of a *measure* lies at the heart of Lebesgue style integration[1]. Because the definition does not employ such concrete entities as intervals, it generalizes easily to functions that do not have the real numbers as their domain. In particular, the notion of measure is very natural in the field of probability theory.

The so-called gauge or Kurzweil-Henstock integral is a strictly stronger concept. That most powerful integral has even been formalized for functions over the reals in the HOL theorem prover by Harrison [6]. However, the simplicity that makes it so elegant in real analysis (especially over compact intervals) seems to get lost in more general cases, as the intuition behind it is very similar to the Riemann

---

[1] A measure is simply a function mapping sets to real numbers, which satisfies a few sanity properties (cf. 2.3).

K. Slind et al. (Eds.): TPHOLs 2004, LNCS 3223, pp. 271–286, 2004.

construction, which depends heavily on the structure of the real numbers as domain.

We begin by declaring some preliminary notions, including elementary measure theory and monotone convergence. This leads into measurable real-valued functions, also known as random variables. A sufficient body of functions is shown to belong to this class. A lot of the theory in this section has also been formalized within the Mizar project [3,4]. The abstract of the second source hints that it was also planned as a stepping stone for Lebesgue integration, though further results in this line could not be found.

The central section is about integration proper. We build the integral for increasingly complex functions and prove essential properties, discovering the connection with measurability in the end. To my knowledge, no similar theory had been developed in a theorem prover up to this point. It enables formalization of results that require general concepts of integration, such as average case analysis of algorithms.

Before closing with a short summary and suggestions for future work, we test our achievements in an application. The first moment method is applied to k-SAT. Though the setup is simple enough in terms of integration, a new primitive is needed to represent the probabilistic programs involved.

As stated before, the formalization is performed in the theorem prover Isabelle [12,11], using the Isar language [14], the HOL logic [10], and the Real/Complex theory [5].

2   Measurable Functions

2.1   Sigma Algebras

theory *Sigma-Algebra2 = Main*:

The **theory** command commences a formal document and enumerates the theories it depends on. With the *Main* theory, a standard selection of useful HOL theories excluding the real numbers is loaded. *Sigma-Algebra2* is built upon *Sigma-Algebra*, a tiny example demonstrating the use of inductive definitions by Markus Wenzel. This theory as well as *Measure* in 2.3 is heavily influenced by Joe Hurd's thesis [7] and has been designed to keep the terminology as consistent as possible with that work.

Sigma algebras are an elementary concept in measure theory. To measure — that is to integrate — functions, we first have to measure sets. Unfortunately, when dealing with a large universe, it is often not possible to consistently assign a measure to every subset. Therefore it is necessary to define the set of measurable subsets of the universe. A sigma algebra is such a set that has three very natural and desirable properties.

constdefs
  sigma-algebra:: $'a$ *set set* $\Rightarrow$ *bool*
  sigma-algebra A $\equiv$

$\{\} \in A \wedge (\forall a. \ a \in A \longrightarrow -a \in A) \wedge$
$(\forall a. \ (\forall i::nat. \ a \ i \in A) \longrightarrow (\bigcup i. \ a \ i) \in A)$

Mind that the third condition expresses the fact that the union of countably many sets in A is again a set in A without explicitly defining the notion of countability.

Sigma algebras can naturally be created as the closure of any set of sets with regard to the properties just postulated. Markus Wenzel wrote the following inductive definition of the *sigma* operator.

consts
   sigma :: $'a \ set \ set \Rightarrow 'a \ set \ set$

inductive *sigma A*
   intros
      basic: $a \in A \Longrightarrow a \in sigma \ A$
      empty: $\{\} \in sigma \ A$
      complement: $a \in sigma \ A \Longrightarrow -a \in sigma \ A$
      Union: $(\bigwedge i::nat. \ a \ i \in sigma \ A) \Longrightarrow (\bigcup i. \ a \ i) \in sigma \ A$

There are a few rather obvious facts to prove about sigma algebras, like the universe itself being contained in them as well as the empty set, but they have to be left out.

2.2   Monotone Convergence

theory *MonConv* = *Lim*:

A sensible requirement for an integral operator is that it be "well-behaved" with respect to limit functions. To become just a little more precise, it is expected that the limit operator may be interchanged with the integral operator under conditions that are as weak as possible. To this end, the notion of monotone convergence is introduced and later applied in the definition of the integral.

In fact, we distinguish three types of monotone convergence here: There are converging sequences of real numbers, real functions and sets. Monotone convergence could even be defined more generally for any type in the axiomatic type class[2] *ord* of ordered types like this.

mon-conv $u \ f \equiv (\forall n. \ u \ n \le u \ (Suc \ n)) \wedge isLub \ UNIV \ (range \ u) \ f$

However, this employs the general concept of a least upper bound. For the special types we have in mind, the more specific limit — respective union — operators are available, combined with many theorems about their properties. It still seems worthwhile to add the type of real- (or rather ordered-) valued functions to the ordered types by defining the less-or-equal relation pointwise.

instance *fun* :: $(type, ord) ord$ ..

---

[2] For the concept of axiomatic type classes, see [9,15]

defs
le-fun-def: $f \leq g \equiv \forall x.\ f\,x \leq g\,x$

To express the similarity of the different types of convergence, a single overloaded operator is used.

consts
  mon-conv:: $(nat \Rightarrow {}'a) \Rightarrow {}'a{::}ord \Rightarrow bool\ (\text{-}{\uparrow}\text{-})$

defs (overloaded)
  real-mon-conv: $x{\uparrow}(y{::}real) \equiv (\forall n.\ x\,n \leq x\,(Suc\,n)) \wedge x \relbar\joinrel\relbar\joinrel\relbar\joinrel\relbar\joinrel\rightarrow y$
  realfun-mon-conv:
  $u{\uparrow}(f{::}'a \Rightarrow real) \equiv (\forall n.\ u\,n \leq u\,(Suc\,n)) \wedge (\forall w.\ (\lambda n.\ u\,n\,w) \relbar\joinrel\relbar\joinrel\relbar\joinrel\relbar\joinrel\rightarrow f\,w)$
  set-mon-conv: $A{\uparrow}(B{::}'a\ set) \equiv (\forall n.\ A\,n \leq A\,(Suc\,n)) \wedge B = (\bigcup n.\ A\,n)$

lemma *realfun-mon-conv-iff*: $(u{\uparrow}f) = (\forall w.\ (\lambda n.\ u\,n\,w){\uparrow}((f\,w){::}real))$

The long arrow signifies convergence of real sequences as defined in the theory *SEQ* [5]. Monotone convergence for real functions is simply pointwise monotone convergence. Quite a few properties of these definitions will be necessary later, but none of them are of intrinsic interest or difficulty.

2.3   Measure Spaces

theory *Measure=Sigma-Algebra2+MonConv+NthRoot*:

Now we are already set for the central concept of measure. The following definitions are translated as faithfully as possible from those in Joe Hurd's thesis [7].

constdefs
  measurable:: $'a\ set\ set \Rightarrow {}'b\ set\ set \Rightarrow ('a \Rightarrow {}'b)\ set$
  measurable $F\ G \equiv \{f.\ \forall g{\in}G.\ f -{'}\,g \in F\}$

So a function is called F-G-measurable if and only if the inverse image of any set in G is in F. F and G are usually the sets of measurable sets, the first component of a measure space[3].

  measurable-sets:: $('a\ set\ set * ('a\ set \Rightarrow real)) \Rightarrow {}'a\ set\ set$
  measurable-sets $\equiv fst$

  measure:: $('a\ set\ set * ('a\ set \Rightarrow real)) \Rightarrow ('a\ set \Rightarrow real)$
  measure $\equiv snd$

The other component is the measure itself. It is a function that assigns a non-negative real number to every measurable set and has the property of being countably additive for disjoint sets.

---

[3] In standard mathematical notation, the universe is first in a measure space triple, but in our definitions, following Joe Hurd, it is always the whole type universe and therefore omitted.

positive:: (*'a set set* * (*'a set* ⇒ *real*)) ⇒ *bool*
positive M ≡ *measure M* {} = *0* ∧
(∀ *A. A*∈ *measurable-sets M* —→ *0* ≤ *measure M A*)

countably-additive:: (*'a set set* * (*'a set* ⇒ *real*)) ⇒ *bool*
countably-additive M ≡ (∀*f*::(*nat* ⇒ *'a set*). *range f* ⊆ *measurable-sets M*
∧ (∀ *m n. m* ≠ *n* —→ *f m* ∩ *f n* = {}) ∧ (⋃*i. f i*) ∈ *measurable-sets M*
—→ (λ*n. measure M* (*f n*)) *sums   measure M* (⋃*i. f i*))

This last property deserves some comments. The conclusion is usually — also in the aforementioned source — phrased as

measure M (⋃*i. f i*) = (∑*n. measure M* (*f n*)).

In our formal setting this is unsatisfactory, because the sum operator[4], like any HOL function, is total, although a series obviously need not converge. It is defined using the ε operator, and its behavior is unspecified in the diverging case. Hence, the above assertion would give no information about the convergence of the series. Furthermore, the definition contains redundancy. Assuming that the countable union of sets is measurable is unnecessary when the measurable sets form a sigma algebra, which is postulated in the final definition[5].

measure-space:: (*'a set set* * (*'a set* ⇒ *real*)) ⇒ *bool*
measure-space M ≡ *sigma-algebra* (*measurable-sets M*) ∧
positive M ∧ *countably-additive M*

Note that our definition is restricted to finite measure spaces — that is, *measure M UNIV* < ∞ — since the measure must be a real number for any measurable set. In probability, this is naturally the case.

Two important theorems close this section. Both appear in Hurd's work as well, but are shown anyway, owing to their central role in measure theory. The first one is a mighty tool for proving measurability. It states that for a function mapping one sigma algebra into another, it is sufficient to be measurable regarding only a generator of the target sigma algebra. Formalizing the interesting proof out of Bauer's textbook [1] is relatively straightforward using rule induction.

theorem assumes *sigma-algebra a* **and** *f* ∈ *measurable a b*
   shows *measurable-lift*: *f* ∈ *measurable a* (*sigma b*)

The case is different for the second theorem, which Joe Hurd calls the Monotone Convergence Theorem, though in mathematical literature this name is often reserved for a similar fact about integrals that we will prove in 3.2. It is only five lines in the book, but almost 200 in formal text.

theorem assumes *measure-space M* **and** ⋀*n. A n* ∈ *measurable-sets M* **and** *A*↑*B*
shows *measure-mon-conv*: (λ*n. measure M* (*A n*)) − − − − > *measure M B*

---

[4] Which is merely syntactic sugar for the *suminf* functional from the *Series* theory [5].

[5] Joe Hurd inherited this practice from a very influential probability textbook [16]

The claim made here is that the measures of monotonically convergent sets approach the measure of their limit. By the way, the necessity for the above-mentioned change in the definition of countably additive was detected only in the formalization of this proof.

2.4   Real-Valued Random Variables

theory *RealRandVar = Measure + Rats*:

While most of the above material was modeled after Hurd's work (but still proved independently), the original content basically starts here[6]. From now on, we will specialize in functions that map into the real numbers and are measurable with respect to the canonical sigma algebra on the reals, the Borel sigma algebra. These functions will be called real-valued random variables. The terminology is slightly imprecise, as random variables hint at a probability space, which usually requires *measure M UNIV = 1*. Notwithstanding, as we regard only finite measures (cf. 2.3), this condition can easily be achieved by normalization. After all, the other standard name, "measurable functions", is even less precise.

As mentioned in the introduction, there have been MIZAR realizations of related material[3,4]. The main difference is in the use of extended real numbers — the reals together with $\pm\infty$ — in those documents. It is established practice in measure theory to allow infinite values, but "(...) we felt that the complications that this generated (...) more than canceled out the gain in uniformity (...), and that a simpler theory resulted from sticking to the standard real numbers." [7, p. 32 f]. Hurd also advocates going directly to the hyper-reals, should the need for infinite measures arise; I share his views in this respect.

constdefs
   Borelsets:: *real set set* (𝔹)
   𝔹 ≡ *sigma* {*S*. ∃ *u*. *S*={..*u*}}

   rv:: (*'a set set * ('a set ⇒ real)*) ⇒ (*'a ⇒ real*) *set*
   rv M ≡ {*f*. *measure-space M* ∧ *f* ∈ *measurable* (*measurable-sets M*) 𝔹}

As explained in the first paragraph, the preceding definitions[7] determine the rest of this section. There are many ways to define the Borel sets. For example, taking into account only rationals for *u* would also have worked out above, but we can take the reals to simplify things. The smallest sigma algebra containing all the open (or closed) sets is another alternative; the multitude of possibilities testifies to the relevance of the concept.

---

[6] There are two main reasons why the above has not been imported like the probability space in the application (4.1). Firstly, there are inconveniences caused by different conventions in HOL, meaning predicates instead of sets foremost, that make the consistent use of such basic definitions impractical. What is more, the import tool simply was not available at the time these theories were written.

[7] The notation {..*u*} signifies the interval from negative infinity to *u* included.

The latter path leads the way to the fact that any continuous function is measurable. Generalization for $\mathbb{R}^n$ brings another unified way to prove all the measurability theorems in this theory plus, for instance, measurability of the trigonometric and exponential functions. This approach is detailed in another influential textbook by Billingsley [2]. It requires some concepts of topologic spaces, which made the following elementary course, based on Bauer's excellent book [1], seem more feasible.

Two more definitions go next. The image measure, law, or distribution — the last term being specific to probability — of a measure with respect to a measurable function is calculated as the measure of the inverse image of a set. Characteristic functions will be frequently needed in the rest of the development.

distribution::
$('a \ set \ set * ('a \ set \Rightarrow real)) \Rightarrow ('a \Rightarrow real) \Rightarrow (real \ set \Rightarrow real) \ (law)$
$f \in rv \ M \Longrightarrow law \ M \ f \equiv (measure \ M) \circ (vimage \ f)$

characteristic-function:: $'a \ set \Rightarrow ('a \Rightarrow real) \ (\chi\text{-})$
$\chi A \ x \equiv if \ x \in A \ then \ 1 \ else \ 0$

Now that random variables are defined, we aim to show that a broad class of functions belongs to them. For a constant function this is easy, as there are only two possible preimages. Characteristic functions produce four cases already.

theorem assumes *measure-space M* **and** $A \in measurable\text{-}sets \ M$
  shows *char-rv*: $\chi A \in rv \ M$

For more intricate functions, the following application of the measurability lifting theorem from 2.3 gives a useful characterization.

theorem assumes *measure-space M*
  shows *rv-le-iff*: $(f \in rv \ M) = (\forall a. \ \{w. \ f \ w \le a\} \in measurable\text{-}sets \ M)$

As a first application we show that addition and multiplication with constants preserve measurability. Quite a few properties of the real numbers are employed in the proof. For the general case of addition, we need one more set to be measurable, namely $\{w. \ f \ w \le g \ w\}$. This follows from a like statement for $<$. A dense and countable subset of the reals is needed to establish it. Of course, the rationals come to mind. They were not available in Isabelle/HOL[8], so I built a theory with the necessary properties on my own. It is omitted for the sake of brevity.

theorem assumes $f: f \in rv \ M$ **and** $g: g \in rv \ M$
  shows *rv-plus-rv*: $(\lambda w. \ f \ w + g \ w) \in rv \ M$
proof −
  from g **have** $ms:$ *measure-space M* **by** (*simp add: rv-def*)
  { **fix** a
    have $\{w. \ a \le f \ w + g \ w\} = \{w. \ a + (g \ w)*(-1) \le f \ w\}$

---
[8] At least not as a subset of the reals, to the definition of which a type of positive rational numbers contributed [5].

```
    by auto
  also from g have (λw. a + (g w)*(−1)) ∈ rv M
    by (rule affine-rv)
  with f have {w. a + (g w)*(−1) ≤ f w} ∈ measurable-sets M
    by (simp add: rv-le-rv-measurable)
  finally have {w. a ≤ f w + g w} ∈ measurable-sets M .
  }
  with ms show ?thesis
    by (simp add: rv-ge-iff)
qed
```

To show preservation of measurability by multiplication, it is expressed by addition and squaring. This requires a few technical lemmata including one stating measurability for squares.

theorem assumes $f \in rv\ M$ **and** $g \in rv\ M$
   shows *rv-times-rv*: $(\lambda w.\ f\ w * g\ w) \in rv\ M$

Measurability for limit functions of monotone convergent series is also surprisingly straightforward.

theorem assumes $\bigwedge n.\ u\ n \in rv\ M$ **and** $u{\uparrow}f$ **shows** *mon-conv-rv*: $f \in rv\ M$

Before we end this section to start the formalization of the integral proper, there is one more concept missing: The positive and negative part of a function. Their definition is quite intuitive, and some useful properties have been proven, including the fact that they are random variables, provided that their argument functions are measurable.

constdefs
  nonnegative:: $('a \Rightarrow ('b::\{ord,zero\})) \Rightarrow bool$
  nonnegative $f \equiv \forall x.\ 0 \le f\ x$

  positive-part:: $('a \Rightarrow ('b::\{ord,zero\})) \Rightarrow ('a \Rightarrow 'b)\ (pp)$
  pp $f\ x \equiv$ **if** $0{\le}f(x)$ **then** $f\ x$ **else** 0

  negative-part:: $('a \Rightarrow ('b::\{ord,zero,minus\})) \Rightarrow ('a \Rightarrow 'b)\ (np)$
  np $f\ x \equiv$ **if** $0{\le}f(x)$ **then** 0 **else** $-f(x)$

lemma *f-plus-minus*: $((f\ x)::real) = pp\ f\ x - np\ f\ x$

theorem *pp-np-rv-iff*: $(f::'a \Rightarrow real) \in rv\ M = (pp\ f \in rv\ M \land np\ f \in rv\ M)$

3   Integration

theory *Integral* = *RealRandVar*+*SetsumThms*:

3.1   Simple Functions

A simple function is a finite sum of characteristic functions, each multiplied with a nonnegative constant. These functions must be parametrized by measurable sets. Note that to check this condition, a tuple consisting of a set of measurable sets and a measure is required as the integral operator's second argument, whereas the measure only is given in informal notation. Usually the tuple will be a measure space, though it is not required so by the definition at this point. It is most natural to declare the value of the integral in this elementary case by simply replacing the characteristic functions with the measures of their respective sets. Uniqueness remains to be shown, for a function may have infinitely many decompositions and these might give rise to more than one integral value. This is why we construct a *simple function integral set* for any function and measurable sets/measure pair by means of an inductive set definition containing but one introduction rule.

consts
  sfis:: $('a \Rightarrow real) \Rightarrow ('a\ set\ set * ('a\ set \Rightarrow real)) \Rightarrow real\ set$
inductive *sfis f M*
  intros
  base: $[\![f = (\lambda t.\ \sum i\in(S::nat\ set).\ x\ i * \chi(A\ i)\ t);$
  $\forall i \in S.\ A\ i \in measurable\text{-}sets\ M;\ nonnegative\ x;\ finite\ S;$
  $\forall i\in S.\ \forall j\in S.\ i \neq j \longrightarrow A\ i \cap A\ j = \{\};\ (\bigcup i\in S.\ A\ i) = UNIV]\!]$
  $\implies (\sum i\in S.\ x\ i * measure\ M\ (A\ i)) \in sfis\ f\ M$

As you can see we require two extra conditions, and they amount to the sets being a partition of the universe. We say that a function is in normal form if it is represented this way. Normal forms are only needed to show additivity and monotonicity of simple function integral sets. These theorems can then be used in turn to get rid of the normality condition. More precisely, normal forms play a central role in the *sfis-present* lemma. For two simple functions with different underlying partitions it states the existence of a common finer-grained partition that can be used to represent the functions uniformly. The proof is remarkably lengthy though the idea seems rather simple. The difficulties stem from translating informal use of sum notation, which permits for a change in index sets, allowing for a pair of indices. .

lemma assumes *measure-space M* **and** $a \in sfis\ f\ M$ **and** $b \in sfis\ g\ M$
  shows *sfis-present*: $\exists\ z1\ z2\ C\ K.$
  $f = (\lambda t.\ \sum i\in(K::nat\ set).\ z1\ i * \chi(C\ i)\ t) \wedge g = (\lambda t.\ \sum i\in K.\ z2\ i * \chi(C\ i)\ t)$
  $\wedge\ a = (\sum i\in K.\ z1\ i * measure\ M\ (C\ i)) \wedge b = (\sum i\in K.\ z2\ i * measure\ M\ (C\ i))$
  $\wedge\ finite\ K \wedge (\forall i\in K.\ \forall j\in K.\ i \neq j \longrightarrow C\ i \cap C\ j = \{\})$
  $\wedge\ (\forall i \in K.\ C\ i \in measurable\text{-}sets\ M) \wedge (\bigcup i\in K.\ C\ i) = UNIV$
  $\wedge\ nonnegative\ z1 \wedge nonnegative\ z2$

Additivity and monotonicity are now almost obvious, the latter trivially implying uniqueness. The integral of characteristic functions as well as the effect of multiplication with a constant follow directly from the definition. Together with a generalization of the addition theorem to setsums, a less restrictive introduction rule emerges, making normal forms obsolete. It is only valid in measure spaces though.

lemma assumes *measure-space M* **and** $\forall i \in S.\ A\ i \in measurable\text{-}sets\ M$
  and *nonnegative x* **and** *finite S*
  shows *sfis-intro*: $(\sum i \in S.\ x\ i * measure\ M\ (A\ i))$
  $\in sfis\ (\lambda t.\ \sum i \in (S::nat\ set).\ x\ i * \chi(A\ i)\ t)\ M$

3.2 Nonnegative Functions

There is one more important fact about *sfis*, easily the hardest one to see. It is about the relationship with monotone convergence and paves the way for a sensible definition of *nnfis*, the nonnegative function integral sets, enabling monotonicity and thus uniqueness. A reasonably concise formal proof could fortunately be achieved in spite of the nontrivial ideas involved — compared for instance to the intuitive but hard-to-formalize *sfis-present*.

lemma assumes $u \uparrow f$ **and** $\bigwedge n.\ x\ n \in sfis\ (u\ n)\ M$ **and** $x \uparrow y$
  and $r \in sfis\ s\ M$ **and** $s \leq f$ **and** *measure-space M*
  shows *sfis-mon-conv-mono*: $r \leq y$

Now we are ready for the second step. The integral of a monotone limit of functions is the limit of their integrals. Note that this last limit has to exist in the first place, since we decided not to use infinite values. Backed by the last theorem and the preexisting knowledge about limits, the usual basic properties are straightforward.

consts
nnfis:: $('a \Rightarrow real) \Rightarrow ('a\ set\ set * ('a\ set \Rightarrow real)) \Rightarrow real\ set$
inductive *nnfis f M*
  intros
  base: $\llbracket u \uparrow f;\ \bigwedge n.\ x\ n \in sfis\ (u\ n)\ M;\ x \uparrow y \rrbracket \implies y \in nnfis\ f\ M$

We close this subsection with a classic theorem by Beppo Levi, the monotone convergence theorem. In essence, it says that the introduction rule for *nnfis* holds not only for sequences of simple functions, but for any sequence of nonnegative integrable functions. It should be mentioned that this theorem cannot be formulated for the Riemann integral. We prove it by exhibiting a sequence of simple functions that converges to the same limit as the original one and then applying the introduction rule. By definition, for any f_n in the original sequence, there is a sequence $(u_{mn})_{m\in\mathbb{N}}$ of simple functions converging to it. The nth element of the new sequence is then defined as the upper closure of the nth elements of the first n sequences.

theorem assumes $f \uparrow h$ **and** $\bigwedge n.\ x\ n \in nnfis\ (f\ n)\ M$
  and $x \uparrow y$ **and** *measure-space M*
  shows *nnfis-mon-conv*: $y \in nnfis\ h\ M$

3.3 Integrable Functions

Before we take the final step of defining integrability and the integral operator, we should first clarify what kind of functions we are able to integrate up to now. It is easy to see that all nonnegative integrable functions are random variables.

lemma assumes *measure-space M* **and** *a* ∈ *nnfis f M*
  shows *nnfis-rv*: *f* ∈ *rv M*

The converse does not hold of course, since there are measurable functions whose integral is infinite. Regardless, it is possible to approximate any measurable function using simple step-functions. This means that all nonnegative random variables are quasi integrable, as the property is sometimes called, and brings forth the fundamental insight that a nonnegative function is integrable if and only if it is measurable and the integrals of the simple functions that approximate it converge monotonically. Technically, the proof is rather complex, involving many properties of real numbers.

lemma assumes *measure-space M* **and** : *f* ∈ *rv M* **and** *nonnegative f*
  shows *rv-mon-conv-sfis*: ∃ *u x. u↑f* ∧ (∀ *n. x n* ∈ *sfis* (*u n*) *M*)

The following dominated convergence theorem is an easy corollary. It can be effectively applied to show integrability.

corollary assumes *measure-space M* **and** *f* ∈ *rv M*
  and *b* ∈ *nnfis g M* **and** *f≤g* **and** *nonnegative f*
  shows *nnfis-dom-conv*: ∃ *a. a* ∈ *nnfis f M* ∧ *a* ≤ *b*

Speaking all the time about integrability, it is time to define it at last.

constdefs
  integrable:: (′*a* ⇒ *real*) ⇒ (′*a set set* ∗ (′*a set* ⇒ *real*)) ⇒ *bool*

  integrable f M ≡ *measure-space M* ∧
  (∃ *x. x* ∈ *nnfis* (*pp f*) *M*) ∧ (∃ *y. y* ∈ *nnfis* (*np f*) *M*)

  integral:: (′*a* ⇒ *real*) ⇒ (′*a set set* ∗ (′*a set* ⇒ *real*)) ⇒ *real* (∫ - ∂-)
  integrable f M ⟹ ∫ *f ∂M* ≡ (*THE i. i* ∈ *nnfis* (*pp f*) *M*) −
  (*THE j. j* ∈ *nnfis* (*np f*) *M*)

A useful lemma follows, which helps lift nonnegative function integral sets to integrals proper. The dominated convergence theorem from above is employed in the proof.

lemma *nnfis-minus-nnfis-integral*:
  assumes *a* ∈ *nnfis f M* **and** *b* ∈ *nnfis g M* **and** *measure-space M*
  shows *integrable* (λ*t. f t − g t*) *M* **and** ∫ (λ*t. f t − g t*) *∂ M* = *a − b*

Armed with this, the standard integral behavior should not be hard to derive. Mind that integrability always implies a measure space, just like random variables did in 2.4.

theorem assumes *integrable f M*
  shows *integrable-rv*: *f* ∈ *rv M*

theorem *integral-char*: **assumes** *measure-space M* **and** *A* ∈ *measurable-sets M*
  shows ∫ *χA ∂ M* = *measure M A* **and** *integrable χA M*

theorem *integral-add*: **assumes** *integrable f M* **and** *integrable g M*
  shows *integrable* $(\lambda t.\ f\ t + g\ t)\ M$
  and $\int\ (\lambda t.\ f\ t + g\ t)\ \partial M = \int\ f\ \partial M + \int\ g\ \partial M$

theorem assumes *integrable f M* **and** *integrable g M* **and** $f \leq g$
  shows *integral-mono*: $\int\ f\ \partial M \leq \int\ g\ \partial M$

theorem *integral-times*: **assumes** *integrable f M*
  shows *integrable* $(\lambda t.\ a * f\ t)\ M$ **and** $\int\ (\lambda t.\ a * f\ t)\ \partial M = a * \int\ f\ \partial M$

To try out our definitions in an application, only one more theorem is missing. The famous Markov–Chebyshev inequation is not difficult to arrive at using the basic integral properties.

theorem assumes *integrable f M* **and** $0 < a$ **and** *integrable* $(\lambda x.\ |f\ x|\ \hat{}\ n)\ M$
  shows *markov-ineq*: *law M f* $\{a..\} \leq \int\ (\lambda x.\ |f\ x|\ \hat{}\ n)\ \partial M\ /\ (a \hat{} n)$

4   Probabilistic Algorithms

To take up a point from the prologue, one major motive for formalizing integration is to formalize expectation. Indeed, the expectation of a random variable is nothing but its integral. This simple fact makes it possible to use all the theorems about integration to manipulate expected values. In the application I chose, only two properties are needed, namely additivity and the Markov inequation. The latter gives rise to the so-called first moment method[9]. Before going into the details of the use case, a concrete probability space is required.

4.1   The Probability Space

theory *ImportPredSet = HOL4ExtraProb+Measure*:

It is at this point that real HOL4 theories from Hurd's thesis [7] come into play. They have been imported to Isabelle/HOL by Sebastian Skalberg using his Import Tool [13]. Joe Hurd has formalized the probability space of independent identically distributed infinite Bernoulli trials, or random bitstreams. It is applied in theorems about probabilistic functional programs employing monadic notation. These can be built from three primitives only: *sdest* hands back a tuple consisting of the first bit of the argument bitstream and the rest of this bitstream. *UNIT* lifts the first argument value to the monad by just pairing it with the unmodified second argument boolean sequence. *BIND* is the monadic equivalent of functional composition.

The main problem in incorporating Hurd's theories (in the imported form) is that in HOL4, predicates are used instead of sets. Therefore, a little work is required to switch between the equivalent but technically different variants of probability space definitions for example.

---

[9] This is a standard technique in the field of randomized algorithms; it may be found in the authoritative textbook on the subject by Motwani and Raghavan [8]

4.2 A New Primitive

theory *Lsdest* = *HOL4ExtraProb*:

It is time to introduce the example application that is being formalized in section 4.3. We will be looking at the most simplistic possible program for finding a satisfying assignment for a propositional formula in conjunctive normal form where any clause consists of exactly k literals. This problem is known as k-SAT. Our algorithm simply selects a random assignment for all of the n variables. We are interested in the probability that the assignment fails to satisfy a given clause. The reasons behind this will become clear in a while.

In the previous section it was stated that one should be able to construct any randomized functional program from the three primitive building blocks defined there. Of course, this also holds for the program we have in mind. Nevertheless, when following the style these constructs suggest, taking one random bit at a time and evaluating somewhere in between, one runs into problems. That is to say, the clauses are not independent in general. A variable may appear in several clauses, and it would be wrong to fetch a new bit from the stream every time it is evaluated. Ergo, the simplest way to perform the evaluation of a clause independently from the rest is to get a list of all n random bits beforehand. A function accomplishing this is not hard to devise. It is elementary enough to possibly support a lot of programs.

types $'a\ seq = nat \Rightarrow {'}a$

consts
  lsdest:: $nat \Rightarrow {'}a\ seq \Rightarrow ({'}a\ list * {'}a\ seq)$

primrec
  lsdest $0 = UNIT\ []$
  lsdest $(Suc\ n) = BIND\ sdest\ (\lambda x.\ BIND\ (lsdest\ n)\ (\lambda l.\ UNIT\ (x\# l)))$

The decisive theorem about this new function is furnishing all we need to know about its results' probability distribution[10].

lemma *lsdest-probs*: $[\![$*finite* R; *card* $R = k$; $\forall r \in R.\ Suc\ r \leq n]\!]$
  $\Longrightarrow P\ (\lambda s.\ \forall r \in R.\ (fst\ (lsdest\ n\ s))!r = b\ r) = (1/2)\ \hat{}\ k$

4.3 The First Moment Method

theory *kSAT* = *Lsdest+ImportPredSet+Integral*:

Formulas are modeled as lists of clauses, which in turn are represented by lists of integers. The absolute value of a number stands for the variable name, the sign signifying negation of the literal. For an illustrative instance, -4 means the 4th variable inverted, and 0 is not allowed. A variable may not appear twice

---

[10] Here, the exclamation mark operator $l!n$ returns the element number n in the list l, while P stands for the imported Bernoulli probability measure from 4.1. Thus, a predicate is measured rather than a set.

in any clause, as ensured by the *absdistinct* predicate. Looking at the following example might clarify the notation.

theorem $[[1,2,3],[-4,-2,1]] \in 4 \ var \ 3 \ SAT$

A formula can be evaluated at an assignment, that is a list of booleans, by primitive recursive functions.

primrec
 clauseeval $[] \ l \ = \ False$
 clauseeval $(x\#xs) \ l \ = \ (if \ (0<x) \ then \ (l!nat \ (x+-1) \ \lor \ clauseeval \ xs \ l)$
                         $else \ if \ (x<0) \ then \ (\neg(l!nat \ (-1+-x)) \ \lor \ clauseeval \ xs \ l)$
                         $else \ True)$

primrec
 CNFeval $[] \ l = \ True$
 CNFeval $(x\#xs) \ l = \ (clauseeval \ x \ l \ \land \ CNFeval \ xs \ l)$

Now we may randomize these functions, obtaining just the simple programs described in 4.2. In addition, an indicator variable is defined that takes the value 1 for exactly those elementary events — or rather bit sequences — where the argument clause is not satisfied.

constdefs
 randCNFeval:: $(int \ list) \ list \Rightarrow nat \Rightarrow bool \ seq \Rightarrow (bool * (bool \ seq))$
 randCNFeval $F \ n \ s \ \equiv \ (CNFeval \ F \ (stake \ n \ s), \ sdrop \ n \ s)$

 randclauseeval:: $int \ list \Rightarrow nat \Rightarrow bool \ seq \Rightarrow (bool * (bool \ seq))$
 randclauseeval $D \ n \ \equiv \ BIND \ (lsdest \ n) \ (\lambda l. \ UNIT \ (clauseeval \ D \ l))$

 indicator:: $int \ list \Rightarrow nat \Rightarrow bool \ seq \Rightarrow real$
 indicator $D \ n \ \equiv \ \chi\{s. \ \neg \ fst \ (randclauseeval \ D \ n \ s)\}$

lemma *randCNFeval-BIND-UNIT*:
 randCNFeval $F \ n \ s \ = \ BIND \ (lsdest \ n) \ (\lambda l. \ UNIT \ (CNFeval \ F \ l)) \ s$

We just saw that both *randclauseeval* and *randCNFeval* can be built from *UNIT*, *BIND* and *sdest* alone. Hence they are strongly independent functions[11] In particular, indicator is a characteristic function for an event.

The next step is to compute the measure of this event, the probability that a given clause is not satisfied. In spite of the preparatory work on *lsdest*, the greatest difficulty lies in here. Though a rough idea should have emerged until now, it is technically demanding to arrive at a setup where *lsdest-probs* may be applied instantly.

theorem assumes $D \in n \ var \ k \ clauses$
 shows *rce-prob*: $P \ (\lambda s. \ \neg \ fst \ (randclauseeval \ D \ n \ s)) = (1/2)\hat{} k$

---

[11] More about the concept of strong independence may be found in Hurd's work [7, p. 70ff]. In this context, it just means that with regard to the first component of the function, the preimage of any set is measurable.

We should take a moment to appreciate this first result. It embodies the gist of the probabilistic analysis for the *randclauseeval* randomized algorithm. What is more, it enables the primal application of integration in the following theorem. Here we encounter an expectation in the true sense for the first time in this paper. Like any expectation it sums up easily[12].

theorem *sum-ind-int*: **assumes** $F \in n$ *var* k *SAT* **shows**
   $\int (\lambda s. \sum m\in\{..(length\ F)(\}.\ indicator\ (F!m)\ n\ s)\ \partial\ ImportPredSet.bern$
   $=\ real\ (length\ F)/2\hat{\ }k$
   and *integrable* $(\lambda s. \sum m\in\{..(length\ F)(\}.\ indicator\ (F!m)\ n\ s)\ ImportPredSet.bern$

The result just obtained contributes all the information about probabilistic programs we will need: The expected number of unsatisfied clauses with our simplistic algorithm is the total number of clauses divided by 2^k. It is only now that the first moment method comes into play. The point put forward by this proposition is that if the expected value of nonnegative random variable is less than 1, then there must be an event witnessing this. The proof turns out to be rather elementary from the Markov inequation.

corollary assumes *integrable* $f\ M$ **and** $\int f\ \partial\ M < 1$
   and *ImportPredSet.prob-space* M
   shows *fmm*: $\exists s.\ f\ s < 1$

In the application we have in mind, a random bitstream that makes the indicator variables sum to a value less than 1 corresponds to a satisfying assignment.

lemma assumes $F \in n$ *var* k *SAT* **and**
   $(\sum m\in\{..(length\ F)(\}.\ indicator\ (F!m)\ n\ env) < 1$
   shows *satisfy*: *CNFeval* F (*stake* n *env*)

In the end we have shown that a satisfying assignment always exists if there are less than 2^k clauses in a k-CNF formula.

theorem assumes $F \in n$ *var* k *SAT* **and** *real*(*length* F) $< 2\hat{\ }k$
   shows *existence*: $\exists l.\ CNFeval\ F\ l$

5   Epilogue

We have formalized a general approach to integration in the Lebesgue style. We managed to systematically establish the integral of increasingly complex functions. Of course, the repository of potential supplementary facts is vast. Convergence theorems, as well as the interrelationship with differentiation or concurrent integral concepts, are but a few examples. They leave ample space for subsequent work.

Though the focus has been on the formal content, another aspect of this research is as an example application of new prover technology. All proofs have been carried out in declarative style using Markus Wenzel's Isar language[13] [14].

---

[12] The *bern* space is a set version of Hurd's Bernoulli predicate space from 4.1
[13] The full theories are available on the web:
   http://www-lti.informatik.rwth-aachen.de/~richter/papers/

Unlike Isar, which has been used in several projects, Sebastian Skalberg's import tool [13] is still under development. It has proven extremely handy as the missing link from Joe Hurd's HOL4 theories, though differences in terminology obviously couldn't be taken care of automatically.

To my mind, the example application conveys its point in a satisfactory manner. As a side effect, another building block for functional probabilistic programming, or what is more, its essential properties, could be obtained. Without a doubt, there is an infinite amount of further examples, including more involved varieties of the first moment method or the run-time analysis of probabilistic quicksort. The latter is work in progress at the time of writing.

References

1. Heinz Bauer. *Maß- und Integrationstheorie*. de Gruyter, 1990.
2. Patrick Billingsley. *Probability and Measure*. John Wiley, second edition, 1986.
3. Noboru Endou, Katsumi Wasaki, and Yasunari Shidama. Definitions and basic properties of measurable functions. *Journal of Formalized Mathematics*, 12, 2000. Available on the web as http://mizar.uwb.edu.pl/JFM/Vol12/mesfunc1.html.
4. Noboru Endou, Katsumi Wasaki, and Yasunari Shidama. The measurability of extended real valued functions. *Journal of Formalized Mathematics*, 12, 2000. Available on the web as http://mizar.uwb.edu.pl/JFM/Vol12/mesfunc2.html.
5. Jacques D. Fleuriot and Lawrence C. Paulson. Mechanizing nonstandard real analysis. *LMS Journal of Computation and Mathematics*, 3:140–190, 2000.
6. John Harrison. *Theorem Proving with the Real Numbers*. Springer, 1996.
7. Joe Hurd. *Formal Verification of Probabilistic Algorithms*. PhD thesis, University of Cambridge, 2002.
8. Rajeev Motwani and Prabhakar Raghavan. *Randomized Algorithms*. Cambridge University Press, 1997.
9. Tobias Nipkow. Order-sorted polymorphism in isabelle. In Gérard Huet and Gordon Plotkin, editors, *Logical Environments*, pages 164–188. Cambridge University Press, 1993.
10. Tobias Nipkow, Lawrence C. Paulson, and Markus Wenzel. Isabelle's logics: HOL, 2002. Unpublished. Available on the web as http://isabelle.in.tum.de/doc/logics-HOL.pdf.
11. Lawrence C. Paulson. Isabelle: The next 700 theorem provers. In Piergiorgio Odifreddi, editor, *Logic and Computer Science*, pages 361–386. Academic Press, 1990.
12. Lawrence C. Paulson. Isabelle: A generic theorem prover. *Lecture Notes in Computer Science*, 828:xvii + 321, 1994.
13. Sebastian Skalberg. Import tool. Available on the web as http://www.mangust.dk/skalberg/isabelle.php.
14. Markus Wenzel. *Isabelle/Isar — a versatile environment for human-readable formal proof documents*. PhD thesis, Technische Universität München, 2002.
15. Markus Wenzel. Using axiomatic type classes in Isabelle, 2002. Unpublished. Available on the web as http://isabelle.in.tum.de/dist/Isabelle2002/doc/axclass.pdf.
16. David Williams. *Probability with Martingales*. Cambridge University Press, 1991.

Formalizing Java Dynamic Loading in HOL

Tian-jun Zuo[1,*], Jun-gang Han[2], and Ping Chen[1]

[1] Software Engineering Institute
XiDian University, Xi'an 710071 China
zuotianjun@sina.com
[2] Department of Computer Science
University of Xi'an Post & Telecomm, Xi'an 710061 China
hjg@xiyou.edu.cn

Abstract. Dynamic class loading is an important feature of the Java virtual machine. It is the underlying mechanism that supports installing software components at runtime. However, it is also complex. Improperly written class loaders could undermine the type safety of the Java virtual machine. Given the importance of security, the current description provided by the Java virtual machine is deficient. It is ambiguous, imprecise and hard to reason about. In this paper, we suggest a model for the Java virtual machine, which includes the main features of dynamic class loading and linking. We formalize the model and prove its soundness in the HOL system. The soundness theorem demonstrates that our model can preserve types indeed. Based on the model, we can analyze the behaviors of loading in the virtual machine.

1 Introduction

Dynamic class loading is an important feature of the Java virtual machine (JVM). It is the underlying mechanism that supports installing software at run time. Although the Java class loading is powerful, it also creates opportunities for malicious codes. Early versions (1.0 and 1.1) of the Java Development Kit (JDK) contained a serious flaw in class loader implementation. Improperly written class loaders could defeat the type safety guarantee of the Java virtual machine. For example, Saraswat [17] published a bug related to type spoofing by use of dynamic class loaders. With the release of JDK 1.2, an important feature, loading constraint scheme, was introduced in JVM specification to fix Saraswat's problem.

Given the importance of Java security, the current specification [18] of class loading is deficient. It is a prose description. Although good by the standards of prose, this description is ambiguous, imprecise, and hard to reason about. One contribution of our work is that we propose a formal model for the Java class loading and linking and prove its soundness. Moreover, we use a theorem

---

* Supported by the National Natural Science Foundation of China under Grant No.90207015

K. Slind et al. (Eds.): TPHOLs 2004, LNCS 3223, pp. 287–304, 2004.
© Springer-Verlag Berlin Heidelberg 2004

prover to increase the reliability and maintainability of the formalization, which is another main contribution of our work.

The paper begins with the overview of class loading and type problems in section 2. The operational semantics of the model is specified in section 3. Soundness theorem and some other lemmas are discussed in section 4. Section 5 relates our work to other research. Conclusions are presented in section 6.

2   The Overview of Class Loading and Typing Problems

Java is the only system that incorporates all of the following features: lazy loading, type-safe linkage, user-defined classing loading policy and multiple namespaces. The notion of class loader plays a critical role in the security of Java. Each class is associated with a specific class loader that corresponds to a specific namespace in the virtual machine. JVM uses class loaders to load class files and create class objects. Class loaders are ordinary objects that can be defined in Java code. They are instances of subclasses of the class *java.lang.ClassLoader*, some methods of which related to the presentation are shown in Figure 1.

```
class ClassLoader {
    public Class loadClass(String name);
    protected final Class defineClass(String name, byte[ ] buf, int off, int len);
    ... ...
}
```

Fig. 1. Some methods of java.lang.ClassLoader

If C is the result of $L.loadClass()$, we say that L initiates loading of C or, equivalently, that L is an initiating loader of C. If C is the result of $L.defineClass()$, we say that L defines C or, equivalently, that L is the defining loader of C. Class loading can be delegated. One class loader may delegate to another class loader for loading class. Thus, the loader that initiates the loading is not necessarily the same loader that completes the loading and defines the class.

A run-time class type is determined not by its name alone, but by a pair: its fully qualified name and its defining class loader. In this paper, we represent a class with the notation $<N, L1>^{L2}$, where N denotes the name of the class, $L1$ denotes the defining loader, and $L2$ denotes the initiating loader. When we do not care about the defining loader, the notation is abbreviated to N^{L2}. When we do not care about the initiating loader, the notation is abbreviated to $<N, L1>$.

Due to class delegation between loaders, a type-spoofing problem was first published by Saraswat [17]. Figure 2 presents the problem. The code itself is totally correct at compile time. However, type inconsistency will occur at the statement $r = rr.getR()$ during run time since r has a type $<R, L1>$ at runtime, but $rr.getR()$ returns a type $<R, L2>$ due to the class loading delegation from $L1$ to $L2$. Thus, the program above can access the private value in $<R, L2>$ through $System.out.println("private value of R in class file R2 = " + r. secret)$, which violates the type system of Java.

```
class RT { // the defining loader of RT is L1
     private R r;
     void test() {
          RR rr = new RR();
          r = rr.getR(); // type inconsistency, fail
          System.out.println ("private value of R in class file R2 = " + r. secret);
     }
}
class RR { // the defining loader of RR is L2
     R getR() {
          return new R();
     }
}
class R { //the defining loader of R is L1          class R {// the defining loader of R is L2
     public int secret;                                      private int secret;
}                                                                   }
```

Fig. 2. The type spoofing problem

3   Formal Model

We propose a state transition system to specify the operational semantics of class loading and linking, which is precise enough to describe and analyze the loading operations of the virtual machine. States in our model contain data structures to specify the inner changes occurring in the virtual machine. These data structures are loaded class cache (LCC) and loading class constraints (LLC). Thus, our states can be represented as *stack* × *LCC* × *LLC* × *heap*. There are two kinds of state transitions in the model: one is to describe the operations of instructions; the other is to specify the process of loading and linking in the virtual machine. These transitions are mutually recursive.

3.1   HOL 4

We formalize our model and prove its soundness in the HOL 4, which is the latest version of the HOL automated proof system for higher order logic. Some frequently used HOL functions are: *EXISTS : ('a bool)* → *'a list*→ *bool* is the predicate of list theory. It determines whether there exists an element in a list, which satisfies the constraint imposed by the predicate *('a → bool)*. *HD :* '*a list* → *'a* is the standard list processing function to get the first element of a list. *TL :* '*a list* → *'a list* is the list processing function to get the tail of a list, e.g. *TL (h::t) = t*. *EL :* '*a list* → *num* → *'a* gets the element of a list which is indexed by the second argument of the function. The index of the first element is zero. Thus, *EL* $(n-1)$ *t* gets the nth element of a list *t*.

3.2   Basic Definitions in HOL

Because of the limitation of space, we cannot present all definitions of our model. Some basic definitions are illustrated in figure 3 and figure 4 respectively.

(1) Names of classes, fields and methods

The definition of *CLASSNAME* and *METHODNAME* are straightforward. The type of field names is defined abstractly.

```
Hol_datatype                                Hol_datatype
  'CLASSNAME = Class |                        'METHODNAME = loadClass |
               ClassLoader |                                 defineClass |
               CLSNM of string';                             MTHDNM of string';

Hol_datatype
  'INSTRUCTION = areturn |
                 getfield of CLASSNAME # FIELD |
                 getstatic of CLASSNAME # FIELD |
                 invokestatic of CLASSNAME # METHOD |
                 invokevirtual of CLASSNAME # METHOD |
                 putfield of CLASSNAME # FIELD |
                 putstatic of CLASSNAME # FIELD |
                 new of CLASSNAME ';

Hol_datatype                                Hol_datatype
  'CLASS = <|Cls_Loader:LOADER;               'FIELD = <|Fld_Name:FIELDNAME;
             Cls_Name:CLASSNAME;                        Fld_Type:CLASSNAME|>';
             Cls_SuperName:CLASSNAME;
             Cls_fld:FIELD list;
             Cls_mthd:METHOD list|>';

Hol_datatype                                Hol_datatype
  'METHOD= <|Mthd_Name:METHODNAME;            'LCC = <|LCC_loader:LOADER;
             Mthd_arg:CLASSNAME list;                  LCC_classname:CLASSNAME;
             Mthd_retType:CLASSNAME|>';                LCC_Class:CLASS|>';

Hol_datatype                                Hol_datatype
  'LLC = <|LLC_L1:LOADER;                      'STACK = <|STK_cls:CLASS;
           LLC_L2:LOADER;                                STK_mthd:METHOD;
           LLC_classname:CLASSNAME|>';                   STK_lvar:VALUE list list;
                                                         STK_pc:num;
                                                         STK_os:VALUE list list|>';

Hol_datatype
  'PROG_STATE = <|PROG_STATE_stack:STACK list;
                  PROG_STATE_heap: VALUE list;
                  PROG_STATE_lcc:LCC list;
                  PROG_STATE_llc:LLC list |>';
```

Fig. 3. Some basic data structures defined in HOL

(2) Instructions

According to the JVM specification, the instruction, *getfield*, *getstatic*, *putfield* or *putstatic*, has two operands generated at compile time. These operands are used to construct an index into the runtime constant pool of the current class. The runtime constant pool item at that index must be a symbolic reference to a field, which gives *the name and descriptor of the field* as well as a *symbolic reference* to the class in which the field is to be found. In our model, *the name and descriptor of the field* correspond the second argument *FIELD* of the instruction; the *symbolic reference* to the class corresponds the first argument *CLASSNAME*. The argument *CLASSNAME#METHOD* of *invokestatic* and *invokevirtual* can be understood similarly.

(3) Class, Objects and Heap

java.lang.Class plays an essential role in the JVM architecture. This class implements the reflection mechanism of Java. An object instance of *java.lang.Class* keeps the meta information of each class of Java. In our model, Class is defined as a record type that consists of a defining loader, a class name, a direct super class name, as well as field and method declarations.

In our model, the type of object is defined abstractly with a type *VALUE*. Thus the type of the heap is *VALUE list* . To talk about the internal structures (such as field and method) of an object, we define an abstract function *objcls* : *VALUE → CLASS*, which models the reflection of Java to return the meta information of an object. Thus we can build a connection between an abstract object with its corresponding Class object.

(4) Loaded class cache (LCC) list

The virtual machine maintains two kinds of consistency. One is temporal namespace consistency; the other is the consistency between the loaded class cache and loading class constraints. Temporal namespace consistency means that the virtual machine must be able to obtain the same class type for a given class name and loader at any time. However, mistakes in the user-defined loadclass method or malicious code may violate the constraint. Therefore, the virtual machine must check the consistency for every loaded class. This is implemented by maintaining an inner data structure, *LCC* list, in the virtual machine. The type of *LCC* is defined as a record type which models a map from an initiating loader and a class name to the corresponding Class object.

(5) Loading class constraints (LLC) list

In Java 2, a loading class constraint scheme is introduced to fix the type-spoofing problem in the virtual machine. It has advantages of ensuring type-safe linkage and preserving lazy class loading. A *LLC* record <L1, L2, N> represents a loading class constraint imposed on the virtual machine, which means $N^{L1} = N^{L2}$.

(6) Program state

From the definition, a program state is composed of a stack list, a heap, a *LCC* list and a *LLC* list. Where the stack consists of the current class, the current method, the program counter, the local variable list and the operand stack list.

The tricky point here is that the types of the local variable and the operand stack are *VALUE list list*. These structures are just to define the model more conveniently. For example, some bytecode instructions require more than one operand to process, thus the top element (a list) of the operand stack (a list list) in the initial state can contain all operands to be processed by the current instruction. Therefore, the operand stack is structured by each of its elements for bytecode instructions. In our formalization, we just model the operand stack and the local variable to be object containers. However, we do not try to impose any constraints on the implementation.

(subtyping)
```
    sub c c' lcc = EXISTS (eq_subc c) lcc ∧ EXISTS (eq_subc c') lcc
                 ⊃ (EXISTS (eq_sublcc c.Cls_Loader c.Cls_SuperName c') lcc);
```

(method resolution)
```
    (mthd_RESOLUTION cls mthd [] = cls) ∧
    (mthd_RESOLUTION cls mthd (x::t) =
    if (EXISTS (eq mthd) cls.Cls_mthd)
    then cls
    else if (cls.Cls_SuperName = x.LCC_Class.Cls_Name) ∧
      (cls.Cls_Loader = x.LCC_loader)
      then mthd_RESOLUTION x.LCC_Class mthd t
      else mthd_RESOLUTION cls mthd t);
```

(LCC list and LLC list consistency)
```
    wf_constraint lcc llc =
    ∀l l' n c c'.
     ¬ ((EXISTS (wf_eqlcc l n c) lcc) ∧
       (EXISTS (wf_eqlcc l' n c') lcc) ∧
       (EXISTS (wf_eqllc l l' n) llc) ∧
       ¬ (c = c'));
```

Fig. 4. Some basic functions and predicates defined in HOL

(7) subtyping

Predicate $sub : CLASS \to CLASS \to LCC\,list \to bool$ defines the subtyping relation between classes. It asserts that if C is the subclass of C' in the context of LCC list, then $C' = C.Cls\_SuperName^{C.Cls\_Loader}$. Where $C.Cls\_Loader$ is the defining loader of C. eq_subc and eq_sublcc are predicates applied to predicate $EXISTS$. The transitive closure of subtyping relation is defined as relation $subtc : CLASS \to CLASS \to LCC\,list \to bool$.

(8) LCC list and LLC list consistency

To preserve the type safety, the consistency between the loaded class cache and the loading class constraints is maintained by the virtual machine. Every time there is a modification of either of them, the virtual machine will consider the both to guarantee the consistency.

Predicate $wf\_constraint : LCC \to list \to LLC\,list \to bool$ defines the consistency between the LCC list and the LLC list. It asserts that the consistency can be satisfied iff the following conditions cannot hold at the same time:

- There exists a loader L such that L has been recorded by the virtual machine as an initiating loader of a class C denoted by N.
- There exists a loader L' such that L' has been recorded by the virtual machine as an initiating loader of a class C' denoted by N.
- The equivalence relation defined by the (transitive closure of the) set of imposed constraints implies $N^L = N^{L'}$.
- $C \neq C'$.

(9) Method and field resolution algorithm

Since the LCC list keeps the linearization of the class hierarchy loaded in the virtual machine, algorithm $mthd\_RESOLUTION : CLASS \to METHOD \to LCC\,list$

$\rightarrow$ *CLASS* traverses the *LCC* list recursively to resolve the specified method. The details of method resolution will be discussed in the next section. The algorithm of field resolution *fld_RESOLUTION : CLASS $\rightarrow$ FIELD $\rightarrow$ LCC list $\rightarrow$ CLASS* is similar to the *mthd_RESOLUTION*.

3.3   Operational Semantics

We have formalized state transitions of instructions presented in section 3.1, as well as class loading and resolution of classes, fields and methods. Because of space limitation, we cannot show all the transitions. We only present such representative transitions as *invokevirtual*, class loading, and method resolution to illustrate the outline of the class loading and linking of the virtual machine. However, we have to refer to some other transitions because these relations are mutually recursive.

In our formalization, these state transitions are defined by pre-defined ML function *Hol_reln*. Since these HOL definitions are too lengthy and hard to read, we take a usual mathematical way to present these transitions which are represented as a conjunction of hypotheses implying a conclusion. In the following transitions, all the terms up the line are the hypotheses and the term below the line is the conclusion. In these definitions, all functions defined in HOL respect their type declaration. To be more readable, all the labels in record types are omitted.

(1) invokevirtual

The bytecode instruction *invokevirtual* invokes instance method. Its semantics is shown in figure 5. We first examine the conclusion. $\rightarrow$ represents the state transition relation of bytecode instructions. The initial state asserts that: the current class is *Curcls*; the current method is *Curmthd*; and the arguments of

PC(Curmthd,pc) = invokevirtual (refcn,refmthd)
E'.ENV_CLS = Curcls
E'.ENV_CN = refcn
E'.ENV_MTHD = refmthd
(E',<|stack; hp;lcc; llc|>) MR (E',<|stack; hp'; lcc'; llc'|>)
mthd_RESOLUTION (objcls objref) refmthd lcc' = c'
subtc (objcls objref) (querylcc lcc' Curcls.Cls_Loader refcn).LCC_Class lcc'
cond

<|<|Curcls; Curmthd; lvar; pc;[argn, ..., arg2, arg1, objref] :: os|> :: stack; hp; lcc; llc|> $\rightarrow$
<|<|c'; c'.Cls_mthd; [objref, arg1, arg2, ..., argn] :: lvar; 0; [[]]|> ::
<|Curcls; Curmthd; lvar; pc+1; os|> :: stack; hp'; lcc'; llc"|>

where
cond = ¬ (subtc c' (querylcc lcc' Curcls.Cls_Loader refcn).LCC_Class lcc') ⊃ (llc" = llc')) ∨
    (subtc c' (querylcc lcc' Curcls.Cls_Loader refcn).LCC_Class lcc' ⊃
    (c'.Cls_mthd override refmthd ∧ wf_constraint lcc' llc" ∧ llc" = t :: llc'))
t = <|c'.Cls_Loader; Curcls.Cls_Loader; refmthd.Mthd_arg|> ::
    <|c'.Cls_Loader; Curcls.Cls_Loader; refmthd.Mthd_retType|>

Fig. 5. The invokevirtual instruction

the invoked method are pushed on the top of the operand stack. The subsequent state asserts that a new active record $<|c'; c'.Cls\_mthd; [objref, arg1, arg2, ..., argn]$ $:: lvar'; 0; [[]] |>$ is created after the state transition. Where c' is the class in which the invoked method is selected; *objref* is the object reference (*this* object in the Java programming language).

The first line of hypotheses asserts the current instruction of the method *Curmthd* is *invokevirtual*; where function $PC : METHOD \rightarrow num \rightarrow INSTRUC$-*TION* is to return the current instruction pointed by the program counter. According to the specification, the invoke of instruction *invokevirtual* is composed of the following processes:

– Method resolution. The named method is resolved by term $(E', <|stack; hp;$ $lcc; llc|>) MR (E', <|stack; hp'; lcc'; llc'|>)$. Where *MR* is the transition relation of method resolution. E' defines the context of method resolution.
– Method selection. This is a process to determine whether there exists method overridden in class declaration. Therefore, let C be the class type of *objref*, the actual method to be invoked is selected by term $mthd\_RESOLUTION$ (*objcls objref*) *refmthd lcc'* = c', which can be summarized as follows:
  • If C contains a declaration for an instance method with the same name and descriptor as the resolved method, and the resolved method is accessible from C, then this is the method to be invoked, and the lookup procedure terminates.
  • Otherwise, if C has a superclass, this same lookup procedure is performed recursively using the direct superclass of C; the method to be invoked is the result of the recursive invocation of this lookup procedure.
– Invoke the selected method.

In the relation, term *subtc* (*objcls objref*) (*querylcc lcc' Curcls.Cls_Loader refcn*).*LCC_Class lcc'* is a type-safety condition. Let's examine three arguments of the predicate *subtc*. The first argument (*objcls objref*) computes the Class object *C* of the receiver *objref*. The second argument (*querylcc lcc' Curcls.Cls_Loader refcn*).*LCC_Class* computes the Class object B denoted by *refcn*. The third argument lcc' represents the *LCC* list that has been updated by the method resolution *MR* . Intuitively, this term requires that Class object C of the receiver should be the subclass of B. To understand the motivation of the condition, let's give an example: if there is a statement *obj.test()* in a Java program, then the type system requires that the run-time type of *obj* should be the subclass of the type of *obj* declared in the program. Since the class loading introduces run-time namespaces, we use *subtc* to express such requirement.

According to the JVM specification, if $<C, L>$ overrides a method T_0 method $(T_1, T_2, ..., T_n)$ declared in $<B, L'>$, then a set of constraints $T_0^L = T_0^{L'}, ..., T_n^L$ $= T_n^{L'}$ should be added to the *LLC* list. Term *cond* is to ensure this requirement. Predicate *override* : $METHOD \rightarrow METHOD \rightarrow bool$ determines whether one method can override another by their method descriptors. *wf_constraint lcc' llc"* checks the consistency between the *LCC* list and the *LLC* list. t is the constraint added to *LLC* list.

querylcc : $Loader \rightarrow CLASSNAME \rightarrow LCC$ returns a record with a specified loader and a class name in the *LCC* list.

(2) Class loading

There are two types of loaders: user-defined loaders and the bootstrap loader supplied by the virtual machine. When the virtual machine starts up, the bootstrap loader is first used to load classes. Although both types of loaders are formalized in our model, the relation *LOAD* in figure 6 only defines the class loading by user-defined loaders. Relation *LOAD* contains multiple loaders.

The class loading relation *LOAD* specifies the process of class loading as follows:

L = E.ENV_CLS.Cls_Loader
N = E.ENV_CN
¬ (EXISTS (eqln L N) lcc)
cond1 ∧ cond2 ∧ cond3 ∧ cond4

(E,<|stack; hp; lcc; llc|>) LOAD (E,<|stack; hp; <|L; N; C|>::lcc"; llc|>)

where
cond1 = PC(prev_m',pc') = invokevirtual (refcn',m') ∧
      m'.Mthd_Name = defineClass ∧
      prev_m'.Mthd_Name = loadClass ∧
      ¬ (EXISTS (eqln L N) lcc) ∧
      (<|C'; prev_m'; prev_lv'; prev_pc'; [N, L'] :: prev_os' |> :: stack; hp; lcc; llc|>
      →<|<|Class; m'; [L', N] :: lv; 0; [[]]|> ::
      <|C'; prev_m'; prev_lv'; prev_pc'+1; prev_os'|> :: stack; hp; lcc; llc|>)
cond2 = PC(m',pc) = areturn ∧
      C.Cls_Loader = L' ∧
      (<|<|Class; m'; lv'; pc; [C] :: os|> ::
      <|C'; prev_m'; prev_lv'; prev_pc'+1; prev_os' |> :: stack; hp; lcc'; llc|> →
      <|<|C'; prev_m'; prev_lv'; prev_pc'+1; [C] :: prev_os'|> :: stack; hp; lcc"; llc|>) ∧
      wf_constraint lcc" llc
cond3 = PC(m",pc") = areturn ∧
      m".Mthd_Name = loadClass ∧
      prev_C" = E.ENV_CLS ∧
      (<|<|C"; m"; lv"; pc"; [C] :: os"|> ::
      <|prev_C"; prev_m"; prev_lv"; prev_pc"; prev_os" |> :: stack; hp; lcc'; llc|> →
      <|<|prev_C"; prev_m"; prev_lv"; prev_pc"; [C] :: prev_os"|> ::
      stack; hp; <|L; N; C|> :: lcc"; llc|>) ∧
      wf_constraint (<|L; N; C|> :: lcc") llc
cond4 = (E'.ENV_CLS = C)
      (E'.ENV_CN = C.Cls_SuperName)
      (E',<|stack; hp; lcc; llc|>) CR (E',<| stack; hp; lcc'; llc|>))
lcc"   = <|L'; N; C|> :: lcc'

Fig. 6. The class loading relation

- Term ¬ *(EXISTS (eqlcn L N) lcc)* in the relation is used to maintain the temporal namespace consistency. It requires *L* not been recorded as an initiating loader of a class denoted by *N* in the virtual machine. In other words, it requires *N* not been loaded by *L*. Otherwise, no class loading is necessary.
- Intuitively, when there are class loading delegations in a program, there exists a *loadClass* method invocation nest which can be written as *loadClass(){...; loadClass() {...; defineClass()}}*. According to the JVM specification, however, the soundness of the delegation model is only determined by the last

loadClass invocation because the last *loadClass* invokes the *defineClass* which defines Class objects. Therefore, we can only formalize the first *loadClass* and the last *loadClass* to prove the soundness of the class loading delegation. The delegation process is specified by *cond1*, *cond2* and *cond3*.

- *cond1* specifies the invocation of the *defineClass* by the last *loadClass*. It is a conjunction of five hypotheses. Informally, hypotheses 1 to 3 assert the current method is *loadClass*, the current instruction is *invokevirtual* and it invokes the *defineClass*. Hypothesis 4 ensures that loader L' has not been recorded as an initiating loader of a class denoted by N. Hypothesis 5 specifies the state transition of the invocation.
- *cond2* specifies the invocation return of the *defineClass*. It is a conjunction of four hypotheses. Informally, the first hypothesis asserts the current instruction is *areturn*. Hypotheses 2 and 3 assert a Class object C is created on the top of the operand stack and the defining loader of C is L'. Meanwhile, a record $<L'; N; C>$ is added to the loaded class cache. The fourth hypothesis checks the consistency between the LCC list and the LLC list.
- *cond3* specifies the invocation return of the first *loadClass*. It is a conjunction of five hypotheses. Informally, hypotheses 1 and 2 assert the active record is *loadClass* and the current instruction is *areturn*. The fourth hypothesis asserts a Class object C is returned to the last active record and a record $<L; N; C>$ is added to the loaded class cache. The fifth hypothesis checks the consistency between the LCC list and the LLC list.

- In the process of the invocation of *defineClass*, the virtual machine determines whether C has a direct superclass. If it has, the symbolic reference from C to its direct superclass is resolved using class resolution relation CR. *cond4* defines such process. It is a conjunction of three hypotheses. Hypotheses 1 and 2 define the context of the resolution. Hypothesis 3 asserts a state transition of the class resolution.
- The conclusion of relation $LOAD$ asserts the state transition of class loading.

(3) Method resolution

Resolution is the process of dynamically determining concrete values from symbolic references in the runtime constant pool. Certain Java virtual machine instructions require specific linking checks when resolving symbolic references. For instance, in order for an *invokevirtual* instruction to successfully resolve the symbolic reference to the method on which it operates it must complete the method resolution with relation MR. Method resolution is defined in figure 7.

Intuitively, if a class refers a symbolic method *refmthd* in *refcn*, then the virtual machine resolves the symbolic references by method resolution. In the relation MR, E is the context of method resolution. C is the current class member of the context E. *refcn* and *refmthd* are symbolic references to be resolved. The resolution process is as follows:

C = E.ENV_CLS
refcn = E.ENV_CN
refmthd = E.ENV_MTHD
E'.ENV_CLS = E.ENV_CLS
E'.ENV_CN = E.ENV_CN
(E',<|stack; hp; lcc; llc|>) CR (E',<| stack; hp'; lcc'; llc'|>)
mthd_RESOLUTION cls refmthd lcc' = C'
wf_constraint lcc' llc"

(E,<|stack; hp; lcc; llc|>) MR (E,<| stack; hp'; lcc'; llc"|>)

where
cls = (querylcc lcc' C.Cls_Loader refcn).LCC_Class
llc" = <|C.Cls_Loader; C'.Cls_Loader; refmthd.Mthd_arg|> ::
       <|C.Cls_Loader; C'.Cls_Loader; refmthd.Mthd_retType|> :: llc'

Fig. 7. The method resolution relation

- If *refcn* is unresolved, then term *(E',<|stack; hp; lcc; llc|>) CR (E',<| stack; hp'; lcc'; llc'|>)* resolves the reference first. Terms *E'.ENV_CLS = E.ENV_CLS* and *E'.ENV_CN = E.ENV_CN* defines the context of class resolution.
- Let the Class object of *refcn* is *cls*, which is computed by term *(querylcc lcc' C.Cls_Loader refcn).LCC_Class*; then the virtual machine invokes algorithm *mthd_RESOLUTION* to look up the method *refmthd* in the class *cls* and its superclasses as following processes:
  - If *cls* declares the method, method lookup succeeds.
  - Otherwise, the lookup is recursively invoked on the direct superclass of class *cls*.
- If method lookup succeeds and the referenced method has a form of T_0 method $(T_1, T_2, ..., T_n)$, a set of constraints, $T_0^L = T_0^{L'}, ..., T_n^L = T_n^{L'}$, is added to the *LLC* list. Where $L = C.Cls\_Loder$ and $L' = C'.Cls\_Loader$. Term *llc"* ensures the constraints.
- Predicate *wf_constraint* checks the consistency between the *LCC* list and *LLC* list.

4 Soundness

We have proven the soundness of the model. The main soundness theorem states that a well-typed state can still preserve well-typedness after being rewritten with the relations. For this what a well-typed state means should be defined first.

4.1 Bytecode Verification

One important feature of the language design of Java is the bytecode verification. It guarantees the runtime well-typedness through the static checks, which allows the minimum type checks at run time.

Bytecode verification has a four-pass architecture. Among these passes, the most complicated is the third one which performs dataflow analysis on each method. It is difficult to model this accurately. To make simplifications, we define a function *verify : CLASS → VALUE list → CLASSNAME list* for bytecode verification, which returns the related class name of the object in the context of current class.

4.2   Well-Typed State

Definition 1 (Well-formed Heap) A heap is well-formed iff any object reference *objref* in the heap satisfies all the following conditions:

(1) The Class object of *objref* is in the *LCC* list.

(2) Let *fld* be a field of *objref*, then the value of *fld* is either null or an object reference that satisfies the condition (1) and (2) recursively.

(3) Let the class of *objref* be *C* , *fld* be a field of *objref*, the class name of *fld* be *fntype*, the value of *fld* be *v*, the class of *v* be *V* and the class returned by resolving *fld* in the context of *(objcls objref)* with algorithm *fld_RESOLUTION* be *C'*, then there exists a transitive closure of subtyping relation between *V* and the class which takes defining loader of *C'* as its initiating loader and *fntype* as its class name.

Predicate *wf_hp : VALUE list → LCC list → bool* defines the condition (1) and (2). Predicate *wf_getval_hp : VALUE list → LCC list → bool* defines condition (3). Table look-up function *querycls : LCC list → CLASS → LCC* is to return a record with a specified class in the *LCC* list. Predicate *fnobj : FIELDNAME → CLASSNAME → VALUE → bool* is to decide whether there exists a field in an object reference. *get_objval : VALUE → FIELDNAME → VALUE* is to return the value of a field in an object.

Definition 2 (Well-formed *LCC* List) A *LCC* list is well-formed iff let *C* be a loaded class in the *LCC* list, *L* be the defining loader of *C* and *N* be the class name of *C* , then there exists a record in the *LCC* list with *L* as its initiating loader, *N* as its class name and *C* as its class type.

Intuitively, definition 2 ensures that the virtual machine have recorded the defining loader of each loaded class as its initiating loader.

Definition 3 (Well-formed *LLC* List) A *LLC* list is well-formed iff it is consistent with a *LCC* list.

Definition 4 (Well-formed Stack Frame List) A stack frame list is well-formed iff all the stack frames in the list satisfy the following conditions:

(1) Let *L* be the defining loader of the current class, *objref* be any object reference in the current operand stack list, *C* be the class of *objref* and *N* be the class name computed by the application *verify objref*, then there exists a transitive closure of subtyping relation between class *C* and class *C'* that takes *L* as its initiating loader and *N* as its class name.

(2) Let *L* be the defining loader of the current class, *v* be any object reference in the current local variable list, *C* be the class of *v* and *N* be the class name computed by the application *verify v*, then there exists a transitive closure of subtyping relation between class *C* and class *C'* that takes *L* as its initiating loader and *N* as its class name.

(well-formed heap)
wfm_hp hp lcc = wf_hp hp lcc ∧ wf_getval_hp hp lcc;
wf_hp hp lcc =
Vobj fn fntype.
  (EXISTS (eq_wfsetvalhp obj) hp) ⊃ ((¬ (querycls lcc (objcls obj) = CNULL)) ∧
  ((fnobj fn fntype obj)
  ⊃((get_objval obj fn = CNULL) ∨EXISTS (eq_wfsetvalhp (get_objval obj fn)) hp)));
wf_getval_hp hp lcc =
Vobj fn fntype c.
  ((EXISTS (eq_wfsetvalhp obj) hp) ∧
  (fnobj fn fntype obj) ∧
  (c = fld_RESOLUTION (objcls obj) <|Fld_Name:=fn; Fld_Type:=fntype|> lcc))
  ⊃(subtc (objcls (get_objval obj fn)) (querylcc lcc c.Cls_Loader fntype).LCC_Class lcc);

(well-formed LCC list)
wf_lcc lcc =
  Vc. (EXISTS (eqwflcc c) lcc) ⊃ (EXISTS (wf_eqlcc c.Cls_Loader c.Cls_Name c) lcc);

(well-fromed LLC list)
wf_llc llc =Vlcc. wf_constraint lcc llc;

(well-formed stack frame list)
wf_state stk =
  (wt (objclslst (HD stk.STK_os)) (verify stk.STK_cls (HD stk.STK_os))
  stk.STK_cls.Cls_Loader) ∧
  (wt (objclslst (HD stk.STK_lvar)) (verify stk.STK_cls (HD stk.STK_lvar))
  stk.STK_cls.Cls_Loader);

(well-typed state)
wt_PROG_state st =
  (wfm_hp st.PROG_STATE_heap st.PROG_STATE_lcc) ∧
  (wf_lcc st.PROG_STATE_lcc) ∧
  (wf_llc st.PROG_STATE_llc) ∧
  (wf_state (HD st.PROG_STATE_stack));

Fig. 8. The definition of well-typed state

Predicate *wt : CLASS list → CLASSNAME list → LOADER → bool* determines the transitive closure of subtyping relation stated in condition (1) and (2).

Definition 5 (Well-typed State) A state is well-typed iff its heap, *LCC* list, *LLC* list and stack frame list are well-formed.

Figure 8 presents all the definitions in HOL.

4.3   Soundness Theorem

We first discuss some non-trivial lemmas related to the proof of the main theorems in figure 9.

During method invocation, the virtual machine requires that if $<C, L>$ overrides a method T_0 methodname $(T_1, T_2, \ldots, T_n)$ declared in $<C', L'>$, then a set of constraints $T_0^L = T_0^{L'}, \ldots, T_n^L = T_n^{L'}$ should be added to the loading class constraints list. Intuitively, lemma 1 implies that the *invokevirtual* rule can impose such constraints correctly.

The hypotheses of lemma 1 are a conjunction of three formulas. Formula 1 asserts the *invokevirtual* rule holds for states *st1* and *st2*. Formula 2 asserts the current instruction is *invokevirtual*. Formula 3 asserts a Class object *c* can be got by method resolution; where the first argument *(querylcc (st2.PROG_STATE_lcc)*

Lemma 1 (correctness of method invocation)

∀st1 st2 refcn refmthd.

  (∃c. (IVKRule st1 st2) ∧

  (PC (HD (st1.PROG_STATE_stack)).STK_mthd (HD (st1.PROG_STATE_stack)).STK_pc =

    invokevirtual (refcn,refmthd)) ∧

  (mthd_RESOLUTION

    (querylcc (st2.PROG_STATE_lcc) (HD (st1.PROG_STATE_stack)).STK_cls.Cls_Loader

    refcn).LCC_Class refmthd (st2.PROG_STATE_lcc) = c)⊃

  (EXISTS (eqlcc <|LLC_L1:=(HD (st1.PROG_STATE_stack)).STK_cls.Cls_Loader;

    LLC_L2:=c.Cls_Loader; LLC_classname:=refmthd.Mthd_arg|>) st2.PROG_STATE_llc));

Lemma 2 (uniqueness of subtyping hierarchy)

∀c1 c2 c3 lcc. (sub c1 c2 lcc) ∧ (sub c1 c3 lcc) ⊃ (c2 = c3);

Lemma 3 (transitivity of field resolution)

∀c1 c2 lcc c fld.

  (subtc c1 c2 lcc) ∧ (fld_RESOLUTION c2 fld lcc = c) ⊃ (fld_RESOLUTION c1 fld lcc = c);

Fig. 9. Some lemmas related to the soundness

(HD (st1.PROG_STATE_stack)).STK_cls.Cls_Loader refcn).LCC_Class computes the Class object denoted by *refcn* that is loaded by the defining loader of the current class of state *st1*. Intuitively, formula 3 resolves the method *refmthd* declared in *refcn*. The conclusion of the lemma asserts there exists a constraint *<L, L', N>* in the *LLC* list of state *st2*; where *L* is the defining loader of the current class in state *st1* and *L'* is the defining loader of the class *c* got by the method resolution. Relation *IVKRule : PROG_STATE → PROG_STATE → bool* defines the state transition of the instruction *invokevirtual*. The proof requires lemmas of the structure of *invokevirtual* rule and method resolution relation, as well as the definition of loading class constraints.

Lemma 2 asserts if *c1* is the subclass of *c2* and *c1* is the subclass of *c3* also, then *c2* equals *c3*, which implies the uniqueness of subclass hierarchy in the loaded class cache list. The proof is mainly by induction on the definition of predicate *sub* and the structure of relations of class loading.

Lemma 3 asserts if there is a transitive closure of subtyping relation between *c1* and *c2*, then resolving field *fld* from *c2* can get the same result as that from *c1*. That is, there exists some transitivity between *c1* and *c2* in the field resolution. The proof requires lemma 2 and the induction on the definition of recursive function *fld_RESOLUTION*.

Theorem (Soundness) A well-typed state will still be well-typed if rewritten with the relations defined in the model.

The soundness theorem implies a well-typed program can preserve type safety in the model. The proof of the theorem is lengthy. It is a case analysis on all the relations. On the top level there are 13 cases, where

- Six cases can be directly solved by induction on the structure of the relations.
- The proof of relation *invokevirtual* requires not only the lemmas on the structure of relation *invokevirtual* and the definition of *mthd_RESOLUTION*, *override* and *wt*, but also lemma 1 and related lemmas of other relations.
- The proof of *areturn* requires some lemmas of rule *invokevirtual* and the induction on the structure of rule *areturn*, as well as the definition of well-formed stack frame list.

- The proof of *getfield* can be mainly solved by lemma 3, the lemma of *getfield* and the definition of field resolution.
- The proof of *putfield* requires not only lemma 3 and lemmas of field resolution but also the lemma of the structure of *putfield* and the definition of well-formed heap.
- The proof of other rules is similar to the above rules.

5   Related Work

Saraswat [17] first published the type spoofing problem and proposed two solutions to it. Dean [4] has discussed the problem of type safety in class loaders from a theoretical perspective. He presents a model of dynamic linking that is closely related to Java prove the soundness in PVS. Drossopoulou [5] proposes an abstract model for dynamic linking and verification in Java. Their account is useful for reasoning about Java source language and their model does not yet treat multiple loaders. Jensen [7] gives a formal specification of the dynamic loading of classes in the Java Virtual Machine and of the visibility of members of the loaded classes. However, they define loading and linking abstractly. Moreover, there exist inaccuracies in [7].

Tozawa [19] proposes a formalization of JVM, which is enough to analyze the loading constraint scheme of Java. Tozawa takes an environment to define the operational semantics of loading and only formalize the invokevirtual and areturn instructions. Moreover, Tozawa does not model loaded class cache explicitly.

Qian [16] proposes a state transition system to describe the loading in the JVM and proves its soundness. The basic differences between theirs and ours are: first, we construct and check our model in HOL. Second, the specification of some important transitions, such as *invokevirtual* and *LOAD*, are totally different. For example, Qian does not consider the method overriding in the *invokevirtual* instruction and defining loader in class loading. Also, Qian does not consider the delegation of class loading. Third, since our model is totally different from theirs, the proof of soundness is totally different from theirs.

Fong et al. [6] propose a proof linking architecture to uncouple bytecode verification, class loading, and linking. They only consider a single class loader.

Liu et al. [11] present a virtual machine simulator which is implemented in a functional subset of Common Lisp. One important feature is their simulator can model dynamic class loading, class initialization and synchronization via monitors. Another striking feature is that the simulator can be treated as a set of formulas in the ACL2 specification language and reasoned about mechanically. However, their model does not simulate multiple loaders. Therefore, there is no run-time multiple namespaces in their model. In essence, their model of class loading is much simpler than the official specification.

Qian [15] presents a static type system for a large fragment of Java bytecode language. To make simplifications, he just assumes all classes are loaded by a single class loader. Pusch [14] follows Qian's work [15] and formalize the specification of the JVM in the Isabelle/HOL.

Nipkow and Klein have done lots of work on bytecode verification. They propose an abstract framework for bytecode verification, which can be instantiated to yield executable verified bytecode verifiers [12, 8, 10]. Klein et al. [9] has proved correct a compiler for Java from source to bytecode language in Isabelle, and has also shown that all well-typed programs of the source language are accepted by the bytecode verifier. Nipkow and Oheimb [13, 20] also formalize the Java language in the Isabelle/HOL. Their proposals are useful for the reasoning of the Java source language. All these work does not consider multiple loaders.

There are also lots of researches on the verification of Java Card [8, 3, 2, 1]. Nipkow and Klein [8], using the Isabelle/HOL, formalize and prove the soundness and completeness of lightweight bytecode verification used in the KVM, one of Sun's embedded variants of the JVM. Barthe et al. [3, 2] formalize the JavaCard virtual machine and the bytecode verification in Coq system. Barthe et al. [1] also describe a package to reason about complex recursive functions in Coq. They also illustrate how to apply the package to the reasoning of the Java Card platform.

6   Conclusion

We propose a model for the Java virtual machine. Our model includes the main features of the Java class loading and linking. Comparing with the prior work, our proposal considers multiple loaders and the concrete implementation of the class loading and linking. We show how the notion of class loaders is related to the Java security model. Therefore, our model is precise enough to specify and reason about class loading formally and most closed to the official specification. To ensure the correctness of the model, we formalize it in the HOL system. The theory files sums up to more than 2300 lines. To our knowledge, there is no such research that formalizes JVM class loading in a theorem prover. The machine-assisted proof eliminates the omissions and inaccuracies, such as type errors and inconsistencies, in the formalizations. The power of automated reasoning in the prover is also of great help. Moreover, the expressiveness of higher order logic makes the model more concise.

We are also working on integrating bytecode verification in our model. Although there is lots of work on the bytecode verification, almost all of them focus on the verification algorithm due to Gosling and Yellin [18]. Also, all the previous work does not consider multiple loaders during bytecode verification. For Java, a most striking feature is that the verification of type soundness is carried out at four different time: compiling, loading, linking and run time. The notion of class loader plays a critical role in Java 2 security model,which relies on name spaces to ensure that an untrusted applet cannot interfere with other Java programs. Therefore, integrating loading, linking and bytecode verification in a unified model and prove the type soundness is a major challenge for the future research.

References

1. G. Barthe and P. Courtieu. A formal correspondence between offensive and defensive javacard virtual machines. In V. Carreno, C. Munoz, and S. Tahar, editors, *Proc. TPHOLs'02*, volume 2410 of *Lecture Notes in Computer Science*, pages 31–46. Springer-Verlag, 2002.
2. G. Barthe, G. Dufay, L. Jakubiec, S. M. Sousa, and B. P. Serpette. A formal executable semantics of the javacard platform. In D. Sands, editor, *Proc. ESOP'01*, volume 2028 of *Lecture Notes in Computer Science*, pages 302–319. Springer-Verlag, 2001.
3. G. Barthe, G. Dufay, L. Jakubiec, S. M. Sousa, and B. P. Serpette. A formal correspondence between offensive and defensive javacard virtual machines. In A. Cortesi, editor, *Proc. VMCAI'02*, volume 2294 of *Lecture Notes in Computer Science*, pages 32–45. Springer-Verlag, 2002.
4. D. Dean. The security of static typing with dynamic linking. In *Fourth ACM Conference on Computer and Communication Security*, 1997.
5. S. Drossopoulou. Towards an abstract model of java dynamic linking and verification. In R. Harper, editor, *TIC'00 - Third Workshop on Types in Compilation (Selected Papers)*, volume 2071 of *Lecture Notes in Computer Science*, pages 53–84. Springer, 2001.
6. P. W. L. Fong and R. D. Cameron. Proof linking: Modular verification of mobile programs in the presence of lazy, dynamic linking. *ACM Transactions on Software Engineering and Methodology*, 9(4):379–409, October 2000.
7. T. Jensen, D. Le Metayer, and T. Thorn. Security and dynamic loading in java: A formalisation. In *Proceedings of the 1998 IEEE International Conference on Computer Languages*, volume 2618, pages 4–15, Chicago, Illinois, May 1998.
8. G. Klein. *Verified Java bytecode verification*. PhD thesis, Technische Universitat Munchen, 2003.
9. G. Klein and M. Strecker. Verified bytecode verification and typecertifying compilation. *Journal of Logic Programming*, 2002.
10. G. Klein and M. Wildmoser. Verified bytecode subroutines. *Journal of Automated Reasoning, Special Issue on Bytecode Verification*, 2003.
11. H. Liu and J. S. Moore. Executable jvm model for analytical reasoning: a study. In *Proceedings of the 2003 workshop on Interpreters, Virtual Machines and Emulators*, pages 15 – 23, San Diego, California, 2003.
12. T. Nipkow. Verified bytecode verifiers. In F. Honsell, editor, *Foundations of Software Science and Computation Structures (FOSSACS'01)*, volume 2030 of *Lecture Notes in Computer Science*, pages 347–363. Springer-Verlag, 2001.
13. T. Nipkow, D. von Oheimb, and C. Pusch. μjava: Embedding a programming language in a theorem prover. In F.L. Bauer and R. Steinbruggen, editors, *Foundations of Secure Computation*, pages 117–144. IOS Press, 2000.
14. C. Pusch. Proving the soundness of a java bytecode verifier specification in isabelle/hol. In W.R. Cleaveland, editor, *Tools and Algorithms for the Construction and Analysis of Systems (TACAS'99)*, volume 1579 of *Lecture Notes in Computer Science*, pages 89–103. Springer-Verlag, 1999.
15. Z. Qian. A formal specification of java virtual machine instructions for objects, methods and subroutines. In J. Alves-Foss, editor, *Formal Syntax and Semantics of Java*, volume 1523 of *Lecture Notes in Computer Science*, pages 271–311. Springer-Verlag, 1999.

16. Z. Qian, A. Goldberg, and A. Coglio. A formal specification of javatm class loading. In *OOPSLA' 2000*, November 2000.
17. V. Saraswat. Java is not type-safe. Technical report, AT&T Rresearch, 1997.
18. T.Lindholm and F.Yellin. *The Java^{TM} Virtual Machine Specification - 2nd edition.* Addison-wesley, 1999.
19. A. Tozawa and M. Hagiya. *New fomalizaion of the JVM*, 1999. http://nicosia.is.s.u.-tokyo.ac.jp/members/miles papers/cl-99.ps.
20. D. von Oheimb. *Analyzing Java in Isabelle/HOL: Formalization, Type Safety and Hoare Logic.* PhD thesis, Technische Universitat Munchen, 2001.

Certifying Machine Code Safety: Shallow Versus Deep Embedding

Martin Wildmoser and Tobias Nipkow

Technische Universität München, Institut für Informatik
{wildmosm,nipkow}@in.tum.de

Abstract. We formalise a simple assembly language with procedures and a safety policy for arithmetic overflow in Isabelle/HOL. To verify individual programs we use a *safety logic*. Such a logic can be realised in Isabelle/HOL either as shallow or deep embedding. In a shallow embedding logical formulas are written as HOL predicates, whereas a deep embedding models formulas as a datatype. This paper presents and discusses both variants pointing out their specific strengths and weaknesses.

1 Introduction

Proof Carrying Code (PCC), first proposed by Necula and Lee [14, 15], is a scheme for executing untrusted code safely. It works without cryptography and without a trusted third party. Instead, it places the burden on showing safety on the code producer, who is obliged to annotate a program and construct a certificate that it adheres to an agreed upon safety policy. The code consumer merely has to check if the certificate – a machine-checkable proof – is correct. This check involves two steps: A verification condition generator (VCG) reduces the annotated program to a verification condition (VC), a logical formula that is provable only if the program is safe at runtime. Then a proof checker ensures that the certificate is a valid proof for the VC. If both VCG and proof checker work correctly, this scheme is tamper proof. If either the program, its annotations or the certificate are modified by an attacker, they won't fit or, if they still do, the resulting program would also be safe. Proof Checkers are relatively small standard components and well researched. The VCG is a different story. In early PCC systems it is large (23000 lines of C in [8]) and complex. The formulas it produces are usually influenced by the machine language, the safety policy and the safety logic. The machine language determines syntax and semantics of programs. These are considered safe if they satisfy the conditions the safety policy demands. The safety logic can serve multiple purposes. First, it provides a formal description language for machine states, which can be use to write annotations or to specify a safety policy. Second, it is used to express and prove verification conditions.

For some safety policies, such as checking that all instructions are used on proper arguments (type safety), a type system could play the role of the safety logic. VCG and proof checking could be replaced by automatic type inference. A typical example is Java Bytecode Verification, which is formally verified by now

K. Slind et al. (Eds.): TPHOLs 2004, LNCS 3223, pp. 305–320, 2004.

[12]. To handle more complex properties, for example checking that programs operate within their granted memory range (memory safety), type systems can be combined with a logic or extended to a logic like system [10,13,7]. Foundational proof carrying code tries prove safety directly in terms of the machine semantics [2,3], without a VCG or safety logic as an extra layer.

Our approach uses a VCG, but keeps it small and generic. We model this VCG as part of an Isabelle/HOL framework for PCC, which can be instantiated to various machine languages, safety policies and safety logics. The machine checked soundness proof we have for this VCG automatically carries over to the instantiations. One only has to show that the instantiation meets the requirements our framework makes explicit. None of these requirements touches the safety policy, which in turn can be replaced without disturbing any proof at all. In addition Isabelle/HOL supports the whole range of code producer and consumer activities. We can generate ML code [5] for our VCG and use Isabelle/HOL to produce and check proof objects for verification conditions [6].

By now we have instantiated various non trivial safety policies, such as constraints on runtime or memory consumption, and verified various example programs, including recursive procedures and pointer arithmetics [1]. In this paper we instantiate a simple assembly language (SAL) with a safety policy that prevents type errors and arithmetic overflows. Both are kept rather simple. This paper focuses on the safety logic, which can be embedded in Isabelle/HOL [16] either in shallow or deep style. In the first one models safety logic formulas as HOL predicates on states. The safety logic automatically inherits the infrastructure of the theorem prover such as its type system and tools for simplifying or deciding formulas. In the second one models formulas as a datatype and defines functions to evaluate or transform them. We discuss both variants and point out their specific strengths and weaknesses.

2   Execution Platform

Our simple assembly language (SAL) is a down sized version of TAL [13], which additionally has indirect jumps, multiple argument passing modes and an explicit distinction between registers and heap addresses. Since we are primarily interested in the safety logic and policy, we rather keep the programming language simple. However, with pointers and procedures SAL already includes major pitfalls of machine languages. We consider programs as safe if all instruction arguments have proper type and do not cause arithmetical overflows. Note that the latter involves reasoning about runtime values and demands an expressive annotation language. A simple type system does not suffice, because it can only express what types the results of an instruction or procedure have, not the relation between input and output values.

2.1   SAL Platform

In SAL we distinguish two kinds of addresses. Locations, which we model as natural numbers, identify memory cells, whereas positions identify places in a program. We denote positions as pairs (pn,i), where i is the relative position inside a procedure named pn.

types $loc = nat$, $pname = nat$, $pos = pname \times nat$

SAL has instructions for arithmetics, pointers, jumps and procedures.

datatype $instr$ = $SET\ loc\ nat$ | $ADD\ loc\ loc$ | $SUB\ loc\ loc$ | $MOV\ loc\ loc$ | $JMPL\ loc\ loc\ nat$ | $JMPB\ nat$ | $CALL\ loc\ pname$ | $RET\ loc$ | $HALT$

These instructions, which we explain in §2.2, manipulate states of the form (p,m,e), where p denotes the program counter, m the memory and e the environment.

types $state = pos \times (loc \Rightarrow tval) \times env$

The program counter p is the position of the instruction that is executed next. The main memory m, which maps locations to typed values, stores all the data a program works on. We distinguish three kinds of values: Uninitialised values $ILLEGAL$, natural numbers $NAT\ n$, and positions $POS\ (pn,i)$.

datatype $tval$ = $ILLEGAL$ | $NAT\ nat$ | $POS\ pos$

The environment e tracks useful information about the run of a program. It is a record with two fields cs and h and equally named selector functions. To update a field x in a record r with an expression E we write $r(\!|x{:}{=}E|\!)$.

record env = $cs :: (nat \times (loc \Rightarrow tval))\ list$
$\qquad\qquad\quad h :: pos\ list$

An environment e contains a call stack $cs\ e$, which lists the times and memory contents under which currently active procedures have been called, and a history $h\ e$, which traces the values of program counters. We use the environment like a history variable in Hoare Logic. It is not necessary for machine execution but valuable for reasoning about execution. We can describe states by relating them to former states or refer to system resources, e.g., the length of $h\ e$ is a time measure.

$OD = [$
$(0,[\ \{A_0\}\ SET\ B\ b_0,$
$\quad\ \{A_1\}\ SET\ C\ c_0,$
$\quad\ \{A_2\}\ CALL\ P\ 1,$
$\quad\ \{A_3\}\ ADD\ B\ C,$
$\quad\ \{A_4\}\ HALT\ ]),$

$(1,[\ \{A_5\}\ SET\ M\ MAX,$
$\quad\ \{A_6\}\ SUB\ M\ C,$
$\quad\ \{A_7\}\ JMPL\ B\ M\ 2,$
$\quad\ \{A_8\}\ SET\ C\ 0,$
$\quad\ \{A_9\}\ RET\ P\ ])]$

Fig. 1. Sample Code

A program is a list of procedures, which consist of a name $pname$ and a list of possibly annotated instructions. With $'a\ option$ we model partiality in Isabelle/HOL, a logic of total functions. It injects the new element $None$ into a given type $'a$.

$'a\ option = None$ | $Some\ 'a$.

types
$proc = pname \times ((instr \times (form\ option))\ list)$
$prog = proc\ list$

For example Fig. 1 shows a program that safely credits the balance B of a smart card purse. A procedure checks whether $B + C$ exceeds MAX. If it does it set C to 0 thus preventing an overflow of the following ADD instruction. For better readability we write $\{A\}$ ins to denote an instruction/annotation pair $(ins, Some\ A)$. Annotations are formulas in the safety logic and have type $form$. To access instructions we write $cmd\ \Pi\ p$, which gives us $Some\ ins$ if a program Π has an instruction *ins* at p, or *None* otherwise. For example in Fig. 1 we get *cmd OD* $(0,2)$ = *Some* $(CALL\ P\ 1)$.

2.2 Program Semantics

To formalise the effects of SAL instructions, we use the transition relation *effS*.

$$effS\ \Pi\ =\ \{((p,m,e),(p',m',e'))\ |\ step\ \Pi\ (p,m,e)\ =\ Some\ (p',m',e')\ \}$$

For this small step semantics we use *step* Π (p,m,e), which yields *Some* (p',m',e') if the instruction at p yields the successor state (p',m',e'). For example *ADD X Y* updates X with $(m\ X)\ulcorner+\urcorner(m\ Y)$, which is *NAT* $(x+y)$ if $m\ X=NAT\ x$ and $m\ Y=NAT\ y$ and *ILLEGAL* otherwise. Here $+$ is addition on naturals (no overflow) and $\ulcorner\ \urcorner$ lifts operators from natural numbers to typed values. Like all instructions *ADD* also extends the history $h\ e$. We formalise this using $\mapsto$ for function update and @ for list concatenation:

$cmd\ \Pi\ (pn,i)\ =\ Some\ (ADD\ X\ Y)\ \longrightarrow\ step\ \Pi\ ((pn,i),m,e)\ =$
$Some\ ((pn,i+1),m(X\mapsto m\ X\ \ulcorner+\urcorner\ m\ Y),e(\!|h:=h\ e@[(pn,i)]|\!))$

The transitions of *SUB X Y*, which subtracts two numbers, and *SET X n*, which intialises X with *NAT* n are similar; just replace $\ulcorner+\urcorner$ with $\ulcorner-\urcorner$ or change the update to $m(X\mapsto NAT\ n)$. The backwards jump *JMPB t* jumps t instructions backwards. The conditional jump *JMPL X Y t* expects numbers at X and Y. If the first number is less than the second it jumps t instructions forward, otherwise just one.

$cmd\ \Pi\ (pn,i)\ =\ Some\ (JMPB\ t)\ \longrightarrow$
$step\ \Pi\ ((pn,i),m,e)\ =\ Some\ ((pn,i-t),m,e(\!|h:=h\ e@[(pn,i)]|\!))$

$cmd\ \Pi\ (pn,i)\ =\ Some\ (JMPL\ X\ Y\ t)\ \wedge\ m\ X\ =\ NAT\ x\ \wedge\ m\ Y\ =\ NAT\ y\ \longrightarrow$
$step\ \Pi\ ((pn,i),m,e)\ =\ Some\ ((pn,i+if\ x<y\ then\ t\ else\ 1),m,e(\!|h:=h\ e@[(pn,i)]|\!))$

The procedure call *CALL X pn* pushes the time (length of $h\ e$) and the current memory onto the call stack, leaves the return position in X and jumps into procedure *pn*. The procedure return *RET X* pops the topmost entry from the call stack and jumps to the return position it expects in X.

$cmd\ \Pi\ (pn,i)\ =\ Some\ (CALL\ X\ pn')\ \longrightarrow\ step\ \Pi\ ((pn,i),m,e)\ =\ Some$
$((pn',0),m(X\mapsto POS\ (pn,i+1)),e(\!|cs:=[(length\ (h\ e),m)]@cs\ e,\ h:=h\ e@[(pn,i)]|\!))$

$cmd\ \Pi\ (pn,i)\ =\ Some\ (RET\ X)\ \wedge\ m\ X=POS\ r\ \longrightarrow$
$step\ \Pi\ ((pn,i),m,e)\ =\ Some\ (r,m,e(\!|cs:=tl\ (cs\ e);\ h:=h\ e@[(pn,i)]|\!))$

The move operation *MOV X Y* interprets the values at X and Y as locations x and y; it copies the value at x to y.

$cmd\ \Pi\ (pn,i)\ =\ MOV\ X\ Y\ \wedge\ m\ X=NAT\ x\ \wedge\ m\ Y=NAT\ y\ \longrightarrow$
$step\ ((pn,i),m,e)\ =\ ((pn,i+1),\ m(y\mapsto(m\ x)),e(\!|h:=(h\ e)@(pn,i)|\!))$

Finally, for *HALT* or in case the premises above do not hold *step* returns *None*, i.e. $cmd\ \Pi\ p\ =\ Some\ HALT\ \longrightarrow\ step\ \Pi\ (p,m,e)\ =\ None$.

2.3   Safety Logic and Policy

To notate and prove safety properties of programs formally we use a so called safety logic. The essential constituents of this logic are connectives for implication $\Longrightarrow$ and conjunction $\bigwedge$ and judgements for provability $\vdash$ and validity $\models$.

$$\bigwedge :: 'form\ list \Rightarrow 'form \qquad\qquad \vdash :: prog \Rightarrow 'form \Rightarrow bool$$
$$\Longrightarrow :: 'form \Rightarrow 'form \Rightarrow 'form \quad \models :: state \Rightarrow 'form \Rightarrow bool$$

At this point we do not specify the syntax of formulas. This will be done later by instantiating *'form* in a deep and shallow style. However, we assume that the formula language is expressive enough to characterise initial and safe states of programs. That is, we assume that one can define functions $initF :: prog \Rightarrow 'form$, which specifies initial states, and $safeF :: prog \Rightarrow pos \Rightarrow 'form$, which yields local safety formulas. Together $initF$ and $safeF$ comprise a so called safety policy. A program is safe if all states (p,m,e) we can reach from an initial state (p_0,m_0,e_0) are safe.

$$isSafe\ \Pi = (\forall\, p_0\ m_0\ e_0\ p\ m\ e.\ (p_0,m_0,e_0) \models initF\ \Pi\ \wedge$$
$$((p_0,m_0,e_0),(p,m,e)) \in (effS\ \Pi)^* \longrightarrow (p,m,e) \models safeF\ \Pi\ p)$$

In this paper we instantiate $initF$ such that it only holds for states (p,m,e) where the program counter p is $(0,0)$, the memory is uninitialised $\forall x.\ m\ x = ILLEGAL$, the history is empty $h\ e = []$ and the call stack has one entry $cs\ e = [(0,m)]$ containing a copy of the initial memory m. The safety formula for a position p, i.e. $safeF\ \Pi\ p$, will be constructed such that it guarantees safe execution of the instruction at p. In our case this means all arguments have proper types and numerical results this instruction yields are equal or below some maximum number MAX. In other words: the instruction is type safe and does not cause an overflow. For example if we have $ADD\ X\ Y$ at program position p, the formula $safeF\ \Pi\ p$ demands that variables X and Y have values $NAT\ x$ and $NAT\ y$ such that $x + y \leq MAX$.

2.4   Verification Condition Generation

Equipped with $\bigwedge$, $\Longrightarrow$, $initF$ and $safeF$ we can define a generic VCG, which transforms a given well formed program into a formula, the verification condition VC, that is provable only if the program is safe. The VCG soundness theorem below expresses this formally:

$vcg :: prog \Rightarrow 'form$ **theorem:** $wf\ \Pi \wedge \Pi \vdash vcg\ \Pi \longrightarrow isSafe\ \Pi$

The wellformedness judgement wf demands that every instruction is annotated and that the main procedure has no RET instructions. In our project [1] we usually work with a VCG that also accepts programs where only targets of backward jumps, entry and exit positions of procedures are annotated. However, in this paper we focus on the safety logic and rather keep the VCG simple.

$vcg\ \Pi = \bigwedge [initF\ \Pi \Longrightarrow \bigwedge [safeF\ \Pi\ (ipc\ \Pi),\ anF\ \Pi\ (ipc\ \Pi)]]@$
$(map\ (\lambda\ p.\ (map(\lambda\ (p',B).\ \bigwedge [safeF\ \Pi\ p,\ anF\ \Pi\ p,\ B] \Longrightarrow$
$(wpF\ \Pi\ p\ p'\ (\bigwedge [safeF\ \Pi\ p',\ anF\ \Pi\ p'])))$
$(succsF\ \Pi\ p))$
$(domC\ \Pi)))$

In addition to the instruction and annotation fetch operations cmd and anF this VCG uses various other auxiliary functions. With $succsF\ \Pi\ p$ it computes the list of all immediate successors p' of a position p paired with a branch condition B. This branch condition is expected to hold whenever p' is accessible from p at runtime. For example assume Π has at position $p=(pn,i)$ an instruction that jumps t instructions forward if some condition C holds, or 1 otherwise. Then we expect $succsF\ \Pi\ p$ to yield two successor positions $(pn,i+t)$ and $(pn,i+1)$ with C or its negation as branch conditions, i.e. $succsF\ \Pi\ (pn,i)$ $= [((pn,i+1),C),((pn,i+1),\neg C)]$. The function wpF is named after Dijkstra's operator for weakest preconditions. It takes a postcondition Q and constructs a formula $wpF\ \Pi\ p\ p'\ Q$, that covers exactly those states where the program Π can make a transition from p to p' such that Q holds when we reach p'.

The verification condition is a big conjunction. There is one initial conjunct and one conjunct for each position in the code domain $domC\ \Pi$, which lists the positions of all instructions in Π. Hence, the overall size of the VC is linear to the program size. The initial conjunct demands that initial states are safe and satisfy the initial annotation $anF\ \Pi\ (ipc\ \Pi)$ where $ipc\ \Pi$ denotes the initial program counter $((0,0)$ in our case). The conjunct we get for each position p in the code domain demands that a state (p,m,e) that is safe and satisfies the annotation at p only has successor states (p',m',e') that satisfy the safety formula and annotation at p'. For example if a position p annotated with A only has one successor p' with branch condition B and annotation A' we get this conjunct inside the VC:

$\bigwedge [safeF\ \Pi\ p,\ A,\ B] \Longrightarrow wpF\ \Pi\ p\ p'\ (\bigwedge [safeF\ \Pi\ p',\ A'])$

So far we have not defined any of the auxiliary functions nor the safety logic and policy. The VCG above is generic. By instantiating the parameter functions one can use it for various PCC platforms. We have proven that the soundness theorem above holds, if these parameter functions meet some basic requirements. The $succsF$ function has to approximate the control flow graph of a program. It can yield spurious successors, but must not forget some or yield invalid branch conditions.

assumption $succsFcomplete$:
$wf\ \Pi \wedge (p,m,e) \in safe_\square\ \Pi \wedge ((p,m,e),(p',m',e'))\in effS\ \Pi \longrightarrow$
$\exists B.\ (p',B) \in set\ (succsF\ \Pi\ p) \wedge (p,m,e) \models B$

This must only hold for all states in the safety closure $safe_\square\ \Pi$, the set of states that can can occur in a safe execution of Π. These are the initial states and states that are reachable from these by only traversing states that are safe and satisfy their annotation.

$(p,m,e) \models initF \ \Pi \longrightarrow (p,m,e) \in safe_\square \ \Pi$

$(p,m,e) \in safe_\square \ \Pi \wedge ((p,m,e),(p',m',e')) \in effS \ \Pi \ \wedge$
$(p,m,e) \models safeF \ \Pi \ p \wedge (p,m,e) \models anF \ \Pi \ p \ \wedge$
$(p',m',e') \models safeF \ \Pi \ p' \wedge (p',m',e') \models anF \ \Pi \ p' \longrightarrow (p',m',e') \in safe_\square \ \Pi$

The wpF operator has to be compatible with the semantics of SAL. That is, the formula it yields must guarantee the postcondition in the successor state.

assumption *correctWpF*:
$wf \ \Pi \wedge (p,m,e) \in safe_\square \ \Pi \wedge ((p,m,e),(p',m',e')) \in effS \ \Pi \ \wedge$
$(p,m,e) \models (wpF \ \Pi \ p \ p' \ Q) \longrightarrow (p',m',e') \models Q$

Another requirement is the correctness of the safety logic. That is, provable formulas must be valid for all states in $safe_\square \ \Pi$.

assumption *correctSafetyLogic*:
$wf \ \Pi \wedge \Pi \vdash F \longrightarrow \forall s \in safe_\square \ \Pi. \ s \models F$

Finally, we require that the logical connectives have their ordinary semantics and that *initF* is consistent with *ipc*.

assumptions
$s \models (A \Longrightarrow B) \longrightarrow s \models A \longrightarrow s \models B$
$s \models \bigwedge Fs = \forall F \in set \ Fs. \ s \models F$
$(p,m,e) \models initF \ \Pi \longrightarrow ipc \ \Pi = p$

Note that these requirements are kept very weak in order to allow for a wide range of instantiations. With $safe_\square \ \Pi$ in the premises verifying these requirements becomes simpler; one only has to consider states originating from a safe execution. A lot of properties, for example the wellformedness of the call stack, can be deduced from this fact.

3 Shallow Embedding

3.1 Syntax

In a shallow embedding logical formulas are written directly in the logic of the theorem prover. In our case this means SAL formulas become Isabelle/HOL predicates on states.

type *form* = *state* $\Rightarrow$ *bool*

We can write arbitrary Isabelle functions from *state* to *bool* and use them to describe machine states. Typically we do this using λ notation. For example $\lambda(p,m,e). \ m \ X = NAT \ 1$ covers all states having the value *NAT 1* at memory location X. Since we have machine states with enviroments, we can also describe states by relating them to former states. For example $\lambda(p,m,e). \ m \ X = (\overline{m} \ e) \ X$ holds for states, where location X contains the same value as it did at call time of the current procedure. Here we use the shortcut $\overline{m} \ e$ for the memory at calltime, which we can retrieve from the environment e, i.e. $\overline{m} \ e = snd \ (hd \ (cs \ e))$. In a similar fashion we can reconstruct the program counter or the environment at call time, i.e $\overline{p} \ e = (h \ e)!k$ and $\overline{e} \ e = e(\!| cs := tl \ (cs \ e); \ h := take \ k \ (h \ e) |\!)$ where $k = fst \ (hd \ (cs \ e))$. The following formulas give some flavour on the style of a shallow embedded formula language. They could be used to annotate the example program OD. The function $incA$ increments the offset of a position, i.e. $incA\ (pn,i) = (pn,i+1)$.

$A_0 = \lambda(p,m,e).\ True,\quad A_1 = \lambda\ (p,m,e).\ m\ B = NAT\ b_0,$
$A_2 = \bigwedge\ [A_1, \lambda(p,m,e).\ m\ C = NAT\ c_0],\quad A_3 = \bigwedge\ [A_1,$
$\lambda(p,m,e).\ \exists c.\ m\ C = NAT\ c \wedge (c < 0 \longrightarrow (c = c_0 \wedge b_0 + c_0 \leq MAX))]$
$A_4 = \lambda(p,m,e).\ True$
$A_{5a} = \lambda(p,m,e).\ m\ P = POS\ (incA\ \overleftarrow{p}\ e) \wedge \exists b.\ m\ B = NAT\ b \wedge \exists c.\ m\ C = NAT\ c$
$A_5 = \bigwedge\ [A_{5a}, \lambda(p,m,e).\ \forall x.\ x \neq P \longrightarrow m\ x = \overleftarrow{m}\ e\ x]$
$A_{6a} = \lambda(p,m,e).\ \forall x.\ x \neq P \wedge x \neq M \longrightarrow m\ x = \overleftarrow{m}\ e\ x$
$A_6 = \bigwedge\ [A_{5a}, A_{6a}, \lambda(p,m,e).\ m\ M = NAT\ MAX]$
$A_7 = \bigwedge\ [A_{5a}, A_{6a}, \lambda(p,m,e).\ \exists c.\ m\ C = NAT\ c \wedge m\ M = NAT\ (MAX - c)]$
$A_8 = \bigwedge\ [A_7, \lambda(p,m,e).\ \exists b\ n.\ m\ B = NAT\ b \wedge m\ M = NAT\ n \wedge n \leq b]$
$A_9 = \lambda(p,m,e).\ (\forall x.\ x \neq C \wedge x \neq M \wedge x \neq P \longrightarrow m\ x = \overleftarrow{m}\ e\ x) \wedge$
$\qquad\qquad (\exists b\ c\ c'.\ m\ B = NAT\ b\ \wedge m\ C = NAT\ c \wedge \overleftarrow{m}\ e\ C = NAT\ c' \wedge$
$\qquad\qquad (c \neq 0 \longrightarrow (c = c' \wedge b + c' \leq MAX)))\}$

3.2   Validity

In the shallow embedding we define validity of formulas simply by application.
$(p,m,e) \models Q \equiv Q\ (p,m,e)$

3.3   Provability

The provability judgement $\vdash$ of a logic is usally defined with derivation rules. However, since we write formulas as HOL predicates, we can use Isabelle/HOL's built in derivation rules as proof calculus. We consider a formula F provable if it is valid for all states in $safe_\square$: $\varPi \vdash F \equiv \forall s.\ s \in safe_\square\ \varPi \longrightarrow s \models F$

3.4   Weakest Precondition

The predicate, which $wpF\ \varPi\ p\ p'\ Q$ yields, computes the successor state for the transition from p to p' in program $\varPi$ and applies the postcondition Q to it. For ADD, $CALL$ and MOV, we define wpF as follows. The remaining instructions are analogous.

$wpF\ \varPi\ p\ p'\ Q = (case\ cmd\ \varPi\ p\ of\ None \Rightarrow \lambda\ (p,m,e).\ False$
$|\ Some\ a \Rightarrow case\ a\ of\ ...$
$|\ ADD\ X\ Y \Rightarrow \lambda(p,m,e).\ Q\ (p',m(X \mapsto (m\ X)\ulcorner\dotplus\urcorner(m\ Y)),e(h:=(h\ e)@[p]))$
$|\ CALL\ X\ pn \Rightarrow \lambda(p,m,e).\ Q\ (p',m(X \mapsto POS\ (pn,0)),e(h:=(h\ e)@[p]))$
$|\ MOV\ X\ Y \Rightarrow \lambda(p,m,e).\ (case\ m\ X\ of\ ILLEGAL \Rightarrow False\ |\ POS\ r \Rightarrow False\ |$
$\qquad\qquad NAT\ x \Rightarrow (case\ m\ Y\ of\ ILLEGAL \Rightarrow False\ |\ POS\ r' \Rightarrow False\ |$
$\qquad\qquad NAT\ y \Rightarrow Q(p',m(y \mapsto m\ x),e(h:=(h\ e)@[p])))) ...$

3.5   Code Generation

Isabelle can generate ML programs out of executable Isabelle/HOL definitions [4]. However, for *wpF* this code generator does not produce the kind of ML program we want. Due to our shallow embedding the code generator also turns safety logic formulas into ML programs. Instead we would like them to be handled as terms of type *state* $\Rightarrow$ *bool*. A way out is to enhance the code generator by a quotation/antiquotation mechanism. We can introduce functions *term* and *toterm*:: $'a \Rightarrow 'a$ that are identities for Isabelle's inference system. For the code generator these functions serve as markers: When it generates code for an Isabelle term and steps into a *term* quotation it treats the following input term as output of the currently generated ML program. If inside this mode a *toterm* antiquotation appears, it switches back to normal mode. For example, consider the following two Isabelle definitions:

$$f = \lambda\, n.\ n + n + n, \qquad g = \lambda\, n.\ term\ (toterm\ n + (toterm\ (n + n)))$$

When applied to operand *5* the ML program we get for *f* would return the integer *15*, whereas the one for *g* would return the term *5 + 10*. Using this mechanism we are able to generate an executable VCG from the definitions in Isabelle.

4   Deep Embedding

4.1   Syntax

In a deep embedding we represent logical formulas as a datatype. At leaf positions we have expressions.

datatype *expr* = *V nat* | *Lv nat* | ⌞*tval*⌟ | *Pc* | *Rp* | *Tm* |
         expr ⌞+⌟ *expr* | *expr* ⌞−⌟ *expr* | *expr* ⌞∗⌟ *expr* |
         ⌞if⌟ *expr* ⌞=⌟ *expr* ⌞then⌟ *expr* ⌞else⌟ *expr* | *Deref expr* | *Old expr*

Following Winskel [17] we distinguish two kinds of variables. Program variables *V 1*, *V 2*, ... denote values we find at specific locations in memory. For example *V 1* stands for the value we find at location *1* in memory. Apart from these we have logical variables *Lv 1*, *Lv 2*, ..., which stand for arbitrary values that do not depend on the state of a program. Quantification will be defined later on only for logical variables. Since these are not affected by machine instructions we will not have to bother about them when we define the *wpF* Operator later on. Apart from variables we have constants ⌞*NAT 2*⌟, ⌞*POS (0,1)*⌟, ⌞*ILLEGAL*⌟, ... and special identifiers for the current program counter *Pc*, the return position of the current procedure *Rp* and the system time *Tm*. These primitives can be combined via arithmetical operators and conditionals. To support pointers, we have the *Deref E* expression. It yields the value we find at address *a*, provided *E* evaluates to *NAT a*. Finally, we have a call state expression *Old E*, which interprets an expression *E* in the call state of the current procedure. This enables one to describe states by relating them to former states.

datatype *form* = $True$ | $False$ | $\bigwedge$ *form list* | *form* $\Longrightarrow$ *form* | $\neg$ *form* |
expr $\rightleftharpoons$ *expr* | *expr* $\leqslant$ *expr*| *expr* $\lesssim$ *expr* | *expr* $::$ *vtype* | $\bigvee$ *nat form*

Formulas are either the boolean constants $True$ and $False$, conjunctions $\bigwedge$
$[A,B,\dots]$, implications $A \Longrightarrow B$ or negations $\neg A$. In addition we have relational
formulas $E \rightleftharpoons E'$, $E \leqslant E'$ or $E \lesssim E'$ and a type checking formula $E :: T$, where
T can either be *Pos* for *POS* or *Nat* for *NAT*.

datatype *vtype* = *Pos* | *Nat*

Finally, we can quantify over logical variables. In $\bigvee v\ F$ all free occurences of
$Lv\ v$ in F are bound and F is expected. Below we have the annotations for our
example program, written in this new style.

$A_0 = True,\quad A_1 = V B \rightleftharpoons NAT\ b_0,\quad A_2 = \bigwedge [A_1, V C \rightleftharpoons NAT\ c_0]$
$A_3 = \bigwedge [A_1, V C :: Nat, NAT\ 0 \leqslant V C \Longrightarrow$
$\qquad\qquad \bigwedge [V B \dotplus V C \leqslant NAT\ MAX, V C \rightleftharpoons NAT\ c_0]$
$A_4 = True,\quad A_{5a} = \bigwedge [V P \rightleftharpoons Rp, V B :: Nat, V C :: Nat]$
$A_{5b} = \bigvee x\ \neg (Lv\ x \rightleftharpoons NAT\ P) \Longrightarrow Deref\ (Lv\ x) \rightleftharpoons Old\ (Deref\ (Lv\ x))$
$A_5 = \bigwedge [A_{5a}, A_{5b}],\quad A_{6a} = \bigvee x \bigwedge [\neg (Lv\ x \rightleftharpoons NAT\ P),$
$\neg (Lv\ x \rightleftharpoons NAT\ M)] \Longrightarrow Deref\ (Lv\ x) \rightleftharpoons Old\ (Deref\ (Lv\ x))$
$A_6 = \bigwedge [A_{5a}, A_{6a}, V M \rightleftharpoons NAT\ MAX]$
$A_7 = \bigwedge [A_{5a}, A_{6a}, V M \rightleftharpoons NAT\ MAX, \neg V C], A_8 = A_7$
$A_9 = \bigwedge [A_{5a}, \bigvee x \bigwedge [\neg (Lv\ x \rightleftharpoons NAT\ P), \neg (Lv\ x \rightleftharpoons NAT\ M,$
$\neg (Lv\ x) \rightleftharpoons NAT\ C)] \Longrightarrow Deref\ (Lv\ x) \rightleftharpoons Old\ (Deref\ (Lv\ x)),$
$\neg (V C \rightleftharpoons NAT\ 0) \Longrightarrow \bigwedge [V C \rightleftharpoons Old\ (V C), V B \dotplus V C \leqslant NAT\ MAX]]$

4.2   Validity

We use *eval*::$(nat \Rightarrow tval) \Rightarrow state \Rightarrow expr \Rightarrow tval$ to evaluate expressions on
a given state and interpretation for logical variables. Program variables stand
for memory locations, logical variables are interpreted via L and constants are
directly converted to values.

$eval\ L\ (p,m,e)\ (V\ v) = m\ v,\quad eval\ L\ s\ (Lv\ v) = L\ v,\quad eval\ L\ s\ ty = tv$

The identifer Pc stands for the program counter, Tm for the system time (number of executed instructions), and Rp for the return position of the current
procedure. It evaluates to $POS\ (0,0)$ if we are in the main procedure or to
$ILLEGAL$ in case of a malformed call stack.

$eval\ (p,m,e)\ Pc = POS\ p \qquad eval\ (p,m,e)\ Tm = NAT\ (length\ (h\ e))$
$eval\ (p,m,e)\ Rp = (case\ length\ (cs\ e)\ of\ 0 \Rightarrow ILLEGAL$
$|\ Suc\ n \Rightarrow (case\ n\ of\ 0 \Rightarrow POS\ (0,0)\ |\ Suc\ n' \Rightarrow POS\ (incA\ (\overleftarrow{p}\ e))))$

Arithmetical expressions and conditionals are evaluated recursively.

$eval\ L\ s\ (E \dotplus E')= (eval\ L\ s\ E) \overset{\ulcorner\urcorner}{+} (eval\ L\ s\ E')$

The cases for $\neg$ and $*$ are analogous.

$eval\ L\ s\ (if\ E_0 \rightleftharpoons E_1\ then\ E_2\ else\ E_3) =$
$if\ (eval\ L\ s\ E_0 = eval\ L\ s\ E_1)\ then\ eval\ L\ s\ E_2\ else\ eval\ L\ s\ E_3$

With $Deref\ E$ we fetch the value at position a, provided E evaluates to $NAT\ a$.

$eval\ L\ (p,m,e)\ (Deref\ E) = (case\ (eval\ L\ (p,m,e)\ E)$
$of\ ILLEGAL \Rightarrow ILLEGAL \mid POS\ r \Rightarrow ILLEGAL \mid NAT\ a \Rightarrow m\ a)$

Finally, we evaluate $Old\ E$ by retrieving the call state from the environment.

$eval\ L\ (p,m,e)\ (Old\ E) = eval\ L\ (\overleftarrow{p}\ e, \overleftarrow{m}\ e, \overleftarrow{e}\ e)\ E$

Next, we define the validity of formulas relative to states and interpretations.

$L,s \models True, \quad \neg\ L,s \models False, \quad L,s \models \bigwedge\ Fs = (\forall F \in set\ Fs.\ L,s \models F)$
$L,s \models F \Longrightarrow F' = (L,s \models F \longrightarrow L,s \models F') \quad L,s \models \Box F = \neg\ (L,s \models F)$
$L,s \models E \rightleftharpoons E' = (eval\ L\ s\ E = eval\ L\ s\ E')$
$L,s \models E \therefore T = (case\ (eval\ L\ s\ E)$
$of\ ILLEGAL \Rightarrow False \mid POS\ p \Rightarrow T{=}Pos \mid NAT\ n \Rightarrow T{=}Nat)$
$L,s \models E \leqslant E' = (case\ (eval\ L\ s\ E)\ of\ ILLEGAL \Rightarrow False \mid POS\ r \Rightarrow False \mid$
$NAT\ x \Rightarrow (case\ (eval\ L\ s\ E')\ of\ ILLEGAL \Rightarrow False \mid POS\ r' \Rightarrow False \mid$
$NAT\ y \Rightarrow x \leq y))$

The case for $\leqslant$ is analogous to $\leqslant$; just replace $\leq$ with $<$. The meaning of $\bigvee v\ F$ is that F holds irrespective of the interpretation of $Lv\ v$.

$L,s \models \bigvee v\ F = (\forall\ tv.\ L(v \mapsto tv), s \models F)$

4.3 Provability

Provability is defined in a similar manner as for the shallow embedding. A formula is considered provable if it holds for all interpretations and states in $safe_\Box$.

$\Pi \vdash F \equiv \forall L.\ \forall s \in\ safe_\Box\ \Pi.\ L,s \models F$

To show provability of a formula, there are two alternatives. One can either expand the definition of $\vdash$ and work directly with the inference rules of HOL. This makes sense if the code consumer's logic is HOL (something that the shallow embedding requires). On the other hand, if the code consumer's safety logic is more specialised, the deep embedding can still model the precise inference system involved. For example, we have derived suitable introduction and elimination rules for our language of formulas that do not rely on λ calculus and HOL. However, proving with deep embedded inference rules inside Isabelle/HOL turned out to be inconvenient. The proof tools are designed to prove HOL formulae not elements of a datatype. In addition the $\bigvee$ elimination rule causes trouble. It says that from $\bigvee v\ F$ we can deduce $F[t/v]$, which is F with all free occurrences of $Lv\ v$ replaced by some term t. We need a form of substitution that renames bounded logical variables in F when they occur as free variables in t. This renaming complicates the correctness proof and turned out to double the size of our deep embedding theories. Nevertheless defining and verifying deep embedded inference rules inside Isabelle/HOL pays off if one wants to use specialised tools for proof search and checking. Since Isabelle is generic one can also think about instantiating the safety logic as a new object logic.

4.4 Weakest Precondition

A big difference between our shallow and deep embedding lies in the definition of the wpF operator. In the deep embedding we express the effects of instructions at the level of formulas with substitutions. For these we use finite maps, which we internally represent as lists of pairs, e.g. $fm = [(1,1),(2,4),(3,5),(3,6)]$. Finite maps enable us to generate executable ML code for map operations like lookup $\text{-}\downarrow\text{-}::\ 'a \vartriangleright 'b \Rightarrow 'a \Rightarrow 'b\ option$, domain $dom:: ('a \vartriangleright 'b) \Rightarrow 'a\ list$ or range $ran:: ('a \vartriangleright 'b) \Rightarrow 'b\ list$. A few examples demonstrate how these operators work $fm{\downarrow}0 = None$, $fm{\downarrow}3 = Some\ 5$, $dom\ fm = [1,2,3]$ and $ran\ fm = [1,4,5]$. Note that a pair (x,y) is overwritten by a pair (x,y') to the left of it. For ADD, $CALL$ and MOV, we define wpF as follows. The remaining instructions are analogous.

$wpF\ \Pi\ p\ p'\ Q = (case\ cmd\ \Pi\ p)\ of\ None \Rightarrow \lfloor False \rfloor\ |\ Some\ a \Rightarrow case\ a\ of\ ...$
$|\ ADD\ X\ Y \Rightarrow substF\ [(Tm,\ Tm \overset{+}{\sqcup} \lfloor NAT\ 1 \rfloor),(Pc,\lfloor POS\ p' \rfloor),$
$\qquad\qquad (V\ X,\ V\ X \overset{+}{\sqcup} V\ Y)]\ Q$
$|\ CALL\ X\ pn \Rightarrow popCs\ (substF\ [(Tm,Tm \overset{+}{\sqcup} \lfloor NAT\ 1 \rfloor),(Rp,\lfloor POS\ (pn,i+1) \rfloor),$
$\qquad\qquad (Pc,\lfloor POS\ p' \rfloor),(V\ X,\lfloor POS\ (pn,i+1) \rfloor)]\ Q)$
$|\ MOV\ X\ Y \Rightarrow substPtF\ X\ Y\ [(Tm,Tm \overset{+}{\sqcup} \lfloor NAT\ 1 \rfloor),(Pc,\lfloor POS\ p' \rfloor)]\ Q\ ...$

The substitution function $substF:: (expr \vartriangleright expr) \Rightarrow form \Rightarrow form$ is the main workhorse for the deep embedding. With $substF\ em\ F$ we simultaneously substitute expressions of the form $V\ v$, Tm, Pc or Rp in a formula F according to a finite map em. It traverses F and applies $substE\ em\ E$ on all expressions it finds.

$substF\ em\ \lfloor True \rfloor = \lfloor True \rfloor \qquad substF\ em\ \lfloor False \rfloor = \lfloor False \rfloor$
$substF\ em\ (\bigwedge Fs) = \bigwedge (map\ (substF\ em)\ Fs)$
$substF\ em\ (F_1 \Longrightarrow F_2) = (substF\ em\ F_1) \Longrightarrow (substF\ em\ F_2)$
$substF\ em\ (\neg F) = \neg (substF\ em\ F)$
$substF\ em\ (E \mathbin{::} T) = (substE\ em\ E) \mathbin{::} T$
$substF\ em\ (\forall v\ F) = \forall v\ (substF\ em\ F)$

Expressions of the form $Lv\ v$ or $\lfloor ty \rfloor$ are ignored by $substE$, because they are not affected by instructions. Here Winskel's [17] distinction of program and logical variables pays off. In wpF only program variables appear in the expressions we substitute in. Hence, we do not have to rename bound (=logical) variables. However, a substitution with renaming is useful when one wants to define deep embedded inference rules (see §4.3). For the remaining primitive expressions $substE$ looks up the expression map and replaces them with their substitute in case there is some. Otherwise $substE$ just recurses down the expression structure.

$E=Lv\ v \lor E=\lfloor ty \rfloor \longrightarrow substE\ em\ E = E$

$E=V\ v \lor E\in\{Pc,Rp,Tm\} \longrightarrow$
$substE\ em\ E = (case\ em{\downarrow}E\ of\ None \Rightarrow E\ |\ Some\ E' \Rightarrow E')$

$o\in\{\overset{+}{\sqcup},\neg,*\} \longrightarrow substE\ em\ (E_1\ o\ E_2) = (substE\ em\ E_1)\ o\ (substE\ em\ E_2)$

$substE\ em\ (if\ E_1 \leftrightarrows E_2\ then\ E_3\ else\ E_4) = if\ (substE\ em\ E_1) \leftrightarrows (substE\ em\ E_2)\ then\ (substE\ em\ E_3)\ else\ (substE\ em\ E_4)$

In case of $Deref\ E$, we have to check, whether E evaluates to $NAT\ v$ where v is the location of a variable $V\ v$ that is substituted by em to some expression E'. In this case the $Deref\ E$ expression needs to be substituted as well. Since the evaluation of E depends on the state we cannot do this statically. A way out is to replace $Deref\ E$ by another expression that incorporates this check, e.g. $if\ E'' \leftrightharpoons NAT\ y\ then\ E'\ else\ E''$ where $E'' = substE\ em\ E$ and $em \downarrow E = Some\ E'$. This check needs to be done for all variables in the domain of em; we fetch them with the auxiliary function $changedvars$.

$$v \in set\ (changedvars\ em) = (\exists\ E'.\ em \downarrow (V\ v) = Some\ E')$$

$$substE\ em\ (Deref\ E) = (let\ E'' = substE\ em\ E;$$
$$res = (foldl\ (\lambda E'.\ (v,E').\ (if\ E'' \leftrightharpoons NAT\ y\ then\ E'\ else\ E''))$$
$$(Deref\ E'')\ (changedvars\ em))\ in\ res)$$

In this definition we use the HOL function $foldl$ wich calls its input function recursively over a list of arguments.

$$foldl\ f\ a\ [] = a \qquad foldl\ f\ a\ (x\#xs) = foldl\ f\ (f\ a\ x)\ xs$$

Since we use $substE$ only to express the effects of instructions on the current state, it ceases to play a role when we come to an expression that refers to another state. Hence, $substE$ terminates when it reaches an Old expression.

$$substE\ em\ (Old\ E) = Old\ E$$

To express the effect of pointer instructions, e.g. $MOV\ X\ Y$, we use the special substitution function $substPtF:: nat \Rightarrow nat \Rightarrow (expr \triangleright expr) \Rightarrow form \Rightarrow form$. It works exactly like $substF$ except that it calls $substPtE:: nat \Rightarrow nat \Rightarrow (expr \triangleright expr) \Rightarrow expr \Rightarrow expr$, when it encounters an expression. The function $substPtE$ is a variant of $substE$ that does additional transformations for variables and $Deref$ expressions. When we execute $MOV\ X\ Y$ it could be that the target location $NAT\ v$ stored in Y coincides with a variable $V\ v$ in an expression. In this case the value of $V\ v$ after the $MOV\ X\ Y$ instruction becomes the value at the location we find in X. To express this effect we can replace $V\ v$ with a conditional expression.

$$substPtE\ X\ Y\ em\ (V\ v) =$$
$$if\ V\ Y \leftrightharpoons NAT\ y\ then\ Deref\ (V\ X)\ else\ (substE\ em\ (V\ v)).$$

For $Deref\ E$ expressions the same technique can be applied.

$$substPtE\ X\ Y\ em\ (Deref\ E) = let\ E'' = substPtE\ X\ Y\ em\ E;\ res = \ldots$$
$$in\ (if\ V\ Y \leftrightharpoons E''\ then\ Deref\ (V\ X)\ else\ res)$$

Finally, we need special formula manipulations for procedure calls and returns. Remember that $CALL$ pushes the current state (call state) onto the call stack. With $popCs$ the wpF function reverses this effect. After the call a new procedure is active and expressions of the form $Old\ E$ have a different meaning. The expression $Old\ E$ evaluated after the call yields the same value as E does before (because $(\bar{p}\ e', \bar{m}\ e',\ \bar{e}\ e') = (p,m,e)$ when $e' = (cs := ((length\ (h\ e),m)\#(cs\ e));\ h := (h\ e)@[p])$. To ensure validity of some formula Q after the call $popCs$ Q replaces occurrences of $Old\ E$ in Q with E. For RET we do the opposite; we replace $Old\ (Old\ E)$ with $Old\ E$.

5   Comparison

Expressiveness

In our shallow embedding we use predicates in HOL as assertion language. These are more expressive than the deep embedded first order formulas. One can quantify over functions, use expressions of any type and has direct and unrestricted access to the state. For example we verified list reversal [1] in our shallow embedding, but we found it difficult to do this example in the deep embedding, which does not offer expressions for lists. However, this shortcoming could be overcome by utilizing a richer assertion language.

Proof Size

Shallow and deep embedding differ in the definition of wpF; one uses λ abstraction, the other substitutions. This difference affects verification conditions and their proofs. For example for the transition from $(0,2)$ to $(1,0)$ in our example program we get these formulas:

$$VC_s = \bigwedge [\lambda(p,m,e).\,True, \lambda(p,m,e).m\ B{=}NAT\ b_0 \wedge m\ C{=}NAT\ c_0, \lambda(p,m,e).\,True]$$
$$\Longrightarrow (\lambda(p,m,e).\bigwedge[\lambda(p,m,e).MAX{\leq}MAX, \lambda(p,m,e).m\ P{=}POS\ (incA\ \bar{p}\ e)\,\wedge$$
$$\exists b.m\ B{=}NAT\ b \wedge \exists c.m\ C{=}NAT\ c \wedge \forall x.\ x{\neq}P \longrightarrow m\ x{=}\bar{m}\ e\ x]$$
$$((0,2),m[P{\mapsto}POS\ (0,3)],e(\!|h{:=}(h\ e)@[(0,2)]; cs{:=}(length\ (h\ e),m)\#(cs\ e)|\!)))$$

$$VC_d = \bigwedge [True, \bigwedge [V\ B{=}NAT\ b_0, V\ C{=}NAT\ c_0], True]$$
$$\Longrightarrow \bigwedge [NAT\ MAX{\leqslant}NAT\ MAX, POS\ (0,3){=}POS\ (0,3), V\ B\ ::\ Nat,$$
$$V\ C\ ::\ Nat, \forall x\ \neg(Lv\ x{=}NAT\ P) \Longrightarrow Deref\ (Lv\ x){=}Deref\ (Lv\ x)]$$

In the formula VC_s, which results from the shallow embedding, we have various uncontracted λ terms. This is because the VCG does not simplify; it just plugs annotations and safety formulas into a skeleton of conjunctions and implications determined by the control flow graph. The contraction of these λ terms is done when we prove them in Isabelle. In VC_d, which results from the deep embedding, these simplifications are carried out by the substitution function, which is executed when we run the VCG. Hence, the proof of VC_s involves more simplification steps than the one of VC_d. For example in VC_s we find after β contraction this subformula:

$$m[P{\mapsto}POS\ (0,3)]\ x = \bar{m}\ e(\!|h{:=}(h\ e)@[(0,2)]; cs{:=}(length\ (h\ e),m)\#(cs\ e)|\!)\ x$$

Knowing that $x \neq P$ and the definitions of $\mapsto$, $\bar{m}$ and record updates, we can simplify this to the triviality $m\ x = m\ x$. In VC_d this triviality is already exposed by the wpF operator, which yields $Deref\ (Lv\ x) = Deref\ (Lv\ x)$ in this situation. The VC we get for our example program can be proven automatically in Isabelle using built in decision procedures for Presburger Arithmetics. The latter is required for the formula we get for the transition from $(1,4)$ to $(0,4)$. There we have to show that the Addition operation at $(0,3)$ cannot overflow. The resulting proof object for the shallow embedding is about twice the size as the deep embedding. Other experiments [1] confirm this fact.

Formula Optimisations
Another advantage we get from the deep embedding is that we can write Isabelle/HOL functions that operate on the structure of formulas. This enables us to optimise VCs after/during their construction. Elsewhere [1] we present an optimizer for VCs in the deep embedding. It evaluates constant formulas and subexpressions, for example $NAT\ MAX \leqslant NAT\ MAX$ can be reduced to $True$. In addition it simplifies implications, for example $A \Longrightarrow True$ or $\bigwedge [\ldots,A,\ldots]$ $\Longrightarrow A$, and conjunctions, for example $\bigwedge [\ldots,True,\ldots]$ or $\bigwedge [A, \bigwedge [B,C],D]$. It can also do some trivial deductions, for example $V\ b = NAT\ b_0$ implies $V\ b :: Nat$. These transformations, which can be done in time quadratic to the formula size, suffice to reduce the size of VCs and their proofs considerably. For example VC_d can be reduced to $True$. Although these optimisations do not always trivialise VCs, experiments [1] show that leads to proof objects that are about 3 times smaller than they are in the shallow embedding. More could be gained by coupling the optimizer to a proof procedure that performs introduction and elimination rules on our first order formula language.

Annotation Analysis
In the shallow embedding we cannot analyse annotations in the VCG or its helper functions. This is because HOL predicates cannot be structurally analysed by other HOL functions (Isabelle does not support reflection). In the deep embedding the structure of formulas is accessible and can be used to handle more complex machine instructions like computed gotos. We simply demand that the possible targets of such jumps, which are runtime values and therefore hard to determine statically, must be annotated. Then we can define a *succsF* function that reads off the possible successors from the annotation. Since annotations must be verified in the resulting VC this approach is sound.

6   Conclusion

As we expected the deep embedded safety logic was harder to instantiate within our PCC framework than the shallow one. One has to define explicit evaluation and substitution functions and prove them correct. This becomes a non trivial task when variable renamings are involved. In addition one has to deal with subtle effects pointer instructions or procedure calls have on formulas. However, once the deep embedding is proven correct it buys us a lot. We can specify and prove correct an optimiser or pre-prover for VCs and handle more instructions (computed gotos). Homeier [11] also works with a deep embedded assertion language and points out similar advantages. Based on these experiences we instantiated our PCC framework to a down-sized version of the Java Virtual Machine [9] using an extended version of our deep embedded assertion language.

References

1. VeryPCC project:. http://isabelle.in.tum.de/verypcc/, 2003.
2. A. W. Appel. Foundational proof-carrying code. In *16th Annual IEEE Symposium on Logic in Computer Science (LICS '01)*, pages 247–258, June 2001.

3. A. W. Appel and A. P. Felty. A semantic model of types and machine instructions for proof-carrying code. In *27th ACM SIGPLAN-SIGACT Symposium on Principles of Programming Languages (POPL '00)*, pages 243–253, January 2000.

4. S. Berghofer. Program extraction in simply-typed higher order logic. In H. Geuvers and F. Wiedijk, editors, *Types for Proofs and Programs, International Workshop, (TYPES 2002)*, Lect. Notes in Comp. Sci. Springer-Verlag, 2003.

5. S. Berghofer and T. Nipkow. Executing higher order logic. In P. Callaghan, Z. Luo, J. McKinna, and R. Pollack, editors, *Types for Proofs and Programs, International Workshop, (TYPES 2000)*, Lect. Notes in Comp. Sci. Springer-Verlag, 2000.

6. S. Berghofer and T. Nipkow. Proof terms for simply typed higher order logic. In J. Harrison and M. Aagaard, editors, *Theorem Proving in Higher Order Logics*, volume 1869 of *Lect. Notes in Comp. Sci.*, pages 38–52. Springer-Verlag, 2000.

7. J. Chen, D. Wu, A. W. Appel, and H. Fang. A provably sound tal for back-end optimization. In *Programming Languages Design and Implementation (PLDI)*. ACM Sigplan, 2003.

8. C. Colby, P. Lee, G. C. Necula, F. Blau, M. Plesko, and K. Cline. A certifying compiler for Java. In *Proc. ACM SIGPLAN conf. Programming Language Design and Implementation*, pages 95–107, 2000.

9. K. Gerwin and N. Tobias. A machine-checked model for a Java-like language, virtual machine and compiler. Research report, National ICT Australia, Sydney, 2004.

10. N. Hamid, Z. Shao, V. Trifonov, S. Monnier, and Z. Ni. A syntactic approach to foundational proof-carrying code. In *Proc. 17th IEEE Symp. Logic in Computer Science*, pages 89–100, July 2002.

11. P. V. Homeier and D. F. Martin. Secure mechanical verification of mutually recursive procedures. pages 1–19, 2003.

12. G. Klein. *Verified Java Bytecode Verification*. PhD thesis, Institut für Informatik, Technische Universität München, 2003.

13. G. Morrisett, D. Walker, K. Crary, and N. Glew. From system F to typed assembly language. In *Proc. 25th ACM Symp. Principles of Programming Languages*, pages 85–97. ACM Press, 1998.

14. G. C. Necula. Proof-carrying code. In *Proc. 24th ACM Symp. Principles of Programming Languages*, pages 106–119. ACM Press, 1997.

15. G. C. Necula. *Compiling with Proofs*. PhD thesis, Carnegie Mellon University, 1998.

16. T. Nipkow, L. C. Paulson, and M. Wenzel. *Isabelle/HOL – A Proof Assistant for Higher-Order Logic*, volume 2283 of *Lect. Notes in Comp. Sci.* Springer, 2002.

17. G. Winskel. *The Formal Semantics of Programming Languages*. MIT Press, 1993.

Term Algebras with Length Function and Bounded Quantifier Alternation

Ting Zhang, Henny B. Sipma, and Zohar Manna[*]

Computer Science Department
Stanford University
Stanford, CA 94305-9045
{tingz,sipma,zm}@theory.stanford.edu

Abstract. Term algebras have wide applicability in computer science. Unfortunately, the decision problem for term algebras has a nonelementary lower bound, which makes the theory and any extension of it intractable in practice. However, it is often more appropriate to consider the bounded class, in which formulae can have arbitrarily long sequences of quantifiers but the quantifier alternation depth is bounded. In this paper we present new quantifier elimination procedures for the first-order theory of term algebras and for its extension with integer arithmetic. The elimination procedures deal with a block of quantifiers of the same type in one step. We show that for the bounded class of at most k quantifier alternations, regardless of the total number of quantifiers, the complexity of our procedures is k-fold exponential (resp. $2k$ fold exponential) for the theory of term algebras (resp. for the extended theory with integers).

1 Introduction

The theory of term algebras, also known as the theory of finite trees, axiomatizes the Herbrand universe. It has wide applicability in computer science. In programming languages many so-called recursive data structures can be modeled as term algebras [19]; in theorem proving it is essential to the unification and disunification problem [18,3]; in logic programming, it is used to define formal semantics [14]. Other applications can be found in computational linguistics, constraint databases, pattern matching and type theory.

In this paper we consider an arithmetic extension of the theory of term algebras. Our extended language has two sorts; the integer sort $\mathbb{Z}$ and the term sort TA. Intuitively, the language is the set-theoretic union of the language of term algebras and the language of Presburger arithmetic plus the additional length function $(.)^{L} : TA \rightarrow \mathbb{Z}$. Formulae are formed from term literals and integer literals using logical connectives and quantifications. Term literals are exactly those literals in the language of term algebras. Integer literals are those that

---

[*] This research was supported in part by NSF grants CCR-01-21403, CCR-02-20134 and CCR-02-09237, by ARO grant DAAD19-01-1-0723, by ARPA/AF contracts F33615-00-C-1693 and F33615-99-C-3014, and by NAVY/ONR contract N00014-03-1-0939.

K. Slind et al. (Eds.): TPHOLs 2004, LNCS 3223, pp. 321–336, 2004.

can be built up from integer variables (including the length function applied to TA-terms), the usual arithmetic relations and functions. This type of arithmetic extension has been used in [10, 11] to show that the quantifier-free theory of term algebras with Knuth-Bendix order is NP-complete.

Our interest originates from program verification as term algebras can model a wide range of tree-like data structures. Examples include lists, stacks, counters, trees, records and queues. To verify programs containing these data structures we must be able to reason about these data structures. However, in program verification decision procedures for a single theory are usually not applicable as programming languages often involve multiple data domains, resulting in verification conditions that span multiple theories. A common example of such "mixed" constraints are combinations of data structures with integer constraints on the size of those structures. In [24] we gave a quantifier-elimination procedure for this extended theory.

Unfortunately the theory of term algebras has nonelementary time complexity [7, 3, 22], which makes the theory and any extension of it intractable in practice. However, as observed by many [20, 8], in consideration of the complexity of logic theories, the meaning of a formula soon becomes incomprehensible as the number of quantifier alternations increases. In practice we rarely deal with formulae with a large quantifier alternation depth. Therefore it is worthwhile to investigate the class of formulae which can have arbitrarily long sequences of quantifiers of the same kind while the total number of quantifier alternations is bounded by a constant number. We call such formulae **alternation bounded**.

In this paper we present new quantifier elimination procedures for the theory of term algebras as well as the extended theory with integers. Our procedures can eliminate a block of quantifiers of the same kind in one step. For the bounded class of at most k quantifier alternations, regardless of the total number of quantifiers, the complexity is k-fold exponential (resp. $2k$ fold exponential) for the theory of term algebras (resp. for the extended theory with integers).

Related Work and Comparison. Presburger arithmetic (PA) was first shown to be decidable in 1929 by the quantifier elimination method [6]. Efficient algorithms were later discovered by Cooper et al [5, 20]. It was shown in [20] and [8], respectively, that the upper bound and the lower bound of the bounded class in the theory of PA is one exponential lower than the whole theory.

The decidability of the first-order theory of term algebras was first shown by Mal'cev using quantifier elimination [17]. This result was reproved in different settings [16, 3, 9, 2, 1, 21, 13, 12, 24]. The lower bound of any theory of pairing functions was shown to be nonelementary in [7]; this result was strengthened in [4] to a hereditarily nonelementary lower bound. This lower bound complexity applies to the theory of term algebras as term algebras with a binary constructor can express pairing functions. Using techniques in [4], [22] showed that theories of finite trees, infinite and rational trees are all hereditarily nonelementary.

Quantifier elimination has been used to obtain decidability results for various extensions of term algebras. [16] showed the decidability of the theory of infinite and rational trees. [2] presented an elimination procedure for term algebras with membership predicate in the regular tree language. [1] presented an elimination procedure for structures of feature trees with arity constraints. [21] showed the decidability of term algebras with queues. [13] showed the decidability of term powers, which generalize products and term algebras. [24] extended the quantifier elimination procedure in [9] for term algebras with length function.

Traditionally, methods for quantifier elimination for term algebras follow one of two approaches: they either perform transformations in the constructor language [17, 3, 16, 12], or they work in the selector language [9, 21]. In the first approach formulae are reduced to a boolean combination of a specific kind of formulae called "solved forms", which include ordinary literals. In this respect [3] is essentially a dual of [16] with the special formulae being universally quantified. In [12] selectors are used to convert solved forms to quantifier-free formulae. In the second approach, formulae are transformed into a form in which the quantified variable is not embedded in selectors and only occurs in disequalities. Methods following the first approach can deal with a block of quantifiers of the same type in one step. They all rely on the "independence lemma" ([17], page 277, also see Thm. 1 in this paper) which states that "there are enough elements to satisfy a certain set of disequalities and equalities." However, this does not hold in the language with finite signature and length function. Methods following the second approach can only handle a single quantifier at a time.

Our elimination procedures are carried out in the language with both selectors and constructors. The method combines the extraction of integer constraints from term constraints with a reduction of quantifiers on term variables to quantifiers on integer variables.

Paper Organization. Section 2 provides the preliminaries: it introduces the notation and terminology. Section 3 defines term algebras. Section 4 describes a new elimination procedure for the theory of term algebras. Section 5 introduces the theory of term algebras with integer arithmetic and presents the technical machinery for handling the length function. Section 6 presents the main contribution of this paper: it expands the elimination procedure in Section 4 for the extended theory with integers. Section 7 concludes with some ideas for future work. Due to space limitation all proofs have been omitted from this paper. They are available for reference in the extended version of this paper at the first author's website.

2   Preliminaries

We assume the first-order syntactic notions of variables, parameters and quantifiers, and semantic notions of structures, satisfiability and validity as in [6]. We explain concepts and terminology important to this paper as follows.

A signature Σ is a set of parameters (function symbols and predicate symbols) each of which is associated with an arity. The function symbols with arity 0 are also called constants. The set of Σ-terms $\mathcal{T}(\Sigma, X)$ is recursively defined by: (i) every constant $c \in \Sigma$ or variable $x \in X$ is a term, and (ii) if $f \in \Sigma$ is an n-place function symbol and $t_1, \ldots, t_n$ are terms, then $f(t_1, \ldots, t_n)$ is a term. If θ is a formula, we use $\Sigma(\theta)$ to denote the set of terms occurring in θ. The length of a term t, written $\text{len}(t)$, is defined recursively by: (i) for any constant a, $\text{len}(a) = 1$, and (ii) for a term $\alpha(t_1, \ldots, t_k)$, $\text{len}(\alpha(t_1, \ldots, t_k)) = \sum_{i=1}^{k} \text{len}(t_i) + 1$.

An atomic formula (atom) is a formula of the form $P(t_1, \ldots, t_n)$ where P is an n-place predicate symbol and $t_1, \ldots, t_n$ are terms (equality is treated as a binary predicate symbol). A literal is an atomic formula or its negation. A variable occurs free in a formula if it is not in the scope of a quantifier. A formula without quantifiers is called quantifier-free. A ground formula is a formula with no variables. A sentence is a formula in which no variable occurs free. Every quantifier-free formula can be put into disjunctive normal form, that is, a disjunction of conjunctions of literals.

We use x to denote a set of variables, say, $x_1, \ldots, x_n$, and $\exists x$ (resp. $\forall x$) as an abbreviation of $\exists x_1, \ldots, \exists x_n$ (resp. $\forall x_1, \ldots, \forall x_n$). When we write $\theta(x)$, we mean that x occur free in θ. Any formula θ can be put into prenex form $Q_1 x_1, \ldots, Q_n x_n \, \theta(x)$, where Q_i's are either $\exists$ or $\forall$ and $\theta(x)$ is quantifier-free. We call $\theta(x)$ the matrix of θ. We say that θ has quantifier (alternation) depth m if $Q_1, \ldots, Q_n$ can be divided into m blocks such that all quantifiers in a block are of the same type and quantifiers in two consecutive blocks are different.

A Σ-structure (or Σ-interpretation) $\mathfrak{A}$ is a tuple $\langle A, I \rangle$ where A is a non-empty domain and I is a function that associates each n-place function symbol f (resp. predicate symbol P) with an n-place function $f^{\mathfrak{A}}$ (resp. relation $P^{\mathfrak{A}}$) on A. We usually denote $\mathfrak{A}$ by $\langle A; \Sigma \rangle$ which is called the signature of $\mathfrak{A}$.

A variable assignment σ (or variable valuation) is a function that assigns each variable an element of A. We use $[\![x]\!]\sigma$ to denote the assigned values of x under σ. We write $[\![x]\!]$ when σ is clear from the context. The truth value of a formula is determined by an interpretation and a variable assignment.

A formula θ is satisfiable (or consistent) if it is true under some variable assignment; it is unsatisfiable (or inconsistent) otherwise. A formula θ is valid if it is true under every variable assignment. A formula θ is valid if and only if $\neg\theta$ is unsatisfiable.

By a theory of structure $\mathfrak{A}$, written $\text{Th}(\mathfrak{A})$, we shall mean the class of all valid sentences in $\mathfrak{A}$. We use $\text{BC}_k(\mathfrak{A})$ denote the subclass of $\text{Th}(\mathfrak{A})$ in which all sentences have at most k quantifier alternations.

A theory T is said to admit quantifier elimination if any formula can be equivalently (modulo T) and effectively transformed into a quantifier-free formula. If a theory admits quantifier elimination, then every sentence is reducible to a ground formula. Therefore, if ground literals are decidable, then a quantifier elimination procedure becomes a decision procedure.

Presburger arithmetic (PA) is the first-order theory of addition in the arithmetic of integers. The corresponding language and structure are denoted, respectively, by $\mathscr{L}_{\mathbb{Z}}$ and $\mathfrak{A}_{\mathbb{Z}} = \langle \mathbb{Z}; 0, +, < \rangle$.

We define $\exp_0(f(n)) = f(n)$ and $\exp_{m+1}(f(n)) = 2^{\exp_m(f(n))}$.

3 Term Algebras

We present a general language and structure of term algebras. For simplicity, we do not distinguish syntactic terms in the language from semantic terms in the corresponding structure. The meaning should be clear from the context.

Definition 1. *A term algebra* $\mathfrak{A}_{\mathsf{TA}} : \langle \mathsf{TA}; \mathcal{A}, \mathcal{C}, \mathcal{S}, \mathcal{T} \rangle$ *consists of*

1. TA: *The term domain, which consists of all terms built up from constants by applying constructors. Elements in* TA *are called* TA-*terms.*
2. $\mathcal{A}$: *A finite set of constants:* $a, b, c, \ldots$
3. $\mathcal{C}$: *A finite set of constructors:* $\alpha, \beta, \gamma, \ldots$ *The arity of* α *is denoted by* $\mathsf{ar}(\alpha)$. *An object is* α-*typed (or an* α-*term) if its outmost constructor is* α.
4. $\mathcal{S}$: *A finite set of selectors. For a constructor* α *with arity* k, *there are* k *selectors* $\mathsf{s}_1^\alpha, \ldots, \mathsf{s}_k^\alpha$ *in* $\mathcal{S}$. *For a term* x, $\mathsf{s}_i^\alpha(x)$ *returns the* i^{th} *component of* x *if* x *is an* α-*term and* x *itself otherwise.*
5. $\mathcal{T}$: *A finite set of testers. For each constructor* α *there is a corresponding tester* Is_α. *For a term* x, $\mathsf{Is}_\alpha(x)$ *is true if and only if* x *is an* α-*term. In addition there is a special tester* Is_C *such that* $\mathsf{Is}_C(x)$ *is true if and only if* x *is a constant. Note that there is no need for individual constant testers as* $x = a$ *serves as* $\mathsf{Is}_a(x)$.

We denote by $\mathscr{L}_{\mathsf{TA}}$ *the language for* $\mathfrak{A}_{\mathsf{TA}}$.

Unless mentioned otherwise, in this paper we assume that $\mathscr{L}_{\mathsf{TA}}$ is finite. However, the techniques presented here can be modified to handle the case of infinite languages. In particular, the decision problems become considerably easier if we allow $\mathscr{L}_{\mathsf{TA}}$ to have infinitely many constants. We leave the detailed discussion to the extended version of this paper.

The theory of term algebras is axiomatizable as follows [9].

Proposition 1 (Axiomatization of Term Algebras [9]). *Let* z_α *be* $z_1, \ldots, z_{\mathsf{ar}(\alpha)}$. *The following formula schemes, in which variables are implicitly universally quantified over* TA, *axiomatize* $\mathsf{Th}(\mathfrak{A}_{\mathsf{TA}})$.

A. $t(x) \neq x$, *if* t *is built solely by constructors and* t *properly contains* x.
B. $a \neq b$, $a \neq \alpha(x_1 \ldots, x_{\mathsf{ar}(\alpha)})$, *and* $\alpha(x_1 \ldots, x_{\mathsf{ar}(\alpha)}) \neq \beta(y_1, \ldots, y_{\mathsf{ar}(\beta)})$, *if* a *and* b *are distinct constants and if* α *and* β *are distinct constructors.*
C. $\alpha(x_1, \ldots, x_{\mathsf{ar}(\alpha)}) = \alpha(y_1, \ldots, y_{\mathsf{ar}(\alpha)}) \rightarrow \bigwedge_{1 \leq i \leq \mathsf{ar}(\alpha)} x_i = y_i$.
D. $\mathsf{Is}_\alpha(x) \leftrightarrow \exists z_\alpha \alpha(z_\alpha) = x$; $\mathsf{Is}_C(x) \leftrightarrow \bigwedge_{\alpha \in C} \neg \mathsf{Is}_\alpha(x)$.
E. $\mathsf{s}_i^\alpha(x) = y \leftrightarrow (\exists z_\alpha(\alpha(z_\alpha) = x \wedge y = z_i)) \vee (\forall z_\alpha(\alpha(z_\alpha) \neq x) \wedge x = y)$.

In general selectors and testers can be defined by constructors and vice versa. One direction has been shown by (D) and (E), which are pure definitional axioms.

Example 1. Consider the LISP list structure

$$\mathfrak{A}_{\mathsf{list}} = \langle \mathsf{list}; \{\mathsf{nil}\}, \{\mathsf{cons}\}, \{\mathsf{car}, \mathsf{cdr}\}, \{\mathsf{Is}_{\mathsf{cons}}\} \rangle$$

where list denotes the domain, nil denotes the empty list, cons is the 2-place constructor (pairing function) and car and cdr are the corresponding left and right selectors (projectors) respectively. It is not difficult to verify that $\mathfrak{A}_{\text{list}}$ is an instance of term algebras.

We use the notation $\alpha = (\mathsf{s}_1^\alpha, \ldots, \mathsf{s}_k^\alpha)$ to mean that α is a constructor with $\text{ar}(\alpha) = k$ and $\mathsf{s}_1^\alpha, \ldots, \mathsf{s}_k^\alpha$ are the corresponding selectors of α. We call a term t a constructor term (resp. selector term) if the outmost function symbol of t is a constructor (resp. a selector). We assume that no constructor term appears inside selectors as simplification can always be done. For example, $\mathsf{s}_i^\alpha(\alpha(x_1, \ldots, x_k))$ simplifies to x_i ($1 \leq i \leq k$) and $\mathsf{s}_j^\beta(\alpha(x_1, \ldots, x_k))$ simplifies to $\alpha(x_1, \ldots, x_k)$ for $\alpha \not\equiv \beta$. We use $L, M, N, \ldots$ to denote selector sequences. If $L = \mathsf{s}_1, \ldots, \mathsf{s}_n$, Lx is an abbreviation for $\mathsf{s}_1(\ldots(\mathsf{s}_n(x)\ldots))$. We say a selector term $\mathsf{s}_i^\alpha(t)$ is proper if $\text{Is}_\alpha(t)$ holds. We can make selector terms proper with type information.

Definition 2 (Type Completion). *θ' is a type completion of θ if θ' is obtained from θ by adding tester predicates such that for any term $\mathsf{s}(t)$ exactly one literal of the form $\text{Is}_\alpha(t)$ ($\alpha \in C$) or $\text{Is}_C(t)$ is present in θ'.*

Example 2. Let $\alpha = (\mathsf{s}_1^\alpha, \mathsf{s}_2^\alpha)$. A possible type completion for $y = \mathsf{s}_1^\alpha \mathsf{s}_2^\alpha x$ is $y = \mathsf{s}_1^\alpha \mathsf{s}_2^\alpha x \wedge \text{Is}_\alpha(x) \wedge \text{Is}_C(\mathsf{s}_2^\alpha x)$. With this type information we can simplify $y = \mathsf{s}_1^\alpha \mathsf{s}_2^\alpha x$ to $y = \mathsf{s}_2^\alpha x$ by Axioms (D) and (E) in Prop. 1.

4   A New Quantifier Elimination Procedure for Th($\mathfrak{A}_{\text{TA}}$)

In this section we present a new quantifier elimination algorithm for the theory of term algebras and show that the algorithm only needs exponential time to eliminate a block of quantifiers of the same kind. The algorithm works mainly in the constructor language while using selectors as auxiliary tools. The algorithm is also the basis for the elimination procedure for the extended theory presented in Section 6.

Normal Form. It is well-known that eliminating arbitrary quantifiers reduces to eliminating existential quantifiers from formulae in the form

$$\exists x(A_1(x) \wedge \ldots \wedge A_n(x)), \tag{1}$$

where $A_i(x)$ ($1 \leq i \leq n$) are literals [9]. We can also assume that A_i's are not of the form $x = t$ as $\exists x(x = t \wedge \theta(x, y))$ simplifies to $\theta(t, y)$, if x does not occur in t, to $\exists x \theta(x, y)$ if $t \equiv x$, and to false by Axiom (A) if t is a term which is built solely by constructors and properly contains x.

Nondeterminism. In this paper all transformations are done on formulae of the form (1). Whenever we say "guess θ", we mean to add a valid disjunction $\bigvee_i \theta_i$ (where θ is one of the disjuncts) to the matrix of (1). When we replace θ by $\bigvee_i \theta_i$ or directly introduce $\bigvee_i \theta_i$, it should be understood that an implicit disjunctive splitting is carried out and we work on each resultant disjunct in the form (1) "simultaneously".

Simplification. For simplicity, in the description of algorithms, we omit tester literals unless they are needed for correctness proof. We may also assume that the matrix of (1) is type complete and basic simplifications are carried out whenever applicable. For example, for a nonempty selector sequence L, we replace $Lx \neq x$ by true and $Lx = x$ by false. Similarly for $t(x) \neq x$ and $t(x) = x$ where $t(x)$ is a term properly containing x.

Notation. In the algorithm we use the following notation: x denote the set of existentially quantified variables; y denote the set of (implicitly) universally quantified parameters; s, t, u denote TA-terms; G, H denote (possibly empty) selector blocks; f, g, h denote index functions with ranges clear from the context; numerical superscripts are parenthesized. Index functions are used to differentiate multiple occurrences of the same variables.

Note that in each step the algorithm manipulates the formula $\exists x : \theta(x, y)$ to produce a version of the same form (or multiple versions of the same form in case disjunctions are introduced), and thus in each step $\exists x : \theta(x, y)$ refers to the updated version rather than to the original input formula.

Definition 3 (Solved Form). *We say $\theta_{\mathsf{TA}}(x, y)$ is in the solved form (with respect to x), if x are not in equalities, not asserted to be constants and not inside selector terms. We say $\exists x\, \theta_{\mathsf{TA}}(x, y)$ is in the solved form if $\theta_{\mathsf{TA}}(x, y)$ is.*

The elimination goes as follows. A sequence of equivalence-preserving transformations will bring the input formula into a disjunction of formulae in the solved form which have solutions under any instantiation of parameters. Therefore, the whole block of existential quantifiers $\exists x$ can be eliminated by removing all literals containing x in the matrix.

Algorithm 1. *Input:* $\exists x : \theta(x, y)$.

1. *Type Completion. Guess a type completion of $\theta(x, y)$ and simplify every selector term to a proper one.*
2. *Elimination of Selector Terms Containing x. Replace all selector terms containing x by the corresponding equivalent constructor terms according to Axiom (E). For example $s_1^\alpha x = y$ becomes $\exists z_2, \ldots, z_k \alpha(y, z_2, \ldots, z_k) = x$ for $\mathrm{ar}(\alpha) = k$. It may increase the number of existential quantifiers, but leaves parameters unchanged. From now on, x never appear inside selector terms.*
3. *Elimination of Equalities between Constructor Terms. Replace*

$$\alpha(t_1, \ldots, t_i) = \alpha(t'_1, \ldots, t'_i) \tag{2}$$

by $\bigwedge_{1 \leq i \leq k} t_i = t'_i$. Repeat until no equality of the form (2) appears.
4. *Elimination of Disequalities between Constructor Terms. Replace*

$$\alpha(t_1, \ldots, t_i) \neq \alpha(t'_1, \ldots, t'_i) \tag{3}$$

by $\bigvee_{1 \leq i \leq k} t_i \neq t'_i$. Repeat until no equality of the form (3) appears. At this point we may assume that each disjunct (that has not been simplified to false) is in the form

$$\exists x : \left[\bigwedge_i x_{f(i)} \neq t_i(x, y) \wedge \bigwedge_i G_i y_{g(i)} \neq s_i(x, y) \wedge \bigwedge_i H_i y_{h(i)} = u_i(x, y) \right]. \tag{4}$$

5. *Elimination of Equalities Containing x*. *Solve equations of the form $H_i y_{h(i)} = u_i(x, y)$, where $u_i(x, y)$ is a constructor term containing x, in terms of $H_i y_{h(i)}$ such that the result is a set of equations in the selector language. For example, with $\alpha = (s_1^\alpha, s_2^\alpha)$, the solution set of $s_2^\alpha y = \alpha(\alpha(x_1, y_1), y_2)$ is*

$$x_1 = s_1^\alpha s_1^\alpha s_2^\alpha y, \quad y_1 = s_2^\alpha s_1^\alpha s_2^\alpha y, \quad y_2 = s_2^\alpha s_2^\alpha y.$$

Solving $\bigwedge_i H_i y_{h(i)} = u_i(x, y)$ and eliminating all x's occurring in solved equations, we obtain

$$\exists x : \Big[\bigwedge_i x_{f^{(2)}(i)} \neq t_i^{(2)}(x, y) \wedge \bigwedge_i G_i^{(2)} y_{g^{(2)}(i)} \neq s_i^{(2)}(x, y) \wedge$$
$$\bigwedge_i H_i^{(2)} y_{h^{(2)}(i)} = H_i^{(3)} y_{h^{(3)}(i)} \Big]. \quad (5)$$

6. *Elimination of Constants. If for some $x \in x$, $\mathsf{Is_C}(x)$ appears in (5), we instantiate x to each constant to eliminate $\exists x$. We still use (5) to denote the resulting formula.*
7. *Elimination of Quantifiers. Rewrite $\bigwedge_i G_i^{(2)} y_{g^{(2)}(i)} \neq s_i^{(2)}(x, y)$ as*

$$\bigwedge_i G_i^{(3)} y_{g^{(3)}(i)} \neq s_i^{(3)}(x, y) \wedge \bigwedge_i G_i^{(4)} y_{g^{(4)}(i)} \neq s_i^{(4)}(y),$$

where x do not appear in $s_i^{(4)}(y)$. Then (5) can be rewritten as

$$\exists x : \Big[\bigwedge_i x_{f^{(2)}(i)} \neq t_i^{(2)}(x, y) \wedge \bigwedge_i G_i^{(3)} y_{g^{(3)}(i)} \neq s_i^{(3)}(x, y) \Big] \wedge$$
$$\bigwedge_i G_i^{(4)} y_{g^{(4)}(i)} \neq s_i^{(4)}(y) \wedge \bigwedge_i H_i^{(2)} y_{h^{(2)}(i)} = H_i^{(3)} y_{h^{(3)}(i)}. \quad (6)$$

We claim that

$$\exists x : \Big[\bigwedge_i x_{f^{(2)}(i)} \neq t_i^{(2)}(x, y) \wedge \bigwedge_i G_i^{(3)} y_{g^{(3)}(i)} \neq s_i^{(3)}(x, y) \Big] \quad (7)$$

is valid and hence (6) is equivalent to

$$\bigwedge_i G_i^{(4)} y_{g^{(4)}(i)} \neq s_i^{(4)}(y) \wedge \bigwedge_i H_i^{(2)} y_{h^{(2)}(i)} = H_i^{(3)} y_{h^{(3)}(i)}. \quad (8)$$

Theorem 1. *All transformations in Alg. 1 preserve equivalence.*

Theorem 2. *Alg. 1 eliminates a block of quantifiers in time $2^{O(n)}$.*

Theorem 3. $\mathsf{BC_k}(\mathfrak{A}_{TA})$ *is decidable in $O(\exp_k(n))$.*

5   Term Algebras with Length Function

In this section we introduce the extended theory and present the technical machinery needed to handle lengths of TA-terms in the elimination procedure.

Definition 4. *The structure of the extended language is* $\mathfrak{A}_{TA}^{\mathbb{Z}} = (\mathfrak{A}_{TA}; \mathfrak{A}_{\mathbb{Z}}; (.)^{L} : TA \rightarrow \mathbb{Z})$ *where* $\mathfrak{A}_{TA}$ *is a term algebra,* $\mathfrak{A}_{\mathbb{Z}}$ *is Presburger arithmetic, and* $(.)^{L}$ *denotes the length function; for a term* t, $(t^{L})^{\mathfrak{A}_{TA}^{\mathbb{Z}}} = \text{len}(t^{\mathfrak{A}_{TA}^{\mathbb{Z}}})$. *We denote by* $\mathscr{L}_{TA}^{\mathbb{Z}}$ *the language for* $\mathfrak{A}_{TA}^{\mathbb{Z}}$.

We call terms of sort TA (resp. $\mathbb{Z}$) TA-terms (resp. integer terms), similarly for constants, variables, quantifiers and formulae. We also use "term" for "TA" when there is no confusion. A TA-term can occur inside the length function. We call this type of occurrence integer occurrence to distinguish it from the normal term occurrence.

If t is a set of TA-terms, we use t^{L} to denote the set of all integer occurrences, in the context, of the form $(Lt)^{L}$ where $t \in t$ and L denotes a (possibly empty) block of selectors.

Example 3. The formula $\exists x \exists y : TA\ (x \neq y \wedge x^{L} = y^{L})$ states that there exists at least two distinct terms $t_1, t_2 \in TA$ such that $\text{len}(t_1) = \text{len}(t_2)$. Note that the first occurrence of x is an ordinary term while the second one is integral. The same for the occurrences of y.

Instead of writing $n = t^{L}$ to indicate the connection between term variables and the corresponding integer variables, we abuse the notation a bit by using t^{L} as formal variables directly in Presburger formulae. For example, $\exists x^{L} : \mathbb{Z}\ \theta_{\mathbb{Z}}(x^{L}) \rightarrow \exists x : TA\ \theta_{TA}(x)$ stands for $\forall x^{L} : \mathbb{Z}\left[\theta_{\mathbb{Z}}(x^{L}) \rightarrow \exists x : TA\ \theta_{TA}(x)\right]$, which in turn is a shorthand for $\forall n : \mathbb{Z}\left[\theta_{\mathbb{Z}}(n) \rightarrow \exists x : TA\ (\theta_{TA}(x) \wedge n = x^{L})\right]$.

5.1   Counting Constraints

As before, to eliminate $\exists x$ from $\exists x : TA\ \theta_{TA}(x, y)$, we first put $\exists x : TA\ \theta_{TA}(x, y)$ into solved form. However, this alone does not suffice as the constraints on the lengths of x may restrict the solution set of x.

Example 4. The truth value of $\exists x_1 \exists x_2 : TA\ (x_1 \neq x_2 \wedge x_1^{L} = x_2^{L} = 3)$ depends on the existence of two distinct terms of length 3.

Hence we need to know the number of distinct TA-terms at certain length.

Definition 5 (Counting Constraint). *A counting constraint is a predicate* $\text{CNT}_{k,n}^{\alpha}(x)$ $(k > 0, n \geq 0)$ *that is true if and only if there are at least* $n+1$ *different* α-terms of *length* x *in* $\mathfrak{A}_{TA}$ *with* k *constants.* $\text{CNT}_{k,n}(x)$ *is similarly defined with* α-terms *replaced by TA-terms.*

Example 5. For $\mathfrak{A}_{list}^{\mathbb{Z}} = (\mathfrak{A}_{list}; \mathfrak{A}_{\mathbb{Z}})$ with one constant, $\text{CNT}_{1,n}^{cons}(x)$ is $x \geq 2m-1 \wedge 2 \nmid m$ where m is the least number such that the m-th Catalan number $C_m = \frac{1}{m}\binom{2m-2}{m-1}$ is greater than n. This is not surprising as C_m gives the number of binary trees with m leaves (that tree has $2m - 1$ nodes).

Lemma 1 ([24]). $\text{CNT}_{k,n}^{\alpha}(x)$ *and* $\text{CNT}_{k,n}(x)$ *are expressible in Presburger arithmetic.*

5.2   Equality Completion

Often formulae do not have all the information required to construct counting constraints. Consider the formula $\exists x : \mathsf{TA}\,(y_1 \neq x \wedge y_2 \neq x \wedge y_1 \neq y_2)$. Without knowing equality relations between the lengths of x, y_1 and y_2, we can not find the integer constraint on the length of x. So in order to construct counting constraints, we need equality information between terms and equality information between lengths of terms.

Definition 6 (Equality Completion). *Let S be a set of* TA-*terms. An equality completion θ of S is a formula consisting of the following literals: for any $u, v \in S$, exactly one of $u = v$ and $u \neq v$, and exactly one of $u^{\mathsf{L}} = v^{\mathsf{L}}$ and $u^{\mathsf{L}} \neq v^{\mathsf{L}}$ are in θ.*

Let θ be a conjunction of literals. We say that θ' is an equality completion of θ, if θ' is a conjunction of an equality completion of $\Sigma(\theta)$ and tester literals in θ. We are only interested in compatible equality completions, i.e., θ is a subformula of θ'.

Example 6. Let $\mathsf{ar}(\alpha) = 2$ and θ be $y \neq \alpha(x, z) \wedge \mathsf{Is}_\alpha(y)$, then $\Sigma(\theta) = \{x, y, z, \alpha(x, z)\}$. A possible equality completion of θ is

$$\mathsf{Is}_\alpha(y) \wedge y^{\mathsf{L}} = (\alpha(x, z))^{\mathsf{L}} \wedge x^{\mathsf{L}} = z^{\mathsf{L}} \wedge y^{\mathsf{L}} \neq x^{\mathsf{L}} \wedge \bigwedge_{t, t' \in \Sigma(\theta); t \neq t'} t \neq t'. \tag{9}$$

5.3   Clusters

Equality completion is an expensive operation and it is hard to maintain if the subsequent operations generate new terms (as in Alg. 6). Revisiting $\exists x : \mathsf{TA}\,(y_1 \neq x \wedge y_2 \neq x \wedge y_1 \neq y_2)$, it is easily seen that we need to know whether $y_1 = y_2$ or not only if we have guessed $x^{\mathsf{L}} = y_1^{\mathsf{L}} = y_2^{\mathsf{L}}$. In fact it suffices to have the equality information between terms of the same length. This leads to the notion of clusters.

Definition 7 (Clusters). *Let $[t]$ denote the equivalence class containing t with respect to term equality. We say that $C = \{[t_0], \ldots, [t_n]\}$ is a cluster if $t_0, \ldots, t_n$ are pairwise disjoint terms of the same length.*

For notation simplicity we may assume that a cluster is a set with each member being an (arbitrarily chosen) representative of the corresponding equivalence class. A cluster is maximal if no superset of it is a cluster. A cluster C is closed if C is maximal and for any maximal C', $C \cap C' \neq \emptyset \rightarrow C = C'$. Two distinct closed clusters are said to be mutually independent. A cluster is α-typed (called α-cluster) if all of its elements are α-typed. The notions of maximality, closedness and mutual independence naturally generalize to typed clusters. Note that an untyped maximal cluster may contain more than one typed maximal cluster. The size of a cluster is the number of equivalence classes in it. The rank of a cluster C, written $\mathsf{rk}(C)$, is the length of its terms. Clusters are partially ordered by their ranks.

Example 7. In Ex. 6, formula (9) induces two mutually independent clusters $C_1 : \{[x], [z]\}$ and $C_2 : \{[y], [\alpha(x, z)]\}$ with C_2 be α-typed and $\mathsf{rk}(C_1) < \mathsf{rk}(C_2)$. In fact any equality completion induces a set of mutually independent clusters. As another example, the formula

$$x \neq y \wedge x \neq z \wedge x^L = y^L \wedge x^L = z^L \wedge \mathsf{Is}_\alpha(x) \wedge \mathsf{Is}_\alpha(y)$$

gives two maximal clusters $C'_1 : \{x, y\}$ and $C'_2 : \{x, z\}$, with C'_1 be a α-cluster. However, neither C'_1 nor C'_2 is closed and their ranks are incomparable.

5.4   Length Constraint Completion

In general, formulae are of the form $\exists x : \mathsf{TA}\left(\theta_{\mathsf{TA}}(x, y) \wedge \theta_Z(x^L, y^L)\right)$, where the lengths of x have been constrained by $\theta_Z(x^L, y^L)$. For the construction of accurate length constraints for x, we need to make $\theta_Z(x^L, y^L)$ "complete" in the sense defined below.

Definition 8 (Length Constraint Completion). *Let $\theta_{\mathsf{TA}}(x, y)$ be a formula of $\mathscr{L}_{\mathsf{TA}}$ and $\theta_Z(x^L, y^L)$ be a formula of $\mathscr{L}_Z$. Write $\theta_{\mathsf{TA}}(x, y)$ as $\theta_{\mathsf{TA}}^{(1)}(x, y) \wedge \theta^{(2)}(y)$ such that $\theta^{(2)}(y)$ does not contain x. We say a formula $\Theta_Z(x^L, y^L)$ is a* **completion** *of $\theta_Z(x^L, y^L)$ in x with respect to $\theta_{\mathsf{TA}}(x, y)$ if the following formulae are valid:*

I. $\forall y : \mathsf{TA} \ \forall x : \mathsf{TA} \left[\theta_{\mathsf{TA}}(x, y) \wedge \theta_Z(x^L, y^L) \leftrightarrow \theta_{\mathsf{TA}}(x, y) \wedge \Theta_Z(x^L, y^L)\right].$

II. $\forall y : \mathsf{TA} \ \forall x^L : \mathbb{Z} \left[\theta^{(2)}(y) \wedge \Theta_Z(x^L, y^L) \rightarrow \exists x : \mathsf{TA}\left(\theta_{\mathsf{TA}}(x, y) \wedge \Theta_Z(x^L, y^L)\right)\right].$

Example 8. Let $\mathsf{ar}(\alpha) = 2$, $x = \{x_1, x_2, x_3\}$, $y = \emptyset$, $\theta_{\mathsf{TA}}(x_1, x_2, x_3)$ be $\alpha(x_1, x_2) = x_3$ and $\theta_Z(x_1^L, x_2^L, x_3^L)$ be $x_1^L < x_3^L \wedge x_2^L < x_3^L$. Consider the following formulae:

$$\Theta_Z : x_1^L + x_2^L + 1 = x_3^L \wedge x_1^L > 0 \wedge x_2^L > 0,$$
$$\Theta_Z^1 : x_1^L < x_3^L \wedge x_2^L < x_3^L \wedge x_1^L > 0 \wedge x_2^L > 0,$$
$$\Theta_Z^2 : x_1^L + x_2^L + 1 = x_3^L \wedge x_1^L > 5 \wedge x_2^L > 5.$$

It is not hard to argue that Θ_Z is a completion of $\theta_Z(x_1^L, x_2^L, x_3^L)$ in x with respect to $\theta_{\mathsf{TA}}(x_1, x_2, x_3)$. However neither Θ_Z^1 nor Θ_Z^2 is such a completion. Though Θ_Z^1 satisfies [I], it does not satisfies [II], as the assignment $\{x_1^L = 3, x_2^L = 3, x_3^L = 4\}$ can not be realized by any assignment for x. On the other hand, Θ_Z^2 satisfies [II], but not [I], as the assignment $\{x_1 = a, x_2 = a, x_3 = \alpha(a, a)\}$, where a is a constant, falsifies Θ_Z^2.

For the construction of length constraint completion, we require that $\theta_{\mathsf{TA}}(x, y)$ $\wedge \theta_Z(x^L, y^L)$ induce a set of closed clusters and be in a special form defined below.

Definition 9. *We say $\theta_{\mathsf{TA}}(x, y) \wedge \theta_Z(x^L, y^L)$ is in* **strong solved form** *(with respect to x) if $\theta_{\mathsf{TA}}(x, y)$ is in solved form and all literals of the form $Ly \neq t(x, y)$, where $y \in y$ and $t(x, y)$ is a constructor term (properly) containing x, are redundant.*

Example 9. In Ex. 6, formula (9) is not in strong solved form. However, it can be made into strong solved form by adding $s_1^\alpha y \neq x$ or $s_2^\alpha y \neq z$.

The following predicates are needed to describe the construction algorithm:

$$\text{Tree}(t) : \exists x_1, \ldots, x_n \geq 0 \left(t^\perp = \left(\textstyle\sum_{i=1}^n d_i x_i \right) + 1 \right),$$
$$\text{Node}^\alpha(t, t_\alpha) : t^\perp = \textstyle\sum_{i=1}^{\text{ar}(\alpha)} t_i^\perp + 1,$$
$$\text{Tree}^\alpha(t) : \exists t_\alpha \left(\text{Node}^\alpha(t, t_\alpha) \wedge \textstyle\bigwedge_{i=1}^{\text{ar}(\alpha)} \text{Tree}(t_i) \right),$$

where t_α stands for $t_1, \ldots, t_{\text{ar}(\alpha)}$ and $d_1, \ldots, d_n$ are the distinct arities of constructors. The predicate $\text{Tree}(t)$ is true if and only if $t^\perp$ is the length of a well-formed TA-term. The predicate $\text{Node}^\alpha(t, t_\alpha)$ forces the length of an α-term with known children to be the sum of the lengths of its children plus 1. The predicate $\text{Tree}^\alpha(t)$ states the length constraint of a well-formed α-term.

Algorithm 2 (Length Constraint Completion). *Input:* $\theta_{\text{TA}}(x, y) \wedge \theta_{\mathbb{Z}}(x^\perp, y^\perp)$, *where* $\theta_{\text{TA}}(x, y)$ *is a conjunction of literals in* $\mathscr{L}_{\text{TA}}$ *and* $\theta_{\mathbb{Z}}(x^\perp, y^\perp)$ *is a conjunction of literals in* $\mathscr{L}_{\mathbb{Z}}$. *Initially set* $\Theta_{\mathbb{Z}}(x^\perp, y^\perp) = \theta_{\mathbb{Z}}(x^\perp, y^\perp)$. *For each term t occurring in* $\theta_{\text{TA}}(x, y)$, *add the following to* $\Theta_{\mathbb{Z}}(x^\perp, y^\perp)$.

a. $t^\perp = 1$, *if t is a constant.*
b. $t^\perp = s^\perp$, *if $t = s$.*
c. $\text{Tree}(t)$, *if t is untyped.*
d. $\text{Tree}^\alpha(t)$, *if t is α-typed.*
e. $\text{Node}^\alpha(t, t_\alpha)$, *if t is α-typed with children t_α.*
f. $\text{CNT}_{k,n}(t^\perp)$, *if t occurs in an untyped clusters of size $n + 1$ and $\mathfrak{A}_{\text{TA}}$ has k constants.*
g. $\text{CNT}_{k,n}^\alpha(t^\perp)$, *if t occurs in an α-cluster of size $n + 1$ and $\mathfrak{A}_{\text{TA}}$ has k constants.*

Lemma 2. *If* $\theta_{\text{TA}}(x, y) \wedge \theta_{\mathbb{Z}}(x^\perp, y^\perp)$ *is in strong solved form and induces a set of mutually independent clusters, then* $\Theta_{\mathbb{Z}}(x^\perp, y^\perp)$ *computed by Alg. 2 is a completion of* $\theta_{\mathbb{Z}}(x^\perp, y^\perp)$ *in x with respect to* $\theta_{\text{TA}}(x, y)$.

Lemma 3. *Alg. 2 computes* $\Theta_{\mathbb{Z}}(x^\perp, y^\perp)$ *in time $O(n)$.*

6   A New Quantifier Elimination Procedure for $\text{Th}(\mathfrak{A}_{\text{TA}}^{\mathbb{Z}})$

In this section we expand Alg. 1 to an elimination procedure for $\text{Th}(\mathfrak{A}_{\text{TA}}^{\mathbb{Z}})$. Since $\mathscr{L}_{\text{TA}}^{\mathbb{Z}}$ has two sorts, namely $\mathbb{Z}$ and TA, we need to show elimination of integer quantifiers as well as term quantifiers.

6.1   Eliminate Quantifiers on Integer Variables

We assume that formulae with quantifiers on integer variables are in the form

$$\exists z : \mathbb{Z} \left(\theta_{\mathbb{Z}}(x^\perp, y, z) \wedge \theta_{\text{TA}}(x) \right), \tag{10}$$

where y, z are integer variables and x are term variables. Since $\theta_{TA}(x)$ is in $\mathscr{L}_{TA}$, we can move $\theta_{TA}(x)$ out of the scope of $\exists z$, obtaining

$$\exists z : \mathbb{Z} \; \theta_{\mathbb{Z}}(x^L, y, z) \wedge \theta_{TA}(x). \tag{11}$$

Now $\exists z : \mathbb{Z} \; \theta_{\mathbb{Z}}(x^L, y, z)$ is essentially a Presburger formula and we can proceed to remove the block of existential quantifiers using Cooper's method [5, 20]. In fact, we can defer the elimination of integer quantifiers until all term quantifiers have been eliminated.

6.2 Eliminate Quantifiers on Term Variables

We assume that formulae with quantifiers on term variables are in the form

$$\exists x : \mathsf{TA} \left(\theta_{TA}(x, y) \wedge \Psi_{\mathbb{Z}}(x^L, y^L, z) \right), \tag{12}$$

where x, y are term variables, z are integer variables, and $\Psi_{\mathbb{Z}}(x^L, y^L, z)$ is an arbitrary Presburger formula. The following algorithm is based on Alg. 1. To save space, we do not list $\Psi_{\mathbb{Z}}(x^L, y^L, z)$ until needed.

Algorithm 3. *Input:* $\exists x : \mathsf{TA} \left(\theta_{TA}(x, y) \wedge \Psi_{\mathbb{Z}}(x^L, y^L, z) \right)$.
Run Alg. 1 up to Step [7]. Apply the following subprocedures successively unless noted otherwise.

1. *Equality Completion (Alg. 4).*
2. *Elimination of Equalities Containing x (Alg. 5).*
3. *Propagation of Disequalities of the Form $Ly \neq t(x, y)$ (Alg. 6).*
4. *Reduction of Term Quantifiers to Integer Quantifiers (Alg. 7).*

The purpose of steps [1]- [3] is to transform (12) to a formula in strong normal form which induces a set of mutually independent clusters. Therefore by Alg. 2 we can construct the length constraint completion for x which allows us to reduce term quantifiers to integer quantifiers.

Algorithm 4 (Equality Completion). *We assume the input formula is in the form (renaming the first part of (7))*

$$\exists x : \mathsf{TA} \left[\bigwedge_i x_{f(i)} \neq t_i(x, y) \wedge \bigwedge_i L_i y_{g(i)} \neq s_i(x, y) \right], \tag{13}$$

where t_i, s_i are: (i) quantified variables x, (ii) parameters y, (iii) selector terms of parameters in the form Ly ($y \in y$), (iv) constants in $\mathcal{A}$, or (v) constructor terms built from terms in (i)-(iv). Let S be all terms including subterms which appear in (13). Guess an equality completion of S. It is easily seen that an equality completion is of the form (omitting integer literals)

$$\exists x : \mathsf{TA} \left[\bigwedge_i x_{f(i)} \neq t_i(x, y) \wedge \bigwedge_i L_i y_{g(i)} \neq s_i(x, y) \wedge \right.$$
$$\left. \bigwedge_i x_{f'(i)} = t'_i(x, y) \wedge \bigwedge_i L'_i y_{g'(i)} = s'_i(x, y) \right]. \tag{14}$$

Algorithm 5 (Elimination of Equalities Containing x). *Let $\mathcal{E}$ denote the set of equalities containing x. Exhaustively apply the following subprocedures until $\mathcal{E}$ is empty. Pick an $E \in \mathcal{E}$.*

A. *E is $x = u$. Then we know x does not occur in u and hence we can remove $\exists x$ by substituting u for all occurrences of x.*

B. *E is $Ly = \alpha(t_1(x, y), \ldots, t_k(x, y))$. Then replace E by*

$$s_1^\alpha Ly = t_1(x, y), \quad \ldots, \quad s_k^\alpha Ly = t_k(x, y).$$

C. *E is $\beta(u_1(x, y), \ldots, u_l(x, y)) = \beta(u_1'(x, y), \ldots, u_l'(x, y))$. Then replace E by*

$$u_1(x, y) = u_1'(x, y), \quad \ldots, \quad u_l(x, y) = u_l'(x, y).$$

Algorithm 6 (Propagation of Disequalities of the Form $Ly \neq t(x, y)$). *We only need to propagate those disequalities of the form $Ly \neq t(x, y)$ such that $(Ly)^L = (t(x, y))^L$ and $t(x, y)$ is a constructor term (properly) containing x. This is done by the following sequence of disjunctive splittings.*

Let $\mathcal{D}$ denote the set of disequalities of the above form. Exhaustively apply the following subprocedures until $\mathcal{D}$ is empty. Pick $D : Ly \neq \alpha(t_1(x, y), \ldots, t_k(x, y)) \in \mathcal{D}$.

A. **Disequality Splitting.** *Remove D from $\mathcal{D}$ and add to $\theta_{TA}(x, y)$*

$$\neg \mathsf{Is}_\alpha(Ly) \vee \bigvee_{1 \leq i \leq k} s_i^\alpha Ly \neq t_i(x, y).$$

Return if we take $\neg \mathsf{Is}_\alpha(Ly)$; continue otherwise.

B. **Length Splitting.** *Suppose we take $s_j^\alpha Ly \neq t_j(x, y)$ $(1 \leq j \leq k)$. Split on*

$$(s_j^\alpha Ly)^L = (t_j(x, y))^L \vee (s_j^\alpha Ly)^L \neq (t_j(x, y))^L.$$

Return if we take $(s_j^\alpha Ly)^L \neq (t_j(x, y))^L$; continue otherwise.

C. **Equality Splitting.** *Suppose the cluster of $t_j(x, y)$ contains $u_0, \ldots, u_n$. Split on*

$$\bigvee_{i \leq n} s_j^\alpha Ly = u_i \vee \bigwedge_{i \leq n} s_j^\alpha Ly \neq u_i$$

In case we take any disjunct $s_j^\alpha Ly = u_i$, return if u_i does not contain x; rerun Alg. 5 otherwise. Note that Alg. 5 can only be rerun finitely many times as each run will remove at least one existentially quantified variable.

The last case is that we choose $\bigwedge_{i \leq n} s_j^\alpha Ly \neq u_i$. This in general will increase the size of $\mathcal{D}$ if some of $u_i(x)$'s are also constructor terms containing x. However if this happens, $u_i(x)$'s will sit in a cluster whose rank is lower than that of the cluster of $\alpha(t_1(x, y), \ldots, t_k(x, y))$. As the rank ordering is well-founded, eventually the size of $\mathcal{D}$ will decrease.

Algorithm 7 (Reduction of Term Quantifiers to Integer Quantifiers). *Omitting the redundant disequalities of the form $Ly \neq t(x, y)$, we may assume the resulting formula be*

$$\exists x : \text{TA} \left[\theta_{\text{TA}}^{(1)}(x, y) \wedge \theta_{\text{TA}}^{(2)}(y) \wedge \Theta_{\mathbb{Z}}(x^L, y^L) \wedge \Psi_{\mathbb{Z}}(x^L, y^L, z) \right], \qquad (15)$$

where $\theta_{\text{TA}}^{(1)}(x, y)$ is of the form $\bigwedge_i x_{f(i)} \neq t_i(x, y)$, $\theta_{\text{TA}}^{(2)}(y)$ does not contain x, $\Theta_{\mathbb{Z}}(x^L, y^L)$ is the integer constraint obtained from Algs. 4, 6 (Step [B]), and $\Psi_{\mathbb{Z}}(x^L, y^L, z)$ is the PA formula not listed before for simplicity. Now let $\theta_{\text{TA}}(x, y)$ denote $\theta_{\text{TA}}^{(1)}(x, y) \wedge \theta_{\text{TA}}^{(2)}(y)$. Call Alg. 2 to get the completion $\Theta_{\mathbb{Z}}(x^L, y^L)$ of $\theta_{\mathbb{Z}}(x^L, y^L)$ in x with respect to $\theta_{\text{TA}}(x, y)$. Now we claim that (15) is equivalent to

$$\exists x : \text{TA} \left[\theta_{\text{TA}}^{(1)}(x, y) \wedge \theta_{\text{TA}}^{(2)}(y) \wedge \Theta_{\mathbb{Z}}(x^L, y^L) \wedge \Psi_{\mathbb{Z}}(x^L, y^L, z) \right], \qquad (16)$$

which in turn is equivalent to

$$\exists x^L : \mathbb{Z} \left[\theta_{\text{TA}}^{(2)}(y) \wedge \Theta_{\mathbb{Z}}(x^L, y^L) \wedge \Psi_{\mathbb{Z}}(x^L, y^L, z) \right]. \qquad (17)$$

Lemma 4. *Algs. 4,5 and 6 produce a formula in strong normal form which induces a set of mutually independent clusters.*

Theorem 4. *All transformations in Alg. 3 preserve equivalence.*

Theorem 5. *Alg. 3 eliminates a block of quantifiers in time $2^{2^{O(n)}}$.*

Theorem 6. *$BC_k(\mathfrak{A}_{\text{TA}}^{\mathbb{Z}})$ is decidable in $O(\exp_{2k}(n))$.*

7 Conclusion

We presented new quantifier elimination procedures for the theory of term algebras and for the extended theory with Presburger arithmetic. The elimination procedures deal with a block of quantifiers of the same type at one step. The complexity of one-step elimination is exponential (resp. double exponential) for the theory of term algebras (resp. for the theory of term algebras with integers).

The double exponential complexity is due to the propagation of literals of the form $Ly \neq t(x, y)$ in a cluster. We believe that more refined length constraint construction will remove this costly operation.

We plan to apply these methods to the first-order theory of queues [21] and to the first-order theory of Knuth-Bendix order [23].

References

1. Rolf Backofen. A complete axiomatization of a theory with feature and arity constraints. *Journal of Logical Programming*, 24(1&2):37–71, 1995.
2. Hubert Comon and Catherine Delor. Equational formulae with membership constraints. *Information and Computation*, 112(2):167–216, 1994.
3. Hubert Comon and Pierre Lescanne. Equational problems and disunification. *Journal of Symbolic Computation*, 7:371–425, 1989.

4. K. J. Compton and C. W. Henson. A uniform method for proving lower bounds on the computational complexity of logical theories. *Annals of Pure and Applied Logic*, 48:1–79, 1990.

5. D. C. Cooper. Theorem proving in arithmetic without multiplication. In *Machine Intelligence*, volume 7, pages 91–99. American Elsevier, 1972.

6. H. B. Enderton. *A Mathematical Introduction to Logic*. Academic Press, 2001.

7. J. Ferrante and C. W. Rackoff. *The Computational Complexity of Logical Theories*. Springer-Verlag, 1979.

8. Martin Fürer. The complexity of Presburger arithmetic with bounded quantifer alternation depth. *Theoretical Computer Science*, 18:105–111, 1982.

9. Wilfrid Hodges. *Model Theory*. Cambridge University Press, Cambridge, UK, 1993.

10. Konstantin Korovin and Andrei Voronkov. A decision procedure for the existential theory of term algebras with the Knuth-Bendix ordering. In *Proceedings of 15th IEEE Symposium on Logic in Computer Science*, pages 291–302, IEEE Computer Society Press, 2000.

11. Konstantin Korovin and Andrei Voronkov. Knuth-Bendix constraint solving is NP-complete. In *Proceedings of 28th International Colloquium on Automata, Languages and Programming (ICALP)*, volume 2076 of *Lecture Notes in Computer Science*, pages 979–992. Springer-Verlag, 2001.

12. Viktor Kuncak and Martin Rinard. On the theory of structural subtyping. Technical Report MIT-LCS-TR-879, Massachusetts Institute of Technology, January 2003.

13. Viktor Kuncak and Martin Rinard. The structural subtyping of non-recursive types is decidable. In *Proceedings of 18th IEEE Symposium on Logic in Computer Science*, pages 96–107. IEEE Computer Society Press, 2003.

14. Kenneth Kunen. Negation in logic programming. *Journal of Logic Programming*, 4(4):289–308, 1987.

15. L. Lovász. *Combinatorial Problems and Exercises*. Elsevier, Horth-Holland, 1993.

16. M. J. Maher. Complete axiomatizations of the algebras of finite, rational and infinite tree. In *Proceedings of the 3rd IEEE Symposium on Logic in Computer Science*, pages 348–357. IEEE Computer Society Press, 1988.

17. A. I. Mal'cev. Axiomatizable classes of locally free algebras of various types. In *The Metamathematics of Algebraic Systems, Collected Papers*, chapter 23, pages 262–281. North Holland, 1971.

18. Alberto Martelli and Ugo Montanari. An efficient unification algorithm. *ACM Transactions on Programming Languages and Systems*, 4(2):258–282, 1982.

19. Derek C. Oppen. Reasoning about recursively defined data structures. *Journal of ACM*, 27(3), July 1980.

20. C. R. Reddy and D. W. Loveland. Presburger arithmetic with bounded quantifier alternation. In *Proceedings of the 10th Annual Symposium on Theory of Computing*, pages 320–325. ACM Press, 1978.

21. Tatiana Rybina and Andrei Voronkov. A decision procedure for term algebras with queues. *ACM Transactions on Computational Logic*, 2(2):155–181, 2001.

22. Sergei Vorobyov. An improved lower bound for the elementary theories of trees. In *Proceedings of the 13th International Conference on Automated Deduction*, volume 1104 of *Lecture Notes in Computer Science*, pages 275–287. Springer-Verlag, 1996.

23. Ting Zhang, Henny Sipma, and Zohar Manna. The decidability of the first-order theory of term algebras with Knuth-Bendix order, 2004. Submitted.

24. Ting Zhang, Henny Sipma, and Zohar Manna. Decision procedures for recursive data structures with integer constraints, 2004. To appear in the Proceedings of the 2nd International Joint Conference on Automated Reasoning.

Author Index

Lecture Notes in Computer Science

For information about Vols. 1–3101

please contact your bookseller or Springer

Vol. 3232: R. Heery, L. Lyon (Eds.), Research and Advanced Technology for Digital Libraries. XV, 528 pages. 2004.

Vol. 3223: K. Slind, A. Bunker, G. Gopalakrishnan (Eds.), Theorem Proving in Higher Order Logic. VIII, 337 pages. 2004.

Vol. 3221: S. Albers, T. Radzik (Eds.), Algorithms – ESA 2004. XVIII, 836 pages. 2004.

Vol. 3220: J.C. Lester, R.M. Vicari, F. Paraguaçu (Eds.), Intelligent Tutoring Systems. XXI, 920 pages. 2004.

Vol. 3208: H.J. Ohlbach, S. Schaffert (Eds.), Principles and Practice of Semantic Web Reasoning. VII, 165 pages. 2004.

Vol. 3207: L.T. Jang, M. Guo, G.R. Gao, N.K. Jha, Embedded and Ubiquitous Computing. XX, 1116 pages. 2004.

Vol. 3206: P. Sojka, I. Kopecek, K. Pala (Eds.), Text, Speech and Dialogue. XIII, 667 pages. 2004. (Subseries LNAI).

Vol. 3205: N. Davies, E. Mynatt, I. Siio (Eds.), UbiComp 2004: Ubiquitous Computing. XVI, 452 pages. 2004.

Vol. 3203: J. Becker, M. Platzner, S. Vernalde (Eds.), Field Programmable Logic and Application. XXX, 1198 pages. 2004.

Vol. 3199: H. Schepers (Ed.), Software and Compilers for Embedded Systems. X, 259 pages. 2004.

Vol. 3198: G.-J. de Vreede, L.A. Guerrero, G. Marín Raventós (Eds.), Groupware: Design, Implementation and Use. XI, 378 pages. 2004.

Vol. 3194: R. Camacho, R. King, A. Srinivasan (Eds.), Inductive Logic Programming. XI, 361 pages. 2004. (Subseries LNAI).

Vol. 3193: P. Samarati, P. Ryan, D. Gollmann, R. Molva (Eds.), Computer Security – ESORICS 2004. X, 457 pages. 2004.

Vol. 3192: C. Bussler, D. Fensel (Eds.), Artificial Intelligence: Methodology, Systems, and Applications. XIII, 522 pages. 2004. (Subseries LNAI).

Vol. 3189: P.-C. Yew, J. Xue (Eds.), Advances in Computer Systems Architecture. XVII, 598 pages. 2004.

Vol. 3186: Z. Bellahsène, T. Milo, M. Rys, D. Suciu, R. Unland (Eds.), Database and XML Technologies. X, 235 pages. 2004.

Vol. 3184: S. Katsikas, J. Lopez, G. Pernul (Eds.), Trust and Privacy in Digital Business. XI, 299 pages. 2004.

Vol. 3183: R. Traunmüller (Ed.), Electronic Government. XIX, 583 pages. 2004.

Vol. 3182: K. Bauknecht, M. Bichler, B. Pröll (Eds.), E-Commerce and Web Technologies. XI, 370 pages. 2004.

Vol. 3181: Y. Kambayashi, M. Mohania, W. Wöß (Eds.), Data Warehousing and Knowledge Discovery. XIV, 412 pages. 2004.

Vol. 3180: F. Galindo, M. Takizawa, R. Traunmüller (Eds.), Database and Expert Systems Applications. XXI, 972 pages. 2004.

Vol. 3179: F.J. Perales, B.A. Draper (Eds.), Articulated Motion and Deformable Objects. XI, 270 pages. 2004.

Vol. 3178: W. Jonker, M. Petkovic (Eds.), Secure Data Management. VIII, 219 pages. 2004.

Vol. 3177: Z.R. Yang, H. Yin, R. Everson (Eds.), Intelligent Data Engineering and Automated Learning – IDEAL 2004. XVIII, 852 pages. 2004.

Vol. 3175: C.E. Rasmussen, H.H. Bülthoff, B. Schölkopf, M.A. Giese (Eds.), Pattern Recognition. XVIII, 581 pages. 2004.

Vol. 3174: F. Yin, J. Wang, C. Guo (Eds.), Advances in Neural Networks - ISNN 2004. XXXV, 1021 pages. 2004.

Vol. 3172: M. Dorigo, M. Birattari, C. Blum, L. M.Gambardella, F. Mondada, T. Stützle (Eds.), Ant Colony, Optimization and Swarm Intelligence. XII, 434 pages. 2004.

Vol. 3170: P. Gardner, N. Yoshida (Eds.), CONCUR 2004 - Concurrency Theory. XIII, 529 pages. 2004.

Vol. 3166: M. Rauterberg (Ed.), Entertainment Computing – ICEC 2004. XXIII, 617 pages. 2004.

Vol. 3163: S. Marinai, A. Dengel (Eds.), Document Analysis Systems VI. XII, 564 pages. 2004.

Vol. 3162: R. Downey, M. Fellows, F. Dehne (Eds.), Parameterized and Exact Computation. X, 293 pages. 2004.

Vol. 3160: S. Brewster, M. Dunlop (Eds.), Mobile Human-Computer Interaction – MobileHCI 2004. XVIII, 541 pages. 2004.

Vol. 3159: U. Visser, Intelligent Information Integration for the Semantic Web. XIV, 150 pages. 2004. (Subseries LNAI).

Vol. 3158: I. Nikolaidis, M. Barbeau, E. Kranakis (Eds.), Ad-Hoc, Mobile, and Wireless Networks. IX, 344 pages. 2004.

Vol. 3157: C. Zhang, H. W. Guesgen, W.K. Yeap (Eds.), PRICAI 2004: Trends in Artificial Intelligence. XX, 1023 pages. 2004. (Subseries LNAI).

Vol. 3156: M. Joye, J.-J. Quisquater (Eds.), Cryptographic Hardware and Embedded Systems - CHES 2004. XIII, 455 pages. 2004.

Vol. 3155: P. Funk, P.A. González Calero (Eds.), Advances in Case-Based Reasoning. XIII, 822 pages. 2004. (Subseries LNAI).

Vol. 3154: R.L. Nord (Ed.), Software Product Lines. XIV, 334 pages. 2004.